ALL THINGS MUST
FIGHT TO LIVE

ALL THINGS MUST FIGHT TO LIVE

Stories of War and Deliverance in Congo

Bryan Mealer

BLOOMSBURY

Published by Bloomsbury USA, New York
Distributed to the trade by Macmillan

All papers used by Bloomsbury USA are natural, recyclable products made from wood grown in well-managed forests. The manufacturing processes conform to the environmental regulations of the country of origin.

Portions of this book have appeared in *Harper's* magazine in slightly different form.

Map on p. xi by Joyce Pendola.

LIBRARY OF CONGRESS CATALOGING-IN-PUBLICATION DATA HAS BEEN APPLIED FOR.

ISBN-10: 1-59691-345-2
ISBN-13: 978-1-59691-345-5

First U.S. Edition 2008

1 3 5 7 9 10 8 6 4 2

Typeset by Westchester Book Group
Printed in the United States of America by Quebecor World Fairfield

For Ann Marie, my parents, and my sisters

Suffer, suffer for world. *Amen!*
Enjoy for heaven. *Amen!*

—Fela Kuti, "Suffering and Smiling"

CONTENTS

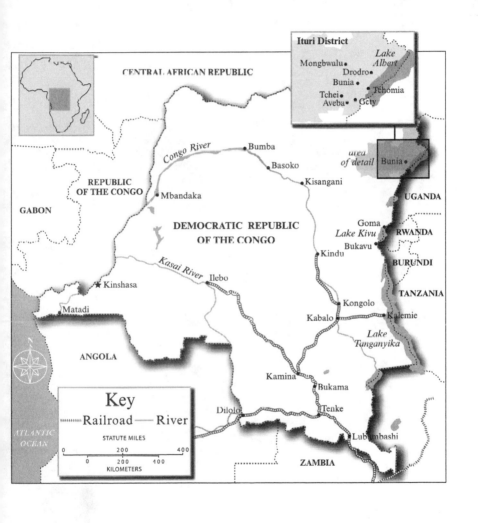

Ituri District

- Mongbwalu
- Drodro
- Bunia
- Tchomia
- Tchei
- Aveba
- Gcty

Lake Albert

CENTRAL AFRICAN REPUBLIC

Congo River

- Bumba
- Basoko
- Kisangani

REPUBLIC
OF THE CONGO

- Mbandaka

GABON

DEMOCRATIC REPUBLIC
OF THE CONGO

area of detail Bunia

UGANDA

- Goma
Lake Kivu
- Bukavu

RWANDA

BURUNDI

- Kindu

Kasai River

- Ilebo
- ★ Kinshasa

- Matadi

- Kongolo
- Kabalo
- Kalemie

TANZANIA

Lake Tanganyika

ANGOLA

- Kamina
- Bukama
- Tenke

Key

~~~~~~ Railroad — River

STATUTE MILES

0 — 200 — 400

0 — 200 — 100
KILOMETERS

- Dilolo

- Lubumbashi

ZAMBIA

ATLANTIC OCEAN

INTRODUCTION

We went in first with soldiers, young and terrified Ugandan kids straight from the villages, whip-thin in their baggy fatigues and wound tight around their triggers even high above the clouds. The Ugandan army flew Antonov-26s into Congo, scrapped by the Soviet bloc and born again for African war, steel Trojan horses loaded with gun-mounted jeeps, barrels of diesel, and crates of banana moonshine. You found a place on the floor and instantly started sweating, nestled between rifles and rocket launchers so close to your eyeballs you could study the paint chips on the grenades. There was little cabin pressure to soothe the landings, and going in fast, you felt like your eyes would pop out of your skull. The soldiers buried their faces in their hats to hide the tears. And all you could do was wince and give a thumbs-up and be thankful the engines were so loud that no one could hear you scream.

Later on it was UN Air, the almighty "move-con," sleek, white 727s that floated in like flying nuns. Inside you were greeted by cordial South African blondes who served Coca-Cola and gave quiet comfort to the malaria evac whose IV drip hung from the overhead compartment. You could read a book or fade out with your headphones or lose yourself in the six hundred shades of green below. Coming in was normal enough, but after returning from the field still plugged into the war, stepping into those planes was like being dunked in pure oxygen, or finding your way to the mother ship after crossing a hostile, unsheltered land.

There were eleventh-hour charter flights and Airbus red-eyes, six-seater Cessnas and the French-army Hercules, where female crew members doled out pizza and left you feeling ashamed by your own filth. There were speedboats across the Congo River, old German warships that ferried you over Lake Tanganyika, and one guy I met rode all the way from Paris on a Honda four-stroke before the border guards rolled him clean.

There were journalists and aid workers, diplomats and diamond dealers, assorted opportunists, and third-world peacekeepers deputized and deployed into hell. You could guess the new guys by the way their eyes never left the window; sitting next to them always made me nervous. There were many ways of going in, and everyone had his own reasons. But when we arrived, there was always the same war. Many came simply to test themselves against the brutal country, and I've learned there is nothing wrong with that. What mattered was what kind of prints you left behind in the red dirt. Five centuries of those bootprints now packed the soil and snaked into the trees, so many they bled into one enormous trail that hid below the camouflage and slowly choked the land.

But get down close and you can see.

One of those trails was mine.

Chapter One

IN THE VALLEY OF THE GUN

I

For me, the war started with the sound of a horn.

On the morning of April 3, 2003, as dawn broke over the green hills of northeastern Congo, several hundred ethnic Lendu warriors gathered along the lip of a narrow valley overlooking the sleeping villages of Drodro, Largu, and Jissa. The villages were mainly occupied by members of the Hema tribe, who'd become archenemies of the Lendu in a macabre conflict hatched amid Congo's larger, ongoing war, which had swept across the vast nation in 1998 and already killed several million people.

The Lendu fighters carried AK-47s held together with duct tape and wire, rocket-propelled grenades, and mortar tubes strapped to their backs. Some had long spears with steel tips whittled to saw teeth, arrows dipped in poison, and broad machetes ground to a razor edge. They'd marched all night from their villages deep in the hills, trailing along their women, children, and elderly, who now gathered in the rear and waited for the signal. Finally it came: the low wail of a horn, of a warrior squeezing his air through the narrow bore of a bull's antler. And at the sound of the horn, the bottom dropped from the hills.

They came in three waves: the first rushed in behind a volley of machine-gun fire, rockets, and mortars. The mud-walled huts of the villages exploded and burst into flame as rocket fire and shrapnel ignited the thatched roofs. Villagers scrambled out of their homes and ran for the trees, only to find that every exit was blocked. Gunmen caught them in the open and cut them down with rifles, while others emptied their guns into the thin walls of homes, then torched the roofs.

The second wave moved through with spears, arrows, and machetes to finish off the wounded. Those found hiding amid the manioc and sugarcane were dragged to the street and their throats cut. The warriors pounced from body to body, their long blades painted with blood, shouting, "Come out, Hema! The Lendu have come!"

Those who managed to hide in the trees lived to watch the massacre unfold. One father watched a group of Lendu boys surround his six children in their yard. The boys carried machetes and AK-47s. One of them took a running kick at the smallest child, a six-month-old infant crawling in the yard. The blow sent the child straight into the air, like a deflated ball, and machete blades caught her tiny body on the way down. The warriors then dismantled the remaining five children in the yard.

Down the road, survivors kept still in their hiding spots while several warriors opened the chest of a dead man, cut out his heart, and ate, blood streaming down their wrists. Other fighters held severed arms over the burning rubble and picked at the charred meat with their fingers. As the warriors dispatched the living, the third wave, the Lendu elderly, women, and children, rounded up cattle in the nearby fields and looted the village food pantries.

Around eight A.M., a second horn sounded and the warriors melted back into the hills. That morning, over a dozen Hema villages and nearby settlements were raided and destroyed. Initial reports estimated nearly one thousand people were murdered in just under three hours.

At the time I was living in Nairobi, eight hundred kilometers to the east and a universe removed. I was two months out of New York

City and still mesmerized every time I stepped outside into all that sunshine. I'd moved to Kenya to find work as a freelance reporter and had been spending my days and nights with detectives patrolling the Nairobi slums, hunting the carjackers and thieves who made that city one of the scariest places I'd ever been. But few editors in the States seemed interested in my African cop saga, and after two months' work, I was going broke with nothing to show for it.

During my first week in town I'd made friends with the bureau chief of the Associated Press. Susan Linnee was a twenty-five-year veteran of the wires who'd seen her share of people like me, guys who rolled in with half a clue about the region and talked as if they were reading from an encyclopedia. But she graciously allowed me to use the bureau to make phone calls and use the computers and never once bristled at my inexperience or naïve comments.

In Congo, the news of the Drodro massacre took two days to travel seventy kilometers south to the small United Nations base in the town of Bunia. Susan received the news flash across the wire, and a few hours later I walked into the office from one of my patrols. She called me into her office

"Have you ever been to Congo?" she said.

I shook my head.

"Do you know anything about Congo?"

I said no, nothing.

"Well, I'm sending Rodrique and Azim on a flight this afternoon."

"Okay."

"You should go with them, see how they work. It'll be a good experience for you."

She handed me an envelope with a plane ticket inside. I looked up, confused. Rodrique Ngowi and Sayyid Azim were seasoned staff who'd been to Congo many times; I had no connection with AP at all, other than loitering in their office.

"Pay me back when you can," she said. "I'm sure you can sell the story somewhere." I rushed home and packed a bag, then paused at the door before finally walking out. By evening, I was sitting in a hotel bar in Entebbe, Uganda, buzzing with paranoia about the morning departure. I thought of the map of Africa that had hung on the wall of my old apartment in New York. I'd marked the places I'd wanted to work, places in Ethiopia, Eritrea, along the Serengeti for the great migration. But Congo remained this green abyss, stitched by lost-looking rivers that snaked through bad jungle. Guys like me disappeared in places like that, I'd thought. There was a small television in the corner of the bar playing CNN, and while I sipped my beer, American tanks were rolling into Baghdad.

The Ugandan army had occupied Congo since 1998, when Uganda and Rwanda invaded the country to oust the Congolese president, Laurent Kabila. They still ran their flights in and out of Congo from the old Entebbe airport, the one that had been attacked by Israeli warplanes in the hostage rescue in 1976. The white concrete terminal remained chewed and peppered with bullet holes the size of golf balls. We piled into one of the old Antonovs parked on the tarmac, piloted by a ruddy, potbellied Ukrainian wearing white athletic socks and sandals. As we climbed the ladder, I saw he'd dismantled the landing gear and had it scattered across the tarmac like evidence at a crime scene. Inside the plane, the reporters and soldiers were pressed shoulder to shoulder. I found a seat on a stack of paint cans in the corner of the hold, and as we lifted off, the pile collapsed and doused the soldier next to me in thick, blue paint. He didn't even flinch, just clutched his rifle and watched the paint dribble down his leg and pool onto his boot. Forty-five minutes later, the pilot nose-dived into Bunia and we emerged into the white light, tears streaming down our cheeks and deaf from the noise.

Bunia was the regional capital of the Ituri district in the sprawling Oriental province, where seven thousand Ugandan soldiers were based. I'd expected Congo to be thick jungle and sucking humidity. But Bunia sat on the western rise of the Great Rift Valley, over twelve hundred meters above the forest, where the landscape was mostly grass-covered hills. The air was hot, but dry. And in the early mornings when the sun was right, the town's dust-choked boulevard looked as lonesome and lawless as in an old John Ford film.

The Ugandan soldiers were scattered throughout the hills of Ituri and, following the Drodro massacre, had moved several platoons to that village for security. The next morning their jeeps drove us the seventy kilometers north into the hills toward Drodro, a spine-shattering ride that took five hours over switchback roads that were rutted and washed from the rains. The soldiers were based at a redbrick Catholic mission tucked amid the trees, where about one hundred half-naked and hungry survivors had staggered from the bush for protection.

Inside the tiny mission clinic, the wounded were doubled up on beds and foam mattresses that lined the concrete floors. There was a woman who'd lost her leg to a machete, her eyelids fluttering like moth wings as she faded in and out from the pain, and a five-year-old boy with a necklace gash from ear to ear where the raiders had tried to take his head. The clinic had no real medicine, and inside the hot, airless chamber, the sickly-sweet smell of infection hung thick and syrupy. After half an hour my vision began to pixelate and I nearly fainted against the wall. I stumbled out into the fresh air and was sick in a nearby latrine, praying none of my colleagues had seen me run. I managed to go back and finish my interviews and came out with a decent story, one I sold to the *Chicago Tribune* for four hundred dollars—my first.

But I wasn't satisfied with just one story. One story had only lifted the lid, and down inside was this dark, forgotten war that grabbed hold and wouldn't let me go. By the time I flew back to Kenya two days later, all I could think about was going back to Congo.

★ ★ ★

In Nairobi, I tapped into AP's archives, borrowed books from friends, and began reading everything I could find. The war in Ituri between the Hema and Lendu was just another front in Congo's years-long war, a devastating conflict entirely orchestrated by outsiders. The war had initially been sparked by the 1994 genocide next door in Rwanda, when Hutu militia had massacred around eight hundred thousand ethnic Tutsi in just one hundred days. When Tutsi-led rebels finally crushed the genocide and took the capital, Kigali, tens of thousands of Hutu killers rushed over the border into the forested mountains of Congo. There they regrouped for further attacks on Rwanda.

Rwanda's new Tutsi-led government began accusing Congo's then dictator, Mobutu Sese Seko, of giving refuge to the rebels. In late 1996, Congolese rebels backed by Rwandan and Ugandan troops seized control of eastern Congo to exterminate the Hutu militia. And once they had a foothold in the east, they marched for seven months across the jungle to Kinshasa in the west and overthrew Mobutu, imposing the rebel leader Laurent Kabila as president. But once in power, Kabila alienated and ousted his Rwandan staff who'd put him in office. So in August 1998, Rwanda and Uganda invaded again with the help of neighboring Burundi, while Kabila mounted a firm defensive with troops from Zimbabwe, Namibia, Angola, Chad, and Burundian rebels.

The country eventually divided into three parts: the regions held by Kabila's government-allied forces; Rwandan-occupied areas shared with their Congolese rebel group Rally for Congolese Democracy (RCD); and the Ugandan-held territories controlled alongside their rebel groups Movement for Congolese Democracy (MLC) and an offshoot of the RCD called RCD-Kisangani. The mercurial allegiances of Rwanda, Uganda, and the government to their various rebel factions caused even greater turmoil and infighting. As a result, these groups splintered throughout the war and produced a dizzying list of acronyms like RCD-G, RCD-K/M, and RCD-N that filled several pages. But civilians were always caught in the middle no matter who was fighting, and over the next nine years, the war claimed over five million lives, most dying from sickness and hunger as they fled the fighting. The death toll from Congo's war would surpass that of any other conflict since World War II.

The armed groups fighting in Congo financed their stay largely by stealing the nation's minerals. The battlefields of eastern and central Congo were full of gold, diamonds, and other minerals such as coltan, which was in great demand to manufacture the cell phones and laptop computers for the dot-com boom of the West. The forests were lush with exotic wood, and the southern plains spilled with copper and cobalt just waiting to be dredged. By 2001, the Rwandan army was estimated to be earning nearly $20 million per month from stealing coltan, and the RCD rebels pulled in $1.5 million a month from diamonds. One rights group estimated Uganda exported over $60 million in Congolese gold in 2003 alone, most of it headed for Switzerland.

To administer their looting of gold, coltan, diamond, timber, and coffee, Uganda and Rwanda used these rebel groups as proxy forces to hold power. They trained them in jungle camps and flooded them with weapons, ultimately creating even more factions when those groups would splinter. And to hold sway over these groups, Rwanda and Uganda exploited the deep well of ethnic tensions that already existed among the tribes. In Ituri, the two foreign armies began salting the wounds between the Hema and the Lendu.

The Hema and the Lendu tribes of northeastern Ituri had lived in strained harmony near the Ugandan border for three hundred years. The Hema had crossed into Congo in the sixteenth century from Rwanda and Burundi, cattle herders who were closely related to the Tutsi of those regions, along with Hema and Banyoro tribes of Uganda. The Lendu were a mix of Nilotic and Bantu peoples, farmers and hunters, and one of the more populous tribes that mostly occupied the vast, remote hill country.

Mobutu had always favored the Hema. Like the Tutsi, they were the educated, landowning, and politically savvy elite. This favoritism had begun with Congo's Belgian colonialists, who'd rewarded Hema with large tracks of grazing land, jobs within the colonial government, and made extra efforts to educate their children—all of which alienated the Lendu, who were regarded as backward stock. During the chaotic last days of Mobutu, a wealthy Hema farmer in the Walendu Pitsu region of Ituri seized a large tract of Lendu land in a backroom deal with government officials and began evicting Lendu residents. The Lendu farmers could do little to stop him, since most of their deeds and documents had disappeared in the crumbling Mobutu empire.

So in 1999, the Lendu assembled their warriors and staged vigilante raids against Hema in the region, killing some ten thousand people in eighteen months. Hema militia then turned to the Ugandan army for help, using them as guns for hire against their enemies. Together, they slaughtered thousands of Lendu. In turn, the Ugandan army began arming the Hema militia to control the region's gold fields and other resources. When that relationship spoiled, the Ugandans backed the Lendu. Over the next several years, the number of slaughtered Hema and Lendu civilians exceeded fifty thousand—the death count spiking as warriors supplemented their spears and arrows with automatic rifles and RPG-7s supplied by their neighbors in the east. Mass killings of civilians like the massacre at Drodro, Largu, and Jissa had been happening in Ituri regularly, yet many were never investigated or even reported.

In July 2002, Rwanda and Congo signed a peace pact in Pretoria, South Africa, that ended the Rwandan army's active role in the conflict. Rwanda pulled its twenty thousand troops from Congo by October 2002, leaving Uganda as the last foreign army still operating in country. Soon after, Ugandan president Yoweri Museveni, under pressure from the international community, gave the orders for Uganda's remaining seven thousand troops to begin their slow exodus home.

The security of Ituri—still angry, factionalized, and armed to the teeth—would now be the job of UN peacekeepers, who'd soon arrive to replace the Ugandan soldiers. Peacekeepers already held positions in North and South Kivu, near the Rwandan border where the war had begun, but the UN had little presence in Ituri. Despite the grisly deaths of over fifty thousand people in the war between the Hema and the Lendu and their sponsors, the UN had only a small contingent of unarmed military observers in the vast area covering over four million people. Because the scale of Rwandan and Ugandan support of Hema and Lendu militias in Ituri was largely unknown until May 2003, many in the UN (and many of us journalists) still considered the conflict merely a "tribal war," with few links to Congo's larger multinational war.

The Ugandan army threw a big parade on April 25, 2003, as they began rolling out of Ituri. All across Bunia, shops closed early, and hundreds of sweaty bodies jammed both sides of the airport road to watch the soldiers march past. A thirty-piece army brass band stumbled through a lethargic rendition of the Ugandan national anthem, followed by a procession of armored personnel carriers, gun-mounted jeeps called "Mambas," and two rattletrap Russian tanks piled with dozens of gaunt, whooping soldiers. The traffic made the dust unbearable, and when the tanks sputtered past, they coated the reeling crowd with an aerosol of hot engine grease.

As several companies of soldiers took up the rear of the parade—weathered Kalashnikovs dangling at their hip, gum boots slapping the yellow dirt—young girls rushed out and loaded them with cigarettes, boiled eggs, and bags of peanuts. Farther up the road, groups of women spit at their feet and shouted for them to just go away. The parade was a colossal event, never mind the size, for it marked the ending of a brutal period of foreign occupation and, much to our collective fear, also kicked off a brand-new era of viciousness and murder.

Anticipating the Ugandan withdrawal, hundreds of fighters, both Hema and Lendu, were gathering in the hills outside Bunia, waiting for the perfect moment to seize the prize. Bunia was already an embattled spoil of war, occupied by several rebel factions over the years who'd vigorously fought to hold it. It was a nexus of trade routes in and out of Uganda, both overland and across Lake Albert, thirty kilometers to the east. Bunia essentially connected the Oriental province to East Africa and Asia, and Lake Albert itself provided a flourishing fish trade. Bunia had a functioning airport, a sprawling and healthy market, and most of all, the hills around Bunia were filled with gold.

Many of the once-nationalized gold mines in the hills north of Bunia, located near the towns of Mongbwalu and Kilo, were seized by Uganda or Rwandan-backed militia when the second war began in 1998, with miners forced to dig for the militia or to pay entry fees in gold or taxes. Alluvial gold is also bountiful in the streambeds of the Shari River on Bunia's outskirts, which provide many local men their living. The tumbledown wooden shacks of gold dealers lined Bunia's main boulevard. Prospectors in mud-crusted clothes filed in with gold dust and nuggets wrapped in cigarette foil and walked out with wads of American dollars. Controlling Bunia went hand in hand with controlling the gold, and whoever controlled the gold carried the better guns.

The Hema militia had taken Bunia in August 2002 and quickly moved to seize Mongbwalu. Earlier that summer, Lendu combatants had killed scores of Hema in the gold-mining town, so the Hema were bent on revenge. They attacked in November, murdering more than two hundred Lendu and ethnic Nande civilians, who they gunned down in the streets or brutally executed by smashing people's heads with hammers and slicing their throats, then burning the bodies.

The Hema militia was led by Thomas Lubanga, a beanpole of a commander, who towered over his militia army, many of them child soldiers whom he'd recruited from villages decimated by Lendu raids. He was charismatic and loved publicity; he would throw marathon press conferences when reporters were in the area, ending his diatribes against his current enemies by dancing atop the tables. (Two years later, he would also be the first war criminal arrested to stand trial in the International Criminal Court in The Hague, charged with conscripting and using child soldiers.)

Uganda's relationship with Lubanga's militia had spoiled in mid-2002, and in March 2003, army commanders had used Lendu fighters to help expel the Hema from Bunia. The Lendu militia itself consisted of two subgroups—one from the north of Bunia, the other from the south. Uganda's relationship with the southern faction—known as the Ngiti—subsequently failed, and the Ugandans had begun trying to push them out in turn.

The Drodro massacre made a puff in the newspapers, but was dead gone the next day. And the UN started saying the death toll was largely exaggerated, even though it hadn't conducted a real investigation. But in reality, the April 3 attacks had been so efficient and macabre that humanitarian workers in Congo were afraid the conflict was spiraling into another Rwanda. I convinced an editor to send me back to chronicle the killings and join a UN forensic team scheduled to uncover the mass graves. I arrived back in Bunia as the Ugandans were pulling out and started trying to arrange rides into Drodro. But once there, it became clear another massacre was unfolding right there in town.

The last Ugandan soldiers were scheduled to leave Bunia on

May 6, two weeks away. When they did, it was almost certain the Lendu Ngiti militia would sweep right in to fill the vacuum. By the time I arrived in Bunia, they were hitting the Ugandans every day, slowly closing in on the town. Bunia's population of Hema took on the mien of the hunted. Everyone feared the raid, it seemed, but the UN.

II

After a few days in Bunia, I quickly fell into the rhythms of the town. I buzzed up and down the broad boulevard on the back of motorcycle taxis and hired a steady driver named Oliver. The 350,000 residents of Bunia were mostly traders and merchants who operated out of the white-stone colonial shops that lined Lumumba Boulevard, the main commercial strip, selling everything from motorbikes imported from China, to radios, jumper cables, and the ubiquitous Blue Band margarine found in every corner of Africa. Along the narrow paths of the town market, plump women sat behind tall mounds of brightly colored beans, manioc root, and spinach, and stacks of salted fish that smelled so strong it stung your throat in the heat. All down the boulevard, little boys walked the road hawking fried chapatis, and women glided in tight lines down the grassy median, balancing bundles of laundry atop their heads and bowls spilling with bananas. Old men rested their tired bones in the awning shade with radios pressed against their ears; chickens scratched in the dirt; moto-taxi drivers waited at the junctions in sunshades and open shirts; and the stoic money changers sat at their stands hovered over cubes of grimy francs.

The Mobutu government had neglected Bunia for decades, leaving the stately colonial buildings along the boulevard to crumble and fade. And numerous battles between armies and militia had left the boulevard scarred with gun pocks and blast wounds. The post office had been locked for three years, and the bank for ten. The water ran cold and brown from the pipes, and electricity was a precious luxury. The roads leading to town were full of sinkholes that reached up to snap the axles of trucks and flatten tires. Gasoline was sold by little boys with jerricans and tin funnels, while down the road, pumps at abandoned filling stations were rusted and stripped for parts. The remnants of better days still whispered in mocking tones: one building along the boulevard bore a faded advertisement from a colonial-era insurance company. OWN YOUR LIFE, the sign suggested.

Just as I arrived, the first cellular tower was being erected, and in the coming days residents would line up at the new office of Celtel for phones and prepay cards that would change how they did business and bring the rest of the massive country much closer. Across the street was the new MONUC headquarters (the French acronym for the UN's Congo mission), where painters were trimming the windows in UN signature blue, a color so mixed up with Congo's blood it would later pinstripe the new national flag.

I had checked into the Hotel Takabeya, just on the edge of the market, where the women wore brassy blonde wigs to serve greasy omelets and tea at six thirty in the morning. During the day I'd stop by the UN to check about rides into Drodro, maybe do some interviews, then have dinner at the Club Hellenique, the only decent bar and restaurant in town, located next door to UN headquarters. At night, it was cold beers on the patio of my room listening to BBC and Voice of America on my shortwave radio.

I'd needed an interpreter for interviews, so the day I arrived at the airport, I'd walked around asking everyone, "Know where I can find a translator?" Only one person had answered in English and said he'd send someone over. It was a dumb rookie move, especially since I didn't know anyone or their delicate tribal affiliations, but it paid off. The next morning I walked out of the dining room at the Takabeya and found Johnny Ngure waiting for me in the courtyard.

Johnny was short and thin with a wispy, boyish mustache and base-ball cap pulled low over his eyes. He was a student at the local teacher-training school and his English was good. I hired him on the spot.

Johnny told me how his father had been murdered by Lendu fighters a year before, shot in the back as he tried to run during a raid north of town. His body lay in the street for three days while Johnny hid in the bush. Johnny had buried him alone in a hand-dug grave. The only story about his father that he seemed to enjoy telling was how he gave Johnny his name. "After Johnnie Walker the whiskey," he said. "I was always walking and running away."

Johnny lived in a dim, mildew-infested dormitory just behind the UN headquarters. His mother had died of illness years before, and after his father was killed, Johnny paid his tuition and rent by pushing wheelbarrows of dried fish from Lake Albert to Bunia, a two-day haul through the mountains.

"I hope that you will be happy with my job," he said that day. "It's important to me. My father was a journalist, too."

I spent my mornings that week having tea with Brigadier General Kale Kayihura, commander of the Ugandan army in Congo. We'd sit under the shade of the small concrete terminal at the airport, from which his men were gradually departing.

What troubled the general most was how the UN was preparing for his withdrawal. The first of 350 Uruguayan peacekeepers had begun trickling in that week, and MONUC was hoping the small force could contain the war slowly creeping toward town. To maintain their international force, the UN was flying in tons of cargo every day, erecting a giant prefab city of good intentions that would soon dwarf the town it'd come to help, a blue-and-white Potemkin village shuttled about in white Toyota SUVs that filled the streets and every parking lot.

The people of Bunia didn't realize it, but the UN had no

intentions of saving them in the event of an attack. The Security Council's mandate for MONUC only allowed soldiers to protect UN staff and property. The mandate worked swell for those areas of the country where fighting had ceased. But in Ituri, the blue flag of the UN only cast a shadow, and not a long one at that.

It was an ugly paradox the Security Council refused to swallow. Everyone agreed the Ugandans desperately needed to leave, but in the same breath they'd acknowledge the troops were preventing further massacres (or helping stage them, depending on whom you asked). The Ugandans were dirty cops, but they were the only law the people had. And during those mornings over tea, the general assured me, over my astonishment, that history would regard the Ugandans as heroes once MONUC dropped the ball and Bunia was awash in blood.

"Does the Security Council think about the security in this region?" he said to me one day. "Their politics seem to be prevailing over human life."

He'd often conclude these rants by squeezing my shoulder and with a long, exhausted look saying, "I'm so glad you're here as a witness."

I mainly spoke with the general because he wasn't afraid of journalists, unlike the UN staff, who seemed to deflect my every approach. The general was good with questions, even if answers were never part of the deal.

"General, some people say your officers are stealing gold."

"*Stealing gold*. Nonsense. You've been here. Have you seen us stealing gold?"

"Personally, no, but—"

"What's with you Americans and Europeans?" He reached out and grabbed my wrist. "I've never understood why you people are so thin in the arms."

On my second day in Bunia, a Friday, the first Lendu warriors appeared on the streets. In an attempt to pacify Bunia before the

Ugandan withdrawal, MONUC had set up talks in town and invited both Lendu and Hema leaders: intellectual types who referred to themselves as "general secretary," along with militia leaders—roguish gangsters who decorated themselves with phony military credentials and carried ivory-tipped staffs. The militia leaders had also brought in dozens of "bodyguards" from the bush, while dozens more combatants had poured into Bunia to join the national army, part of a power-sharing deal recently brokered between the government and the rebels the previous year. But the government disarmament camp wasn't up and running, and none of the boys were asked by MONUC to surrender their weapons. By the end of the week, four different groups patrolled the streets with guns. Thus the fall of Bunia began from within.

I first saw them walking down Lumumba Boulevard with a sickening swagger, drinking beer outside the gates of the Hotel Musafira, and getting stoned in the shade. The Lendu boys carried taped-up Kalashnikovs hiked across their shoulders and slid their fingers across their throats as they passed young Hema girls. Some wore ill-fitting uniforms stripped from dead Ugandan soldiers, while a few younger boys dressed in sequined ball gowns that dragged in the dirt, clear-plastic fright masks and punked-out yellow wigs. Around their biceps were strips of leopard skin and animal teeth tied with vine, and amulets full of strange milky liquid dangled from their bandoliers.

The boys believed the trinkets and dresses protected them from bullets during battle, a belief they seemed eager to test again. The dresses and wigs conjured a magic ruse, a second identity, that confused their enemies and shielded them from harm. Cross-dressing in Ituri wasn't as widespread as in other African wars; later that year in Liberia, stoned gunboys in drag would pack the front lines as government forces battled encroaching rebels. The battle armor was also intended to frighten and intimidate, and that first time I caught eyes with them on the streets of Bunia, I quickly looked away. Those weren't the eyes of boys, not anymore.

Little by little, the gunboys took a piece of Bunia each time the sun went down. For three straight mornings after they appeared, a different moto-taxi driver was found dead, shot or hacked up in a ditch on the outskirts of town. At the same time, I began getting regular visits at my hotel from Jean-Pierre, a boxy troll of a man who claimed to be a local journalist. He'd wear the same black suit and blue, button-down shirt and carried a leather briefcase full of photos of dead bodies. Most were massacre victims from the villages, people emptied of all their organs lying in wooden coffins; people missing heads, arms, testicles, and strips of flesh from their buttocks. He charged twenty dollars for each photo, which he sold to passing journalists, though I never knew anyone who'd actually bought one. One morning I was interested in a shot of a guy sprawled in the road, his pond-water eyes staring blankly at the clouds. There was a gaping, sinewy gash in his neck from a machete blade.

"That is the taxi driver killed this morning," Jean-Pierre said. "Thirty dollars American."

"Thirty? Why thirty?"

"*Monsieur*, he is still lying in the road."

The morning the first taxi driver was killed, Oliver didn't show up at my hotel with his bike. I didn't hear from him all day and soon began to worry. Two days passed and I became scared that Oliver would appear in one of the photos in Jean-Pierre's briefcase. Late that afternoon, Johnny came by and said he'd just seen Oliver by the roundabout.

"So when is he coming?" I said.

"Oliver said he won't be driving you anymore," Johnny said. "He's afraid the Lendu will kill him if he's seen driving a white man, a journalist."

By Tuesday the following week, the taxi drivers would stop working altogether, partly out of protest against their colleagues being killed, but mainly out of fear. Few cars were in Bunia at the time, so without the motorcycles, the streets grew quiet and sinister. Many people took this as a sign and just stayed home.

During my first days in Bunia, I also began hearing rumors about other massacres out in the villages, or in the bush just outside of town. Since it was unwise to travel outside Bunia, I often relied on two UN press officers, Leo and Christophe, to confirm or deny these reports. On Friday, I heard about a Lendu attack on the town of Kasenyi, on the shores of Lake Albert, where many people were reportedly killed. I found Leo in the Hellenique eating lunch.

"Oh, yes, big massacre," Leo said, never turning from his spaghetti. When I pressed him further, he looked up, annoyed, and said, "I don't know, call Kinshasa," referring to UN headquarters in the capital about eighteen hundred kilometers to the west.

But most frightening were the increasing reports by residents of massive numbers of Lendu and Hema militia congregating on the edge of town, preparing for a fight. It was impossible to know when or how this would happen, how many warriors there were, or if it was even true. And asking the UN only confused me more.

"Yes, yes, things are tense," Leo would say.

"Don't worry," said Christophe. "Things are fine."

On Saturday I found the general pacing the airport runway as heavy guns echoed from the northern hills, near Rwampara. "We pulled our men out of there as the UN instructed," he said. "Now these Lendu are shooting civilians." He walked out past the tarmac into the high elephant grass. "You hear that? They're using a fifty-caliber." He ordered two gun-mounted Mambas toward the shooting, and a few minutes later the hills rumbled with mortar blasts and antiaircraft guns as the soldiers made contact.

The day before, he said, one of his soldiers had been shot through the chest while guarding a bridge north of town. "They stole his uniform. And then, those Lendu cut out his tongue!" A voice crackled over the radio saying the Lendu had been pushed from Rwampara. "Did I tell you that we found the head of one of our soldiers?" he continued. "It was lying in the bush. The rest of him had been eaten. I tell you, these Lendu are like animals. They have no remorse!"

Just about then, a cargo plane touched down full of more Uruguayan peacekeepers. They stepped out into the white sun and adjusted their eyes to the blinding light. Each wore a blue flak jacket and clunky helmet. "The UN is sending these people into a trap," the general said. "What business do these men have dying here?"

Later that same day, a UN military observer was killed in Komanda, a little village sixty kilometers southwest of Bunia, when his vehicle ran over a land mine in the road. Another observer traveling with him had his legs blown off.

The unarmed military observers had been the first UN presence in Congo back in 2000, sent in to monitor the cease-fire between warring factions. Like the UN's mandate, they were effective in places where war had ended, but in Ituri, their deployments were often like tossing meat to a cellar of dogs.

I met one observer that week in the Hellenique, a Uruguayan named Juan, who'd recently returned from a long mission in the northern hills. He explained how he'd been dropped with three other soldiers deep in the bush with just their packs and radios. They were given crude maps and little intelligence, and none spoke any of the local languages. They were instructed to find the local chief and ask permission to set up a small command post. If the chief refused, he said, they were to inform him the UN was already sending the rest of their gear in choppers. "And if we were attacked," Juan said, "they told us, 'Just use your radios.'"

The following month, two more observers—Major Safwat Oran from Jordan and Captain Siddon Davis Banda from

Malawi—would be gunned down by Lendu fighters near the gold mines of Mongbwalu. I'd later watch peacekeepers load their black body bags onto planes in Bunia and ship them home. One had been shot in the head, the other in the stomach; the UN had recovered their remains a week after villagers buried them.

As I sat there that night drinking with Juan, I looked down and noticed his hands vibrating against the bar. He told me, "Out on observation, I imagined my own death, and it was more clear than in a dream." He was putting back beers in rapid succession. "Each night I went to bed, I watched it play over again in my mind. Every night I died."

On Saturday night, heavy shooting began on the edge of town. It woke me up at two A.M., sustained burps of machine-gun fire, followed by a series of single rounds. The gunfire came every night afterward; one evening, I lay wide-awake for hours following single shots that popped fifteen minutes apart and, each time, inched a little closer to my window.

On Sunday, Johnny and I were taking a motorbike into Mudzipela, a Hema neighborhood just north of my hotel, where Johnny's father had been killed. He wanted to show me the grave. But on the way there, a group of boys stopped us in the road. "Please, don't travel any farther," one said. "The Lendu are killing people in the streets." A couple of rifle rounds echoed through the trees, but nothing more. Back at the UN base, no one knew anything about it, and I was too afraid to return and check myself.

Steadily, paranoia began working its way into everyone. One night I sat at the Hellenique with two South Africans who claimed to be UN intelligence officers sent to monitor the Ugandan withdrawal. Unlike most other UN military staff, though, they didn't wear uniforms or badges and were always vague about their "mission." They didn't have a vehicle, nor did they stay in rented homes or nicer motels like other UN staff. They stayed at the Takabeya, next door to me, endured the cold bucket baths and blackouts, and frequently invited the brassy, wig-wearing women into their rooms. I liked them a lot.

The three of us sat on sofas in a dark corner of the restaurant, sharing a large bottle of Primus beer. The radio behind the bar crackled with old soukous love ballads, and the lights flickered from Bunia's shaky current. A few tables were filled with the UN's mostly Euro staff in their jeans and T-shirts, barking orders in French to Jean, the long-faced waiter, to bring their brochettes and plates of toasted cheese. The intelligence officers began talking about "the Conflict" in whispers, and I marveled at the things coming out of their mouths. That morning, I'd heard a woman working in the fields had been hacked in the head by a gang of Lendu. When I said the word *Lendu*, one of the officers threw a finger in front of his lips and told me to quiet down.

"Please," he said, and motioned to a table of Congolese, all non-English speakers. "We only use the terms *the H* and *the L* when discussing the Conflict."

He surveyed the bar, then leaned in and whispered, "You never know who is listening. For instance, be careful around Jean the waiter. We're still not sure if he belongs to the H or the L."

Soon it became too dangerous to leave even the main boulevard at night. Hit-and-run gangs of Lendu and Hema teenagers were kicking down doors in the outer neighborhoods, looting homes, raping women, and killing. The UN had banished the remaining Ugandan soldiers from patrolling Bunia's streets and would often be called out to intervene during these violent attacks. One morning after a night of heavy shooting, two UN employees stood outside the Hellenique smoking cigarettes. One said he had been awakened that morning by a little girl pounding on his door.

"She said the Lendu were in her house and were about to kill her parents," the guy said. "What the fuck am I supposed to do? I called security to go check it out."

"We're not here to protect civilians," his friend snapped. "You can't save the world, mate. As far as I'm concerned, let the bastards kill each other."

The other guy looked up and said, "Then what are we doing here?"

Each night the gunfire grew heavier and louder, and residents said they were the shots of execution squads. At first I tried drinking myself to sleep, but it only made matters worse. After a while, I made a habit of packing my bag before going to bed in case I had to run out in a hurry. At the end of my second week in town, I'd started switching hotels every few days and not telling anyone where I was staying: one night at the Takabeya, a couple nights at a guesthouse behind MONUC, and finally I settled in a hotel near the airport called the CAPA. It was the safest hotel in town, Leo told me, because several MONUC officers also stayed there. Therefore, chances of being evacuated in the event of an attack were good.

Then one evening over many beers, one of the South African intelligence officers' local "contacts" said he had information I should hear, something about my translator. "I know this person Johnny," he said. "Johnny works for the Hema. Your friend is a rebel."

Deep down, I didn't believe a word of it, but the idea still nagged me. Johnny was an Alur, a neutral majority tribe, though they sometimes got grouped with the Hema when the Lendu were cutting the cards. Over a Coke at the Hellenique the following day, I grilled him about his allegiances.

"Johnny, this guy says you're a rebel," I said. "I know that's a stupid word, but tell me the truth. It's my safety here."

I watched his body deflate like a balloon as he stared down at his lap. *"Please, no . . . ,"* he said. It was all he had to say. I'd hurt his feelings, and it was then I realized how deeply the fear had soured my own judgment.

Paranoia ruled, it engineered our thoughts and actions, guided our conversations, poked us out of bed in the morning and tucked us in at night. Contingency plans, evacuation rosters ("Who's on the UN's evacuation list? Hey, journalist guy, have you seen the evacuation list? Was my name on it?"), and half-baked theories on when and where the enemy would finally strike—this was the repartee of frightened military men, hardened souls whose nightmares were cast with African boys in prom dresses carving them up in their beds.

During these weeks, there was a theory the UN officers in Bunia followed like gospel: that the gunboys, full of beer and howling for blood, never attacked before eleven in the morning, on weekends, or when it rained. This theory had held true so far, and it certainly eased my mind as I sat in the Internet café on Lumumba Boulevard. *Three for three,* I thought. *In the clear.* It was morning, a Saturday, and the sky was the color of lead and threatening rain.

Over the past ten days in Bunia, my e-mails to friends had grown cryptic and detached, mostly uncensored descriptions of what was taking place. "Twelve shots last night, closer to my hotel than before . . . man found hanging from tree this morning, woman hacked up in a ditch . . . Just another day in Paradise. Funny, huh?"

I was sending my mother a standard "I'm safe, gotta go" note when the manager of the café walked over to my computer, flipped the power, and shouted, "Go now, we're closed!" I got pissed off and reached to turn the machine back on, but saw that I was all alone and stopped. The other customers were in the next room by the tall windows, peeking out at the boulevard, which had suddenly filled with Lendu warriors.

There were hundreds of them, more than I'd ever seen. They carried beat-up Kalashnikovs and rocket-propelled grenades, long spears, and sharpened machetes. One boy had on a 2Pac T-shirt and a different sneaker on each foot. Others wore wigs and were shirtless and wrapped in bullets. Most were barefoot and their toes were dusted in the boulevard's yellow dirt. Their eyes were narrow and catlike from the joints that bounced in their lips as they marched past.

An older man standing next to me looked terrified. From his expression, I guessed he was Hema. He cocked his head to hear the Swahili words the boys chanted in the streets, then turned to me. "They're saying it's time to pay."

After the last fighter passed the window, I ran outside with a few others. We stood together at the edge of the empty boulevard and saw more boys tearing toward us. Someone said they were Hema soldiers coming to fight the Lendu. As they approached, the air around me filled with gunfire. I turned to run as three bullets smacked into the building behind me, kicking out puffs of dust and concrete. I tried to hit the ground, but something propelled my legs forward.

People came running down the street as gunshots popped at their backs. They wore crazy electric smiles on their faces, the same gimme-danger grins worn by people who run from bulls. I was headed back inside the café when a Congolese woman in a yellow dress grabbed my hand and said, "You better hide. It's not safe for you here," and led me to a house off the road.

We ducked into a ground-level apartment just behind the café and she closed the door. The living room was dark, with thin shoots of sunlight cascading through the curtains of a nearby window. Several other women sat on sofas and foldout chairs, whispering soothing words to a few children at their feet. The women were immaculately dressed in bright floral skirts and smelled of strong perfume. Their breezy French mixed with the rolling gunfire and was punctuated by cackling laughter and elaborate hand gestures.

"This happens all the time," said the woman in the yellow dress, in English. She noticed my leg trembling, gave a small laugh, and said, "Are you afraid?" Then she stood up, smoothed the wrinkles in her dress, and disappeared into the kitchen to make tea.

I sat there for twenty minutes while thoughts formed in my head and quickly blew apart, until there was nothing but gunfire and brief lapses into silence. At my feet, two children played like kittens on the floor. Even as the fighting grew more intense and rumbled like a train in the bathroom, they never made a sound.

The front door then suddenly swung open, sucking every bit of wind from my lungs. But when I saw who was there, I jumped from the sofa and nearly kissed him on the mouth. It was Johnny, sent straight down on heaven's rope from the warm kitchens of my mother and grandmother. I'd given him the morning off and now he was standing in the doorway, winded and smiling.

"I have a motorbike," he said. "Let's go."

We waited while the shooting moved down the street, then ran to the back of the house where Johnny'd stashed a Honda he'd borrowed from a striking taxi driver. I got on the back and Johnny kicked the engine.

"Johnny, how'd you know I was there?"

"I just asked someone."

We lit off down a back road, through leafy tea fields, and within seconds we'd moved beyond the shooting. Once we were safe, the panic and fear released their grip and I began to laugh so hard I nearly fell off the bike.

So that's what it's like, I thought. I knew I should be more afraid, but for some reason I felt a calm so sharp it spooked me. It certainly wasn't from bravery, but whatever it was, it left me with the clearest tunnel vision I'd ever experienced. It could've been a lot worse (weeks later, Rodrique Ngowi would be pinned down on the same street as .50-caliber rounds passed inches from his head). I knew that I'd been kissed with luck, saved by a rainy-day reserve of prayer and a woman I'd never met. But as we drove back to my hotel, the thing that kept running through my mind was *Yes, yes. That's it exactly.*

I'd made friends the week before with a Swiss doctor from the aid group Médecins Sans Frontières (MSF—or Doctors Without Borders) who'd recently arrived at the Bunia hospital to operate on the war wounded. When I arrived at the hotel that night, I found the doctor sitting at a table on the front lawn, badly shaken. He'd had a tough week. On his second day in town, he'd announced on the radio that there were fifty empty beds, and those wounded outside town should make an effort to get treated. One of his first patients was a teenage girl who'd been shot in the leg and waited ten days to come to the clinic because the roads weren't safe to travel. Her entire leg had turned black and crawled with caterpillars. "Who knows how many more are still out there?" he'd told me. "When they learn about the beds, you can expect a line out the door." The hospital was terribly understaffed, and on the day of the gunfight, I'd actually made plans to assist him while he performed amputations, which had become common procedures.

He'd been at the hospital performing surgery that afternoon when the battle along the boulevard shifted right in front of his door. The local staff had bolted immediately and left him alone with fifty patients. For three hours he crawled on the floor and radioed the UN for help as mortar rounds and grenades shook the foundation, but none arrived. The Ugandans had finally swung by and carried him out. He now sat in the courtyard, his breathing still labored from the stress. The hotel had no beer because the market was destroyed, so I went into my bags and brought out a pint of whiskey I was saving for a rainy day. I gave it to the doctor.

"What's stopping these militia from coming into my hospital and killing everyone?" he said, draining a full glass with one gulp.

The year before, in nearby Nyakunde, Lendu warriors had entered the large village hospital, searched for Hema patients, then butchered them in their beds. The slaughter continued for ten days until twelve hundred people were dead.

"I promised my wife I'd be safe. We just bought a house." He poured another drink and turned it over, then buried his face in his hands and whispered, "Shit, shit, shit." Two days later they pulled him out.

In the wake of the gunfight, more people began to leave. Most of the Hema who could afford a ticket rushed to the airport and tried to board flights to Beni, Goma, or Kinshasa, anywhere but Bunia. They waited patiently for hours in the sweltering lobby dressed in their best clothes—the women in their colorful *pagne* wraps, clutching little boys in suits that swallowed their shoulders. Once a plane landed, any plane, they rushed the runway, dragging children and suitcases and cardboard boxes bound in tape. One afternoon a group of them mobbed a cargo plane headed for Kinshasa. About six people managed to grab hold of the open doorway as a stocky Ukrainian pulled the ladder and the plane taxied toward the runway. The crewman scrambled to push them off with his feet, kicking several men to the pavement. A woman carrying a baby was pummeled in the face, but managed to squeeze through his arms and steal aboard.

The people who couldn't afford flights still flocked to the airport, which quickly became a massive camp of the displaced as the Ugandans prepared to leave town. People jammed the airport road and massed around the one-story terminal, and from a distance it appeared the airport itself was ablaze from all their cooking fires. Many came from surrounding villages and carried what they could manage: a few pots, some clothes, jugs of water. Several thousand were choosing to march four days to the border with the army, rather than stay behind and risk the odds. In the end, tens of thousands streamed into western Uganda. But while they waited at the airport, most of them ran out of food and water, and sanitation was spiraling into an emergency.

In the early afternoon of May 5, the day before the Ugandans left, a rowdy gang of children assembled by the loading ramp. In the center was a young Ugandan soldier clutching a box of rations he was trying to distribute. As he handed out the first few, the children rushed him and ripped the box from his hands, sending the shiny tins of canned beef rolling across the dirt. The mob seized the scattered loot, then hurried back to their camps with their prizes.

Just then a UN cargo plane thundered onto the runway and taxied toward the ramp. As it swung around, its exhaust jets kicked up a stinging dust storm that sent the children and the soldiers running for cover. A crew of workers rushed over to the plane's rear cargo hatch, but the only thing to unload were a few steel rods. Easy trip. Then the engines fired again and the empty plane took off as quickly as it landed. And with the returning quiet, the gang of children returned for more rations. The soldiers were now giving away their beans.

As Bunia descended into chaos, the UN forensics team finally arrived to investigate the April 3 massacre. The team was made up of two independent Argentine forensic anthropologists who'd unearthed mass graves everywhere from South America to Bosnia. Today they'd travel to the hills of Ituri. Along with seven Uruguayan peacekeepers and a dozen UN staff, we boarded the white UN chopper and traveled thirty minutes over the electric green until we arrived at the redbrick Catholic mission at Drodro. Because of the volatile security in the area, the UN instructed the pilot to drop and leave—don't even stop the engines.

Several hundred people now packed the sandy courtyard of the church, and hundreds more were sleeping in the bush. It was damp and cold, too wet for fires. Our delegation was greeted by a silent mob of children with bloated stomachs, hacking and wheezing from chest infections, sick from the weather and severe diarrhea. The situation had only gotten worse since I'd last been there. One of the priests said there'd been attacks in the surrounding settlements every day since the massacre, despite the unit of Ugandan soldiers stationed there to protect them. He opened a ledger that contained a list of people killed in the past three weeks. I counted forty-seven names. "When the Ugandans leave here," the priest said, "the population is going to disappear. Today they're here, tomorrow they're gone."

In Largu, a few kilometers up the road, the forensics team zeroed in on a grave at the base of a small cliff, surrounded by manioc and banana trees. The wooden cross staked at the head of the grave indicated twenty-six bodies buried underneath. Five local men grabbed shovels and hoes and began digging into the heavy red dirt, while the village chief and a flock of residents stood behind a cordon of white tape and watched in silence. I stood near the edge of the hole, pressing a bandanna soaked in whiskey against my face; the UN had warned the smell of decay would be overwhelming. After an hour of digging, the workers reached a thin layer of banana leaves in the soil. Just beneath lay the body of a woman who'd been hacked with a machete through the skull. In the hook of her arms was the decomposing corpse of an infant.

The forensics team snapped a few photos, and as a steady afternoon rain began to fall, the grave was filled with dirt and our group returned to Drodro to meet the chopper. No exhumation, no examination. According to the UN, they just wanted to confirm dead people were really in the grave.

In Drodro, the village chief called a meeting with the UN officials. "How can you spend so much time and resources examining our dead, while doing nothing to protect the living?" he asked. He explained that once the Ugandans left, everyone would be slaughtered. Was it possible, he asked, to get a small unit of peacekeepers to protect the village when the Ugandans withdrew? The UN told him to write a formal request and take it to Bunia, and later, Kinshasa would be notified of his concerns. "But the rains have washed out the roads," he answered. "Can I have a lift in your chopper?" The UN told him no, but agreed to deliver the request. Before any further discussions could be had, a Uruguayan captain rushed in and demanded we evacuate immediately. Seventy Lendu warriors had just entered Largu, where we'd been only minutes before. Gunshots pattered in the distance. "They're coming to attack us!" the captain said. Seconds later the chopper touched down and we clambered aboard. Then it whisked us away, up and over the hundreds of faces still looking to the sky when they finally disappeared.

On May 6, the day Uganda pulled its last soldiers out of Congo, I arrived at the airport at dawn, determined to get a seat aboard the general's plane back to Entebbe. I didn't like leaving so soon, but I simply didn't trust MONUC to protect me. The night before, the UN had ordered all their officers to vacate their rooms at the CAPA and move to the main headquarters. I'd spent the evening mostly alone in the hotel, then lay there all night fully clothed waiting for the raid. I didn't know if I could handle another night like that.

As I arrived at the airport that morning on the back of Johnny's motorcycle, I wondered what would happen to the people I'd met, the hotel staff, the boy who sold me cigarettes on the street. Most of all, I worried about Johnny. Before we parted at the airport, I gave him a few packs of smokes, my French-English dictionary, a wad of cash, and a firm lecture on staying safe. "I'll be fine here," he said. "I have to stay for my school. And besides, where else can I go?" I gave Johnny a hug and watched him disappear into the crowds, kicking myself for not buying him a cell phone when I had the chance so I could keep in touch.

Just then, someone tapped me on my shoulder. "Hey!" a voice said. "Are you an American?"

I turned around to find a tall man holding a backpack and camera, looking somewhat overwhelmed. Samson Mulugeta was an Ethiopian-born American reporter based in Johannesburg. He'd just stepped off a Ugandan cargo plane from Entebbe, and now he was here. "I'm from *Newsday*," he said, half-yelling over the engine noise. "Hey, are you Mealer? I read your AP story about the gun battle. I'm here to cover the Hema-Lendu thing."

I could hardly make out what he was saying over the roar of machinery; for a minute I just stared at him, convinced he was some kind of hallucination.

"You're here . . . *what*?"

"*The tribal war.* The UN told me a forensics team was coming. When's the forensics team coming?"

"Man, they're gone. That was five days ago."

"They're *what* . . . ?"

"Man, I'm *leaving*, I'm getting out of here. It's not safe here."

"It's *what* . . . ?"

"You need to leave with me, *now*!"

I tried to convince the guy, told him everything I could, even made it sound a whole lot worse than it was. But he wouldn't listen. He'd come a long way already, and with everything I was telling him, he probably smelled a good story. I didn't blame him. The least I could do was try to help. I gave him the telephone number of one of Johnny's friends, who Johnny had told me would be able to get in touch with him, then told him about the Hotel CAPA. "It's the closest hotel to the airport," I said. "You might be safe there." Then I watched him disappear as well.

The general was sitting in the shade nearby, watching his men load the last remaining gear into trucks and a few idle planes waiting on the runway. His face was pinched and exhausted. He'd come down with malaria the night before. "More reason for me to get out of this place!" he said. He stood up and paced awhile, then sat back down. "I just got a call saying these Lendu are on their way. What am I supposed to do? I wash my hands of this place. Let MONUC figure it out."

When the last soldier was ready to leave, we boarded a small twin-engine plane and the general sat alone. As the plane circled up and over Bunia, I looked down and saw the group of Lendu, like a column of ants, marching toward the town.

III

Two hours later, a band of Lendu fighters raided the Catholic mission in Mudzipela and murdered ten people in their rooms. One of them, a priest named Raphael Ngona, was a contact of mine, who'd survived the Drodro massacre only weeks before. Bunia then fell with ease. The Lendu had it by the throat the next afternoon, and by evening it was carrion.

For the next several days the Lendu went house to house looking for Hema. They painted their stomachs and faces coal black and kicked down doors. They pulled families from their beds, from behind furniture, out of closets, then dragged them to the streets and shot them through the head. "Come out if you are Hema!" they screamed as they swept through bedrooms and over back fences. "The Lendu have come!"

One woman who managed to hide witnessed several warriors enter her neighbor's home and drag an old woman to the backyard. The boys lived down the road and everyone knew them well. "Spare me, I've done nothing wrong to you," pleaded the woman. The boys were drunk and informed her she belonged to the wrong tribe, then hacked off her hands and feet. Finally they killed the woman and cut her body into small pieces, which they scattered in the road outside her home. When they were finished, they went inside the woman's kitchen and washed their hands of her blood.

Others saw friends beheaded by young boys amped on liquor,

and one watched a lone warrior crouched in the road, feasting on the open organs of a man he'd just killed. Another looked out from her window as militia apprehended nine people on the streets, including three women holding babies. Militia stripped the children from their mothers' arms, cut the kids' throats, and smashed their heads in the dirt. Then they shot the adults. Around the same time, militia attacked Bunia's Nyakasunza parish, slaughtering two more priests and twenty civilians who'd fled there for refuge.

When the killing was done, the painted gunboys howled and sang as they paraded down the empty boulevard waving the severed hands of their dead. They wore the ears of their victims strung around their necks, and some festooned their bandoliers with kidneys and bladders.

Then, on May 12, the Hema militia broke through the Lendu defenses and pushed them out of town. Over the preceding five days the Hema had vigorously fought from their base north of town and had been hammered back each time. Hundreds of civilians had been killed in their cross fire, but their final assault had proved victorious. But soon as the Hema militia won control of Bunia, they simply looted what was left and began raping and killing Lendu civilians.

The entire week I sat at home in Nairobi and stared at the radio, waiting for some kind of news. Over and over I called the mobile phone of Johnny's friend and tried repeatedly to get through to the number Samson, the reporter, had left me. Nothing. I called the Hotel CAPA, but could never decipher what was happening on the other end. People I didn't know kept answering the phone and hanging up, and at times I heard gunfire like popcorn in the background. A BBC reporter got through to one of the UN press officers at headquarters, who said they were under attack and living on the floor. Finally I saw a *Newsday* story describing a similar scene inside the UN compound and knew that Samson was safe. But the story told me nothing about Johnny.

★ ★ ★

The first real lull in the fighting came on May 15, and it was then I found myself on a flight with American missionaries headed back into Bunia. Ten minutes before landing, our copilot, Dave, a handsome, leather-skinned missionary, walked out of the cockpit and sighed so loudly I could hear it over the engine. More bad news.

"They're sayin it's still pretty rough down there," he shouted. "Lot of shooting this morning."

I pressed my forehead against the cool window glass and watched the clouds part to reveal the green hills of Ituri. I couldn't believe I was going back. All week I'd convinced myself I'd never go there again, repeating it over and over, until I packed my bags and caught a taxi to the airport. Now at ten thousand feet over the border, the notion was slowly becoming real.

The missionaries were running the first available flight back into Bunia: a six-seat, single-engine Cessna that would sit on the ground for ten minutes, then fly out carrying church members waiting to be evacuated. My group of reporters—Helen Vesperini from Agence France-Presse, Rodrique from AP, and a few others—had spent all the previous day in Kigali, Rwanda, waiting on a rumored MONUC plane, but when that fell through, we'd driven thirteen hours back to Entebbe. As the missionary plane began its descent, I saw the familiar mud huts of Bunia and slivers of smoke rising from breakfast fires. Dave then informed us we were going to circle the airport before diving in—he was afraid the plane might get shot. He bowed his head and led us in prayer.

At the airport I grabbed my backpack and jumped out into a throng of UN military hardware and people clamoring to leave. The tarmac was now choked with chalk-white armored personnel carriers, mountains of sandbags, and dozens of Uruguayan peacekeepers wrapped in flak jackets and helmets.

Mahmadou Bah, a UN press officer, ran up and grabbed my

hand, shouting over the din of departing planes, "Don't go any-where. The road's not safe. We'll have to take you in under guard."

I saw another familiar face near the terminal building—it was Juan, the Uruguayan military observer I'd met at the Hellenique a few weeks before, the soldier who'd just returned from the long observation mission in the bush. He was now on his way out, his green duffel resting at his feet. God knows what his week had been like. I flapped my arms and screamed his name.

Juan saw me, hiked his bag over his shoulder, and ran over. Be-fore I could even say hello, he tossed the bag onto the tarmac and grabbed me in a powerful hug. When he pulled back, I looked in his eyes; they were like staring into a river. Without saying a word, he grabbed his bag, ran to a waiting C-130 cargo plane, and disap-peared inside. I walked back to the terminal and watched the mis-sionaries help a few old women and kids board the plane. Then I watched them leave.

I caught a ride into town with a convoy of aid workers tailing a fast-moving UN armored vehicle. Before pulling out of the air-port, the driver told me to prepare myself for what I was about to see. "It's all gone," he said. "They've destroyed it all." The first place we passed was the Hotel CAPA. Through the gates I could see the doors kicked open and trash strewn across the parking lot. Six teenagers sat out front smoking cigarettes, each one cradling a Kalashnikov across his lap. And when we finally turned onto Lu-mumba Boulevard, the lifeline of the city, I sank in my seat.

The shops along the boulevard were gutted shells: doors busted off hinges, windows raked with bullet holes, heaps of garbage spilling out of entrances. The wooden kiosks of gold dealers and cigarette salesmen had been turned on their sides and smashed to splinters. Greasy black circles now stained the roads from burning tires, and everywhere you looked there were empty sandals.

The boulevard now belonged to the young Hema fighters. They wore loose army jackets over scrappy T-shirts and grimy blue jeans.

A small group of them gathered outside a deserted shop, laughing at a joke someone told. Farther down the road, one of them walked out of a shop carrying a looted office chair over his head. As we passed, he cocked his chin in our direction and grinned. I caught his eye and felt my face start to burn.

The UN headquarters now looked like a maximum-security prison. The squat, concrete fence surrounding the building had been crowned with silver mantles of razor wire. Five armored vehicles sat parked outside the gate like stone pillars, set between barricades of more wire and steel. A dozen Uruguayan soldiers stood guard, arms ready.

The Lendu had overrun the peacekeepers almost immediately. As soon as the militia stormed the town, the UN soldiers retreated to protect their base. Three days into the battle for Bunia's streets, one of the two groups (it's not clear exactly who) attacked the UN headquarters with heavy machine guns and mortar rounds that exploded in the yard. The soldiers could do nothing but fire rounds over the heads of militia, even as they watched them attack people in the street with machetes. And there were many reports of Uruguayan soldiers buckling under the strain as bullets flew around them, including one captain who retreated inside the compound to hide. "I don't have my helmet," he screamed. Several logistics officers grabbed his arms and threw him out the door. "You're a fucking soldier," they told him. "Now go do your job!"

During the fighting, people had fled their houses and massed outside the UN gates—only to find they were locked out. To escape the shelling, some attempted to run headlong through the wall of razor wire. A woman desperate to get inside tossed her baby over the wire then barreled through herself. They were both cut to shreds. When the people realized the UN had no intention of protecting them, they rioted. Stones and garbage were hurled at the building. A corpse was tossed over the fence. Tires were set ablaze in the boulevard and roadblocks were erected from rubble and large rocks. This lasted two days until the mob grew big enough and strong enough to finally crash the gates.

Once inside, they left the UN no choice but to distribute the basics of aid: plastic sheeting, medicine, food. Four thousand displaced now lived around the headquarters in a space the size of a city block. Aid groups such as UNICEF, Oxfam, and German Agro Action were feeding them high-protein biscuits and trying desperately to repair the town's water main, which had been cut during the fighting. There was already an outbreak of cholera.

Since the hotels were all destroyed and occupied by gunmen, our group of reporters had to sleep at UN headquarters. But UN staff occupied every inch of floor inside, so the journalists were put outside with the displaced. We set up our tents under a tarp along the side of the building, which had served the previous day as the mission's triage center. Bloody gauze and shattered syringes littered the dirt, and a Canadian UN officer chuckled when he saw me spread my bedroll. "You guys are sleeping on a lot of DNA," he said. A snaking coil of razor wire hemmed us in, and just beyond it the edge of the displaced camp began. Nearest us, several middle-aged women hovered over small charcoal burners cooking pots of rice. A group of kids sat around them pitching bottle caps.

As I unpacked, I looked up and noticed our neighbors staring through the wire. I didn't know how to interpret their gaze, but it wasn't friendly. It was ice-cold and vacant, and I was even getting it from the kids. Not knowing what else to do, I smiled and waved. I then looked down and noticed our collective inventory of junk scattered across the dirt: satellite phones and computers, generators, cases of water, canned meats, imported cheese, whiskey bottles, chocolate bars, cartons of cigarettes, an espresso maker. Embarrassed, I quickly gathered my own things, crammed them back into my bag, and hurried off.

When I stepped out from under the tarp, I saw Johnny walking across the grass. A rush of relief swept over me. "You're okay,"

I shouted, and threw my arms around him. "Things are not so good," he said. "I can't go home. They've stolen everything I had."

Samson had found Johnny soon after leaving the airport and hired him right away. Johnny was still driving the motorbike he'd borrowed from his friend, so he checked the reporter into my old room at the CAPA, and they spent the morning doing interviews. That afternoon, fighting in Mudzipela emptied the town and the two parted ways. The next day, Johnny stayed behind at Hellenique while Samson walked next door to MONUC headquarters. Not long after Johnny entered the bar, the Lendu attacked the town. Johnny ran outside and flagged down a moto taxi and headed toward the CAPA, determined to grab Samson's luggage before the militia sacked the hotel. He'd also stashed his borrowed motorcycle there in the courtyard for safekeeping. But several warriors blocked the road and told them to halt. Terrified, Johnny emptied his pockets and the gunboys turned them loose, but by this time, the fighting had grown so heavy they turned back and returned to the Hellenique. Just outside the bar, Johnny saw a friend's small child running alone and petrified down the street as bullets cut the air around him. Johnny raced outside and grabbed hold of the kid, then sprinted toward the UN base. Finding the gates locked, the two joined several others and squeezed through the razor wire. Hours later, militia reached the CAPA and beat down Samson's door with an ax, stealing his luggage and passport, along with Johnny's bike.

Gunmen had also ransacked Johnny's dorm room and looted what few things he owned. When he finally made it home a week later, a family had invaded his room and taken over. He was now living in the displaced camp with some friends who'd cleared some room in their tarpaulin shelter.

During a brief lapse in fighting, he'd left the camp to investigate, and near the market came upon several Lendu carrying out their killing. Now, as we stood in the grass, Johnny leaned in and rested his hand on my shoulder. His eyes were tired and swollen. "I saw them do it," he said. "I never believed it was true, but when I was hiding, I saw them kill an old man and eat from his heart. I saw them do it." I did what little I could for my friend: gave him some cash and hired him for the week.

An emergency hospital ward was set up in one of the deserted buildings across the street from the UN headquarters. The hospital was a place I returned to every day, sometimes several times, even though I knew what I'd discover each time: that sharp, sickly smell of fluid and infection, the dead glaze over the eyes of a kid coming to terms with the fact he no longer had legs; the way they stared straight through you, so you averted your eyes and still asked questions; the emptiness that crawled through your head as you hurried out the door and stepped back into the sun that was much brighter than you remembered.

In one bed a young woman named Neema rewired whatever ideas I thought I had about that war and what it had done to these people. Neema lay there unconscious, her body sprawled sideways across one of the foam mattresses in the center of the cement floor. Her arms were spread at her sides, and the top of her head was wrapped in a crown of bandages. During the first hours of the Lendu attack, Neema had gone into labor and rushed to a clinic down the road. Just as her baby was being delivered, a mortar round hit the roof and rained shrapnel through the ceiling of her room. The baby survived, but Neema's brains had to be scooped back into her head.

The first time I saw Neema, I stared at her for a long time, trying to process why she was even alive. Then she began to move, at first just her lips, then a twitch in her cheeks. Then her body began to writhe on the bed. Her palms slapped the concrete and she emitted a guttural moan, as if lashing out against a nightmare. I realized she was saying something—it was in Lingala and I couldn't make out the words. "What's this woman saying?" I asked the doctor. He walked over and we watched together. "She's saying, 'I'm dying,'" he said, and turned to see my reaction. "She needs a neurosurgeon desperately. But there's just no way."

Neema's baby had been taken to a house next to Hellenique. One afternoon, Helen Vesperini walked inside and discovered the baby languishing on a sofa, getting fed powdered milk once a day. The incident haunted her for the duration of our trip. Finally she was so mortified she drew up adoption papers on her laptop and told the doctor she was taking the baby home.

Dozens of other people had horrific wounds, but every time I passed the hospital, I only thought of Neema. I made excuses to visit the hospital even more, just to see how she was doing. I'd stand at a distance, pretending to look for someone in her direction, or just lean against the far wall and study her face. Sometimes it had a serene rapture, almost a smile. Other times it was full of spirits. Her eyebrows would lift, as if she were about to sneeze, and from the bottom of her stomach came a low moan that built to a peak, then faded to a heavy pant, leaving her face slack. The sound of her voice leached into my brain like a bad song on a loop, and I heard that voice every time I passed the gunboys in the road.

"I'll tell you what we need," a MONUC officer told me one night. He was former military and had come to Congo with noble intentions, but had quickly become a calloused and bitter man. We'd sit on the front steps of the UN headquarters sipping warm bottles of beer, and he'd often tell me things in strict confidence for fear of his job. During the attack, Lendu fighters had stopped his truck and shoved a gun barrel up his nose. An arrow had even rattled through his driver-side window and stuck in the passenger seat, narrowly missing him. Once, he said, a kid stood in the road with his gun leveled, so he hit the gas and ran over him with his truck. "I'll tell you what we need," he said, drunk, his face as ungiving as stone. "We need an army that can come in here and kill off an entire generation of these fuckers. I mean, what are they gonna grow up to be anyway? These kids are worse than animals."

* * *

"I'll show you the body," said the young boy, and ran off ahead of me. I heard a corpse was on the road near the UN compound, so I ventured out to investigate. The boy and his two friends, all around ten years old, had raced to see it, as any kid would've done when there was a dead body to look at. I knew we were getting close because the smell hit my throat and hung there. The boys gathered by the side of the road and stared into the ditch, leaning over as if held back by an invisible railing. "It's here," said one of them, pointing down. I saw a black, pulsing mass that erupted in a swarm of flies as I got closer. It was the body of a boy, I think, and the entire lower half of him had been eaten by dogs.

Bunia was full of dogs. I'd never really noticed them before, but now they were everywhere. They scurried in and out of open shops and slept in the awning shade. And wherever there was a pack of dogs, there was usually a body nearby.

I'd first noticed the dogs when a few colleagues and I took a walk one day to Yambi Yaya, a neighborhood south of Bunia, which had been emptied by the fighting. We approached Yambi and were greeted by a man leaning casually on a berm, holding a sandal in one hand as if using it to gesture. But as we drew closer, I could see the man had no head. We reached the village center and found another half dozen bodies sprawled in the dirt. We chased several dogs from the body of a young girl, around fifteen years old, who lay flat on her back in front of a small, concrete house. There were no signs of machete wounds or bullet holes; it was as if she'd walked outside and fallen dead in her steps.

One of the girl's legs twisted out from a pink dress, and the other had been chewed off at the knee. As we got closer, I saw something that turned my marrow cold. Five yellow ducklings were gathered at the base of her knee, picking at the flesh.

That sight spooked us all and became an obsessive topic of conversation for the rest of the trip, most often at night when passing the whiskey bottle on the front lawn of MONUC headquarters. Even weeks later some of the same guys, seasoned correspondents, would stop whatever they were doing, look up, and mutter, "Ducks, man. *Fucking ducks*."

Soon after the trip into Yambi, I started checking out. All week we'd shared the town with the young killers who roamed the streets, puffed and arrogant, while the Red Cross body crews came back each day with their litters full (except the times they were murdered and didn't come back at all). More confusing was that the UN not only tolerated their crimes, but had also invited them into the town for talks. The same men commanding the kids who'd gutted people like fish, strung human kidneys across their bandoliers, and raped old women sat in the Hellenique that week drinking beer on the UN's tab. (Further attempts at "pacification," MONUC had claimed.) Bunia became a world without second thought, a town so lost in its own madness that no one was good anymore.

And trying to work the streets had become more volatile than ever. One day we were touring the empty market and stopped to interview a ten-year-old Hema soldier named Chipe. The other militia said that Chipe had watched his parents massacred in Drodro and the trauma had caused him to lose his mind. His eyes now flared and trembled, as if he were bugging on amphetamine, and he'd developed a gasping stutter. Thomas Lubanga, the reedy commander of the Hema militia, had taken the orphaned warrior and made him his personal bodyguard. The other gunboys were wary of Chipe and often kept their distance. As we walked through the market, where corpses lay putrid and bloated under the empty stalls, Chipe spotted two women rummaging through a shop and ran after them. He pulled the women from the doorway and began whipping them with the barrel of his gun, swinging it like a truncheon, his eyes feral with rage. We threw ourselves to the ground, terrified the boy was about to unload his magazine. Karel Prinsloo, a streetwise AP photographer who'd been standing next to me, summed up our fear perfectly: "Put me in Gaza any day. At least there I know where I fucking stand."

The tipping point came that afternoon while we were visiting the makeshift market near the UN headquarters. (The militia had looted all the stalls and shops, then made the vendors buy their merchandise back at twice the price.) On the way I passed several militia mugging for a knot of news photographers. One of them proudly puffed his chest and displayed an Osama bin Laden T-shirt. Next to him was a teenage girl, tall and gorgeous with a model's smile, wearing a chain of bullets and tossing a grenade in the air like an apple.

Back at the camp, things were tense. A few Lendu had been caught sneaking in, attempting to clear old vendettas. A Hema kid was busted with a grenade and a couple of people had been stabbed. The UN was cutting back its food rations, and people were getting angry. ("We're trying to get the people to return to their homes," a UN staffer told us. "But they'll be killed," we replied.)

I sat down on a milk crate while the others quietly filed their stories. I tried to read a book, but couldn't concentrate. Some woman was screaming into the camp from just over the fence. At first I brushed her off, until I realized she was screaming at us. She was stretched practically through the razor wire, pointing her finger at each of us in turn. The veins bulged from her neck and her eyes danced with hate. What she screamed was in Lingala, so I never knew what she actually said. But her sentences were punctuated with *"Journaliste! Journaliste!"* and I soon got the message.

But I didn't care anymore. I just wanted her gone. I wanted to grab her by the shirt, look her in the eyes, and tell her I was only doing my job, that it wasn't my fault, ask her to please shut up and stop being so *goddamn pitiful*.

I walked out on the grass and found a spot to lie down. It wasn't seeing the suffering Congolese that chipped away at me, but the way they took their beatings, the way they woke up each day to viciousness and abuse and still sang songs while they walked down the road. *Suffering and smiling.* I guess the woman in the camp finally got tired of singing.

The tenacity of the Congolese both impressed and confused the hell out of me. In America we made mourning such a public affair, pored over the virtues of our dead, and placed great significance on dates and remembering them. It wasn't like that here. Despite everything that had happened in those weeks, I'd yet to see mothers wail over their dead in public, or children cry at all for that matter. I'd certainly see it later, but here the trauma was so malignant it had ravaged everything soft inside and left them numb. I remembered the way the man from Drodro had described how gunboys kicked his six-month-old baby in the air and sliced her in half with a machete. How they rounded up the rest of his kids and butchered them in the yard. He'd watched it all from his window, yet when he told the story, you'd think he was recounting something he'd read in a newspaper.

"This happens all the time," the woman in the yellow dress had told me during the gun battle. Ravage was a disease perched constantly in the corner, and hunger was part of growing up. They endured because it was all they knew. In Congo, people just died, and over the next five years, the war would kill them at the rate of twelve hundred per day.

I thought of this as the dozens of white UN Land Cruisers passed by, as their massive logistics base was being built near the airport, as their staff drank beer all afternoon in the Hellenique, as cargo planes landed each day loaded with photocopiers, steamrollers, forklifts, guns and ammo, lumber and steel beams.

I thought about Johnny and Neema and this town I'd grown attached to, only to see it ransacked and destroyed, and for what? There'd been no struggle, no uprising against a despot, not even against those who pillaged their country's wealth and turned their children into beasts. There was no collective sacrifice for a greater cause, for anything. There was only poverty and a savage lust for gold and plunder. The point of it all was that there was no point. People just died, and they died for nothing.

For the next hour I lay in the grass, letting the hot sun sting my face. I closed my eyes and drifted off to sleep, hoping to wake up just as a plane landed to take me home, anywhere but Bunia.

The following month, the European Union deployed a rapid-reaction force to Bunia, eleven hundred troops under the command of the French army. The soldiers of Operation Artemis had a fleet of Mi-24 and Mi-17 gunships and a shoot-to-kill mandate. Once the first gunboy took one in the chest from a well-trained French infantryman, the militia realized their game was up. They retreated back to their hillside camps and the violence abated in town.

Over five hundred people had been murdered in Bunia in the week after the Ugandan withdrawal, most of them executed in the streets, and hundreds more were severely wounded or missing. The UN received enormous criticism for failing to anticipate the carnage, and editors and human rights workers pointed to the UN's bumbling in Rwanda as an example of their continuing ineptitude. Even the UN commissioner for human rights, Sérgio Vieira de Mello, expressed outrage and horror at their failure and blamed the war in Iraq for drawing away attention from Congo.

"People are dying there by the hundreds, and that is not happening anywhere else in the world. But who is paying attention?" he told reporters during the siege. "There is an urgent need to demonstrate that the lives of Congolese are as important as the lives of Iraqis or any other life on this planet." (In a sad twist of events, de Mello himself would be assassinated in Iraq three months later when a terrorist bomb ripped through the UN's Baghdad headquarters.)

On June 28, the UN Security Council voted to give its soldiers in Congo a mandate to protect civilians and, by November, had sent in forty-three hundred additional troops. But attacks and massacres continued in the remote villages throughout the summer. Thousands poured into Bunia to escape, collecting at the airport, where the camp had swelled to 14,250 people by August and would remain for years a permanent suburb of grief. But with the town relatively stable, aid workers were able to treat the new arrivals, including hundreds of skeletal, starving children carried in from the bush on the verge of death.

On June 30, 2003, President Joseph Kabila officially announced the beginning of Congo's transitional government, which had been formed following the signing of an ostensibly final cease-fire with rebels in April. The transitional government would be presided over by Kabila and four vice presidents. Two of the men hailed from the political opposition and the former government, while the others had commanded the war's largest rebel groups, the RCD and MLC. The mandate of the transitional government was to integrate the rebels into the national army and hold elections in two years' time.

In the weeks and months following the Ugandan withdrawal, journalists and human rights researchers confirmed that Uganda had left behind tons of weapons for militia. The southern Lendu Ngiti faction had carried out the attacks on Bunia, but their northern compatriots were still being propped up by the Ugandans to control the region's gold. In August, MONUC forces intercepted more shipments of weapons bound for the northern Lendu fighters near the gold mines of Mongbwalu. (In the days before they left, the Ugandans actually turned over Mongbwalu to Lendu commanders in a signing ceremony. Listed as a witness on the signed document was UN military observer Safwat Oran, who would be executed by the same Lendu group the very next week.)

It was a long summer for everyone. Johnny continued living in the camp on a straw mat on the ground, until he was able to return to his dorm. But he was at least getting lots of work. All the violence in May had pulled in the international press, and Johnny soon became everyone's favorite translator. The AP even hired him as the resident stringer, until one afternoon when a militia lieutenant threatened to kill him for helping journalists. Azim, who was in Bunia at the time, quickly put Johnny on a plane to Beni, where he holed up with his sister while the situation calmed.

My colleague Helen Vesperini spent the summer living in Bunia covering the French army for Agence France-Presse. In August she completed the adoption of Neema's baby, named Lea, and took her home to Kigali, Rwanda. The last I heard, Neema was still alive but severely brain-damaged; she slowly recovers. And as for the woman in the yellow dress, I never saw her again.

I returned home to an empty house in Nairobi and too much time to sit around remembering things. I didn't know what to do with any of it, all the bodies and faces. I'd taken rolls of photos in Bunia after the siege—the headless man in Yambi, the teenage girl lying serene in the road, gunboys in hollow-eyed repose—and plastered them across my wall. I locked the doors and didn't leave the house for days, just sitting there in a little room at the end of the hall, staring up at these photos that gave me nothing, told me to either come a little closer or back up for good. It was Susan who finally pulled me out by giving me a job and sending me back to Bunia.

Susan got word that the Hollywood actress Jessica Lange would be touring the airport camp as a UNICEF goodwill ambassador, and since half the Nairobi bureau was in Iraq, Susan sent me to cover it. Lange was flying in to highlight the hunger crisis and that over two hundred women had been raped in Bunia that summer, along with countless others who'd probably never come forward.

The actress arrived at the camp at nine A.M., then made her way to the general hospital, where an emergency therapeutic feeding center had recently opened. Inside the center's dark rooms were three hundred children in various stages of starvation. They lay in cribs shadowed against the light, their temples sunken and disfigured, and skin so tight against their delicate bones they no longer appeared human. Their eyes told you everything, round and filled with terror, or glazed and slipping, but whatever they were suffering, they did it in silence, hardly even a whimper.

The UNICEF officer leading the tour had been caring for them from the beginning. I'd seen her at the airport right after the siege, days since her last sleep, and on the verge of tears or collapse. She now led the actress to each crib and peered inside, and in the depths of her eyes you could see the scabs that had bled and dried somewhere within. They spent the next hour at the giant scale, hoisting the emaciated figures into the slings, while the officer explained in clinical terms the stages in which children slowly died from hunger.

In the afternoon the group came to a cluster of tents in the hospital compound. Passing one, the officer explained it was the temporary ward for patients who'd recovered, children who had just weeks before been hopeless and feared for dead. About thirty children now sat inside the large tent holding cups of juice and biscuits, and out of nowhere they all began to sing. I didn't know the song they were singing, only that every child knew the words, and the sound of their living voices was so hauntingly beautiful, so pure and good in that awful, evil place. The actress and I stood at opposite ends of the tent watching them sing, sitting up on their knees, smiling with bright eyes and juice mustaches, singing the song over and over again, their voices looping and harmonizing, the sound of it like a single flame in a place too dark to see. And as they sang, I looked over and saw the actress weeping behind her tinted shades, and I felt my own throat tighten and the tears come at last. I recorded everything in my tape recorder, and in later months when the depression would find me back in my room looking to the dead for answers, I'd play that song again and again until I could hear it in my dreams. I can summon that music like recall, and even now it plays.

Chapter Two

DAILY BLOOD

In late September, I stepped out of a taxi on Sixth Street in Brooklyn and looked up at the apartment number matching the one in my notebook. I rang the buzzer, and in a minute out stepped this beautiful woman who walked down the stoop and put her arms around me. Our relationship had started the year before as a real whirlwind affair, and after dating only three weeks, we'd decided one night in a bar we were "moving to Africa." Five months later we were on a plane to Nairobi.

But Ann Marie was a playwright, and two months into our African adventure, before Congo, before anything, one of her plays was produced in Manhattan and pulled her back to the States. She'd returned for a brief visit, right after the fall of Bunia, but I'd been so completely out of my head, so wired into what I knew was taking place. I'd stayed up nights sitting by the radio, and since her French was better than mine, I'd open my Bunia notebooks and dial every random number people had given me, then make her talk to the strange, petrified voices who answered. When the taxi had arrived to take her back to the airport, she'd left me in the back room of that big house surrounded by photos of dead Congolese on the walls.

She'd returned to New York and rented this apartment in Brooklyn, hoping soon I'd find whatever it was I was looking for, then come home and share it with her. And now, there I was. I hadn't seen her in nearly five months, and I'm sure we both wondered if I was the same guy who'd once circled the Serengeti on the African map during those fever-pitched months of planning the getaway, who'd plotted epic trips involving long and bumpy bus rides, the peak of Kilimanjaro, and long weekends in Zanzibar. The ro-mance had been so thick during those months we'd practically floated all the way there. In the end, we'd done none of those things, but I'd certainly found what I was looking for, plus a whole lot more. And now, as I said, there I was.

I was home, and I was thrilled and grateful to be there. I embraced the everyday routines and amenities: visiting friends, long dinners at restau-rants, autumn in the trees. The newspaper delivered on the stoop each morning nearly brought me to tears.

In New York, no one seemed to know anything about what had hap-pened in Bunia. I'd meet people in bars or at parties and they'd casually say, "So I hear you were in Congo. What was that like?" But every time when I started on the war, the memory slipped out so raw and blood-soaked I often had to stop. Each moment became another opportunity to explain it to myself, hoping it would make a little more sense. And since most Amer-icans knew little about Congo ("Now that was Zaire, right? Wasn't there a movie called Congo?"), they never saw it coming. By the end of the night I'd be slant-eyed drunk, while some unlucky stranger had gotten dragged through the blood and gristle at Drodro and Nyakunde and knew in vivid detail how women were raped and dismembered. After a while I didn't talk about it at all or would just smile and say, "It was alright, just glad to be home."

I was glad to be home, for the idea of home, the idea of coming home, had violently been redefined. But I had no idea what to do with it. All the gangsterism and murder still remained tangled into a question I couldn't resolve. So when the AP called and offered me the staff job of West Africa correspondent, based in Congo, I took it hoping to understand something I'd missed before. I was going back because Congo was now part of me, dug in beneath the skin and all I ever thought about. The only way to get clean was to bring the terrible tale to a conclusion that made some kind of sense.

Ann Marie and I agreed the job was too good an opportunity to pass by. She would follow me to Kinshasa in a few months, we decided. Or maybe she wouldn't. I left New York with my guts in a bag, convinced I'd made some permanent, drastic mistake, yet completely unable to stop myself from getting on the plane.

I

My first assignment in December 2004 was to cover the presidential election in Ghana. When that was done, I flew to AP's funky West Africa bureau in Dakar, which pushes up against the blue-green Atlantic, where I sat at a desk staring at the pounding coastline from a wall of windows, anxious to leave for Kinshasa. I had a hundred questions about living and working in the capital, but no one to ask. Daniel Balint-Kurti, the previous Congo correspondent, had been shipped to Nigeria after only a few months in Kinshasa. The guy he'd replaced had stayed a total of twenty days before being sent to cover the war in Ivory Coast. So no one really knew anything, least of all me.

The only thing I knew about Kinshasa was that Daniel had rented a palace on the edge of town, an old mansion built by Mobutu's former foreign minister that would serve as my new home and office. A driver had also been called to pick me up from the airport. And knowing little more, I boarded a plane. I made it to Kinshasa without incident, walked into the terminal, and was arrested almost immediately.

My eyes must've flashed bright green lights because the police pounced on me as soon as I stepped in the immigration line. At the time, Kinshasa's N'Djili Airport was one of the most lawless and corrupt places on earth, and this was my first go-round, my breaking in. The police and immigration officials were wily professionals at shakedowns and outright theft. Their most successful ploy was enforcing a made-up law that forbade foreigners to leave the country with local (or sometimes any) currency, which they would enforce by pocketing your cash. Once you understood their behavior was motivated by poverty, aggravated by months without pay, you didn't get so upset and soon figured out the local games. But that night, they really put the screws on me good. They dragged my bags across the airport and up a flight of stairs, into a dim office occupied by the chief of airport police.

"Why are you in this country?" he demanded. He wore a light blue uniform and black beret. His eyes were bloodshot and chewing me alive.

"I'm a writer," I said. (Daniel's advice, as saying *journalist* might raise flags.)

"Then why did your driver tell the police you were a journalist?"

"Well, I am a journalist—"

"Aha! So you lied!"

"No, I meant—"

"Perhaps you aren't a journalist or writer at all. Perhaps you're here in the service of someone else, someone like Rwanda."

"You mean a spy?"

"Yes! You are a spy!" And so on. We sat in the room staring at one another for two hours until I finally broke. I handed the chief five dollars and was promptly released.

It was a stupid and minor incident, but the whole ordeal sent me into a spin, which only became worse when we pulled onto the road toward town. The road was a gnashing panorama of gridlock and belching exhaust, screaming taxi touts, cripples hobbling in the dirt in rags, garbage and sewage seeping out of gutters and filling the potholes, and crowds pulsing through it all. The airport road is also one of Kinshasa's major nerve centers, where the trademark *Kinois* bravado is in glorious display along the taxi stands and market stalls. But first-timers rarely see this deep, and I certainly didn't see it then. I made my driver go straight to a grocery store for beer, and when I arrived at the mansion, my new home, I found it was nothing but a shell of a building. The construction had stopped long ago when the foreign minister died, leaving only a sad little kitchen and two upstairs bedrooms. White columns curled up the second-floor balcony like legs of a dead spider, and gaping black holes covered the façade where doors and windows were never installed. It was full of mosquitoes and smelled of mildew. The electricity was also out, making the whole place feel condemned. As the taxi pulled out of the gate, I stood in the dark driveway taking stock of it all, and as I stared at the broken walls and holes in the ceilings, all my luggage lying in a heap in the dirt, not a friend to be found, I suddenly became worried I'd die here, tragically and alone. But I'd asked for it all, and with little else to do, I grabbed my bags, took my flashlight, and climbed the crumbling staircase.

I spent that night sitting on the balcony of my little room, pounding through a six-pack and giving myself a good talking to. And after a couple days, the feeling of doom seemed to lift as I came to appreciate where I'd landed. I'd brought with me the 1951 *Traveler's Guide to the Belgian Congo*, which I'd found in New York before leaving. Flipping through those black-and white photographs and looking out the window, all my previous Congo reporting suddenly took on greater dimension. I'd arrived in the capital, this distant kingdom we'd pondered in theory all those weeks in Bunia. To the people in the east—eighteen hundred kilometers across the great wall of jungle—the capital existed more as an article of faith than heaven itself. But here I was; I breathed deeply and took in the heavy smells of ozone and moist earth, exhaust fumes and garbage fires that burned down the block, and listened to the cackle of women on the road outside my compound. I rented a taxi and spent hours riding through the old boulevards, around immense traffic circles where centerpiece statues no longer stood. The city seemed to have frozen in time and crumbled with the thaw. I realized I'd only glimpsed Congo's tragedy on its surface, but here in the capital, those faded boulevards could take you down deep.

★ ★ ★

Kinshasa, or Leopoldville under the colony, was founded by the British-born American explorer Henry Morton Stanley in 1881 as a trade station for Belgium's King Leopold II. For years, the king had been searching for a colony for Belgium to compete with the rest of Europe's expanding empires.

Stanley was the right guy to find it for him. He had become an international celebrity several years earlier by becoming the first explorer ever to navigate the Congo River, which he did as part of an epic march across the African continent that took nearly three years and killed over half of his expedition. Stanley's bestselling account of the journey had piqued the interest of the king, who arranged a meeting. Stanley passionately explained to Leopold his dream of developing the Congo River and using it to open up central Africa for trade. Congo, the king knew, was full of ivory, and it was just the treasure he wanted. The Belgian government itself had no interest, so Leopold went to work in claiming Congo for himself, his personal empire in the heart of darkness.

To avoid suspicion from his neighbors, Leopold established the International Association of the Congo, whose professed objective was to open the continent to missionary work, free international trade, and eradicate the Afro-Arab slave traders from Zanzibar who were operating in the eastern forests. With his empire-building thus wrapped in altruism, Leopold gave Stanley a five-year contract and sent him back to Congo to lay the groundwork for the new colony, convincing even the explorer of his selfless aims. Stanley arrived at the mouth of the Congo on August 14, 1879, and over the next five years, in two separate trips, established trade agreements with many local chiefs and opened a series of stations along the river, the largest being Leopoldville.

Leopold finally acquired Congo for his own at the Berlin Conference in February 1885. There, he was granted the 2,345,000-square kilometer territory and promptly went to work pumping the forests of ivory, and later rubber, which he did for the next two decades with catastrophic results. Leopold named his new territory the Congo Free State, though it was nothing of the sort, as the king imposed an immediate trade monopoly on two thirds of the colony—his plan all along. The principal trading post and capital was established at Leopoldville, located five hundred kilometers from the Atlantic Ocean up the Congo River, which became the commercial highway for the burgeoning empire.

In 1908, amid controversy over the colony's murderous rubber and ivory gathering practices, the national government of Belgium assumed control over Congo from King Leopold and began transforming the capital from a bustling river post into a modernized metropolis. Throughout the late 1950s, when Belgian Congo was in its prime, Leopoldville was billed as "the city of contrasts" and marketed to thrill-seeking tourists and outdoorsmen as an outpost of luxury hemmed by the darkest wilds. The Belgians built beautiful hotels, museums, and sidewalk cafés, stadiums, cathedrals, and bronze monuments to the king. The boulevards of "European City" were wide and flanked by white colonial buildings like rows of perfect teeth. Africans were prohibited from straying into the Western quarter without a special pass. Yet tourists and the nearly seventeen thousand white residents could walk off their steak au poivre in "Native City," where the blacks would smile for photos with mortar and pestle and bang the tom-tom on cue. "Civilized and savage, Nordic and tropical," said my guidebook, "Leopoldville is the spectacular intersection of two civilizations, which after avoiding each other tend to integrate more and more."

Integration, however, was the farthest thing from reality. Throughout the 1950s, colonized Africans across the continent began demanding their independence, and after anticolonial riots broke in Leopoldville in 1959, Belgium realized it was powerless to resist. On June 30, 1960, Belgium granted Congo its freedom, and five days later, the country fell apart. The colonial army, known as the Force Publique, mutinied outside the capital, and soon the violence spread to several cities. For decades the colonial administration had corralled the Force Publique like attack dogs, keeping them demoralized, uneducated, and hungry. So it was no surprise the soldiers went for the throats of their white masters, targeting first the officers in the Force, then moving into the streets. For the Europeans, their most haunting nightmare was finally manifest as wild African soldiers crashed the forbidden color line into the palm-lined neighborhoods, ransacking homes and gang-raping white women.

Belgian paratroopers immediately swooped into all major cities to protect their citizens, but it mattered little. The whites fled in waves across the river to Brazzaville, down into Rhodesia and Tanzania, and into every empty seat on any airplane they could find. In ten days, around twenty-six thousand whites had vanished, and only a fraction would return, leaving their crops, factories, businesses, and homes for the locals to pick apart, and for the long arms of the viny earth to begin their eternal embrace.

The rioting and collapse of the country was now the problem of Congo's newly appointed prime minister, Patrice Lumumba, and its president, Joseph Kasavubu. Lumumba was a firebrand in the mold of Kwame Nkrumah, the Ghanaian who'd sparked the great independence movement that swept Africa in the 1950s and '60s. A former postal clerk, Lumumba started the first Congolese political party, Mouvement National Congolais (MNC), and ascended rapidly in party politics that gained momentum during the run-up to independence.

Lumumba appealed to the UN to help calm the crisis, and on July 15, UN secretary-general Dag Hammarskjöld sent several thousand peacekeepers into cities throughout Congo to replace Belgian paratroopers and help maintain a semblance of order. It didn't take long for the mutiny to spark other crises across the country. The mineral-rich southern province of Katanga seceded, and Baluba tribesmen in northern Katanga were staging massacres against the army and white settlers. In the central, diamond-mining province of Kasai, a tribal chief announced his territory's secession as well. Lumumba had, meanwhile, given the job of crushing the mutiny and insurrections to a former journalist and army sergeant named Joseph-Désiré Mobutu, who'd been made chief of staff. Amid this chaos, Mobutu was handed an indefinite amount of power, which he used to his advantage.

By September, the mounting chaos finally caused Congo's fledgling government to fracture and split. Kasavubu dismissed Lumumba as prime minister, prompting Lumumba to attempt to start his own rival government. Mobutu had Lumumba, his former boss, arrested in December 1960, and the following month, the former prime minister was executed in Katanga. In November 1965, as chief of the army, Mobutu seized power in a bloodless coup and took Congo for himself.

The capital, Leopoldville, maintained its charm for several years into Mobutu's reign, and the president used it as a showpiece to trumpet his version of the modern African state. In 1971, he changed the country's name to Zaire as part of a wide-sweeping "authenticity" movement meant to reclaim African pride and identity. Leopoldville became Kinshasa; *monsieur* was replaced by *citoyen*; suits and ties were replaced by Mao-ish, high-collar shirts and wool jackets designed by the Big Man himself; and all the Belgian street names and monuments were stripped and taken down.

Yet the Belgian-built mining and forestry industries still poured revenue into the national coffers, and as the Cold War began, Congo was heavily financed by the United States, France, and Belgium, who sought a democratic foothold amid socialist governments in surrounding Tanzania, Angola, and Congo-Brazzaville. During Angola's civil war, the United States funneled aid to UNITA rebels through Congo, which acted as the rebel's rear base.

But the city fell into decline in the 1970s as Mobutu began siphoning off the treasury to hold power. Over a span of years, Mobutu personally sucked dry the nation's operating budget in boondoggle projects, personal luxuries, and kickbacks to political rivals ("Keep your friends close," he liked saying, "but your enemies closer still"). The culture of corruption and extravagance was encouraged at every level of government until the system finally destroyed itself. The flourishing mining sector collapsed along with other industry, loans reared their heads, and with the end of the Cold War, handouts from Western countries and Bretton Woods institutions dried up and vanished.

In the waning years of Mobutu, Kinshasa became almost unlivable. The Big Man's thievery had bankrupted the country many times over. By 1990, the presidency alone accounted for 80 percent of the country's spending. Zaire's national debt was $14 billion at one point, and by 1994, inflation had rocketed to an unheard of 9,800 percent annually. Prices on essential goods soared out of reach, the public sector vanished, and while Mobutu's circle of sycophants and elite businessmen zipped around in Mercedes, drinking champagne in French restaurants, and chatting on their boxy Motorola mobiles, the city's residents suffered the weight of ruin on $120 per year.

When Kabila's rebel army captured Kinshasa in 1997, it was largely without a fight, and a rebel advance during the second Congo war got as close as the eastern outer neighborhoods, but never penetrated the town. The city had never been shelled. There were no bombed-out buildings or craters in the earth, no land mines left in the roads. Kinshasa wasn't flattened like Dresden or Tokyo. But the war and decades of festering neglect had poisoned the city from the inside. It was crippled, as if by a long, drawn-out illness.

When I arrived in December 2004, unemployment was still nearly absolute, with jobs reserved mainly for those with family or government connections. Most people scraped along by selling cheap wares in the markets, or walking the streets hawking whatever random items they were fortunate enough to come across: one pair of shoes polished to window-glass shine, two dog collars, packs of facial tissue, a miniature dollhouse, and a single dishrag. Basic government services were a distant memory: Kinshasa's main post office hadn't received mail in years, but as in every other government office, rank-and-file employees still turned up for work every day hoping to be paid. Most of the city remained without regular water or electricity, and the streets ran with green sewage, an incubator for the malaria that killed countless children in the city.

But as in Bunia, a tough resilience still managed to prevail. The people certainly suffered, but they did it with grace and humor, chins up, stepping out each day with swagger and personal style, which they upheld like a badge of defiance. Kinshasa was still in deed the city of contrasts, civilized and savage, opulent and bleak, so rich with character that my neck nearly snapped every time I drove the streets.

Kinshasa was live music all night long, every night of the week, brash and thumping and spilling down the street at four A.M. It was legions of street children groping to stay alive in a city that couldn't care if they died, abandoned by parents who believed them witches, devils, and sorcerers, and made to scavenge and hide like rats. It was sirens at midday and government Mercedes racing reckless through the slums; it was a fat man in a French suit mopping sweat with a silk handkerchief; soldiers squeezing out bribes on the intersection; and boys walking through traffic hawking puppies that dangled by their napes, neither dead or alive. It was clouds of exhaust parting on the boulevard to reveal a bombshell in a shiny gown and perfect hair, not a spot of dirt or wrinkle on her. It was families dressed for Sunday services, girls with long copper extensions and boys in boxy suits; the young *sapeur* (one of Kin's mod fashionistas) in the *shawarma* shop with bleached Afro, "Billy Jean" glove, and IRON stenciled on the back of his designer hoodie. And it was thousands of young men standing on corners all over town with no work to do or books to study, so disillusioned and eternally conquered it was a wonder they ever smiled at all.

In a country three times the size of Texas, Bunia and Kinshasa sat on opposite ends, separated by the world's second-largest rain forest. The two cities could've occupied different planets altogether. I'd only experienced the east, and almost everything about Kinshasa was different: the tribal makeup, local languages (they spoke Lingala in the west, Swahili in the east), and attitudes. In the east, people were characteristically mellow (when they weren't being killed), while the *Kinois* could be snobbish and curt. Even the food and music were different. The slow, sad soukous ballads fit right in with Bunia's doomed, frontier vibe, while the capital— wound tight, constantly on edge—demanded as much hipshake per second as possible.

Kinshasa was wholly different from the east, but during my first months living in the capital, the east still dominated my coverage. In Ituri, Hema and Lendu militia were still battling over gold fields and taxation rights to Lake Albert, and in the ongoing conflict hundreds of people were being killed and tens of thousands driven from their homes. Near the border with Rwanda, packs of Hutu rebels were massacring villagers before rounding up the women and gang-raping them while family members were forced to watch. The aid group Global Rights estimated forty-two thousand women and girls were raped over twelve months in South Kivu province alone, and those were just the ones who'd sought treatment.

The already horrific epidemic of rape became worse in May 2004, when renegade soldiers loyal to Laurent Nkunda and Jules Mutebusi had seized the city of Bukavu, provincial capital of South Kivu. Nkunda and Mutebusi were ethnic Tutsi and former commanders in the RCD, the Rwandan-backed rebel group. They'd bucked the government's army-integration program in

2002 and fled to the hills with a cadre of ex-militia. After government soldiers murdered over a dozen Congolese Tutsi in Bukavu in late May, the renegade commanders attacked the town, under the auspices of protecting their people.

Uruguayan peacekeepers, disobeying direct orders, had allowed the invaders to march right into Bukavu rather than fight. For days the renegade soldiers battled the army and raped scores of women across town—including a mother and her three-year-old daughter—and executed people in the streets. The UN's inaction sparked riots in Kinshasa, where residents torched UN vehicles and tried to sack the headquarters. Government soldiers finally drove Nkunda and Mutebusi's men from Bukavu, but not before thousands of residents had fled town and the surrounding villages. And all across the east, the UN estimated over two million people were displaced from the assorted violence, many sick and slowly starving to death in the bush.

In mid-March 2005, UN humanitarian chief Jan Egeland announced Congo had become "the world's worst humanitarian crisis." For the few Western journalists based in the capital, this was fantastic news, meaning we'd somehow edged out the tsunami in Asia and genocide in Sudan in the race for absolute misery. The announcement did wonders in getting my stories printed in American papers, which had previously been like kicking in a hailstorm. If the story involved something exciting such as cannibalism, endangered gorillas, or little girls being raped with machetes, it might have big enough wings to survive its journey across the Atlantic. Everything else left the desk and crashed straight into its watery grave, where a half century of dispatches of bothersome African despair boiled at the bottom.

Following the UN announcement, I'd had a few good weeks of nonstop work, and I was grateful for that. Congo and its grinding troubles seemed to radiate a low-grade depression that settled deep in your lungs like a flu, and I agreed with my new friend Dave

Lewis, the Reuters and *Economist*'s man in Kinshasa, that busy weeks shielded us from this malaise. You got one or two stories in the morning and rode the wave through the afternoon, till it was time for sundowners, or a hearty dinner to put you off to bed. Slow weeks lifted this shield and left you suddenly vulnerable, left you pacing your bedroom with all that murder and mutilation of the past weeks' stories stirring around in the air-conditioning. The depression made you paranoid and suspicious, kept you out at degenerate nightclubs until the sun rose over the palms, and one of these typical weeknights we found ourselves in the VIP Saloon.

The bar was just off Kinshasa's main boulevard and usually filled by midnight with Lebanese diamond dealers, French and Belgian soldiers, and the few Congolese who could afford the five-dollar beers and sodas. The buzz created by the UN's announcement had ended, leaving me and Dave restless and manic. It had been four days since our last story—even the east was quiet that week—and neither of us had really left our apartments.

We ordered two bottles of local Skol at the lamplit bar and watched long-legged prostitutes in red-flame boots dance before the wall of mirrors. The Euro pop on the speakers was loud and monotonous, but punchy enough to lift us from our doldrums. Across the bar at VIP, a group of Belgian businessmen sipped J&B while bar girls sat like smiling mannequins in their laps. Two Germans stood in the far corner, twitchy and bug-eyed, taking turns doing bumps of cocaine in the bathroom.

Dave was one of those far-flung Brits born out in the empire, raised in Kenya and Tanzania and schooled in England. He'd kicked around South America after university, eventually finding his way back to Africa and landing in Kinshasa, where he'd been spellbound by the violent country as much as I was. He was a slick operator, rolling in late for dinner or drinks after greasing one of the government or embassy sources he cultivated like some section-five spook. "Just someone I met somewhere," he'd say, shifting to the menu. "So, what are you having?" I learned a lot by watching Dave Lewis work, and those first couple months he must've scooped me weekly.

He'd just returned from an assignment in Congo-Brazzaville, traveling with UNICEF to gauge the humanitarian situation in the bush. The war in Congo-Brazzaville—just a boat ride across the Congo River from Kinshasa—had ended years before, but rebels known as Ninjas still operated freely in the deep interior. On this last trip, a small wolf pack of Ninjas had ambushed Dave's convoy, guns blazing in the air and lots of shouting. No one had been hurt, but a stoned, crazy Ninja had jumped into Dave's truck, held two grenades to his head, and stolen his cherished jungle boots.

"Two grenades in one hand, and a bloody *joint* between his fingers," he said, demonstrating with a cigarette. We laughed about it now over beers. Sometimes even the most rotten assignments seemed like holidays once back in Kinshasa.

"The UN's saying the Mai Mai are sporting fetuses around their necks," he said.

"Oh, lovely. The Lendu wear human kidneys on their bandoliers. I think I saw it once."

It was our usual blowing-off-steam banter, tasteless and maybe too loud. But something about it must've tapped a nerve in Dave, who went quiet for a minute, then said, "I haven't written one story in six months where someone didn't die."

"Same here," I said. "I'm thinking of counting all the dead people in mine. I wonder how many I'll get."

News of the dead found you in several ways, and often when you wanted it least—two beers into the night after filing all day, or just when you reached the restaurant and put in your order. If Dave was there, and it was something small like a plane crash (those Soviet-era Antonovs fell out of the sky almost weekly), we'd exchange a haggard look and start making deals. "If you wait, I'll wait," we'd say, just to finish our food like normal people. We never waited long; the desk and telephone controlled us like tin men. But while we sat there with a mouthful of food, the dead now among us to sort out, one of us would shoot a glance and repeat our sacred news-grunt mantra: "If we don't file, it doesn't exist."

Many reports of attacks, rapes, and massacres came through confidential sources within the UN, and to them by humanitarian officers, local government officials, or residents—often those who'd escaped attacks, walking several days with children and festering wounds to a military post. One UN contact shuttled information to me through instant message, usually bloody and rancid by the time it flashed on my screen: *Hear about the attack near Tchomia? 18 Hema lost their livers.*

With my contact in the UN, things were never serious, even on those rare occasions when I desperately wanted them to be. Most often the jokes came out of boredom, or those dark recesses where coping mechanisms had terribly malfunctioned after years of being in the bad bush: *Have you thought much about the* Ituri Cookbook? *I have an addition: stewed hearts of Hema in mother's milk. Or perhaps, kidney brochettes with peacekeeper pie?*

One day after one of those unrelenting weeks of sitting in Kinshasa filing daily blood from the east, hardly ever leaving the house, I'd said something that must've sounded naïve, about never having time to write positive, hopeful stories. The reply was quick and barbed: *There aren't any happy stories here, pal,* the message read. *This place is a Viking holiday. It's all blood, rape, and gore.*

II

Even knowing what we were in for, every couple months it was necessary to leave the relative quiet of Kinshasa, the restaurants, nightclubs, and pool parties, and experience the war up close. I'd turn up at MONUC headquarters before dawn and board the white UN bus to the airport, the one with steel grates over the windows for the rocks and garbage often hurled from the road-sides. I'd squeeze in among the Congolese officials in double-breasted suits; the local human rights workers returning wearily to the field. There'd be Indian and Uruguayan peacekeepers laden with boxes of food shipped from home, and UN officers with gelled hair and roller briefcases like software salesmen on the shuttle. We'd all board one of those 727s and leap across the green, sucking carpet.

The personnel planes had become more crowded since I'd last been in Congo. By the time I arrived in Kinshasa, the tiny UN mission that began in 1999 with ninety staff observing the cease-fire was now the largest, most expensive peacekeeping effort in the world, with 16,700 soldiers and an annual budget of over one billion dollars.

Congo's peacekeepers, along with UN agencies, were now saddled with trying to eradicate some twenty thousand militia in the east and assist the two million people displaced by the raids and war. But most important, there was now a massive movement to hold presidential elections.

This was the pinnacle the UN had been building toward. These would be the first elections since Congo's independence from Belgium, and the hopeful vanguard for peace and recovery. Elections were a new beginning, a chance to right all the wrongs, purge the corruption that had plagued the nation since its birth, create accountability in government and state-run enterprises. Elections could make way for a judiciary to prosecute war criminals and corrupt officials, one that wasn't swayed by political payoffs. They would deliver a rightly elected parliament that could function properly and draft laws, and a national army that wasn't as predatory as the militia they were supposed to fight.

Of course, in the vast, forest-covered nation, one empty of roads, electricity, telephones, or local municipal governments, this also entailed some difficulties. Elections meant taking a largely un-educated population of over fifty million people and explaining democracy and how to vote. It meant ordering tens of thousands of ballot boxes and taking them by boat, 4x4, motorcycle, bicycle, and small plane into the jungles and mountains, along with armies of election workers who themselves had to be trained. It meant raising money from wealthy Western nations to finance nearly all of it, since corruption had left the Congolese government no money for its own. And most of all, it meant purging the country of armed groups so people could vote in peace. Battling militia and planning elections, UN officials said, had unexpectedly become the single most ambitious project the world body had ever undertaken in its sixty-year history. And it came at a high price.

As the elections neared, UN soldiers in Ituri were making use of their robust mandate to hunt and disband militia, ripping down bases, making arrests, and engaging them whenever resistance was met. And before long, the strategy took its toll. On February 25, 2005, a gang of Lendu ambushed a foot patrol of Bangladeshi sol-diers near a tiny village called Kafe and killed nine. During the well-coordinated attack, the other peacekeepers fled the scene, and in their retreat, militia stripped the dead UN soldiers' uniforms and mutilated their bodies.

The peacekeepers had been sent to Kafe—part of a vast, hill-swept territory in the northern part of Ituri called Djugu—in late January to protect more than one hundred thousand people who'd fled battles between Hema and Lendu militia over taxation rights to Lake Albert. The villagers, who'd managed harrowing escapes from these attacks, walked dozens of miles to four separate camps in the remote hills and, once there, started dying by the hundreds from cholera, dysentery, and measles. Two weeks after the ambush, peacekeepers gunned down some sixty Lendu militia using armored vehicles and Mi-25 attack helicopters. The assault was led by Pakistani ground troops, hardened from fighting Al Qaeda in the mountains of Pakistan, and assisted by Indian helicopter pilots. Locked in a years-long face-off on their own borders, the two armies now combined to create a rolling killing machine along the bloody hills of Ituri.

In late March, I took one of the twice-weekly UN flights from Kinshasa to Bunia, which had become the headquarters for the five-thousand-strong UN Ituri Brigade. A rush of cold nostalgia hit me as I stepped off the plane and rode into town, which had drastically transformed since the bad days of 2003. The UN mission had tripled in size, and teenage gunboys in wigs and painted fingernails were no longer prowling the streets with rocket launchers. Several new restaurants and hotels had even opened, including an enterprising Indian joint at the Hotel Ituri that catered to Indian and Bangladeshi troops, plus the massive influx of international press and foreign aid workers.

There was a lopsided pool table in the bar of the Indian restaurant, and every night a dozen Italian aid workers would line up to play two hefty Congolese girls who'd established themselves as local sharks. The girls played for bottles of beer, knocking back one after another, yet they never weaved or staggered, and I never saw them lose.

The Italian men wore their hair long and kept it clean and bouncy, even in Bunia's thick dust and heat. They wore tight designer jeans and pointy leather shoes and thundered through town on silver Ducatis, which they had shipped from Italy. The women were young and loud and would fall down drunk in front of tables of staring Congolese.

My first night in town, I had a beer in the restaurant with an old friend, the hardened UN officer whose truck had been shot with arrows during the siege. We watched the aid workers spilling their drinks and running into tables, just another night now in Bunia. "Look what's happened to this town," the officer said, his face twisted in disgust. "These kids don't have a fucking clue what happened here."

Along with the aid workers, Bunia had also become a backwater for cowboy journalists looking for action. You'd see them at dinner, outfitted with GPS systems and dressed in the latest tactical gear, talking about cannibals, gunfights, and child-raping peacekeepers. The ones who rolled in hot from New York were the best, like this American photographer whose business cards were shaped like dog tags, metal and all. I guessed it was only a matter of time before one of them finally walked into the airport camp and shouted, "Anyone here been raped and speaks English?" (It was a classic line passed down as lore among the Africa hacks, only because once in Congo, in 1960, someone had actually said it.)

A few days later I landed a seat on a UN chopper that was taking Ross Mountain, the UN deputy in charge of Congo, on a tour of three of Djugu's camps, where more than seventy-five thousand people now stayed. Before arriving in Kinshasa in December 2004, Mountain had served as Kofi Annan's special representative in Iraq through the elections. He was a straight-talking Kiwi who never tried to sugarcoat the UN's mistakes or bad calls, and there'd been many. Every week Mountain would take trips into the thick of Congo's misery to get a look for himself, and this week he'd asked to see the great catastrophe of Ituri.

Staring down from a chopper over eastern Congo was like glimpsing a prototype of earth during the first days of creation. *Where are all the people?* I always wondered. The camp in Tche was located 161 kilometers north of Bunia in the sweeping, green hills—countryside so stunning it flipped your stomach if you really knew what happened on the ground. About twenty-five thousand people had congregated in the crook of a narrow valley, which quickly became an ideal container for disease. At least twenty kids were dropping every day from measles and drinking dirty water, and groups such as MSF were working days without sleep just to quell the death. About 350 Pakistani peacekeepers were dug into the valley with tons of steel and firepower, but it wasn't enough to stop kids wasting away from diarrhea.

The helicopter landing zone was on a ridgeline overlooking the camp, and as we approached, I could see the Pakistanis had arranged some sort of welcoming ceremony nearby for the guests. The camp had also spread up onto the ridge, and hundreds of its weary residents stood below to watch the helicopter land. But as we touched down, the rotor wash from the chopper blades blew the thatched roofs off several huts and sent a wall of red, stinging sand into the crowd. Children screamed and scattered in all directions. The plastic tables and chairs meant for our ceremony sailed through the air and slammed into people's backs. As the wheels bounced and settled, someone from Mountain's entourage shook his head and yelled, "Jesus Christ, what have we done?"

The people had returned when I stepped out of the chopper. They now crowded together, pressed behind a high wall of razor wire, while others sat perched in trees, watching and waiting. The eyes stopped us cold, even long after the blades had finished spinning. We stood frozen in the awkward silence, waiting for someone to say something. Mountain broke the ice for all of us. "My God," he said, walking forward, "look at all these kids who aren't in school."

A Pakistani colonel escorted Mountain and his staff away, so I headed down into the camp to get my story. And to my surprise, there amid the haze of cooking fires, was Johnny. He'd landed a job as a UN interpreter a few months before and had even sent me an e-mail about the good news. I'd suspected he was kicking around these hills somewhere, but never expected to actually bump into him. I ran over and tackled him with a giant bear hug. I hadn't seen him in nearly two years. He looked healthy and happy, if a little tired and dirty from living in a tent camp with a battalion of Pakistani soldiers, maybe four of whom spoke any English. "I *knew* you'd be back," he said. "I *knew* you couldn't stay away from Congo!"

I immediately enlisted him to translate Swahili for me, and we made our way through the camp, speaking to people who'd escaped the village raids with little but their lives. One man, named Ali Mohammed, had walked outside his hut in Loga just in time to watch Lendu teenagers butcher his mother and two children with machetes. He'd escaped by throwing himself down a mountain and tumbling to the bottom. He was still dressed in the long, torn nightgown he'd been wearing during the first shots of the raid, now his only material possession.

I didn't have time for many interviews. The chopper stayed no longer than thirty minutes in each camp, long enough for Mountain and his staff to speak with aid workers and military, get off some snaps, and declare that, yes, this was indeed the world's worst humanitarian crisis. We then climbed back into the bird, fired up the blades, and sailed off again like a white ghost over the hills.

A week after Mountain's visit, UN peacekeepers pulled out of the camps at Tche, Gina, Tchomia, and Kafe, leaving over one hundred thousand people in the hands of poorly paid, ill-equipped Congolese soldiers, who promptly began looting the tents as soon as the blue helmets were out of sight. A cholera epidemic had already descended on two camps, so when hundreds of people fled the marauding troops, many also carried their deaths with them into the tall grass.

No one understood the delicate dance of warfighting and peacekeeping better than Major General Patrick Cammaert, who was having his own troubles in the mountainous provinces of North and South Kivu, near the Rwandan border. I met Cammaert in early June 2005 in a flower-decked hotel bar in Bukavu, which had become the UN's command post in dealing with the scourge of Rwandan Hutu rebels. The Dutch general was in charge of over twelve thousand peacekeepers in the eastern sector, stretching from the Sudanese border to the southern province of Katanga. And with Ituri alone, there was never a moment when his command wasn't hot.

After peacekeepers had initially allowed Bukavu to fall the previous year, government soldiers had managed to push Nkunda and Mutebusi's men into the hills, where they remained a threat to be watched. But the general wasn't worried about Nkunda or Mute busi now. He'd just returned from the dense forests west of Bukavu, where Hutu rebels had sliced up the village of Ihembe, hacking off hands and feet of their victims and removing their kidneys. The killings had partly been the work of Rasta militia, an even more macabre group consisting of Rwandan Hutu *geno-cidaires*, renegade government soldiers, and Mai Mai warriors, regional minutemen who'd formed in the vacuum left by Mobutu's crumbling army. Rastas had kidnapped fifty young girls during the raid and most likely taken them to mountain camps and raped them day after day before abandoning them in the forest to die. During the attack, panicked villagers had fled into the mountains, where many were likely to die from exposure and disease.

The general removed his blue beret and rubbed his temples. He'd toured the scene of the killings, and seeing that kind of evil had really twisted his head. "The brutality, it's beyond comprehension," he said, the words trailing off. "Innocent kids, two years old, just beaten to pulp."

I'd come to Bukavu myself to see the damage from the Hutu raids. The previous day, I'd visited a halfway house for women and girls so brutally raped by Hutu rebels they'd needed reconstructive surgery. I'd entered with a few stock questions and left three hours later, having listened to an entire room full of victims explain precisely how they were ravaged with gun barrels, sticks, and knives and left to die on the forest floor, how insects had entered their bodies, and how they could never bear children or look at their husbands again. They'd lined up to tell their stories, their eyes digging through the walls, and by the time I walked outside I was soaked with sweat and cursing like a scared child.

What was heavy on the general's mind that night was how to send troops into the jungles to protect these people, and how to keep his men from being ambushed in the process. The only way to safeguard the population was to purge the ten thousand Hutu and Rasta fighters from the jungles, which would need to be done before elections could ever take place. With the recent murders of the nine Bangladeshis, Cammaert had already lost twelve peacekeepers in combat in Ituri that year, and the terrain there was mostly treeless and ideal for open-ended assaults. The mountains and jungles near Rwanda were an altogether different war game, where the probability for ambush was extremely high.

But the general had just pulled a brilliant maneuver, convincing the UN brass to bring in units of Guatemalan special forces, trained jungle fighters who could creep through the dense terrain to stage surgical strikes on unsuspecting Hutu. Once the rebels were flushed into open territory, Mi-25 attack helicopters could dispatch them. It was certainly one of the most ingenious tactics the UN had proposed. The general, a decorated soldier who'd just got done serving as Kofi Annan's top military adviser in New York, now found himself a lead player in Congo's confusing nightmare. But the general had his own bad dream, more vivid and horrifying, the one where he was auditioning for the role of UN commander in the world's next Mogadishu.

"I'm losing sleep," he said, staring off into nothing. "I can't stop thinking about those forests."

He was right to be worried. The following January, eight of those Guatemalan special-ops soldiers were killed in action, not in the forests as the general feared, but on the open plains of Haute Uélé district, north of Ituri. In a secret operation entirely unknown to New York headquarters, eighty soldiers were sent to Garamba

National Park to arrest a top lieutenant in the Lord's Resistance Army, a Ugandan rebel group who'd crossed over from neighboring Sudan. Little is known about the actual mission, but most sources conclude the Guatemalans had been tracked early on, then walked right into an ambush. The general was later summoned to New York to explain why eight men were killed and mutilated on the prairie, hundreds of kilometers from their sector. A UN investigation into the operation yielded few results, or certainly none that were shared with the press.

The mystery surrounding the Guatemalan operation would serve as a later example of the difficulty in reporting the UN's military actions in Congo. For instance, the March operation in Loga—when peacekeepers killed around sixty militia—had also resulted in a number of civilian deaths, according to villagers. Peacekeepers had taken small-arms fire as they'd approached a crowded market and responded by pounding the market with mortars, while gunships hovered overhead and emptied their cannons. The militia had used the market vendors as human shields, the UN said, and women and children were also seen firing guns. As with most peacekeeping operations, there was no way to confirm the UN's information.

In fact, most of my reporting days were spent trying to decipher the cryptic bits of information provided by UN headquarters while somehow remaining credible. To sell the world body's new method of peace enforcing to the world press, the UN relied on Kemal Saiki, a tough, chain-smoking Algerian and bona fide Sergeant Slaughter for the struggling blue helmets. Kemal would routinely lay down the law for the gunboys during his weekly press conferences, issuing ultimatums and barbed threats. Dave and I often joked about petitioning MONUC to just give Kemal a rifle and pocketknife and turn him loose in the hills to clean up. He was a former spokesman for OPEC, leagues better than most UN press officers in Congo, and always good for a beer. But still, when it came down to numbers and hard facts, you filed at your own risk.

One Friday night I'd called Kemal to follow up on a raid that had begun that morning south of Bunia. The blue helmets were tearing down another Lendu camp, and we knew they'd made contact.

"How many dead?" I asked.

"Eighteen casualties," he said.

"No, I mean dead. How many militia killed?"

"Yeah, eighteen," he said. "Eighteen fatalities."

I ran with the story. Hours later, Dave called and said he got thirty-eight dead, and Radio France International was reporting ten killed, all from different sources within the UN. At the weekly press conference days later, Dave and I cornered Kemal to get an explanation.

"Look, we're all getting different numbers," I said. "Which is it: eighteen, thirty-eight, or ten?"

"It's eighteen," he said. He then leaned in and whispered, "Look, what really happened was the helicopter fired eighteen shots, and it got mistaken for eighteen *shot*. Get me? We don't really know."

"But you told me eighteen," I said.

"Yeah, or it was eighteen militia standing on the roof of a house when the helicopter released its rockets. The roof collapsed, the people disappeared. Boom. Eighteen."

He pulled out a cigarette and made his way for the door.

"Why are you so obsessed with death counts?" he said. "This isn't Vietnam."

Kemal was right. It wasn't Vietnam. This was worse. And we knew because we had the Number, the count. Every couple of years, the International Rescue Committee, an American aid group, gave us the gift of the official death count. They'd divide the country into health zones and actually send nurses with clipboards into the hills and jungles asking families to count their dead. Their 2005 report estimated 3.9 million killed between 1998 and 2004, about "38,000 excess deaths per month," caused mostly by "easily preventable and treatable illnesses rather than violence." The report went on to suggest that "if the effects of violence were removed, all-cause mortality could fall to almost normal rates."

We recited the official death count at the end of every story, along with a few tight summary sentences of the conflict that I could magically produce without even thinking about it. The death count was the boilerplate, the one thing you dropped into every conversation, lecture, or e-mail to those who didn't know the score. It differentiated Congo from everything else, from Korea, Vietnam, Bosnia, and Iraq. It had killed more than all of them, and every day the count grew bigger and bigger.

Sexed-up homicides came almost daily: death by bullets or machetes or sledgehammers to the head; the steady sequence of plane and train crashes and boats sinking in the rivers. These stories made the papers. But most people passed away in quiet obscurity—of starvation, cholera, diarrhea, malaria, measles, a hacking cough that just wouldn't quit—usually on the muddy floor of the forest where they'd finally run out of strength, or some stranger's home far from their own. Those rarely made the news; they were just the Number. We'd have to get creative with those or sneak them in whenever ten people died of Ebola or plague and the desk went nuts.

Before I could blink, I'd passed six months in Kinshasa and all I seemed to do was file away this ugly depredation. On top of it all, in April my editors had sent me to Togo to cover the presidential election, where the son of the country's dead ex-dictator was sure to win. And when he finally did, the streets exploded in violent riots and army crackdowns. For three weeks I reported that story, and nearly every day I'd get chased through the streets by mobs swinging machetes and nail-studded clubs. One French reporter was doused in gasoline and chased with a lighter. And when it wasn't the mobs, it was jackbooted soldiers pumping the streets with tear gas and wild firing down the alleys. When the desk finally pulled me out, I'd gone straight home to Congo and plugged right back into the war and that foul-smelling machine, mostly telling the stories from my desk in Kinshasa instead of the red-dirt roads themselves, adding color from a box of blood-slaked observations resupplied on those infrequent trips to the east. And after months and months of that work, the mind begged to be released, to find the autopilot and hand over the controls. It was almost too easy to do, shut it down and let the eyes glaze back while you assembled the generic beast from your repertoire of menacing words, drew some teeth and beady eyes, slugged it "CONGO-FIGHT," and flung it on the wires before the ketchup could dry. It was hard as hell to remember that each story deserved the same attention because the people and crimes were real and you were the record. And for those millions who died nameless and afraid, each had a story that would go untold if you didn't tell it, and the very idea would spin you tight if you gave it too much thought. It was the greatest job I'd ever had. But after a while it wore you down, nothing like trauma or shell shock (not from the desk, anyway), but a creeping emotional atrophy, and loneliness so intense on sun-bleached mornings it erased every thought in your mind. After a while I began to cultivate a little getaway daydream, of flying to Paris and checking into the nicest hotel I could find, then lying in bed with blackout curtains drawn, just staring into the dark.

But there was no time for Paris, because little by little, the two worlds of east and west gradually began to merge and the violence arrived in the capital. Gradually our cocktail and dinner parties, and then our lives in general, became weighted down by one encompassing subject: June 30, the day many predicted Kinshasa would crumble in a wave of blood and terror.

The date marked the end of the country's transitional govern ment, which had been established in 2003 by government and rebels at the end of the war. The agreement also made clear that June 30, 2005, must be the date of presidential elections, the goal the UN and everyone else were struggling to meet.

But anyone expecting elections in June was living a fantasy, because the UN couldn't plan them alone. They'd need help, and from the one person least able to offer it: Joseph Kabila. President Kabila had come to power after his father, Laurent, was assassinated by his own bodyguard in 2001. He'd immediately made strides in ending the war and coaxed back Western donors and the World Bank, which over the next five years gave Congo $2.3 billion in loans. And doing so, he'd played lip service to the Western diplomats and UN officials who advised him to hold elections.

But Kabila's government was in constant disorder, gutted by corruption, and hamstrung by allegiances within the president's inner circle, and those of his four vice presidents, two of whom were former rebel leaders. Over a quarter of the national budget was still unaccounted for; 80 percent of all taxes and customs revenue disappeared (up to $1.7 billion a year); in the east, that missing revenue directly funded the plague of armed movements. And of the $8 million set aside each month to pay and feed the army, more than half was disappearing before it ever reached the men. The president remained surrounded by people intent on keeping these systems in place, lawmakers and army officers with too much money and power to lose in a transparent, corrupt-free state. As one American diplomat once told me, "Kabila is alone in a lake of piranhas. He knows the second he puts the first toe in, his whole body will follow."

The government promised to contribute $70 million to elections, but by June had produced only $4 million. There was obviously little political will within the establishment to hold elections. So as expected, in late April, the president extended the transitional government and delayed the vote until June 2006. The first hint of a postponement back in January had sparked massive rioting in the capital, which ended when police opened fire into the crowds. I'd only been in town a couple of weeks and didn't venture out into the mobs alone, knowing how easy it would've been for some kid to put a rock in my face and be lost underfoot.

But after the official April declaration, the country's main opposition party, the Union for Democracy and Social Progress (or UDPS, their French acronym), called for protests on June 30, and rumors quickly spread they'd be much worse than the January riots, that mobs would run wild through the streets. It was billed as "Congo's apocalypse," a Y2K in the heart of darkness that would terminate and delete in a rain of bullets and machete blades, and I knew I'd be right at the middle with little place to hide.

I had, however, convinced the AP to let me move apartments. After a few weeks of settling in, the mansion had worked out fine. There was no electricity much of the time, and water worked only two hours per day, but it was livable. The problem was that the house was too close to the Kintambo market, which was a popular staging area for opposition demonstrators. Riots and demonstrations had swept through Kintambo the previous May when UN peacekeepers allowed Bukavu to fall to renegade soldiers. It had been Daniel Balint-Kurti's first month, and gangs of rioters had streamed down our street and mobbed around the compound walls, looking to get inside. Soldiers nearby had to fire rounds over their heads to scare them off. The UN listed Kintambo outside its "safe zone" and forbade its own staff to live there. Worried, I called the U.S. embassy's head of security and asked him what I should do. "Are you kidding?" he said. "Move."

So I'd found a two-bedroom apartment just off the main boulevard in Gombe, the relatively safe commercial and diplomatic quarter. The UN headquarters was a five-minute drive, and the U.S. embassy just a mad dash across the boulevard. Water and electricity were more reliable in Gombe, though never constant. Several times a week I still tiled from outside next to my generator, which was like typing while you mowed the lawn. The Indian landlord even provided me with a housekeeper, a shrunken, toothless man named Kasango, who cooked marvelous chicken dinners and prepared hot oatmeal in the mornings, yet insisted on keeping my laundry detergent in the refrigerator.

Gombe was home to most of Kinshasa's expat community, and even with their private security guards, their high walls topped with razor wire and broken glass, and a compound of UN soldiers nearby, the June 30 fear still crept its way inside. Aside from UN and humanitarian staff, Kinshasa had many Belgians who'd stuck around after independence, having invested everything in a falling star. There were also many French, Israelis, and Lebanese, who owned much of the city's commercial center, and Indians who'd returned after Mobutu had booted them out in the 1970s.

The expats' fear was rooted in the city's long history of mass lootings, or *pillage*, mainly carried out by government soldiers. Lootings had marred the capital in the late 1950s in the last days of colonial rule, then again after independence, and twice in the 1990s. In each one of these instances, Belgian or French paratroopers had been dropped in to restore order and evacuate foreigners. The worst of the *pillages* had been in September 1991, when several thousand soldiers rioted in the capital to protest missed wages. Residents quickly joined the melee, barging into homes in the expat quarter and stripping them of everything, including sink fixtures and wallpaper. The mobs picked apart the city like ants—factories, car dealerships, groceries, boutiques—even as French commandos fired bullets over their heads. Mobutu loyalists simply gunned the looters down in the streets. The looting then spread nationwide. Foreigners who'd sank decades into farms and factories lost them in minutes. Fears of famine and epidemic spread since no food or medicines were left anywhere. Hundreds were killed, and from all across the country reports flooded in of foreigners being raped by soldiers.

Kinshasa was rocked by another round of mass lootings in 1997 after Mobutu fled the city in advance of Kabila's rebels. The city still bore the nasty scars of all these events. In government offices, workers sat in darkness since all the fixtures had been ripped from their wires. At the Ministry of Information, for instance, the elevator worked only sporadically, and inquiries into your press credentials often meant climbing sixteen flights of stairs in pitch-darkness since there was no electricity. The walk was best done with a cigarette lighter since many of the steps had crumbled and fallen off. They were slippery, too, since workers used the stairwell as a urinal after the building's restrooms stopped functioning long ago.

We'd sit around and listen to the old hands talk about the *real* crazy days, about watching the city disappear piece by piece in the gunfire and looting while they bravely fought to maintain their small stake. "There were two days between the time Mobutu fled in 1997 and Kabila's rebels advanced onto Kinshasa," my friend Moi would tell us. He was a Congolese businessman married to a beautiful Polish woman, and they'd lived in a large house on the outskirts of town. The city had gone mad after Mobutu's retreat, with ravenous mobs of residents and soldiers looting every quarter. For two days, Moi sat on his roof with a pump shotgun and a case of shells, scattering the crowds that gathered at his gate. Government soldiers would cruise by and listen for the gun blast; the heavier the weapon, the better the chance they'd keep going. Other security forces raced down the block, gunning down looters and lining bodies on the roadside. While Moi blasted away on the roof, his wife, Nesh, kept the NBA play-offs on the television below, poking her head out the window every half hour to announce the score. "I was up there trying to save our house," he'd say, "and there was Nesh yelling, 'Heat 67, Knicks 55' *Boom! Boom!*"

Toward the end of April 2005, Congo's army chief of staff appeared on state television to announce something that had alarmed him. Businesses throughout the city were reporting mass buyouts of machetes, and he suspected the surge in sales had something to do with June 30 plans. Average Congolese were buying the Tramontina blades as fast as shop owners stocked them on the shelves, he said, and someone in power was behind their distribution. The opposition party was vowing to shut down the streets June 30 with thousands of supporters, but even they denied distributing weapons.

The machete scare was made worse by a spate of grotesque murders throughout Kinshasa's Lingwala slum. People started turning up dead with their legs, heads, arms, and even lips missing. Residents started blaming the killings on the mysterious Kata-Kata, which means "cut-cut" in the local Lingala. Kata-Kata was one of several things, or many things all together: Angolan soldiers dressed in Congolese uniforms, Tanzanian and Zambian agents who'd come to overthrow the government, or perhaps members of Kabila's presidential guard, who were killing to make people too afraid to protest on June 30. A few even guessed Kata-Kata was some kind of mutant werewolf who'd crawled out of the forest, an agent of the devil who'd arrived as a harbinger of the end of days.

Rush hour suddenly started two hours earlier because residents didn't want to be caught in the dark. Gas stations also closed earlier, causing a backup of taxis that left throngs of terrified people still stranded at dusk. Ask people what was happening, and they'd tell you, *"C'est Kata-Kata."*

After a pregnant woman was found butchered in the weeds, my housekeeper, Kasango, asked for his entire month's salary to buy a television. I refused again and again, hating the idea of his family not eating for weeks because Kasango wanted to watch TV. I'd say something stupidly paternal like "You can't eat a television!" and he'd reply, *"Patron, c'est Kata-Kata."* I finally gave him the money, only discovering later the TV wasn't for him, but for his daughter, who walked two miles every night to watch television at a friend's house. Buying the television was Kasango's way of keeping her safe at home.

The gas stations were also closing earlier due to a string of violent robberies committed by a gang of rogue policemen (and one woman). They'd zip into the parking lots and rob people at the pumps, then cut them down with machine guns before spraying rounds in every direction, sometimes killing passersby. I'd visited one of these stations to report the story, and as the owner was showing me bullet holes in his walls, a drunken policeman bulled inside and stood leering in the doorway until everyone became afraid and stopped talking to me.

And on May 17, riots broke out in Mbuji-Mayi, the opposition stronghold deep in the central forests. Angry over the election delay, mobs looted the commercial center, burned tires in the streets, and set fire to Kabila's political campaign headquarters. Other mobs then torched the opposition office, finally convincing MONUC to rush in dozens of blue helmets to put down the anarchy. Only two people had been killed, but in the capital the news was received as a chilling omen.

The fear spread through the city, affecting both the rich and the poor, those with everything to lose and those with nothing. The multitude of beggars that plied Kinshasa's traffic suddenly turned more violent in their panhandling, and friends began reporting of mobs of *shegue*—the ubiquitous street kids—jumping onto their cars and pounding the windshields until each one was paid.

I also noticed the change in Kinshasa's roving bands of cripples, who already formed one of the toughest and meanest gangs in the city. Kinshasa was full of cripples: you'd see them every day asking for money in traffic—men with legs corkscrewed behind their backs from polio, war vets missing shoulders, legs, and arms; blind women being led from car to car by ragtag *shegue*. They congregated on street corners and under shade trees with their wheelchairs and hand-peddled carts, a mass of shining steel like freaky Hells Angels. They'd gather in front of businesses, thirty and forty at a time, and demand money. If the owner refused, the mob would hurl bricks through windows and smash cars with steel pipes. Many business owners paid them off, which also gave their stores protection from thieves and miscreants.

I was having breakfast at the Hotel Fontana, next door to my apartment, when they staged an ambush on two police officers. One of the cops had stolen money from a young, legless man at some point earlier in the day, so he'd collected his pals to get some payback. Within ten minutes, about forty people had gathered against a concrete wall across the street. They were screaming and jabbing their fingers toward the cops, really threatening trouble.

Finally the legless man took it alone. With powerful arms, he thrust his torso forward across the dirt road and reached the cop in seconds. The cop saw him coming, threw his AK-47 behind his shoulder, and braced himself, terrified. The legless man lurched forward and wrapped his arms around the officer's shins and held on. The cop tumbled onto his back, reaching up to his buddy with pure animal fear. Once the officer was down, ten more cripples pounced him, pelting him with punches and fistfuls of gravel.

The Indian manager of the hotel ran out and pulled the gate closed, fearing a riot. "Oh, God, not again," he shouted. The restaurant was filled with gruff UN officers and Polish UN civilian cops, who stood with me at the window and watched the poor guy try to save himself. All he had to do was start smashing skulls with his rifle butt or use his boots. But a dozen pairs of UN eyes were on him, and about twenty more wheelchairs were rolling across the street to get a piece.

"Maybe someone should do something," one of the men said.

"Nah," said another, closing the drapes. "These assholes have it coming."

III

While the Congolese waited for some unknown evil to land on June 30, the UN was nailing down contingency plans for an all-out collapse. Warehouses and empty office space, equipped with cots and a week's supply of food, were being prepared to hold over a thousand expats. Secret messages were being encoded into popular UN Radio Okapi broadcasts, giving UN officers instruction on riots and crowd gatherings. The UN also staged an ambitious weekend evacuation drill for hundreds of its staff, only to realize a week later they'd forgotten to inform fifty-five ranking officers.

It was no secret to the Congolese that the *mundele* could leave when things got bad, and they hardly trusted the UN to save them from marauding soldiers. It was true that many Congolese thought the UN was only there to collect their big salaries and thousand-dollar-per-month "hazard pay," and to hell with the rest. And at the end of the day, weren't we all UN? Why else would a *mundele* be in Congo other than to preach or profit?

As June 30 approached, I began buying dozens of cans of tuna and sardines, twenty-gallon jugs for water, and extra fuel for the generator, in the event I was trapped at home while the streets burned outside. I also bought water jugs for Kasango and Eddy Isango, my Congolese colleague, and gave them money for emergencies, but it didn't change the reality of who would stay and who would get ferried away in an armored vehicle. All the expats were stocking up on supplies, or finding ways out, but ask any Congolese on the streets and he'd tell you, "Yeah, I'd love to buy more bread, but who's got the money for that?"

The desperation could only stay pure for so long before it soured and mutated into panic and rage, which was the next logistical step for this place. I'd look at the people on the boulevard and wonder when that last straw would break. In the end, we wondered, what would spark the madness? A soldier shooting someone? Some kind of announcement on the radio? A coup? And how bad would it get? I'd look at the people and wonder quietly, *Will it be you? Or you?* The desperation shined on the faces of the street kids when they suddenly appeared in your open window, tugging at your arm and moaning in that put-on devil voice, *"Boss, boss, j'ai faim, boss, boss."* It was in the policemen who guarded the restaurant when you stumbled out drunk, fumbling for your cigarettes. It was in the eyes of the peanut sellers, the old mamas painting stripes on the road, the countless men lined up under the shade without a job or a pot to piss in, watching you, *le blanc*, walk down the boulevard with your notebook and pen, thinking to themselves, "five thousand dollars a month. *You fucking UN prick.*"

I was having a beer with Dave one night at a local Greek restaurant and pool hall. He'd just returned from covering a soccer match at the stadium, where the Simbas had given a sound beating to the Uganda Cranes. Tens of thousands had filled the stadium, already amped by the matchup between one of Congo's former invaders and the uncertainty of June 30. When one of Congo's vice presidents, Zahidi Ngoma, entered to take his seat, the entire stadium bellowed, *"Thief! Thief! Kill him! Kill him!"* And as Dave later drove off in his car, crowds of teenagers pounded on his hood, sliding their fingers across their throats, "We have our Tramontinas waiting for you, *le blanc*," they shouted. "June thirtieth will be your day!"

About then Nico and Nick, two Greek businessmen we knew, stumbled into the bar already drunk. Nick worked in the steel business and wore a ponytail. He was in his early thirties, kept a loaded .45 in his truck, and was very into his own movie. In his basement he'd already prepared several cases of Molotov cocktails, ready to ignite and hurl at the natives when they climbed his gate. "And if that's not enough," he said with a grin, "I got a dozen gas grenades yesterday from the Belgians."

Nico, the other Greek, owned an Acropolis-themed nightclub in Victoire, an opposition neighborhood we all knew would be among the first to pop. Nico had a crew of muscled bodyguards protecting him at the club and always traveled with a hired Congolese soldier with a Kalashnikov. Days earlier he'd predicted nothing would happen June 30, but tonight the fear had broken him.

"They're saying the government will cut the power, and there won't be water for weeks," he said. "I listen to the staff at the club. They're saying everyone has a machete hidden at home. They're preparing for slaughter."

"Who knows," I said, pretending. "Never trust rumors."

"I hired four more policemen for my apartment," he said. "I can't get enough policemen."

The big Greek took his beer off the bar and walked toward the pool tables. Halfway there, he turned around and pointed to Dave, "If you find my body in the street," he said. "Please send it home to my mama."

As we waited in anticipation for the looting mobs and street violence, I took comfort in knowing I'd had a little preparation. The newswires never sent their grunts into danger without plenty of heavy protection and training. Earlier in the year, the agency sent me through a week of "hazardous environment training," held on a grassy farm outside London, where Royal Marine commandos guided us through the dangers of our trade. The commandos were top-rate special-forces soldiers, steely country boys who quoted poetry and served in both the Falklands and Northern Ireland. They taught us how to dodge bullets and incoming mortars, how to train the eyes to notice land mines, booby traps, and trip wires rigged to grenades. They showed me how to distinguish light-weapons fire from the burp of automatic, long-range assault weapons. I learned how to prod the dirt for bouncing bettys, child-killing butterfly mines, and how to spot a claymore antipersonnel mine, the worst. I learned how to use a compass and determine my bearings, then find my way home with the sun, moon, and stars, and tell north with rocks and sticks and shadows. I learned that brick walls disintegrate under one burst of .50-caliber fire and watched videos of protesters being shot point-blank with shotguns (this to demonstrate how not to challenge third-world riot cops).

Then they taught us how to patch ourselves up in case any of the above weaponry did indeed get us: how to treat a sucking chest wound, how to plug a bullet hole with a tampon, and how to stanch the blood spray from an arterial gash. I learned that when you're being mortared at close range, you must always open your mouth and scream to balance the blast pressure in your body so your innards don't turn to jelly. I learned the best way to dry wet socks is to stick them under your armpits while you sleep, and the best way to treat food poisoning is to drink water laced with iodine.

The first hour we arrived they piled us into a van and sent us through a "make-believe checkpoint" to get a feel for the training. Instead we were ambushed by several men wearing ski masks, who detonated a flash-bang grenade and rushed from the trees firing pistols (blanks, of course). They threw open the doors of the van, yelling, *"Get the fuck out of the car motherfuckers get the fuck out!"* and hurled us violently to the dirt. Our hands were tied and heads covered with flour sacks, the kind you saw in pictures from Guantánamo. It was difficult to breathe, and the fear and adrenaline caused a few people to hyperventilate. They emptied our pockets and marched us in circles through the forest in our hoods to throw off our balance. Occasionally people were led away from the group and farther into the trees, where a marine fired a pistol over their heads to simulate their execution. The marines filmed it all, and later we went to the classroom and watched in wonderment how we reacted to being kidnapped by terrorists.

Other days they sent us down lonely wooded paths and opened

fire on us from the trees and detonated large explosions, just so we could practice hitting the deck. I dove into thorn bushes and sliced up my arms, crab-walked through the mud behind trees and hills and anything that provided cover. The exercises were exciting and terrifying, because the moment you realized you'd messed up (hid behind a thin pile of leaves instead of the ditch three feet away), a great weight swelled in your stomach. I must've died twice, once after stepping on a land mine, and the second time after the guy next to me snapped a trip wire rigged to a claymore buried in the bushes. It was the best money anyone ever spent on me.

Back in Kinshasa, I'd put my driver through a similar course in first aid and kept kits in the car stocked with pressure pads, shock blankets, and syringes for makeshift field IVs. In my room I kept a Kevlar vest with porcelain plates at the front and back, and a helmet to shield my brains from shrapnel. I had all of this gear and training, but doubted it would ever save me from mobs with machetes and nail-studded clubs, or soldiers kicking down my bedroom door.

Over the past six years, my agency had had two staffers killed in West Africa, and two others critically wounded. The region was among the most dangerous in the world, aside from obvious places such as Iraq and Afghanistan. The nerves of New York editors had long been frayed over African wars, and some felt it wasn't even worth the risk at all. When I arrived in Dakar, before I moved to Congo, my boss immediately sat me down, put a gin and tonic in my hand, and told me flatly, "Don't be a cowboy. If you're killed in Congo, they'll shut down this whole operation."

My group of friends dealt with the stress and boredom in different ways. Some of us played squash in the mildewed courts of the Grand Hotel, while others went running along the river road, where brilliant sunsets bounced off the slow current like glass and gave the ugly city an almost wholesome glow. Many lost themselves in the dark, dreary bars or took advantage of cheap dope sold in bushels by nearly every kid who hawked cigarettes on the streets. There were extravagant costume parties with James Bond themes, or where you came dressed as your favorite dictator. Music helped as much as anything, and the Congolese embraced their music as the only national treasure that still belonged to them. We'd stay out all night at the balmy rooftop bars, dancing to live, six-piece soukous bands, or deep in the local clubs where Werrason and Papa Wemba and Koffi Olomide delivered the multitudes each week. Back at home, it was Fela Kuti's "Coffin for Head of State," with its spacey, resonant darkness; Iggy Pop howling, "Baby, wanna take you out with me, come along on my death trip"; or Chan Marshall in the headphones while storms ripped over the river and kicked out the lights, that straight-razor voice like a spirit in the room: "Oh, come, child, in a cross bones style . . . come rescue me."

But during the maximum paranoia of June, our methods of escape began to reflect the violence pressing in. Every Saturday, often after staying out all night, we'd gather in my friend Andy's backyard, strap on gloves and headgear, and fight until we collapsed from pain or exhaustion. It became known as Fight Club Kinshasa.

There were about ten of us, including Dave, some aid workers, and a few guys from the French embassy. Together we had five pairs of boxing gloves, headgear, and leg pads, and usually enough people showed up so you could fight someone your own size, or with the same level of skill. But before any fighting took place, we endured an hour of grueling warm-ups to break the sweat and get us loose, led by Moi and Nico, who'd also been a professional kick-boxer in Greece before opening his nightclub in Kinshasa.

Moi got us started with two-minute drills of jump rope, push-ups, aerobics, and crunches, often coming by and whacking us in the gut with a foam bat, screaming, "You must feel the pain!" Nico helped us develop our punches and maintain our guard, often in punishing ways. He'd dance around us, his broad chest running with sweat, yelling, "Protect yourself!" The second we dropped our guard, he pounded us in the face. "What ah' you dewing? I said protect yourself!" One week Dave got hit so hard in the forehead he went behind a tree and vomited. After warm-ups, Moi and Nico picked two people to fight while the others watched. The fights were ragged and sloppy, all adrenaline and little skill. Once you got hit in the face the first time, everything you'd just learned flew out of your head. Someone would shout, *"Doucement, douce-ment!"* Gently, gently. But everyone swung his hardest, even when fighting a good friend. We'd back one another into trees with stomach shots or sweep the legs and send them tumbling down. There were few rules, and sometimes people had to be pulled away, those who'd momentarily lost their heads in the violence. It was a fine rush, until all the poison from the previous night raced to your head and turned you green. Each fight lasted only two minutes, but left us so exhausted we didn't speak for long periods afterward. We walked away with bruised ribs, busted lips, and bloody feet since we fought without shoes or socks. It was something few of us would've done back home in Europe or America, but for many reasons it made sense in Kinshasa.

After months of rumors and paranoia, June 30 finally arrived. I set out early that morning with Eddy, my Congolese colleague at the agency, and our driver. The main boulevard was heavily patrolled by UN armored vehicles and trucks of Congolese police, whom the government had finally paid a few days earlier in an attempt to avoid a mutiny. Businesses were shuttered throughout the city, and few cars ventured on the roads, leaving the wide boulevards open for groups of barefoot children to play soccer. It was eerie and silent as the city waited for something to happen.

Once we hit the ramshackle neighborhood of Victoire the quiet was shattered. Large crowds surrounded our car, with young men pounding their fists on the roof and hood, and stuffing the windows with opposition flyers. They were wild-eyed and wound tight, but at least they were keeping their cool. They were saving their hatred for the police. The crowd swelled to several thousand and marched toward parliament, so we raced ahead to meet them. When we arrived, dozens of riot police were already lining up in formation, cutting off the boulevard in a tight phalanx. These were new units trained by the Europeans for crowd control; they wore all-black riot gear, including molded chest plates and helmets and black gas-grenade launchers. Sleek, disciplined killers filing onto the boulevard like Darth Vader's storm troopers. Several French policemen with European Union badges stood quietly behind the formation, filming their minions with handheld cameras.

We parked the car, and Eddy and I ran toward the police, making sure to stay close to the French. I'd already been arrested a dozen times in Kinshasa for reporting on the streets, and today I expected no less. In Kinshasa, you'd get arrested for anything. I'd be detained by police for simply entering the market, pulling out my notebook, and asking questions. Crowds would immediately swarm and begin screaming, "Pay us! Pay us!" and before I could explain I didn't pay for interviews, someone would get the police, who smelled a quick buck. Each detainment, like the one at the airport my first day in town, ended when I passed along some small cash or threatened to call the minister of information.

Eddy and I found a safe place along the road just as thousands of demonstrators poured out of the neighborhoods and headed toward the police lines. The lead marchers held long white banners of the UDPS, and hundreds waved giant palm leaves as a gesture of peace. They reached the wall of security in minutes, and once there, all raised their arms with palms to the sky.

"Our brothers, why do you kill for these thieves?" they yelled at the police. "They give you nothing, and your children are still dying!"

The police began rapping batons against their shields in a slow, steady rhythm that grew faster and faster, until a blow from a whistle silenced them. The police took four steps back and leveled their gas guns against the crowd. The first round of grenades hit the closest demonstrators directly in the chest, and the second round bounced off their backs as they fled in panic. As the demonstrators scattered in the haze of smoke, the police drew their Kalashnikovs and chased them into the narrow streets of Victoire, spraying rounds into the air. Police later returned dragging prisoners behind them, who were taken to the street and beaten in the stomach with batons.

I'd been shooting photos between the lines, trying to work through the gas. (With tear gas, your eyes locked shut and gushed water, and your throat and lungs contracted and burned, like you'd just inhaled a mouthful of bleach.) And just as I managed to open my eyes, I noticed the French policemen had left and, just then, heard Eddy screaming from the roadside. Eddy was a small man, barely 110 pounds. The police had him by the arms and legs and were carrying him into a vacant field of tall grass. I raced over and threw myself between the police, grabbing Eddy's legs to pull him free. "We're American journalists," I shouted. "Let him go now!"

As I struggled with Eddy, I was swallowed in a crush of police, who threw me to the ground and dragged me through the grass by my shirt. Hands dove into my pockets and ripped out my money and ID. They planted us in the dirt and a policeman stood guard. After we sat there for half an hour, the commander walked over and pulled the memory cards from both our cameras, tore the pages from Eddy's notebooks, and told us to leave. I argued and screamed, but when I noticed Eddy's body shaking from fright, I shut my mouth and walked to the car. Only I was an American and had the luxury of arguing without fear.

Throughout the day, Kinshasa police opened fire into large crowds and beat people with impunity. Demonstrations in Mbuji-Mayi and Tshikapa were put down in similar ways, with police beating people and shooting live rounds into crowds. Aside from Eddy and myself, many Congolese journalists working that day were arrested and jailed, and there was no one to plead for them. But to the United Nations and every foreign embassy in Congo, June 30 was a smashing success. Howling mobs didn't kick down gates to loot and rape white women, and the city—or the area of the city that really mattered, anyway—had been spared the wave of destruction.

"We live in a violent country where there are violent clashes every day," Ross Mountain told me the next day. "The situation ended much better than we'd feared."

Days later at a Fourth of July party at the American ambassador's residence, I spoke to an American security officer who praised the professional conduct of the police, going on about how they did a "fine, fine job" at crushing the demonstrations, and how he wished he could "be there cracking skulls right with 'em." Standing nearby was a Congolese priest from Mbuji-Mayi, who'd been trapped at his church as police shot into crowds outside.

"They fired tear gas into my church," the priest told the official. "I saw people drop from bullets."

"Aw, come on, Father," the American said with a shrug. "It wasn't all that bad."

The American was right, and so was Ross Mountain. Things could've been much worse, and lives were spared by the heavy security presence, which stopped crowds from getting too large and looting the city. What had also helped was a voter-registration drive the government kicked off June 20 in Kinshasa, which had, by June 30, already registered a million people to vote for the first time in their lives. The people finally saw progress, and they spared the city as a result. A rare bit of hope and reprieve had touched the plagued country. Kinshasa had been saved. A week later, militia raided a village in the east and burned forty women and children alive, plunging the whole stinking place back into the cellar of the world.

By then I was already on a plane back to New York. My reason for quitting was mostly personal and had been planned for some time. I was anxious to return to Brooklyn, where Ann Marie was waiting. She'd taken a job and had no plans of moving to Kinshasa. Except for a brief rendezvous in London, we'd been apart for months, and by now there'd been way too many terse exchanges over my scratchy satellite phone. I was worried she'd leave me and all I'd have left was Congo. That scared me more than anything, because I knew I'd stay for years.

But it wasn't just the girlfriend. I also felt I'd failed, not just in my job, but in a much larger sense. I'd failed to trumpet loud enough, been so bogged in the mud I'd never called my editors in London and New York and said, *"This is what we'll do! I have a plan!"* During the 2003 war in Liberia, my bureau chief had become so sick of watching helpless people die that she began an assault of stories built around the central question "Why isn't the U.S. government helping?" And within weeks, marine choppers were landing in Monrovia. It was a different country—a country settled by Americans as a home for freed slaves—and there'd been other reporters there doing the same, but I'd taken away the message. And I'd dreamed of doing that in Congo, really causing a rally (stopping that insanity couldn't be *that* hard, could it?). But my voice had barely cleared the trees.

Earlier that summer, I'd got an e-mail from a friend who'd read some of my stories, wanting to know if there was more to Congo than just people dying. He'd ended the note asking, "Why can't you write more stories we can all relate to?" It was an honest question and one I couldn't answer. It was easy to kick yourself for not writing what you thought should be written. All we really had time to do was make some record of the killing and dying and hope to tell it the right way. I'd been there maybe a year, covered a war and followed it through. It wasn't a long time by any stretch, but long enough to understand that total comprehension was impossible, no matter how long you stayed. No one really understood how twenty-five thousand people could walk twenty kilometers, meet in the same remote valley, and start dying there immediately. No one really understood what drove someone to behead a five-year-old girl with a farm tool, or to wipe out an entire village for the sake of a few dollars in gold or loot. It was all too abstract, even as I think of it now. It was much easier to pretend they didn't exist, and maybe they really don't. Maybe when that white UN bird lifted off the LZ and out of sight, all the dying people simply melted back into rocks and grass. Maybe if one of them pulled out a *People* magazine or said Hollywood kept their hope alive, perhaps that would make them human again, give their misery a song we all know. Maybe then we could relate.

Dave and I had a joke we liked to tell the aid workers and UN flacks after we'd had too much beer, that there wasn't a single person in Congo who had any idea what was really going on. It wasn't a joke where anyone laughed, but one we could both agree on, and that offered a little relief. No one had the slightest clue, top to bottom.

As my plane lifted off and over the river, I looked around at all the people who were leaving, the preachers and profiteers, the doom junkies and cowboys, all the people like me. I imagined we could all use the break, put the death and dying out of sight and out of mind. But I knew what we all knew, that somewhere in that plane the dead were still with us, and no matter who we were, it was still up to us to sort them all out.

Chapter Three

WAITING FOR COBRA

I arrived home to Brooklyn in mid-July, and six weeks later Hurricane Ka-trina struck New Orleans. In a matter of days I was in Houston, where the city had arranged for over twenty-three thousand evacuees to be housed at the Houston Astrodome. Most were being bused over from the New Or-leans Superdome, and off crowded interstate overpasses, where they'd fled after the city's levees had broken and water flooded their neighborhoods.

I'd spent some memorable afternoons in the Dome as a kid, sitting up in the nosebleed seats squinting my eyes to see Nolan Ryan on the mound, or standing to join the rowdy chorus of "C-R-U-U-U-U-U-U-Z" when the legendary outfielder Jose Cruz stepped up to bat. Now I entered the Dome from the second-row stands and was slapped frozen by the im-age. Down below was this churning sea of black bodies, their faces ex-hausted and bewildered under the hard stadium lights. Most were dressed in donated, secondhand clothes that hung awkwardly on their bodies. Many lay on cots and covered their faces to sleep, while others sat alone in a trance and grieved without privacy for those who'd died or gone missing in the flood. And weaving through the rows of beds were dozens of nurses and doctors, journalists and camera crews, cops and volunteers, all with a look of gravity in their faces, and all mostly white. My mind seemed to skip for a second. I was suddenly back, staring into the valley of Tche or Tchomia or Bunia after the siege. At first glance, the only thing missing was the haze of cooking fires and the red African mud, and it was the last image I ever thought I'd see at home. And just like in Congo, this misery had spawned

its own kind of carnival. In addition to the many preachers and Scientolo-
gists and dreadlocked masseuses, there were clowns and magicians who
pulled flowers from hats to the delight of children, while parents stood by
staring into the walls. And each day the politicians and celebrities net-
worked their way inside making promises few could keep.

A few months later I reported from New Orleans itself, where the
flattened neighborhoods were full of well-meaning young people bused in
for too brief periods of time, and the flooded streets had been reclaimed by
contractor pickups with out-of-state plates. At night, gunshots popped in
the dark and the law couldn't be trusted. This story occupied me for
months after my return because it was so similar to the one I'd left. After-
ward, I pitched other stories hoping to point myself in new directions, but
those stories never panned out, probably because my heart just wasn't in
them. When Congo's election commission announced the presidential vote
would take place July 30, 2006, something urged me to go. But there was
something I had to do first, and in June, Ann Marie and I threw a big
wedding on a farm in Minnesota. We spent a quiet honeymoon in the Sea
Islands of South Carolina. And two weeks later, I caught a plane to
Bunia.

I

There was little hard information to be had about Commander
Cobra, yet in the summer of 2006, his legend seemed to permeate
the hills like creeping fog. Villagers, soldiers, and former gunboys
who'd come in from the bush, all had different versions of Cobra's
history. Everyone agreed Justin Banaloki Matata was a former soldier in Mobutu's army who'd lost the job after the Big Man fell.
He'd fought with Lendu militia during the war and possessed a
penchant for butchery that had earned him respect in battle. Cobra
had helped lead one of the most savage attacks to date in Ituri, the
sacking of Nyakunde in September 2002. There, Lendu fighters,
along with members of the rebel group RCD-Kasangani, entered
the Centre Médical Évangélique hospital and hacked to death

every Hema they could find (this chilling incident had haunted the Swiss doctor in Bunia). The militia then closed off every exit and trapped the town, and over ten days, methodically butchered twelve hundred people and stuffed them into latrines and wells or left them dismembered in the roads. The leader of the Nyakunde massacre was a commander named Khandro, who many claimed was Cobra's mentor in the field. Not long after the raid, Cobra murdered Khandro and took the crown of the gunboy army, one of the largest and most feared in all of Ituri.

Cobra had something greater than his reputation that he used to drill fear and loyalty into his boys, a weapon as ancient as the red clay itself. The commander had black magic, wielded by an eighty-year-old sorcerer named Kakadu, who many believed could shift his face from old to young and speak through animals and trees. In a country where Christ and Lucifer were merely two flavors in a much larger soup, the gris-gris magic was the spoon that stirred the pot.

Kakadu had found his place among warriors back in 1972, when he led attacks against Ugandan Hema over a border dispute near the Semliki River, just south of Bunia. Then, like now, the sorcerer's gift was a potion that delivered on every gunboy's bulletproof dream: drink the water, become unkillable, dart through the hail of death like an invisible string. After the Ugandan government complained about the attacks, Mobutu's troops arrested the magic man and threw him in prison for ten years. There, locals say, he honed his craft and stewed in his own powers, walking out virtually a god. He'd lived the past two decades deep in the bush on a farm near Sazi, which became a site of pilgrimage for mystics and those seeking guidance. Payments were taken in livestock, and Kakadu had built himself a veritable kingdom. One of those pilgrims was Cobra Matata, who came seeking power as he seized control of the militia army. In late 2005, government soldiers began sweeps through Lendu villages hunting militia, looting and raping as they went. And to repel this assault, Kakadu joined the gunboy army as prophet and sorcerer and brought with him the black magic of war. Every so often he'd appear in a village market, like a specter in a white robe and wooden staff. His sermons drew hundreds.

"He held a meeting once in Kagaba," said one UN translator from Aveba, seventy kilometers south of Bunia. "He put a microphone in a tree and different voices came through the speakers. That day all militia came seeking their destiny, and the magic leader told each boy his fate in battle."

To the gunboys, especially the younger ones, Kakadu was like a mythic lord who carried death and retribution in his pouch. The boys told how Kakadu planned and sanctioned every battle they fought. Inside a closed hut, the magic man would scrawl a crude map of the hills into the dirt floor, then slice the throat of a white cock. The wounded bird would shudder and bleed across the room, and wherever it fell dead was where the militia would attack. Later, he'd arrange the fighters in formation and prepare them for war, smearing their chests with a putrid ointment made from castor beans, and presenting them with a cloth pouch stuffed with herbs and trinkets, the antibullet.

Together, Cobra and the magic man controlled an army of two thousand militia, many of whom were child soldiers, in a wooded mountain empire known as Tchei, a name that rolled like a tombstone off the tongues of the UN's hardened leaders. The territory of Tchei (not to be confused with Tche, the displaced camp north of Bunia) was sixty-five kilometers southwest of town, a sixty-kilometer expanse of dense, tree-covered mountains and deep hollows where the morning mist gathered like cream in a bowl. For the UN, Tchei was a tactical nightmare. The mountaintop base-village offered invaluable views of a huge swath of surrounding land. The base was totally self-sustaining, with nearby streams for water and fields for growing food. The rugged terrain made access by vehicle impossible, and the dense cover hindered air operations. Whoever controlled

Tchei controlled it all. And the UN, under extreme pressure to clean out militia and protect an election, desperately needed control.

At the time, the attention of MONUC, aid groups, and donors was again focused on pulling off elections. The preparation alone had been historic. In a country with only five hundred kilometers of paved roads, no real census for the past forty-five years, and a largely illiterate population with no national IDs, the UN had hired three hundred thousand election workers and sent them into the jungle by boat, dugout canoe, motorcycle, bicycle, and foot to register twenty-five million people. It took some workers weeks to make the journey, and on two occasions, several were kidnapped and taken hostage by local militia bent on derailing the vote. Nevertheless, they'd established 50,045 polling stations throughout the country, an accomplishment every bit as admirable as Stanley's historic trek across the continent.

The list of candidates measured the size of the nation: thirty-three presidential contenders (including Oscar Kashala, a Harvard-educated Congolese oncologist living in the Boston suburbs) and 9,632 parliamentary candidates representing 218 political parties. Five hundred seats in parliament would be chosen. The ballots themselves were as large as broadsheet newspapers and featured photos and symbols of the candidates and their parties for those who couldn't read. Over five thousand tons of election materials were shipped on fifty flights from South Africa at the cost of $50 million. The bill for the election itself, funded almost entirely by the EU, totaled nearly $500 million, around $3 million per day, making it the largest and most expensive ever attempted in Africa.

It was a grand achievement, and precisely the right way forward. But a century of colonialism, war, and despotism had so isolated the Congolese that the aim of elections flew over the heads of most people. Election workers had reached many areas in the forest, but the size of the country made widespread education and training impossible. A common misconception was that elections alone would be the silver bullet into the heart of war and corruption, that once the ballots were cast and winners announced, a new standard of living would suddenly blossom from the ruin. And of the thousands of candidates, few had even been into the jungles and introduced themselves. If candidates had even bothered laying out political platforms (and most hadn't), they were unknown to the people. In the virtual absence of government for so many years, personal politics had evolved around tribe, local alliances, and graft. People would by and large vote for whomever the village chief instructed them to, or for the candidate who passed through with the best hats and T-shirts.

Of the thirty-three presidential candidates, the true contest was between President Kabila and Vice President Jean-Pierre Bemba. Everyone suspected Kabila would sweep the east, and especially Katanga, from where his ancestors hailed. Kabila was a Swahili speaker, and son of the man who'd toppled Mobutu. He'd ended the war and welcomed peacekeepers who had, like them or not, paved the way toward elections and allowed a semblance of normalcy to return in places like Bunia.

His adversary Bemba was the leader of the Ugandan-backed rebel group MLC, which had nearly defeated the government-allied troops of Kabila's father during the war. He was the son of a wealthy businessman whose family was loved in Kinshasa and throughout the central jungles of Equateur province. In the jungles, Bemba was seen as a patriot son battling the outsiders who'd hijacked and derailed the country. The biggest outsider of them all, in their opinion, was Kabila, who they claimed was born in Tanzania to a Rwandan mother (the president was raised in Tanzania, where his father was in exile, but he claimed to have been born in Fizi, South Kivu). It was their explanation for why the president—a foreigner—had auctioned off the country's mineral wealth in shady deals with international conglomerates.

Bemba was loved in the west, but hated in the east, where he was regarded as a megalomaniac and warmonger. In November 2002, his forces had assisted the Hema militia in attacking the gold-mining town of Mongbwalu, where two hundred civilians were murdered. Bemba's gunboy army was so vicious they named their push into Ituri *Effacer le tableau* (Operation Erase the Blackboard) and were grimly referred to by locals as the "Effaceurs." During his recent campaign stop in Bunia, the vice president had even threatened to pick up the gun if he lost the vote.

For the sake of the power-sharing, transitional government, Kabila and his four vice presidents seemed to endure one another in public, but the fact remained that two of the men—Bemba and Azarias Ruberwa, leader of the Rwandan-backed RCD—had once sought to overthrow Kabila's father. And during the war, the president himself had fought against them as a major general in his father's army.

Militia activity and idle threats by war-drumming politicians made protecting the polls on election day the UN's biggest priority. Militia leaders had publicly expressed willingness to support elections, but in private, they knew its mandate was designed to wipe them out. After seven years of hard-earned advances and just as many setbacks, with billions of dollars spent and the stability of all of central Africa hanging on its shoulders, the last thing the UN needed was villagers massacred on their way to vote.

The area was far from serene, though. Various militia still controlled vast swaths of eastern Congo. Mai Mai militia were attacking villages in northern Katanga, Rasta and Rwandan Hutu *genocidaires* continued their rape and pillage in North and South Kivu, and Cobra's men—along with other Lendu factions—still battled Hema (and one another) for resources in Ituri. The combined instability had left over one million displaced and continued to kill over a thousand people each day.

Success depended largely on strengthening the Congo army, a

task even more onerous than planning the elections themselves. The FARDC (Armed Forces of DR Congo) consisted mostly of former militia who'd disarmed—part of the 2003 power-sharing deal between government and rebels at the war's end. By the end of 2005, the UN boasted over twenty thousand militia had surrendered in Ituri, many of them joining the army. The integration of warring factions into Congo's army was crucial in securing the polls, both by removing gunboys from the bush and training and using them to assist MONUC with joint patrols. The government had promised eighteen brigades of newly integrated troops for this task, but by election day, only six brigades were delivered, most of them untrained and malnourished, and many without uniforms or weapons.

In December 2005, a human rights group discovered most of the government money set aside for integration and training had been stolen, with millions embezzled to pay for (among other scams) hundreds of thousands of "ghost soldiers" who never existed. Soldiers received a paltry salary of twelve dollars per month (later raised to twenty-four dollars), which they often never saw. Cholera epidemics killed scores of soldiers across Congo in 2005 and 2006 because of poor sanitation and lack of medicine, and in Katanga, over twenty men starved to death after ration money was repeatedly stolen by their commander. Conditions were significantly worse on the front lines where troops battled militia, as food and clean water rarely reached their positions. As a result, the new recruits fell back on their old militia tactics and lived by the gun.

All across the country, soldiers sacked villages and looted displaced camps they were sent to protect, and crime waves swept through larger towns once soldiers arrived. Congo's Fourth and Sixth Brigades settled into Ituri in early 2006 to prepare for joint operations with the UN to clear militia and immediately went berserk on the local population. Soldiers looted livestock and burned homes, kidnapped and executed young men in the fields, and raped countless women.

Confronted with this mess, the UN threatened to end all support of the local army. But in reality, no matter how great a liability the soldiers were, the UN had no choice but to use them. The militiamen lined up against the elections were just too numerous for the UN forces to face alone, and UN commanders still hoped to instill a modicum of training and discipline into the Congo troops in the event of the UN's eventual withdrawal.

Which perhaps explains why, only months away from the country's first elections, a time that desperately called for peace, the UN and Congo army went ahead with joint offensives, the most robust military operations since the mission began in 1999. Their main target was the massive Lendu force commanded by Cobra Matata.

The first major campaign was in late February 2006, when around 750 Congolese commandos punched the main axis into Tchei as UN forces reinforced them with mortars and Firebird helicopters. On the second day of fighting, the commandos expelled Cobra's militia and took the mountain with ease. But their commanders were late to resupply them, and by the time their ammunition was dropped the following morning, thousands of militia were surging up the mountain. The commandos retreated all at once, taking withering fire and dropping as they ran. Looking back, they could see the gunboys pounce on their fallen comrades like dingoes on the kill, ripping and carving their trophies. When the commandos finally reached the UN-run forward base, bloody and demoralized, they rioted for three days and looted the base clean.

A second push in late May was victorious. Bangladeshi peacekeepers pounded the mountains with mortars and helicopter gunships while UN and Congolese troops walked straight in. But the threadbare army could only hold the position a month. Just ten days after UN forces left the Congolese in control, a small band of Cobra's soldiers approached one of their positions. The gunboys were unarmed and waved a white flag of surrender. When the

Congo troops dropped their guard to investigate, thousands of militia swooped over the mountain and routed them within the hour. The magic man himself had orchestrated the ruse.

The loss of Tchei was an embarrassing blow for the UN; not only had they wasted months of planning and resources and strengthened the militia's resolve, but the combat operations (including several skirmishes with militia between the battles for Tchei) had also killed dozens of villagers and forced thousands more to flee their homes. By the time of elections, the UN found itself with a worsening security situation in Ituri, along with 230,000 displaced people who desperately needed attention.

I flew into Bunia in mid-July hoping to piggyback on the next joint operation before elections. During the May offensive, Dave had embedded with UN and local troops and couldn't believe the things he'd seen: Congolese soldiers looting villages and taking slaves to hump their food and ammo, their Bangladeshi officers watching it all in stunned disbelief.

Hoping to sweeten my chances for a mission, I'd stopped into an Indian grocery in Queens before leaving home and bought a box of sweet rice balls for the UN force commander, Brigadier General Mohammad Mahboob, a very homesick Bangladeshi. He'd taken the gift with a forlorn sigh and asked me where I wanted to go. "Tchei," I said, and heard it echo off the walls. "Very well," he answered. "I'll put you as close as I can. But as you know, we no longer hold the mountain."

It would be several days before the next patrol left Bunia for the hills, so I spent some time getting back into the swing of the country. I rented my old room at the Hotel Ituri and took meals at the Hellenique, happy to see Jean the waiter still scuttling across the floor and forgetting my order. The heavy UN presence had halted nearly all militia activity in Bunia and the immediate neighborhoods. The fighting up north in Djugu had also subsided from the previous year, and the Ugandan trade routes were once again open. Bunia's shops were full and business was strong, and for once people seemed to be contently lost in the routine of everyday living. Despite the problems with Cobra's militia in Tchei, the upcoming elections had struck the town as a jolt of excitement instead of the death sentence it would've been in earlier times.

The UN had even built a massive Rec House on the edge of town, replete with a gym, tennis courts, and wood-fired pizza oven. (The bathrooms also had the only working flush toilets I'd seen in Ituri.) Each night the back lawn was filled with the usual mix of Euro staff and third-world soldiers, ordering gins and eating pizza while waitresses in white vests sauntered across the grass. The lawn doubled as the UN's evacuation landing zone in the event the town was overrun again.

I also used this time to visit the displaced camps near Tchei that had sprung from the fighting. For this I hired Pastor Marrion P'Udongo, a circuit preacher based in Bunia, and the ace fixer for the passing journalists. The pastor was already a legend throughout Ituri, a kind of black Moses who'd served the years of war and displacement as a lighthouse for the broken and scattered. He was a roly-poly man with a megaphone voice and goofy belly laugh, which, when triggered, caused his round eyes to vanish behind thick, black-framed bifocals. The pastor's sermons stirred people into dancing frenzies. Women ran out of houses to kiss his cheek whenever he passed through villages, and men on the roads bowed to him and waved. Militia commanders softened in his presence, and even the most bogey-eyed gunboys dropped the mask when he passed, regarding him like a fun-loving uncle up from the city. That charisma had saved not only the pastor's life, but the lives of many others.

He'd been the assistant pastor at the Pentecostal Chrisco Church in Bunia when the town fell to Lendu warriors in May 2003. Like Johnny, the pastor belonged to the Alur tribe, which the Lendu often pitted alongside the Hema. As Lendu death squads marched from house to house, dragging people out and executing them in the streets, about seventy Hema, many of them members of Chrisco Church, sought refuge at the pastor's house. Among the Hema was the pastor's wife, Julienne.

For four days they huddled inside a large living room with little food and water, praying and singing quietly as gunfire and rockets rumbled through the nights. At one point, the pastor's four-year-old son peeked outside the gates and saw the mutilated bodies of neighbors being eaten by dogs. On the afternoon of the fifth day, a gang of militia finally broke through the gates and discovered them. The gunboys ordered several people into the yard and stripped them naked while others watched in horror. But the execution was halted when a top commander named Pichu entered the house, along with a low-level lieutenant known as Gorilla.

Months earlier, Gorilla had attended one of the pastor's sermons in nearby Mongbwalu, and now he began pleading with Pichu to spare his life. "This pastor can't die," he said. "He is too good a man to be killed like this." After a long debate, Pichu finally ordered the gunboys away and looked at the pastor. "I should kill you and everyone here," he said. "But for some reason I'm not. Something is telling me no."

Instead, Pichu ordered the militia to escort the pastor and his congregants to the UN headquarters, where they'd be safe. And once the group was gone, the militia returned and looted everything in the house.

Two years later, Pichu was arrested for war crimes by UN and Congolese soldiers and placed in Kinshasa's notorious Makala prison. One of his first visitors was Pastor Marrion, who now periodically made the eighteen-hundred-kilometer journey by plane to bring Pichu money and spiritual counsel. "The reason I am alive is because of him. God sent him to rescue us. And you know, Pichu's wife is now a member of my church at Chrisco." He laughed until his eyes disappeared beneath his round cheeks. "My chief, we are living *because of the grace of God!*"

The displaced camps were scattered amid thick-wooded mountains where roads were easy for ambush. It was far beyond the UN-designated "no-man's-land," but the pastor had been running these roads throughout the war. He'd escorted teams of foreign journalists and even traveled here alone with a bullhorn, passing himself off as Lendu to gain trust of the young militia, many of whom he convinced to surrender.

These winding routes had circumscribed the pastor's life, and he'd developed an instinct for their dangers. The pastor had been born and raised in the town of Panyimur, on the Ugandan shores of Lake Albert. When he was fifteen years old, Ugandan soldiers gunned down his father, and three days later, his mother died from illness. "It was high blood pressure," the pastor said. "She died from grief." Like Johnny, he was left alone to his wits to survive in a perilous and rapidly dissolving region. He made money ferrying gasoline back and forth over the Congo border and, for a while, smuggled gold from the fields of Mongbwalu to businessmen in Kampala, traveling at night to avoid soldiers who hunted smugglers and stripped their wares.

In 1990, he'd followed a girl to a church in Bunia run by Swedish missionaries, and there he gave his life to Christ. The call to preach was sudden and strong, and by chance he happened upon a group of Texan evangelists in Uganda who trained him in the gospel. After the Rwandan genocide, he ministered to thousands of refugees who poured over the Ugandan border and helped open churches in their camps. And after several years, he was running those roads again, preaching from village to village and offering a rare hopeful message as war swept the country.

The pastor had a piece of scripture he'd clung to during the days of war, as militia flooded the hills and spread their plague. It was Romans 14:7—"For none of us liveth to himself, and no man dieth to himself . . ." Those words had saved him from execution squads and gunboys in the hills, and they'd given him hope back in 1998, when he'd fallen terribly ill and nearly died. He'd been preaching in Tchomia village on Lake Albert, getting things organized to marry Julienne the following day, when his kidneys and liver suddenly failed. Family rushed him to a hospital in Kampala, where he fell into a coma. Doctors couldn't determine the cause, but the pastor was convinced he was poisoned by fellow preachers in Tchomia. ("They were jealous because people loved me too much," he said.) After eight months in the hospital with no improvement, the pastor was taken back to Bunia to die at home, his body emaciated and weak. And as family and congregants prayed and wailed in the living room outside, the pastor mustered a deathbed prayer, pleading to live. And then came a vision: There he was, standing on a dark stage before a large crowd of people. "And I was *preaching!*" he said. "I was *strong!* I was preaching how God saves us and heals us, and *praise God,* I got out of bed the next week and preached *all the way back to Uganda!*"

The words from Romans continued to guide him as he ministered from camp to camp, connecting with his flock, who'd scattered at the teeth of wolves. And I hoped they'd guide us still as we left the sandbags and razor wire of Bunia and ventured into Cobra's realm. I felt a measure of invincibility when traveling with the pastor, as if his front-seat sermons and warped gospel cassettes supplied a force field as we passed through the valley of gunboys with death in their fingers.

"God promises to bless and protect us coming in and coming out, and I expect him to keep that promise," he said as our Land Rover rattled through the dark forest. "But oh, *my chief,* someone could *really* disappear here! *Oh, yes!*"

The most recent fighting around Tchei had emptied many villages into the pine-covered hills, where they gathered at a village called Gety. Over forty thousand people had collected there by the time we arrived, and hundreds more continued to stagger from the bush barely strong enough to walk. Aid workers had recently arrived and distributed plastic sheeting for shelters, but it did little against the cold mountain air and daily seasonal rain. As we entered the camp, all we saw was a gray, dismal tableau of ragged-looking people, shivering and covered in mud.

A small team of doctors from MSF had set up in an old house at the edge of the camp with no water or electricity. Along with a few aid workers from the French group Solidarités, they were trying to hold back a wave of malnutrition and diarrhea. About forty people were dropping dead each day, most of them children.

The aid workers—fewer than a dozen—had swept in and halted a massive humanitarian fiasco almost by sheer will. In just three weeks' time, they'd already immunized for measles (the first thing you always do in camps, since an outbreak could wipe out everyone), handed out sheeting, blankets, and emergency food rations, and hired one thousand camp residents to help, among other things, dig latrines, purify drinking water, and build bamboo triage centers for the sick.

The person heading the MSF team was my friend Olivier, who'd worked in Bunia with the Swiss doctor trapped in the hospital. I walked in and found him sitting at a wooden table in the dark, sipping cold instant coffee and poring over the latest camp figures. He was exhausted and hadn't showered in days.

The doctors and aid workers had finally stabilized the camp, he said, before the population more than doubled in three days. The death was now overwhelming, and the faces of the doctors who passed through the room were pale and troubled.

"It's been hard on the staff," he said. "They feel they can't save the kids." He sighed heavily and stared off into the chipped and peeling walls. It occurred to me I'd never seen this man at ease. "It's been a tough week for all of us."

Whereas other camps I'd visited were smaller and more

concentrated in a large field or valley, the camp at Gety had swallowed an entire village. A large Catholic mission was the only remaining space (it would later be used for elections); just outside, the
camp stretched for several kilometers in every direction. Shelters
made from plastic sheeting, clay, and tree branches jammed both
sides of the village roads. Once you stepped off the path and into
the maze they created, the suffering was outward and unmistakable.
Here the morning fog mingled with woodsmoke, and inside the
haze, babies wailed and children's lungs seized with wet, bubbling
coughs. My steps became instinctively delicate and my voice lowered to a whisper, as if to respect the soft exit of life around me.

The pastor found several people to interview, and one by one we
took them back to the truck to speak in private. The tales of rape
and murder actually lined up at my notebook. First came Adjove
Anyotsi, a preacher from nearby Tchekele. Militia had captured his
family and shot his young daughter in the neck while she stood beside him. The following day they raped his other daughter, who I
interviewed next. Next came a farmer named Kandro, who spent
two months hiding in the forest with his wife and seven-month-
old son, until his wife died of hunger. He'd held her in the seconds
before she passed and said, "I have nothing to give you." Days later,
his son died, too. He'd buried their naked bodies in shallow holes
in the forest, but now couldn't remember where.

After Kandro left the truck, I spoke to a seventeen-year-old girl,
who'd been gang-raped by four army soldiers on the road near
Tchei. "I couldn't stand up when they left," she said, her eyes
wounded and wild. "It was my first time to be with a man." She
was in such obvious physical pain that we stopped the interview
and the pastor guided her to the clinic.

Afterward, the pastor and I walked through the camp and passed
the funeral of an old woman who'd died in the night of diabetes.
Her body had been wrapped in grass mats and hoisted on the
shoulders of men, who led a long procession of women singing

and waving palm branches. Just beyond the funeral, a young boy came running up and spoke to the pastor. "His brother just died," the pastor said. "Just now, twenty minutes ago." The boy led us to a nearby hut, where a young woman sat rocking a bundle of blankets in her arms, slack-eyed from shock. The infant's name was Zapatista, and for days he'd withered from diarrhea and vomiting. That morning he'd developed a violent cough, then stopped breathing. His temples were sunken from starvation and his skin was taut and sickly bronze. The mother looked up and lifted the dead boy like an offering. "Take a picture," she said. I snapped the death portrait and backed away, capturing probably the only image of the child in its entire short life. Standing in the doorway, we were told another boy had just died. But it was getting late and we needed to head back to Bunia, and I didn't think I could handle seeing any more dead children.

But about twenty kilometers outside Gety we noticed another cluster of tents at the bottom of a rippled valley. We were making good time, so I told the driver to pull in. Once we reached the camp itself, I begin to wonder if anyone was left living at all. Little by little, though, the people began to emerge from the tumbledown grass huts at the sound of our engine. Their squinted faces gave them the look of survivors who'd been plucked from the guts of a mine shaft.

The chief of Manji-Sona told us about two thousand people were living there, all area residents who'd fled during fights between the government and Cobra's militia. They'd been there six months; aid workers had managed to visit only once. With no food or medicine, they'd survived by collecting firewood and selling it in nearby Kasenyi. The old people who couldn't work were left to starve and were easy targets of the cholera that spread with the rains.

"There are two dead children today," said the chief, whose name was Kanombe. "Would you like to see them?" The children had both died that morning of diarrhea and now lay rigid in the hook of their mothers' arms. The father of the second child, two-year-old Guillaume, was making plans for a funeral. Where will you bury him? I asked. He hadn't thought of it. He pointed to a nearby scrub field. "Just here, I guess," he said, and went to look for a spade. On the edge of the tent, the dead boy's brother was catching termites in the mud because there was nothing else to eat.

Several tents down, a mother's voice called for the pastor. She sat inside the darkness clutching her three-year-old son, who was slowly withering away from diarrhea. The boy's eyes barely registered any signs of life, and his arms and legs trembled under a blanket from fever. I stood there scribbling notes, then stopped because it felt so absurd. For a second I froze, then realized, *I can save this kid's life.*

I ran back to the truck and grabbed my big medical kit and turned it upside down in the backseat. Sifting through, I found half a dozen packets of rehydration salts, antidiarrheal tabs, and some ibuprofen for fever. Simple things. I gave the mother two packets of salts and a bottle of clean water. The rest I gave the chief to distribute, then we climbed into the truck to leave. Our driver was restless to get back to Bunia; only bad things happened on these roads at night. (When I returned to Manji-Sona two days later, the boy was still alive, but his grandmother was unconscious from dysentery and not expected to live. There was nothing I could do; all my medicine was gone.)

During our visit to the MSF compound in Gety, Olivier had pulled the pastor aside and offered him a job. The team of doctors desperately needed a local person to translate and organize the staff, someone they could trust. The request had touched the pastor deeply, and now on the road back to Bunia, he stared ahead in silence.

The aid group couldn't pay as much as journalists—the pastor's sole source of income since the church gave no salary—but he saw their work as morally superior and guided by the hand of God. They'd treated the pastor's children during the war and given him medicine when his kidneys became reinfected, a problem that still caused him constant pain. It touched him that MSF doctors left six-figure salaries in Europe and America to be frontline medics in places most people didn't even bother pronouncing right; that in places where all hope and sanity were lost, these people were always first to arrive, blood up to their elbows and never asking thanks. And in Congo, their staff had been kidnapped and held hostage for doing it.

As we drove, the pastor's eyes darted around behind his thick glasses, and drops of sweat pooled on his bald head as he discerned his message. The Swahili praise music warbled like a warped record as we bucked over the mud-slicked roads. Finally, the pastor turned:

"God put us here on this earth *to live*, to have a successful life, *and to be healthy!* We are not here by accident. We should not just preach that people who believe in God go to heaven. We should know how to spare their lives when they're still on *earth!*

"If it is God's will for us to live a healthy life, to escape the bondage of death and poverty, then MSF is doing the work of God. They are doing a kind of sacrifice. I respect you journalists because you give me money, but I respect MSF because they are saving the lives of us, they are *doing great work, God's work!* In the name of God I will join MSF, *even if they will pay me nothing!*"

Sacrifice in this period of struggle meant a great deal to the pastor, and he clearly believed it measured a person's place in heaven. The peacekeepers who came to Congo and gave their lives for another man's country, for another man's tribe, that was sacrifice. The aid workers who left their blessed homes and families and sank themselves in the mud and excrement of a place that would never appear on a map, to hold a frightened child as it died because the government couldn't be bothered, that was sacrifice.

I sensed that working for MSF would certainly ease the pastor's mind, both in deepening his own sense of duty and safeguarding his dignity. Because on this scale, journalists existed somewhere further down, and that his children depended on them to eat probably cost him many a night's sleep. He'd had some bad experiences recently with foreign reporters, real Hemingway types who'd cursed him in front of locals and bullied the village chiefs. Some had caught their UN flights home without paying, others had embarrassed him by getting too drunk or bringing prostitutes into their hotels. There were also many dedicated, kindhearted guys who passed through to balance that weight, but still, our lot was a gamble.

I never felt I was sacrificing anything other than a few comforts and luxuries I'd grown accustomed to, and whether our stories did any good was a question I still couldn't answer. We'd been sending the reports out of Congo for years now, but how much had really changed? How much did the millions in food aid flown in every year actually change, or the legions of small foreign NGOs committed to their myriad contraceptive programs, mosquito-net drives, and hygiene seminars?

The war was so big and had a hundred different answers to the same few questions. The food aid filled stomachs, but didn't create economies. For every child saved in a camp, three hundred died in the forest. Journalists wrote the truth, but they also lied and took advantage and distorted. And all of us made by Congolese standards a fortune in pay.

It seemed the longer you stayed, the stranger the questions became. And the next day, two of my photographer colleagues, Lionel Healing and John Moore, saw just how strange it had all become. They were driving back from shooting in Gety when they passed a smaller displaced camp near a place called Kotoni. And rising from the heart of the squalid camp was a manifestation of all those questions that had no answers, a freak totem of the savior-destroyers. There, in the middle of the forest was, impossibly, a bright blue neon sign. The two looked at one another, then looked back again. Its message was written in English, in bold letters that read:

PLEASE ENJOY POVERTY

A tall white man in his early thirties sat at the base of the sign, clutching a video camera while preaching to a gathered crowd. His white shirt was yellowed with sweat and tucked into a pair of khakis, and his long hair was greased against his head. He was Renzo Martens, a Dutch artist and filmmaker. He'd spent the year traveling the country and filming the crisis—the UN press conferences, committee meetings, sorrow and hunger in the camps—and the neon sign was a blazing billboard for his message of deliverance, one meant to expose the grand conspiracy behind this deceitful humanitarian front: that misery was Africa's largest export, more than diamonds and gold, and the millions of dollars it generated each year for aid groups and news organizations was too great a boon for them to work toward its end. The system was entrenched and there to stay, so Africans should embrace their poverty and learn to enjoy it, and through this acceptance, be set free.

The film was a montage of Renzo lecturing impoverished villagers on the value of their suffering, throwing drunken parties in the camps at night, where hundreds whooped and danced in frantic drum circles around the blinking totem. His previous film was set in the bleak refugee camps of Chechnya, where he'd interviewed war victims at ration stations—frail old women and a man who'd been mangled by fire—and asked them, "What do you think of me? Do you think I'm handsome?"

As Lionel and John pulled in and stepped out of the truck, Renzo swung his camera toward them and announced, "Ah, the journalists have arrived. Tell me, guys, how much money do you earn from your photos in Africa?" As with the sign, Renzo spoke in English when the camera rolled, never mind that French was the official language. "This exhibit is a resource for the local people," he said. "You might call it an emancipation."

He worked the crowd like a sideshow tout and goaded the photographers toward rage. And when John and Lionel finally left, Renzo chased after the truck with his camera, screaming, "Typical journalists, just take the photos and leave!"

The UN had escorted Renzo to Kotoni in one of their vehicles, and everyone knew he traveled on UN flights. They'd issued him press credentials, probably never asking what in hell he was actually doing, and even flown his neon sign across the country from Kinshasa. And now there he was, crucifying the UN and aid workers in front of hundreds of people who desperately needed them to survive. The UN escort had stood there dumbstruck.

The next afternoon, the pastor and I traveled together to the camp in Tchomia. I'd visited the previous year and wanted to see if there'd been any progress. The camp had survived numerous outbreaks of cholera, and once UN peacekeepers had turned it over to government soldiers, the local troops had raped women and looted the camp. Tchomia was the pastor's old turf, where he'd preached in the village church (and perhaps been poisoned). He'd visited the camp many times over the past year and was well-known and loved. But when we arrived this time, the crowd rose up against him, waving their arms, shouting, and demanding to be paid. Renzo, it seemed, had visited a few days before and given one of his sermons.

"Journalists and aid workers are no longer welcome in this camp," said the chief. "Not unless they pay!" The pastor explained how the children needed the aid workers to eat and help them go to school. And journalists only helped to expose their story.

The pastor told him, "The journalists are not getting rich and they cannot pay."

The old chief just waved him off. "That's not what Renzo told us. And he paid us well."

II

After several days of waiting, the UN informed me I could join one of their units in the hills. General Mahboob explained there were no planned "operations" this close to elections, mainly for fear of further destabilizing the population. But if anything happened, I would have a front-row seat.

Sensing I was headed into a classic "hurry up and wait" situation, I invited Lionel along to keep me company. As it turned out, he'd arrived in Kinshasa just a couple of months after I left. I'd met him over beers my second night in Bunia and liked him immediately. He was a tall, even-keeled Londoner with a rank sense of humor, the kind of guy who'd hand you a gin and tonic and, ten minutes later, casually tell you he'd spiked it with noxious Congo tap. He'd been a shooter for the local news when his wife quit her teaching job to join Save the Children, and they'd assigned her to Congo. Lionel was picked up by AFP shortly after arriving and hurled himself into the story, learning quickly how to operate in the lawless hills.

In Ituri, several weeks had passed without any militia attacks, and the relative quiet had boosted confidence among the residents. Already thousands of people who'd been scattered in camps began walking home to vote where they'd registered. But the calm worried some of the UN commanders. While high voter turnout was the dream, it could also play into the perfect trap.

A rumor had started circulating about a massive election-day assault by Cobra's boys on the Gety camp, coinciding with another attack north of Bunia by another Lendu group. The Catholic mission at the Gety camp was a major polling station, and as the rumor went, the gunboys would wait until the voting lines were long, then sweep down from the hills.

The camp at Gety wasn't regularly guarded by UN or government troops, and the Congolese soldiers nearby had pillaged the area so much that residents felt safer alone. Unable to trust anyone for security, the doctors at MSF were ordered to temporarily evacuate their Gety base, leaving behind only a skeleton crew of local staff. The pastor had hoped to work on election day, and he took the news hard. He'd steeled himself for his heavenly call, but in the end, Cobra and the magic man had been closer to the earth.

The morning after receiving the green light from General Mahboob, after six days in Bunia, Lionel and I hired a Land Rover and were driven to a secluded mountain camp occupied by a company of South African peacekeepers. The camp was a no-frills crash pad for the worked and weary, nothing but a few canvas mess tents and lean-to shelters scattered across the muddy hills. The only adornments were two 82 mm mortar positions and a half dozen minesweeping Casspir APCs parked in the back lot.

The South Africans were a scrappy and salty bunch. Most all had grown up poor in South Africa's dire slums, where violence and early death were always in the wings. A few of the older commanders had been soldiers with the African National Congress (ANC) armed wing, who'd fought against apartheid and survived the horrific township wars of the mid-1990s. But even the younger guys had been touched in some way by the country's turmoil.

"You see that vehicle?" a young captain said to me that first day. He was pointing to one of the tall Casspirs, once an iron horse of the apartheid government and the Angola campaigns. "When I was a boy, they used to chase me through the streets. Now I'm the one chasing people!" He took a drag of his cigarette and just laughed.

The South Africans had seized and occupied Tchei back in May, only to watch their position later disintegrate in the hands of the Congolese troops. They'd fought hard for that mountain, slogged through the mud and rain, and losing it pissed them off. But not long after the operation, they'd engaged Cobra's militia again. The gunboys had tried to cut the supply road from the peacekeepers' base to Bunia, then march into town. But the South Africans had stopped their advance and, after two weeks of daily fighting, had driven them back to Tchei.

When I arrived, the troops were exhausted and still buzzing from the fight. But it was evident they saw beyond the rush of combat and viewed the mission in broader, historical terms. Many of these young grunts saw their mission as a way to uplift the troubled continent by taking on the insurgent rogues, brother against brother, killing as a kind of vital surgery. "It is our responsibility as Africans to help our people here," they'd say in casual conversation. They saw liberating Congo as a necessary humanitarian duty, and their idealism seemed to come directly from their solemn commander, a headstrong man who'd proved himself to be one of the UN's most effective military leaders.

Colonel Joseph Tyhalisi had come to Congo from the UN's mission in Burundi, where his South African unit had assisted in brokering peace talks between rebels and the government. The colonel had a natural gift of speaking on the level to rebels and insurgents in the bush, gaining their trust and bringing them around, since, for much of his life, he'd been one himself.

He'd grown up in Cape Town during the oppressive days of Afrikaner rule, when race laws were brutally enforced and the only education offered to black children prepared them for servitude. In 1985, at the age of eighteen, he'd joined the ANC's military wing, Umkhonto we Sizwe (or MK), which had been staging guerrilla attacks against the apartheid government since 1961. Throughout the eighties, the guerrilla fighters bombed police stations, assassinated officials, and, near Cape Town, attacked a nuclear power plant. Soon after joining, Tyhalisi was arrested by the police and severely tortured, and upon his release, he went into exile in Tanzania and Uganda. There, squads of MK guerrillas received military training for covert attacks inside South Africa, often slipping across the border for two days at a time. Tyhalisi spent the next decade in exile, often living rough in the bush. In 1996, two years after Nelson Mandela won the presidency on the ANC ticket, ending apartheid, Tyhalisi returned as an officer in the national army.

The period spent living in exile in the bush had not only given the colonel an insight into the minds of the boys he now fought, but also a firm command of Swahili. That combo gave him a decided edge over other UN commanders when dealing with Congo's militia. He was also handsome and extremely fit, a model soldier with level-straight posture and eyes that always caught you looking.

He'd scared the hell out of me the first time I met him. He was standing at the gates when I first arrived, so I handed him my credentials and rattled off my big important mission. He'd taken the documents and just stared at me, those eyes digging around inside until I ran out of things to say. Then he turned and walked off. A captain standing nearby just laughed and started giving me the tour. Later, I'd turn around to find the colonel just watching me like some predatory bird, lines of confusion or disgust drawn across his brow, I never could tell which, and I'd have to make some gesture of excuse and leave.

If anyone else felt those eyes on them, it was Cobra. Over the past two weeks, it seemed, whenever Cobra turned around, the colonel was right behind him, humping his weapon and gear through the cold rain with his men. He'd foiled the militia attack, secured the supply road to Bunia, and trapped the gunboys in the hills and, over the past two weeks, had never allowed them to rest.

"Every time I heard they were somewhere, I'd hit them," the colonel said. "Then I'd hit them again and again, until they could feel me in their blood. This Cobra, he's like a fever around me."

The heaviest fighting had occurred on the grassy highlands near the village of Bavi, a militia stronghold where the gunboys operated a gold mine and kept a base. With the colonel in the lead, the two platoons of South Africans had reached the top of the rise and were attacked by gunmen. There was no cover besides the tall grass, leaving the soldiers pinned down as bullets zipped just inches above their heads. With no other options, the colonel switched his weapon to automatic, lifted it above his head, and fired blindly at the enemy, praying his hands wouldn't get blown off.

The South Africans thwarted the attack and pushed the militia back to Tchei. And in the following days, the colonel dropped leaflets from a high-flying chopper with his mobile number listed and a warning: "If you don't surrender, I'm coming after you." He'd also worked diplomatic angles by organizing Lendu elders from Bunia and the vicinity to venture into Tchei and convince Cobra to disarm.

When Lionel and I arrived in Kagaba, the elders had been inside Cobra's mountain camp for several days discussing the deal and were scheduled to come out that afternoon. As soon as we put our bags down, the colonel called his men together. He was organizing a patrol to meet the elders at a rendezvous point six kilometers outside Tchei, then transport them to Bunia to speak with government and UN officials. The mission seemed fairly routine, and the South Africans expected little to happen. But just for assurances, a unit of Bangladeshi peacekeepers stationed in nearby Aveba would join us for reinforcement.

The rendezvous point was near the village of Kamatsi, which was the highest and nearest vantage point to Tchei. After two hours of driving, our convoy was finally called to a halt along a broad, grassy hill where the wind blew heavy and warm. Down below, the soldiers could see the road to Tchei leading into the trees, dissolving against jagged hills and streams where vehicles could no longer pass.

The APCs parked in a half circle and the platoon jumped out and readied their weapons: automatic rifles, rocket and grenade launchers, and two mounted fifty-caliber guns. The colonel shouted, "Get into position!" and his men fanned into a perimeter along the hill. They disappeared inside the neck-high elephant grass, their bodies concealed except for their UN-issued body armor that left them glowing like blue gas flames in the reeds.

There was a rumbling of diesel engines down the road. Seconds later, several white Bangladeshi APCs barreled through the brambles and stopped on the hill. Sitting atop the first vehicle was Johnny, my old translator. It seemed like everywhere I went he was there, like some Forrest Gump in the *Charge of the Blue Helmets*. He wore a grimy, well-worn flak vest over his parka and an oversized helmet that slid over one eye.

Johnny was now translating for the Bangladeshi officers in Aveba and had seen a lot of fighting in the past six months. But each deployment lasted five weeks, and when there were no operations, the days were long and painfully boring. The comfort of the translators also depended on the base officer in charge, and he'd had some real assholes. A Pakistani commander once locked him outside the APC during a firefight, and in Aveba, the commanders were actually charging him room and board. "We eat MREs and live in tents, man, where it rains through the floor. And they charge me ten dollars a day! To eat MREs! I hired an old woman from the village to cook *pondu* because my stomach couldn't take it."

But he'd managed to save enough money to buy a small house in Bunia. He'd also found a girlfriend named Aline and paid a marriage dowry to her father, who'd given his blessing to marry. "Four goats and three cows," he said, "and a suit for her father. Even socks and shoes!" But with all the fighting, he'd had little time to think about marriage, much less a wedding. "Oh, man, and she wants a *big* wedding."

The colonel had given the tribal elders two-way radios before sending them into the bush, and now his handset squawked with voices. "Where is this translator?" the colonel shouted, and motioned Johnny over. The elders were close, the colonel said, and handed Johnny a radio and megaphone and sent him down the hill to greet the delegation.

After a few moments, Johnny radioed back saying the elders were coming but were surrounded by militia. "There are many of them, and they're heavily armed!" The Bangladeshi soldiers rushed behind their armored vehicles for cover. We could see nothing from where we stood, only the road directly in front of us. "Tell them to come slowly," the colonel said. "I want their hands in the air."

"They say Cobra is with them," said Johnny. "And he wants to greet you."

The Bangladeshi commanders protested, fearful of an ambush. They shouted at Johnny, "Tell them to stay back!" But the colonel waved them off and marched toward the road. "Johnny, tell them to come," he said. "If Cobra has come himself, then I must trust him."

As the colonel marched toward the road to meet Cobra, he knew he had the advantage. In the end, even if the colonel couldn't bring Cobra down from the mountain, at least he'd broken his magic. During the militia attack at Bavi, after the colonel had lifted his weapon and fired through the grass, something strange had happened. The incoming rounds suddenly stopped, and the gunboys turned around and fled. The following day, through one of the Lendu elders, the colonel learned one of his rounds had struck and killed the militia's top lieutenant, Cobra's second-in-command. The lieutenant, it turned out, was Kakadu's son.

When the militia had seen the magic leader's son dead with a bullet through his chest, they'd panicked. Their antibullet magic had failed. They dragged the lieutenant's body back to Tchei and revolted against Cobra, shouting for an explanation of how their commander had died, how their magic shield had been breached. Panic spread through the camp, and as they buried the lieutenant, some distraught boy opened fire and kicked off a barrage. When the shooting finally stopped, fifteen of them were dead.

As the peacekeepers braced themselves for the meeting, a forward party of young militia emerged from the bush and lined both sides of the road. They carried their rust-eaten AK-47s slung over their shoulders with shoestring and vines, and long wooden spears tipped with jagged blades. Many wore the uniforms and berets of dead Congolese and Ugandan soldiers. Their very presence now was enough to quicken the pulse of every UN soldier, for the enemy had rarely been this close. Seeing them was like glimpsing something wild, something rare and nimble that had strayed into the open. Their eyes now locked on the South African soldiers, who, with their jacked bodies and heavy steel, must've seemed like Minotaurs in the reeds.

Johnny pointed the group toward the colonel, who was fast approaching. But as the gunboys crossed our perimeter, the jittery Bangladeshi soldiers chambered their weapons. The unmistakable sound of live rounds locking into place was like a hole being punched in the sky. For a second everything went still. Gunmen from both sides froze in the tall grass, weapons clutched tightly, fingers stroking the triggers. One nervous bullet could spark a wild slaughter.

"So where is Cobra?" the colonel finally said, speaking to one of the elders. The man appeared unable to move. "He's at the end of the road waiting," he said, then waffled. "But maybe he should meet you next time."

"Nonsense," the colonel said. "Take me there now."

The two men led the rabble of militia and peacekeepers down the road and through the tall grass. There at the end, a group of militia parted and Commander Cobra stepped forward. He was a short, dark-skinned man dressed in camouflage fatigues and an olive-green beret. His chest and arms were surprisingly thin, with barely enough meat to hold a silver watch that hung on his wrist. But his eyes were like dead coal, and when they caught me, they told something different. The colonel stepped to Cobra and stared into those eyes. The two men embraced.

"I wanted to meet the South African I'd thought so much about," said Cobra.

"I'm glad you came," the colonel said, "because I've been thinking a lot about you."

The meeting lasted only a few minutes. The two men discussed the militia's surrender, and for the first time Cobra said he was open to negotiations. "You will hear from me," Cobra said, and squeezed the colonel's hand. And for the next half hour, the two armies who'd battled one another across the green hills stood arm in arm and posed for photos.

Walking back to the vehicles, a Bangladeshi captain could hardly contain his joy. "This is the greatest thing to happen in a year," he said. "You were just a witness to UN history."

For the next two nights, the South African soldiers unwound with a deep freeze of Nile Special beer and hard *kwaito* beats pumped from boom boxes. They watched American movies on portable DVD players and cleared pallets of bottled water and onions in the supply tent to make a crude dance floor. On the second night, a lashing storm sent flash floods through the camp and shredded most of their tents. Everything they owned was soaked and scattered in the bush. So the soldiers crowded into the supply tent and kept on drinking, wrapping themselves in ponchos and soggy sleeping bags to fend off the mountain chill. A well-oiled captain stood atop a stack of pallets and raised a bottle. There wasn't a dry stitch of clothing on him. "Remember troops," he said, and the chorus of soggy soldiers chimed in, "there is no reign in the army, only army in the rain!"

"Hey," one of them said to us, "how come you guys are so dry?" It was true, we hadn't left the tent for hours. Still, I was freezing through three layers of clothes. A group of soldiers crowded around Lionel, with his golden beard and blue eyes, and started calling him Chuck Norris. "Mr. Chuck," they said, "you missed the battle, man, we done cut the head off the Cobra."

One of the commanders had instructed the men not to speak to the journalists, so I didn't expect any war stories. Sure enough it came up. "We can't be talking to no reporters, man," they said, just to get it out of the way. Because when the beer finally ran dry, the men started to talk. They huddled around a fire of C-ration heat tabs, boiled pots of instant coffee, and reflected on their days in the violent east.

There was a white soldier named Smith who manned the big .50-caliber guns. When the South Africans had marched into Tchei, he said, one of the first things that greeted them were the boneyards along the roads, the bleached skeletons of dead militia lying in the open grass where they'd fallen. But the shallow graves in Tchei stayed with him the most. "The arms and legs stuck up from the ground," said Smith. "And the dogs stripped them to the bone." He couldn't sleep the whole time he was there, he said, those graves seemed to make their own restless noise.

The soldiers spoke of their colonel with both loathing and supreme love. He was like a god who revealed himself only through pain and sacrifice. "The colonel is hard," said one soldier. "When you speak to him, he just stares at you like a jackal. *I think I will be eaten.*"

"Yes," said another. "But he's always there with us. When he says fight, he is the man who leads the way."

They would follow their colonel anywhere, they said. And the next morning, as the soldiers awoke in puddles of cold rainwater, the colonel arrived to inform them they were going back to Tchei.

In the early-morning chill, the South African soldiers filed into formation and the colonel stood before them. He wore a knit cap pulled low over his head and a grenade clipped to his flak vest. He explained the latest developments to his men, speaking loudly and clearly and without any expression. After lengthy negotiations via satellite phone and radio, Cobra Matata had agreed to surrender with two thousand soldiers. He'd demanded amnesty for his boys and a smooth integration into the national army. Cobra also wanted legitimacy himself, demanding the government admit him into the army with the rank of general.

Cobra would surrender with his boys, the colonel explained, but one last condition was to be met. The South Africans would have to enter Tchei and get them. They would drive until they couldn't drive anymore, then walk into Cobra's boneyard.

The risks were so clear. Everyone knew it was six hard kilometers into Tchei, through mud banks, steep hills, and swollen streams. Much of the journey was under a thick canopy of trees, making support or rescue by chopper impossible. Once inside, your flesh and bone took on cartoonish expendability, worth only as much as a stoned twelve-year-old saw fit.

"We're going to walk inside and bring him out," the colonel said. He'd taken the grenade off his vest and now held it behind his back, fingering the smooth steel like a rope of prayer beads.

"If I tell you to do something, you don't analyze, don't attach any emotions to it. You just do it." The soldiers stared firmly ahead, beyond the colonel to where the green hilltops touched the lead-colored sky.

"What's important is not to panic. Don't think about what's going to happen to you, think only about what you have to do." Beyond the hills were the slopes of Tchei, and along the scarp they saw their bodies lying dead in the tall grass, a still life as innocent as if they'd walked past it in a museum.

"And if something happens while we're there, give each other your backs, you hear me? Give each other your backs and shoot everything in front of you."

The colonel paused. A pair of magpies screeched overhead and swooped to the ground. "Just trust me," he said. "But if you walk with me, make sure you're not very close."

When the colonel dismissed his men, we quietly loaded the vehicles and pulled the convoy onto the road. Sitting in the back of the Land Rover was a sweet-faced soldier who clutched his rifle and stared calmly out the window. I asked if he was afraid, and his lips parted into a smile. "Everything will be just fine," he said. "I believe in Jesus Christ."

The overnight rains had washed out the roads, slowing the convoy to a maddening crawl that only heightened the anxiety. The dense forest reached in and clawed at the windows, and somehow I was certain we were being watched from the trees. I focused on the headlights of the APC a hundred meters behind us, barely visible through the sheen of dirt and mud. I must've zoned out for a while, because when I came to, the first thing I realized was the headlights were gone. I turned to Lionel. "Where's that last APC?"

The major in the front seat must've realized it, too, because he told the driver to stop. The convoy ahead of us continued moving, and soon we were alone on the trail. The major called into his radio for the missing vehicle, but got no reply. *It's an ambush*, I thought, *they've split the convoy*.

The driver whipped the vehicle around and sped back the opposite direction looking for the missing APC, slamming into sinkholes that smashed our heads into the roof. We drove faster and faster. Around each bend we craned our heads and saw only red mud and trees. *Christ, how long ago did we lose them?* The colonel called from the lead vehicle, saying he was also turning back. Nobody in the truck said a word.

Finally, after a half hour of driving, we found the APC turned over in a ditch. Everyone was okay; the driver had taken a hard turn and spun the wheels off the road. We all just kind of laughed and cursed his skills, and no one acknowledged a thing.

When the other vehicles joined us at the wreck, we cracked open the MREs and ate breakfast on the trail. The colonel sat in the lead Land Rover, his boots propped up on the dash. He dug into a can of lentils with a pocketknife and ate from the blade. Loud Swahili hip-hop thumped from the speakers, but the colonel seemed to ignore it. Instead he appeared deep in thought and utterly alone.

We stood watching the colonel from the road, then Lionel leaned in and whispered, "That's my knife, mate, he borrowed it." He was proud as a boy and knew that I was jealous.

★ ★ ★

At the rendezvous point in Kamatsi, the soldiers fanned out once again in a broad perimeter. They carried heavier weapons this time, grenade launchers shaped like oversized tommy guns with multiple rounds strapped to their chests; spare RPG rockets sticking out of backpacks like deadly wands; and you knew the Casspir's guns were live and ready. The colonel sat atop one of the APCs and gazed across the valley with a pair of binoculars. The militia had promised to send escorts to meet the colonel and his men, so we waited for them to show. The wind whipped through the tall grass where the soldiers stood, and the morning sun was already strong overhead.

We waited for an hour, and then another, until every muscle became sore from standing so still. Silver clouds of cigarette smoke rose from the tall grass as soldiers crouched and waited. Otherwise no one moved. A few soldiers talked near the road, and I could see the colonel pointing to the hills and mouthing something to the major. But something about that hilltop and all its empty space sucked away all sound, leaving only wind. And silence like that only left you with yourself. Since I had no flak vest, I spent most of my time behind the APC, leaning against it, sitting in its shade, always within arm's reach.

Somewhere along that wind, around ten A.M., the first militia arrived. I never heard their approach, just looked up and saw them standing there on the road, a dozen of them, maybe twenty. Then within minutes there were hundreds, so many they filled the road and grassy field where we stood. They walked in small squads with four boys leading each pack. Two boys held the ends of a belt-fed machine gun while the others draped chains of bullets across their shoulders like ropes of brass garland. Fetishes were now tied to each boy's biceps, some with glass amulets and bits of herb protruding from their cloth bundles. The air was thick with dope, as rows of gunboys tugged off joints that turned their eyes yellow against their coal black skin. The battle armor and magic were all in place, suggesting a display of power or a readiness to fight — certainly not to give up. I'd seen militia disarm over their years, and no one had dressed up for that.

At news of the impending surrender, the UN brass in Kinshasa had organized a formal signing ceremony with Cobra as he emerged from Tchei. It would be attended by a delegation of senior UN civilian and military officials, plus FARDC generals and representatives from the Ministry of Defense. The UN and government needed every victory they could squeeze out before the elections, and a major warlord surrendering with two thousand militia was the stuff of dreamy PR. Earlier that morning, Bangladeshi soldiers had arrived and erected two giant canopies along the hill with tables and rows of chairs, along with urns of cold water, hot tea, and biscuits.

Around noon, several APCs thundered up the road with the delegation huddled inside. The vehicles stopped along the hill, and when the hatch opened, a UN cameraman scurried out and rolled the film. Delegates emerged dressed in sharp clothes and carrying clipboards under their arms. They were half-blinded by the sun and smiling, but once their eyes focused, their faces seemed to drop at the sight of the young killers glaring back from the high grass, smoking joints and polishing their gun barrels with dirty T-shirts.

The head of the UN office in Bunia, a dapper Ivorian named Charles Providence Gomis, made his way through the soldiers and militia and found the colonel. He was impeccably dressed in a tailored suit and smelled of expensive cologne. "Colonel," he said with burning sincerity, "you've showed a lot of courage and determination and the delegation is proud of you. Without you, we'd have no mission."

The colonel beamed and dug his boot into the dirt, and for the first time I saw his expression break. As the colonel briefed Gomis, other members of the delegation mingled and chatted with the peacekeepers and officers, with the delegates throwing wary glances at the militia in the perimeter. Several approached the militia and attempted conversation, but the gunboys only muttered a few nervous words, a childlike coyness I found almost encouraging. Up the hill, a small crowd gathered under the canopies as Bangladeshi soldiers served tea and biscuits and offered to light cigarettes. The UN cameraman weaved through the crowd shooting it all, his Palestinian *kaffiyeh* flapping in the wind. Lionel and I stood back in the grass just taking in the scene. "This has got to be the strangest party I've ever attended," he said, and there was no denying that.

An hour after the delegation arrived, the colonel reached Cobra by satellite phone. Cobra explained he was having second thoughts about meeting the delegation. He didn't trust the government's promise of amnesty and felt the UN was planning to betray him. He was afraid he would be arrested. "Cobra, you must trust me," the colonel pleaded. Cobra suggested he was still willing to talk, but only if the colonel came into Tchei alone.

Again, the Bangladeshi commanders balked. "It's a trap," they said. "You can't go in there alone. They're setting you up to die." The colonel looked up the hill at the delegates, who were guzzling water and starting to wilt in the heat. "We have only two days before elections," he said. "There are people in these houses that need to vote, and if we ruin a day, then it's over."

The colonel turned to his major. "I'll park the vehicle and walk in," he said. "If I'm not out in three hours, send everyone to get me."

The colonel climbed into the Land Rover with his driver and we watched them disappear around the bend and into the dense bush. Sometime later, the colonel's radio went dead. We waited two hours without word, sending call after unanswered call. The sun was brutal and the breeze had given way to sucking heat. The delegates slumped under canopies, fanning themselves and looking faint. Finally, embarrassed and a little more than worried, they announced they were returning to Bunia. It would be dark in an hour, and no one wanted to be stranded in the dark. With no word from the colonel, everyone started imagining the worst.

"We can't dwell on these options," said the South African major, rubbing his hands along his face as he stared at a silent radio. "For now we must trust him. Just wait for now."

The Bangladeshi commander suggested they go find him. "We'll just go in and stay the night. If someone shoots at us, we'll have plenty of our own to answer back."

"But we don't even know where he is," said the major. "Look, we just have to take it easy." The major walked away still staring at the dead radio, which had by now started to tremble in his hands.

The setting sun threw an auburn glow across the hills of Tchei, and the cool wind returned to chase off the heat. In the orange haze of dusk, the major looked up the road and noticed most of the militia had vanished. Something had happened, it suggested, something was complete. Still, we waited.

At near dark, the major's radio rumbled to life: "Ten-nine, ten-nine, do you read, over?" It was the colonel, alive, and instructing the major to send Land Rovers to the end of the road. "I have the package," he said, meaning Cobra was with him. The major sent the vehicles, and half an hour later, they emerged with the colonel walking briskly in between. He carried his service pistol in one hand at his side. When he reached the hill, his body was shaking so violently he could hardly speak.

"They have two brigades up there, almost a division of people," the colonel said, breathing heavily. "The man himself has like three hundred bodyguards."

The Bangladeshi commander ran over. "We thought you were dead."

The colonel had switched off his radio. "If I communicated at all, I would've taken a bullet."

The colonel explained how, after traveling two kilometers, his driver had parked the vehicle at the end of the road and stayed behind, while the colonel began walking the four kilometers into Tchei. He was soon greeted by twenty bodyguards sent to escort him to the militia base, where Cobra waited. The colonel gave them his rifle, pistol, and grenade, but kept a spare grenade tucked inside his underwear. "If anything happened," he said, "I wasn't going down alone." As he walked in, hundreds of gunboys packed both sides of the road. The militia were unaware the colonel himself had killed Kakadu's son, yet they saw him as the leader of warriors who'd beaten their magic. Most were drunk on corn liquor and their eyes danced crazy. "Here is the meat!" they shouted. "Give us your heart, colonel, it will make us strong!" The boys leveled their rifles at his head, while others reached through the bodyguards with clubs and knives, hoping to throw off their balance and take the colonel down. The colonel refused to look at them and continued walking.

They passed through thick forest, an open field, and finally reached the base itself. It was a village of mud and clay houses, busy with children and families of the militia. Many of the women were also drinking in their courtyards and cried out, "Here he comes!" The bodyguards led the colonel to a thatched hut and told him to wait. After fifteen minutes, Cobra and Kakadu emerged. The magic man had white hair and wore a white robe. He turned to Cobra and said, "Here is the son of the soil I spoke of. He is one of us. He comes in peace." Kakadu turned to the colonel and said, "I'm happy to see you made it," then assured the colonel he wouldn't be harmed.

Cobra took the colonel aside and said he was now willing to speak with the delegation. The colonel's lone march into Tchei had been a test to see if the UN and government were serious. No strangers had ever entered Tchei before and lived, Cobra said. After retrieving his weapons from Cobra's bodyguards, the colonel radioed his major at Kamatsi and ordered the extra vehicles to transport the party of militia to the rendezvous point. The group reached the vehicles and Cobra and one of his lieutenants climbed inside with the colonel. The driver started back toward Kamatsi, but before they got far, the bodyguards rushed forward and blocked the road with their rifles raised. They were afraid Cobra would be arrested and couldn't allow him to continue. Cobra grabbed a weapon from his lieutenant, jumped out of the truck, and aimed it at the boys. "I'll kill you if you don't move," he screamed. The colonel pulled him aside and told him it wasn't worth it. It was getting late, he said, and while they'd been walking toward the vehicles, he'd received word over the radio that the delegation had gone home.

"There's really no point now," said the colonel. "We'll have to talk next time."

The colonel left Cobra on the trail with his boys and a gun in his hand and drove toward Kamatsi. When we'd spotted the colonel approaching on foot, it was because he'd stepped out of the vehicle to speak to some of Cobra's guys on the road, to tell them the meeting was canceled. And after he explained everything to us, he lined the boys up and doled out his rations, then sent them back to Tchei.

III

With Cobra's militia still at large, we entered elections with the specter of violence still heavy in the hills. The UN responded by sending Bangladeshi APCs to Gety to guard the camp and the Catholic mission, where polling would be held. If there was an attack, the Bengali soldiers would be the first responders. Knowing this, Lionel and I grabbed our gear and moved to their base in Aveba. There I could sit and wait for Cobra, whether he surrendered or made his stand. I took comfort in knowing the wait, however long, would be conducted in luxury; the Bangladeshis ran one of the finest camps in all of Congo, a lavish pleasure dome (by UN military standards) that had generated its own lore among the Kinshasa-based correspondents.

Even the South Africans who'd dropped us off in one of the big Casspirs had said farewell with a longing sigh, for this was no mud-slicked bivouac. The Bengali soldiers lived in spacious, World War II–era center-pole tents rigged with electricity and set on prim rows of packed earth, which several soldiers were scouring with brooms when we arrived. A smiling captain greeted us at the door of a converted schoolhouse, which served as the officers' quarters and recreation hall. He handed our bags off and told someone to arrange our tents, then led us inside. "You're just in time for breakfast," he said.

The South Africans had given us MREs to eat, many of them so waterlogged the heat tabs just exploded when put to flame. Lionel and I had resorted to eating cold cans of lentils, pulled from soggy green ration boxes labeled HINDU. After days of this food, our stomachs were caving in, and we'd begun trading food fantasies like castaways.

At Aveba, the table inside the rec hall was spilling with food: omelets, stewed meats and vegetables, and fried parathas smeared with jam. About four officers sat digging in, while an army of cooks rotated out the empty plates for more heaps of steaming food. Each officer had his own personal servant—called a battle man or batman and traditionally taken into combat—who stood patiently behind him while he ate. When the meal was finished, the officer would flick his wrist and shout something in Bengali, and the batman would fetch him tea, fresh fruit, or cigarettes. Outside, two officers sat in the sun while their batmen shaved them with razors and boiled water for their bath.

Lionel and I ate like dogs, looking up every so often to exchange a nod of victory. The hot food and spices warmed our stomachs and lapsed us into a narcotic trance, abetted by the odd Bengali music videos playing on a nearby television, streamed in from a satellite dish outside. At night the officers watched westerns on DVD, such as *Quigley Down Under* and *Silverado*, plus episodes of *The Three Stooges* and *Tom & Jerry*. Their favorite cartoon had Tom and Jerry in combat with egg mortars and carpet bombs made of lightbulbs. The men howled with delight at every stunt and narrow escape, shouting, "I can't believe he did that!" and applauding madly.

After two gluttonous days of eating and napping, I'd almost forgotten about Cobra, the colonel, and the elections. I suddenly remembered the night before, while watching cartoons and sipping tea, the importance of the event, and how everything I'd reported since Bunia had led up to this day. Tomorrow the Congolese would come one step closer to reclaiming their nation from the cesspool of corruption and violence. But across the country in Kinshasa, the dawn of better times still looked a lot like the punishing days of old.

The EU had flown in a thousand French, German, and Spanish soldiers to secure the capital, with another thousand on standby in Gabon. Yet despite the extra manpower, violence had still plagued the city in the last days of campaigning. Vice President Bemba threw a campaign rally at the stadium that drew forty thousand people and ended with his supporters clashing with police outside. Six people had been killed, including two policemen who were shot and stoned to death by mobs. The next day, one of President Kabila's bodyguards shot and killed the bodyguard of Vice President Azarias Ruberwa, himself a presidential candidate, as the two politicians' details crossed paths on the road. And a mysterious Belgian army drone crashed into a crowded Kinshasa neighborhood, injuring five people and burning homes. The drone was intended to fly around the city taking photographs on election day. The army blamed the crash on software error.

As election morning arrived in Aveba, I left my tent and walked to the metal gates of the UN camp and saw hundreds of people streaming down the road. They carried their bundles of belongings on their heads—pots and pans, buckets and blankets—or pushed them on bicycles and oxcarts. Any other time such a procession would suggest something terrible, a militia raid or massacre that would empty the villages and fill the camps again. But now the exodus was reversed, as the camps and villages around us emptied and people hit the roads to vote.

We traveled twenty kilometers down the road to Gety camp and pulled into the Catholic mission. The compound was already crowded and thrumming with eagerness as residents poured in. It was like a different place from the camp I'd seen only days before. The sun was high and warm and had dried away the mud that choked the roads. Women wrapped in bright-colored *pagnes* stood in the voting lines, holding their children and chatting to the crowds that passed. The suffering and sickness no doubt remained in the narrow corridors of the camp, but here, now, something more powerful and hopeful had gained a foothold.

I stood and watched the voters enter the Catholic mission and drop their ballots, and when they emerged into the bright morning sunshine, each had the strangest look on their face, one of deep abatement, as if every muscle had relaxed for the first time in years. It was then, while staring across this place so overrun with death only days before, that the significance of the day finally set in.

In Gety we were joined by Pastor Marrion, who arrived to help us with interviews. For the past week he'd worked with the crush of correspondents in Bunia, hopefully making a good chunk of pay. That morning in Bunia he'd awoken before dawn to stand in line to vote, finally getting to experience the moment he'd anticipated and spoken about for months. By the time he pulled up to Gety in the Land Rover, his face was dancing. "Hello, my chief," he said, his arms opened wide and hands in a fist. "Today is a *great* day for Congo, one of our *greatest* days, praise *God!*"

All around the Catholic mission in Gety, families spread blankets in the grass and shared food. A mother and son carried trays of peanuts and cigarettes atop their heads for sale. Children played soccer with Bangladeshi peacekeepers, who snapped photos and chased them around the pitch with video cameras. The Congolese soldiers even kept to themselves, smoking cigarettes and dozing in the shade.

The pastor and I sat in the courtyard eating peanuts and watching the children play, and from his silence I could only guess the cathartic journey that had to be taking place in his mind as he revisited all the tragic milestones of his life—the death of his father; gunboys kicking down his door—a journey that accounted for all the pain, but eventually led here, to a sunny day in July, watching his nation vote. All across that courtyard those same sorrowful paths were remembered and relived, and I imagined them all fusing together into a splendid arch that spanned the blue sky and allowed those four million souls to finally cross over.

Across the giant country, election day was a peaceful and celebrated event. Even in Kinshasa, all the bleak predictions fell away as polls closed without incident. And despite the setbacks with Cobra's surrender, it appeared that all the UN's hard work and investment had finally paid off.

Negotiations with Cobra were ongoing in the following days, and while Lionel returned to Kinshasa, I stayed behind in Aveba with hopes of entering Tchei with the colonel. Each morning I'd walk down the road from the UN base to a space the size of a pitcher's mound we called Telephone Hill—the only place within twenty kilometers with cellular reception. Each morning I'd call the colonel at his base in Beni, and he'd guarantee that we'd soon be bringing out Cobra. "Just one more day," he'd say. "Tomorrow is looking very good. And when it happens, we'll go in together."

But after three full weeks of waiting, Cobra never came down from the mountain, and I began to doubt if he'd ever come down at all. Three weeks was a long time to wait, but it wasn't all bad. I'd gotten a good dose of rest and mountain air and ridden on patrols deep into the hills, past lush, green hollows where the floor of the world had dropped into an expanse of vines and trees. Johnny had been on duty the first week of my stay, so the two of us hung out in his tent, reading Stephen King novels and watching kung fu DVDs on his portable player. A few more militia managed to escape from Tchei and find their way to the base, and Johnny and I would sit with them and see how much they'd talk. One kid, nineteen years old, explained the cannibal ritual without hesitation: "We eat the livers of the dead Congo soldiers. We eat it fresh and raw, and after the first time, you're never afraid again. You no longer see fear. It's like your eyes are covered with blood. And the taste, I find, is very good."

With election results scheduled to be announced soon in Kinshasa, and absolutely nothing moving in Tchei, I made plans to leave Aveba and travel to the capital. I spent the morning saying good-bye to new friends, trading e-mails and numbers, then caught a ride back to Bunia with a French aid group. Once there, I boarded a UN Boeing and returned to my old home.

The politics surrounding the election told me Kinshasa would be the best place to cover the winner, no matter who it was. It didn't take a creative leap to guess Kabila would win it all. It was just the consequences that were interesting. Kabila may have controlled the east and majority vote, but Bemba was still king in the Lingala-speaking west, where the vice president had pulled thousands to his rallies.

My trip to Kinshasa was also my own little homecoming, my first time back since I'd left the previous year. I was looking forward to seeing the old gang and working the streets together. And a steak and several bottles of wine at Château Margaux would restore my sense of taste after three weeks of Bengali chili peppers.

At one point during dinner in the officers' mess, my throat had actually seized up and refused to swallow. For the past several days, I'd eaten only rice, bananas, and parathas with jam.

I was leaving Aveba a bit disappointed, having waited for something that never materialized. But for the first time, I was leaving eastern Congo feeling something other than dread and fatigue. The election had made me optimistic, elated, as if the sun had finally broken through after a long, brutal winter.

My UN jet landed at Kinshasa's N'Djili airport on a Friday night, and within an hour I was on Lionel's balcony mixing gin and tonics with Lionel and Dave Lewis. After five weeks of living clean in the mountain air, the dirty tropical heat now leeched into my blood and made me thirsty and took me back to some dark days I sure didn't miss. And Kinshasa never disappointed. The mood in town was as peaked as ever, and the vine was full of festering rumors of how the boulevard would soon run with blood.

Once again, Dave had been left to sort through this slush pile of doomsday predictions and report back to London, hoping his tone of voice hadn't taken on the ring of a believer. "Like I've always said, not a single person in this place has a bloody clue what's going on," he said. "Myself included."

Of course, all the scenarios ended with Congo spiraling back to war. If Kabila won, Bemba would declare war in the west, have the president assassinated, and stage a coup; if Bemba won, the rebellion would flame in the east, with Europe and America backing Kabila's troops to salvage deals they'd brokered with the president. After all, the former political-affairs officer at the U.S. embassy in Kinshasa had just become an executive at Phelps Dodge, which had recently been granted a $900 million mineral concession in Congo. Those were just a few scenarios, and with four vice presidents on the verge of unemployment, two of whom were former rebel leaders with standing armies on call, anything was likely.

All the rumors had ratcheted up the antiforeigner sentiment

considerably, and several times Dave had been caught alone at Bemba's rallies after the fat man had spewed his xenophobic poison. Mobs had smashed Dave's windows, tipped his vehicle, and nearly taken his head with a club. He laughed it off in typical fashion, but I could tell he was bone-tired. "My career could probably use a long vacation from Congo," he told me.

But knowing how rumors in Kinshasa thrived like kudzu, I blew them off and focused on having fun. "Nothing's gonna happen," I said. "And if it does, I'll probably miss it."

We ate steak dinners under the shaded veranda of Margaux and listened to the fistfights of *shegue* outside the gates and copped ten-dollar bags of grass from taxi drivers that rolled your head until you swore it would come right off. One of Dave's college friends, Henry Burnand, was a med student in Britain who was doing an internship at the Kinshasa General Hospital. My second night in town, he invited all of his fellow Congolese intern pals out for beers, and we had a big night. We hit the rooftop clubs of Bandal, drinking tall bottles of Skol and dancing with the plump mamas, who pressed us into their bosoms and incited roars of laughter from the tables.

The election results were scheduled to be announced Sunday night, and all of us had agreed to just listen on the radio and skip the drive over to election HQ. But half an hour before the announcement, my cell phone lit up. "Hurry, mate," Dave said, "we've got shots fired on the boulevard."

A UN vehicle had been en route to election headquarters when bullets strafed its side; steel plates in the door panel had saved the passengers. It was unclear who'd fired the shots, but everyone suspected they'd come from the jittery troops of Jean-Pierre Bemba, who were garrisoned in the center of town near the vice president's sprawling riverside mansion. If you included armed loyalists living within a day's drive from town, Bemba had about a thousand men at the ready. It was beginning to feel like the east all over again.

Everything was silent as Lionel and I drove the boulevard toward the election headquarters. It was dark now and the streets were windblown and empty. Lionel floored the jeep and we raced through the eerie stillness, forgetting to breathe until we saw the lights of the election commission office. We whipped around to the side of the building and were stopped by a roadblock. Out stepped a white guy dressed in T-shirt and jeans, strapped with full body armor, night-vision goggles, and a short-barreled Israeli machine gun. "Get the *fuck out of here!*" he screamed. He was American, most likely UN private security. A single gunshot echoed a block away, sending the soldier's eyes skipping off the street corners and rooftops, then finally back to us. "Did you fucking hear me? I said get the fuck out of here *now!*"

The guards at the election commission wouldn't allow us to park inside the compound and motioned for us to turn back. But before we could argue, the air around us rippled with machine-gun fire. A crowd outside the gate panicked and mobbed the entrance. *"Get out of the way!"* Lionel screamed. *"Get out of the way!"* He gunned the motor, nearly crushing people under the wheels. We plowed inside before the steel gates rattled shut.

The election commission was housed inside a local Catholic parish, just across the boulevard from my old apartment. Once inside the gates, we found ourselves in a large courtyard hemmed by the parish buildings. A white UN APC was parked with its cannon facing the gate and manned by a couple of Tunisian peacekeepers, who'd jumped inside their armored vehicle. They now stood halfway inside the hatch, clenching their rifles and lighting one cigarette off the other.

We weren't inside five minutes before the boulevard exploded in heavy gunfire, a metallic caterwaul like an avalanche of rocks over a tin roof. Kabila's Presidential Guard were now fighting Bemba's men right outside the parish. Artillery shook the gates as Congolese tanks fired their cannons, and mortar and rocket rounds rumbled from the riverbank behind us. Soon the whole courtyard was one frantic war room as UN, EU, and Congolese officers tried to determine how to keep the whole capital from splitting apart.

A Uruguayan officer in soccer shorts (he'd probably run straight from his barracks) had a map spread on a wooden table in the grass. "Bring the reinforcements around this way," said the officer, pounding a pencil onto the map.

"That will never fool them," a Congolese officer chimed in. "I know these rebels!" Cell phones and radios chirped incessantly, causing a sonic wall of babble as they were answered in twenty different languages.

From the courtyard, a French officer shouted, *"Attention! Attention!"* and pointed to the roof of the parish. "There's someone with a gun!"

We all dove behind vehicles, as officers fumbled for their helmets and scanned the black sky with their pistols. One female Congolese soldier jumped behind a pickup with our group. I heard Henry Burnand say, "It's gonna be okay," and turned to find the soldier tugging his shirt like a blanky in the night. As every pair of eyes searched the rooftops for the alleged sniper, the tense silence was interrupted by ringtones of "Lambada" and "Scotland the Brave."

The gunfire and cannons continued until early morning, but the Congolese journalists handled it with aplomb. They'd somehow brought in sandwiches, fried chicken, and beer, and when I walked inside headquarters to investigate the aroma, I found them gyrating to heavy soukous.

In the midst of all this chaos, the chairman of the election commission was rushed into the compound inside an APC. The shooting seemed to stop long enough for him to announce that the election was too close to call, and a runoff between Kabila and Bemba would have to decide who would lead the Congo. We were oddly relieved, for a decisive victory in either direction, we feared, would usher in even greater violence than what we were hearing now.

Most of the gunfire had come from the direction of Lionel's apartment, making it too dangerous to go home. So around three A.M., we deemed it safe enough to make a dash across the boulevard to the Memling Hotel, where the nervous guards whisked us inside the gates. The surly desk clerk, keenly appreciating the extraordinary circumstances, charged us three hundred dollars for several hours in a dingy room.

The fighting had eventually shifted toward Bemba's residence, which was four blocks from Lionel's apartment. All night Lionel had been calling to check on his wife, Nathalie, who'd been stuck at home alone while explosions rocked their windows.

So as the morning came without incident, Lionel was anxious to get home. Back in the car, we passed streets littered with shell casings, cars with windshields blown out from gunfire, and discarded uniforms of soldiers who'd stripped and fled. We rolled past the first roundabout at a crawl, too afraid to stop and photograph the lone policeman lying with his head against the curb. If not for the blossoms of dried blood across his chest, you'd think he'd lain down to sleep.

Nathalie was awake when we got home. She was a short, fiery Portuguese woman who wasn't easily rattled. If anything, the night of constant gunfire had left her cranky about missing her sleep.

"Ay, those men kept shooting all bloody night!" she said. "Nothing but *pa-pa-pa-pa-pa*! I could not sleep one *minute*." She was especially pissed about having taken down the curtains from their windows the day before, which had left her exposed during the barrage. "I didn't even need to take them down, why did I take them down?"

The morning remained quiet so we ventured out again. Lionel kissed his wife before walking out the door, telling her, "Going for a quick look around, be back in a couple hours." People were slowly returning to the boulevard, which was reassuring, but as we got downtown, a menacing wind came up, as if to announce more trouble was on the way. Men and women dashed across the side streets and hid in buildings, people poked their heads out of doorframes, and shoes lay abandoned in the road. My ears began to ring and I tasted metal.

"This is bad," I said. "We need to find somewhere now." Trucks full of black-clad Presidential Guard rumbled past, belching fumes out the back. We hit the backstreets and raced toward Dave's apartment at the Grand Hotel, the closest place where we knew it was safe.

Dave and Henry were already outside, along with Jean-Philippe Remy from *Le Monde*. They were about to leave, but we told them what we'd seen on the boulevard. "Come on, just a little spin," they said, and we reluctantly agreed. Dave and Jean-Philippe pulled out first in one car, while we followed behind with Henry at the wheel. ("Make yourself useful with the journalists," Lionel had told him, and thrown him the keys.)

But even before we could leave the compound, a dozen different machine guns erupted a block away. Dave had jumped out to speak with someone on the street just as it had happened and now sprinted through the gates at a full clip, not stopping until he was safe inside. Jean-Philippe followed in the jeep, jumping the driveway ramp as he screeched past. "Never leave the hotel," we said, and whipped the car back around.

The wraparound windows of Dave's ninth-floor suite offered a sweeping view of the city. Many nights I'd sat on his balcony drinking beers and watching the sunset sparkle off the Congo River. The green tops of palm and mango trees seemed to cover the poverty and crumbling neglect, and if you scissored the reel of history in your mind and let your eyes wander, Kinshasa from above was actually a beautiful place.

The Reuters office at the Grand Hotel was as hardwired into the history as anything else. Legend had it that George Foreman had lived there the summer of 1974 while training to fight Muhammad Ali. Whether or not it was true (and we didn't check that hard), the great Rumble in the Jungle still sparkled like a clean space on the country's sordid time line. It was probably the last time Congo wasn't seen through a prism of violence, and even that fight went eight rounds.

From Big George's room we watched the time line extend along the treads of government tanks that rolled down below, wondering when it would finally grow so tangled it hung the country in its own noose. And that afternoon, as tanks and rockets pushed inky plumes across the skyline, I thought it finally had.

Earlier that morning, the head of the UN's mission in Congo, William Lacy Swing, along with the American and British ambassadors and ten other diplomatic envoys and UN officials, had met with Bemba at his riverside mansion. The delegation had come to convince the vice president to call down his men and hopefully meet with Kabila to negotiate a truce. Halfway through their meeting, government tanks had rolled up and surrounded the house.

We'd seen the black columns of smoke from the river and started calling around. One UN officer on the phone with Dave confirmed what we'd feared: "The tanks opened fire with the delegation inside. Swing and the ambassadors are trapped."

Over the next several hours, a fierce and chaotic gun battle unfolded outside Bemba's home while the UN scrambled to rescue the diplomats. Everything at that moment seemed to twist in the heavy air: the seven years of work and planning, billions of dollars, two dozen dead peacekeepers, and the patience of the Security Council, which had already begun to evaporate. If anything happened to any of those men, the whole show was over. So when a chalk white APC finally made it to the door to evacuate the team, you could almost hear the collective sigh whistle through the razor wire at HQ.

But the anxiety seemed to dissipate from one place only to settle in another. Soon Lionel's phone rang, and when he answered, I watched the color bleed from his face. The gun battle around Bemba's residence had again spilled into the surrounding streets, and this time the front lines were just below his bedroom where Nathalie lay cowering on the floor. The gunfire and explosions were so loud I could hear them through the phone across the room.

He screamed over the noise, "Darling, please move away from the windows. Pull the mattress into the corridor and stay there. *Do you hear me? Hello?*" The line was shaky. Their conversation slipped in and out.

"She says she's fine," he said, hanging up. "She's only worried about running out of cigarettes if this keeps up." He laughed, but he was thinking what we were all thinking. Tonight the gunboys would get drunk and go marauding through the neighborhood, just as we knew they would, just as we'd always written about. But we said nothing.

"We'll get her as soon as this shit dies down," we told him, then all agreed it was best to go downstairs for a meal and some fresh air.

Downstairs, dozens of tanned, leather-skinned foreigners lounged around the pool in the late-afternoon sun. Children splashed in the water and leaped off the diving board. Two Chinese businessmen played tennis nearby, and American hip-hop pulsed over the raucous bar, stifling the sound of cannons outside.

It was as if the battle for Kinshasa were only happening within the walls of our upstairs suite, and our nerves were a little raw as a result. (Earlier that morning, we'd mistaken the *sssssp* of blue jeans brushing a potted plant for a stray bullet through the open window. We'd all hit the floor, hearts in our throats.) When our waitress dropped a beer tray and sent Dave two feet off his chair, we finished our drinks and hurried back to our chamber. In the elevator up, we'd stared nervously at one another while "Strangers in the Night" piped softly through the speakers.

I awoke on the sofa before dawn the next morning and saw Henry standing at the wall of windows. Red tracer rounds arched from one side to the next, followed by the staccato reports of gunfire. Ten minutes later, Nathalie called to say the fighting hadn't stopped all night again. Lionel hung up the phone, then joined us by the windows. "She ran out of cigarettes," he said.

The shooting cleared enough that afternoon to attempt a short drive outside the gates, but nothing farther. We found three soldiers lying in the roundabout near the hotel, killed in the morning fight. A poisoned silence seemed to radiate from their open arms. Families from the neighborhood were using the momentary reprieve to leave town. One family walked up holding suitcases and bundles, and as they passed, the mother shielded the eyes of her young daughter as they stepped over the corpses.

Half an hour passed and we were still among the dead, until the strangest moment, when all of us looked up together and said, "We should go." Seconds later, a pair of machine guns popped down the block and sent us sprinting to the truck.

As darkness fell again that night, we sat together on the balcony and watched tracer rounds arc against the sky like red Roman candles. The gunboys were firing wildly.

Lionel's phone kept ringing. You could hear the bullets hitting walls over Nathalie's strained voice. "Just hold on, darling," he'd say. "Please just hold on." After the last call, his body seemed to collapse. "What am I supposed to do?" he whispered, then looked at each of us. *"What the fuck am I supposed to do!?"*

We sat in silence for a long period of time, listening to the battle, until someone asked the inevitable question: "I wonder if it'll kick off again tomorrow. You guys think it'll kick off?"

I'd always loved that question, so pregnant with possibility. It was the reason I'd come to Congo and kept on coming back, and for the past two days I'd seen some of the heaviest fighting yet. I'd come looking for war and found it, and here it was again in its purest and most savage form. But it wasn't the sexy tracer rounds against the night, or the pulse-quickening whoosh of rockets—but a cell phone that sent waves of nausea through my guts every time it rang. The war was ours now, and I felt truly sorry for ever wishing it at all.

"I hope not," I said finally. "I really hope not."

That night I decided I never wanted to see it again, not there anyway, and if I continued to pursue this death and decay, then death and decay would forever be my memory of Congo. A folder of blood-soaked pages would be the only thing I left behind in that place, and that bothered me even more. As a reporter in Congo, I'd always bristled at the nagging question "Why do you only focus on death and never the positive?" It usually came from Africans themselves and struck me as naïve. And working for the wires, there was no time for that anyway. You wrote about the death because if you didn't, who would?

But it was true that in three years I'd rarely ventured beyond the massacres and displaced camps. And now, despite what was happening below in Kinshasa, or in small pockets of the east, the war had ended inside the vast country, and I wanted to see those places that weren't bleeding or blown to hell. I wanted to find the recovery I'd momentarily glimpsed that afternoon in Gety, to meet people whose lives were moving a little ways forward. I needed to see this for my own conscience, and it was the least I could do for the Congolese, who only seemed to suffer and bleed in the news.

As I sat there on the balcony, four new tracers hooked across the darkness without a sound, then disappeared just before the broad river. There was no moon, and the sparse city lights shimmered off the water. My journey would begin there.

Chapter Four

THE RIVER IS A ROAD

There is, despite the myriad difficulties it presents at every hand,
an element of fascination about a tropical forest unlike anything
else, though the chief pleasure lies in looking forward to getting
out of it.

—Captain S. L. Hinde, *The Fall of the Congo Arabs* (1897)

I

The early Kongo people called it *nzere*—"the river that swallows
all rivers," and the Congo River is indeed massive; in all the world,
only the Amazon carries more water. It stretches forty-seven hundred kilometers from Congo's southern highlands, slicing upward
through the second-largest rain forest on earth and hooking twice
over the equator before barreling out to sea, emptying into the Atlantic at a rate of over one million cubic feet of water per second.
The sheer ferocity of that union has created grooves in the ocean
floor a mile deep.

The 1,734-kilometer voyage upriver from Kinshasa to
Kisangani—the river's longest navigable route—was one of the
great journeys of the world. This stretch of water had brought ac-
claim and glory to explorers like Henry Morton Stanley, who
became the first European to breach its uncharted waters, and it

delivered King Leopold a fortune in ivory and rubber that fueled the industrial revolution. But to the Congolese, who were hunted, enslaved, raped, and murdered in this quest for empire, it delivered only oppression and terror, an African holocaust that by the early twentieth century had wiped out roughly half the country's population. A journey upriver was like breaching the very vine-choked memory of the land.

I'd glimpsed its far reaches once before. In August 2003, just after my trip to Bunia to follow up on the fighting, I was on a UN flight to southern Congo for another story when the plane made a scheduled stop in Kisangani, the country's third-largest city along the Congo River. After deboarding and eating an egg sandwich at the airport snack counter, I was told my continuing flight had been canceled. It was typical, especially back in MONUC's chaotic early days. But since there wasn't another flight going south for four more days, it meant I was stranded in Kisangani.

Kisangani had been crippled by the war, both physically and economically. Soldiers, rebels, and bandits had overrun the river and choked all commercial traffic from Kinshasa. The roads in and out of town had crumbled years before, and the airport was now a rebel trophy. With all routes sealed, the city slowly began to starve.

In June that year, President Kabila had announced the official beginning of the postwar transitional government. In July, given this hopeful occasion, six river barges loaded with much needed food and merchandise set out from Kinshasa and landed in Kisangani the day before I arrived. Except for a lone barge in February, they were the first commercial vessels anyone had seen in over five years. As the first boats appeared in the morning fog, hundreds of people rushed into the river and started dancing in the shallows. When I showed up the following day, many were still packed along the banks, helping unload boxes or simply staring at the long, rust-eaten flotillas with laundry drying along their rails. The barges brought not only precious sugar and salt and bags of cement, but two thousand river traders and Kisangani residents who'd been stranded since the war, caught on the wrong side of the jungle and unable to get home. And when the boats appeared from the mist, it was as if they'd traveled from another time, figments of that good dream where the country was at peace and the family was whole, except this time the flesh was alive and the voices real.

Not many barges followed in the years after. Congo's economy remained a wreck throughout the fitful period of transitional government; imports and exports slowed to a drip, and the river captains remained gun-shy and jittery. But that day in August, after five years of war, the divided country had finally come together.

I'd always wanted to make that same journey when I lived in Kinshasa, but never had the time. I'd heard it could take six weeks by barge, possibly longer, but I didn't know anyone who'd actually done it. Plenty of reporters and travelers had made the trip before the war, but after that it became pure suicide, and you wouldn't have found a local guide to take you up anyway, not for any amount of money. But the river after the war, after the nation's first elections, that was now uncharted territory.

The election commission had announced the runoff between Kabila and Bemba would take place on October 29, 2006, and I planned my trip so I could cover the polls deep within the trees. Where exactly, I wasn't sure yet. There were a few towns far upriver where polling stations had been established, places like Bumba and Lisala, but everything else was forest and villages that hadn't changed in centuries. But after the elections, I sensed that change was inevitable and coming soon, or perhaps I just told myself this and believed it true.

In early October, with that plan in mind, I boarded a KLM flight to Entebbe, Uganda, where I caught a UN Boeing to Kinshasa. Once there, I immediately went to work searching for a boat. I was prepared to catch one of the commercial barges I'd seen in

Kisangani that were like the great Freightliners of the river, hauling hundreds of tons of goods within their steel hulls and atop their flat, rust-covered decks. Passengers and river traders squeezed amid the topside cargo, often as many as five hundred on one vessel, living and doing business as the barge crawled up the river. These barges had no timetables and were often plagued by disaster. Sandbars marooned some boats for weeks, others sank from collisions in the night or overcrowding. It was an often dangerous way to trade and travel in a country without roads, and airfare out of reach. But the resilient Congolese sucked it up and endured. I would, too.

I'd done some preliminary work before leaving the States. Through a colleague, I got the name of a local fixer in Kinshasa, whom I e-mailed and asked to ply the river ports in my advance. Séverin Mpiana was a trained electrical engineer with a university degree, but like many Congolese professionals in a city with absolute unemployment, he'd found work in other places, in his case with foreign journalists.

I'd already decided that if he found a boat before I arrived, I'd offer him a job as my translator and fixer on the river. Unlike in the cities, the people upriver spoke mainly Lingala and local, tribal dialects. Séverin was fluent in Lingala, French, and English and had a firm command of Swahili, which would prove useful as we made our way eastward.

I found him in the busy Lebanese *shawarma* shop on the main boulevard, where we'd agreed to meet. He was immaculately dressed in a crisp white shirt, pressed jeans, and designer leather sandals. His features were soft, almost fawnlike, and his speech was quiet and contemplative. I tried to imagine him on the river and couldn't. After a brief introduction, he skipped the small talk and pulled out a notebook.

"I found you a boat," he said. "It leaves in two days."

Perfect, I said, and offered him the job.

★　★　★

We caught a taxi to the public docks where the big barges came in, and where Séverin had been the previous day. On the ride over, he said he was eager to travel upriver and revisit Kisangani, where he'd lived as a child and still had family. His father had worked for the Belgian-run Commercial Bank of Zaire during the Mobutu years and had been posted all over the country, including Lubumbashi, where Séverin was born, then later Kisangani, where Séverin had picked up his Swahili. They'd moved back to Kinshasa in 1988 when he was twelve years old, just in time for the collapse and everything that followed. His father managed to find a job with Rawbank, owned by an Indian family, where he was now an officer.

His father's position meant Séverin's family was solidly middle class, a rarity in Congo. Two of Séverin's other brothers and sisters had completed college, and his youngest brother was now studying to be a lawyer. The family wasn't wealthy by any means, but they were free of the desperation that plagued so many others in Kinshasa. And while Séverin had lived elsewhere, he'd never traveled through the interior of his own country, so the trip would be as much an adventure for him as it was for me.

The sun was already brutal when we arrived at the port, cooking off the expanse of concrete and rusting steel tied up to the docks, much of which hadn't moved in decades. About a hundred people—mainly market women going upriver to trade—were camped on straw mats in the dirt, where they'd been for over a week, just waiting for barges to be loaded. They sat under bright-colored umbrellas, fanning themselves, all their belongings wrapped in cloth bundles at their sides and children running in every direction.

We asked one of the dockworkers about our boat, the *Eben Ezer*, and he shouted something in Lingala to a man nearby, who called to another man, who then conferred with several workers unloading a pallet of hair tonic. That way, he pointed, and led us to the water's edge. He motioned toward a white tugboat at the far end of the port.

Two crewmen lay dozing in the shade of a paint-chipped lower deck. They said that, yes, this was the boat to Kisangani, but there'd been a small holdup. The remaining merchandise hadn't yet arrived, and even when it did, it could take days to finish loading, or as long as two weeks. I asked when they expected the merchandise.

"Two days," he said. "But maybe four." I was also told there were no cabins to store my bags and computer, only space on the deck, which I'd have to wrestle from the gang of women waiting in the sun. From the tomcat look in their eyes, I didn't like my chances. "But we do have a deep freeze," he added. "If you wish to carry any large quantities of meat."

No, I said, but supposing I do get aboard, how long was the trip to Kisangani?

He looked at his friend and they laughed. "Who knows," he said. "After all, it's the river."

For the next three days, Séverin and I returned to make inquiries, also checking other ports and finding nothing. And after all this time spent in the sun with no prospects, I began feeling a bit hopeless. But on the fourth afternoon, Séverin called saying he'd found another boat: "A much better boat, so *beautiful* you won't believe it. And we'll ride in luxury! No sleeping on the dirty ground."

The boat was housed at a private commercial dock, where several armed security guards opened the gates and led us inside. At the end of the dock sat a giant, barrel-chested river tug called the *Ma'ungano*. She was ninety feet long with three decks, which included the engine room, the wheelhouse, and what appeared to be first-class cabins. The boat looked sturdy, almost new, and sparkled bone white in the sun. The national flag was hoisted atop the wheelhouse, unfaded and fluttering in the breeze.

The captain of the *Ma'ungano* was a stout Frenchman named Albert-Henri Buisine, an old soldier who'd been raised in Congo and served two decades in the service of Mobutu, whom he'd considered his closest friend and a genius the world was cruel to dismiss. After the Big Man's kingdom finally collapsed, sending its minions scattering to Europe and elsewhere, Buisine had turned to the river.

The captain, now in his late fifties, owned six commercial tugboats that plied the country's many rivers, all thirteen thousand kilometers of which snaked and splintered across weathered maps along his office walls. He'd been one of the few captains to brave the river over the past couple of years, and sitting behind his desk, he explained just how much the war had taken from the people in the forest. After fighting closed the rivers and tributaries, freezing all movement of merchandise that sustained the jungle economy, gunmen moved into the villages. They pillaged, raped, and murdered, so people fled deep into the forests like hunted animals, living in the rough so long their clothing simply rotted off their bodies. Several million had escaped to the capital, abandoning a way of life they'd nurtured for centuries. They'd walked hundreds of kilometers through the jungle to get there, leaving a wake of dead along the trail, and doubling Kinshasa's population. "And you should see them all now," the captain said. "Starving in the slums while still dreaming of the forest. *C'est catastrophique!* And those in the forest . . . well, if you go deep enough, you might still find them naked, hiding behind the trees."

But there was good news, he said. The recent elections had been a vanguard for hope and recovery along the river. For the first time in a century, the potential for prosperity had been introduced to the Congolese. Boat captains were braving the river again, people were returning home, and money was changing hands. As for the captain, he'd be pushing twenty-six hundred tons of freight on two barges all the way to Kisangani, which is where I wanted to go.

After spending days at the docks looking for a boat, sucking in the dust and exhaust and finding no luck, I was so relieved to have ended this task that I began to gush, explaining how anxious I was to finally pierce the interior and be with the people, see the ways they really live—"Live instead of die!" I said, regrettably.

"*Bon.*" The captain smiled and walked around the desk. "But tell me something. Will you prefer local or European cuisine? It's important I give the chef plenty of notice."

In addition to Séverin, I'd invited an old friend to travel up the river. Riccardo Gangale was based in Kigali, Rwanda, part of a free-bird fraternity of photographers who toured the sub-Saharan on motorcycles with girlfriends perched on the back, selling photos to whoever would take them. He was AP's man in eastern Congo, since it was easy for him to catch a bus in Kigali and be in Goma in two hours. We'd worked together a couple times in Ituri, where he'd first introduced me to Pastor Marrion, and I trusted him as a solid operator on the road. He was an Italian with a hot streak a mile long and a gung ho love for Deep Purple and testing his limits, sometimes to calamitous ends.

Six months earlier, Riccardo had taken the same voyage from Kinshasa to Kisangani by himself, jumping commercial barges, hiring dugout pirogues, and biking through the jungle. Halfway upriver he'd contracted malaria and run out of food. And jungle-fly bites he'd received then became infected, only compounding the malarial fevers and hallucinations. He'd stopped at a small town and holed up in a house, where he lay shivering and slipping out of consciousness. He was saved only after a pirogue full of diamond dealers passed by and paddled him two days to an MSF camp near Kisangani. When he heard about my plans to travel the river, he'd written me straightaway. He couldn't wait to do it again.

Our plan was to ride with Buisine as far as Mbandaka, about a week's journey upriver, then jump to the public barges that carried hundreds of traders on their decks. Riccardo was certain there'd be barges in Mbandaka headed upriver when we arrived, just as there'd been when he'd passed through six months before. "Yes, there were boats," he said, his Roman accent richly melodic. "Still, I wait five days for the crew to load this *focking* boat. You will see. Five days Mbandaka is five days too long."

With the *Ma'ungano* leaving in two days, we set to work preparing for our journey. We spent a sweltering afternoon in Kinshasa's central market purchasing the necessary gear, like a durable orange tarp for slapdash shelters, nylon rope, foam mattresses, pots and pans, plastic cups and buckets, pills for pain, malaria, and worms, and dozens of cans of sardines, beans, and corned-beef hash. For days, Riccardo and I had already dedicated ourselves to our own rigorous Get Fat Diet, gorging on steaks, doughnuts, and lots of cold beer, trying to gain weight we'd inevitably lose through sweat and diarrhea.

I also brought along my *Traveler's Guide to the Belgian Congo* from 1951, a year when the Belgian Congo was a gem of the African colonies. For seventy years, the colonial masters had ruled the Congolese with barbarism and oppression behind the curtains. But they'd also built sleek European cities connected by packed-gravel highways, luxury trains, and river steamers. How quickly all of that vanished in the forty-six years since independence.

The *Ma'ungano* (which meant "unity" in Swahili) was the last vestige of the era, and it was only fitting I begin my journey along its decks. So far my collective experience in Congo had been looking down, from UN choppers and APCs, from balcony apartments shielded by razor wire and guards, from the Land Rovers and press cards we used to escape the misery and smell of disease when it all became too much. Oddly, I thought, it would take a journey by river to finally plant my feet on the ground.

The evening before departure we stayed aboard the *Ma'ungano* drinking cans of Castle beer on the decks, gloating over our good fortune. Not only did we have a personal chef, but also a private cabin equipped with soft beds, a hot shower, and an air conditioner more efficient than most I'd owned in the States. I went to bed wired tight from anticipation and awoke to the rumble of engines in the pink haze of dawn. Running outside, I saw the river bubbling from the rudders the color of clean motor oil. We were moving seconds later, but so slowly that landmarks stayed in view for hours. By late afternoon, we could still see Kinshasa.

The capital sits along the tail of a wide, oval-shaped expanse in the river known as Malebo (or Stanley) Pool. In 1877, Stanley reached this lakelike area after his journey across the entire width of the African continent, having started from Zanzibar nearly two and a half years before. The core of Stanley's mission had been to discover the source of the Nile River, which several European explorers had claimed lay somewhere along the Great Lakes of central Africa and eastern Congo. One theory was the Congo River was the Nile's source, but the waterway had yet to be fully navigated. Ever since Portuguese mariners had discovered the Atlantic mouth of the Congo in 1482, the river was traveled by explorers and merchants and combed heavily by slave ships working the jungles of western Congo. But because of disease, starvation, hostile tribes, and about 350 kilometers of impenetrable cataracts between Stanley Pool and the sea, none of these ships ever breached the heart of the country. And from the east, no European had ever sailed west toward the sea. As a result, much of central Africa remained a vacuous hole on the map even four centuries after the river's initial discovery.

Born John Rowlands in 1841 in Wales, Stanley was abandoned by his single mother as a young boy and made to live in a workhouse. He fled to the United States in 1859 and worked as a store clerk in New Orleans. Stanley later joined the Confederate army during the Civil War and fought in the Battle of Shiloh before being captured by Union soldiers and thrown into a prison camp. To ensure his release, Stanley then defected to the Union army.

All along this journey he'd changed his name and much of his life story to better fit his intrepid alter ego. Claiming to be American, he became a newspaper reporter and covered the Indian wars on the western frontier. In 1868, the *New York Herald* sent him to cover the British military campaign against Emperor Theodore in Abyssinia. Before Theodore's capital Magdala fell to the Brits, Stanley managed to bribe a telegraph clerk to send his stories first, a journalistic coup that ensured news of the event reached New York before London. A year later, he convinced James Gordon Bennett, editor of the *Herald*, to send him to Africa after the vanished Scottish explorer David Livingstone, possibly the greatest story a journalist could ever hope for. Stanley's book about the journey was a bestseller that made him one of the most famous men on the planet.

Stanley's voyage across Africa began in November 1874 in Bagomoyo on the East African coast with a caravan of 228 people (including thirty-six women), mainly picked up in Zanzibar two months prior. The caravan carried eight tons of food, supply, and weaponry, and a forty-foot cedar boat they portaged in five sections weighing 280 pounds each.

After circumnavigating both Lakes Victoria and Tanganyika—the largest lake in Africa and the longest freshwater lake in the world, respectively—Stanley headed west into the forests toward the Lualaba River (the Upper Congo), which Livingstone once suspected to be the source of the Nile. For days the caravan slogged through soupy mud and quicksand, swarms of biting flies and malaria-carrying mosquitoes that dropped the men on the trail. After finally reaching the Lualaba near Nyangwe, the convoy was attacked by hundreds of warriors who suspected them of being slavers. In his best-selling book about the voyage, Stanley claimed to have fought legions of hostile tribes for the remainder of his journey, many of them cannibals who launched attacks from the riverbanks chanting, "Meat! Meat! Meat!" By the time his convoy reached the sea—exactly 999 days after leaving Zanzibar—disease, starvation, desertion, and skirmishes with natives had wiped out 132 of his original 228 crew members, including three of his British companions. Stanley's heavily armed convoy had themselves left behind a bloody trail of warriors and villagers, killed in berserk defensives that often spun into slaughter.

Stanley's successful navigation of the Congo River was a grand achievement, one that would forever change the African continent. First, it resolved one of its most puzzling questions: the source of the Nile River. His exploration of Lake Victoria confirmed an earlier theory by British explorer John Hanning Speke that the lake was the true source of the Nile. Stanley also debunked the theory by explorer Richard Burton that Lake Tanganyika actually fed the Nile from a northern outlet, which it did not. Livingstone had suggested the Lualaba eventually became the Nile, but as Stanley proved, the Lualaba was in fact the Congo and emptied into the sea. The origin of the Nile was one of Africa's last remaining geographical pursuits, and by solving the riddle Stanley closed the book on four centuries of exploration. But by illuminating the dark spaces, he in turn made room for King Leopold.

The *Ma'ungano* cleared Stanley Pool by nightfall and entered a chain of islands so immense that I often mistook them for shoreline. The first night was moonless and dark, so the *Ma'ungano* tied to shore rather than risk the sandbars. We were still in the open, low-lying scrub near the capital, nothing like the jungle we'd soon enter, yet the still, pitch-black night was like standing in a torrential downpour where every raindrop was a chirp or buzzing of wings. One of the crewmen stood in the wheelhouse and shone the powerful spotlight onto shore, sweeping the dark vegetation and drawing a thick tube of bugs that crawled in sheets across our window screen. Opening the door for even a second allowed in swarms of mosquitoes.

I woke up before dawn the next morning and climbed to the wheelhouse to watch the sunrise, kicking away the thousands of silver-winged moths that had perished in the searchlight. A large breakfast of omelets, bread, and avocado was served on the terrace, and afterward Séverin and I walked to the tip of the first barge to take in the view. The two barges stretched nearly the length of a football field and were fully loaded—both inside the airless holds and atop their rust-covered decks—with sacks of flour and sugar, cheap rubber flip-flops stuffed in bundles the size of hay bales, lawn chairs, crates of Italian tomato paste, Crème Top Claire hair cream, Tiger Head batteries, and two Indian-built Tata passenger vans bound for a customs station deep in the trees. The merchandise was piled up in rounded humps covered with brightly covered tarps. We tiptoed delicately over the ropes and tie-downs that crisscrossed our path, the water just inches from our feet. It was at this moment Séverin informed me he couldn't swim.

Once we reached the end of the barge, the rumble from the engines faded, leaving only the bright splash of water against the slow-moving steel. The river stretched several kilometers across in front of us. Patches of puffy green hyacinth floated past, along with colossal hunks of grassy earth ripped from the shore by the fierce current. The best seat in the house, I thought, but I wasn't the only one. One of the crewmen already occupied a chair at the edge of the barge. He was fast asleep, with one hand tucked lazily down his pants.

His name was Kalu, and for the past two years he'd worked as a loader and deckhand, traveling the river with Buisine about five times a year. His true field of expertise was botany, which he'd studied as a forestry student at the University of Kisangani.

He pointed to the floating chunks of vegetation in the water, which in Lingala were known as *Congo ya sika*, meaning "new Congo." They were a product of the rainy season, he explained, which rejuvenated the land, but also caused the water to rise and shear off the banks. The floating pieces of land were sometimes so large, he said, that antelope were spotted thrashing around on them.

While at university, Kalu had sung lead vocals in a band that gigged the dark and sweaty nightclubs of the city. "My friend and I played all the time. We loved to sing," Kalu said. "I wrote songs about everything: love, disappointment, the slave trade."

Singing was Kalu's first love, but the pressures of a career and family had forced him to postpone the dream. "For four years I worked in the forest studying, involving my mind with science," he said. "And now I'm on the river. I don't have much time for music."

He felt the muse slipping away, so he often spent time on the tip of the boat, waiting for inspiration to strike. "Maybe the view will make me want to write a song," he sighed. And after two minutes of absolute silence, he sat up with a jolt of revelation and calmly proclaimed, "The Congo River is a road. And I am only a witness on this road."

One of his old bandmates, Papi, also took a job with Buisine and worked aboard the *Ma'ungano*. And although they saw one another every day on the river, they never reminisced about old times. Kalu hadn't even sung a note in two years. But this was just a rough patch, a thirty-two-year-old man going through one of life's transitions.

"My music is still in my blood," he said, pausing to gather his thoughts off the soft river sheen. "Maybe it's not over. I figure all I need to do is record two songs, really big songs, and then my voice will become immortal."

The "grand highway" of trade that Stanley had extolled to the king had opened following the Berlin Conference of 1885, allowing Leopold to begin turning a profit on the exportation of ivory from the interior. To maximize the quantity of ivory taken from the forest, Congo Free State officials began paying their agents a profit percentage, which spurred the men to collect more. The gathering parties relied on caravans of local porters to carry equipment and tusks, and to guide agents around the rapids. Soon the crushing demand for porters led to wholesale village raids, where people were enslaved and made to work, often chained by the neck and force-marched down forest trails. Anyone stepping out of line or refusing orders would be beaten with the *chicotte*, a long whip made of dried hippo hide that cut the skin like jagged glass. The weak and the dead were simply kicked off the path and left to rot in the jungle, and reports from that period describe piles of skeletons in the grass and a permanent stench of decay.

The bulk of atrocities were committed by the Force Publique, whose elite soldiers were largely from the Bangala tribe that dominated the inner jungles along the equator. Many were slaves themselves, and many were also children, as Leopold pushed for trained columns of young boys, who were often kidnapped from their villages and made to serve, which they would do through all of Congo's wars. By the late 1890s, the Force Publique numbered nearly twenty thousand soldiers, who were being used heavily in eastern Congo to battle Afro-Arab slave traders for control of the forests. During the First World War, they'd also fight German colonial forces in Rwanda, Burundi, and Tanzania, while other units fought Italians in Ethiopia.

If the wealth of ivory in the forests didn't bring enough foreign interest to the Congo and misery to the Congolese, a worldwide rubber boom soon did. By the 1890s, with the second industrial revolution in full flush, rubber was in demand for everything from automobile tires to telegraph wires. To Leopold's delight, the Congo forests were carpeted in wild rubber vines, which, unlike rubber trees, required no maintenance or expensive cultivation. By the turn of the century, the Congo Free State produced more rubber than anywhere else in Africa and, by 1904, had increased its rubber profits ninety-six-fold since the boom had begun in 1890.

As with ivory, colonial agents were given a share of rubber profits, which encouraged the same brutal means of collecting it. Villagers were enslaved and sent into the forests to tap the wild rubber vines that snaked hundreds of feet up the towering trees, requiring them to climb to the top with buckets. Each person was given a quota, and failure to meet one resulted in whippings or death. But money being made from rubber far surpassed the proceeds from ivory, and soon the vast majority of Congo's forest population were conscripted to collect rubber. To ensure participation, Force Publique soldiers kidnapped women and children and held them in stockades until the village men delivered their required amounts of raw rubber. Many of the women died while in custody or were raped by soldiers, even as their men toiled in the forests. Settlements and villages that categorically refused to collect were simply massacred by the Force Publique. To guarantee the guards were carrying out their orders, soldiers were instructed to sever the right hands of their corpses, and sometimes those of living people. The hands were then smoked and delivered in baskets to regional headquarters as proof of death.

Swept away by such power, the white colonial officers would often order massacres for smaller infractions. One officer whose troops were denied fish and manioc in one village described his reaction: "I made war against them. One example was enough: a hundred heads cut off, and there have been plenty of supplies at the station ever since."

When one of the crewmen on the *Ma'ungano* told me they still hauled raw rubber on the barges, I launched into a long speech about the atrocities along *these very banks*, the amputations, the village raids, heads on pikes. But when Séverin finished translating, the crew stared at me as if I'd just asked how to buy a MetroCard.

"No," the guy said, looking at his friends for reactions. "We don't know about this stuff. You might want to ask the old people."

Walking back, Séverin shook his head and gasped. "So many people here, they have no idea of their own history."

To Buisine, history was everything, and it all connected right here. "To understand Congo," he'd say, "you must first understand the river."

During the afternoons when the heat would drive us indoors, the captain would stand at the wheel and mix the bad lessons with the good. His eyes would break focus on the channel and he'd explain the things he knew, like how the water silver-plated at dusk and hid the sandbars, or how the bank appeared dangerously close in the cool morning air. He'd point out whirlpools roiling in the deep spots or crocodiles camouflaged in the mud. On afternoons after the rains, we trained our eyes upriver and watched ghost ships hover above the water. Low pressure from the storm can play tricks on your eyes, the captain explained, and through a pair of binoculars, the boats returned to earth as the rust-eaten barges they were.

Other times he'd point to the distant bank where a brick building stood shrouded in vines and decay, a remnant of the old empire, and tell the story of the hospital or timber mill the locals allowed the forest to reclaim. He told how during the grand days of the colony there was lots of traffic on the river, with rivermen pushing hundreds of thousands of tons of product a year up and down Congo's rivers and tributaries; now they're lucky if they move a fraction of that. And because there were more boats, the river was dredged regularly, and a well-trained captain was easy to find. Signs were posted along the banks indicating sandbars and snags, depth and direction of tributaries, signs telling the rivermen they weren't alone on the black water at night. The captain would wax sentimental about these years before the collapse, when he was young and the country made sense, and during these times his eyes never left the river.

He'd been there from the beginning and watched it all fall apart; his life alone was like a window into the decline. He'd grown up in the eastern town of Bukavu, where his family owned a quarry and cinchona plantation on Lake Kivu. He later served in the French navy and, once discharged, returned to Bukavu looking for quick money and adventure, organizing gorilla tours in nearby Kahuzi-Biega National Park, and leading tourists up the smoldering Nyiragongo volcano near Goma in the Virunga Mountains.

But the government seized the family's plantation in the mid-seventies during Mobutu's nationalist land-grab campaign known as Zairianization. Buisine's uncle walked into his office one morning and found an African sitting in his chair, a midlevel government official from Kinshasa who'd never picked up a shovel. Cinchona (the natural source of quinine) requires meticulous pruning and cultivation, but the new owner rushed the harvest and the entire crop died. "People whose families had worked there a century committed suicide right then," said Buisine. Years later, Buisine was working as a supervisor at Kinshasa's Palace of the People when he received a phone call one morning at five A.M. It was President Mobutu, screaming over the line, "Buisine! From now on you work for me." Mobutu had been impressed by the Frenchman's military background and family history in Congo. Buisine took the job. "Despite everything that had happened," he explained, "when the president calls, you can't say no."

Buisine served as Mobutu's personal superintendent for sixteen years, organizing the dictator's daily schedule, security, and logistics. He was chained to Mobutu's shadow at all times, even living four straight years aboard his lavish, hundred-meter yacht, the *Kamanyola*, as it drifted aimlessly down the Congo River.

Aboard the *Kamanyola*, Buisine's living quarters were directly below the president's. "Each day would begin at four thirty in the morning, with Mobutu stomping his foot on the floor to wake me up," he said, laughing. "I'd shower and run up as quickly as possible, and he'd be fully dressed with a list of the day's events, sipping his morning Guinness from a coffee cup.

"Mobutu never felt comfortable on land," Buisine added. "He was most happy just floating the river and stopping for barbecues, having friends flown in to join him."

Sometimes, when the Big Man's mood was right, Buisine would mention his family's land. "He'd tell me, 'We'll fix that, we'll fix that. *C'est pas grave,*'" Buisine remembers. "Other times he'd say, 'Look at everything Europe lost during the world wars, and it's doing fine now. Don't make such an issue of this Zairianization.'"

After Laurent Kabila's rebel troops entered Kinshasa in May 1997, Buisine was arrested at his home, along with many of Mobutu's inner circle. "They had a list," said Buisine. "And they were out to get every person on it." With his family safely in France, Buisine spent nine months in jail, serving out the last portion of his sentence in Kinshasa's hideous Makala prison—a death sentence for most Congolese. But because of Buisine's political status, he was able to negotiate with the guards for better food and a nightly ration of beer and whiskey. He was in jail when he received the news that Mobutu, then exiled in Morocco, had died from prostate cancer.

"I didn't cry," he added. "I'm a soldier."

On August 2, 1998, someone came to Makala prison and ordered Buisine released. It was Kabila himself, who'd just learned that Rwandan and Ugandan troops—his old allies against Mobutu—had just invaded Congo. The following day, the Rwandans managed to load hundreds of soldiers and rebels onto hijacked planes and get within striking distance of the capital. The rebels would eventually reach the city's eastern suburbs before Zimbabwean, Namibian, and Angolan soldiers, summoned by Kabila, finally halted the full-on assault. So as the five-year war began, Buisine retreated to his home in the capital. There, he waited out the war as it ravaged everything Mobutu hadn't already destroyed.

Buisine's way of life for the past two decades soon vanished for good, and most people were happy to see it go. ("I don't miss it, either," he said, "especially hearing Mobutu shout, *'Buisine! Buisine!'* a thousand times a day.") In those initial years after Mobutu, he took long vacations with his family, navigating the rivers around France, Poland, and Russia, weaving through the interiors and out to seas. But after years of this, he returned home to the river he loved so well.

Buisine now led the simple life of a river rat who ran the stretch six or seven times a year. Each trip was spent in the company of his commander, Abraham Bukasa, a tall, slender man with pepper-gray hair, whose own military career had also been destroyed by the Big Man's many whims. In 1978, gendarmes arrested the young navy sergeant after suspecting him of aiding a failed coup. He spent months in a dank, underground prison in the port town of Boma, where rats chewed on inmates' flesh at night and lice infested their clothing and pubic hair. Many of his friends were executed or died from abuse.

Bound by military experience and their own place in Congo's tragic history, the two friends now spent their days in quiet comfort along the river, one place in Congo that had never cast judgment against them. "The river was created by God," said Bukasa. "It won't change. Only men change."

By the third afternoon, we'd reached the Ngobila stretch, exactly 171 kilometers upriver from Kinshasa. Five kilometers long, Ngobila was the most dangerous region of our journey, where the river was faster (8 kmh as opposed to the average 5 kmh) and over sixty meters deep, and where deadly whirlpools stalked the waters during the rainy season when the river was high.

"Sometimes smaller boats can even see the whirlpools coming," said Buisine, pointing toward the shores, where they were most often found, "and they can't do anything about it until it's too late. There are many boats on the bottom." But the *Ma'ungano* was loaded down and heavy and pushed through Ngobila without incident.

Shortly afterward we began noticing streaks of orange and brown in the river, clay-colored, silty and thick. An hour later we reached Kwamouth, at the mouth of the great Kasai River. Here the Kasai and the Congo meet in a clash of speed and color. The village of Kwamouth looked lovely along the banks: no cars, only pristine huts and homes, groves of mango and avocado trees, large gardens and courtyards, pirogues tied up and bobbing on the shore, and children playing along the banks. And just as Stanley must have done before me, I peered at this native village for signs of God or civilization, and *lo and behold*, there was a cellular tower! It would be the last traces of the modern world we'd see for the next four days.

When peacekeepers arrived in 2001 to help maintain an early cease-fire, Buisine volunteered to help pilot the first UN boats up-river to assess the damage; in recent years as river traffic slowly increased, he's helped the UN draft the first modern navigational maps of the Congo River. Many of the earth's navigable bodies of water have been mapped using satellite images, which can be downloaded into onboard computer systems on discs. The resulting charts, now used by most captains in the world, reflect new construction of levees or bridges and account for bank erosion and shifts in sandbars.

As Buisine explained this, he picked up a thick, spineless book of weather-beaten pages and slapped it down on a nearby stool. It was a set of hand-drawn charts issued by the old Belgian-run river authority, meticulously drafted in black and white, and last updated in 1936. "This is all we have in Congo," he said.

But Buisine said the UN had recently provided him with military satellite images of the river, which he ran through a global-positioning program. On a large monitor inside the wheel-house, a red-boat icon chugged up the bend. Buisine updated the digital map with each trip, recording changes in current speeds, shifts in sandbars, and average depth in rainy and dry seasons. Village names and coordinates appeared in pop-up windows, along with tribal affiliations, and logistical data in the event of UN intervention. The information would someday combine to form a massive data-base of the river, which he hoped to make available to the public.

Each morning I ducked into the wheelhouse to check the progress of the tiny red boat, and each morning the jungle squeezed a little closer in. Outside, the uniform brick settlements of the old colony disappeared and gave way to moldered huts, set high above the river on stilts of bamboo. Smoke from breakfast fires crept through their porous roofs, giving the huts the appear-ance of giant animals steaming in the mist.

But the solitude along the river was alleviated by the local traders who flocked the *Ma'ungano* day and night as she passed. They'd strike out from shore in long dugout canoes filled with fish and vegetables, four or five people in each one, stabbing the current with hand-carved paddles the shape of raindrops. We'd watch them from a kilometer out, standing upright as they pumped their arms in perfect unison to make the interception.

The river traders supplied the crew with their meals, and it was also how we supplemented ours. We'd buy huge, ten-pound tilapia and give them to the chef, along with spinach, roasted peanuts, green onion, plantains, papaya, and exotic white apples. I bought wild honey so fresh that bees still clung to the arm of the old man who poured it. And we bought mangoes to store in the ship's deep freeze, taking them out on hot afternoons and peeling them with pocketknives. It was like eating ice cream.

When the river people came aboard, Riccardo became absorbed in a world of lighting and angles, rushing down the steps to capture their dramatic approach to the boat, or the way the shadows fell on a pile of tomatoes. Other times I'd find him on the barge snapping sunset portraits of some ragged fisherman whose clothes were half rotting off, both their faces as serious as stone. *"You see his eyes, man? Did you see his eyes?"*

In my old guidebook, the "natives" were dressed in rows of beads and colorful loincloths, their bodies covered with sprawling mutilation tattoos, their lips and ears adorned with brass hooks and trinkets. It was as if nothing had changed from the days of the old monarchies, when the Kongo and Bakuba kingdoms of this region were among the strongest and most advanced in all of Africa before the surge of European interference and slavery forced them into decline.

Alongside a photo of a group of Gombe tribal dancers, the guidebook explains, "The Negro has a rugged constitution. His torso is broad and well proportioned, his hips rather narrow, his limbs well developed, but his legs are sometimes too thin . . . the Negro in his youth has a very quick intelligence. He learns easily, but this facility quickly degenerates because of sexual excess and the abuse of fermented beverages . . . The traveler must see to it that his Negro staff does not drink beer or alcohol during the hours when its services will be needed . . . The Negro is called lazy because he is a firm believer in the policy of as little effort as possible. However, when he is well trained and judiciously employed, his output is good."

While many sections of the river I was seeing seemed bountiful with food, and the people healthy, others areas appeared destitute and starving. No grass skirts or ornamentation like in the guidebook, just secondhand rags that barely hid their nakedness. The children would rush out of thatched huts and wave when they saw white faces, their bellies bloated from malnutrition. Their mothers often stood behind them, rubbing their stomachs and asking for money. The farther we went, the worse off they appeared. Buisine explained how villages along the river and in the forest specialized in different trades. Some were farmers, while others were known for fishing or hunting bush meat. The latter villages, he said, were generally worse off because of their meager, unbalanced diets.

The captain joined me on the deck one afternoon as we passed a group of people living on one of the large middle islands. They looked particularly thin and rangy. The war really leveled these people, I offered. He shrugged and said, "They had nothing even before the war. This is the new generation you're seeing. All the old ones are either dead or fled to the city. These ones, they have no education, and their diet—nothing but fish and alcohol from cradle to the grave. Nothing has changed for hundreds of years. I mean, they still make fires by rubbing sticks together."

I'd often tease Séverin about moving out to the "country" and settling down, living the simple life with the river people, but the joke would fall flat. "To think we had one of the greatest civilizations in Africa," he said once, shaking his head the way he did. "Ah, but now . . ." Séverin had grown up with some of the world's nastiest poverty just outside his door in Kinshasa, and like me I think he was hoping to find something better in the vast, green interior. "Now these people can't even read, only count," he'd say, echoing Buisine. "No school, no prospects for the future. What will become of their children?"

Unlike the workers on the barge, Séverin was hungry to know his own history, and anything he could read, any conversation with Buisine or the commander, with the crew, or the river people themselves, was like adding a missing piece to a puzzle he was slowly putting together in his head. Every morning he'd pull out his copy of *King Leopold's Ghost*, Adam Hochschild's definitive chronicle of the Belgian atrocities, and make copious notes, while using the text to also practice his English. Other times I'd find him alone on the terrace, hunched over Buisine's old river charts, studying the maps and symbols with unshakable concentration.

My past translators, Johnny and the pastor, had been products of the war, rugged and scarred individuals who'd seen immeasurable horror and became deft survivors. Johnny had buried his murdered father with his own hands, and the pastor had risked his life to save his congregants and heaped the suffering of thousands onto his shoulders. For me, their lives had redefined what it meant to be brave.

Then there was Séverin: middle-class city boy, egghead and academic, president and founder of the Kinshasa English Club, content with spending his time lying in bed studying maps or poring over his *Kid's Life Application Bible*. He was indeed the strangest Congolese I'd ever met, and it was the very reason I was so drawn to him. You got the sense that Séverin had a future outside Congo and this war. Some path would lead him somewhere great, and each missing piece to that puzzle allowed him to see it more clearly. You could tell he sensed some mission within himself, but didn't know how to define it, not yet anyway. One morning, to my surprise, he told me he was considering running for local office, perhaps a place in the new legislature.

"Be a *politician*?" I said.

"The people in my neighborhood are always encouraging me," he said. "I tell them it's too crazy, but seeing these people here on the river, perhaps one day that will be in my future." After that, he never mentioned it again, though Lionel and I began to refer to him as *Monsieur Président*.

On the morning of the fourth day we entered Sandy Beach Pool, a wide section where the current was slow compared to the channel we'd just left, and the *Ma'ungano* could punch through it at the breakneck speed of seven kilometers per hour. But we had to beware; as its name suggested, sandbars filled the Sandy Beach Pool like waiting land mines, ready to beach a rig that wasn't careful. Fortunately for us, a scout named Freddy from the local river authority La Régie des Voies Fluviales, or RVF—paddled out in a pirogue, climbed aboard, and helped steer the ship around the sandbars, which shift with every rainy season. "The river is like a book and you must learn to read it," said Freddy, who wore no shoes and smelled of wet leaves. He spun the wheel with gentle precision, staring down the pool with the focus of a fighter pilot. "The dangers are always shifting. It's like a temperamental woman, always changing with the rain and wind." About fifty kilometers later, a new scout jumped aboard and relieved Freddy, who left to meet boats coming from the opposite direction.

Sandy Beach Pool had some of the most beautiful scenery so far: marshy finger islands with fisher birds swooping down to snatch small fish off the topwater. A silver mist hung over the islands, themselves like patches of wayward jungle, and each island was dotted with a few small huts and thatched canopies. Buisine and the commander told us about the trees that lined the shore, how many of them could be either medicinal or deadly, depending on their use. One tree he pointed out was popular with women who wished to shrink their vagina after giving birth. They boiled the ground bark of the tree into a soup, poured it into a basin, and sat in the brew for hours at a time. When Buisine was with Mobutu once in Gbadolite, an old woman noticed Buisine was walking with a grimace. "Do you suffer hemorrhoids?" the woman asked. "Why, yes," he answered, blushing. The old woman mixed this same brew and made the Frenchman sit in it for an hour. "Voilà, the hemorrhoids disappeared."

Speaking about the trees and islands, Buisine became animated. He began to explain an elaborate plan he'd been pondering for years, a plan to turn the Congo River into a national park for tourists. I laughed at first, since anything tourist-related in Congo was a fantasy. But he was serious. "I used to speak with Mobutu about this for hours," he said. "Mobutu was very passionate about the land and environment."

The plan, even if it existed only as an old man's dream, was indeed wonderful. The river would be transformed into a sprawling nature preserve that stretched from Kisangani to the sea. The vast chain of hundreds of river islands would be stocked with wild game, which would be imported from South Africa, where private game parks were becoming overpopulated. Rather than kill the animals, Buisine said, the businessmen who owned the reserves were eager to partner with people in Congo, where the wildlife had greatly been reduced by war.

"The islands on this river represent all the ecosystems of central Africa," said Buisine. "You have primary and secondary forests, swamps, savanna, everything."

There'd be antelope and zebra, leopards and lions, elephant and hyena. Villagers living along the river would be appointed game wardens and rangers to maintain the park and guard the animals from poachers and harm. Tourists would spend days cruising the park by riverboat, stopping at rustic lodges along the way to camp, barbecue, and sip cocktails while overlooking the river. Villagers would visit the boats during the day for "cultural lessons," teaching people how to fish, weave casting nets, or carve masks, which this section of Congo was famous for.

"It would be the greatest, most unique national park in all the world," Buisine mused. "And every person who lives on this river would be part of its glory."

He explained how he'd been pitching the plan for the past decade, first to Mobutu, then various environmental groups. The South African business partners were already lined up. Everyone agreed it was a good idea, but nothing was ever done. It would cost billions to implement, but it was necessary for the river to maintain its virgin ecosystem before democracy and peace brought development and ruin.

"The Congo River is the great lungs of the world," he said. "We must preserve and maintain this living thing. It's the only good thing we have left."

★ ★ ★

That evening we docked in Bolobo, 323 kilometers upriver from Kinshasa, and stayed the night. A lightning storm engulfed both sides of the river, kicking up monsoonlike winds to announce the coming rain. When we arrived in Bolobo, we'd planned to hop off and see the village. Buisine said it was beautiful and the people were friendly to strangers. But where we docked was two kilometers from town, on the opposite side of a long point. There was also no electricity, which meant that for us, Bolobo was just another black mass along our night passage we'd never see.

The port turned out to be an ominous little way station, with no lights except those of an oil tanker that had also moored for the night. A powerful spotlight illuminated the steel platform, where several workers in grease-slicked overalls sat on steel drums and listened to the storm roll in. Lights flickered through the cabin windows of the tugboat, dancing different shades of dirty yellow from a sputtering generator within. A few pirogues were pulled up onshore, some fires twinkled far up a hill, and that was all. The only sound was the low rumble of diesel engines competing against the wind.

We were docked maybe a full minute before a gaggle of government officials raced up the iron stairwell of the *Ma'ungano* and shouted for us to come out. There were eight of them, like a pack of wide-eyed mice who'd come to feed. "Show us all your papers right this moment!" one of them shouted. We politely obliged and went to retrieve our papers. When we got back, Buisine had booted half the group off the boat and was screaming at the only man who seemed to have a badge. "I only deal with actual officials," he shouted, "not your cronies looking for a beer! What do you really want?"

They insisted on switching on the fluorescent light of the deck to study our documents, which they did for over an hour. And the light brought bugs, millions and millions of bugs, as if the forest had emptied her arms to let her children play on the deck of the *Ma'ungano*. We stood there answering their questions, battling the insects flying into our mouths, down our shirts, squirming in our ears, dive bombing into our eyes, ducking, swatting, and cursing while the officials bellowed, "What airport did you land? Where is your entry stamp? Where is your vaccination card?" They pored over our *ordre de mission* statements from our employers and copied every word into their notebooks, even from mine, which was written in English. They accused me of being in Congo illegally, fingering several of the old visas in my passport (I had six), and refusing to flip to the visa that was current. *"Attend! Attend!"* they shouted every time I attempted to validate myself. "I can see your visa! And I can see this is a problem!"

It went on and on, until they finally satisfied themselves and left. We gave them no money, and surprisingly they didn't ask. In the end, they turned out to be pretty nice guys. But we'd have more encounters like this one in Bolobo, not all so benign.

By the fifth day I began to notice subtle changes in the land and people. The daily storms became heavier and swept in with little notice, and people along the bank seemed cagey and suspicious, replacing the friendly waves we'd come to expect with a steel-eyed gaze. That night, the captain commanded the crew to tie off along the bank and wait for the moon, as the stars weren't bright enough to illuminate the rocks and drifts. As the boat edged slowly toward shore, small fires glimmered behind the jungle fronds, only to disappear once the high beam raked the trees. The engines sputtered to a halt, and I lay in bed listening to the sound of monkeys howling like deranged children from the dark. The next morning a pirogue full of women jumped aboard carrying a plastic bucket of charred monkey meat. The monkey had been quartered and its parts stuffed tightly inside. A rib cage hooked around the lip of the bucket, and next to it, a long, disfigured arm reached out from the top, its fingers curled and blackened from fire.

A while later we heard Buisine screaming from the deck at a

group of traders below. A yellow jerrican sat in the bottom of their pirogue, full of fermented palm wine. They were selling booze to the crew and the boss had caught them. "No alcohol on this boat, you hear me?!" the captain screamed. He pointed to the tall man with a grizzled beard and tattered pants who'd paddled the boat. *"Keba na yo!"* Buisine told him in Lingala, which meant "Watch yourself!" Shamed in public by the white captain, the men didn't get mad. Instead, they hung their heads in silence, carefully untied their pirogue, and drifted off.

The following morning, our sixth day on the river, the *Ma'ungano* was intercepted by two motorboats carrying men with guns. They'd set off from shore as we passed Gombe, a small village with a few rows of huts peppered along the shore. Once the boats were attached, several muscled men with AK-47s and aviator sunglasses jumped aboard and ran toward the captain's room. I was sitting on the terrace when they ran past; my first thought was we were getting hijacked by pirates, or simply robbed by the army.

They turned out to be soldiers loyal to Vice President Bemba, whose rebel army had controlled the forests during the war. The soldiers told Buisine they had a prisoner that needed transporting to Mbandaka, another soldier who'd been arrested for stealing guns. They needed a ride, a free ride. Buisine cringed and agreed, and one of the soldiers signaled for the prisoner to come aboard. He was barefoot and dressed in fatigues, his arms flexi-cuffed behind his back. His face was swollen and red from a heavy beating. The jack-booted soldiers pushed him into a metal shed on the barge and sat guard out front, eating bananas and tossing the peels into the river. With guns now aboard the *Ma'ungano*, the mood quickly darkened throughout the ship and everyone became tense and agitated. No matter how far you ran, I thought, the war would always find you.

A major dressed in a crisp uniform was aboard the prisoner's boat, and after instructing his men, he walked up the stairs and toward the captain's room, where Buisine sat at the wheel. The major was short with a round belly that hung over his belt, and medals decorated his uniform. He stood in the doorway and said nothing. Buisine looked up, expecting to see another jackbooted soldier, but instantly beamed. He jumped up and grabbed the major's hand. *"Mbote,"* the captain said warmly—"hello" in Lingala. The two men clasped shoulders and exchanged a local greeting, touching heads three times as if cheek-kissing with skulls. "How the hell are you?" Buisine said. "I wondered if you were still alive."

The major, it turned out, had once been a Mobutu bodyguard during the heyday of pink champagne and Concorde flights. When Kabila's rebels stormed the interior in 1997 to oust Mobutu, the major's position was overrun, and he was forced to join or be killed. He joined and proved his loyalty by attacking his own troops as rebels took Kinshasa. He later deserted and joined Bemba's thriving rebel army in the jungles in their fight against President Kabila's government troops. Despite being national army himself now, the major still considered himself a rebel officer.

Buisine hadn't seen him for years, and for the next few hours the two old dinosaurs did some catching up. Have you seen so-and-so? No, he's dead. What about so-and-so? Dead, too. And so-and-so? He's in Europe, couldn't find a place in the new government. They talked about the upcoming runoff, how a Kabila victory could spell disaster for these soldiers sympathizing with Bemba. The major's men were scared of their fate. "Do yourself a favor," Buisine told the major. "Keep a low profile. In six months, this whole place could be fucked."

Buisine instructed the chef to prepare a meal and a bed for the major, and once the captain was alone, I asked him if the army had a satellite phone in Gombe. It was just a small fishing village with no cellular network for hundreds of miles. No, he said, I don't think they have a sat phone.

"Then how did the major know you were coming?" I asked.

"The neighboring village told them," he said. "With drums."

II

We reached Mbandaka on the next evening, seven days and seven hundred kilometers from where we began. There was no electricity in the town, and dozens of oil lamps flickered ashore in the inky darkness. As we pulled into port, we saw what appeared to be a floating refugee camp with hundreds piled aboard, living under tents made from tattered plastic sheeting labeled UNICEF. Plumes of smoke from charcoal burners shrouded the steel surface, and somewhere a radio blared a wobbly tune as its batteries slowly died. Men danced drunk in the shadows, and toddlers rolled naked in the coal dust. She was called the *Ndobo* and her barges pointed upriver, toward Kisangani. We immediately knew: *That's our boat.*

The three of us leaned over the rail when the *Ma'ungano* touched its barge against the *Ndobo* to tie together. And when the crowds of people camped below saw our white faces, they roared and chanted, "*Mundele! Mundele!* You've arrived!"

Séverin sighed. "These people are waiting for us," he said, his face pinched with dread. I asked him what *ndobo* meant in Lingala. "The hook," he answered, and walked back into his room.

The boat would travel to Ndobo, its namesake town, located 578 kilometers upriver from Mbandaka. It was operated by a Lebanese-owned logging company called Trans-M, which was logging over one million acres of forest between Mbandaka and Kisangani. The *Ndobo* had come from Kinshasa with passengers loaded on its three barges and, after reaching its destination, would return to the capital loaded with timber bound for Europe.

Logging was now the boom business of the forests, with exotic wood such as mahogany, afrormosia, and tola fetching hundreds of thousands of dollars per barge-load in European markets. During the war years, Congo's government doled out logging titles to dozens of multinational firms, signing away over 107 million acres of rain forest, an area larger than California. Before 2003, companies were buying half-million-acre contracts for only $286 a year in taxes, never mind what was handed under the table. Zimbabwe received over eighty-four million acres in exchange for sending troops to assist Kabila's army during the war.

Environmental groups such as Greenpeace estimate that by 2050 over 40 percent of Congo's forests will be gone. And while the government had recently frozen new logging contracts and reviewed existing ones, the companies operated entirely without environmental standards. To appease the natives, they would sign "social responsibility" contracts that promised schools and clinics, but these were often meaningless and unenforceable. Like many of the companies, Trans-M had promised a lot in the forest and delivered little. But I didn't know any of this as I stood looking at the barge that would take us upriver. A couple hundred more passengers were expected to board that day, and they'd already started arriving. The fare was ten dollars each.

We needed to stake out a location on the barge, so the next morning we hurried down the market road, looking for a vendor who specialized in the long wooden poles used for barge shelters. Mbandaka was a river town, and everything bought, sold, and traded in the market somehow catered to the steel that drifted by. It was also one of the most haunted cities in all of Congo, and I'd felt it since we'd arrived.

I'd heard stories about Mbandaka, none of them very good: boat sinkings, mutinies, cholera. It floated on the map like some lost outpost adrift from the constraints of the world; the last exit before things turn wild for good.

Mbandaka straddled the equator at the junction of the Congo and Ruki rivers and was founded by Stanley in 1883 as one of the colony's first stations. First called simply Equator, then Coquilhatville, the city was a thriving port and military post during the days of the colony, with hundreds of Europeans living in rows of brick villas along bamboo-paved streets shaded by groves of coconut palms. The old steamers bound for Kisangani (then Stanleyville) would stop for the day in the Equator station, allowing passengers time to visit the Eala Botanical Gardens, a sanctuary of over four thousand species of local flora, including sections devoted to experimental strains of rubber vine. Large colonial plantations and farms surrounded the town center and in turn gave way to the "native quarters" in the trees. After independence, most of the whites fled the town, leaving their farms and plantations to rejoin the surrounding jungle.

When Rwandan soldiers and rebels seized eastern Congo in late 1996, they targeted the sprawling refugee camps along the Rwanda-Zaire border packed with hundreds of thousands of Hutu refugees. Many of these people had participated in the ethnic slaughter, and others were innocent civilians who'd fled Rwanda fearing retribution from the country's new Tutsi government. When rebels and soldiers attacked the camps, thousands of the refugees, innocent and guilty alike, fled west into the dense jungle of Congo as rebels pursued them. They were chased for seven months through the forest, dying along the way from malaria, cholera, and starvation, until finally they reached the Congo River near Mbandaka. From there, they hoped to cross over to neighboring Congo-Brazzaville, where they'd seek immunity.

But the river was too swift and wide to cross over. Dozens tried to swim and vanished in the current. The rest simply collapsed along the banks and awaited their fate. When rebels arrived soon after, missionaries working nearby stood helpless while hundreds were shot and hacked to death with machetes and bayonets, their bodies then flung into the river. Residents downstream in Kinshasa say the bloated corpses floated past for days.

I found no memorials for the dead in Mbandaka, but their

ghosts seemed to riot on the streets to agitate the living. As we walked in search of materials for our shelter, crowds along the market road soon pressed all around. Several plump, red-cheeked women pushed their way to the front. They held carcasses of smoked monkeys, hog-tied with bellies flayed open and fangs exposed in horrific death mask. A small crocodile was flung at our feet, its jaws bound with vines, its eyes like dark, smoky windows. Children ran forward and beat it with sticks, while others tormented the beast with stones. "*Mundele! Mundele!*" they shouted. The croc thrashed wildly, beating its powerful tail against the mud in its final stand. Then it was snatched away and tossed into the grass, where a group of reptiles were slowly dying in the sun.

"Ah, the Mbandaka people are *crazy*," Séverin said as we walked away. "They're Bangala tribe, very tough and confrontational, and they enjoy fighting." A famous story in Kinshasa explained everything about the Mbandaka mentality, Séverin said, and perhaps the river people in general. In the 1980s, Mobutu made one of his grand, infrequent tours of the forest and stopped in Mbandaka. "A very big crowd came to hear Mobutu," said Séverin. "Mobutu asked them, 'What do you need from me? What can I get for you? A school, a hospital perhaps?' The people shouted, '*Beer! Beer! Beer!*' So Mbandaka got a brewery."

At the end of the market road we turned into the narrow maze of wooden stalls. Like any grocery or department store, African markets are divided into sections, and we were headed toward the section that sold poles. But along the way, several women selling raw peanut butter screamed for us to stop. "*Mundele,* buy some peanut butter," one said. "No, *mundele,*" screamed another, just across the aisle. "Buy *my* peanut butter. My peanut butter tastes the best!" I bought some from both women, smeared it on several fried beignets, and drowned it with wild honey.

We found the wooden poles near the river's edge. Hundreds were arranged in pens according to height, some stretching ten feet. After sketching the kind of shelter we needed in my notebook, we bought eight poles for forty-five hundred Congolese francs, about nine dollars. Back at the barge, we claimed a small, empty space near the tug and set to work building our house. Riccardo had served a year in the Italian army and was proficient in knots. Under his supervision (and a nattering gang of busybodies crowded around giving advice), we lashed the poles together with nylon rope to form a reinforced A-frame, which we secured to railway ties along the barge. Our roof was constructed from the orange tarp and woven grass mats we'd bought in the market. It was sturdy and every bit cozy. Inside, there was barely room for three of us to sit, much less sleep.

We celebrated that night with cold beer and steaks at the one good restaurant in town. The dim fluorescent lights of the Métropole drew swarms of insects so large they cast slow-moving shadows across the empty tables. A dance floor sat in the middle of the outdoor patio, where a fat woman waltzed with a man too drunk to keep time. Slow soukous ballads played from an old cassette deck that ebbed and flowed with surges in the generator and sometimes blew static so loud everyone shielded their heads from some unseen attack.

The waitress sat drinking at a dark corner table with a large white man who spoke fluent Lingala—Belgian, I guessed, an importer, or one of the last romantic holdouts—dressed in a starched oxford with several empty bottles in front of him. His skin was the color of ash, with pasty liver spots creeping up his neck and cheeks. There was something already dead about him, the way his face moved in and out of the shadow but never really took shape. Watching him was like staring at a scarecrow from a fast-moving car. Like the town, he seemed to float in some restless space, cut off long ago and unable to find his way back. He put the chill on me. I ordered a beer and shifted my chair, keeping my back to the colonial ghost in the corner.

★ ★ ★

The next morning, around four hundred people crowded the barges of the *Ndobo* as we pulled out of port and waved good-bye to Mbandaka, and us, the luxury of the *Ma'ungano*. Our little shelter offered a wide-open view of the left bank, but as the hours slowly passed, the sunlight and calm disappeared, never to return. Plastic sheeting and threadbare tarps were pulled from the heaping bundles, poles materialized from nowhere, pots and pans rattled on the deck, and radios thundered to life. In a matter of hours, a small village had risen up around us.

These were the river traders, the men and women who moved Congo's jungle economy like a great army of ants. Every journey was a toss of the dice, a chance to double down or wash up in the backwater. But they took the risk because life in the city was far more unforgiving. Traveling the river was the good life, and they basked in its pleasures, an extended business trip aboard a floating disco that never closed.

"*Ay, mundele,*" my neighbor yelled. "Put away your notebook and come drink some wine!" It was eleven A.M., an hour after we left port, and the party aboard the *Ndobo* was going full throttle. Our neighbors to the right, Lucy and Toni, were pouring milky palm wine into plastic mugs. A new camp began every four feet, and in every camp a different radio blasted its buoyant rumba. The sun radiated through our orange tarp like a heat lamp, sucking our energy. Small chores, such as filtering water or washing dishes, stole our breath and left us wilted. I finally put away my notebook and focused on not passing out.

The three barges were so crowded that corridors soon formed through the floating village. One walkway barreled past our tent, and most people passing by stopped to stare at the two *mundele* who'd come aboard. "*Bonjour,*" we'd offer, like freaks in a cage, until the people laughed and sauntered off.

The barges were like giant floating supermarkets, and one could buy almost anything in the great bazaar that spread itself along the deck. Walking through the narrow corridors you found essential items such as lye soap in blue and pink blocks, Angola-brand toothbrushes sold in packs of six, safety razors, plastic mirrors, lead spoons, needle and thread, travel-size bags of raw sugar, beads and necklaces, women's panties with LOVE embroidered on the crotch, rubber sandals, nylon fishing nets, Betasol lotion, Tiger Head batteries that lasted exactly four hours in the cheap cassette players sold and used on the barge.

In its aisles you could find quinine and chloroquine for malaria, hydration salts for diarrhea, and pills for intestinal worms and pain. There were nurses and midwives, witch doctors and preachers, and a man for just about every trade. Our neighbor Lucy sold the secondhand clothing worn by most everyone on the barge and along the river, the ubiquitous American T-shirts donated to charities and dumped on the African market. Everywhere I looked was a strange remnant of home, the old grandmother who advertised the strip club in Kentucky, or the stoic fisherman whose shirt read, I'M THE BIG SISTER.

Lucy was from Kinshasa, with pretty green eyes and short dreadlocks wove with decorative blue thread. For hours each day, despite the brutal sun, Lucy would sit on a little stool outside her camp with her used T-shirts, shorts, and jeans spread on a blanket in neatly folded piles. Whenever a buyer with cash would come around, usually one of the other traders or passengers, Lucy would make change from a thick wad of francs she pulled from under the folds of her dress. With the river people themselves, Lucy would trade for dried fish, which were smoked black and secured between handwoven racks, like tennis racquets bound together with vine. Each rack cost three dollars on the river and would fetch five times the price back in Kinshasa.

Lucy had traded along the river for the past decade, through war and peace and all the trouble in between. During the war, when the river was closed, she often walked nearly eight hundred kilometers through the jungle from Kinshasa to Basankusu territory in the north. Soldiers and rebels prowled the skinny trails. Soldiers raped her friends in front of their children, and everyone was taxed and robbed for the "war effort." Lucy had already lost everything twice to storms and thieves. "When you lose your stuff, there's nothing for you," she said. "They don't sell insurance on the river."

With every trip, Lucy would sink her savings into merchandise in Kinshasa and hope to double her investment along the river. Everything on the barge was part of her hustle, including the plastic chairs she rented to us for a dollar a day, and the small money she made each morning selling cups of coffee boiled with gingerroot. Other traders supplemented their income by selling fried beignets smeared with peanut butter, or bowls of fresh catfish soup. Even in the dead of night, someone was always cooking.

I could tell the river traders made an impression on Séverin, who'd warmed up to our neighbors considerably. Their brassy resilience and resourcefulness impressed him, and soon he counted many friends on the barge, joking and debating politics and religion. He later discovered Lucy even lived on his street in Kinshasa and was friends with his mother.

"They are loud and uneducated, but the river people are teaching me many things," he said one night. "How to make money from nothing and survive. In many ways, their life is better than Kinshasa. Notice they eat five meals a day! Only the rich can eat like this in the city."

The second day on the barge, we passed the small village of Malela, another uniform cluster of thatched huts wrapped in a dense wall of trees. One of the *Ndobo*'s crewmen, Albert, came by our tent and pointed to the banks. "This was the front line during the war," he said, "the 810-kilometer mark. From here to Kinshasa was Kabila's men, and from Malela to Kisangani was rebels."

The 810-kilometer mark had divided the river and run like an electric fence through the forest. Traders such as Lucy who'd braved the water during the war knew the 810 mark as if it blinked bright yellow on the current. Albert had sat at home in Kisangani until 2001, he said, when many small-time traders attempted to return to work. "Soldiers would be standing along the banks in every village," he said. "They'd call out for you to come, and if you refused, they'd open fire. Neither side was better, but you'd better know who you were dealing with."

Later that day, I met an army lieutenant who was traveling back to Kisangani after reuniting with his family after eight years. In 1998, Pierre Kitebo had joined the Rwandan-backed rebels who pushed their way west toward Kinshasa, only to get knocked back by government-allied troops. When Rwanda pulled out of Congo in 2002, Kitebo was sent to Kisangani and put through the army integration process, where he remained as an instructor. His wages were never enough to travel to Basankusu, where his family waited, and few barges or trains were operating to take him. But a few months before, the army had granted Kitebo his leave, and with some money he'd saved, he set out to find his family, carrying only an old photo of his wife to keep him warm and a vague idea of where they now lived. He spent three weeks on a barge from Kisangani to Basankusu, where he finally found his family in a small hut deep in the jungle. When Pierre had left eight years before, his youngest daughter, Benedite, was still in her mother's stomach. She didn't recognize the tall, beaming man in army fatigues when he walked out of the trees.

"They all ran out and hugged me," he said. "They were happy to see their daddy."

He now sat in a cramped, ragged lean-to surrounded by his wife, two sons, and daughter, who were finally going to Kisangani to live with him at the army camp. He pulled the little girl close to his chest and kissed her head. "They were naked when I found them," he said, "but there'll be no more suffering now."

Here, I thought, I was finally seeing some hopeful signs. I'd also glimpsed it in people such as Lucy and Solange Kobo, another neighbor, who was making her first journey on the river with her husband. They were from Kinshasa, and both had university degrees in teaching and literature, but had been unable to find jobs. Solange instead worked as a hairdresser, and her husband was an occasional mechanic, but there was hardly enough money to support their two kids and still live in the city. So they decided to roll their dice on the river. After six months they'd saved four hundred dollars and bought a new bicycle, bags of sugar and salt, along with batteries, soup mix, spices, and biscuits. When I met them after my third day on the barge, the only thing left was the bike, which they hoped to sell in Ndobo. "But even without the bike," Solange said, "we've already doubled our money."

I recognized this emerging confidence in such guys as Jean Kalokula, whose last river journey was with a convoy of pirogues during the war. Despite the soldiers patrolling the banks, Jean and a few other traders would risk voyages to villages upriver, where he'd bring essential items like salt and flour that didn't otherwise get through, then trade them for smoked meats and fish. They'd set out for weeks at a time, traveling at night to avoid checkpoints, and sleeping in the jungle during the day, until malaria and cholera finally killed many of his party. Their bodies were buried on the lonely middle islands, and Jean limped back to Kinshasa to wait for the war to end. He was now traveling the river again for the first time, a man who was proud to be going back to work.

I was delighted to hear some good news on the river, and the traders all seemed elated to be running their old routes and having a party. And I was grateful they'd embraced us like one of their group. I couldn't walk the length of the barge without someone holding up a ladle of palm wine with a warm, drunken grin, or one of the fat, white caterpillars that were such a popular staple in the forest, looking at my reaction while the grub squirmed between their fingers. And every time I stood up, it seemed, I was hailed with a chorus of *"Mundele!"* (or at night, *"Mundele moto!"*—which meant "turn off your light!")

An order seemed be revealed as we floated east. The racks of oily smoked fish, the charred monkeys and bushes of manioc, the palm wine, and the way the traders squatted by their wares and haggled so intensely over a sale I thought they would fight—all of this had remained the same through the cataclysmic horrors of the past century, and I wondered if perhaps that was a good thing.

Watching the river traders strike out from shore in their long pirogues, five people exactly aligned and pumping against the current, racing five hundred horsepowers of engine, and catching it nearly every time, was as primal and graceful as the fisher birds that skimmed the middle current and arched back into the trees. Even their wipeouts seemed like ancient, well-rehearsed rituals. The pirogue might catch a bad wake after releasing from the barge and spin like an oil drum, spilling everyone into the river, vegetables and racks of smoked fish slowly vanishing beneath the water. But no one ever seemed worried. Instead, crowds would gather along the side of the barge and cheer. The dumped passengers would give an embarrassed wave and swim ashore, leg strokes so powerful they sent their bodies bouncing chest-high through the current. Often the pirogue would drift aimlessly downstream, where someone would pick it up and safeguard its return.

And after a few days, we began to adapt. We'd wake up in the morning, always right at dawn, and join the dozens of others quietly brushing their teeth over the side, leaning to spit into the mist that hung on the water. I'd head to the back of the barge near the toilet and stand in line with the other men, using my plastic bucket to collect the steaming water that poured off the engines and out the side spout, then strip to my underwear and lather up. At any given time, a dozen men would be bathing off the back, their black bodies covered head to toe in white suds.

After breakfast and a stiff cup of ginger coffee, Séverin and I would make the rounds and talk to people before the sun became too hot. As we walked along the usual rows of toothbrushes, medicines, sandals, and razor blades, the river people would climb aboard carrying ten-foot pythons in bamboo cages to sell as food, or rare, prized Congo African Gray parrots they'd trapped in the forest with rubber gum and sold to traders for ten dollars apiece. There were catfish as big as bathtubs, monkeys and wild pigs tethered with vine and thrashing against the deck, and the random severed hog leg just lying in the path.

But after only two days, the novelty of the good times began to wear thin and I just craved some quiet. I wanted to sleep without music blasting from ten directions around my head, without people dancing into my sleeping bag or the pastor who waited until four A.M. before pulling out his megaphone and starting his sermon. ("One cannot know the hour of the Lord," the preacher said, while the sleepy, drunken voices chanted, "Aha.") It would be days, maybe even weeks, before we reached Kisangani. It suddenly dawned on me that everything I'd wished for had come true: I had passed the point of no return. The river now owned me, and the sound of its chains was a hundred radios dying in the night.

It was so hot during the day that I'd sit in my tent for hours just stoned on the humidity, watching the molecules behind my eyes ignite like tiny starbursts, until something came along to distract me. The third afternoon on the barge, a particularly wicked aroma straightened me in my seat. I swore someone's head was on fire. The heat made the smell come alive and dance, gave it a flavor in the back of my throat. I followed a pale cloud of smoke to where a woman sat flipping a giant dead monkey over a charcoal stove, scorching the fur and scraping the char with a broad cutlass. Its innards were still intact and boiling out of its mouth. The woman sensed me staring and stopped, looked up from her work, and gave me a big, toothy grin.

The next morning, while rolling up my mattress, I discovered tiny, pea-shaped objects writhing beneath my bed. *Maggots*, I thought, the words flashing like a JumboTron in my mind: *Maggots on my pillow. Maggots on my pillow.* They'd dropped from the racks of rancid smoked fish that Lucy had stored right above my head. The previous night, I swore I'd heard the popping sounds of them feeding. But how could I make a scene? I'd asked to be there, had come a long way to get up that river, and now was *definitely* up that river. I simply kicked the maggots away with my boots and went in search of breakfast. That same afternoon, while eating a stick of beef jerky, I looked down to find a matted wad of pubic hair resting on my arm. I shrugged, blew it back into the wind, and finished my lunch.

After dinner on our fourth night, I sat on the tie post near the water's edge and watched the river. The sun was sinking fast the way it does along the equator, sending cascades of orange and reds shooting from behind the green wall like a bright solar bomb. And with the darkness came the first cool breezes of the day. For some reason the radios were quiet, and for once I could hear every sound of the forest, every chirp and whistle and shrill monkey scream, as if every tree were full of beans and rattling off its roots. Despite the loud music at night, little sleep, and even the maggots, I was feeling pretty good that night, feeling positive about the rest of the journey, however it would unfold. I'd even pulled out my notebook and written these words: *Watching the river moving past—this is what keeps the spirit strong when you get low. This is when I love this place the most.*

Just as I finished writing, the engines faded and I felt the barge veer to the bank, where it eventually stopped. I then watched aghast as the tugboat *Ndobo* disembarked from the barges, turned around, and disappeared downriver, stranding us on the riverbank in jet-black darkness. The vanishing taillights seemed to hold my optimism by a thread. And when they were gone, I panicked.

Riccardo stood nearby, aiming his flashlight into the black vacuum of the jungle's edge. He smiled. "What do you call it?" he said. "The white man's grave? Well, man, they left us in the white man's grave."

I walked back to our tent, where Séverin had just returned from his nightly rounds, talking to friends and trying to negotiate a price for some fish to sell in Kinshasa. "It's the captain's son," he said. "He was burned very badly. They had to find a hospital."

"The nearest hospital is two days away," I said. I looked for panic in his eyes but found none, not even the slightest hint of irritation. He was maddeningly calm. "No one seems to care," he said, shrugging. "This is their life."

It was true. Instead of panicking, the Congolese only amped up the party. The saucy soukous of Werrason now roared behind an arsenal of fresh batteries, and jugs of palm wine sloshed from camp to camp. Stranded on a remote stretch of river in the middle of Congo, they reacted by dancing as if it were the last night on earth.

I shone my light down the barge and saw several men pissing in the river. This was normal; with only one toilet for all four hundred people, the guys usually did their minor business over the side. But now, near the bank, the current was stagnant, and just a few feet downstream, half a dozen women were scooping the same water and drinking it.

The year before, a barge had been hit with cholera in the same remote stretch east of Mbandaka. By the time it reached the next town, dozens were dead on the deck. Yes, I thought, it would happen like that, here and now. And by the time we were discovered, it would be too late.

Riccardo was standing next to me, and I turned to him with panic in my eyes. "We've gotta get off this boat," I said. "We've gotta get off this boat or we'll all die of cholera."

He shoved a handful of whiskey packets into my hand, the kind that were sold all over the barge. "Relax, man," he said. "You are just paranoid. These people, they do like this for hundreds of years."

And after a few whiskeys, I began to feel better. I still wanted to get off, and I could tell Riccardo agreed, if only for the sake of progress. We decided our only prayer was flagging down a passing boat, but we hadn't seen one in two days. "What about Buisine?" I said. "He can't be more than twelve hours behind." Yes, we decided, Buisine would save us! We began to fantasize about the *Ma'ungano* chugging past and sending its dugout to rescue us. "So long, suckers!" we'd yell, using our boots to beat away the doomed crowds who tried to tag along, tried to weasel in on our air-conditioning and hot showers. These soothing thoughts calmed my panic, and all night I lay awake listening for the sound of diesel engines passing by.

The next morning, some fishermen informed us the *Ndobo* was only a few kilometers downriver in Mankanza, which had a small clinic. Riccardo, Séverin, and I hired a passing canoe to take us there and, upon arriving, found the captain's three-year-old son, Gus, sprawled on a thin mattress and his worried father kneeling beside him. Gus had been running through the crowded barge and accidentally tipped a pot of boiling cooking oil all over his body, scorching his chest, arms, and back. The pain was so great he couldn't even cry.

"His wounds are already infected," the doctor whispered. There was no medicine in Mankanza, he added, and the best option was to return to the barge and rush him to the hospital in Bumba, sixty kilometers from Ndobo. For now, the best the doctor had to offer was talcum powder.

For the next three days, as we chugged toward Ndobo, Riccardo and I occupied ourselves by stopping in to visit Gus and treat his wounds. Both of us carried antibiotic ointment in our medical kits, and we gently applied it to the boy's blistered skin, which began to appear like the scales of a dead fish. We gave his mother ibuprofen to give Gus for the pain, but like the doctor in Mankanza, we could do little else.

On our sixth night we pulled into Ndobo and docked there until morning. When the sun rose, we saw the gargantuan stacks of felled lumber lying like dead giants in the red mud. We were at the Trans-M logging camp, just outside the village, where the trees would be loaded and sold in Europe, and the logging would likely continue until the forest no longer went on forever.

By dawn the traders had disassembled and packed up their floating city as quickly as they'd built it. And when it became light enough to see, they flocked off the barge and into the village to trade the remainder of their merchandise in the market. I was glad to leave the barge, and after packing all our gear, we watched with indifference as the traders picked apart our shelter down to the very last rope. They could have it.

III

We hitched a ride with the timber company to Bumba, where we'd cover the runoff elections, due in three days. Since the *Ndobo* was returning to Kinshasa, we hoped to find another boat to Kisangani once we arrived in Bumba—a motorized pirogue, anything but a barge. We'd now traveled 1,337 kilometers in fifteen days, with only four hundred kilometers of river left to go. Surely, we thought, the worst was over.

Bumba is the origin for one of the first roads ever built in Congo, the Route Royal Congo-Nil, which spanned over thirteen hundred kilometers and connected the Congo River with the Nile in Juba, Sudan. The road cut through the northeastern corner of Congo near present-day Garamba National Park and was once a transport route for European goods shipped down the Nile and into the colony. It also accessed the Lado Enclave, one of the major elephant-poaching grounds for the Free State's trade of ivory, allowing poachers to bring their haul to the sea. In later years, ships would unload at

Bumba, where merchandise would be taken into the northern stretches of the colony via the Juba road or Vicinaux railway, which the Belgians built in the mid-1920s.

Once the colonial masters pulled out, Bumba was left to fade like the rest. Many of the white-stone shops along the riverfront boulevard stood shuttered and empty, with market women now selling pineapples and cigarettes on the ground out front. There were two bars, where the beer was cool and plentiful, but no restaurants or cafés to kill the time. We took our meals in the Hotel Mozulua, where the heat and mosquitoes kept us awake at night and only encouraged us to press forward.

At Bumba, the Congo stretched twenty kilometers across at its widest point, but this majestic view was blocked by chains of wooded islands that only seemed to throttle the great river. Shortly after we arrived, despite Séverin's earlier deftness at finding a boat, we discovered nothing in town to carry us to Kisangani. There were no pirogues with working engines, and even if there had been, the fuel alone—so rare in the jungle—would've cost us hundreds. One barge was docked at port, but the captain was waiting long after the runoff elections to decide his departure. After the gunfights in Kinshasa following the first round of voting, the threat of sudden violence was heavy on everyone's mind. Caution prevailed, and for the moment the river would be empty. If we wanted to advance soon, it would have to be through the trees.

We weighed our options carefully. If we stayed and chose to go by river, we could easily be stuck in Bumba for two weeks. The only other option was to cross through the jungle, and the only way to do that was on bicycles. Riccardo had found himself in a similar spot on his journey six months before. He'd rented bikes in Bumba and gone three days through the jungle. On the bike he'd become sick with malaria, plus gotten the fly bites that eventually became infected. It seemed like a grueling journey, and I knew I wasn't in good enough physical shape to pedal a bike over four hundred kilometers through the forest. But Riccardo was persistent.

"Come on, man, you think the river is wild? Wait until you see the *jongle*. The people there, they never saw a white man before me. You are like some kind of UFO."

If anything, he was right about getting off the river. Between Buisine and the *Ndobo*, I felt I'd seen as much as I could. Another barge journey, I feared, would feel redundant at best and tip me toward madness at worst. And if the forest was as isolated as Riccardo described, it would be the perfect place to see how the war had truly affected the country. I'd seen the ruin in the cities, but nothing like the remote forests, which covered over half the country. Thinking about that isolation brought to mind the naked people Buisine had described, frightened and hiding behind the trees. As I did with many things, I turned to Séverin and asked him what we should do.

"Yeah, the bikes will be a good experience," he said. "The most important thing is forward progress. Bumba is no place to hang around."

So with that decision made, we spent the days before the election looking for a convoy of men to move us on bikes through the world's second-largest rain forest.

Bicycles were certainly not hard to come across in Bumba. They'd long replaced vehicles as the sole means of transporting people and product through the jungle and town. Many of these bikes were driven by a well-organized group of taximen called *tolekas*, who comprised the Association de Cyclistes Transporteurs de Bumba, the biker's union.

When the river was closed during the war, the *tolekas* had routinely braved the rebel-infested forest to bring back essential goods such as salt block, sugar, and used clothing from Kisangani. Many left and never returned. For years, they single-handedly kept the town from starving and for good reason were still considered local angels.

The union headquarters was in a small concrete building near the busy central market. There we met with the president, Dominique Lisobe, and made our requests: we needed six bicycles, two for Riccardo and me to pedal, and the rest to porter Séverin and our burden of gear. For this we needed four of his strongest men who were familiar with the trails to Kisangani. And the bikes, we insisted, had to be in top condition and have spare parts for the trip.

Lisobe adjusted his thick-framed glasses and scribbled careful notes. He warned us first about the extreme hardship of riding through the forest; the trails were now flooded from heavy seasonal rains, and given the fragile political climate, the entire region could quickly become a death trap for foreigners.

"Nonetheless, my boys are well prepared for this sort of journey," he said finally. "My only concern is you will slow them down. Perhaps hire two more riders just in case."

"No, no," Riccardo said, "we pedal the bikes."

"Right," I said, completely ignorant. "How hard can it be?"

"You will see," Riccardo said to me. "To ride in the forest, it feels *great*, man. None of these *focking* barges to delay us. Just you and the forest!"

We agreed on a price of fifty dollars per bike. We'd depart immediately following the next morning's vote. In four days, we estimated, we'd be eating steaks at the finish line.

The runoff election was the most significant step toward peace and stability in the country's history. But we'd become so impatient to keep moving that it became little more than a distraction. The vote was no mystery, either, not in that part of the country. All along the river we'd been hearing nothing but praise for Bemba and scorn for Kabila. Even though Bemba's soldiers had terrorized these people all throughout the war, the fat man was regarded as the patriot son. Kabila was just a puppet crook hired by white men. And with no real newspaper or radios for hundreds of miles, rumor was king.

The morning polls went smoothly enough, with people lining up at schoolhouses that had been converted to voting stations. Riccardo and I toured the various stations and interviewed people, and I found myself having the same conversations I'd had in every African election I'd covered.

"What kinds of changes will you demand from the winner?"

Silence. "Hmmm."

"So you're demanding peace, electricity, and better schools for your kids?"

"Oh, yes, yes . . . peace. Peace and schools."

It was afterward, when we were riding bike taxis back to the hotel, that everything went wrong. The crowded streets were now empty, void of dogs and children and women ferrying to the market. Looking around, I saw people staring out windows and sheepishly standing in doorways, all the bad signs. A government lorry rumbled past loaded with soldiers with readied guns. And when we turned a corner toward the hotel, it was like being dropped into the madness of Kinshasa all over again.

A mob of about a hundred young men rumbled down the street carrying machetes, sticks, and jagged stones. Earlier that morning, a Kabila supporter had been caught stuffing a ballot box in one of the stations. The mob then burned the ballots in the streets and set fire to several buildings. They now rioted through the empty town, spewing venom against Kabila and thieving foreigners. When they saw us, it was as if we'd walked right into their trap. *"Ay, étranger!"* they shouted, and quickened their pace. Riccardo raced toward them with cameras held high. And whereas I'd usually follow, this time I froze.

It was everything I'd been running from since that night at the Grand Hotel. And here it was again, kicking up a cloud of dust straight toward me. The mobs terrified me the most. I'd been through some bad ones in Togo and Kinshasa, but that morning in Bumba, I suddenly felt my luck had run its course. A voice, diamond sharp in my mind, told me to turn back immediately. There were no lives left. If I stayed, only bad things would happen.

"Allez! Allez!" I screamed at my driver, just a small boy whose body had gone rigid. "Séverin, tell this kid to go!"

We turned onto a backstreet and moved parallel with the crowd, struggling for speed on the sandy streets. Some of the mob caught up and held rocks near our heads, leering and shouting threats. But we finally found our turn, and luckily no one followed us. We raced down empty streets where voting ballots still smoldered in the road. After a short while, we arrived safe within the high walls of the Hotel Mozulua.

The rioting had scared away the taximen who'd agreed to take us to Kisangani, and after several hours of waiting, we received a visit from Lisobe, the union president. Soldiers had stormed the mobs with guns and tear gas, he told us, and three people had been killed. One of the dead was his fifteen-year-old nephew. "He was only throwing rocks," the president said, "and they shot him in the head. His brains aren't even there anymore." Despite his tragedy, he'd come down to reassure us the drivers would be ready the next morning.

Depressed and frustrated, caught again by the shadow of the war, we spent our last night in Bumba getting stone drunk in the dark courtyard of the Mozulua, blasting the Stooges from my portable speakers. We drank liter bottles of beer and sent out for more, ending the evening with highway songs and Riccardo standing on the table singing "Smoke on the Water" to the Congolese watchman laughing in the shadows.

The shrill sound of bells stirred me from my poisoned sleep at six the next morning. I drew back the curtains and saw, one by one, a line of taximen pull up to the outer wall. After the previous day's violence, the president had sent word out to all *toleka*, hoping at least a few would heed the call. By the time I was dressed and downstairs, a dozen bikes were waiting.

Like most bikes found in African villages where motor vehicles had vanished along with paved roads, these were all steel, double-framed machines built for hauling passengers and cargo. They'd come off boats from India and China with brand names such as Avon Country Bike and Hobo Champion. Each weighed about forty pounds, and in *toleka* tradition, they were tricked with pink and yellow roses that bloomed from the spokes and rear reflectors.

But as we lined them up for inspection, we noticed that all were in terrible shape. The wide tires were bald and cracked, brake pads replaced by scrap rubber, and chains fastened by bits of wire and greased with bright-red palm oil. None of the bikes seemed capable of carrying us across town, much less through the unforgiving forest. But with little alternative, we chose six bikes and hoped for the best. We also picked four of the tallest and fittest-looking riders, men who knew the route and seemed capable and trustworthy, four strangers whom we'd follow like children into the unknown.

And with our gear strapped and covered, we said good-bye to Bumba and headed east toward the boiling sun. As we rolled past the final remnants of civilization, shouts arose from the sandy yards:

"To where?!"

"Kisangani!"

They smiled and waved their arms. *"Courage, camarade, courage!"*

Five minutes later, we had our first flat tire.

From Bumba, Kisangani lay just four hundred kilometers by river, at the end of the line where navigation ends as the river dissolves into rapids and hooks south. According to villagers, the journey by forest trail was over a hundred kilometers farther, though the trails didn't even appear on my map. I'd only reached Kisangani by air, and flying in, it looks like there isn't enough space in that thick carpet of trees to squeeze in a human being, much less land a plane. Then something in those trees pulls you against the window. There below is the Congo River, snaking through the tangle, catching the sun like a coil of glass and lighting up the dark, murky blood of the forest. It zigzags through the green until the vegetation opens into rows of tin-roofed shacks and white-stone relics of the old colony. This civilization appears almost temporary against the jungle, as if the river itself had licked a clean place against the shore before slowly taking it back. Stepping out, the air is heavy and wet and attacks all vigor and zeal like a parasite to a cell, leaving only torpor and a thirst for beer.

You've now reached the fabled Inner Station in Joseph Conrad's *Heart of Darkness*, where Kurtz, the star agent at the ivory-trading company, is sending more ivory downriver than anyone at headquarters has ever seen. When the narrator, Marlow, journeys upriver to the Inner Station, he discovers Kurtz has become the overlord of a savage kingdom, where natives bow at his feet and rows of shrunken heads are spiked on the fence posts.

The image of Kisangani as a way station of madness was hardly a fiction. In 1890, Conrad himself made the four-week voyage upriver to Kisangani as a ship captain's apprentice in Leopold's Congo. There he witnessed the barbarous greed that would later poison agent Kurtz, as ivory hunters enslaved and murdered countless people in their binge for white gold. Conrad would arrive in Kisangani (then Stanley Falls station) five years before Captain Leon Rom of the colonial army, who, while stationed there, kept twenty-one severed heads as decorations around his flower garden. Rom, it's believed, was agent Kurtz.

Afro-Arab slave traders had also used the area as a base for their village raids, capturing millions who were sent to slave markets in the Middle East. Following Congo's independence, the city was the setting for a string of bloody uprisings and massacres. In 1964, hordes of cannibal anticolonialist rebels sacked the city and slaughtered thousands of civilians while taking two thousand American and European hostages. The uprising was put down only after a dramatic rescue operation by Belgian paratroopers and hired white mercenaries.

Rebels captured Kisangani in August 1998 and effectively divided the nation in two from the government-held west. Rwanda and Uganda supplied their allied troops in Congo from bases in Kisangani, and the two armies finally parted allegiance here in three separate battles that left the city in ruins. The last fight, in June 2000, ended when Rwanda finally pushed Uganda out of town. The six-day battle, the UN estimated, sent over six thousand mortar and artillery shells raining down on the city, killing more than five hundred people.

We raced toward the battered city along a red-clay trail that first morning, muscles pumping, lungs wheezing for breath, shouting greetings of *"Mbote!"* to the traders who passed on foot. This was the low forest, where the undergrowth slammed against the trail like a wall of sheet metal, yet offered no shade or shoulder to rest. Just a winding chute through the scrub, so we took the blind curves with a chorus of handlebar bells, craving speed and fifty kilometers a day if we could get it.

In the convoy, Séverin rode passenger in the lead with Nzimbe, the strongest of the crew and the most familiar with the trail. Riccardo rode second, a nest of camera gear strapped like the Hope diamond on the back. I was third, followed by Simon and Raifin, tall and swanlike, who pedaled entire days standing straight up. Last was Thomas, the shy and able mechanic. They humped our gear and carried nothing of their own, just an ancient set of wrenches wrapped in a plastic bag. I could hear them singing softly as we rode, and in those moments when the trail was smooth and quiet, I realized they were singing the same song in chorus.

We'd shot out of Bumba like hell's raiders, but after a few hours in the topless forest, the rays of the sun sapped our will. The trail narrowed to one winding lane, pockmarked by pits of deep sand that erased all momentum. The handlebars were also too short for my arms, causing the front wheel to pitch in the sand and send the entire bike careening into the bush.

By midafternoon we'd pushed our bikes half the distance, each man dragging sixty pounds of steel and gear through sand so deep the wheels no longer turned. Here the low Congo Basin began its gradual rise toward the western mountains of the Rift Valley, meaning most of the journey would be uphill. When we finally stopped for lunch, I laid my head against a shade tree and fell into comalike sleep, waking up fifteen minutes later. Once we were back on the road, lightning split the heavy sky and rain poured down like daggers. We pushed the remainder of the day through rivers of silt and mud.

By nightfall we'd reached a small village called Yalingemba, a few kilometers shy of the Itimbiri River. We pushed our bikes to the home of the chief, where we were given chairs under a thatched canopy. The rain and fatigue had stripped our social graces, and we insisted they build a fire since our clothes were wet and the temperature was dropping. After Nzimbe, our lead rider, screamed at some men standing in the dark, a few boys dug a pit and struck a fire. We stripped off our shirts and draped them over our knees to dry, then Riccardo prepared a pot of canned beef and sauce.

Word of our visit had spread throughout the region, and within an hour crowds of people were circled around our chairs watching us eat. Most were children, who mimicked our movements like mimes and scattered when we approached. The strobe light on my headlamp sent them all screaming into the trees.

"Please forgive them," said the chief. "This is their first time to see a white man."

The next morning, feeling rested, we entered the old-growth forest, where teak and umbrella trees now towered overhead and snaking tangles of vine smothered the sun. When we reached the banks of the Itimbiri, we loaded our bikes into two canoes operated by four young traders, who paddled us several miles through dense mangroves.

The boats glided into an oval-shaped door in the brambles, and inside the dark theater the air turned cool and every sound exploded as if piped through amplified stacks. The teardrop paddles beat against the canoe with the rhythm of timpanis, and the warbling birdsong of the boatmen was so hauntingly beautiful it nearly peeled me out of my skin. There were no posted signs or visible landmarks. We zigzagged through the thorny brush and tangle, guided by the boatmens' internal compasses. I looked across the mangrove and saw no land, only the shine of black water. I had the curious urge to jump, then wondered how long it would take for the forest to kill me. The scenarios played on a reel.

The second day on the trail was much like the first, yet the forest now shielded us from the direct rays of the sun. But without sun there was only mud, and much of our ride was spent pushing through ankle-deep channels along the trail. After two days of this torture, the enthusiasm of the great reporter-explorer had given way to simple survivalism, and the intrigue and very pursuit of knowledge in such a place just seemed like hubris. *What was I thinking?* I thought. *How did I ever get roped into this?* As I pushed the pedals through another pit of sand, gasping for breath, trying to see through the stinging haze of sweat pouring into my eyes, I looked back to see Riccardo, shirtless, bouncing along the trail like some Juicy Fruit commercial, and smiling.

"Hey, man!" he yelled. "Take my picture! Take my picture on the bike!"

That evening we arrived in Yalimbongo, six bicycles rattling down the trail near dusk and yelling, *"Where's the chief?"* As in the first village and every one after, crowds quickly gathered around our bicycles to point, laugh, and gawk. Others stood studying us in wide-eyed wonderment, not laughing, not smiling, just watching. "I told you," said Riccardo. "They think you are from Mars or something."

The chief was away from the village, but his wife built a fire in the yard and cleared a room for us to sleep. As in many of the villages, the forest trail acted as Main Street, with square mud homes with thatch roofs scattered on both sides. Each home had a large dirt courtyard that was neatly swept. Some villages even had brick chapels, weathered but sturdy, most likely built by missionaries decades ago.

The chief's house in Yalimbongo, like most of the homes where we stayed in the forest, was a four-walled hut made of mud and thatch with several enclaves shooting off a large central room. The floors were dirt and the delicate mud walls crumbled to the touch. Like other huts belonging to chiefs, this one had handmade wooden beds and tables. Cooking was done in a covered patio out back, with hand-carved wooden loungers set up in the yard for guests. A thatched outhouse and separate hut for bathing sat farther in the trees. Lots of people were around, cooking and weaving hair, talking and smoking. It didn't seem like a bad way to live, except they were all extremely poor, more destitute than the river people.

In fact, the river people seemed almost wealthy now compared to those in the forest, simply because there were fish and the proximity to fruits and vegetables. But here, despite the blossoming jungle all around, there was nothing. Most families, like the ones in Yalimbongo, survived mainly on bush meat and *chikwangue*— cassava flour cooked to a doughy mass, fermented in the sun, and wrapped in banana leaves. It was an ideal traveler's food, portable and filling, but contained no nutrients. So the children quietly suffered from malnourishment, their bellies bloated and hair tinged a golden bronze. Every family we encountered spoke of dead children. "No one is here to help us," one mother said. "The world doesn't look into the forest."

We rolled through villages every few hours on the trail, stopping at many to repair a flat tire, a broken pedal, or to look for food and refill our water jugs. And as we stopped, people would run out to greet us. Some were thrilled to have visitors or intrigued by the rarity of white skin, but many clearly expected us to help them, to pull some magic from a pouch that would end their suffering. Women would run out and hold up babies and outstretched palms, and one old man cried out in Lingala, *"Mundele, salisa ngai!"* ("Help me!"), clutching his foot that was dripping with sores.

I supposed it was something leftover from the missionaries, but one old man in a village told me they'd left over a decade ago. "A white man walked through in 1995," he said, "but he was with a logging company, and he didn't really stop to talk." None of these people had voted in the election, and UN observers hadn't penetrated these parts. Yet when we rolled through, they shouted, *"Mundele,* you've arrived!"

But we had nothing to give these people. We were running out of food ourselves. After finding no fruits and vegetables that night in Yalimbongo, we ate one of our last cans of beef and filed off to bed just after sunset. We slept on tarps on the dirt floor, and at one point in the night a rat darted across my chest. We awoke exhausted and covered in fleabites. Riccardo had even developed a rash, his arms and chest covered in tiny sores. We sat in the courtyard at first light eating our leftover dinner. As the riders were maintaining the bikes and preparing to leave, we heard them grumbling and asked Séverin what they were saying.

"They're saying you guys are slow," he said. "They want you to hire some more riders in the next village."

When we protested, Nzimbe pushed back. "Soon we'll reach the swamps," he said. "If you think this forest is hard, wait until we reach the swamps."

Later that day we pushed through rivers that rose to our knees, up incredible mud-slicked hills, and over fallen logs that had obstructed the path for hundreds of years. Instead of clearing the log with a few men and a saw, travelers had simply bored a new road into the jungle around it. By noon we'd traveled thirty kilometers and reached Yahila, where we hoped to eat lunch, refill our water jugs, and rest. But we found only pigs and naked children swimming in the same stagnant river. The villagers there offered us *chikwangue*. We were so weak from lack of food we chewed mouthfuls of raw sugar to keep us going and, when that ran out, bought stalks of sugarcane and chewed it for juice.

We finally stopped for the night in Yalikambe, depleted and weary as we stumbled in. There, I was delighted to find some tomatoes, onions, and limes, which I squeezed into the cool water we dipped from the village well. The chief also sold us a chicken for two dollars, and we slaughtered and divided it among the men.

From Yalikambe, it was only seventy kilometers to Basoko, which had become in our minds the great Shangri-la of the jungle. It was a medium-size trading town much like Bumba, and while we harbored no grand expectations, we knew Basoko could at least offer a hot meal, warm bath, and soft bed to sleep in. Maybe we'd find a motorized pirogue in Basoko, maybe even Captain Buisine and the glorious *Ma'ungano*. Basoko became the light in the forest, the great savior of us all.

But before we reached Basoko, we had to cross the swamp— fifteen kilometers of shin-deep mud. It was such a nuisance the locals just called it *mayi*—"the water" in Lingala. The previous evening in Yalikambe, Riccardo and I heeded Nzimbe's advice and hired two additional men to help cross the swamp. It was a minor blow to our pride, but for the first time, we were able to walk while someone else pushed our bikes, and the extra hands sped our progress tremendously.

Despite my hunger and fatigue, I felt a sudden swell of energy as we entered the great swamp, fueled by delirium and our proximity to food and bed. My face began to tingle and my lungs opened wide, drawing deep, charged breaths. I raced ahead, jumping into trenches that swallowed my boots and singing, "I'm a rolling stone, all alone and lost . . ." The forest rippled in waves of color, sound, and smell. Spectacular clouds of butterflies exploded from the trail in plumes of blue and white. "For a life of sin, I have paid the cost . . ." The rotting earth belched under every step and smelled oddly of beef bouillion and mushrooms. Giant, horned-billed toucans cried from the treetops warning danger was on its way. "When I pass by, all the people say . . . just another guy on the lost highway . . ."

By the time we exited the swamp we were barely able to stand. Since morning, all we'd eaten were a few bananas and avocados, which we spread among ourselves. The two new men now pedaled the bikes, allowing Riccardo and I to ride on the back and rest. From there the road was smooth and straight, and by late afternoon we coasted into the cradle of Basoko.

The town, located at the confluence of the Congo and Aruwimi rivers, was established as a Belgian military garrison in 1888 during a period of epic battles with Afro-Arab slave traders, built to safeguard navigation along the river and stop slavers who were slowly pushing west. But it was Stanley who'd first arrived here in 1877 on his maiden voyage down the Congo. According to Stanley's written account of the journey (which was later proved to be exaggerated for the sake of his audience), Stanley's fleet of boats had been assaulted by hostile tribes twenty-seven times since they'd entered the forest. But one of their largest fights came at the mouth of the Aruwimi near the camp of the Basoko cannibals, who attacked with fifty-four canoes, led by an eighty-man battleship carrying warriors with crimson headdresses and broad-tipped spears. "Boys, be firm as iron," Stanley ordered his men. "Don't think of running away, for only your guns can save you."

During the deafening barrage of rifle fire, a fed-up Stanley lost his last compunction. "It is a murderous world," he wrote, "and we feel for the first time that we hate the filthy, vulturous ghouls who inhabit it." So instead of fending off the assault as usual, he ordered his men to lift anchor and chase the warriors into the village, slaughtering them as they fled into the trees. When the warriors were finally routed, Stanley's men looted everything in the village, including a holy temple made entirely of ivory. Stanley soon realized he stood in a cannibals' lair, where numerous skulls "grinned on many poles" and half-gnawed human bones lay scattered in the garbage heap.

We limped into Basoko with better hopes, needing only food and rest, and if we were lucky, a boat to end our misery. Basoko had also been where Riccardo, during his last trip upriver, had finally collapsed from fevers and malaria, before being rescued by the pirogue of diamond dealers coming off the Aruwimi. And now, as I rolled into town, I was also experiencing fever and a sore throat and was terrified it was early malaria. We arrived at the only guesthouse in town, a little cottage with six rooms operated by the local parish. We told the manager we were famished and needed to eat immediately. "Not to worry," the manager said, and sent out for fish, plantains, spinach, and cold beer. How delighted we were! We gave him ten dollars, a fortune in Basoko, and said, "Buy everything you can!"

But after three hours there was still no food, and no one around to explain. I lay in my stifling room, lapsing in and out of fevered sleep, then heard screaming from the courtyard. I ran outside and saw Riccardo had the manager pinned against the wall. Riccardo turned to me, his face twisted with hate. "There's no food! There was never any food. They stole our money and gave us *nothing!*"

Séverin stood nearby, exasperated, "The manager says there's only *chikwangue*," he said.

I tried to find some solution, listening to the manager explain how the market had closed early and food was impossible to find. Bad luck, I concluded, but then noticed a group of other guests being served fish, our fish. They also had plantains and rice. I blacked out with rage and joined the tantrum in the courtyard, kicking chairs against the wall and screaming, since screaming was the only thing that felt any good.

Séverin tried to intervene: "Please, please, getting angry won't help anything."

For a couple days now, Séverin had been working on my nerves, the way he never bargained aggressively for our pirogues, always accepting the first offers; the way he covered the damp logs with palm leaves before sitting down in the forest; the way he peeled the skins off peanuts before eating them, separating the loose husks with a gentle puff of breath. And a couple of days before, as we'd slogged through the slime, I'd looked back and seen Nzimbe straining to push the bike with Séverin perched on back, his leather sandals held high above the muck.

They were stupid, little things, undeserving of criticism, but all the frustration from the forest suddenly welled forward. "Just whose side are you on, Séverin? Angry? Yeah, why don't you get angry . . . why don't you stand up and see this guy's walking right over you?"

"I can see everything clearly," he said, turning now to walk inside. "But I will never scream at these people for you."

That night we ended up getting fish and plantains, even eggs for an omelet. It had really been a ploy to take our money, but it didn't matter. By the time the food arrived, I felt too sick to eat anyway. I lay in bed sweating through my clothes, the mosquito net like an incubator over my fevered skin. That night we also discovered there were no boats to take us upriver. Tomorrow would be just like today, another eleven hours spent trudging through the jungle.

We awoke at dawn and crossed the Aruwimi River. There was some sort of fight at the riverbank over the price of our boats, but I couldn't quite follow it, I was still so sick. A syrupy, septic film shrouded my vision. People around me seemed to move robotically as if under strobe light, their faces vibrating in the heat waves. My head throbbed and thoughts faded before they formed. I remembered the immigration official who'd held our passports for ransom, until we jerked them from his hands and ran. And the crowd of people who'd watched us leave, their voices like a flock of cockatoos plunging off the steep, muddy bank: "*MUndeLE . . . MuNdele . . .* why you give me nothing, my bigeeeeee?"

We'd crossed the wide river against heavy wind and now paddled through the quiet mangroves. The soaring trees became the walls of a hidden, primordial cathedral. Tiny holes of sunshine pierced the high ceiling like a galaxy of stars, each one wired into the white roar of heaven, so loud it could rip the skin from bone. The sky reflected precisely onto the placid water, as if the forest had split in half and allowed us safe passage through the middle. I let the cool river glide over my hand. We must have been there for hours.

We'd hired two more bikes in Basoko and kept the two additional riders from Yalikambe, expanding our convoy to eight bikes and nine men. I rode lead with Nzimbe after crossing the river, though we ended up pushing the bike most of the morning. I soon noticed how crushing Basoko had been for the whole party. I could see Nzimbe was now weak and listless, slumped over his handlebars, and Raifin, another rider, now complained of a fever.

Around three o'clock we reached the outskirts of a large, populated village. The narrow trail opened to a wide, sandy boulevard. And in every direction, we noticed rows of banana trees spilling with fruit. A small crowd of villagers rushed out to greet us, helping push our bikes down the boulevard, which was flanked by columns of palms. The Aruwimi River sparkled through the trees in the distance, and the setting sun painted the huts and smiling faces in a warm, benevolent glow. "*Mundele,*" someone shouted. "Welcome to Baonde!"

The chief of Baonde sat weaving a fishing basket under a tree when we arrived. He greeted us quizzically and ordered his men to fetch chairs. "We're sick and desperately need to eat," we told him. I was prepared to demand food as we'd done in previous villages. But without hesitation the chief turned to the large crowd who'd gathered behind us. "Go to your homes and bring everything you have," he said. "These men have had a difficult journey, but they're willing to pay for your things." I asked his name and the location of the village, but he waved me off. "In time, son," the chief said. "First rest and get your strength."

For the next half hour, a procession of villagers passed by our chairs. They carried bowls of tomatoes, bananas, papaya, onion, eggplant, and baskets of duck eggs and salted fish. They presented goats, chickens, pigs, and a freshly killed monkey swinging by its tail. We slaughtered two chickens and prepared a bubbling stew full of vegetables. We ate and ate, and slowly the fever released its grip and returned some of my strength.

I rested well that night in Baonde, a ten-hour, narcotic death sleep courtesy of a little grass and some sleeping pills we'd bought at a clinic in Basoko. We were feeling good when we pulled out the next morning, laughing and joking once again, basking in the giddy relief that comes with having escaped something dire. We felt confident we'd take the last two hundred kilometers in three days' time.

But the forest provided no rest, and broken chains, flat tires, and snapped pedals constantly slowed our progress. For three days, we inched through the forest, nursing our bikes and bodies on short rations. Then, late on the third afternoon after leaving Baonde, the convoy pushed its way up a steep rise and stopped at the top. The trees suddenly vanished and the trail was plowed wide and flat. Three Caterpillar bulldozers sat parked on the roadside, shadowed by tangled heaps of rooted and shattered trees. It was the Trans-M logging road. A woman passing nearby said it went all the way to Kisangani, now just a day's journey on bikes. We paused to bask in this violent and open expanse, then thanked the Lord for deforestation.

After seven days in the forest, the convoy spent its last night in Yaosuka, a small settlement just eighty kilometers from Kisangani. Being so near civilization, we expected to find a great bounty when we arrived, but the villagers there refused to sell us any food. Instead of arguing, we sent Séverin and Nzimbe on a bike to another nearby settlement, where they were able to buy some rice and a chicken, which we grilled over a fire and shared among the nine of us. We were hungry when we turned to bed, but it didn't matter now. Tomorrow we'd receive our great reward in the city. As we drifted off to sleep, a steady rain began to fall.

The downpour continued through the night, with sheets of wind and rain slapping the tin roof where we slept and shooting gullies across the dirt floor. The next morning we hurriedly packed our wet gear, not even bothering to talk about the storm, so accustomed were we now to the punishing weather. We wheeled our bikes to the crude highway as a light rain fell, speaking only of beautiful things to come.

But after a few hundred feet, our bike tires began sinking into the road, slowing us to another agonizing crawl. The new logging road had yet to pack into hard shell. The all-night storm had poured inches of rain into the freshly turned soil. And while the forest mud had been a slimy soup, we now struggled through clay-like cement that caked our boots and clung to the tires, leaving us heavier with each step. Soon the fenders were so clogged the wheels ceased to turn. Behind me, the entire convoy was paralyzed and the rain was heavy once again.

"You've gotta help me push!" Riccardo said. He'd stripped off his clothes and now strained against the handlebars, his legs sinking in the mire. We'd come this far. "Stand at the back and push!" he said, but pushing only dug us deeper. The bike felt rooted like a tree. "The worst," I managed. "It must be . . . after everything . . . the worst day."

We now dragged the overturned bike like a dead animal through the mud. The drilling rain shrank our eyes into cold, vapid holes. Riccardo lost his grip when the bike caught a snag and toppled into the muck. As he sat there, he noticed the large crowds who'd gathered on the roadside to watch our exercise in misery. We called to them, *"Quelque aide, s'il vous plaît?"* But instead of helping, they only pointed and laughed.

The Italian's curses began with a slow, fuming whisper before his gut spewed them forward, *". . . porco dio porca MADONNA DIO CANE,"* curses against baby Jesus and Joseph, God the Pig and Dog, and Mary the Whore-Fucked Saint of Congo, a torrent of boiling lead aimed straight at heaven and the pissing rain, until the words themselves disintegrated into a tirade of gibberish.

The crowd roared with laughter. Children ran into the road and cheered. They spun around and swatted their asses. I tasted the warm rain on my teeth and my breathing quickened. I found a heavy stick and hurled it into the crowd of children, praying it would miss as soon as it left my fingers. *Bravo!* The crowd howled even louder. *Mundele, you've arrived!* It was indeed a rare, spectacular show. I followed the script to the letter, even bowed before picking up the bike and soldiering on, no greater a man. "You shouldn't have done that," Riccardo said. "I know," I told him. "Believe me, I know."

That afternoon we reached the banks of the Lindi River. Across its choppy waters sat Kisangani, yet it was hard to muster the expected surge of joy. Minutes after arriving at the river we had another fight with immigration officials, who seized our riders' ID cards and demanded their money. "River tax," they said, their breath heavy with wine. But their authority meant nothing. Riccardo stormed the office, yelling, collected the cards, and calmly instructed the riders to load the boats for Kisangani. "Arrest us," we said. We must've looked insane.

After experiencing the same ordeal on the other side of the river, we finally rolled into Kisangani in the late afternoon. At the hotel we toasted our riders and paid them out, clapping as each man took his first sip of something cold. "To the end," we said, raising our glasses high. "To the end!"

But the end sat cold and awkward. There was something unsettling about the end.

Riccardo grabbed my arm, saying, "We did it, man, we survived the *jongle*! Eight days on the bikes!"

All of my emotions from the past few weeks now rioted inside me, peaked and heightened by exhaustion. I wanted to punch the walls, fall down laughing, or walk into a dark room and not come out for days.

"Yeah, man," I said. "We did it. We did it."

I'd traveled upriver and crossed through jungle and come out unscathed, triumphant even, but I wondered now what it was I'd found. The traders on the river had shown a glimmer of something like hope, but the rest had been a fool's errand, and the jungle had broken me in half and given nothing. I realized I'd risked life and limb looking for something that didn't exist, some modern notion of progress that didn't even apply. Like Buisine had said, there was nothing even before the war. And there was certainly little now, except a few naïve ideas I'd left on the forest floor. All I wanted now was to close my eyes and sleep, then go home and remember what it was about this country I'd loved so much. A good part of me wanted to climb back on the bike and just keep riding.

There was something funny down the table because the riders began to laugh. Nzimbe said to Riccardo, "We loved how you screamed at the officials. You handled them like a man!" The riders would've certainly been arrested. "The people in the villages thought you were mercenaries," he added. "They were very afraid!" The riders laughed and one of them stood up and duckwalked along the table, barking orders. I forced a smile and finished my beer, then ordered another. Outside the sunset thinned the busy streets and pulled shadows over the table. We raised our glasses a few more times until the light finally faded, leaving us exhausted in the dark.

Chapter Five

"UN PETIT DÉRAILLEMENT"

I left Kisangani two days later on a UN flight to Uganda, caught my connection, and arrived home in a wicked funk. I'd spent five weeks traveling fifteen hundred miles through some of the most brutal terrain on earth, and it certainly felt good to have finished. But I'd found few signs of promise along the way, no grand harbinger of revival or reform. Instead, I spent the winter frustrated and empty-handed.

Even if there were some markings of progress along the path, I probably missed them anyway. Because once in the jungle, my own basic needs and level of comfort had stood in the way of learning anything. I didn't even know my riders' last names or anything about their families. I'd simply been too exhausted and hungry to care. It wasn't my proudest moment, and even now, those last days on the trail leave a sting of regret.

In any case, whatever enthusiasm I may have gathered would've evaporated quickly after getting home. Twice during the winter and spring, I turned on my computer and saw Kinshasa paralyzed by more fighting between Kabila's and Bemba's men. The last battle in March 2007 killed around four hundred people, many of them civilians, and sucked dry any postelection optimism that might have remained.

It was the perfect opportunity to call off this fruitless wandering and just stay home. Except there was one last place I wanted to go, one last adventure through the vast, beckoning country. The old railway network in the southern province of Katanga was finally running for the first time in a decade. The rails were connecting market towns and villages shattered by war

*and long forgotten, and it was possible now to buy a ticket and ride along.
Perhaps something good would emerge down that long steel road, some
kind of beacon rising out of the jungle and over the plains, something to
point the way forward.*

I

I'd fallen in love with the trains back in August 2003 on a reporting trip to Kalemie, a trading town on the shores of Lake Tanganyika. One day after work, I happened to pass the brick rail
station of the Societe Nationale des Chemins de Fer du Congo
(SNCC), the national rail company. The old station looked so regal there at the bottom of the hill, the lake shining behind it, so I
walked inside to see if anyone was home. Inside, the windows
were smashed and boarded, and an inch of dust covered every
surface. I managed to find the director sitting alone in an empty
office, nothing on his desk but a piece of bread, a few papers, and
a Bible.

"There are no trains, *monsieur*," he said. "The last one was in
1998, and I believe you've missed it."

Until the war started, Kalemie—formerly called Albertville—
had been a railway hub ever since the arrival, in 1915, of the
Chemins de Fer du Congo Superieur aux Grands Lacs Africains, or
Upper Congo-Great African Lakes Railway (CFL). The network
that ran through Kalemie linked the rest of Congo to Lake Tanganyika, where ferry boats and ships closed the gap into Tanzania,
East Africa, the Indian Ocean, and Asia. It also connected to lines
into Kisangani and the Congo River, thus providing access to the
Atlantic.

But in 1998, the province fell to the Rwandans. Since then, the
director said, Congo's national rail company had mainly been used
to ferry troops and rebels, depending on who controlled the region. In Kalemie, there hadn't been a passenger train since the
Rwandans swept across the border. Every few months, there was

an occasional freight train loaded with palm oil and salt, but only if there was enough merchandise to make it worth the effort. And since there were no passenger trains, hundreds of people would jump the roof of the freight as it passed, oftentimes to be scraped off and killed when it hit the bridges and low clearances. Derailments were catastrophic.

Worse, in March 2000, Zimbabwean MiGs had blown up a strategic rail bridge about three hundred kilometers west of Kalemie, destroying it before it could wind up in the hands of rebel forces, who were looking for any means to push toward the capital. The bombed bridge at Zofu crippled the two-thousand-kilometer north-south river and rail network that connected Katanga to the Congo River in the north and Zambia in the south. And the old CFL railway into Kalemie had been made defunct when another bridge over the Niemba River collapsed in 1998 from soil erosion, severing Congo's link to Lake Tanganyika and the Indian Ocean.

Now, every train that left Kalemie had to stop at the washed-out bridge, unload onto pirogues to cross the river, then change to another locomotive waiting on the other side. More often than not, the locomotive never appeared on the other side, stranding freight and people for days, often weeks. With just two bridges out of commission, the entire province slowly began to starve.

"And if you can imagine," the director said, "there was a time when you could catch a train all the way to South Africa from Kalemie, enjoy a nice meal and a beer. The scenery from here is breathtaking. You could actually be a tourist here in Congo."

We walked out into the sun-baked yard, now overrun by tall elephant grass that released swarms of grasshoppers as we cut a path across the rusty rails. At the back of the lot, behind a few freight cars, sat an old first-class car painted red with silver runners. Its windows were smashed and splintered. A few bullet holes decorated its broadside, but it still appeared beautiful and so completely lonely, like a washed-up racehorse collecting flies in the back stable.

I jumped inside and marveled at the old wooden bar, complete with a cracked mirror behind the shelves. There were shower rooms and deluxe sleepers, the beds and tables long ripped out by passing soldiers. The Rwandan troops had used the cars as barracks during the first months of the war, the director said. He pointed at mounds of calcified excrement in the toilets and charred holes in the floors. "They actually built fires in the corridors," he said, shaking his head.

To me it was like finding an old abandoned cabin deep in the woods, a true and proper explorer's fort and clubhouse. As the director continued explaining the larger disrepair and decay of the train company, I imagined people on the train dressed in their Sunday clothes, lighting cigarettes at the bar with a cold Tembo, *haridi sana*, sitting down to a steak as the savanna rushed past in a golden blur, imagined falling asleep to a cool breeze through the window and the gentle rock and whine of those steel wheels in the dark.

So you can imagine my excitement, nearly four years later, when I learned both bridges had been repaired and the rail system was up and running. Never mind that "up and running" meant about three trains left Lubumbashi station each month, with no certainty when they'd come back, or how far they'd get. The trains were running, so I called ahead to Kinshasa and recruited Séverin for one last mission. And this time I asked Lionel to come along as photographer.

Katanga was the largest province in all of Congo, stretching south to Zambia and east to Tanzania, which lay just across Lake Tanganyika. Here the rain forests thinned as the elevation rose, the siphoning jungle giving way to open savanna and cool breezes. Here the melodic Swahili of the east replaced the sharp Lingala of the west, and the people themselves seemed to mellow as the air became lighter. Even the beer tasted better in Katanga. But it wasn't just the high altitude that made it different, though it reached sixty-five hundred feet in places. Nor was it the crisp breezes that whipped into the lower valleys, creating a force field against the swampy jungles in the north.

It was money, almost an endless supply of it thanks to one of the largest and purest deposits of cobalt and copper in the world. So much copper was bulging under the surface in Katanga that the earth actually glowed from space.

The mining industry certainly gave the people of Katanga a sense of pride, especially when comparing themselves to their fellow countrymen. But as in Ituri, the minerals carried with them a curse locked inside the blessing. While the minerals made the province a titan in central Africa, they'd also sparked bloody secession attempts and sucked the UN into its first enterprise in Congo back in 1960. Even now, the minerals continue to drive the wholesale pillage of the province by foreigners and corrupt state officials.

And of course, it all began with Leopold. From the moment Leopold had first acquired Congo, he'd heard of the mineral wealth in Katanga, so plentiful the tribes used small crosses made from copper as currency. Securing copper, in addition to rubber, would no doubt fortify his empire. And while he'd sent Stanley in 1879 to secure agreements with local tribes in the river provinces, Katanga remained open and untamed.

The pressure to settle Katanga built suddenly in 1890, when Leopold found himself in a race for the territory with the formidable Cecil Rhodes, the British-born South African tycoon and empire builder. As prime minister of the British-held Cape Colony (now South Africa), Rhodes had already annexed and lent his name to Northern Rhodesia and Southern Rhodesia, the areas now known as Zambia and Zimbabwe. Now he was looking to claim territory farther north, part of his scheme to connect the British empire's African colonies by railroad. Intent on pushing north toward Egypt, he ignored Leopold's borders and sent his agents into Katanga to negotiate with village chiefs. Rhodes, who had already founded De Beers Mining Company and would later control 90 percent of the world's diamonds, was as hell-bent as Leopold on claiming Katanga's copper. "I would annex the planets if I could," he once famously said.

At the time, Leopold was broke. Building a railroad along the Congo River had left him deep in debt, and the project was only in its first year of construction. And half the Free State's funds were tied up in the Force Publique, which was staging its murderous sorties into the jungles to extract the colony's quotas of rubber. And farther east, other Free State troops were becoming mired in battles with Afro-Arab slavers along the Congo River south of Kisangani.

And there was another obstacle: Msiri, chief and supreme ruler of Katanga. A savvy and cunning chief, Msiri had used the region's minerals to build a sizable army of warriors and arm them with guns purchased from Portuguese traders. With these weapons, he'd launched a series of tribal wars in which he'd seized surrounding chiefdoms and incorporated the armies of his enemies, many of them taken as slaves, building an empire that was feared and respected throughout central Africa. Msiri was known as a cold-blooded sadist, who enjoyed locking his estimated hundreds of wives in huts full of starving ravenous dogs, and executing prisoners—but not before feeding them a meal of their own ears.

Rhodes approached him first, sending a delegation to bargain with Msiri, offering the chief bolts of cloth, beads, and a few cases of gin for all of Katanga. Insulted, Msiri refused and sent the delegation away. Hearing this, Leopold saw his chance. Despite being strapped for men and cash, he sent his own teams to negotiate with Msiri before the Brits could rally another attempt. Leopold would not be as diplomatic.

The Belgian king sent three military expeditions into Katanga and built a garrison near Msiri's village. With a small army in place, he then dispatched William Stairs—one of Stanley's former men—to win an agreement by force, if necessary. Stairs's method was direct: he simply marched into Msiri's village with a hundred men and planted a Free State flag in the ground. Msiri fled to a nearby settlement, so Stairs sent one of his officers to drag him back. When the chief resisted, the officer shot him three times with a revolver before being gunned down himself by the chief's bodyguards. With Msiri dead, Belgium imposed its own handpicked chief over Katanga, thus sealing their stake in the region, and for that matter, in Congo as a whole. Because once Belgium organized itself around the mines, they never stopped producing.

The red dirt, it turned out, was also filled with cobalt, tin, diamonds, coal, silver, magnesium, uranium, and other minerals in huge demand as nations built themselves for the industrial age. Even more than rubber, the mines brought wealth to the colony, built the European-style cities that sprouted along the southern savanna, with the largest and proudest of them being Elizabethville, or modern Lubumbashi. The mines financed the hospitals and roads that set the Belgian Congo apart from other colonies and gave jobs and pensions to thousands of Congolese. As a result, Katangese were healthier and better educated and also more worldly, as the mines also attracted Africans from elsewhere in the continent, in addition to one of the largest populations of Europeans in central Africa.

All that would change on June 30, 1960, when Congo was granted her emancipation from Belgium. The mutiny and rioting of the Force Publique that followed independence spread rapidly across the country in days, with Belgian paratroopers helping evacuate the thousands of foreigners who fled in panic as soldiers raped and looted in the cities. In Katanga, the Congolese governor, Moise Tshombe, vowed to keep business operating and safeguard European residents, who were largely employed by the mines. When the mutiny finally reached Katanga on July 9, Tshombe called in additional Belgian paratroopers to restore order, a move bitterly opposed by the freshly appointed premier, Patrice Lumumba, who wanted no more association with the former colonialists.

Worse, in Lumumba's eyes, Tshombe allowed Belgian officers in the Force Publique to remain in command of their Katangan troops. Tshombe even hired hundreds of white mercenaries, who poured in all summer long from Europe, Rhodesia, and South Africa, thus creating a separate standing army for the territory.

Perhaps no one in Katanga was more grateful to the paratroopers than officials at Union Minière du Haut Katanga, the Belgian-British-owned mining company that had essentially built and owned all of Katanga, who were desperate to protect their holdings from the raving mobs. Two days later, these men got an especially pleasing announcement: Katanga was seceding from Congo.

The announcement came as Lumumba and Joseph Kasavubu, Congo's president, were involved in heavy damage control, traveling around the country trying to reel in their troops and impose their authority. Lumumba appealed to Dag Hammarskjöld, then secretary-general of the UN, to send troops to invade Katanga and crush the secession and remove the foreign invaders by force. The UN cannot invade Katanga, the secretary told him. But with anarchy threatening to destroy the Congo government, Hammarskjöld sent several thousand peacekeepers on July 15 to replace Belgian troops in other parts of the country, hoping to maintain some semblance of order.

Determined to outflank Tshmobe, Lumumba traveled to Washington to request American tactical support, but was rebuffed. The Canadians also balked, so Lumumba appealed to the Soviets, who obligingly sent dozens of Ilyushin transport planes and trucks and about a thousand technicians to Leopoldville. Washington, fearing a Soviet foothold in Africa, ordered the Soviets out and parked an aircraft carrier at the mouth of the Congo. The CIA went as far as hatching a plot to slip poison in Lumumba's food or toothpaste, but the agent, Larry Devlin, had a change of heart and wound up pouring the poison into the river.

The CIA then went to work on Mobutu and Kasavubu, pressuring them to rid themselves of the erratic Lumumba, who they saw as a Fidel Castro in the making. In September 1960, Mobutu went further and declared martial law, neutralizing Kasavubu. He gave the Soviets forty-eight hours to leave Congo, then placed Lumumba under arrest. After the former premier was caught trying to escape, Mobutu put him on a plane and sent him to Katanga, dishing him right onto Tshombe's plate.

Mobutu's soldiers reportedly beat Lumumba so badly on the plane ride into Elizabethville that the Belgian pilots closed the cockpit so they wouldn't be ill. Several versions exist of what happened next, but the most likely is that Lumumba was executed on arrival by a Belgian-led firing squad while Tshombe stood witness. It's believed his body was then chopped into pieces and dissolved in a barrel of acid.

Meanwhile, talks between the government and Tshombe had gone nowhere. Eventually Hammarskjöld decided the white mercenaries were in violation of Congo's new sovereignty, and an unacceptable threat to security. In August 1961, thousands of Indian, Swedish, and Irish UN soldiers launched Operation Rum Punch, fanning into Katanga and arresting several hundred white military officers and mercenaries. The UN followed the next month with Operation Morthor, where UN troops battled Katangan forces. It was a rout: Katangan fighter jets destroyed UN planes and military camps, and 130 Irish peacekeepers surrendered and were taken prisoner.

Tshombe fled over the border into Zambia during the attack, so Hammarskjöld flew to meet the governor with hopes of persuading him to allow peacekeepers to replace his Belgian troops. But before he could reach the meeting, Hammarskjöld's plane crashed into the hills just across the Zambian border, killing everyone aboard. A cease-fire reached in the wake of Hammarskjöld's death quickly fell apart.

Over the next year, the UN continued to hammer Katanga, and after successive battles late in 1962, the Katangese resistance broke. The central government assumed control again on January 14, 1963, and two years later, Mobutu staged a coup and took Congo for himself. When Laurent Kabila's forces reached the capital in 1997, the rebel leader announced his presidency from a stage in Lubumbashi—just a few hundred kilometers south of his ancestral home in Manono.

So much of the country's history had played out in Katanga, collected in that bottom crevice and pushed into the heart by all the money buried in the dirt. William Stairs's murderous expedition into Msiri's kingdom undoubtedly secured the vast mineral fields for the cause of Western civilization. But the droves of fever-driven men couldn't have moved an ounce of copper until another crucial milestone was passed: September 27, 1910—the day the Chemin de Fer du Katanga, or Katanga Railway, finally rolled into Lubumbashi. If the copper gave birth to the cities along the plains, the railroads fed them and kept them growing. As Stanley once said, "Without a railway . . . Congo isn't worth a penny."

When Leopold sent Stanley up the river to negotiate treaties in 1879, one of the explorer's first tasks was to build a service road around the 350 kilometers of rapids to Stanley Pool, then portage two disassembled steamships to take him upriver. A railway would then follow, allowing unhindered access from the jungles to the sea. Traveling with him were a crew of porters and laborers from Zanzibar, along with a handful of British, American, French, Danish, Belgian, and Italian volunteers who would help maintain the stations. They established a camp at a village called Vivi along Congo's estuary with the sea, then began chipping away through the Crystal Mountains toward the Pool.

After five years, which included a brief stint back home due to illness, Stanley completed the road and established a series of stations along the river—including Kinshasa, Mbandaka, and Kisangani—luckily experiencing none of the tribal hostility that had plagued his maiden journey in 1877. But due to a lack of cash, Leopold couldn't begin the promised railroad until 1890. The great railway project took about sixty thousand men, mainly slaves from Congo, Zanzibar, Senegal, and Sierra Leone shackled and dragged into service. Leopold also brought in five hundred Chinese laborers, many of whom died from disease or deserted. Several who managed to escape were later found five hundred miles in the jungles, trying to walk home to China by following the eastern sun.

The railroad followed along Stanley's rugged wagon trail through the jagged cliffs of the Crystal Mountains. Without the aid of heavy equipment or steel cables, workers hauled materials on their backs up the steep cliffs, which climbed as high as six hundred feet in just a few miles. In all, ninety-nine bridges and over twelve hundred aqueduct canals were required. After the first two years, crews had completed only five miles of rail. The punishing terrain, tropical heat, disease, starvation, and beatings from colonial guards took scores of lives each week and littered the service road with hundreds of corpses. In 1890, Joseph Conrad spent nearly two months walking this road around the rapids en route to the steamer that would carry him upriver. Along the way, he described in his diaries seeing "at a camp[in]g place the dead body of a Backongo. Shot? Horrid smell"; further along, he encountered "a skeleton tied up to a post." The railway from the Atlantic to Stanley Pool stands as one of the shining benchmarks of Belgian atrocity in Congo. But after its completion, what had been a twenty-day hike along Stanley's road now only took two days by train and allowed the ivory and rubber to flow as if from a spigot.

Cecil Rhodes had died in 1902 without ever having acquired Katanga or his Cape-to-Cairo railroad, but his deputy Sir Robert Williams managed to find his way inside Katanga. Desperate for funding to begin mining, Leopold partnered with Williams's company Tanganyika Concessions Ltd., granting them a stake in mineral rights in exchange for helping finance a railroad to the mines (this merger would later become Union Minière).

To build the railway, Williams brought in British-owned contracting firm Pauling & Company, who'd built railways in South Africa and Rhodesia. The nearest rail station to Katanga was 212 kilometers south of Lubumbashi at Broken Hill mine in Northern Rhodesia. The station was the northern terminus of a railroad that extended east to the Indian Ocean port city of Beira, Mozambique. The objective was to extend this railroad into Katanga, thus connecting Katanga to the ocean.

The work was fast and efficient, with crews of 15 white foremen and 350 Africans laying track in assembly-line fashion, while locomotives followed behind loaded with material. The Greek, Italian, and British contractors drank heavily, packed pistols, and often wagered their pay on how many kilometers they'd push the following day, as bonuses were given to quick teams. In December 1909, the tracks crossed the Congo border, and nine months later, reached Lubumbashi. (Once inspectors closely examined the tracks, however, they discovered only half the bolts had been fastened to the rails.)

Belgium's priority of connecting the mines to the Beira seaport had been realized. But Katanga's main mineral markets were in Europe, which meant boats leaving Beira's Indian Ocean port had to travel north, around the Horn of Africa, and pass through the Suez Canal, where heavy taxes were levied. The route quickly became a financial drain.

What Congo needed was a river and rail route completely within its own borders that could reduce the overhead. So the Belgians immediately began building the Great Lakes Railway to extend the line north from Lubumbashi, connecting it with the Congo River at Stanleyville, where goods could flow downstream to the Atlantic. The network also connected the Congo River with Kalemie and Lake Tanganyika. But this internal route wasn't ideal: freight leaving Katanga and out the Congo River went through seven transshipments through the thick forest and river and often took months to reach its destination.

The ultimate goal was the National Route, finally opened in 1928, an all-Congo rail and river network from Katanga to the Atlantic, which extended the line from the town of Bukama (the railhead along the Congo River) westward to Ilebo, which sits along the muddy Kasai River, 820 kilometers east of Kinshasa by river. From Ilebo, steamers shipped goods down the Kasai, linked with the Congo River, then headed toward the Atlantic.

The National Route would be Congo's principal network until the Second World War, when demands for copper and minerals tripled for the Allied effort (even as Belgium itself was occupied by the Nazis). During the war, Katanga provided British and American troops with the bulk of their copper, cobalt, industrial diamonds, tin, gold, silver, and uranium. In fact, the mines in Shinkolobwe supplied the uranium for the U.S. atomic bombs dropped on Hiroshima and Nagasaki. By the 1950s, Katanga was the fourth-largest copper producer in the world, and minerals constituted nearly 70 percent of Congo's export revenue (aided by gold fields in Ituri and more diamonds in central Kasai).

By that time, Sir Robert Williams had achieved a dream of his own, the 1,348-kilometer Benguela Railway across the barren landscape of Angola, Congo's southern neighbor, which provided Katanga with an even shorter route to the Atlantic. Congo had built a link with the Benguela line in 1931, so by the time of the war, the colony divided a large chunk of its export between the Benguela's all-rail network and Congo's own National Route.

However, the Benguela Railway was lost in the 1970s during the opening salvos of Angola's civil war, which lasted until 2002. And much of Congo's network slowly crumbled under the weight of neglect and unremitting conflict. Two separate secession attempts in Katanga during the late 1970s caused severe damage. And when the great war settled over the copper belt in 1998, it emptied the railroad towns of the men who kept the machine alive, scattering them over the borders into squalid camps and across the plains where those big giants once rolled. But now with peace, elections, and the resulting flood of foreign investment, the old network was struggling to return, and I had plans to meet it.

In late April 2007, I caught an SN Brussels flight straight into Kinshasa, met up with Séverin and Lionel, and began looking for a train. Since I'd ended my previous journey in Kisangani, I was hoping to follow the Great Lakes line that ran from nearby Ubundu down to Lubumbashi, with a river-barge ride in between where the trains didn't operate.

With this plan, Séverin and I visited the Kinshasa bureau of the SNCC, the national rail company. As we entered its musty office just off the boulevard, we began to get our first glimpse of the company's decline. Here the gold wallpaper peeled off the Sheetrock and drooped to the floor, and threadbare carpet revealed the cement underneath. Light fixtures had been ripped from the ceiling during the last *pillage*, and an absence of electricity explained why the secretary's computer wasn't plugged into the wall. On further notice, I realized she didn't even have a monitor.

The bureau's director was a polite, well-spoken man named Mulapu, who wore a pink silk tie and French cuffs. The train schedules were so erratic it was impossible to plan for them, he said, and usually his office was never even informed of trains on the other side of the country. In fact, the route from Ubundu through the forest that had looked so pretty on the map wasn't possible now because the train was broken, and Mulapu didn't know when it would be repaired.

Mulapu offered to call the other bureaus in Lubumbashi and

Kalemie and get some answers. But since the government owed him many months' salary and didn't pay his bills, his phone had no credit. I loaned him mine. Mulapu called several people for short conversations in rapid French and Lingala then handed the phone back. "It will be difficult," he said, "but I think we have something in terms of a freight train."

A World Food Programme train was leaving Lubumbashi early the next week, hauling food aid to Kindu in the north. The year before, fighting between Mai Mai rebels and government troops had left two hundred thousand displaced in northeastern Katanga, and since then the WFP humanitarian trains had made regular runs to ferry food to the isolated reaches. Mulapu said there wasn't a passenger carriage attached, but maybe we could ride in the locomotive with the engineer.

"That's perfect," I said.

"But along the way, many people will pile on top and force their way inside."

I nodded. "Okay."

He laughed, resting his hands on his round belly. "This is a dangerous way to travel. The people have destroyed these trains. Sometimes you wonder if they're meant for humans or animals."

I looked at Séverin. Horror shot from his eyes like sparks on a broken rail.

"That's exactly what we're looking for," I said.

The river and bike journey through the forest had been punishing on my body and I'd lost nearly fifteen pounds. I was determined to never run out of food again while on the trail, so this time I came extra-prepared. I'd gone shopping in the States and stuffed a nylon sack full of canned milk, potted meat, tuna, powdered cheese, and enough beef jerky to survive for weeks. I'd also brought along two backpacks full of every piece of gear I could ever need, and some I would not, including three hundred yards of nylon rope and a gadget that heated buckets of cold bathwater (this last one I never even took out of my pack). And I'd also stopped by the REI out-fitter store and bought Bug Huts for Lionel and myself, which were simple, pop-up mesh cocoons the length of a man's body, and quite possibly the greatest Africa gear ever invented besides the head-lamp. No more torturous, sleepless nights with faulty mosquito nets. And given their compact size, we were certain we could use them on the trains. "We'll just toss our racks on the roof and sleep in the open," said Lionel. "Mate, the Congolese will be so jealous of our Bug Huts."

Two days later, Lionel and I were thoroughly prepared, packed and repacked and reduced to sitting in his apartment, whiling away the four days before we caught our freight train. On a whim, Li-onel decided to call the station director in Lubumbashi just to check in. Mulapu had given us the director's number, and Lionel had called the day before, just to introduce himself and make it known we were serious. Everything had been sorted. But when Lionel called back, the director had startling news: the WFP train had just left without us.

"But we had an agreement," Lionel told him.

"I would've called you," said the director, "but my phone had no credit."

After the river journey, I'd grown indifferent to these kinds of delays and disruptions, expected them even. So I'd returned to Congo with a new attitude, a new way of facing down stress by simply tuning out. And now as we careened into the first barricade of our journey, I didn't mind at all, actually felt relieved to have it out of the way.

"There isn't another train for seven days," Lionel said, hanging up. "A passenger train going to Kalemie. He said something about it being express."

Express, I thought, and the memory of that abandoned dining car in Kalemie came knocking by. We immediately decided to travel to Lubumbashi and wait there before another train slipped past. We would go to Katanga and try to literally catch a train.

II

I'd always wanted to visit Lubumbashi. The very name bounced off the tongue like fingers on a drum. The copper mines, the history, the arrogant swagger from having something the others didn't. Even while supporting Mobutu's ravenous hunger for decades, Lubumbashi had played second only to Kinshasa. But in the 1980s, the state-owned mines known as Gécamines (the former Union Minière) collapsed from neglect, causing the city to finally fall on hard times like the rest of the struggling country.

But all of that changed once China came along.

With its economy growing faster than milkweed, China had swooped into Katanga and begun hauling out commodities at enormous rates, pushing the price of copper to three dollars a pound and cobalt to thirty—the highest in a decade. China's demand for cobalt—used to manufacture rechargeable batteries in cell phones—rose tenfold from 1997 to 2005, when up to 90 percent of China's imported concentrates and ores were coming from Congo. And with the demand set high, over 150,000 local informal miners answered the call, squatting on the old government-owned Gécamines mines that had collapsed or others that were abandoned during the war. The peaceful elections also brought other companies that had anxiously been waiting in the wings. Phelps Dodge, the American mining firm, began developing a sixteen-hundred-square-kilometer, $900 million concession that encompassed two villages, Tenke and Fungurume, and sat on one of the largest copper and cobalt deposits in the world. Other companies such as Anvil Mining, from Australia, and Forrest Group, a Belgian firm, had concessions worth hundreds of millions more.

The big multinationals had to operate on the up-and-up since many eyes were scanning their affairs, especially Anvil, which had been busted several years earlier for letting government troops use their vehicles to assault a local rebel group, a battle in which many civilians were killed. These companies met regularly with aid groups and consultants about how to better serve the community. They built schools and publicized their numbers, which only accounted for about 20 percent of all mining in Katanga, a mere sliver of the money being pumped out of the ground.

The rest of the mining was illegally done by local men with pickaxes and shovels, many of them digging atop the concessions recently acquired by the big multinationals such as Phelps Dodge, which now faced the dilemma of removing them. The local miners were scattered across the province, working shirtless in their broken flip-flops and living off manioc in the sun, earning five dollars a week selling to Congolese middlemen who often disappeared on payday. The middlemen then sold the minerals to the foreign trading houses and Chinese businessmen who lined the mining roads, and they in turn set the market price and made a fortune off these holes that never ran dry.

So where did all that money go? In Katanga, the ore was smuggled out in the dark of night, across the border in beds of covered trucks and railcars, past the eyes of police who hadn't been paid in months and so were hard-pressed to refuse the hush money. It went down through Zambia, Tanzania, and South Africa, where it was processed, then put into giant containers and shipped east into Asia. By the end of 2005, an estimated three quarters of Katanga's minerals were shipped out illegally, greasing the palms of government officials and police on many levels before finally hitting the sea.

The bulk of profits from informal mining never saw the sunlight in Congo, but an estimated $37 million still trickled into Lubumbashi each month, and as a result the city became a boomtown—for some. You felt that money as soon as your plane hit the tarmac, saw it at the customs desk where the official demanded to see the *ordre de mission* of the portly South African, who instead slipped a crisp bill under the window and boarded the mining-company van. It was in the baggage claim, where white men in safari vests stood smoking in rows, their faces like old leather gloves stiffened by sun and whiskey. You felt it on the ride into town, the blacktop smooth as a sheet of marble, with first-world rail guards and streetlights that actually worked at night. It was in the giant billboards advertising Caterpillar tractors and extractors, in the neon signs that blinked from the commercial façades, and in the smell of hot grease that wafted from the chain of KFCs, Lubumbashi's famous Katanga Fried Chiken.

If there was one thing you couldn't find in Lubumbashi, it was a hotel room. The once-stately Leopold II Hotel, now called the Park, was full of miners and Belgian investors, and if you did cadge a room, it would cost you two hundred dollars a night. A soda in the bar was three dollars, served on trays by black waiters in white coats and gloves. With every hotel booked or too expensive, we threw ourselves at the mercy of the Catholic Church, which operated a procure near the grand cathedral. The priest had informed us there were no rooms there, either, until Lionel practically dropped to his knees and begged, explaining how we "were good practicing Catholics and servants of the Lord," until the priest felt sorry for us and offered the floor of his own apartment. When he heard our plan to ride the trains to Kalemie, he laughed so hard he had to brace himself against the wall. "Oh, we shall see!" he howled.

We waited a full week at the procure but I was never bored or sorry to be there. The place was a catchall for the new players in town because the room rates were cheap and included two hots a day. It was a clean way station for foreigners looking for middle-man deals, men who left in the early morning and returned well past dark, putting in their time in hopes of leaving on a first-class upgrade with a full wad of cash and never looking back.

The local diggers operated there, too, trolling the long, shaded corridor like trench-coated pushers at the junior high. One morning after breakfast, I walked out of the dining room and was approached by a guy in a tank top and Kangol cap. His eyes pointed down to his pants pocket, from which he produced a small film canister. He popped open the lid, and inside I saw something that looked like a blob of silver.

"What is it?" I said.

"Liquid mercury."

"Huh?"

"I can get four tons by tonight. Interested?"

That same afternoon while we were walking through town, two men approached us wanting to sell us three tons of coltan. They'd dug it out of a mine eight hundred kilometers north of town and were looking for a buyer to load it onto trucks to Tanzania, then by boat to South Africa. The price was seventy-five thousand dollars.

"It's an open mine," the guy said, "and there's lots more where that came from."

"What about taxes to the government?" I asked.

"Maybe a few hundred dollars to the local chief," he said. "The government doesn't even know it exists. And we have people who can get it across the border, no problem. So are you interested?"

I told them no, and after talking to them a while longer, I learned they were both medical and law students at the local university, trying to sell black-market coltan just to pay their tuition. As they said, "Everyone there does it."

At breakfast the next morning at the procure, I explained the coltan deal to Leo, a Chinese miner who worked for a Canadian firm, or who lived in Canada and worked for a Chinese firm; he was never very clear, and I liked that about him.

"Seventy-five thousand dollars?" he said, tipping the jar of instant coffee into his cup, then drowning it in steaming milk. *"Oh man."*

I'd first seen Leo the day we arrived, walking into the procure with a group of local men, hired translators dressed in starched shirts with threadbare collars and holding clipboards. They'd disappeared into a conference room, where I could hear their conversation as I sat reading in the courtyard outside. Leo was loud and arrogant with the Congolese, bragging in his strangled accent about how much money he was making in Katanga. "We buy twenty thousand tons of copper and ship it to warehouse in China," he'd said. "Twenty thousand tons. Tons! Tons! Then we sell, sell, sell! My friends, we work three months out of year, and rest of time—drive cars and lots of girls! Ha! Ha! Ha!"

So at breakfast, I was anxious to hear his opinion on the coltan deal, more as just a conversation piece. He dumped six spoonfuls of sugar into his coffee and, before he could finish what he was saying, held up his palm. "I explain everything after prayer." He bowed his head and his lips moved in rapid silence. He finished his prayer and looked up. "Seventy-five thousand dollars?" he said. "You get ripped off, man. I get for you much cheaper. Ha! Ha! Ha!"

An Indian named Sibu also usually ate with us. He'd been in Lubumbashi for five months but hadn't been so lucky. The day I met him, Sibu was wearing a bandage over his eye, blood still seeping through the gauze, and his cheek was purple and swollen. He'd been badly beaten by the mayor's soldiers two days before, he said, after a mining deal gone sour. He'd gotten mixed up with some Chinese newcomer looking for easy contacts and, with nothing of his own cooking at the moment, agreed to accompany the Chinese guy to a cobalt mine outside town. Soldiers stopped them on the road and asked for their mining certificates. They only had tourist visas, and an hour later they found themselves in the police station facing the commander. "We can make all of this go away for two thousand dollars," the commander said.

"It's worth it," Sibu told the Chinese guy, but he refused and demanded to see the mayor.

The soldiers brought the two men to the mayor and separated them. Sibu was a citizen of Tanzania, an African. So instead of risking trouble with the Chinese embassy, the mayor ordered his men to beat Sibu instead. Sibu eventually paid them four hundred dollars of his own money just for them to stop. The Chinese miner was released and now ignored Sibu on the streets. This was a small and not unusual price to pay for doing business in Lubumbashi, and for small-time guys, these risks were part of the gamble.

A few days later, Sibu got a job with a Canadian looking to land a contract with Gécamines, the government-mining agent. The Canadian needed someone to shepherd the process, someone on the ground who would smooth things along for a cool 10 percent. The contract was for one hundred tons of copper.

"The price on the London market is nearly eight grand a ton," the Indian said. "Multiply that by a hundred, then factor my cut." He smiled and bobbed his bloodied, bandaged eyebrows. "Not bad. *Not bad at all.*" The contract was still tied up with the government by the time I left, and I never heard whether Sibu ever landed the big score.

The passenger train wasn't arriving for several more days so we used the time to explore the station and the yard. The SNCC had carefully maintained the colonial architecture of the station, everything from the cobblestone on the platforms, to the giant station clock that still kept the time, and the café with bonewood chandeliers draped with silver garland. In a way, the café itself resembled an old dining-car saloon, so cool that Lionel and I found ourselves returning there every day for beers, tall bottles of Simba that we drank slowly as the crisp Katanga breeze called down the night. Once the waiter even dragged a couple of beer crates onto the platform itself and let us drink there, right atop the giant copper arrow pointing north, toward where we hoped to go.

The station sat at the end of a wide cobblestone square, where three old locomotives sat high on earthen platforms like sentinels, proud trophies of the glory days. The steam, diesel, and electric engines—progressive touchstones along the time line—were painted blue and yellow, shimmering in the sun, and looking mighty. They were the first things you saw when rounding the corner from the Park Hotel, and the sight of such beautiful machines made me want to run toward them, made me want to hear the locomotive blow its high, brassy whistle, made me thirsty for a cold beer in the old café.

Many of those same proud machines now sat idle and rusting on the rails, and the sight of them boiled the blood of Fabien Mutomb, whose office overlooked the central yard. Fabien was the director of logistics at SNCC, a company man who kept the president's stoic portrait above the calendar on his wall, but over the years he had become a dispirited patriot. He now chaired the local chapter of the opposition party, and during our regular visits that week to his office, we'd be audience to his venom-fueled soliloquies against the plague of corruption.

"How can we redevelop this country when all of its people are looking to steal?" he said one afternoon. "We have one of the biggest mining industries in the world, but no real contracts to feed back into the country. We send men to check the validity of these contracts, to weed out the fake ones, but the people we send can't even afford a bicycle ride to work. You show these men one hundred dollars and they bend like everyone else. We're talking billions of dollars in contracts. Even the mayor of Lubumbashi has a concession."

Fabien pointed out the window, where nothing had moved all morning. "I can show you what leaves this station in the middle of the night, all that cargo on its way to Zambia, and it's a scandal. I can show you what the average Congolese eats in one day, and your dog probably eats more. Years ago you could get a well-paying job here at the mines, benefits and everything. Now the dream of young people here is to make it to South Africa and wash the streets. People are now saying, 'Let's bring back the white man.' Can you believe that? 'Bring back the white man because we can't do it ourselves.' There is no more dream in this country, no more ambition. The dream here is dead."

The railroad employed thousands of people in company towns all along the line, but still owed these workers two years of back pay, and most hadn't seen a cent in months. As a result, they'd clustered in the SNCC company camps and slowly gone down with the ship. That afternoon, Fabien wanted us to see these people, for no other reason, I guess, than to remind himself they were still around.

We climbed into Fabien's pickup and crossed the wide railyards that once served as the final bulwark between the city's whites and blacks. Across the tracks was the *cité indigène*—the colored town of old Elizabethville, where black colonial police ensured no one left unless to work, or unless they held the card of the *évolué*, the badge that certified an extra effort to adapt had been made.

We tore down a straight dirt road, kicking up red dust behind our wheels, until we arrived at the workers' camp. The road divided two sections of trim brick cottages, once prim and efficient, now derelict and crumbling in the sun. Manioc gardens grew in plots inside the maze of homes, and down the road a young boy ran dragging behind him a tattered kite made of black plastic bags.

As we sat in the truck with Fabien, a frail old man emerged from the warren of houses and walked over. He carried a bundle of documents under his arm, and I thought of all the men you saw in every town and city across Congo, men who put on their one good suit or collared shirt each morning, briefcase in hand or a bundle of documents under their arm, and set out to search for a job that didn't exist, until the act of searching, of walking around the same blocks with that same look of purpose on their faces, became the vocation itself.

As the old man approached the truck with his documents, I hoped that's what he'd been doing that day, out looking for a better job in the boom, getting his piece of that gleaming $37 million a month. But as the old man stepped forward and Fabien rolled down the window, he reached his wrinkled hand inside the cab and said, "Boss, we're starving." Fabien looked at him and said nothing.

"Boss, please, we need—"

"I know," Fabien snapped, and took the man's hand off the wheel. He clasped it for a second, then said, "We'll take care of you. Just be patient."

It must have been all the old man needed to hear; he withdrew his arm from the cab, turned, and walked away. Then Fabien rolled up the window and the truck moved forward. "Like I was telling you," he said, his eyes nailed to the road, "those are the camps."

As the sun continued to rise every morning over Katanga, the rail workers left the squalor of those company camps and returned to work, out of duty and a dog-blind faith in the boss who told them, "Just be patient," and from a knowledge deep in their marrow that if they ever quit, death wouldn't be far behind.

So the morning we were scheduled to depart, the rail workers awoke before dawn as usual, ate their meager breakfast of manioc and tea, and filed down the long dirt road and across the tracks, hoping perhaps today the payroll boss would be there smiling. But the payroll boss wasn't there, so they slipped into their green coveralls anyway and prepared for the morning train to Kalemie.

We'd arrived there at six thirty, just as the workers were trickling in and the first soft light was creeping across the iron tracks. I sat on a pile of luggage against the station wall and watched four women begin their daily chore of sweeping the platform. They bent their backs toward the ground and slashed their short straw brooms against the concrete like scythes, flinging the dust in every direction. Just as one woman scoured a patch clean, another would come alongside and cover it back with dirt. Down a ways, another woman swept a pile of gravel for an hour. There seemed to be no end to their work other than the work itself, since the cloud of dust would no doubt settle again and guarantee more work tomorrow.

I was thinking long and hard about what Charles Diamba had told us the previous day when we'd visited his office to inquire about our trip. Diamba was the station manager of Lubumbashi, the same man who'd sent the World Food Programme train on without telling us. He'd called the day before to say there was good news about our train to Kalemie. After stewing in Lubumbashi for days, and after visiting the workers' camp, I was ready for some good news. We'd walked into Diamba's office and exchanged the standard Congolese greeting.

"*Ça va?*" we'd said. How's it going?

"*Ça va un peu,*" he replied. It's going a little.

Then, also in standard Congolese form, Diamba began by telling us the bad news first. He sat behind his desk and read out a list of things gone wrong. How the SNCC had only thirty working locomotives to serve over three thousand kilometers of track, how the newest engine dated back to 1975, the year of my birth, how they only kept the trains running by cannibalizing one to fix another. The state of the tracks was deplorable, he said, with just about every kilometer of rail needing to be replaced. "North of Kamina," he said, "part of the track is actually missing, so the engineer just hits the gas and prays."

Over the past year, residents along the 750 kilometers of electric track between Lubumbashi and Dilolo had ripped down twenty-five hundred tons of cable, using tree branches as tools, and sold it to foreigners for scrap, causing the entire system to shut down for weeks for repairs. And if that wasn't enough—"If the traders feel they haven't sold enough product during our station stops," he said, "they'll rip out the brake systems. It may take days to fix. And our workers haven't been paid in months, so how do you expect them to keep an eye on things and enforce the rules?"

He paused and leaned forward. "Once you get outside Lubum-bashi, it's the Wild West. *Vous comprendez le Wild West, monsieur?*"

I'm afraid so, I said. But wasn't there some good news?

"The good news," he said, "is you won't have to deal with much of that. You'll be traveling aboard the *Rénové*, our luxury express. If all goes well, you could be in Kalemie in three days. *But that's if all goes well.*"

We'd been hearing about the *Rénové* for days, but weren't harboring any expectations. We'd seen another passenger train leave a couple of days before going to Dilolo, just off the Angolan border, with hundreds of bodies crushed inside, arms and faces pressed against the glass and dangling out windows. The whole caravan had the whiff of smoked fish and warm urine. I asked one of the workers what kind of train that was considered, and he'd replied, "Second class."

We'd also heard nightmare stories about the *Kambelembele*, a passenger train that had recently left and taken three months to reach Kindu. There'd been twenty carriages and two thousand people crammed inside. The day the train left, two children had been crushed on the platform as people rushed the doors. That was in Lubumbashi. No telling how many had died along the way.

So in Diamba's office, I didn't know how to interpret what he meant by "luxury." And I certainly wasn't comforted to hear him say, as he rushed out to catch a meeting, "It's true. This company should've shut down years ago."

As I sat on the platform that morning amid the cloud of broom dust, I was wondering what kind of luxury train would roll in the Congo, and if the *Rénové* was as much a harbinger of revival as its name suggested. It was all speculation, of course, until I heard the screeching feedback of an announcer on a microphone and the faint whistle bellowing down the yard.

The several hundred people who'd arrived to board the train were corralled inside an airless waiting room just off the main platform.

When the whistle sounded down the yard, the iron gates opened and the people spilled forward into the cool air, lugging several tons of bags and boxes atop their heads and dragged behind. They flooded onto the platform, where a fat man greeted them with a microphone and a sweep of his arms. "Ladies *a-a-a-a-nd* gentlemen," he shouted. "*Welcome* to the *Rénové!*"

The fat man, whom everyone called the *animateur*, was the showman and jester hired to keep our spirits high on the long journey ahead. He was also the company tout, the snake-oil salesman sent to promote the *Rénové* to the people along the route, to convince the frail and dispirited masses that change was finally here. Now, like a ringleader in a juggle of spotlights, the *animateur* swept his stubby arm into the air and the *Rénové* rumbled into the yard.

She was an electric locomotive pulling three sleeper cars behind, bright blue and yellow birds like the one I'd seen that day in the Kalemie yard, plus a copper-sided dining carriage straight out of *Bonanza*. As the train rolled to a stop, the powerful sun blasted through the windows on the opposite side, bending starbursts of golden light out the other.

"This is no ordinary train," cried the *animateur*. "This is the luxury express going straight to Kalemie. No, no, people, this is not the train of yesterday . . ."

"It's quite beautiful," Lionel said.

"Yeah, so it was true."

We pulled our tickets from our pockets, for which we'd paid a staggering $140 each (ticket prices started at $75), and found our assigned carriage: *565 Première Classe Deluxe*. Our car was the rear caboose, and the two of us jumped aboard.

Inside, I found myself back in that discovered fort deep in the woods, reliving that same dream as that day in the Kalemie yard. Was this the same car? No, it was better. Open the wood-panel doors and there was the restroom with a stainless-steel toilet with a step-flush contraption and sink. I ran down the long corridor, bathed in brassy light by a wall of windows, and found cabin B, our home for the journey. The eight-by-eight-foot room had a fold-down table in the center, flanked by bunk beds on either side, with soft leather mattresses dressed in pink sheets and blankets, all monogrammed with the SNCC logo.

We threw our bags onto the beds and walked two carriages down to the restaurant car, still holding out the dream of cold beers at sunset watching the savanna. And upon reaching the corridor, I saw a man loading crates of Simba into the train, hoisting the black plastic boxes onto his knees and stacking them in the pantry. He was skinny as sugarcane and wore a white apron.

It was our chef, Andre, who shook our hands and welcomed us aboard. He told us he'd spent fifteen years cooking for a big-shot Belgian brewery executive and his family. When that job ended, he was picked up by the SNCC, which, judging by his expression, had been like moving back home to care for his parents, who'd turned senile and diaper-bound.

"But be assured," he said, "I can prepare recipes for every na-tionality." He smiled and gave a dignified bow. "Please request any-thing you wish, it will be a pleasure."

On the way back to our room, we caught a glimpse of the dark kitchen and looked at one another in wide-eyed amazement. "Look, he cooks on coals!" Lionel said.

Séverin was standing in the room when we entered, still holding his bags. What do you think? I asked him. It certainly beats riding a bike through the jungle.

"It's good," he said, and surveyed the room. "But I still don't be-lieve it."

"What's not to believe?" I said. "Look at these beds. And we just met the chef, Andre, who's gonna cook big dinners for us."

"I'll believe it when we move," Séverin said. "If you notice, we're already two hours and twenty minutes behind schedule."

Lionel smiled and popped him on the shoulder. "Welcome to Congo, bro."

Séverin cringed. We'd tried that joke on him all week, much to our own amusement, but it never seemed to land. He'd just grit his teeth and smile. Sometimes we suspected he hated us.

All week in Lubumbashi we'd teased Séverin about a girl named Nanu, a strong-headed waitress we'd met in the Versailles bar. Lionel and I had gone there one afternoon and she'd chatted us up, told us how she was from Kinshasa but had come to Lubumbashi after high school to work in her aunt's bar. "I miss Kin," she said, breathless. "Lubumbashi is . . . uh, so boring." She was cocky and kind of obnoxious, so naturally we thought she was perfect for Séverin.

We brought him there the next afternoon and introduced him. "He's a really sweet guy," we said, pointing at Séverin, whose face was as close to beet red as possible, all smiles and teeth, and probably cursing our cold graves under his breath.

A few weeks before, Séverin had been accepted to the University of Liège in Belgium to study education and computer science that fall, an accomplishment we'd been celebrating all week. So of course we laid it on thick to Nanu. "He's going to Belgium on a scholarship," we said. "He's very intelligent, wants to learn Chinese so he can make a lot of money. He's very industrious like that. He'll be a big-shot banker one day, maybe even president."

Nanu stepped back and studied him for a long beat, then made small talk in Lingala: where are you from, what's your last name, and so on. When she walked back into the kitchen, we prodded him to make his move: "Get her number, man." And when she returned, he pulled a pen and notebook from his back pocket and, as cool as peppermint ice cream, said, "Give me your number. I'm going to call you." She took a breath and cocked her head, beaten at her own game, then dished out the digits.

Every day after that we'd teased him about marrying Nanu,

insisted he was stealing away in secret after work to the Versailles bar to see his new girlfriend. He'd just grit his teeth and smile. Until one day he said flatly, "I don't see her. Her phone is turned off." It turned out he'd been calling every day and stopping by the bar, only to be told she was home sick.

We started giving Séverin tips about wooing Nanu, making him listen to Fela Kuti late at night, Lionel saying, "Mate, to get the girls you need good music."

He nodded. "Like Phil Collins—"

"*No, man*, not Phil Collins. Play Fela, and turn the lights down."

He'd finally gotten through to Nanu after a week of calling her phone. But minutes into their conversation, she'd mentioned she needed to go, then asked for Lionel's phone number. Séverin had even called Lionel at the bar and asked permission to give out his number. Lionel never picked up when Nanu called, but the damage had been done.

From then on, we were always trying to get a rise out of Séverin. What usually worked was my reenactment of our hellish day in the mud near Kisangani, where I'd tie a Rambo bandanna around my head, fists knotted toward heaven, and scream, *"Porco Dio PORCA MADONNA DIO CANE!"* until he snorted from laughter.

Séverin was right about being late. After adding four additional carriages, the train sat there in the sun all morning and afternoon, while we sweated in our room and paced the crowded platform. Then a whistle would blow and send us running, just to be told to wait some more. Finally around five o'clock, the whistle gave one long whine. The station agents scudded people into the carriages and we lurched forward. We'd just about cleared the platform when the baggage car snapped loose from the locomotive and stranded us again.

An old mechanic standing near the locomotive said the first day of our journey would be along the electric lines, the best section of track on the network. If we punched it through the night, we could keep up over fifty kilometers per hour and make some time. After that, the track was old, so old it had busted loose from the ballasts. For this stretch we'd switch to the diesel and crawl down the line on our hands and knees. As he spoke, I watched the tracks in the station bounce up and down as the locomotive pushed the new baggage car into place. Even here at home base, the rails weren't bolted to the ground.

But before I could register that fear, the long whistle sounded and it was time for us to board. Hanging out the window, I saw how the setting sun struck the station and illuminated the darkened letters of ELIZABETHVILLE, still visible where decades of dust and bleaching African sun had yet to blot out the colonial name. And as the *Rénové* rolled away from old Elizabethville, the agents and family members left standing on the platform cheered and waved good-bye and sent us into the falling night, knowing they might never see anyone on that train again.

I remained in the window as the train rumbled out of the yard, feeling the cool wind whip through my clothes and hair, and marveled at how even ten seconds of true forward progress was enough to clear away the fog of a week's wait. I stood there breathing in all those charged, electric molecules that swim in the air of virgin darkness and couldn't seem to remember anything that had happened before then. The adventure had begun, and I sucked the moment down into the very floor of my being, and as I did, I felt a slight stab of sadness in my guts, for I knew this was my last adventure across the great country.

We sat on our bunks and kept the windows open, rocking back and forth as the train collected speed, spinning on electric tracks in a land where most had never owned a lightbulb. As Séverin snored from the upper bunk, Lionel and I brought cold beers from the dining car, rolled a joint, and passed it in the dark, zoning out to the way the steel wheels sounded like swords clashing underneath.

About thirty kilometers outside town we stopped at a small station platform, and in the stillness I heard the hum of wilderness in the trees, not the biblical swarms of insects like on the river, but the shrill whistle of nothingness, that white noise that fills truly empty expanses of space. A single fluorescent bulb flickered on the platform, casting silhouettes of the power lines above. We heard the sounds of the crew, men shouting in Swahili, "*Wanakuita!* They're calling you," their flashlights darting along the tracks like lightning bugs. The whistle sounded twice, a short and friendly tap on the shoulder that said, "Look out, a train is coming." And sure enough, a whistle screamed on the opposite track and a train rumbled past, gliding by slow like a black, sparkling beast breathing through our open window. All I could see were white T-shirts emerging in the dark, the rest concealed by night.

"*Tika, tika*, Dilolo, Dilolo!" they shouted from the passing train. Séverin stirred from his sleep long enough to hear their shouts and explained they were former child soldiers who'd recently disarmed. But instead of joining the army, they'd gone to work in the maize fields of Dilolo in service of the government, migrant field hands now rolling across the vast country at night.

"*Tika, tika*, Dilolo Dilolo," they shouted in Lingala ("Losers stay put, we're from Dilolo"), until their taunts faded and were swallowed by the night.

The whistle blew a labored wheeze as we cut the darkness toward Kamina. As the train gained speed over the open tracks, we lay on our backs and stared up through the open windows, where the heavens froze and pulsed with the flush of my lungs.

"The sky is unbelievable."

"Yes, you can see everything, every single one of them."

Lying there, it dawned on me we weren't alone inside this little box, where beer bottles clanged in the dark and the Specials played quietly from small speakers on the table—but were attached to a living chain of hundreds of souls, all silent now from the chilly wind and lullaby of forward motion, that great regulator of the road. It was one of those rare unspoken moments, I thought, when all of us people came a little closer to being one and the same.

But who were all these people? I told myself I'd find out tomorrow.

I awoke the next morning with the sting of warm sun on my face, forgetting where I was for a moment, until I felt the rumble of wheels and the groan of the old caboose as it reckoned with another day. Rising in my bed, I saw the door slid open and Séverin standing in the corridor by the wall of windows. We'd reached Tenke, he said. Looking out, I saw the brown hills surging from the savanna like camel humps and remembered reading how they indicated the cobalt deposits below.

Tenke, 237 kilometers northwest of Lubumbashi, was a smattering of brick mining homes with tin roofs surrounded by hills and brown scrub. The area had been developed around the 1920s after the mine was discovered, and where studies would later reveal contained ore ten times as rich in copper than most similar ores found around the world. Phelps Dodge estimated the site would produce around four hundred thousand metric tons of copper over the next decade.

Tenke was also the junction for trains heading west to Dilolo, where they once linked with Angola's majestic Benguela Railway, which after the war only had about thirty miles of functional track, near the Atlantic port of Lobito. But a new $30 million project, funded by Hong Kong–based China International Fund Ltd., had begun to rehabilitate the entire network, reconnecting Congo's quick link to the Atlantic. Repairing the railway also guaranteed the Chinese financiers lucrative concessions in oil fields off the coast of Angola, which was being prepped to become a major world producer.

As we rolled through Tenke, I heard a clanging sound somewhere in the next compartment. A few seconds later, an old man stumbled down the corridor ringing a large yellow bell, bracing himself against the windows as the train jerked around the turns. He rattled it like a Salvation Army Santa, shouting, *"Karibu, karibu."* Everyone was welcome to the dining car, breakfast was ready.

And what a breakfast! It was almost too good to believe, riding that decrepit rail network through a country as broken as it was, and here I was being seated at a table dressed with clean, red cloth and white china, each table situated near windows that opened to the sweeping, aurelian plain. The rising sun was on the right and warmed our faces after the brisk and chilly night, and the breeze pulled in soft notes of wild eucalyptus and jasmine blooming on the prairie.

The waiter burst out of the kitchen balancing ten plates of omelets in his arms, each dish wobbling to the jerks and jolts as if spinning on pencils, and set them down on tables with a clatter. Another man followed with hot milk and packs of Nescafé, and while he poured the frothy milk, we steadied our cups and watched it steam in our hands. That morning, as dishes rattled off tables and most of my coffee ended up in my lap, the two dozen war-weary passengers in that dining car ate quietly in a sheen of sublime content—so normal, it was almost boring. Looking back, I regard that first morning aboard the *Rénové* as one of my happiest moments. Because it was the first time out on the road where, for a brief moment, I felt I could've been anywhere in the world.

So again, who were these people?

In Congo, war and peace acted like the mighty arms of a hurricane. One arm would be wrapped with gunboys and death and send thousands into the bush, and meanwhile, across the country, another arm carried providence and relief and guided the lost ones home. Tens of thousands in, tens of thousands out. War and peace always seemed to sync. At that particular moment to pick out one instance, fighting in North Kivu between Rwandan Hutu rebels and the army was pushing droves into the mountains, while here in Katanga, hundreds of thousands who'd fled the great war were fi nally looking homeward.

When the second war began in August 1998, the fighting had emptied villages and towns between Kalemie and Kabalo and pushed people south toward Lubumbashi, while countless others fled over the borders into Zambia and Tanzania, where the refugee camps became permanent little cities. Those who'd fled to Kamina and Lubumbashi also remained in camps, where conditions had improved little.

All throughout that spring, UNHCR (UN High Commissioner for Refugees) was repatriating thousands from Zambia on ferryboats and trucks across the border. I'd wanted to meet some of those people, but could never align my own trip with their convoys. But at the same time, that benevolent arm of the storm was returning all those who'd fled Kalemie and villages in the north. My best option, I thought, was to meet them once I arrived in Kalemie.

That morning after breakfast, Séverin and I walked eight cars to the front of the train, where I began meeting everyone aboard. And by the time I'd made it halfway through the first carriage, I realized my search for the homeward-bound had in fact found me.

Almost everyone aboard the *Rénové* had fled the war and was returning home for the first time, going home to reunite with family, going home to check on friends and property, to reclaim jobs, to start again.

They'd all left in similar ways when the gunfire had sounded on the shores of Lake Tanganyika, signaling the Rwandans had arrived and the country was at war. They'd scattered south in blind pandemonium, coming together in small groups on nameless dirt roads, and started walking. They walked for days and weeks, across the barren scrub and over the hills, into battlefields shifting and destroying, and like the countless others I'd asked to relive that horror, they watched their children, husbands, and wives murdered by soldiers, starve to death in the tall grass, or simply vanish from sight. The dead were laid to rest without ceremony in hand-dug graves along the trail, and the dead who are buried this way do not glow like the fields of copper.

For nearly a decade they'd lived in the squalid camps of Lubumbashi and Zambia, or with relatives if they were lucky, scattered across the windswept plain with one eye always on the road back home. So when the trains finally started running, they jumped aboard the first ones to leave, knowing there might not be another train again. Many had been saving money for years for the ticket in case the opportunity arose.

Inside the *Rénové*, the company had packed them ten deep in the second-class compartments. They sat buried in children and luggage and took turns sleeping on the two sheetless beds. The carriages were hot and already smelled of moldered vegetables, the way humans tend to smell when they sleep and sweat too close together.

"They told us three days to Kalemie," one man said. "And what's three days when you've already waited this long?"

Séverin and I spent the afternoons going from compartment to compartment, making friends while standing in the doorways taking down notes. In compartment 3211C, Jeanne Mbuyi was going to Kalemie to see her five kids for the first time since that day in August. She'd been selling salt and soaps in Moba, near the Zambian border, when the Rwandans crossed the lake. Her husband fled with the children without her, catching a boat across to Tanzania, where they lived five years in the camps. Jeanne herself had ended up in the camps of Zambia. For years they didn't even know one another was still alive, until a family member heard the kids were still in Tanzania, somewhere near Kigoma. So Jeanne was setting out to find them. "I don't even have an address," she said. "Just an idea, a feeling where they might be."

In 3211C, a man named Floribert Tumbwe was going home to see his wife and two children. They'd lived outside Kalemie and waited out the initial invasion, until one early morning, when Tumbwe awoke and stepped outside to relieve himself. While in the outhouse, government soldiers appeared at his door, shouting, "Where is your husband?" It was a sweep of suspected rebels, he said, and many men were being killed. "So I decided to run," he said. "I didn't even say good-bye." Through friends, he later learned soldiers had returned two days later and killed his two oldest sons.

Overcome by shame and guilt, he remained in Lubumbashi where he'd fled and was only now attempting to contact his wife and two other children. "I need to see what's become of them," he said. "If they're even there at all."

All down the line the stories were similar, the same stories I'd heard in Bunia, Drodro, Bukavu, Aveba, and every place where people had awoken one morning unaware that at some point during the day their livelihood would crumble to dust, everything they owned would be lost, and they'd be force-marched into a years-long struggle to survive where every day was a new blade on the heels.

The train was full of those people, from the woman in 3214A who said to me, "You ask me if I'm happy to be going home? My family will never be the same after what happened, how can I be happy?" to the man so filled with anticipation at going home to see his mother, he worried she might not recognize him. "I'm fatter now and lost all my hair," he said. When he finally got home, he said, "I will ask her to make my favorite dish. Peas. My mother makes really good peas."

★ ★ ★

In the late afternoon we arrived at Bukama, where the Congo River met the rails. If you depended on news searches to tell you anything about Bukama, you'd know that eleven people had been killed by a recent outbreak of cholera, the scourge that crawled out of the ground every few years to take its fill. You'd know about the displaced camp nearby that had been attacked by Mai Mai rebels the year before, forcing tens of thousands to pick up and run, losing step with their lives all over again. And how a train had derailed around that same time, flipping over and crushing eighteen *clandestins* who'd been riding on top.

So of course I thought of these things when Séverin shouted, "Bukama!" and we rolled to a stop. But when I stepped off the train, bracing for a newfound patch of misery, all I heard was music. Haunting, ethereal music that grabbed hold and spun me around. A children's choir was standing on the platform, no doubt pulled together when they'd heard the whistle down the track. They'd struck into song as soon as the wheels stopped rolling, sang through the chaos of passengers coming and going, and the mobs of sellers who swarmed the platform hawking *chikwangue* and dried fish and shouting *"Mayi hapa!"* waving bags of chilled, boiled water for sale. Passengers who remained inside hung their bodies out the windows and listened to the chilling music, carried in full by a young girl soprano whose bright voice gave the songs great, razor-tipped wings. I even watched as the *animateur* readied his microphone and bullhorn, only to sit down near the young girl and shut his eyes to the sound.

We rolled out of Bukama with the setting sun and crossed the great river, where orange light bounced off the top and brought back memories of the *Ma'ungano*, standing in the captain's room with Buisine watching the river silver-plate at dusk, hoping the night sky would be clear enough for us to keep moving on.

Construction on the Bukama-Ilebo route, known as the Chemin de Fer du Bas-Congo au Katanga, or Bas-Congo to Katanga Railway

(BCK), began in 1923 with separate teams beginning in the north and the south and slowly working their way toward the middle. Southern crews began in Bukama and were blessed with flat, arid terrain, while teams working from Ilebo slogged their way through thick equatorial jungle and heavy seasonal rain. The construction of the line drew many of the same Greeks and Italians who'd built the Katanga line into Lubumbashi years before, and also attracted a large number of young Europeans looking for adventure in dark, untamed Africa. For those who were hired, the journey to Congo was probably as surreal as anything they'd ever done.

From Europe, workers embarked on a three-week journey by ship to the port of Matadi, then boarded a train on Leopold's railway over the rapids and arrived in Kinshasa two days later. This was followed by a two-week boat ride up the Congo and Kasai rivers, with stops each night to load tons of lumber cut from the dense forests to use on the railroad's construction. At night they slept under mosquito nets in airless cabins, losing the first of many nights' rest to the sucking tropical humidity, listening to the chatter of Congolese crewmen below in the holds and the jungle vibrating outside. Once in Ilebo, the new recruits were put into *tipoyes*, small, basketlike chairs, which porters carried on their shoulders through the jungles to the camps.

Tools and building materials bound for Ilebo followed a similar route through jungle and river, usually taking months to arrive, sometimes an entire year. And when they did finally arrive, workers would amuse themselves by watching the Congolese try to adapt to the foreign equipment. In one account, white contractors arrived at a work site to the spectacle of natives scooping dirt with their hands and placing it into shovels, which they hoisted on their heads to unload. Full wheelbarrows of dirt were unloaded the same way.

Food and medical supplies arrived on average once per month. The Congolese crews were given six kilograms of manioc and maize, along with pieces of dried fish and beef taken from the colony's herds near the mouth of the Congo. Whites, by contrast, received monthly "medical comfort" boxes from Belgium, loaded with canned meats and vegetables, along with many luxuries shipped in from the modern world. One such medical-comfort inventory listed four boxes of pâté, two cartons of Camembert cheese, chocolate, whiskey, cognac, and two full cases of Bordeaux.

The construction through the jungle was exhausting and slow, food supplies ran low, and heavy rains often destroyed several days' progress, forcing crews to begin all over again. White foremen also found themselves in tricky negotiations with local chiefs for permission to proceed through tribal land. In one account, a local chief forced a young Belgian foreman into nightly drinking marathons, where the chief would agree to allow the railroad, then withdraw his approval the following morning. This went on for weeks before the chief finally gave in, but not before seriously depleting the "medical boxes" the foreigners so dearly cherished.

The north and south lines finally converged on February 13, 1928, in a stretch of jungle 762 kilometers northwest of Bukama and 359 kilometers southeast of Ilebo. A small ceremony was attended by the European workers, dressed in pith helmets and starched white shirts, and native laborers, in their bare feet staring stoically into the camera. A white-stone pillar was erected at the site, indicating the time and date of the union, and the chief of the BCK Railway was present to drive the last bolt. As the first train crossed the junction at 2:40 P.M., a priest popped a bottle of champagne. The entire ceremony took place under a driving equatorial rain.

On our second night on the train, just after dark, we arrived at a village called Mulundu, where another choir of children gathered at the base of our window shouting for *"Copo! Copo!"*—wanting bottles or cans they could use for toys. We tossed some empty water bottles out the window and the kids danced at the wheels, then tore away in fright when the *Rénové* blew three short whistles, a call of distress. It was a sound I'd grow accustomed to in the days ahead. For here in Mulundu, we experienced our first breakdown.

The cable that supplied power to the electric engine had snapped. And after several hours of waiting, the engineer came by and said, "If we can't fix the power line, we'll have to switch to the diesel." The diesel locomotive was being pulled behind the electric for later use. "But that will mean we'll run out of fuel before Kalemie."

We waited at Mulundu for eight hours and tried to sleep, despite the gang of children who returned outside our window to demonstrate their gangly kung fu moves and sing goofy songs like, "Mzungu likes chicken and eggs, mzungu likes chicken and eggs. Ooh ooh ooh, mzungu . . ." Around two in the morning, the broken cable was fixed and we continued with the electric locomotive pulling us toward Kamina. It was a good thing we weren't forced to switch to the diesel engine, because the following day we discovered it had a busted alternator. If we had switched, we would've broken down minutes later, stranded with two dead engines. And while waiting in Mulundu, we'd stepped out into the dark to get some air and found out the tracks were still stamped with the signature of the BCK Railway and hadn't been touched since their construction in 1925.

But the true condition of the railway didn't register until the next morning when we pulled into Kamina. There, lined up for half a mile, sat boxcar after boxcar loaded with freight that hadn't moved in months, some even a year, simply because there weren't enough locomotives to haul them.

Just like on the river, the war had stopped the movement of essential goods and merchandise along the railway, severing market towns one from the other and isolating them on the plain. Farmers and traders were displaced and removed from their fields and stalls, and even if there were goods to ship, rebels and soldiers had commandeered locomotives for moving troops and supplies. All of this created a massive hunger crisis, and basic goods such as salt, soap, oil, and used clothing were in extreme demand. Like the folks I'd met on the river, the traders in Katanga braved countless obstacles just to get flour, sugar, and medicines into the villages, risked soldiers and rebels, bad weather and bandits, and the myriad other traps that lie hidden during war.

Now peace had returned to Katanga and people were going home. The traders were back in their stalls, and farmers in the mostly barren province were enjoying a bumper crop of maize. But amid all these hopeful things, the economy remained stalled because the railroad was in shambles. As we rolled into Kamina, it became clear that peace and goodwill alone could not revive Congo's economy, not without the infrastructure to move it along.

Back when I'd visited in 2003, everyone was saying how the problem was structural: just repair the two blown-out bridges at Niemba and Zofu and all those cars would ride again with prosperity in their hulls. "Fix those bridges," an American aid worker had told me, "and the markets will blossom."

So the American government and the Belgians fixed those bridges for a million dollars apiece, nothing compared to how much it cost to fly in C-130s loaded with food aid. (It cost one thousand dollars per ton to send a UN cargo plane nearly a thousand kilometers from Lubumbashi to Kindu, while a train would cost one fifth that much. The WFP estimated transport ate 60 percent of its budget.) And just like with the elections, once those bridges were finished, we all stood back and waited for greatness.

But what we forgot (or I did) was that decades of neglect and corruption had killed most of the locomotives needed to pull freight over those beautiful bridges. And so the freight backed up and the economy backed up, just as the debt and loss of wages backed up, until the entire network was backed up and filled with stranded boxcars in every station. After all the hungry and barren years of war, the fruit had finally blossomed on the vine, only to hang there and rot in the sun.

III

At Kamina, the lines of stranded boxcars didn't deter the *animateur*. For him, every station was a stage. The fat man waddled off the train in his crisp khaki suit, microphone in hand. An eager assistant followed close behind clutching a remote speaker under his arm like a pet chicken. *"Ladies and gentlemen, this is the* Rénové," he cried. "This is an express train to Kalemie, made for our clients who need to get to their destination quickly. *This is no ordinary train.* This is one seat, one person. We don't stack people and merchandise inside or on the roof. Don't embarrass yourselves, people, this is a special train and she's pulling out soon . . ."

As I jumped off the train and walked under the shadows of the stranded boxcars, a man walked up and stopped. "So this is an express train to Kalemie?" he asked.

"Yes," I said. "The *Rénové*."

He slapped the steel broadside of one of the cars. "You mean my maize has been sitting here for three months and the *Rénové* just rolls on through? *Incredible!*"

The trail of boxcars wasn't a promising sign for the many traders who also rode the *Rénové*. As the *animateur* had stated, this was a luxury express train—which meant that the *only* train to Kalemie had no room for the mountains of cargo afforded on the river barges, or the rat-infested third-class trains, or the rooftops of freights that so many rode. So instead of taking their cargo with them, the traders had loaded it into separate freight cars in Lubumbashi with hopes of meeting it down the line.

"That's how precarious this life is," said one woman, who'd left boxes of used clothing in a freight car in Lubumbashi, which she prayed would meet her in Kabongo, some 750 kilometers north.

"It could take two months to get there, but then again, it used to take one year. So I'll wait again. It all depends on the goodwill of the SNCC."

Down the tracks in the mechanics' depot, where our locomotives were taken for repairs, goodwill was about the only thing left to spare, and even that was full of cracks. The depot sat half a kilometer down the yard, so Séverin and I walked along the rails, through oil slicks and thornbushes and ancient rusted steamers like dinosaur bones in the tall grass, past the young soldier who clicked his tongue and told me in Swahili, "*Mzungu*, here you go enjoying all our money when we have nothing." We continued down the tracks until we arrived at a giant aluminum hangar opened on both ends, where locomotives sat on rails while men tinkered with them from service pits below.

The depot was like stepping into my great-grandfather's old farm shed, a museum of midcentury, American-made heavy machines, still being maintained and used. The four mechanics stared up into the bellies of the engines, their coveralls jet-black from grease, just like every other surface left exposed in the old garage. Even the men's lockers were coated with an inch of gunk. The depot was loud and smelled like work, and after five minutes you realized that within those walls, greater decisions were being made regarding the nation's future than inside the president's chamber itself.

As I stood watching the workers service the *Rénové*'s locomotive, Joseph Tshibangu, the chief mechanic, walked up beside me. "That's a 1972 General Electric V-eight," he said. "American-made. We used to have fifty like these all along the line, now we're lucky to have ten. They're so old we can't even get parts anymore, so we build the parts ourselves."

It was like a trauma ward for the old network, and it had been that way for years. During the war, the government troops controlled Kamina and kept the depot open to carry soldiers and equipment to the front. But fighting the rebels—who'd seized most of the east, including the Kalemie station—took its toll on the haggard troops, and in turn on the beleaguered railroad employees. "They would hit us with their guns if things didn't work," he said. "They even stabbed one of my mechanics. They were so messed up from the front lines."

Tshibangu's mechanics were now harassed by traders whose goods were stranded at the station. But some of that stranded cargo, mostly boxcars of maize, would be leaving shortly for up north, Tshibangu said. He pointed to a second locomotive being serviced near ours. "We'll send that one soon. But it's the only train from Kamina all month.

"If I had ten strong diesel engines and four electric engines," he added, "I could turn this country around. If these trains were fixed, it would improve everything, everything, especially the conditions in these villages you'll see along the line. If these rails were working, Congo could be a powerful nation."

After a while, the mechanics signaled they were finished with our diesel, then carefully began rolling it into the yard. I watched as the harsh sunlight fell on the engine and exposed its ugly sores as if it were an infirm patient being wheeled out for some air. As I turned to say good-bye to Tshibangu, he shook my hand and said wistfully, "We grew up in better conditions than this. We had a lot of dreams about the future. Back then it was okay to dream big things."

"I'm hearing that a lot," I said, then hesitated. "Maybe things will get better."

He smiled and released my hand. "Maybe so."

We waved good-bye to the mechanics and climbed aboard the diesel, which belched a column of inky smoke and crawled toward the station. But a few hundred feet from the platform, we reversed direction and returned to the depot. After fidgeting with the engine, a mechanic determined we had a busted plug.

"What do we do?" asked one. The others sighed and shook

their heads, then pointed to the second locomotive in the garage, the one scheduled to pull the maize. "Take it from there and we'll fix it later," said Tshibangu. Everyone nodded and agreed, and within minutes we were moving again.

Around noon we finally rolled out of the Kamina yard, leaving the marooned boxcars behind, along with a long trail of peanut shells, empty plastic bags, and mounds of toilet paper and shit where the toilets dropped their loads. Once out of Kamina, the plains stretched far until the earth bent south like the fields of West Texas where I grew up, punctuated now and then with tall, bright flowers, Popsicle red, that stood regal and alone on the expanse. We crawled at ten kilometers an hour over rails that were buried and concealed in the sand, traveling so slowly that a man on a bicycle hugged our tail for an hour, complaining because there wasn't room for him to pass.

That night in the dining car, Andre served us a heaping dinner of fresh *capitain* with vegetables and rice, which he'd artfully sculpted into two rising towers on the plate. *"C'est bon!"* we shouted into the kitchen. *"C'est super, magnifique!"* Andre poked his head around the corner and gave a little bow. "I manage with what I have," he said.

The electricity had disappeared somewhere past Kamina, so we ate by the light of a candle melted to an overturned saucer. And with the orange, dancing light, the creak and moan of the wooden car, and the smell of coal smoke wafting from the kitchen, I expected the Duke himself to swagger by at any moment.

Just after dinner, the wheels screeched to a halt in a station called Lusenji. The diesel's whistle gave three short distress blasts, and we knew the rest. After a few moments, Pancha, the *chef du train*, stopped by our room to say there was bad news. Some workers in the next town had just radioed to say a section of track was missing up ahead. We'd have to send the locomotive back to fetch some technicians. "We'll be here for the night," the chief said, his voice quivering with frustration. "In the meantime, I present to you lovely Lusenji."

In the meantime, the villagers of lovely Lusenji—industrious and on their toes—were seizing an opportunity, bursting out from the bush carrying bowls of *chikwangue*, roasted peanuts, and freshwater, crying *"Mayi hapa!"* through the darkness. Fires flickered through the trees, as snaking lines of sardine-can torches bobbed along the trail toward the *Rénové*, not an ordinary train, but one that stammered and suffered *à la Congolais*, never sure when the rail would be missing for good and the bottom would fall away.

So the diesel disconnected and left us there. And as it disappeared down the black rail, the mechanics and engineers waved good-bye from the tail. "Be back in a few hours," they shouted. *Ça va,* the crowd answered, *ça va un peu,* we'll be waiting here as always, playing music softly through the window for when you return.

We awoke at first light the next morning, our fourth day on the train, and jumped down to explore Lusenji. Like many of the small rail towns along the way, Lusenji had a small brick station that was the center of everything, with a few grass-topped huts in the distance and not much else. A few village women were selling peanuts and food outside, so I paid a woman one thousand francs (about two dollars) to wash some of my clothes, which had gotten a bit gamy on the trail. She also returned with fresh buckets of water. Since there were no showers on the *Rénové*, we used them to take quick bandanna baths on the back of the caboose.

The railyard was empty and quiet, and a warm, stiff wind whipped the dust into my teeth. At Lusenji, the stranded sacks of maize were stacked as high as my head. A group of men sat atop the bags drinking cups of maize beer (it was good for something), and as I walked passed, they shouted the usual greeting: "Ay *le blanc*, give me money!" They were ragged and filthy, with a layer of dust and grass tangled in their hair. Looking around, I realized they belonged to the long freight train parked next to ours, which I hadn't noticed in the night. It was a freight hauling some of the maize west to Kananga, someone said, and a small city had formed on its flat roof. Amid heaps of bags and bundles sat scores of tired and rangy-looking people, wind-beaten and gaunt. It was a true river barge of the open rails.

Around ten that morning the locomotive rumbled back into the station and rejoined the train. The broken track was fixed, they said, but we'd have to go slow. The engine gave a long, farewell whistle and jerked to life. And as we left the station, everyone ran to the windows to feel the cool breeze drive away the vapor of last night's sewage that rose from the tracks below. It was always good to be moving, for moving was an instant pill that cured everything.

We basked in that liberating breeze for about half an hour. Then the train derailed.

At first there was a screech and guttural sound of grinding steel, then the train lurched to a halt, slinging all the cups and bottles from our table onto the floor.

"Something bad just happened," Lionel said, then we heard someone down the carriage yell, *"DÉRAILLEMENT!"* Everyone poured out of the train into the sun. Sure enough, carriage 32110 had jumped the tracks and been dragged about five hundred feet, plowing a trail about six inches deep. The tracks below the train were completely buried in the sand. The carriage had simply lost traction and skidded off.

One by one, the train passengers made an obligatory pass of the damage like mourners at a wake. Each stooped low to get a good look, then shook their heads to the side. But instead of throwing a fit, cursing, or even giving it a second thought, they simply grabbed their charcoal stoves and moved under the trees to make lunch.

Pancha, the train chief, strolled up behind us and stared at the wayward carriage, its wheels sunk in the sand. *"C'est un petit déraillement,"* he said, waving his hand. "Not a big deal." He said the locomotive would soon leave for Kabongo, fifty kilometers away, to fetch a derailment crew. "We'll be out of here soon. Trust me, it could be worse."

All throughout the trip, I'd been waiting for the derailment. I'd waited for it in the dining car, while doing interviews in the doorways of second class, and especially while sitting on the toilet. I'd obsessed about it those nights lying in bed as the train pounded the turns and tipped the caboose, worrying if I was lying in the right position on the bed, on the right side of the cabin, trying my best to anticipate the physics of a crash, the jagged path of flight for a six-foot breakable object in a tiny metal box. And now that it had happened, almost without my noticing, I felt a giant sense of relief

But I knew my level of patience, for it had been field-tested the hard way along the Congo River. So after leaving the chief, I set out to occupy my time. A small village was down the road, where I found a girl selling ripe green oranges and bought a few for the cabin. The prairie had now given way to forest, so the three of us ventured into the trees and found a stream to refill our water jugs, guided by a young boy named Idrissa, who strummed a homemade reed guitar as he walked.

Three hours passed, then six. We finally went to find Pancha. Maybe he had a radio, maybe he had some answers. He'd pulled his mattress out into the shade of the carriage and now lay there with his wife, staring up at the clouds. We asked him how long this would take.

"Ten minutes if we had a crew on board," he said. "But we don't."

Everyone got along with the chief. He was a straight shooter like Fabien, a company man from back in the good ol' days whose loyalty had earned him a bellyful of vinegar.

"You want to know why we're taking so long?" he said, and propped himself up on his elbows, still looking away. "The workers in Kabongo haven't been paid in twenty-five months. They probably started running as soon as they heard our train.

They ran because they knew they had to work. Our crew is probably somewhere in the village now trying to convince them to help one last time. Or they can pretend to be working in the fields and not hear the whistle. And how can we blame them for working in the fields, how else are they going to survive?"

It had gotten so bad, Pancha said, that in places like Lubumbashi, the authorities even threatened to arrest the crews if they didn't come back to work.

"Back when things were good," he said, and I watched his eyes shrink, for we'd reached that storied green pasture of history, never as lush as everyone remembered (how could it be?), but good enough to now make their tired feet throb a little harder, the empty stomach growl a little louder, the marrow in their bones grow a little stiffer. Everyone had his own version of history, and how he'd fit inside it. And everyone had his own reasons why things had gone so bad.

"Back in the good days," Pancha said, "well—it was when the white man ran things."

I'd been hearing it all week, starting with Fabien. I'd heard it again from a pastor going to Kongolo, standing outside during the long Lusenji breakdown, asking me, "When is the white man coming to fix this train? When is he coming back to fix this mess?" Then again from the old man who rang the breakfast bell, who told me with those same pinched eyes, "The black man can't run this company because he lacks compassion. The black man lacks love."

"Whites have the same problem," I said. "Believe me."

"No, no," he shot back. "A black man laughs at his countryman who's suffering. White men would never do that. If a black man continues to run this company, the end is certainly near."

Everyone had his own history. Ask an old man in Kinshasa what he thought of the white man, and he'd spin you a picture of Stanley snapping a whip and taking heads, ol' Bula Matari, the rock breaker, or show you the statue of Leopold now facedown in the city dump. The white man was the UN, the fleshy figure behind the tinted glass with a weakness for Tintin and tight, young girls. And on the river he was *l'étranger*, the thief and mercenary, the cloaked shadow who controlled their leaders with fingers that pulsed with war.

But in Katanga, the bejeweled trough of empire itself, where the international firms took their 80 percent on the straight, and where that strange, warm breeze at midnight was the anxious breath of hundreds more waiting to pounce—well, the people couldn't wait to bring them back.

I understood where it came from, even if I became confused when I gave it too much thought. Yes, life was tough under the colony, especially in the interior, and Africans had few rights or privileges, including in Katanga. But in Katanga there'd been real industry that had required many hands. The people had jobs and contributed to a system that functioned and turned a profit. They'd learned and utilized technologies and reaped the fruits, and as the world spun on its axis, they felt they were part of it. Their fathers and grandfathers fought and toiled during both world wars, helped protect the world from fascists and Nazis, for Belgium's future was theirs as well. They'd even been taught to drive those big locomotives and trusted to move them down the line, only to trade places with white drivers once they crossed into Rhodesia, where a black engineer was still unthinkable.

And when black men had finally taken power in Kinshasa, the whites had fought to keep the system intact in Katanga, before finally giving up and watching it all swirl down the drain—a black man in a leopard-skin hat holding the plug.

That's what Pancha was talking about, same with the pastor and the old man in the dining car, when he said that the "black man" was greedy and heartless and let them down at every turn. To them, Mobutu was just a later cast of the old tribal chiefs in Congo who'd sold their own people into slavery, and just a touch above the *genocidaires* who'd killed so many in Rwanda. That black man was always in the game for himself and couldn't be trusted. And when that black man took the reins, things just fell apart. I couldn't blame them for being bitter. In the end, a man just wants to go to work and be paid.

Pancha was also remembering a brief period, from 1995 to 1997, when South Africans and Belgians had operated the trains under a group called Sizarail. Mobutu had let the rail network grind down to absolutely nothing, until the South African rail company Spoornet brought in Belgian managers and took control of the Lubumbashi-Dilolo line, adding $50 million worth of locomotives and freight cars. It had been one of the only state-run companies under Mobutu that operated well. Freight moved on time, employees were paid quickly and in full, and there were regular, weekly trains. But Laurent Kabila's rebels seized the company in 1997 as they marched toward Kinshasa. They booted the foreigners out and nationalized Sizarail as Mobutu had done with so many foreign companies two decades before. The company quickly went under, and when the war swept through the following year, all those good times everyone remembered limped toward the green pasture and died.

"There's something about the Congolese," Pancha said. "We suffer and endure and never act like it bothers us. People can sleep here in the dirt for four or five days. They'll complain but they won't act. And because they don't act, the company and government let it go by as usual. This mentality developed during the Mobutu years when everyone was forgotten and left to survive on their own through war and everything. We're all so traumatized, yet we don't even know it."

Pancha turned his head and motioned down the tracks, where the afternoon shade was shifting, leaving the hundreds of people to wait in the hot sun.

"Don't you find it bizarre that there are pregnant women, sick people, elderly on board, and they'll sit like this without food for three days and not do anything? The normal travelers will bring three days' worth of food, but in the end it takes eight days to get to the destination. Years ago there was a medical team on board, doctors, nurses, and medicine. Now there's nothing, not even aspirin. Recently we lost one of our own employees, a ticket collec tor who contracted typhoid on the train. We could do nothing for him and he died. We buried him in Kabongo, just buried him without a funeral. These are the cases we know. No one knows what happens on those freight trains loaded with people. But no matter what happens, there are no demonstrations, no protests, no revolts, nothing from nobody. They just say, 'It's God's will.' That's the mentality. But with this mentality we'll never improve. We simply cannot keep going with this mentality. It's a miracle we're still even a company. How long do we have before the bottom drops? My friend, it could happen tomorrow."

And really, what could I say to that? I walked down the length of the train, where the sun was now in full, hoping the bottom wouldn't drop until we got to Kalemie, until everyone at least got that fair shot to make things better, people like Jeanne and Floribert, who only wanted to find their kids and hold them high above the floor, because we all knew the bottom would drop again.

I'd also met another woman on the same quest. Fatuma Luzingo had boarded the train in Kamina and, like Jeanne, was on a quest to find her three children. When the war swept into Kalemie, Fatuma and her husband had been washing clothes on the shore of the lake. They hurried home to check on their kids, only to discover Fatuma's father had already taken them away. As the shooting got closer, neighbors ran past saying the soldiers were killing people in the streets. With little else to do, Fatuma and her husband followed the crowds into the bush. "We left everything in the hands of God," she said. "I'd never felt so out of control."

They walked for weeks and were finally picked up by Zimbabwean soldiers, who were fighting Rwandan rebels in the area. The soldiers shared their rations and took them to Kamina, where they lived in a camp until the day they boarded the *Rénové*.

Fatuma was thirty-three years old, with long, immaculate braids, and buxom in a way that gave her a deep, throaty voice. It had only been a few months that she was able to speak to her father on the phone and learn about her kids. The children had been one, three, and four years old when she'd seen them last. Nine years will do a lot to kids at that age. "My kids are my blood," she said, undeterred. "I'll recognize them."

And now as I walked down the train, saying hello to people, walking just to walk, I saw her sitting alone on a blanket, fidgety, impatient, all that anxiety and nowhere for it to go. "What is happening?" she snapped. "How many hours can we wait?" She'd run out of money the day before and now depended on her neighbors to feed her and her husband.

Just as I stood there, I heard a long, booming whistle, looked out, and saw the *Rénové* rolling down the track. Everyone leaped up and jumped with joy and sang, *"Wanatukumbuka! Wanatukumbuka!"* SNCC remembered us!

But it wasn't so. The crew said the derailment technicians weren't in Kabongo after all, but aboard that freight train to Kananga, the one we'd passed back in Lusenji. We'd have to intercept them quickly before they got too far away. Standing there, I could almost feel the freightliner drifting farther and farther away, as if our hopes were stuck there on its windswept roof, slowly losing grip.

I went back into the cabin to try to sleep, and when I did, I noticed everything had changed. The cabin now looked small and dingy, and the table was covered with grit. My blankets were scattershot with pollen and grass from the open window, as if someone had emptied a lawn bag onto my bed. Inside the bathroom, there was no running water and had never been. The toilet was caked with hardened shit that snailed over the lid, with ten inches of piss coagulating in the bowl. It was true, we were riding on the last train in Congo, and here's where it finally stopped. Here's where the strong one finally failed to fix the broken one, where the cog in the system finally slid backward and threw us all off the tracks. I needed to sleep. I went into my bag and pulled out a bottle of Jim Beam, took three long pulls, and lay down. When I woke up, it was dark, but that's the only thing that was different.

For several hours we lay on our bunks in the dark listening to music from the battery-powered speaker on the table, the guitars fusing with a rhythm section of insects out the window. After a while, the entire carriage began to gently rock from someone having sex down the hall.

"I think it's Patrick," said Lionel. Patrick was the security guard assigned to the *luxe classe deluxe*, who had told us the day before that Congolese women were the wildest on the continent. "The way they move," he said, "you'd think they had no bones." He'd pulled out a pouch of white powder bought in a shop in Kamina and swore of its powers over women. "Just massage it into your penis forty-five minutes before action, and it's like a tree trunk," he said, clutching his forearm as if pumping a shotgun.

"The black African can last a long time with a woman. But the Congolese woman—she'll destroy a *mzungu* in under two minutes."

Around ten thirty, as I drifted in and out of a hot sleep, I heard a faint whistle and the voices of men, then realized the derailment crew had arrived to fix our train. We ran outside and saw several men jump off a single diesel engine parked behind our caboose. They'd come from Kipokwe, just north of Kamina, and traveled nine hours to get here. The crew wore greasy blue coveralls and shuffled down the rails like tired, old men, calling out in Swahili to the *Rénové* crew, "We've come to help you, so be real men and get to work. No standing around!"

The *Rénové* crew scrambled to help carry their equipment, enduring their gripes all the way down the line. "We haven't eaten since this morning. We're starving! And do you know how dangerous it was to rescue you? We risked derailing ourselves. *Then where would you be!?*"

Standing next to the derailed car, Lionel pulled a camera from his bag and started shooting. As he pressed in close, one of the derailment crew barked, "You're just here to take pictures? Why don't you do something useful," then handed him a flashlight.

With deft efficiency, the crew dug two deep holes in the sand beneath the derailed car, then filled them with wooden blocks. One man followed behind with heavy steel jacks, groaning *"Yah!"* as he swung them atop the wood. They cranked the jack and the train's belly popped and moaned as it rose. The air was thick with diesel exhaust and dust that hung like a white sheet against the engine's bright lights. When the diesel revved, fountains of fire and spark shot into the darkness.

The men cranked the jack. *"Yah! Yah!"* With each pump, the steel wheels lifted off the sand. Another man attached a winch to the undercarriage and anchored it to a thick acacia tree. The winch tightened— *"Polepole!"* they cried, easy, easy—and the train pulled left. *"Polepole."* The train jerked once, tipped off the jack, and landed perfectly on the rails. *"Yah!"*

Just like that, we were saved. The whole operation had taken just under two hours. And when it was finished, the crewmen collected their tools and walked back to their train for the long journey home. Once again, the railway inched forward into another day of life. We thanked the crew and waved good-bye, the same way we once waved at firefighters and don't anymore. And as we watched the crew disappear down the line into darkness, true heroes tonight, we could hear them calling into the windows of the *Rénové*, begging for something to eat.

As the *Rénové* lurched forward, I imagined the crew's nine-hour journey home, imagined them cold and hungry in their thin, blue coveralls as they rolled against the Katangan chill, and at every desolate station along the way, under every dim lamp in the night, having to stare at all that rotting food.

The insult would've been triple had they gone to Kabongo, where we arrived at dawn the next morning, our fifth day. There at the station was a giant pavilion stacked to the roof with fourteen thousand tons of maize. The white sacks rolled and cascaded like a snowdrift, two stories high at least.

The same farmers who'd harvested and bagged the maize now sat drinking it at the base, while others sprawled out atop the pile and slept.

"How long have you been here?" I asked one man.

"Thirteen months," he answered.

One of them scaled the heap with a pad and pencil and meticulously, almost obsessively, tried to count each sack, and I wondered how many times he did that in a day. Looking at the sacks more closely, I noticed they were all teeming with bugs.

While the farmers waited for their train, the *Rénové* dropped two carriages of passengers and picked up more. And in less than half an hour, we blew the whistle and pulled out.

(Later back in Kinshasa, I told the story of Kabongo to a friend at the U.S. embassy, about stacks of maize rotting like manna in the sun. My friend shook his head and laughed and said only this: "Forty million." That was how much the U.S. government sent Congo that year in food aid.)

Every company town we passed that day told the same story, stacks of grain bags waiting in waste. Meanwhile, someone said, Lubumbashi was experiencing a great shortage of maize. Most of it had to be imported from Zambia, causing the price to triple in the market. Nothing was connecting.

At Kitunda, angry farmers and rail workers jumped aboard the

Rénové and kept the train from leaving, not until the company paid them some back wages. A few workers even climbed aboard our carriage and stood at our door, holding their hats and saying with swallowed pride, "Please, if you can spare a little something."

At every station, whether we stopped there or not, dozens of people rushed to the platform just to watch us pass, as if to confirm the company was still alive. Despite not paying the crew and allowing their crops to spoil, the SNCC was still the mortar that bound the community, if only on promises and history.

In Kitunda, when Lionel casually repeated what a mechanic in Kamina had said, that the company was on its knees and could close within the year, one of the men in our doorway nearly jumped out of his shoes.

"Close?" he said, aghast. "What do you mean, *close?*"

"Nothing," Lionel said, quickly realizing his mistake. "Nothing—I was just being stupid."

By the time we got to Kabalo that night, the mountains of rot had become so common I hardly noticed, until I saw the swarm of people ready to lynch the *animateur*. A mob of farmers and traders and angry passengers now crowded around him, screaming a blue streak. I had to smile.

"I paid three thousand dollars to move this maize and it's still here," one farmer said. "And now you're asking me to pay again?!"

"The carriages are too crowded!" said one woman.

"Yeah," shouted another. "You call this an express train?"

The *animateur* just sat there doing nothing, looking exhausted and depressed. His pressed khaki suit and polished shoes had long vanished, replaced now by a stained white tank top and flip-flops. He wiped his sweaty brow with a handkerchief and panted in the heat like a tired hound. I realized he'd gone missing during the entire derailment. When the crowd finally parted, I walked over to say hello.

"The farmers are very mad," he said, wiping his neck. "They

want to know who's in charge, why won't we take their maize down to Kamina. Hey, I don't know who's in charge anymore. There are just no locomotives. Someone should fix this problem."
I asked him when he personally thought the goods would get delivered. Prompted by a serious question, he somehow summoned back a professional veneer. "The products will get delivered within the month . . . or maybe next year . . . but the SNCC . . . we're doing our utmost . . ." Finally he gave up even trying. "Look, that's just the way it is, okay?"

Kabalo was a key rail junction where the route continued north all the way to Kindu, and east to Kalemie, where barges and ferries still made regular trips across Lake Tanganyika. Kabalo itself sat on the banks of the Upper Congo River, known here as the Lualaba, but had limited use as a port. Just ninety kilometers north, near Kongolo, the broad river collapsed into a deep, narrow gorge known as the Gates of Hell, rendering navigation impossible. So from Kabalo, a small spit of track connected our route to the Great Lakes Railway, the network of rails and barges that ran all the way north to Kisangani, then downriver toward the Atlantic. It was still the main route for the informal traders riding the barges and rails.
Many traders aboard the *Rénové* were headed north to Kongolo to sell items on the river, so the officials decided to send the locomotive and two carriages on the eighty-five kilometer journey. They would drop the passengers and return to Kabalo by dawn, then continue east to Kalemie. Pancha found us on the platform and gave us the choice of staying or riding along to Kongolo, just to kill the time.
We'd arrived at the point where the pleasant savanna finally slammed into the wall of jungle and vine. Being back on the river again, even in the dark, I could hear the familiar din of the forest. Mosquitoes now swarmed thick around my ears, and the tropical heat had smothered the crisp air of the plateau. We decided to ride

along to Kongolo. At least there'd be forward motion and the breeze that came with it.

"Fine, I'll alert the crew," said Pancha. "But understand, the stretch of track is very bad. If anything happens, we'll have to call for help at Kamina, and depending on the problem, that could take weeks."

We boarded the second-class carriage they'd set aside for Kongolo and, to no one's surprise, waited two hours for the locomotive to be serviced. Our compartment was small and smelled like it had been used to breed horses. In the far corner, the floor was freshly scorched where someone had built a fire between Lubumbashi and here.

For two hours we sat there, swatting mosquitoes and sweating through our clothes, Basoko blues once again, but in another sink-hole way upriver, in the swamps where centuries ago the exploring caravans had been bogged and slain by disease, moved along by countless Africans who'd portered them and died with no name. All around I could hear the radios with their fading batteries, blasting that warbled anthem of the river that cooed like night birds for the restless presence. I could feel myself begin to recede, to tip and lose balance, slide toward the deeper darkness that had crept in from outside. It happened so quickly and took me by surprise; sometimes I just turned around and found it there—*ah, camarade*—unaware it had been waiting for me for days. And just as this was about to happen, as the twitch of despair crawled up my arm, the *Rénové* blasted her whistle down the tracks, so brash and strong it lifted the top of my skull and brought me back around. I looked out the window and saw her light tunneling down the tracks, so bright it burned away the mosquitoes and promised its own breeze.

"*On y va!*" screamed Pancha, and the train pulled away.

As those first breezes rinsed the cabin clean, Lionel and I sat on the bottom bunk taking turns with the bottle of bourbon, until finally the drink and gentle motion rocked us to sleep. I awoke two hours later when the train jolted to a stop. The cabin was now thick with the smell of deeper jungle, the tang of a million years of moist, dead earth. I felt something jerk violently next to me, then heard Lionel struggling, *"Fck-fck, get it off! Get it off!"* he shouted. He was swatting his head as if it were on fire. Clearing my eyes, I saw the walls around our bed were solid black and pulsing with flying insects. When he moved, they exploded.

Séverin leaped off the top bunk, screamed once, and ran out of the room flapping his arms. Lionel and I burst into the corridor, where the black swarms seemed to drip off the pale yellow lights. We buried our heads in our shirts and plowed through, feeling them snap between our fingers as we ran.

Outside, they swarmed even thicker around the lone fluorescent lamp of Kongolo station. A gang of fat geckos sat perched on the wall in the escaping light, snatching up the easy prey. The lamp was attached to the station pavilion, and beyond the light there was nothing—no candles, no torches, only the muffled voices of strange shadows. And somewhere in the outer darkness, the river hummed its savage music. Lionel turned to me, foreboding in his eyes, and said, "Well, mate, I believe we've arrived at the Gates of Hell."

Séverin smiled and popped him on the shoulder. "Welcome to Congo, bro."

Just then I heard a low moan, like a man crawling on his belly toward me in the dark. I spun around and heard it coming from a small building behind me. From a square hole in the wooden door, a hand came fingering the air. "Help me," the voice said. "Please help me. They've locked us up."

I shrieked a bit, then realized it was the station jail. The man inside the door said he'd been standing on the platform the day before, waiting for a freight train to arrive. But when the freight arrived, the police arrested many of the *clandestins* riding on top, and he'd been caught in the sweep. "They'll release me for fifteen hundred francs," the voice said. "Please, there are nine of us here."

Then someone emerged from the dark pavilion, another man. There'd been a terrible train accident a few kilometers away, he said. That same freight train, the one the prisoner had been waiting for, had left the station a few hours before and crashed nearby. Many people were riding on top. The station manager appeared and said it was the WFP train.

"The humanitarian train," said Lionel. "The one we were supposed to catch last week. That means—"

"Yeah," I said. "We would've been on the roof."

The carriages had disconnected from the locomotive as the train climbed a hill, sending everyone racing backward. The train was a runaway for nearly five kilometers before flipping over into the bush.

"There were people scattered all over the ground," the manager said. "We fear many are dead."

All I wanted to do was leave Kongolo. The place put the creep all over me. I then remembered I'd been there before, at that same station, back in August 2003. It was during the same trip as when I'd seen the trains in the Kalamie yard. At the time, the Rwandan-backed rebels who'd controlled the area had eased their grip following Rwanda's exit from Congo the year before. Fighting had mellowed and movement on the roads was slow, but finally possible. During that grace period, the WFP began a series of food deliveries by airplane into the region, and I'd tagged along. It was the first humanitarian mission in the region since the end of fighting, and many of the villages we visited that week were hanging to life, entire streets full of children with bowling-ball bellies and hair turned yellow from hunger. We'd flown into Kongolo our second day and I'd got out to walk around. The station, the jailhouse, all of it had been falling down then. Many families were living under the pavilion, children with ballooned bellies and peeling rashes running up and shooting me with finger pistols, holding the aim just a little too long. *This is misery,* I'd thought. *This is what real misery looks like.*

I knew the station had been renovated since then, and the people

I now saw were healthier and not as desperate-looking. But that feeling of dread still hung on the humidity. It was one of those places like Mbandaka, where you seemed to cross through an invisible door you could never find again. Beyond Kongolo you entered the wild.

The crew finally motioned for us to reboard the train for our journey back. I felt a rush of relief to be leaving. But seconds later, the idling locomotive sputtered and stopped. "Oh, no," someone said. And when the engineer started the engine back up, it sounded as if someone had tossed a handful of screws into a clothes dryer. *No—!* Quickly we all crowded around the sick diesel, staring into its guts with horror and anticipation. *"Toujours!"* someone shouted. *"Toujours! Toujours! Toujours!"*

We peered inside the locomotive's cabin and saw the engineer with a flashlight in his teeth, jerking out wires and fuses as if he were pulling weeds. The locomotive refused to start. The engineer then came out and said flatly, "Technical problems. Who knows when we can fix this," then disappeared back inside, unaware of the weight of his words.

As we walked back toward the station, defeated once again, I heard it like a clap of thunder, like a dead fish swinging down from heaven to slap my face. Somewhere under the pavilion, barely alive on the battery's last drop, a radio was singing "Another Day in Paradise."

"Hey, guys," Séverin shouted. "It's Phil Collins!"

And I knew then, without a doubt, we would never leave Kongolo.

The three of us huddled on a bench in the dark and waited for the sun to rise, and when it did, we saw the Congo River sparkling like a glass-topped canyon in front of us. Across the river to the east, the purple outline of the Mitumba Mountains rose above the jungle. Lone fishermen rowed past one by one in long pirogues, standing tall in the stern and stabbing teardrop paddles into the still current, their black silhouettes drifting silently on the pink.

Near the water's edge lay the rusted hulls of old steamers and passenger ferries, more relics from the great industrial age, now half-sunk and dead in the mud. And up the bank near the station I found something unexpected: the remains of the legendary Ocean Pacific.

During the war when nothing moved on the rails but soldiers and guns, the Rwandan rebels had attached a single red railcar to a Caterpillar tractor engine and used it to ferry troops and supplies between the towns of Kongolo and Niemba. In 2000, two local mechanics had taken over the railcar—by now known to all as the Ocean Pacific—and used it instead to save their people. They ferried salt, soap, oil, and essential food items between these two market towns, and like the *toleka* taximen in Bumba, they risked life and limb to keep the villages alive and the economy breathing.

For years I'd heard their story like legend, but never figured out what the name meant or what had become of the men and the train. I'd even asked around a few years before, hoping to maybe catch a ride, but no one knew where it had gone. Now here it was at my feet, the words OCEAN PACIFIQUE handwritten in white paint on the corner of the car. The engine itself was missing. All that remained was the boxcar alone in the yard, with grass and weeds growing through a hole in its belly.

As I stood there, I watched a woman lead her young son by the hand toward the river. They stopped at the water's edge, where the river beyond them was covered in a frost of mist. The mother turned loose of the boy's hand to fetch some water, and when she did, the boy staggered backward and held out his arms, grasping for balance. I then noticed his eyes were badly infected and swollen shut.

"He woke up this morning like this," she said, her voice taut with panic. "We've been waiting here for days on a train to Lubumbashi, but I don't even know when it's coming."

It would be a week or longer, I thought, when ours returned.

But I didn't know for sure so I said nothing. The mother then bent down, scooped water into her hand, and let it drip over the boy's eyes. As the water rolled down his face and soaked his shirt, his head tilted skyward and arms reached for the river. And as the boy stood in his own darkness and mimicked the motions of the blind, his mother covered her mouth and cried.

Back at the station, the crew informed us the engine problems were far more severe than expected. We'll have to bring another locomotive, they said, and in my head I heard the nightmarish echo of Pancha saying, "If anything happens . . . *that could take weeks.*"

Don't worry, the engineer said, the locomotive was close and would arrive this afternoon.

"Which locomotive is it," asked Lionel.

"The one that crashed," said the engineer.

The locomotive was sitting just a few kilometers away on the tracks, where it had finally reunited with its wayward carriages, several of which were lying in the bush. Three people had been killed, two of them children, and nine others badly wounded. But that wasn't enough to keep the locomotive from working another day. In the end, we'd catch that WFP train after all.

We decided to get a few hours of sleep and found a larger cabin this time with four beds and no bugs. I slept deeply and woke up in a daze, our sixth day on the rails, soaked in sweat as the train cooked in the rising sun. The smell of sewage rose from the tracks and danced in the heat, and I knew we couldn't stay there all day.

I remembered seeing a white Land Rover at the station earlier, one of the only vehicles I'd seen in town, and knew it belonged to the Catholic procure. We could go there, I thought, and they'd have to take us in. There we'd find showers, hot food, and maybe even a beer. We'd wait in comfort until the train rode again.

But on our way to the procure, we had a spectacular realization. We remembered there was a UN base in Kongolo. And look, there it was just down the road from the station, an old colonial mansion with that powder-blue flag flapping in the wind, and two white SUVs with antenna the size of surf rods. The options now seemed immense.

Lionel gasped with joy. "Mate, if there's a Bangladeshi in there, we're laughing!"

"Oh, yes," I said. "Parathas and jam, chicken and rice. Tea, coffee, and biscuits."

There were no Bangladeshis, we discovered, but there were equally hospitable Nepalese, Peruvian, Bosnian, and Kenyan military observers who welcomed us like brothers. "What in hell are you guys doing *here*?" they asked. And we told them about the train. Well, take a rest, they said. Would you like a cold soda? *Yeah!* Shower? *Yeah!* Stay for lunch? *Definitely!*

We spent a pleasant afternoon with the UN officers, who seemed happy just to see new faces. The men had been on tour for six months and seen little action, an easy hitch compared to military observers like Juan whom I'd met in Bunia during the siege. The Kongolo officers acted mostly as town cops but without guns, settling disputes and facilitating any gunboys who wanted to surrender their weapons and join the good guys.

That morning, a few of them had visited the local hospital to check on the victims of the derailment. "It's dreadful in there," said the captain, a Bosnian with a thick, meaty face and hands like raw hams. "Their injuries are horrible, and there's not one X-ray machine in the whole town. No medicines, nothing." They discussed putting them aboard our train and sending them to Kalemie, then decided it posed a greater danger than the hospital itself.

The Peruvian had sent one of the servants into the market for some chickens for lunch, and just as we were about to feast, we heard a train whistle blow long and loud. It was our signal to leave, so we bid our UN pals good-bye and ran back to the station, where the cursed locomotive was rolling into the yard.

Pancha hurried us aboard a third-class compartment, saying,

"You guys barely made it." Then we sat another two hours. The splintered windows were missing their glass, and the tin walls and roof were covered in rust-eaten holes. I dozed in the heat and woke up to the river passing by as our train left the yard.

About ten minutes outside town, we passed the scene of the derailment. Luggage and clothing were scattered in the trees as if tossed by a cyclone. Several carriages were tipped into the high grass, while others stood upright with mountains of cargo still stacked on the roof. The three of us looked at each other in a way that said, *We would've died.*

And then, as if the ghosts themselves had appeared and winked at him from the wreckage, the driver punched the gas and the crazy train rocketed toward Kabalo atop the worst tracks in Congo. The carriage pitched and tipped as we sped faster and faster, and grown men bowed their heads and prayed. The scrub forest had grown too close to the track and now reached over both sides of the rails. As the train cut a path through the brambles, branches and tall grass snapped in the windows and sent clouds of pollen and dust swirling inside. I closed my eyes, and when I opened them again, I saw thick smoke filling the car just before we blasted through a brush fire that had jumped the tracks. *Whoosh!* And right as we exited the flames, rain started pouring through the windows.

We arrived back to Kabalo to find the station in a rage. "Where have you been?" people screamed, and I realized they knew nothing about the problems in Kongolo.

"We broke down," Pancha said.

"Toujours!"

The officials sent both locomotives to the station depot to be serviced, which took five more hours. I sat on the ground and watched the *animateur* pace the length of the platform, his eyes now cold as marble. He still wore the stained tank top and flip-flops and now held both the microphone and speaker in his arms. His assistant was nowhere to be seen. He paced the platform in the fading sun and locked his eyes on each official who passed, then at some chosen moment unleashed his torrent of rage. *"What's taking so long?"* he began, increasing his pace and breathing heavily, as if all that frustration would kill him if he didn't get it off. *"Why are we still here? Why won't SOMEONE ANSWER ME?"*

The shop boy had become a magpie for the masses, the voice of the people. The rage fit him well.

"These clients pay way too much to be treated this way! We're staying way too long in these stations. Why are we still in this station? I can't take it anymore! Hurry! Hurry!"

As I walked down the length of the train toward the engine, I saw that the passengers and cargo from the derailed WFP train had been transported to the *Rénové* for the journey to Kalemie. Luggage and cargo now spilled out the doors and was stacked against the windows. The corridor in the first-class compartment squawked with chickens tethered at the feet, and a pig stared me down from the doorway of second class. As I reached the front of the train, I saw dozens of *clandestins* perched on the roofs amid their grimy piles of luggage. I shone my light down the tracks and saw dozens more standing in the tall grass, wrapped in blankets with bundles on their heads, waiting to pounce on the train once it rolled out of the station.

The locomotive finally emerged from the depot and I understood what had taken so long. Every empty space in the diesel had been stuffed with merchandise—sacks of maize, salt, dried fish, everything that wouldn't fit inside the overstuffed carriages. Even the engineer's room was stacked to the ceiling with grain, so full the driver was pinned against his instrument panel.

Lionel yelled up to the engineer, something about the overloading, the *clandestins*, everything. The engineer shot him a look. "What do you expect us to do, *monsieur*?" he said. "Do you have a better idea? The last train to Kalemie was a month ago, and who knows when the next one will be."

I stood there taking in all that chaos—all the frayed nerves and strange energy of yesterday's crash still clinging to the clothes of those who'd survived it; the pigs and chickens; the *animateur* still screaming, *"People are shitting directly on the tracks now! Move this train before it gets any worse!"* Standing there before this scene, it was as if the *Rénové* weren't even a train anymore, but some living animal born of this very soil, now in a desperate struggle to either adapt or die.

All those dreams of the luxury express coasting atop the ashes, a harbinger of better times to come, all those dreams now seemed to fade. It had been such a tall order for the times. The *Rénové* had rolled out with such noble intentions, too, with men like Andre and Pancha trying so hard to make the experience real, all of them trying to resurrect some of that big-hearted pride and glory from days long gone. But in the end, not even the express train could outpace the avalanche of ruin. In the end, the *Rénové* became just another battered part in the vast faulty machine, a barge on wheels, just an ordinary train rolling through Congo.

But none of that seemed important now. Sure, it would've been cool to race through the old war zones eating steak with cold beer, and I might've let myself put that feather in my hat. But in the end, it didn't matter. In the end the *Rénové* still moved forward. In the end, it still took all those people home.

It rolled slowly out of Kabalo with a long, brassy whistle, then leaped into the darkness, as if to chase down all the time we'd lost. Faster on the straightaway, chewing down every second, so fast I gripped the table to keep from falling off the bed. Faster, as the driver pushed the limits of train and track, all that anxious energy tunneling under the floors and through the cars and pressing on his back like the tall stacks of maize, all the collective weight of hopes and wishes too strong a force to let him slow down.

Faster, so fast I began to lift off the bed from the sheer momentum. Faster, as we hit the curves with terror speed, tossing water buckets against the walls and sending a tidal wave down the corridor. (Somewhere inside a dark compartment, the *animateur* smiled.) Faster, listening for the dreaded snap of carriages leaving the loco, that fade of the whistle as we slid backward and down. Faster, as Nigerian psychedelic blasted loud on the speakers, Ofo the Black Company telling us, "Love is you, love is me." Faster, as the forest gave way to the dark plains of Tanganyika, the crunching guitar galloping with the blur of voices in villages racing by, or were they the screams of *clandestins* clinging to the roof? How on earth, I wondered, were they surviving this furious dash to the lake? Faster into the night we sped, hell-for-leather, the wheels grating like a kettle about to blow, until we reached that speed that would wash away all memories of ever having waited.

I woke to the same velocity churning under my bones and Séverin screaming, "Get up, look!" I shot upright, still fully clothed, the bed still made, and threw myself against the window, too dazed to understand what I was supposed to be seeing. "The Niemba Bridge!" he said. "There!" And sure enough, there it was, the little bridge that had reconnected Congo to the lake and its neighbors in the east. I stuck my head out the window just as we passed over the seemingly inconsequential span that had been repaired, nothing but a small patch of fresh tar and steel to distinguish it from the rest. That was it, that's all it took. One million dollars, and because of it, the train rumbled over the river and the route to Kalemie was open.

An hour later we hit the Mitumba hills, green as a golf course and iridescent in the morning mist. We crawled up the hills and raced down, winding along the course of the narrow Lukuga River. We passed villages buried behind the reeds, tossing *copo* bottles out the windows for the children to use as toys. In every village we passed, and in company towns the same, crowds of people rushed out to greet us as if heaven had split apart and laid down this train. The *Rénové* then let out a long-winded blast of the whistle, the longest and hardest yet, as if reaching up to punch the sky. Looking out the window I could see the blue, shimmering waters of Lake Tanganyika in the distance.

A minute later, we pulled into the Kalemie station.

Crowds were waiting to greet us on the platform. Women held up their arms as if to catch the train as it rolled to a stop, their faces igniting when they saw their loved ones in the windows. They shouted, *"Karibu Kalemie! Umeshafika!"* Welcome to Kalemie, you finally arrived! And ran to the doors.

All down the platform people were hugging their loved ones, looking around, then around again, as if to confirm they'd actually made it home. I rushed down the platform and looked for Fatuma and Jeanne, not wanting to miss them before they left to find their kids. I found them both near the customs office, where they waited to clear their belongings. Jeanne was planning to stay in town a week to gather some things, then set out across the lake, into Tanzania to search the villages for her kids. I wished her good luck and said good-bye.

Fatuma and her husband scanned the crowd outside the gates for any signs of family, and not seeing them, grabbed their things and went to find a taxi. They couldn't wait. "I'm so full of joy," she said, wiping a few tears that streamed down her cheek. "Did you know they held funerals for me and my husband? My children thought we were dead. And now here we are. I can't believe I'm standing here."

"You made it," I said, and hugged her good-bye.

As I turned away from Fatuma, two young girls raced past and threw their arms around a tall, gray-headed man behind me. The old man hadn't seen them coming, and the second those arms touched his body, his cheeks puffed once with air and he let forth a buckling sob. The girls pressed their heads against his chest, weeping and clutching him tightly, as if he were a ghost ready to spirit himself away. The whole scene almost dropped me to my knees.

The old man was named Albert Janga, a railroad employee who'd been working in Zambia when the war had started. He'd been stuck in the south ever since. His two girls, Gentille and Elena, were only babies when he left. "I haven't seen these girls in so long," he said, fighting to speak. "I could feel them here, even when I didn't see them. I could feel them near me."

The girls closed their eyes and squeezed their father. They held on and wept, and as their tears fell to the cobblestones below, they repeated over again this one thing: "You're home, you're home, you're home."

EPILOGUE

Three months later in September, in Providence, Rhode Island, where Ann Marie and I had moved the previous summer, I got an incredible piece of news. The Chinese government had announced a remarkable plan to refurbish thirty-two hundred kilometers of railway in Congo, and to construct a highway that would span the nation nearly top to bottom. In addition, they would build 31 hospitals, 145 clinics, 2 universities, and 5,000 government housing units across the country. The $5 billion loan for the project would be repaid in mining concessions, and everything, they vowed, would be completed in under three years. It was a project Leopold, Belgium, and Mobutu couldn't have imagined doing in over a century.

A new railway would connect Katanga's mines directly to the Atlantic Ocean by adding seven hundred kilometers of missing track between Ilebo and Kinshasa. That project had been part of Belgium's Ten-Year Plan, drafted in 1952 for the long-term development of the colony, but was abandoned at independence. The existing track from Lubumbashi to Ilebo—almost a century old—would be completely overhauled, and new locomotives and railcars would be purchased. The proposed thirty-four hundred kilometers of new road would include a fifteen-hundred-kilometer highway that would barrel through the jungle, connecting Kisangani to the Zambian border in the south.

The Chinese plan for Congo would rival some of the greatest public works projects in the world, and the new road and railway alone had the potential to turn the entire economy around, connect markets, reunite families, and create jobs—even while China settled in over the mines and satisfied its growing appetite. It would certainly move some of that maize, along with the countless people who were still stranded and waiting to go home.

Around this time, Séverin said good-bye to his family in Kinshasa and boarded a flight to Belgium. He arrived in Liège, where he moved into a small apartment near the university and began his degree in education and computer science. He'd never been out of Congo, and when I called him on the phone, he sounded a bit overwhelmed. "The sofa in my room," he said. "Do you know it also folds into a bed? And where I live, there are more than forty bridges! And the highways, wow. I've now seen the true world."

Seeing the true world, and looking down at Congo from its high vantage, had filled in many of those missing pieces in his mind. "I feel ashamed to see how we're so behind," he said. "And I see now how much of their wealth came from our country. The young people here don't even know what happened in Congo. All they seem concerned about is maximum pleasure." But Séverin was having no trouble adapting: soon after arriving in Liège, he'd caught the attention of a cute Italian exchange student, and as we spoke on the phone, she was on her way over.

In Ituri, Cobra Matata finally came down from Tchei and reported to Kinshasa in October. Two other Lendu leaders joined him, men who'd ordered the deaths of hundreds of civilians and reaped terror across the province for nearly a decade. One of them was Mathieu Ngudjolo, who'd led the May 2003 attack on Bunia. Like previous warlords who'd surrendered to the government, the three men were given rooms at the Grand Hotel, welcomed into the national army, and awarded the rank of colonel.

However, the surrender brought a much needed respite in Ituri, and the hills remained quiet throughout the fall. And with nothing happening between the gunboys and blue helmets, Johnny was transferred to MONUC headquarters in Bunia, where he spent much of his day sitting in an office. He'd gotten married a few months before, but his fiancée's father had insisted on a big religious wedding, so they'd eloped instead. He was lying in bed the night I called him, his wife asleep beside him. "She's putting me to work ever since I've been home," he said, laughing. "You were right, man. My fun is over."

With the hills quiet around Bunia, Pastor Marrion renewed his zeal to save the lost and broken. He set off down those roads he'd journeyed all his life, this time recruiting souls for a massive, healing revival, something he called the Ituri Gospel Crusade. "God has given me a new vision for Ituri and Congo," he said. "My chief, I was with Pygmies last weekend and God's *power* started moving *beyond* my expectations!"

In August, Lionel and Nathalie left Kinshasa and moved to Goma, where Nathalie took a new position with Save the Children. They arrived just as Congo's army launched a major offensive against rebel leader Laurent Nkunda in the hills above town, resulting in the heaviest fighting since the 1998 war. The heavy shelling emptied villages and towns across two provinces, and by early December the UN estimated nearly eight hundred thousand were displaced or living in camps across North Kivu. Doctors were treating hundreds of cases of cholera, and diarrhea and starvation were taking their usual toll. Cease-fires came and went, and the battles continued into the winter. The last I spoke with Lionel, his voice was tight and shaky and he was headed out the door. "Look, mate, got to run," he said. "It's really kicking off." I told him to take care of himself and be safe, but by then, he was already gone.

The crush and stress of working in Congo had finally chiseled away on Dave Lewis. In early November 2006, he'd gotten pinned down under heavy rocket and mortar fire between Kabila's and

Bemba's men, then found himself diving into a ditch two weeks later when it happened again. By the end of the month, he told his editors he was done. He flew out in mid-December, kicked around New Zealand for a few weeks, then resettled in Dakar. There he could regain perspective and watch Congo from afar, pop back every couple months for the longer view, but always have a ticket out. The last I heard he was trudging through Guinea-Bissau working on a documentary about cocaine smugglers, and happy for the fresh soil under his boots.

As for me, I was left with all these stories of the past four years just waiting to be sent home. I'd collected them from all those dreadful places, carried them with me over river and forest, through town and village, through a marriage and into our home. I'd memorized each one, and together they'd cut the road that now defined my life. So I gathered them up for one last hurrah, and led them down that path to the dark place at the end. And there on the trail sat the box I'd opened so long ago. I folded each story into the collective memory and placed them down inside, then closed the lid. And without looking behind me, I walked off into the trees.

ACKNOWLEDGMENTS

Special thanks goes to Kiley Lambert, the first person to read these stories and help shape them in their raw and nascent form, and Roger Hodge at *Harper's*, who first gave them a home. Anneke Van Woudenberg at Human Rights Watch, one of the foremost experts on the Congo conflict, graciously read over much of this material and offered invaluable advice, and to her I'm grateful. Thanks to Susan Linnee, Ellen Knickmeyer, and Todd Pitman of (and formerly of) the Associated Press, all great bosses and friends alike. Also, thanks to my agent Heather Schroder at International Creative Management and to my editors Colin Dickerman and Nick Trautwein at Bloomsbury, whose thoughtful and poignant insight into the work made it twice the read, and me a better writer. And most of all, thanks to the many proud people of Congo who offered their hospitality, friendship, and told me their stories, mainly with hopes that such tragedy would never be repeated again. This book is for them.

A NOTE ON SOURCES

Most of what appears in the book came from my own reporting and the countless interviews I've conducted with residents and officials over the past four years. To fill the gaps in history, I relied on a variety of sources. Some of the background material on Ituri came from several reports written by human rights groups over the past decade. The International Crisis Group's (ICG; www.crisisgroup.org) "Scramble for the Congo: Anatomy of an Ugly War," published in 2000, gives an extensive breakdown of the conflict and its players. And two reports by Human Rights Watch (HRW; www.hrw.org) are must-reads for anyone interested in the link between minerals and war: "Ituri: Covered in Blood" (2003) and "The Curse of Gold" (2005). I also took material about the pillaging of resources from *The African Stakes of the Congo War*, edited by John F. Clark (Palgrave Macmillan, 2002).

For the general history on Congo, I drew mainly on *In the Footsteps of Mr. Kurtz: Living on the Brink of Disaster in Mobutu's Congo* by Michela Wrong (Fourth Estate, 2000), a vivid, sharply written journey through the last days of Mobutu; *King Leopold's Ghost* by Adam Hochschild (Houghton Mifflin, 1998) is the definitive account of the rubber atrocities and gives a startling, even cinematic view into Leopold's lust for power; and Tim Jeal's biography *Stanley: The Impossible Life of Africa's Greatest Explorer* (Yale University Press, 2007) offers the most authoritative, reliable rendering thus far of Stanley's life and travels. Stanley's own accounts of his trans-African journey, *Through the Dark Continent: Volumes One and Two* (Harper & Brothers, 1878), were somewhat exaggerated for his readers, as Jeal demonstrates, but a spellbinding read nonetheless. I also drew from Joseph Conrad's *Congo Diary* (Doubleday, 1978); Peter Forbath's excellent *The River Congo* (Harper & Row, 1977); Robert B. Edgerton's *The Troubled Heart of Africa: A History of the Congo* (St. Martin's Press, 2002); *The Irish Army in the Congo, 1960–1964: The Far Battalions* edited by David O'Donoghue (Irish Academic Press, 2005); *Rebels, Mercenaries, and Dividends: The Katanga Story* by Smith Hempstone (Frederick A. Praeger, Ltd., 1962), and my trusty field book, *Traveler's Guide to the Belgian Congo and Ruanda-Urundi* (Tourist Bureau for the Belgian Congo and Ruanda-Urundi, 1951).

Further background on Mobutu and Kabila's government came from news reports and ICG's 2006 report "Escaping the Conflict Trap: Promoting Good Governance in Congo" and HRW's "Elections in Sight: Don't Rock the Boat?" (2005). Information about mining and logging came from interviews, news reports, and two recent studies: Greenpeace's 2007 report on the timber trade, "Carving Up the Congo" (www.greenpeace.org), and Global Witness' report on the state of the mining sector, "Digging in Corruption," published in 2006 (www.globalwitness.org).

Background on the rail networks came from interviews, news reports, and a beautiful treasure I picked up while in Lubumbashi: the two-volume *Le Rail au Congo Belge* (G. Blanchart & Cie, 1993 and 1999). Other information came from various reports: "Africa's Strategic Minerals During the Second World War" by Raymond Dumett (*The Journal of African History* 26, no. 4 [1985]) and "The Port of Lobito and the Benguela Railway" by William A. Hance and Irene S. Van Dongen (*Geographical Review* 46, no. 4 [1956]).

A NOTE ON THE AUTHOR

Bryan Mealer was born in Odessa, Texas, and spent his childhood in West Texas and San Antonio. He graduated from the University of Texas at Austin and spent time as a city reporter for the *Austin Chronicle*, then as an assistant editor at *Esquire* in New York City before moving to Nairobi, Kenya, to become a freelance reporter. He later was the Associated Press staff correspondent in Kinshasa, Congo. He is a regular contributor to *Harper's* magazine and several other publications.

(History up to 1960's)

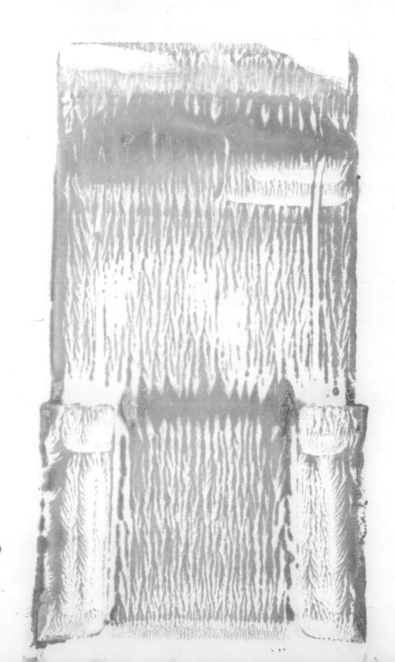

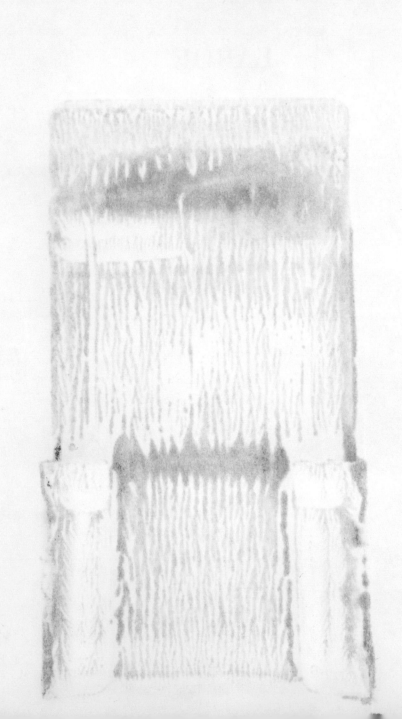

XXX

LABOR

IN AMERICA

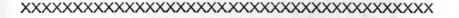

XXXXXXXXXXXXXXXXXXXXXXXXXXXXXXXXXXXXXXXXX

LABOR
IN AMERICA

A History

THIRD EDITION

FOSTER RHEA DULLES

THOMAS Y. CROWELL COMPANY
NEW YORK · ESTABLISHED 1834

PREFACE

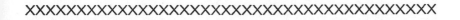

IN THE FIRST EDITION of this book, published in 1949, I suggested in my preface that organized labor, at that time a force of some fifteen million wage earners, was bound to exercise a vital influence on the future economic and political development of the nation. The record of succeeding years has certainly borne out this not very daring prediction. Labor has played a tremendously important role in helping to raise the standard of living for wage earners in the United States; today it is higher than industrial workers have ever before enjoyed in this or any other country. Yet at the same time organized labor has had to face in recent years new problems and new challenges in a society that has in many ways changed more rapidly since World War II than in any comparable span of time.

The unions have found it difficult not only to maintain their anticipated rate of growth but in many instances to prevent a persistent erosion in their membership. They have not been entirely successful in adapting unionism to the structural changes in the economy or in meeting through collective bargaining the problem of job displacement consequent upon technological advance and automation. No satisfactory answer has been found to the problem of industry-wide strikes which may threaten the entire economy as labor and management fight their private wars. These are today's problems—vital to organized labor and vital to the entire country.

It is not the purpose of this book, however, to examine the present for itself but rather to place it in historical perspective. The present, of course, can never be understood without some knowledge of the past and this fact is particularly true of the labor movement in the United States. The long, hard-fought, and on occasion, bloody struggle of the unions to win recognition of their rights—to organize, bargain collectively, and strike—provides a background of labor history that still directly affects all industrial relations.

This background, then, is the stuff of which this book is made. It seeks to give a general and comprehensive account of the rise of American labor since colonial days. The emphasis throughout has been placed on the national organization—the National Labor Union, the Knights of Labor, the A.F. of L., the C.I.O., and, more recently, the merged A.F.L.-C.I.O. It is impossible to cover in a single volume every phase of labor activity. The history of individual unions, the role of women and minority groups in labor organizations, the growth of workers' education and union welfare activities, the relationship of the American labor movement to that in other countries, and other specialized topics have had to be subordinated to the general record.

In this third revision I have left virtually unchanged the chapters dealing with the course of labor history through the dramatic events of the 1930's that led to passage of the National Labor Relations Act and the rise of the C.I.O. The subsequent chapters on the war and postwar years have been reorganized, rewritten, and brought up to date. It has proved to be very difficult to thread one's way through the complicated maze of developing labor relations in the 1950's and early 1960's. I have tried to do so with such objectivity and perspective as the immediacy of these recent developments may allow. Again I would stress that any thorough economic or political analysis of labor's current position is quite beyond the province of this book; it remains a history of labor in America over nearly two centuries of time.

The bibliographical notes have been entirely recast. They were originally designed to indicate the major sources on which the book was based and to give some measure of my debt to earlier writings on labor history. I would once more like to express my appreciation for the help derived from such sources. In rearranging the bibliography as suggestions for further reading, I have included all the basic material noted in both the original and previously revised editions, drawn heavily on the great mass of more recent literature, and tried to provide what is at once a highly selected list of readings and yet one which adequately covers the subject.

January, 1966   F.R.D.

CONTENTS

I: COLONIAL AMERICA

THE PRINCIPAL SOURCES of labor in colonial America were indentured servants and slaves. Free workers were a small minority in the seventeenth and eighteenth centuries. As the little towns scattered along the Atlantic seaboard gradually grew and prospered, however, mechanics and artisans who had either come directly from the Old World or risen out of the ranks of bound labor to build their own lives in freedom became of increasing importance. There were carpenters and masons; shipwrights and sailmakers; tanners, weavers, shoemakers and tailors, smiths, coopers, glaziers, printers.

The skilled craftsmen among these workers at first plied their trades independently, but as the centers of population grew, master workmen set up small retail shops and employed journeymen and apprentices to work for them for wages. By the close of the eighteenth century, these journeymen were beginning to form local trade societies—the genesis of the first unions and of what was to become in time the organized labor movement.

The simple economic pattern of those distant days provides no real basis for comparisons with the complex industrial scene of the twentieth century. The status of a small handful of independent artisans and mechanics does not have any valid relation to that of the huge mass of industrial workers in our modern society. The occasional and sporadic instances of labor protests in the colonial period could hardly be further removed from the nationwide strikes which in recent years have halted production in the coal mining, steel fabrication and automobile manufacture on which our closely knit economy is so wholly dependent. Nevertheless certain underlying conditions were operative in colonial days that were strongly to influence the whole course of American labor.

A constant scarcity of workers served to maintain wage rates well above European levels in the seventeenth and eighteenth centuries;

the opportunities for advancement in the New World nullified the hard and fast class lines that were the feudal heritage of the Old World, and the frontier generally fostered a spirit of sturdy individualism. While industrial revolution was to transform completely the old economic order, these basic factors in the American way of life, affecting not only labor but all the other elements in our society, were to endure. They served to bring the workers into the broad current of democratic advance that has characterized our history and played an important part in giving to the organized labor movement in America its distinctive and unique character.

The early settlers had no more than landed in Virginia and Massachusetts than they realized the imperative need for workers in the forest wilderness that was America. In both the first voyage to Jamestown and three succeeding expeditions, the Virginia Company had sent over to the New World a motley band of adventurers, soldiers and gentlemen. In growing despair of establishing a stable colony out of such unsatisfactory material, Captain John Smith finally entered a violent protest. "When you send again," he wrote home emphatically, "I entreat you rather send but thirty carpenters, husbandmen, gardeners, fishermen, masons, and diggers of trees' roots, well provided, than a thousand such as we have."

Plymouth fared better. Artisans, craftsmen and other laborers largely made up the little band of Pilgrims and the Bishop of London rudely characterized even their leaders as "guides fit for them, cobblers, tailors, feltmakers, and such-like trash." The Puritan settlers of Massachusetts Bay in 1630 also had a majority of artisans and tillers of the soil. But in spite of this advantage, the founders of New England soon felt, as had those of Virginia, the scarcity of persons content with performing the humble tasks of society. Governor Winthrop of Massachusetts wrote despairingly in 1640 of the difficulty of keeping wage earners on the job. They were constantly moving on to frontier communities where pay was higher or else taking up land to become independent farmers. Cotton Mather made it "an Article of special Supplication before the Lord, that he would send a good servant. . . ."

While tillers of the soil and "diggers of trees' roots" were a first and primary consideration in these early days of settlement, the demand for skilled workers rapidly mounted. The colonists were perforce compelled to become carpenters and masons, weavers and shoemakers, whatever their background, but both on southern plantations and in New England towns, trained artisans and mechanics were always needed.

The ways in which the labor problem was met varied greatly in different parts of America. The circumstances of early settlement and natural environment led New England to rely largely on free workers. The south was ultimately to fall back almost wholly on Negro slaves. In the majority of colonies during the seventeenth century, and continuing on through the eighteenth in the middle colonies, the bulk of the labor force was recruited from indentured servants. It has been estimated, indeed, that at least half, and probably more, of all the colonists who came to the New World arrived under some form of indenture and took their place as wholly free citizens only after working out their terms of contract.

There were three sources for such bound labor: men, women and children whose articles of indenture were signed before leaving the Old World; the redemptioners, or so-called free-willers, who agreed to reimburse their passage money by selling their labor after landing in the colonies, and convicts sentenced to transportation to America. Once in the colonies, these various groups coalesced into the general class of bound servants, working without wages and wholly under their masters' control for a set term of years.

So great was the demand for labor that a brisk trade developed in recruiting workers. Agents of the colonial planters and of British merchants scoured the countryside and towns of England, and somewhat later made their way to the continent, especially the war devastated areas of the Rhineland, to cry abroad the advantages of emigrating to America. They distributed handbills at country fairs extravagantly describing the wonders of this new land where food was said to drop into the mouths of the fortunate inhabitants and every man had the opportunity to own his own land. The promises held forth were often so glowing and enthusiastic that the ignorant and the credulous gladly signed articles of indenture with little realization of the possible hardships of the life upon which they were entering. The "crimps" who worked the English countryside, and so-called "newlanders" operating on the continent, did not hesitate at fraud and chicanery.

Thousands of persons were "spirited" out of England under these circumstances, and far from trying to prevent such practices the local authorities often encouraged them. The common belief that England was over-populated led them to approve heartily of the overseas transportation of paupers and vagabonds, the generally shiftless, who might otherwise become a burden upon the community. Indeed, magistrates sometimes had such persons rounded up and given the choice between emigration and imprisonment. It was also found to be an easy way to take care of orphans and other minors who had no means of support: the term "kidnaping" had its origin in this harsh mode of peopling the colonies.

In 1619 the Common Council of London "appointed one hundred Children out of the swarms that swarme in the place, to be sent to Virginia to be bound as apprentices for certain yeares." The Privy Council inquired into this matter, and after commending the authorities "for redeeminge so many poore Soules from misery and ruyne," authorized the Virginia Company to "imprison, punish and dispose of any of those children upon any disorder by them committed, as cause shall require; and so to Shipp them out for Virginia, with as much expedition as may stand for convenience."

Some forty years later, the Privy Council appears to have become aroused over the abuse of this practice by the Virginia Company. Two ships lying off Gravesend were discovered to have aboard both children and other servants "deceived and inticed away Cryinge and Mourning for Redemption from their Slavery." It was ordered that all those detained against their will—"a thinge so barbarous and inhumane, that Nature itself much more Christians cannot but abhor it"—should be at once released.

Under these circumstances the line between voluntary and involuntary transportation—especially when it involved the ignorant poor and young children—was very hard to draw. There were undoubtedly many bound servants in the colonies who might have echoed the pathetic lament of the young girl described in the "Sot-Weed Factor, or, a Voyage to Maryland," a tract published in London in 1708:

> In better Times e'er to this Land
> I was unhappily Trapann'd;
> Perchance as well I did appear,

As any Lord or Lady here,
Not then a slave for twice two Year
My clothes were fashionably new,
Nor were my Shifts of Linnen Blue;
But things are changed, now at the Hoe
I daily work, and Barefoot go,
In weeding Corn or feeding Swine,
I spend my melancholy Time.
Kidnap'd and Fool'd, I thither fled,
To shun a hated Nuptial Bed,
And to my cost already find
Worse plagues than those I left behind.

As time went on the prison and the gaol contributed an increasing number of emigrants who crossed the Atlantic as "His Majesty's Seven-Year Passengers." They were at first largely made up of "rogues, vagabonds and sturdy beggars" who had proved "incorrigible," but during the eighteenth century more serious offenses were added to the list for which transportation overseas was meted out. The pre-revolutionary roster of such immigrants in one Maryland county, adding up to 655 persons and including 111 women, embraced a wide range of crimes—murder, rape, highway robbery, horse-stealing and grand larceny. Among the women, there were many whom contemporary accounts succinctly described as "lewd."

The colonies came to resent bitterly this influx of the refuse from English prisons—"abundance of them do great Mischiefs. . . . and spoil servants, that were before very good"—and they found it increasingly difficult to control them. But in spite of their protests, the practice was continued, and in all some fifty thousand convicts are believed to have been transported, largely to the middle colonies. In Maryland, which seems to have been a favored dumping ground, they made up the bulk of indentured servants throughout the eighteenth century.

"Our Mother knows what is best for us," a contributor to the *Pennsylvania Gazette* ironically observed in 1751. "What is a little House-breaking, Shoplifting, or Highway-robbing; what is a son now and then corrupted and hanged, a Daughter debauched, or Pox'd, a wife stabbed, a Husband's throat cut, or a child's brains beat out with an Axe, compared with this 'Improvement and Well peopling of the Colonies?'" Benjamin Franklin bitterly declared that the policy of "emptying their jails into our settlements is an insult and contempt the cruellest, that ever one people offered another." Its consequences were reflected, from quite a different point of view, in Dr. Samuel Johnson's famous remark on Americans: "Sir, they are a race of convicts, and ought to be content with anything we allow them short of hanging."

Whether convicts, vagabonds, children "spirited" from the countryside, or redemptioners, both voluntary and involuntary emigrants to the New World experienced discomforts and suffering on their voyage across the Atlantic that paralleled the cruel hardships undergone by Negro slaves on the notorious Middle Passage. They were indiscriminately herded aboard the "white guineamen," often as many as three hundred passengers on little vessels of not more than two hundred tons burden—overcrowded, unsanitary, with insufficient provisions. Typhus and other diseases invariably took a terrible toll of lives. The mortality rate was sometimes as high as fifty per cent, and young children seldom survived the horrors of a voyage which might last anywhere from seven to twelve weeks.

"During the voyage," reads one account of the experiences of redemptioners recruited from the German Palatinate, "there is on board these ships terrible misery, stench, fumes, horror, vomiting, many kinds of seasickness, fever, dysentery, headache, heat, constipation, boils, scurvy, cancer, mouth rot, and the like, all of which come from old and sharply-salted food and meat, also from the very bad and foul water, so that many die miserable. . . . Add to this want of provisions, hunger, thirst, frost, heat, dampness, anxiety, want, afflictions, and lamentations, together with other trouble, as e. g., the lice abound so frightfully, especially on sick people, that they can be scraped off the body. The misery reaches a climax when a gale rages for two or three nights so that everyone believes that the ship will go to the bottom with all human beings on board. In such a visitation the people cry and pray most piteously."

Nor did the hardships of the immigrants necessarily end when port was finally reached. Those for whom contracts had already been arranged, were handed over to their unknown masters. If the redemptioners did not immediately find employment themselves, they were put up for sale by the ship captains or merchants to whom they owed their passage money. Families were often separated under these circumstances when wives and offspring were auctioned off to the highest bidder. The terms of servitude varied with age and might run from one to seven years. More generally, those over twenty without specific articles of indenture were bound out for four years "according to the custom of the country."

The colonial newspapers often carried notices of prospective sales. On March 28, 1771, the following announcement appeared in the *Virginia Gazette:*

> Just arrived at Leedstown, the Ship Justitia,
>   with about one Hundred Healthy Servants.
>
> Men, Women and Boys, among which are many
> Tradespeople—viz. Blacksmiths, Shoemakers,
> Tailors, House Carpenters and Joiners, a
> Cooper, several Silversmiths, Weavers,
> A Jeweler, and many others. The Sale will
> commence on Tuesday, the 2nd. of April, at
> Leeds Town on Rappahannock River. A
> reasonable Credit will be allowed, giving
> Bond with Approved Security to
>   Thomas Hodge

If the sales were not concluded at the port of entry, groups of the redemptioners were taken back country by "soul drivers" who herded them along the way "like cattle to a Smithfield market" and then put them up for auction at public fairs.

The importation of servants was highly profitable. A fifty acre headright was granted the planter in some of the colonies for each immigrant, and there was always the sale of the indenture. In the case of sturdy farm hands and particularly skilled artisans, prices might run to high figures. William Byrd reported to his agent in Rotterdam, in 1739, that he was in a good position to handle heavy shipments. "I know not how long the Palatines are sold for who do not pay passage to Philadelphia," he wrote, "but here they are sold for Four years and fetch from 6 to 9 pounds and perhaps good Tradesmen may go for Ten. If these prices would answer, I am pretty Confident I could dispose of two Shiploads every year. . . ."

The treatment accorded bound servants varied a great deal. In John Hammond's seventeenth century account, "Leah and Rachel, or, the Two Fruitfull Sisters Virginia and Mary-land," their labor was said to be "not so hard nor of such continuance as Husbandmen, nor Handecraftmen are kept at in England." The hours of work were reported as those between the rising and setting sun, but with five hours off in the heat of the day during the summer, Saturday half holidays and "the Sabbath spent in good exercises." George Alsop, himself an indentured servant, wrote home in 1659 almost glowing accounts of life in Maryland. "The servants of this province, which are stigmatiz'd for Slaves by the clappermouth jaws of the vulgar in England," he declared, "live more like Freemen than the most Mechanical Apprentices in London, wanting for nothing that is convenient and necessary."

Other accounts, however, give a harsher picture of general conditions. While colonial laws called upon masters to provide their servants with adequate food, lodging and clothing, there were many instances where the diet was as meager as the labor was exhausting. Moreover, the servants were rigidly confined to the immediate vicinity of the place where they were employed, tavern keepers were not allowed to entertain them or sell them liquor, their terms of service might be extended for a long list of minor offenses, and they were subject to whippings and other corporal punishment by their masters for disobedience or laziness. Servant girls could be held in longer bondage because of bastardy, and their masters were sometimes not above conspiring to this end. "Late experiments shew," read one report, "that some dissolute masters have gotten their maides with child, and yet claim the benefit of their services."

The indentured servants were recognized as fellow Christians and were entitled to their day in court—in these respects, at least, their status being quite different from that of Negro slaves. But their masters' quasi-proprietary rights naturally made it extremely difficult for them to secure redress for any injuries or indignities. While humane masters undoubtedly treated their servants well, it is not difficult to believe the report that they were often subjected to "as hard and servile labor as the basest Fellow that was brought out of Newgate."

Court records are concerned with instances of willful ill-treatment and are revealing if not typical. A certain Mistress Ward whipped her maidservant on the back so severely, with the added pleasantry of putting salt in the wounds, that the girl shortly died. On the finding of a jury that such action was "unreasonable and unchristianlike," Mistress Ward was fined 300 pounds of tobacco. In another case, Mistress Mourning Bray defiantly told the court that under no circumstances would she allow her servants to "go to play or be Idle" and the unlucky complainant was stripped and given thirty lashes. A third trial resulted more favorably for another maidservant. She was discharged from the further employ of a master who had climaxed frequent beatings by hitting her over the head with a three-legged stool when he found her reading a book on Sunday morning. "Youe disembling Jade," the court records report him as having shouted, "what doe youe doe with a booke in your hand?"

One sorely beset servant took his own revenge. According to his story, he had "an ill-tongued Mistriss; who would not only rail, swear and curse at me within doors, whenever I came into the house casting on me continually biting Taunts and bitter Flouts, but like a live Ghost would impertinently haunt me, when I was quiet in the Ground at work." Driven to distraction, he one day seized an axe and murdered not only his ill-tongued mistress but also his master and a maidservant.

Advertisements often appeared in the colonial newspapers for runaway servants. One such notice referred to an English servant-man who had "a pretty long visage of a lightish complexion, and thin-flaxen hair; his eye tooth sticks out over his lower teeth in a remarkable manner," and another to a shoemaker and fiddler who "loves to be at frolics and taverns and is apt to get in liquor and when so is subject to fits." Others offered special rewards for runaway bricklayers, tailors, carpenters, and even schoolmasters. Occasional descriptions of their clothes give a vivid glimpse of multi-colored vests and blue, green and yellow coats. One runaway was said to have been wearing "a double-breasted cape coat, with white metal buttons, and an old jacket of bluish color, good shoes, and large white buckles, and no stockings except he stole them."

A more cheerful notice appeared in the *Maryland Gazette* on September 6, 1745. John Powell was able to report that the man who had previously been advertised as a runaway had been found to have "only gone into the country a cyder-drinking." Since he had returned to his master, the notice continued, all gentlemen and others with watches or clocks needing repair could now have them done "in the best manner, and at reasonable rates."

For the servant who faithfully served out the term of his indenture there were substantial rewards. Grants of land were the exception rather than the rule, but in some cases at least the industrious were given "a competent estate" and there was universal provision for some form of "freedom's dues." In Massachusetts, for example, the law specifically stated that all servants that had served diligently and faithfully for seven years should not be sent away empty-handed. What this meant varied, of course, not only from colony to colony but in terms of individual articles of indenture. The freedom's dues generally included at least clothing, tools of some sort, and perhaps such livestock as would enable the servant to start farming on his own account. Typical indentures called for "a pigg to be pay'd at every years end" and "double apparell at the end of the term."

Throughout the seventeenth and eighteenth centuries indentured servants, both men and women, could thus look forward to establishing a life of their own. Once they had obtained their freedom, Hugh Jones wrote in 1724, they may "work Day-Labour, or else rent a small Plantation for a trifle almost; or turn overseers, if they are expert, industrious and careful, or follow their trade. . . . especially Smiths, Carpenters, Taylors, Sawyers, Coopers, Bricklayers, etc."

Many of them made the most of these opportunities, their earlier status forgotten as they became independent farmers or workingmen; others drifted off to the back country, shiftless and unenterprising, to create in the southern colonies an unhappy class of poor whites. But whatever their individual destiny as the country grew and expanded, indentured servants played a vital part in the building of colonial America.

Free labor in the colonies was made up of immigrant artisans and mechanics who had been able to pay their own passage money and of recruits from the ranks of bound servants who had served out their terms of indenture. The available supply of such workers nevertheless remained highly limited and the towns along the Atlantic seaboard continually suffered from an acute labor shortage. Even this early, high wages and relatively favorable working conditions could not stop the steady migration westward. The frontier with its cheap land constantly drained the seaboard.

"The genius of the People in a Country where every one can have Land to work upon," a colonial official reported to the Board of Trade in 1767, "leads them so naturally into Agriculture, that it prevails over every other occupation. There can be no stronger instance of this, than in the servants imported from Europe of different trades; as soon as the Time stipulated in their Indentures is expired, they immediately quit their Masters, and get a small tract of land, in settling which for the first three or four years they lead miserable lives, and in the most abject Poverty; but all this is patiently borne and submitted to with the greatest cheerfulness, the Satisfaction of being Land holders smooths over every difficulty, and makes them prefer this manner of living to that comfortable subsistence which they could procure for themselves and their families by working at the Trades in which they were brought up."

This situation bore most heavily upon New England, where relatively few indentured servants were available, and led to such high wage rates and such an independent attitude on the part of both skilled and unskilled workers that the colonial authorities felt compelled to act. The result was the first labor legislation in America affecting free workers. Maximum wages were established by law, changes in occupation prohibited, and various class distinctions in dress and deportment prescribed to keep the lower classes in a subordinate role.

As early as 1630 the General Court in Massachusetts undertook to enforce a wage ceiling of two shillings a day for carpenters, joiners, bricklayers, sawyers, thatchers and other artisans, and of eighteen pence for all day laborers, with the further provision that "all workmen shall worke the whole day, alloweing convenient tyme for food and rest." To combat what appears to have been a prevailing practice of supplementing such wages with allowances for liquor ("without which it is found, by too sad experience, many refuse to worke"), the Court further decreed that anyone who gave wine or strong liquors to any workmen, except in cases of necessity, would be fined twenty shillings for each offense.

Forty years later, another law reaffirmed these general wage rates, stating more specifically that the working day should be "10 houres in the daye besides repast," and extended its provisions to additional artisans. Carpenters, masons, stonelayers, coopers and tailors were to be paid two shillings a day, special piece rates were established for shoemakers, coopers and smiths, and, finally, the new statute declared "that whereas it appears that Glovers, Sadlers, Hatters, and Several other artifficers doe at present greatly exceed the rules of equitie in their prizes, they are all required to moderate the same according to the rules prescribed to others. . . ."

These maximum wages were in part compensated by price regulation of certain basic commodities to hold down the cost of living, but the clear intent of the General Court was both to help employers and to keep the workers in their place on grounds of public policy. "The excessive deerenes of labour by artifficers, Labourers, and Servants" was felt to have highly unfortunate consequences in the puritanic eyes of the New England fathers. "The produce thereof" they sternly declared, "is by many Spent to mayntayne such bravery in Apparell which is altogether unbecomeing their place and ranck, and in Idleness of life, and a great part spent viciously in Tavernes and alehouses and other Sinful practices much to the dishonor of God, Scandall of Religion, and great offence and griefe to Sober and Godly people amongst us."

Economics and morality walked hand in hand with our forebears. Their high-minded ideal of low wages and long hours as conducive to the workers' wellbeing had a pragmatic value that was not lost upon later generations. The nineteenth century—if not the twentieth—would find long working hours defended in this same puritanic spirit as necessary to combat idleness and to safeguard labor from the temptations to which it might otherwise be dangerously exposed. The "wholesome discipline" of factory life was in time to be sanctified by employers as an antidote to the lure of the saloons and beer parlors which replaced colonial taverns.

An even more direct restriction on what might be called conspicuous consumption by the workers was laid down in another law regulating just what they should wear. "We declare our utter detestation and dislike," this edict read, "that men and women of mean condition should take upon themselves the garb of gentlemen." The ban included "wearing gold or silver lace or buttons, or points at their knees, or to walk in boots, or women of the same rank to wear silk or tiffany scarfs, which though allowable to persons of greater estates, or more liberal education, yet we cannot but judge it intolerable in persons in such like conditions."

These laws could not be enforced. Although the authorities continued to link the demand for higher wages with intemperance, sabbath-breaking, gaming and mixed dancing as among "the Mischievous Evils the Nature of Man is prone unto," they could not control the situation. The General Court ultimately relegated the task to the local town governments, but even then the scarcity of labor proved to be a more decisive factor than arbitrary legislation in determining wage rates and social customs.

Although the bulk of settlers tilled their own land and provided through home manufactures most of their immediate needs, making their own clothing, household furniture and many of the tools and utensils essential for everyday life, craftsmen and artisans played an increasingly important economic role as the eighteenth century advanced. Many of them were itinerant workers, going from town to town to work at whatever job offered or making on order anything the farm families might need. One man sometimes plied several trades. A blacksmith would be also a toolmaker, a tanner a shoemaker, or a soap boiler serve as a tallow chandler. How far a craftsman might be prepared to extend his services is suggested by an advertisement in the *New York Gazette* in June, 1775. John Julius Sorge announced that he could make artificial fruit; do japan work; manufacture cleaning fluid, toilet water, soap, candles, insecticides, and wine, and remove hair from ladies' foreheads and arms.

With the further growth of colonial towns, the demand for artisans increased. There were more and more of the small retail shops in which a master workman employed a number of journeymen workers; that is, artisans or mechanics who worked for wages, and also trained boys as apprentices to whatever trade was being practiced. Printing shops, tailoring and shoemaking shops, hat shops, cabinet-making shops and bakeries were among such establishments. The work was generally done on order—so called "bespoke work"—and the shop might often be the master's home where the journeymen and apprentices could board as well as work. At the same time, the expansion of the building trades led master carpenters and master masons to employ journeymen and train apprentices.

In both New England and the middle colonies, there were also all manner of little mills needing both skilled and unskilled wage earners, and shipyards, ropewalks, distilleries, breweries, paper and gunpowder factories. On the large plantations of the south, home manufactures created a need for skilled labor. Robert Carter had a smithy, a fulling mill, a grain mill, salt works and both spinning and weaving establishments on his plantation where he employed free white workers as well as Negro slaves.

There was at least a beginning of manufacture on a larger scale. By the middle of the eighteenth century, ironworks had been established in Pennsylvania, Maryland, and New Jersey which employed a considerable number of men. One set up by Peter Hasenclever, the best known colonial ironmaster, included six blast furnaces, seven forges and a stamping mill, and he is said to have brought five hundred workers over from Germany for their operation. The glass works of Henry Steigel, at Mannheim, Pennsylvania, must have had a considerable labor force for they included a plant so large "that a coach and four could turn around within the brick dome of its melting house." Linen factories with as many as fourteen looms foreshadowed mounting employment in textile mills. In 1769 a "manufacturing house" in Boston had four hundred spinning wheels, and six years later the United Company of Philadelphia for Promoting American Manufacture employed four hundred women in the production of cotton goods. Some of these latter enterprises provided work for the indigent and for orphans—without wages —as a service to the community.

In addition to the workers in manufacturing establishments, moreover, other groups of wage earners were of growing importance. The most numerous were sailors and fishermen, and every town also had its quota of day laborers. Household servants were never available in sufficient numbers to meet the needs of the more wealthy members of the community. "Help is scarce and hard to gett, difficult to please, uncertaine . . ." remained a familiar complaint in colonial society.

With the approach of the Revolution, the increasing opportunities for wage earners and a diminishing labor supply as men were drafted for military service drove up wages. The earlier attempts to fix maximum rates and control prices were consequently renewed. The Articles of Association adopted by the Continental Congress stressed the importance of such regulations and several of the new state governments undertook to enforce them. At a convention held in Providence in 1776, attended by delegates from Massachusetts, New Hampshire, Rhode Island and Connecticut, agreement was reached on a general program of price and wage control. Farm labor was not to be paid more than three shillings and four pence a day (almost three times the rate a century earlier) and the wages of artisans and mechanics were to be so fixed as to maintain their normal relationship to farm wages at this new rate. The states concerned acted promptly on this resolution—an early example of an interstate compact—and when the matter was brought before the Continental Congress, it referred to the remaining states "the propriety of adopting similar Measures."

Other conventions, however, were not as successful as that held at Providence in reaching mutual agreement upon prices and wage scales. The south was already showing its reluctance to fall in line with standards set in the northern states and the experience of different sections was confused and conflicting. While further action was taken locally in some instances, the Continental Congress finally decided that the whole program was not only impractical "but likewise productive of very evil Consequences to the great Detriment of the public Service and grievous Oppression of Individuals." It advised the states to repeal existing laws and this first attempt at a controlled economy made no further headway.

Although conditions of colonial life made for a greater measure of social and economic equality in America than prevailed anywhere in the Old World, the workers still did not enjoy political liberty. The franchise was restricted to property owners and the skilled artisans and mechanics were as helpless in asserting their rights as day laborers. By the 1780's, however, there was a growing demand for broader privileges on the part of workers in seaboard towns. In supporting the movement that led to American independence, these workers were protesting not only against oppression by a distant England, but against the controls exercised by the ruling class at home.

The role of small tradesmen, artisans and mechanics in promoting the revolutionary cause was particularly important in Massachusetts. Again and again when the ardor of merchants and farmers appeared to be subsiding, the "rage of patriotism" was stimulated by the zeal of those whom the Tories derisively called the "Mobility" or the "Rabble." The popular party in Boston, so astutely led by Samuel Adams, was in large part made up of wharfingers, shipwrights, bricklayers, weavers and tanners who were equally opposed to rule by British officials or colonial aristocrats. The Sons of Liberty, and later the local Committees of Correspondence, were generally recruited from workers from the docks, shipyards and ropewalks. The famous "Loyall Nine," which was to instigate the mob action that led to the Boston Massacre and the Boston Tea Party, included two distillers, two braziers, a printer, a jeweler, a painter and a ship captain.

Such an alignment of forces was also true of other colonies. The Ancient and Honorable Mechanical Company of Baltimore, the Firemen's Association of Charleston, the Heart-and-Hand Fire Company of Philadelphia were the nuclei for the Sons of Liberty in those cities. In each instance their muster rolls show that their membership was primarily made up of small tradesmen and artisans.

This is not to say that other elements in colonial society did not play their full part in the revolutionary movement. The first protests against British taxation came largely from the merchant class and it provided the original leadership in organizing the Sons of Liberty. But the mechanics, artisans and small tradesmen voiced the more radical demands in support of colonial liberties and kept up their agitation when the merchants were willing to compromise. Their zealous activity, indeed, often aroused conservative fears that the revolutionary movement was getting wholly out of hand. "The heads of the mobility grow dangerous to the gentry," Gouverneur Morris wrote agitatedly on one occasion, "and how to keep them down is the question."

They could not be kept down. Their demonstrations, sometimes leading to riot and disorder, both reflected and intensified an increasing hostility toward the British authorities on the part of the common people. The Boston Massacre, for example, grew directly out of a dispute that had arisen between colonial workingmen and British troops. "A particular quarrel happened at a Rope-Walk with a few Soldiers of the 29th. Regiment," General Gage reported; "the Provocation was given by the Rope-Walkers, tho' it may be imagined in the course of it, that there were Faults on both Sides. This Quarrel it is supposed, excited the People to convert a general rising on the Night of the 5th. of March."

While the role of artisans and mechanics in the Revolution has long since been recognized, it is more difficult to determine their part in the adoption of the Constitution. As far as establishment of the new government reflected a conservative trend whittling away the democratic gains made during the struggle for independence, emphasizing the protection of property interests rather than individual liberties, the workingmen might be expected to oppose its acceptance. They had been neither directly nor indirectly represented at the Constitutional Convention, and little consideration was given in its deliberations to either their rights or those of the common people generally. Nevertheless there were workers' demonstrations in favor of ratification in some cities, and their support has been held partly responsible for the Federalists' victory in New York city.

Whatever their contribution to the movement for independence and the establishment of the United States, the workers did not win any substantial gains during these years. It is not necessary to quote the conservative views of such a strong advocate of government by the rich and the wellborn as Alexander Hamilton to demonstrate how far removed the United States was from a democratic society at the close of the eighteenth century. There were everywhere fears of the "levelling spirit" which had seemed so pronounced during the Revolution, and of the threat to national stability in any further concessions to the democratic masses.

Even Thomas Jefferson, stoutly declaring that "the influence over the government must be shared by all the people," had no idea of including the propertyless workers within the scope of those to be granted the franchise and allowed to hold public office. The democracy which he supported was a democracy of small freehold farmers and he gravely doubted whether artisans, mechanics, and laborers, without the stabilizing influence of being land owners, could ever develop the republican virtues which he felt essential for the functioning of a free society.

He strongly opposed the development of manufactures in the United States because he was afraid of the influence on our institutions of an increasing number of urban workers. He would have had our workshops remain in Europe rather than risk the creation of a wage-earning class whose principles and manners he held in suspect. "The mobs of great cities," Jefferson wrote in fearful contemplation of what he felt was happening in Europe, "add just so much to the support of pure government, as sores do to the strength of the human body."

In spite of the high promise of the Declaration of Independence, the political status of the wage-earning class in American society had thus not materially improved. Its standard of living remained high in comparison with conditions in Europe, but with advancing prices in the post-revolutionary period, workers in the little towns strung along the Atlantic seaboard seldom had very much of a margin over extreme poverty. While John Jay complained bitterly in 1784 of "the wages of mechanics and labourers, which are very extravagant," the pay for unskilled workers hardly ever exceeded fifteen shillings a week—less than the equivalent of $4.

"On such a pittance," John Bach McMaster has written, "it was only by the strictest economy that a mechanic kept his children from starvation and himself from jail. In the low and dingy rooms which he called his home were wanting many articles of adornment and of use now to be found in the dwellings of the poorest of his class. Sand sprinkled on the floor did duty as a carpet. There was no glass on his table, there was no china in his cupboard, there were no prints on his walls. What a stove was he did not know, coal he had never seen, matches he had never heard of. Over a fire of fragments of boxes and barrels, which he lit with the sparks struck from a flint, or with live coals brought from a neighbor's hearth, his wife cooked up a rude meal and served it in pewter dishes. He rarely tasted fresh meat as often as once in a week, and paid for it a much higher price than his posterity. . . . If the food of an artisan would now be thought coarse, his clothes would be thought abominable. A pair of yellow or buckskin or leather breeches, a checked shirt, a red flannel jacket, a rusty hat cocked up at the corners, shoes of neat's-skin set off with huge buckles of brass, and a leather apron, comprised his scanty wardrobe."

For all the hardships such a way of life implied—and it must be remembered that the wealthy also lacked many comforts that today would be considered essential—America was still a land of magnificent opportunity. Artisans and mechanics could confidently hope to improve their living conditions and the fluidity of classes meant that there were no barriers holding back the industrious and energetic from further advancement. In a society still based upon agriculture and handicraft industries, moreover, the craftsman had a recognized and respected status that served in part to compensate for meager economic resources. His way of life may have been simple, but he lived in a simple society untouched by industrialism.

Over the horizon were far-reaching changes that would vitally affect both the society in which he lived and his own status. They would in the name of progress open up the possibilities of a far higher standard of living than wage earners had ever before enjoyed in this or any other country. But these changes also demanded adjustments which were to prove highly difficult, and nineteenth century labor often felt itself cut off from the benefits that industrial progress appeared to promise. In the face of new barriers to the realization of their hopes and aspirations, the nation's workers were to find that only through organization could they secure the rights and privileges to which they felt entitled.

II: THE FIRST UNIONS

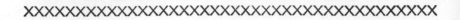

THE REAL BEGINNINGS of labor organization awaited the transformation in economic society brought about early in the nineteenth century by the rise of merchant capitalists who established business on a wholesale basis. The master workmen in the colonial period, bringing together journeymen and apprentices for work on common projects or joint enterprises, and paying them wages, had not created an employer-employe relationship in any modern sense. There was no real differentiation between the interests of the journeymen and those of the masters who labored side by side with them. The price lists set up for "bespoke work" determined wages, and to a very considerable extent the functions of merchant, master and journeymen were united in the same person.

Under such circumstances, masters and journeymen acted together to maintain the standards of their craft, uphold price lists and generally protect themselves from unfair competition. There were occasions when the journeymen protested against the controls exercised by the masters in their capacity as employers. In occupations that did not bring them together in close and natural association, disputes sometimes arose that led to sporadic strikes and incipient labor revolt. But generally speaking, the extremely simple economic organization of the seventeenth and eighteenth centuries precluded any significant concerted action on the part of workers. Before considering the changes effected by the rise of the merchant capitalists, however, such labor protests or strikes as did occur during the colonial period may well be considered for the light they may throw on the conditions that ultimately led to union organization.

The earliest record of what might be considered a labor disturbance goes back to 1636. A group of fishermen employed by one Robert Trelawney at Richmond Island, off the coast of Maine, were reported to have fallen "into a mutany" when their wages were withheld. Some forty years later the licensed cartmen of New York, ordered to remove the dirt from the streets for threepence a load, not only protested such a low rate of pay but "combined to refuse full compliance." Other comparable incidents occasionally were noted in the colonial press during the eighteenth century and in 1768 a "turn-out" of journeymen tailors in New York—perhaps the first really authentic strike against employers—has an almost modern ring. Some twenty workers struck because of a reduction in their wages and publicly advertised that in defiance of the masters they would take private work. They would be on call at the Sign of the Fox and Hound, their notice in the papers read, at the rate of three shillings and six pence per day, with diet.

The masters themselves sometimes joined forces to protect their interests as revealed in a somewhat earlier account of trouble among the Boston barbers appearing in the *New England Courant*. Thirty-two master barbers "assembled at the Golden Ball, with a Trumpeter attending them," and jointly agreed to raise their rates for shaving from 8s. to 10s. per quarter, and "to advance 5s. on the Price of making common Wiggs and 10s. on their Tye ones." It was also proposed that "no one of their Faculty should shave or dress Wiggs on Sunday morning," a resolution that led the *Courant* to observe censoriously that "it may be concluded, that in times past such a Practice had been too common among them."

The Revolutionary period, with its wartime inflation, stimulated further protests on the part of workers who found living costs rising much faster than wages. The New York printers were a case in point. In November, 1778 the journeymen demanded—and received—an increase in pay under circumstances which again have a very modern flavor except for the courtesy with which the printers voiced their demands.

"As the necessaries of life are raised to such an enormous price," read the journeymen's protest as it appeared in the *Royal Gazette*, "it cannot be expected that we should continue to work at the wages now given; and therefore request an addition of Three Dollars per week to our present small pittance; It may be objected that this requisition is founded upon the result of a combination to distress the Master Printers at this time, on account of the scarcity of hands; but this is far from being the case; it really being the high price of every article of life, added to the approaching dreary season. There is not one among us, we trust, that would take an ungenerous advantage of the times—we only wish barely to exist, which it is impossible to do with our present stipend."

To this letter James Rivington, the well known Tory printer and publisher of the *Gazette*, briefly replied: "I do consent to the above requisition."

There were other concerted protests or strikes in these and the immediately following years—on the part of seamen in Philadelphia in 1779, New York shoemakers in 1785, and journeymen printers in Philadelphia in 1786. "We will support such of our brethren," these printers declared, "as shall be thrown out of employment on account of their refusing to work for less than $6 per week." The employers at first refused to meet their demands but the turn-out was ultimately successful.

The members of the building trades were also restive and a long smoldering conflict broke out in 1791 between journeymen and master carpenters in Philadelphia. The former declared that their employers were trying to reduce wages "to a still lower ebb, by every means within the power of avarice to invent." They specifically demanded a shorter working day and additional pay for overtime. They bitterly complained that they had heretofore "been obliged to toil through the whole course of the longest summer's days, and that too, *in many instances,* without even the consolation of having our labour sweetened by the reviving hope of an immediate reward."

What settlement may have been reached in this dispute is not known. The masters blamed the conditions of trade for the low wages and declared that they "had in no instance, discovered a disposition to oppress or tyrannize."

These strikes and turn-outs did not in any case involve an organization that could be termed a labor union. The workers merely got together on some temporary basis to press their demands or to take joint action to protect their interests. Such trade societies as did exist, and there were a number of them in the latter part of the eighteenth century, had been formed not to promote economic aims but for philanthropic purposes. They were mutual aid societies, often including both journeymen and masters, which provided various sickness and death benefits for their members. Almost every important trade in such cities as New York, Philadelphia and Boston had such a society by the 1790's and in some instances there were organizations of broader scope—the General Society of Mechanics and Tradesmen in New York, the Association of Mechanics of the Commonwealth of Massachusetts, the Albany Mechanics' Society.

In supporting such members as might by accident or sickness be in need of assistance and aiding the widows and orphans of those who died in indigent circumstances, these societies sought to free both masters and journeymen from "the degrading reflection arising from the circumstances of being relieved . . . by private or public charity." The workers were self-respecting and proud. Thus early in our history they were prepared, as stated in the charter of one society, "to demand relief . . . as a *right*."

Many mutual aid societies also had social features and provided meeting rooms and recreation. The house rules of the Friendly Society of Tradesmen House Carpenters, organized in Philadelphia in 1767, reveals both the scope of such activities and also the strict regulations governing the deportment of members. A fine of sixpence had to be paid into the common stock of the society by any member who "presumes to curse or swear, or cometh disguised in Liquor and breeds Disturbance . . . or promoteth Gaming at Club Hours."

While in general, economic activity fell wholly outside their scope, the charter of the New York Society of Journeymen Shipwrights stipulating automatic dissolution if the organization made any attempt to fix wages, it was inevitable that these societies should in time become concerned over employment problems. The line between mutual aid and bona fide trade associations thus becomes almost impossible to distinguish. The Federal Society of Journeymen Cordwainers, established in Philadelphia in 1794, has, however, been called the first "continuous organization" of wage earners in the United States and is perhaps entitled to be considered the original trade union. Its membership was solely made up of journeymen shoemakers, it conducted a strike and picketed the masters' shops in 1799, and remained in existence for twelve years.

A few months after the Philadelphia cordwainers organized, the journeymen printers in New York formed what was to be the first of a long line of unions in that trade, and two years later there was also established in New York a relatively long-lived society of Journeymen

Cabinet Makers. The latter organization published in the papers a complete price list—which in effect meant wage scales—with the further provision that the journeymen chairmakers would "work ten hours per day; employers to find candles."

These tentative beginnings of organization pointed the way toward the more general growth of trade societies—as the first unions were long called—that followed upon the rise of the merchant capitalists. It was not until the retail shop and custom-order work gave way to wholesale business and the old easy relationship between master and journeyman was broken down that the workers really felt compelled to combine against their employers. But with the beginning of the nineteenth century, the skilled artisans and mechanics in trade after trade followed the even earlier example of printers and shoemakers in forming societies whose avowed purpose was to guard their interests against "the artifices or intrigues" of employers and to secure adequate reward for their labor. These societies might still have mutual aid features but the major emphasis had shifted to economic action.

The merchant capitalists were interested both in importing goods from abroad and in setting up larger manufacturing establishments at home. They sought to develop broader markets and to introduce the cheap goods which would sell in such markets. With the capital at their command they could secure raw materials in bulk, provide the working places and eventually the tools for the artisans and mechanics they employed, warehouse the finished products, and then transport them to all parts of the country. The small retail shops with their emphasis upon quality and highly skilled craftsmanship could not meet the competitive conditions such large-scale operations fostered.

These trends were increasingly emphasized as the opening up of the country created ever more favorable opportunities for business expansion. The development of improved means of transportation—canals, turnpikes, and steamboats—widened the market which was accessible for the manufacturers and merchants of the Atlantic seaboard. The highways leading to the west were crowded with high-peaked, canvas covered wagons carrying to the new communities of western New York and the Ohio Valley the clothes, shoes, furniture, kitchenware, tools, and iron utensils turned out in eastern towns and cities. A national market was in the making which overshadowed the old local markets dependent upon retail trade and bespoke work, and it set the pace for economic progress. On a small scale, there was taking place the same sort of development that would result from mass production in the later stages of the industrial revolution. The eclipse of the retail shop by the wholesale establishment foreshadowed that of the local manufacturing plant by the industrial combinations and mergers of the 1880's and 1890's.

Under constant pressure to reduce costs in meeting the highly competitive conditions of this new world of business, employers sought to hold down wages, lengthen the working day of their employes, and tap new sources of cheap labor. They tried to break down the restrictions of the traditional apprenticeship system; they began to employ both women and children wherever possible; they introduced the sweat shop and the practice of letting out contracts to prison labor. For skilled craftsmen, whatever their trade, such moves were a threat not only of lower standards of living but of loss of status. They were at once aroused to combat such developments and realized that only through concerted action could they hope to protect their rights.

For a time the artisans and mechanics were able to meet their employers on relatively equal grounds. The scarcity of skilled labor that had been so characteristic of the colonial period was still a basic fact in American economy. "The objections to the pursuit of manufactures in the United States," Alexander Hamilton had stated in his famous *Report on Manufactures,* "represent an impracticability of success arising from three causes; scarcity of hands, dearness of labor, want of capital." Moreover, the expanding frontier still continued in this period to draw off many workers attracted by the easy availability of cheap land or the greater opportunity for plying a trade in the western settlements. The new towns springing up along the land and river highways in the Ohio Valley often offered even higher wages than the older communities in the east.

Newspapers of the period afford constant evidence of this demand for workers. There were frequent advertisements of jobs: "Wanted, two or three journeymen coopersmiths; liberal wages will be paid," "Wanted, six or eight carpenters; will be allowed the use of tools," and "Wanted, four or five journeymen bricklayers." The contractors building the City Hall in New York in 1803, were forced to advertise for stonecutters in the papers of Philadelphia, Baltimore and Charleston, promising high wages, repair of all tools, and assurances that although there was yellow fever in other parts of the city, the workingmen need have no fear of it.

Nevertheless the skilled workers soon found themselves fighting a defensive war against the mounting resources of the employers. Their wages did not keep up with the cost of living in the first decades of the nineteenth century, nor even maintain their relative level with the wages of unskilled workers. The general average about 1818 was probably not more than $1.25 a day except in a few special trades such as that of ship carpenters. New York typesetters, for example, were earning $8 a week and journeymen tailors in Baltimore $9. In comparison, the great demand for laborers on canals and turnpikes, in the construction of buildings and on other comparable projects, had driven up the wages of day laborers from about $4 a week at the close of the revolution to $7 a week and sometimes more. When they were fed and lodged, their actual pay might amount to more than artisans and mechanics could command. An advertisement for men to work on the road being built from the Genesee River to Buffalo, promised $12 a month, with food, lodging and whiskey every day. Although the skilled craftsmen could still live in relatively comfortable circumstances, especially in the eyes of foreign visitors who compared their status with that of workers in Europe, they realized that conditions were changing to their disadvantage and that it was going to grow harder rather than easier for them to maintain old standards.

The organizations that sought, under these circumstances, to safeguard the status of the skilled workers were most general among printers, cordwainers, tailors, carpenters, cabinetmakers, shipwrights, coopers and weavers. Especially important were the journeymen printers and cordwainers. It has already been noted that they were union pioneers, and succeeded in maintaining active societies throughout the first twenty years of the nineteenth century, not only in New York and Philadelphia, but also in Boston, Baltimore, Albany, Washington, Pittsburgh and New Orleans. The members of the building trades were also organized in almost every city, and among other societies were those of millwrights, stone-cutters, handloom weavers and hatters. Prior to 1820 there were no organizations among factory operatives—although some 100,000 persons were employed in cotton mills by that year—and there is no evidence of women taking part in the burgeoning labor movement.

These early trade societies were in effect closely restricted craft unions, wholly local in character and necessarily small in membership. The workers who belonged to them were bound to conform to strict rules and regulations: to keep union proceedings secret, agree under oath to abide by established wage scales, and always to assist fellow members to get employment in preference to any other workers. Initiation fees were about fifty cents with monthly dues amounting from six to ten cents. Attendance at regular meetings was required, with fines for un-justified absence. Moreover, rigid discipline was enforced and union members could be expelled for such lapses as frequent intoxication, gross immorality or "giving a brother member any abusive language in the society-room during the hours of meeting." The societies were deeply concerned with maintaining the standards of the crafts they represented and thereby providing assurance that their membership included all the best workmen in the community.

The basic objectives remained those which have ever since been of primary concern for organized workers—higher wages, shorter hours and improved working conditions. The attempts on the part of em-ployers to lower standards by hiring untrained workers—foreigners and boys, eventually women—also led to vigorous efforts to enforce what today would be called a closed shop. The New York Typographical Society complained bitterly that the superabundance of learners, run-away apprentices and half-way journeymen undermined the wage rates of "full-fledged workers." In common with many other societies—proba-bly with most of them—it maintained a strict rule that none of its mem-bers should work in any shop which employed workers who did not belong to the organization. There were many turn-outs in this and later periods against employers who tried to take on artisans or mechanics who were not union members in good standing, and the society regula-tions were rigidly upheld. The pressure being exerted against the craftsmen appears, in fact, to have led to a more concentrated effort to establish the principle of the closed shop than in any later period. The Journeymen Cordwainers of New York not only had a specific provision in their constitution against working in any non-union establishment, but were prepared to impose fines upon any journeyman coming to the city that did not join the society within a month.

In their dealings with employers, the societies introduced the principles of collective bargaining. In the case of the Philadelphia shoemakers, a deputation had "waited upon the employers with an offer of compromise" as early as 1799, and many instances might be cited of journeymen submitting a price list and coming to terms after protracted negotiations. When agreements had been reached between a society and the employers, a member of the former was often designated "to walk around" from shop to shop to see that it was being kept. In other instances, "tramping committees" were set up to supervise enforcement of the contract.

The strikes or turn-outs, as they were more frequently called—whereby the workers sought to uphold their interests when wage negotiations failed, employers refused to abide by the terms of an agreement, or non-members of the society were employed—were generally peaceful during this period. The employes simply quit their jobs and stayed at home until some sort of a settlement could be reached. The struggle appears often to have been fought out in the newspapers rather than in violent action. Workers and employers would put their respective cases before the public through notices in the press. Appeals and counter-appeals for popular support reflected a general acceptance of the important role of public opinion in determining a proper basis for labor relations.

There were, however, occasions when more forceful measures were taken by strikers. Six journeymen stayed on the job during a turn-out of Philadelphia shoemakers and were kept hidden in their employer's garret. The strikers kept up a sharp eye for them and when they briefly emerged one Sunday night to visit a near-by tavern, beat them up severely. On another occasion when a shop was boycotted because of refusal to accept the prescribed wage scales and the employer advertised for fifty new journeymen, the strikers established what was in effect a picket line and forcefully maintained it. There was deep resentment against non-union workers who would take the place of strikers and attacks were not unusual upon persons already being called "scabs."

Noisy demonstrations and sometimes violence marked the rather frequent turn-outs of sailors. During one strike in New York, in which the seamen demanded an increase in wages from $10 to $14 a week, so much disturbance was created that a parade of strikers had finally to be broken up by the constables. Another time the sailors tried to board and rifle a vessel whose owner had especially aroused their ire. Learning of the planned assault, a group of citizens took over the defense of the vessel and when the strikers moved in behind a drum and fife corps, with colors flying, "they were three times repulsed, with broken and bloody noses." The seamen were not organized and were an especially obstreperous lot. Artisans and mechanics did not approve of tactics that they felt unbecoming to skilled craftsmen.

The growth of journeymen societies and their militant activity were matters of mounting concern to employers. They in turn soon began to cooperate to block demands for higher wages and to combat the closed shop. While the journeymen had organized in self-defense as changing economic conditions undermined their former independent status, the masters also found themselves hard pressed to maintain their position in an increasingly competitive capitalist society. When they were unable to meet the challenge of organized employes on their own ground, they sought protection from the courts and attacked the journeymen societies as combinations or conspiracies in restraint of trade.

The first of such actions was the prosecution, in 1806, of the Journeymen Cordwainers of Philadelphia. The case grew out of one of the recurrent strikes for higher wages on the part of these aggressive shoemakers, and the trial judge proved to be a sympathetic supporter of the employers. In his charge to the jury he characterized the strike as "pregnant with public mischief and private injury" and left the twelve good men and true little choice as to the verdict he expected them to bring in.

"A combination of workmen to raise their wages," he declared, "may be considered in a two-fold point of view; one is to benefit themselves . . . the other is to injure those who do not join their society. The rule of law condemns both. . . ." The grounds for such a decision were found in the old common law principle that wherever two or more persons conspired to do something jointly, even though they were individually entitled to take such action, the public interest was endangered. While its application to labor organizations seeking no more than an increase in wages would appear to have raised some doubts even in the judge's own mind, he quickly brushed them aside. "If the rule be clear we are bound to conform to it," he stated, "even though we do not comprehend the principle upon which it is founded. We are not here to reject it because we do not see the reason for it."

Four years later the Journeymen Cordwainers of New York, and then in 1815 another organization of Pittsburgh shoemakers, were indicted on similar charges of criminal conspiracy. On both occasions the court again found for the employers. The emphasis, however, had somewhat shifted from outright condemnation of any combination for raising wages. The New York judge did not wholly deny the right of working-men to organize for such a purpose, but he declared that the means they were employing "were of a nature too arbitrary and coercive, and went to deprive their fellow citizens of rights as precious as any they contended for." In the Pittsburgh case a further point was stressed. A combination of workingmen attempting to enforce their demands by concerted action against an employer was said to be an illegal conspiracy not only because of its injurious effect upon the employer, but because it was prejudicial to the interests of the community. The judge in this instance dismissed the question of whether the journeymen or the masters were the oppressors as irrelevant and condemned the former's society because it tended "to create a monopoly or restrain the entire freedom of trade."

These conspiracy cases aroused widespread resentment among the workingmen. Were all other combinations, among merchants, among politicians, among sportsmen, among "ladies and gentlemen for balls, parties, and banquets" to be permitted, they asked, and only the poor laborers combining against starvation to be indicted?

"The name of freedom is but a shadow," read one appeal to the public, "if, for doing, what the laws of the country authorize, we are to have taskmasters to measure out our pittance of subsistence—if we are to be torn from our firesides for endeavouring to obtain a fair and just support for our families, and if we are to be treated as felons and murderers only for asserting our right to take or refuse what we deem an adequate reward for our labor."

The issue was injected into local policies. Federalists and Jeffersonian

Republicans were at the time engaged in a bitter controversy over the general use of English common law in the United States, and the latter considered the application of what they termed its undemocratic principles to labor unions a challenge to the whole cause of liberty. The right of association could not be divorced from other fundamental rights, the Republicans declared, and they zealously took up the workingmen's cause.

". . . Would it be believed," an editorial in the *Philadelphia Aurora*, the leading Jeffersonian paper, stated in 1806, "at the very time when the state of the negro was about to be improved attempts were being made to reduce the whites to slavery? Was there anything in the Constitution of the United States or in the Constitution of Pennsylvania which gave one man a right to say to another what should be the price of labor? There was not. It was by the English common law that such things became possible."

The controversy was to continue for many years to come but the decisions against the workingmen stood. They did not stop the further organization of labor societies nor wholly prevent the use of strikes and boycotts. When the employers resorted to the courts, however, the workingmen were hard pressed to defend themselves against conspiracy charges.

If these cases were a first blow at the early movement for labor organization, the new unions were soon confronted by a much more serious threat to their existence. In 1819 the country suffered a serious depression. As business activity was curtailed and the demand for labor automatically declined, even skilled workers found it increasingly difficult to get jobs. They could no longer afford to hold out for higher wages or seek to enforce a closed shop. They were driven to accept whatever jobs were offered, regardless of wages or working conditions. Under such circumstances, the young labor unions could not maintain their membership and rapidly broke up. While some of them managed to survive, the great majority fell by the wayside as economic distress spread throughout the country.

This was to be a recurrent phenomenon during the nineteenth century. Labor unions throve in periods of prosperity when the rising demand for workers gave their members effective bargaining power. They dwindled away whenever depression and the scarcity of jobs forced every man to look out for his own interests no matter how it might affect those of workers generally. The first time that labor succeeded even partially in maintaining union strength during hard times was in the 1890's.

This was far in the future, however. The newly organized unions of the opening years of the century were so local in scope and so inexperienced, that they had no chance whatsoever of holding the line when employers aggressively took advantage of every opportunity to break down wage scales and undermine the closed shop. But in what was to become a familiar pattern, returning prosperity after 1822 led to a re-emergence of unionism. The few societies of artisans and mechanics that had somehow managed to survive depression took on a new lease of life as the bargaining position of their members was strengthened, and new organizations sprang up to replace those that had succumbed.

Not only were the societies of journeymen printers and cordwainers, tailors and carpenters, and other skilled workers revived, but for the first time there was a tentative beginning of organization among factory workers in the textile mills of New England. Moreover these new unions were especially active and did not hesitate to resort to strikes and boycotts to enforce their demands. Successful turn-outs for both higher wages and shorter working hours were reported in contemporary newspapers on the part of tailors in Buffalo, ship carpenters in Philadelphia, cabinet makers in Baltimore and journeymen painters, tailors, stonecutters and even common laborers in New York. The organization of mill hands also led to a first strike on the part of female workers when the weavers at Pawtucket, Rhode Island turned out in 1824. The meeting at which the women agreed on this action was reported in the *National Gazette:* "It was conducted, however strange it may appear, without noise, or scarcely a single speech."

Even more significant than the revival and militancy of these local labor societies was a further step in the organization of labor, going beyond limited craft lines. In 1827 there was established in Philadelphia a Mechanics' Union of Trade Associations. In the terminology of today, this meant rather an association of unions, or a city central. It was the first labor organization in the country which brought together the workers of more than a single craft, and it was to make possible concerted action on the part of the workers in Philadelphia on a citywide basis.

This new association grew out of a strike of carpenters who were demanding a ten-hour day and had obtained the support of such other members of the building trades as the bricklayers, painters, and glaziers. The strike failed, but the experience in working together led to a call for more permanent organization. All existing labor societies were asked to join the association and those trades that had no unions were re-quested to organize at once and send delegates.

The Mechanics' Union was not primarily concerned with such limited goals as higher wages and shorter hours even though it had grown out of a strike for the ten-hour day. A new note was introduced into the activity of labor societies by raising the broad issue of equality for producers generally. The changes effected by the new economic order had aroused among the workers increasing concern over their social as well as economic status. The Philadelphia labor leaders sought some means to maintain the position of workers in the face of what appeared to be newly developing class lines. They did not think of themselves as wage earners arrayed against employers, but rather as members of "the productive and mechanical classes" whose goal was to promote the prosperity and welfare of the entire community.

"If the mass of people were enabled by their labour to procure for themselves and families a full and abundant supply of the comforts and conveniences of life," the preamble of the new organization's constitution stated, "the consumption of articles, particularly of dwellings, furniture and clothing, would amount to at least twice the quantity it does at present, and of course the demand, by which employers are enabled either to subsist or accumulate, would likewise be increased in an equal proportion. . . . The real object, therefore, of this association, is to avert, if possible, the desolating evils which must inevitably arise from a depreciation of the intrinsic value of human labour . . . and to assist, in conjunction with such other institutions of this nature as shall hereafter be formed throughout the union, in establishing a just balance of power, both mental, moral, political and scientific, between all the various classes and individuals which constitute society at large."

Such aims, already suggesting the purchasing power theory as an argument for higher wages, had definite political implications. The Mechanics' Union of Trade Associations, indeed, never engaged in direct trade union activity but turned at once to politics. It appealed to the artisans and mechanics of Philadelphia to "throw off the trammels of party spirit, and unite under the banner of equal rights." It called for the nomination of candidates for local office who would represent the interests of the working classes.

III: THE WORKINGMEN'S PARTIES

IN URGING ITS MEMBERS to nominate candidates for public office, the Mechanics' Union of Trade Associations in Philadelphia broke fresh ground for labor and inaugurated what was to become a widespread political movement of workingmen's parties. It soon spread to other towns in Pennsylvania; to New York where wide popular support developed not only for local parties in New York city itself but in many upstate localities, and into Massachusetts and other parts of New England. Ultimately workingmen's parties were established in at least a dozen states. As far west as Ohio, as well as along the Atlantic seaboard, local groups of farmers, artisans and mechanics named their own political candidates and in some instances elected them. For a brief time they were highly important, and sometimes held an actual balance of power between the major parties in local elections.

An equally widespread growth of labor newspapers took place in the early 1830's, with no less than sixty-eight such journals upholding the workingmen's cause and agitating for labor reforms. Their enthusiasm and assurance knew no bounds. "From Maine to Georgia, within a few months past," commented the *Newark Village Chronicle* in May, 1830, "we discern symptoms of a revolution, which will be second to none save that of '76." "Throughout the vast republic," the *Albany Working Men's Advocate* stated shortly afterwards, "the farmers, mechanics and workingmen are assembling . . . to impart to its laws and administration those principles of liberty and equality unfolded in the Declaration of Independence."

These developments were both a first expression of the awakening forces of Jacksonian democracy, with which the workingmen's political activity was gradually to merge, and a further demonstration of that demand for equal citizenship first voiced in Philadelphia. The country

35

was rapidly expanding in these years. The opening up of new western territory, the building of turnpikes and canals, the steady growth of manufactures, and the rise of cities everywhere created a spirit of buoyant confidence. What the workers of the country basically sought was the right to share fully in the benefits of national growth and development, and they felt that under conditions as they had developed in the 1820's they were being shut off from opportunities to which they were entitled. Having newly obtained political power through the removal of voting property qualifications, they were ready to enter the lists in support of their own interests.

There was little question that the general status of labor was continuing to deteriorate as a result of the changes wrought in our economy by the rise of merchant capitalism. The ordinary divisions within society were deepening. Contemporary critics saw on the one hand the producing masses, made up of the laboring poor, and on the other a wealthy non-productive aristocracy bulwarked by special privilege. Banking and other monopolies accentuated this cleavage, and the great majority of the country's workers saw little improvement in the conditions under which they labored even though trade and commerce expanded and the nation as a whole grew more prosperous.

Wages rose but not in proportion to the rise in the cost of living. Twelve and fifteen hours remained the usual day's work. During the summer, artisans and mechanics were on the job as early as four in the morning, took an hour off for lunch at ten and another for dinner at three, and then quit work only with sunset. They were often paid in depreciated currency whose value was constantly fluctuating. Should their employer fail and be unable to pay them, they had no redress and yet when they could not meet their own obligations, they were liable to imprisonment for debt.

Moreover the workingmen felt that government was wholly on the side of the aristocracy and that its policies were helping to perpetuate the conditions which were depressing the position of all labor. They had no faith in either major party, whatever its professions of goodwill, because the men chosen for public office were invariably representatives of the class that they had come to believe was oppressing them. Heretofore they had been politically helpless to do anything about redressing a balance of power they saw swinging steadily against them. Armed with the vote, they declared themselves unwilling any longer to accept passively policies which in government, finance or business sought to reserve special privilege for the favored few at the expense of the great majority.

In forming their own parties, the workers tried to secure participation in government by members of their own class—the producers—and they were convinced that in doing so, they were serving the best interests of the people as a whole. Their party platforms vigorously attacked every instance of special privilege, and particularly banking monopoly, but indicative of their general objective of establishing equal citizenship, their foremost demand was invariably free public education. Seeking to secure representation for "the plain people" in every governmental process, they recognized that education for the masses was a first step toward an effective democracy. On more specific grounds, the workingmen also demanded abolition of imprisonment for debt and mechanics' lien laws; the revision of a militia system that bore heavily upon the poor; the direct election of all public officials; greater equality in taxation, and the complete separation of church and state.

The political agitation of the workers and the formation of their local parties thus reflected a spirit of liberal reform that was actually much broader than any labor movement. The revolt of the workers in eastern cities was to become more and more closely linked with that among farmers in the new western settlements in the great upsurge of democracy that on the national stage led to the election of Andrew Jackson as spokesman for the interests of the common man. While the workers may not have universally supported the Democrats in 1828, there can be no question but that they swung heavily behind Jackson as he demonstrated his mounting concern in the issues they put forward. In championing the cause of "the humble members of society," he pointedly included mechanics and laborers as well as farmers. Jacksonian democracy had a broader basis than Jeffersonian democracy, and was compounded both of the individualistic spirit of the frontier and the equalitarianism of eastern workingmen.

The local parties formed by the workers were to become inextricably involved in the complex and shifting political patterns of the 1830's.

Whatever their ultimate fate, however, their influence in quickening the demand for reform and promoting progressive principles was important. Commenting on the course of one workingmen's party in Massachusetts, a Whig newspaper sourly charged that there was no distinction between "Working-Menism and Jacksonism." If this was not always true, it was sufficiently close to the mark to suggest that the victories won by the advance of Jacksonian democracy were in many instances victories that owed a great deal to the workers' support.

The significance of the growing political power of the workingmen was demonstrated in other ways. In opposition to Jackson's espousal of the cause of the common man, the newly organized Whigs for a time sought to uphold Federalist traditions favoring government by the rich and the well-born. They especially attacked the proposition of "throwing open the polls to every man that walks." But when they found themselves unable to stem the growing political power of small farmers and urban workers, they began to shift their ground. Attacking Jackson for emphasizing class distinctions—as later day conservatives were to attack Franklin D. Roosevelt—they maintained that there was no warrant for setting off aristocracy and democracy as opposing forces in our national life. "These phrases, *higher and lower orders*," one Whig editor declared, "are of European origin and have no place in our Yankee dialect." However conservative their ideas might still be, it was no longer politically feasible for them to uphold aristocratic principles and they were compelled to recognize the right of all classes in society to share in government.

By the close of the Jacksonian period, the original workingmen's parties had long since fallen by the wayside, but the producing masses of the nation had won the political recognition that had been their first objective. Both major parties were continually angling for labor support. When in 1836 the editor of the *Ohio People's Press*, to cite a single example, shifted his political allegiance from Jackson to Harrison, he called for support of the latter on exactly the same grounds on which he had originally backed the former. The program advocated by Harrison, he maintained, would "restore to the farmer, the mechanic and the working-man their proper station and influence in the Republic." The extension of the franchise and growing political awareness of the workers had made labor for the first time a political power.

Among the various local workingmen's parties, the experience of the one organized in New York is at once most revealing of the influence they were temporarily able to exert and of the complicated factors that brought about their collapse. This party grew out of a meeting of "mechanics and others" that had been summoned on April 23, 1829, to protest against any lengthening in the prevailing ten-hour day already won in that city by the early trade unions. Deciding to broaden the scope of their activity, the delegates sent out a call for a larger meeting. It was attended by some 6,000 persons and a set of resolutions was adopted dealing with the broad principles of workingmen's rights. Consideration of ways and means for implementing this program was then delegated to a Committee of Fifty, and on October 19 it brought in a report, of which 20,000 copies were subsequently circulated, that vigorously attacked the existing social order and called for a convention to nominate for the New York assembly political candidates from among those "who live by their own labour *And None Other*." Four days later this convention was held. After all non-workers "such as bankers, brokers, rich men etc." had been expressly warned to leave the hall, the workingmen agreed upon an assembly slate which included a printer, two machinists, two carpenters, a painter and a grocer.

From the very first, however, rivalry and intrigue over the leadership of the new workingmen's party threatened to split its ranks. It was to be dominated by several highly individualistic reformers whose philosophy and ideas went far beyond the practical demands in which the workers themselves were primarily interested. Four such persons stand out especially for their influence on the labor party in New York, and on the course of the workingmen's general political activity.

In its earliest stages, the party was largely under the control of Thomas Skidmore, a machinist by trade, who had been instrumental in persuading the workers to broaden their program as a means of "coercing their aristocratic oppressors" into maintaining the ten-hour day. Wholly self-educated, he was a violent, fanatical devotee of the workers' cause and had developed an agrarian philosophy that questioned the entire basis for existing property rights. He believed that in giving up his original and natural right to land to become a smith, a weaver, a builder or other laborer, every man was entitled to a guaranty from society "that reasonable toil shall enable him to live as comfortably as others." Any system that failed to provide such social security was inherently wrong in his opinion, and he hoped to lead a workingmen's revolt in favor of basic political reforms.

His views were shortly to be set forth in a formidable treatise which he comprehensively entitled "*The Rights of Man to Property; Being a Proposition to Make it Equal among the Adults of the Present Genera-tion; and to Provide for its Equal Transmission to Every Individual of Each Succeeding Generation, on Arriving at the Age of Maturity.*" Skidmore specifically proposed that all debts and property claims should be at once canceled, and the assets of society as a whole sold at public auction with every citizen having equal purchasing power. After such a communistic division of property, the maintenance of equality would be assured by doing away with all inheritance.

Without fully understanding all the implications of this radical pro-gram, the members of the New York Workingmen's Party allowed Skid-more to draw up their original platform. It was based upon the forth-right premise that "all human society, our own included as well as every other, is constructed radically wrong," and condemned both the private ownership of land and the inheritance of wealth. Its more specific pro-visions, however, set forth the objectives which were fundamental to the workingmen's movement everywhere. The platform demanded com-munal education, abolition of imprisonment for debt, mechanics' lien laws and the elimination of licensed monopolies.

A second leader, who accepted at least in part the Skidmore program but was to be far more influential in the workingmen's movement in these and later years, was George Henry Evans. A printer by trade, he founded the *Working Man's Advocate,* perhaps the most important labor journal of these years, as the organ for the New York party, and turned out a continuous stream of articles and editorials promoting the workers' interests. Reflecting the influence of Skidmore, his paper first carried the slogan: "All children are entitled to equal education; all adults to equal property; and all mankind, to equal privileges." But his views were to be later modified although he remained throughout his life a strong advocate of basic agrarian reforms.

As if such leadership were not enough to condemn the Workingmen's Party in the eyes of all conservatives, it was further damned by the participation in its activities of another brace of radical reformers:

Robert Dale Owen and Frances Wright. Having but recently moved to New York from the cooperative community at New Harmony, Indiana, where the former's father, the English reformer Robert Owen, had attempted to put into practice his socialistic program for replacing the factory system, these two naturally seized upon the workingmen's movement as a medium for promoting their own particular brand of reform. They had founded a paper, the *Free Enquirer*, to publicize their ideas and it was soon campaigning vigorously in support of the new party.

Robert Dale Owen was twenty-eight at this time, a short, blue-eyed, sandy-haired young man whose idealism and earnest sincerity gave him a very real influence. In spite of a rasping voice and clumsy gestures, he was a forceful speaker at workingmen's meetings and he was also a prolific and able writer. He believed strongly in a more equitable distribution of wealth, was opposed to organized religion, and advocated more liberal divorce laws, but his primary interest was in free, public education. He single-mindedly felt that it was the only effective means for regenerating society and had developed an elaborate educational program which called for a system of "state guardianship."

All children, whether of the rich or of the poor, according to this scheme, were to be removed from their homes and placed in national schools where they would receive the same food, be dressed in the same simple clothing, and taught the same subjects in order to promote the general cause of democracy. "Thus may luxury, may pride, may ignorance be banished from among us," read one report on state guardianship; "and we may become what fellow citizens ought to be, a nation of brothers." While the workers were not wholly to approve this particular program, Owen contributed a great deal to their educational ideas.

Frances Wright was at once the most zealous, the most colorful and in the eyes of contemporaries, the most dangerous of these reformers associated with the Workingmen's Party. Although a free thinker, and so outspoken an advocate of women's rights and easy divorce that she was generally accused of advocating free love, she did not look the part of a radical agitator. Tall, slender, with wavy chestnut hair, she completely dazzled the workingmen's audiences she was constantly addressing. Conservatives were as much shocked by the daring effrontery of a female in appearing on the lecture platform as by her unorthodox

views, but few of those who actually heard her speak were wholly im-
mune to her charms. "She has always been to me one of the sweetest of
sweet memories," Walt Whitman, taken to one of her meetings by his
carpenter father, was to write in later years: "we all loved her; fell down
before her: her very appearance seemed to enthrall us . . . graceful,
deerlike . . . she was beautiful in bodily shape and gifts of soul."

Fanny Wright was born in Scotland and falling early under the influence of Jeremy Bentham became even as a young woman the militant
champion of reform that she was to remain throughout her life. On
first coming to this country, she had taken up the cause of the enslaved
Negro and established at Nashoba, Tennessee, a colony where she tried
to prepare groups of slaves, purchased at her own expense, for freedom
and eventual colonization outside of the United States. When this project
failed, she joined the community at New Harmony and then accompanied Robert Dale Owen to New York to cooperate with him in editing
the *Free Enquirer*.

Undaunted by her disappointments at Nashoba and New Harmony,
with her zeal for reform in no way abated, she enthusiastically adopted
the workingmen's movement. She saw in it not only a protest against
social inequality but a basic revolt on the part of the oppressed for
which history offered no parallel. "What distinguishes the present from
every other struggle in which the human race has been engaged," she
wrote in the *Free Enquirer*, "is, that the present is, evidently, openly and
acknowledgedly, a war of class . . . it is the ridden people of the earth
who are struggling to throw from their backs the 'booted and spurred'
riders whose legitimate title to starve as well as work them to death will
no longer pass current; it is labour rising up against idleness, industry
against money; justice against law and against privilege."

The newspapers railed against Fanny Wright. They attempted to
dismiss her as "an exotic of some notoriety"; they called her "the great
Red Harlot of Infidelity." But no matter what abuse they flung at her,
she shamelessly went on expressing her "alarming principles" on public
platforms and in the press.

When the Workingmen's Party took the field under such sponsorship
in the New York elections of 1829, with its slate of tradesmen and
artisans, the conservatives were nonplussed. They at first attempted to
dismiss any possible threat to their own interests, but as the vote of

the laboring classes appeared to be swinging heavily behind the new party, they became thoroughly aroused. "We understand with astonishment and alarm," the *Courier and Enquirer* protested, "that the 'Infidel Ticket,' miscalled the 'Workingmen's Ticket,' is far ahead of every other Assembly ticket in the city. What a state of things we have reached! A ticket got up openly and avowedly in opposition to social order, in opposition to the rights of property, running ahead of every other!" Even more shrill were the outcries of the *New York Commercial Advertiser:* "Lost to society, to earth and heaven, godless and hopeless, clothed and fed by stealing and blasphemy . . . such are the apostles who are trying to induce a number of able-bodied men in this city to follow in their course. . . ."

In the result, such fears proved to be exaggerated. The Workingmen's Party did not sweep the city. Nevertheless, it polled some 6,000 votes, out of a total of 21,000 cast in the election, and sent one of its candidates, a carpenter, to the assembly. "The sun of liberty has not pursued his steady and unchanging course for half a century in vain," George Henry Evans started a rhapsodic editorial in the *Working Man's Advocate,* and then, abruptly dropping his metaphor, observed more moderately that the result has proved "beyond our most sanguine expectations, favorable to our cause—the cause of the people."

Nevertheless a growing divergence in the views of the party's self constituted leaders, and a revolt on the part of the rank-and-file membership against the extreme radicalism of Thomas Skidmore, soon led to internal dissension and factional fights. At a meeting in December, 1829, a resolution was adopted in which the workingmen explicitly stated that they had "no desire or intention of disturbing the right of property in individuals, or the public." As Robert Dale Owen then moved in to try to take over Skidmore's repudiated leadership, opposition also arose to his program of state guardianship. The workingmen were ready to make education their foremost party plank, but they would not support "any attempt to palm upon any man, or set of men, the peculiar doctrines of infidelity, agrarianism, or sectarian principles." They declared that the school system should be based "upon a plan that shall leave to the father and the affectionate mother the enjoyment of the society of their offspring."

The consequences of these inner conflicts, in part promoted by politicians seeking the workingmen's support for their own purposes, was a three-way split in the original organization. Skidmore and the few followers he could hold in line established a straight-out Agrarian Workingmen's Party. Another faction, whose interests were promoted by George Henry Evans in the *Working Man's Advocate* and which was still supported by the Owenites and Fanny Wright, struggled to maintain the original party. A third group broke away under new leadership, with the support of the *Evening Journal*, another labor news sheet, and became known as the North American Party after the name of the hotel where its meetings were held.

Between the last two groups especially there was embittered and continuing strife. They were soon endorsing rival politicians, putting rival tickets in the field, flinging verbal brickbats at each other through the pages of their respective organs, breaking up each other's meetings. The original Workingmen's Party, finding itself under attack because of the radical views of Owen and Fanny Wright, frantically denied the implications of these charges. "The cries of Infidelity and Agrarianism are mere political scarecrows," it asserted, "such as were formerly set up to terrify the democrats of 1801." The North American Party was accused of selling out to local politicians and the workingmen were called upon to avoid "the political trimmer, the pettifogger, the office hunter." Unity was essential if they were to make their influence felt—"Yoke not, therefore, the noble war horse with the ignoble ass."

While the intra-party contest raged in New York, local parties sprang up in such cities as Albany, Troy, Schenectady, Rochester, Syracuse and Auburn. Plans were made to hold a state convention of workingmen and to nominate candidates for governor and lieutenant governor. It was finally summoned, with seventy-eight delegates from thirteen counties, but the split in New York city proved disastrous when rival delegations attended the convention. The professional politicians took over and succeeded in winning the workingmen's vote in support of a Democratic office seeker. "The Working Men Betrayed," shrieked the *Advocate*, and declared its adherents would nominate their own slate.

In the resulting confusion, the election of 1830 found three factions of workingmen each putting forward its own nominees in the city elections and endorsing rival candidates for the governorship. Without cohesion or unity, an easy prey to professional political influences and the blandishments of Tammany Hall, the Workingmen's Party as originally constituted broke up. The Democrats won both the state and local elections and there was an end to any further effective organization among the forces of labor in New York. The *Working Man's Advocate* insisted that nothing could so effectually prevent the final accomplishment of labor's objectives as a coalition with any other party for the temporary purpose of electing particular men. The workers' votes, however, had already swung over to Tammany.

If the experience of the New York artisans and mechanics in trying to set up an independent political organization was short-lived, very much the same story might be told of the activities of other workingmen's parties. In many instances, particularly in Pennsylvania and Massachusetts, they succeeded for a time in aligning the labor vote behind their own candidates and exercising an important and occasionally decisive influence in local politics. But just as in New York, internal friction and external pressures led to factionalism and gradual disintegration. Self-constituted leaders sought to promote their own individual panaceas of reform, which as in the case of the programs promoted by Skidmore, Evans, Owen and Fanny Wright, were often at variance with the real interests of the workers. And when reformers were ousted, politicians were quick to move in to take over control and try to swing the workingmen's votes for one or another of the major parties.

In Massachusetts an attempt to bring about a broader political organization of workers was made in 1832 with the formation of the New England Association of Farmers, Mechanics and Workingmen. The successes won by this group in local elections inspired the nomination of a governor, but the association was soon deeply involved in the major political struggles of the day with its own gubernatorial candidate urging the working class to rally in support of the Democrats.

In spite of the failure of the workingmen's parties themselves, wide acceptance of many of the principles for which they stood marked the final stages of their merger with the larger forces of Jacksonian democracy. Both major parties were greatly influenced, as we have seen, by the new political power of the workers. However, it was the Democrats rather than the Whigs that most directly supported labor's aims. When

Jackson launched his war against the United States Bank, vigorously attacking monopoly and special privilege on a score of fronts, artisans, mechanics and laborers naturally rallied behind him. If the labor vote was not wholly cast in favor of a single party—as, indeed, it never has been—the workers generally hurrahed for Jackson in 1832 as the foe of monopoly and the friend of the people.

The conservatives gave warning in terms that were to be repeated a century later in another period that found marked class divisions in a presidential election. "Elect Jackson," one factory owner told his employes, "and the grass will grow in your streets, owls will build nests in the mills, and foxes burrow in the highways." But the workers turned out nevertheless to help return him to office. In New York they marched to the polls singing:

> Mechanics, cartmen, laborers
> Must form a close connection,
> And show the rich aristocrats,
> Their powers at this election. . . .

> Yankee Doodle, smoke 'em out
> The proud, the banking faction
> None but such as Hartford Feds
> Oppose the poor and Jackson.

The twists and turns of politics in the 1830's are one thing, however, and another is the steady growth of progressive principles and the practical achievement of the reforms the workers sought. As the popular support for the original aims of the workingmen's parties gathered increasing force, and the liberal elements in the community as a whole took them up, steady progress was made in meeting the demands that first flared forth on the mastheads of the labor press.

A first case in point was education reform. At the head of the editorial column in almost every workingmen's newspaper, there had been placed the demand figuring so prominently in the campaign of the New York party—Equal Universal Education. At this time, only the vaguest consideration was being given to the needs of children whose parents were unable to afford private institutions. New England was ahead of the rest of the country in having tax supported schools, but even in such populous and wealthy states as New York, New Jersey, Pennsylvania and Delaware (to say nothing of the new states in the west or the backward states of the south), the only provision for the children of workingmen and other poor families was the charity school—inadequate, inefficient and socially degrading. The Public School Society reported, in 1820, that there were over 24,000 children between the ages of five and fifteen in New York who had no schooling whatsoever, or almost the same number as that enrolled in all charity and private schools. Some years later, a more extensive report in Pennsylvania declared that 250,-000 out of the 400,000 children in that state did not attend school. For the country as a whole, over-all estimates placed the total at over a million, with a corresponding measure of complete illiteracy.

The workingmen resented equally the lack of opportunity for an education as reflected in these figures, and the odium attached to such public schools as there were because they were charitable institutions. Without going so far as to accept all the doctrines of Robert Dale Owen and Frances Wright, they universally agreed with them in insisting upon the importance of free, republican education which would be available on terms of complete equality for the children of both rich and poor. The workingmen based their position on the philosophy of equal rights inherent in the Declaration of Independence, and bulwarked it with the unassailable argument that as future citizens, it was imperative that all children have the education that would enable them to vote intelligently. Never have a people had greater faith in education—"the greatest blessing bestowed upon mankind"—than this generation of Americans. The workers could not have been more determined in demanding it for their children as a right to which they were morally entitled.

"It appears, therefore to the committees," read a typical report of a workingmen's group in Philadelphia, "that there can be no liberty without a wide diffusion of real intelligence; that the members of a republic, should all be alike instructed in the nature and character of their equal rights and duties, as human beings, and as citizens. . . ." It was also argued in this report that only an effective system of public schools could prevent children from being exposed too early to the pernicious

influences of society and thereby "yield an abundant harvest for mag-
dalens and penitentiaries" or fall victim to intemperance—"that assas-
sinator of private peace and public virtue." The major emphasis was
invariably placed, however, on the importance of education as the
very foundation of the democratic forms of government which America
exemplified. "A system that shall unite under the same roof the children
of the poor man and the rich, the widow's charge and the orphan," was
the demand put forward by the reorganized Workingmen's Party of
New York in 1829, "where the road to distinction shall be superior
industry, virtue and acquirement, without reference to descent."

Opinions differed as to the type of education which should be provided, but stress was in most instances laid upon the importance of
practical training as well as the liberal arts. Public institutions, it was
urged in another report of the Philadelphia workingmen, should be
"so located as to command health, exercise at the various mechanic
arts, or agriculture, at the same time [that] a knowledge of the natural
sciences, and other useful literature is taught."

The educational campaign had of course other than working class
support. It was taken up by many reformers and awoke progressively
wider attention. At the same time, it was long opposed by conservatives
who felt that the advantages of schooling should be closely restricted
and that it was wholly unwarranted to tax the rich for the education
of the poor. "Universal, Equal Education," the National Gazette declared, "is impossible, if the trades, manufactories and manual labor
are to be successfully prosecuted,—unless the standard of education be
greatly lowered and narrowed."

Nevertheless this campaign waged so vigorously for Equal Republican, Scientific, Practical Education began to bear fruit. State legislatures
took the issue under more serious consideration than they ever had
before, and new laws were gradually adopted, first authorizing and then
requiring local communities to levy taxes for public education. The
turn perhaps came when Pennsylvania, where the workingmen had
been so active, finally adopted a free, tax-supported system in 1834. The
bill embodying this program narrowly missed defeat. In response to
a protesting petition with 32,000 signatures, the senate tried to substitute a provision "for the education of the poor gratis." But the principle
of a public school system free to all on terms of equality triumphed.

Other states fell in line and the victory for which the workingmen had so long contested was ultimately won.

Another issue for which labor battled valiantly and successfully during this period was abolition of imprisonment for debt. The antiquated practice of throwing a man into jail when he could not meet his financial obligations was still in almost universal effect in the 1820's. The Boston Prison Discipline Society estimated, at the close of the decade, that some 75,000 persons were being imprisoned annually for debts, and that in at least half of the cases, the sums involved were less than $25. In one instance, a woman was taken from her home and the care of her two children for a debt of $3.60, and in another a man was thrown into jail for a $5 debt owing his grocer, even though it had been contracted while the debtor was ill. Thirty-two persons were found in one prison for debts which in every case were less than $1.

Obviously this system bore most heavily on the poor and its injustice rankled deeply. "A law that makes poverty a crime," one workingman political candidate declared, "and a poor man a felon, after these very laws have made poverty inevitable, is not only cruel and oppressive, but absurd and revolting." Adding to the miseries of the situation, the debtors' jails were shockingly overcrowded and insanitary, and there was often no provision for feeding the prisoners, who remained wholly dependent upon private charity. In New Jersey, according to one report, there were "food, bedding and fuel" for criminals, but for the debtors only "walls, bars and bolts."

Reform was long overdue yet it still awoke opposition from the business community. Even John Quincy Adams felt obliged to point out what he considered would be the dangerous effects of doing away with debt imprisonment upon the security of property and the sanctity of contracts. These considerations were felt by merchants and lawyers to be more important than what President Jackson declared to be the injustice of exerting such a "grinding power over misfortune and poverty."

The workingmen's drive first led to the passage of laws whereby the poor debtor could win release by taking a bankruptcy oath, and then to limitations upon the amounts for which he could be imprisoned. But soon the states were one by one forced to accept the inescapable logic of abolishing the system altogether. Ohio took this step in 1828 and the next decade saw its example followed by New York, New Jersey, Connecticut, Virginia and other states. The practice still lingered on in some parts of the country, but its complete disappearance was clearly foreshadowed by the end of the 1830's.

The attack upon the militia system, largely promoted by the workingmen's parties, was also successful. In most states, attendance at annual drills and parades, generally lasting three days, was compulsory for every citizen. The militiamen had to pay all their own expenses and provide their own equipment, while failure to attend was punished by fines or imprisonment. For the workingmen such regulations meant not only a loss in wages while attending the drill, but what were for them heavy expenses. The rich, on the other hand, could easily afford to escape their obligations by paying the same fines without difficulty. After 1830, compulsory service was either modified or completely abolished. President Jackson called attention to the issue in his annual message in 1832, urging that wherever the old system still prevailed—as in New York— its inequalities should be carefully examined.

Other instances of economic or social advance owed much to the workers. Their demand for mechanics' lien laws, at once taken up by Tammany Hall in New York, led to widespread adoption of such legislation. Their opposition to the existing auction system, to general incorporation laws, to the issuance by local banks of small currency notes, and to other economic abuses was an important factor in the passage of remedial laws.

The rise of the workingmen's parties did not at all represent a class movement and it was not completely a labor movement. The workingmen were confused and baffled by the changes that were taking place in their social status, and they sought somehow to establish greater equality between producers and those who lived on the fruits of the producers' toil.

As their movement fell into the hands of doctrinaire reformers or professional politicians, they began to feel that their entry into politics was wholly futile. The broad and distant goal of equality seemed to be a glittering mirage. They gradually returned to more practical aims—

higher wages, shorter hours—which had been neglected in their new absorption in politics. Economic action to attain these immediate objectives now appeared to the rank and file of trade union members to hold far greater possibilities for enabling them to maintain their standard of living. "The Trades' Unions never will be political," the *National Laborer*, of Philadelphia, declared in characteristic expression of this new attitude, "because its members have learned from experience that the introduction of Politics into their Societies has thwarted every effort to ameliorate their Conditions."

The social gains inspired by the original workingmen's parties were at least a partial denial of this emphatic statement. Nevertheless, labor was unable throughout the nineteenth century to organize with political effectiveness in party battles. When later attempts were made to establish a national party, they completely failed. The experience of the 1830's was a first demonstration that labor had no real basis for setting up a distinctive party. Its aims were broadly liberal, and taken over by the major parties whenever the workers were able, directly or indirectly, to exercise sufficient pressure. The flirtation of the New York Workingmen's Party with the radical agrarianism of its original leaders was brief. The workers themselves were basically conservative in their views, and the equality they sought was within the framework of the existing political and economic structure of the country. They wanted to share in the benefits of emerging capitalism rather than to overthrow it. Fanny Wright might declaim upon a war of classes. Such sentiments did not echo the views of the workingmen themselves.

There was no single unifying principle to hold the workers together. Unlike their contemporaries in Europe, they were not inspired to common political action to obtain the franchise, because they had already won the vote as part of the nationwide triumph of democratic principles in the 1820's. Nor were they drawn to the support of socialism, as were workers in England and on the continent. The interests of American wage earners were too closely allied with the interests of the people generally to provide a basis for a distinctive class solidarity that would find political expression in a third party. The opportunities afforded by an expanding economy, the continued fluidity of class lines, and the individualism of the frontier carved out the channels along which the

American labor movement was to develop in sharp contrast to the situation in Europe.

If for a time the workingmen's parties of the 1830's seemed to foreshadow the possible creation of a labor party, their absorption in the general advance of Jacksonian democracy marked the sharp reversal of any such trend.

IV: LABOR STRENGTH IN THE 1830'S

THE ORIGINAL WORKINGMEN'S PARTIES rose and fell within a very brief span of time. Whatever may be claimed for their political influence, their existence as distinctive political organizations was too ephemeral to bulk very large in the history of the labor movement. The return of the trade societies to economic action was in many ways a far more significant development. During these years in which such marked progress was being made in social reform in the country as a whole, and particularly during Jackson's second administration from 1833 to 1837, union activity was more widespread and more militant than it would be again for several decades.

The workingmen continued to feel, as their excursion into politics had already demonstrated, a sense of degradation in their changing social position. The revived trade unions were to be primarily concerned with wages and hours, but they also reflected the desire of their members to regain status in the community. As the old society they had known appeared to be dissolving, with onetime independent craftsmen sinking to the level of wage earners, artisans and mechanics more than ever hoped through union membership to reaffirm the dignity of labor and to win greater public recognition of its social as well as economic values.

"As the line of distinction between employer and employed *widened*," wrote one labor leader in 1834, "the condition of the latter inevitably verges toward a state of vassalage . . . hostile to the best interests of the community, as well as the spirit and genius of our government." The trade societies sought to combat this trend by creating a solidarity among the workers that would safeguard them from any such complete and helpless subordination to the employing class.

Conditions within the country in the early 1830's encouraged the growth of unions. On the one hand mounting prosperity strengthened the bargaining power of the workers, and on the other determined

efforts on the part of employers to hold down wages in the face of
rising prices forced them to organize in self-defense. Not only did trade
societies among almost all classes of workers multiply rapidly, but
further attempts were made to link these local unions in citywide federations which would promote labor unity. A beginning was even to be
made in still broader organization that foreshadowed establishment of
a truly national labor movement. Moreover the aggressive attitude of
the members of these unions led to a wave of strikes that provided a
dramatic chapter in the long struggle of the workers to establish their
rights.

So general did this activity become that no trade appeared to be im-
mune to its contagious militancy. "The barbers have struck," the *New
York Times* exclaimed in April, 1836, "and now all that remains for
Editors is to strike, too."

Never before in time of peace had there been such a rapid increase in
the cost of living as resulted from the wild-cat boom of the early 1830's
with all its speculation and extravagant inflation. The easing of bank
credit and the profligate issue of paper money, which were the immediate consequences of President Jackson's successful attack upon the
United States Bank, forced prices up all along the line. In New York,
flour went from $5 a barrel in 1834 to $8 in April, 1835 and then to $12
a year later. Other foodstuffs followed the same upward spiral, clothing
and household goods rose phenomenally, and the advance in rents
was from twenty-five to forty per cent. It was generally estimated
that the cost of living increased some sixty-six per cent between 1834
and 1836.

Wages invariably lagged behind in this upward march, and the
further measures taken by employers to hold down their own costs
constituted an even greater threat to the workers' living standards. With
the virtual collapse of the apprenticeship system in many trades, young,
half-trained boys were taken on at lower wages than the prevailing rate
for journeymen. Women were brought in, again at lower pay, to replace
male workers. They were most widely employed as tailoresses, seamstresses and shoe binders (contemporary estimates stating that 12,000
of the 20,000 engaged in such work earned no more than $1.25 a week),

but they also offered new competition to printers, cigar makers and other workers. The report of a Philadelphia committee, in 1836, declared that "of fifty-eight societies, twenty-four are seriously affected by female labour, to the impoverishment of whole families, and the benefit of none but the employers." Finally, there was widespread resort to convict labor. Mechanics and artisans complained bitterly that through this developing practice of letting out contracts to prisons, whatever the benefits for the convicts themselves, articles were manufactured at prices "from 40 to 60 per cent below what the honest mechanic, who supports himself and family, can afford."

Under such circumstances, there was hardly an urban community in which the workingmen were not driven to act together in mutual defense of their interests. In Philadelphia, the cordwainers reorganized, the handloom weavers formed a new society, and bricklayers, plumbers, blacksmiths, cigar makers, comb makers and saddlers, among other trades, were unionized. The older societies in New York were revived, with the printers, cordwainers and tailors once again in the lead, and cabinet makers, hat finishers, basket makers, locksmiths, pianoforte makers, and silk hatters joining the union ranks. The organizations in Baltimore included bootmakers, stonecutters, coopers, carpet weavers and coach makers. The same story could be told of every other city on the Atlantic seaboard, and also of upstate New York, Washington, Pittsburgh, Louisville and other manufacturing centers in the west.

The further organization among workers other than the traditional mechanics and artisans was making at least some headway. By this time there was a rapidly developing textile industry in Massachusetts and Rhode Island, factories in Connecticut were turning out clocks and watches, and iron foundries in Pennsylvania presaged the further growth of large-scale industry. In addition to the employes in such establishments, other new groups of wage earners included machinists and engineers, freight handlers, firemen on steamboats, stage drivers, gatekeepers on turnpikes and canal bridges. While these workers still remained largely unorganized, pioneering unions among the cotton factory operatives, tinplate and sheet iron workers and many other groups won increasing support.

Women were also brought into the labor movement with their own trade societies. Baltimore had a United Seamstresses Society; New York its Ladies' Shoebinders and Female Bookbinders, as well as a Female Union Association, and in Philadelphia there was a Female Improvement Society. As an early sign of organized activity among the women employes of the New England textile mills, there was formed, in 1833, the Female Society of Lynn and Vicinity for the Protection and Promotion of Female Industry, and, a year later, the Factory Girls' Association.

A picturesque view of the trade societies as they existed in New York about this time is found in the description of a spectacular demonstration in that city celebrating the triumph of the French revolution in 1830. Although Tammany Hall took over control of the affair, the unions dominated it. Their delegations were the most prominent feature in a parade whose line of march was some three miles long and which was joyfully watched by crowds estimated at thirty thousand persons.

The elaborate floats, as described in the *Working Man's Advocate,* were the sensation of the day. The printers had two elegant presses ("tastefully gilded and ornamented") which they had borrowed from the manufactories of Messrs. Rust and Hoe and set up on two separate cars drawn by four horses. The butchers, in dress described as characteristic of their profession and mounted on prancing white horses, were also on hand. On one of their floats the skin of an ox had been so stuffed as to take on a life-like appearance and had been gaily decorated with ribbons and cockades. On another a butcher's stall had been erected where "sausages were manufactured to the great amusement of the people."

The cordwainers had made extensive and elegant preparations for the demonstration and on one of their floats two young ladies were busily engaged in binding shoes. The manufacturers of steam engines exhibited a perfect steam engine ("the smoke from the pipes ascended, the water wheels revolved"), and the cabinet makers had such splendid specimens of furniture that the *Advocate's* reporter found himself unable to describe them. The carvers and gilders were in the line with portraits of Jefferson and Lafayette in superb gilt frames; the tobacconists won the applause of the admiring crowd by distributing small plugs of tobacco; the saddlers and harness makers had mounts furnished with the most shining examples of their ware; the bookbinders boasted a float in the form of a mammoth book hauled by four sturdy horses;

and the chair makers graciously built on route a "Grecian Post Maple Chair."

The shouts and huzzas, the waving pennants, tricolored cockades and "star spangled banners," made for a great occasion. Only a small part of the throng could be accommodated about the reviewing stand where the venerable ex-President Monroe had the place of honor until the "chilly state of the atmosphere" compelled him to leave. There were fervid speeches and an ode written by Samuel Woodworth, printer, was sung to the tune of the *Marseillaise* with the accompaniment of the orchestra from the Park Theatre:

> Then swell the choral strain,
> To Hail the blest decree.
> Rejoice, rejoice, the Press shall reign
> And all the world be Free.

That night the various societies held commemorative banquets (a dinner was sent in to the inmates of the debtor's prison by the sympathetic delegates of the ninth ward), and a great concourse of workingmen foregathered at the Masonic Hall. After a sumptuous entertainment had served as prelude "for the enjoyment of the mental repast," a glowing panegyric was delivered on the success of the French revolutionary movement and the part played in it by workingmen.

"Move on then, mechanics and working men," the speaker of the evening declared in his eloquent peroration, "in your glorious career of mental independence, with republican education for your polar star, union and firmness your sheet anchor, and the day is not distant which shall crown your noble effort with victory, and your country shall stand redeemed from the poison of fashion and the canker worm of party— and in their place shall spring up the tree of pure republicanism, yielding the choice fruits of real equality of rights; then man shall be judged by his actions and not by his professions; by his usefulness to society as an industrious citizen and not by the texture of the garb which covers him."

The address was followed by toasts—fourteen formal toasts and thirty-one volunteer toasts—happily "interspersed with appropriate songs, odes and recitations." The enthusiastic diners toasted the workingmen of Paris, and the workingmen of New York; they drank to the memory of Jefferson and Lafayette, to Bolivar, to true democrats, universal education, free enquiry; they toasted "the Original Working Men—May they not oblique to the right or the left," and the "Simon Pures—May they not be frightened by the cries of Fanny Wrightism, Agrarianism or any other *ism*, but stick to true republicanism."

Forty-five toasts, as the bottles circulated and the workingmen cheered. "The greatest hilarity and unanimity," concludes the account of the *Working Man's Advocate* "characterized the proceedings of the evening, and the company separated at an early hour, much gratified with the manner in which they had been entertained."

The rapid growth and development of the trade societies led naturally to the movement for closer association in promoting their common aims. A precedent for such cooperation had been established by the Mechanics' Union of Trade Associations in Philadelphia, but as we have seen, this group had almost immediately become absorbed in politics. What the workingmen now sought in forming "trades' unions"—that is, unions of local trade societies that represented in modern terminology central trades councils—was a basis for joint economic activity.[1] The trades' union, in the words of the constitution of one of these new organizations, was a "compact, formed of Societies and Associations of Mechanics and Working Men, which, having discovered that they were unable to combat the numerous powers arrayed against them, united together for mutual protection."

The General Trades' Union of New York was the most important of

[1] The terminology of labor organization in this period is admittedly confusing. The "trade societies," as suggested in the text, were the equivalent of modern "trade unions," and the new "trades' unions" corresponded more nearly to today's "central trades councils" established in the cities by the A.F. of L. and the C.I.O. At this very time, however, the "trade societies" were beginning to be called "trade unions" although "trades' unions" were the association of the local societies.

One of the earliest examples of the use of union in the modern sense of the term, in a pamphlet published in 1836 which was called *Dialogue Between Strike and Steady*, had this interesting comment: "My objection to your Union is, that you wish to use the very compulsion, you will not yourselves endure."

these new central trades councils, and there were comparable organizations in Philadelphia, Boston, Baltimore, Washington, Cincinnati, Pittsburgh, Louisville and other manufacturing cities. Their number had grown to thirteen by 1836, with fifty-two associated societies in New York, fifty-three in Philadelphia, twenty-three in Baltimore, and sixteen in Boston.

The final coordinating step in this activity was taken in 1834 when the summons went out to establish a national organization embracing all trades. Representatives of local societies in New York, Brooklyn, Boston, Philadelphia, Poughkeepsie and Newark met in the first named city and formed the National Trades' Union. Its purposes were to advance the welfare of the laboring classes, promote the establishment of trades' unions in every part of the country, and publish such information as would be useful to mechanics and workingmen. In the light of the failure of the workingmen's parties, its leaders were determined that the new organization should not be drawn off into political activities. The workingmen "belonged to no party," one Massachusetts labor leader declared; "they were neither disciples of Jacksonism nor Clayism, Van Burenism nor Websterism, not any other ism but workeyism."

National organization of the workers was not to be really effective at this time. It was to wait upon the nationalizing of business in the years following the Civil War. But the attempt to form such a federation attests the strength and vitality of the labor movement of the 1830's. As the result of the zeal of local societies, city trades councils and the National Trades' Union, there were in the country as a whole an estimated 300,000 unionized workers. On a relative basis, so large a number of wage earners would not again be enrolled in union ranks for half a century. In New York, some two-thirds of all the city's workers were said to be members of one or another of its fifty-odd labor unions.

In increasingly active defense of their rights, trade union members did not hesitate either to threaten or actually go out on strike when their employers refused to meet what they felt were their legitimate demands. When the latter tried to hold down wages or bring in untrained workers at lower pay, there were turn-outs in almost every trade and in every city. Printers and weavers, tailors and coachmakers, masons and bookbinders walked out. The carpenters in New York earning $1.50 a day struck for $1.75 and having won it, promptly struck again for $2.

The girls working in New England cotton mills again went on strike. "One of the leaders mounted a pump," the *Boston Transcript* reported, "and made a flaming . . . speech on the rights of women and the iniquities of 'monied aristocracy' which produced a powerful effect upon her auditors, and they determined to have their own way, if they died for it." As in the first waves of strikes instigated by the original trade societies, such turn-outs were almost always peaceful, but they became so general that the business community became increasingly alarmed. Between 1833 and 1837 no less than 168 were recorded in contemporary newspapers.

As in later periods, the employers sought to attribute these disturbances not to labor's legitimate grievances, but to the activity of radical and subversive agitators, generally supposed to be foreigners. "I fear the elements of disorder are at work," a conservative New Yorker, Philip Hone, onetime mayor, noted in his diary; "the bands of Irish and other foreigners instigated by the mischievous councils of the trades union and other combinations of discontented men, are acquiring strength and importance which will ere long be difficult to quell." Whatever the workers' complaints (and Hone noted himself the tremendous increase in the cost of living), he felt that any strike, however orderly, was an "unlawful proceeding."

The demand of workers throughout the east for a ten-hour day came to a head during this exciting period in a concerted outbreak of strikes. There had been earlier agitation for such a reduction in the hours of work. It had been the background for the formation of the Mechanics' Union of Trade Associations in Philadelphia in 1827, and of the Workingmen's Party in New York two years later. But the workers were now ready to use their strongest weapon as a means of coercing employers to grant their demands.

"All men have a just right, derived from their creator," stated a resolution of the journeymen carpenters in Philadelphia, "to have sufficient time each day for the cultivation of their mind and for self-improvement; Therefore, resolved, that we think ten hours industriously imployed are sufficient for a day's labor."

On this same note demands were also made by New England work-

ingmen for a shorter day and surprisingly enough found support from
such a conservative paper as the *Boston Transcript*. "Let the mechanic's
labor be over," it urged, "when he has wrought ten or twelve hours in
the long days of summer, and he will be able to return to his family in
season, and with sufficient vigour, to pass some hours in the instruction
of his children, or in the improvement of his own mind."

In other periods of labor's long struggle for shorter hours, stress would
be laid upon the ill effects of prolonged, exacting toil on the workers'
health and well being, or upon the importance of spreading work to
combat the danger of unemployment. In the 1830's, however, the emphasis upon time for self-education, which was considered so essential
to enable the newly enfranchised laboring classes to fulfill their obligations as citizens, was a great deal more than merely a facile argument
to bolster their cause. There is every evidence that the workers were
deeply interested in education for themselves as well as for their children.
The crowded workingmen audiences at the popular lyceum lectures of
these years, the growing vogue for circulating libraries, and the insistent
demand for free, public schools all attest a deep concern born of the
idealistic belief that education alone could provide the basis for a successful democracy.

"We have been too long subjected," a circular of striking workingmen
in Boston in 1835 stated, "to the odious, cruel, unjust and tyrannical
system which compels the operative Mechanic to exhaust his physical
and mental powers. . . . We have rights, and we have duties to perform as American citizens and members of society, which forbid us to
dispose of more than Ten Hours for a day's work."

Such arguments did not, however, carry much weight with employers.
The proposal for a ten-hour day, one newspaper declared, "strikes the
very nerve of industry and good morals by dictating the hours of labour.
. . . To be idle several of the most useful hours of the morning and
evening will surely lead to intemperance and ruin." A statement
published in the *Boston Courier* by a group of merchants and shipown-
ers further emphasized the serious loss to the community in any reduction of the working day and deplored the "habits likely to be generated
by the indulgence of idleness." However deeply grounded the real
objection to shorter hours in its effect upon business profits, it was,
indeed, this professed fear that leisure would undermine the workers'

morals and foster intemperance, already noted in the attitude of employers in colonial New England, that became the chief stock in trade of the conservative opposition to any change in the traditional sun-up to sunset system.

The organized workingmen in city after city refused, however, to be persuaded by such arguments and stood their ground. Their universal demand was for a working day from six in the morning until six in the evening, with an hour off for breakfast and another for dinner. In Baltimore, the members of seventeen trades joined forces in a strike for this reform in 1833, and two years later the carpenters of Boston, with the support of masons, stonecutters and other workers in the building trades, walked-out with similar demands. Both of these movements failed. In Philadelphia, on the other hand, an even more widely organized and popularly supported strike was to win a resounding victory in 1835 that had wide reverberations.

It was initiated by the coal heavers and other common laborers but they were soon joined by cordwainers, handloom weavers, cigar makers, saddlers, printers and members of the building trades. A circular relating the experiences of the Boston workers had an electric effect in unifying those of Philadelphia, and strengthened their determination not to give in. A popular demonstration was staged in which workers of all trades paraded through the streets, with fife and drum, and banners inscribed "from 6 to 6."

"We marched to the public works," wrote their leader, John Ferral, a handloom weaver and fiery labor agitator, "and the workmen joined in with us. . . . Employment ceased, business was at a standstill, shirt sleeves were rolled up, aprons on, working tools in hand were the order of the day. Had the cannon of an invading enemy belched forth its challenge on our soil, the freemen of Philadelphia could not have shown a greater ardor for the contest; the blood-sucking aristocracy, they alone stood aghast; terror stricken, they thought the day of retribution was come, but no vengeance was sought or inflicted by the people for the wrongs they had suffered from their enemies."

The common council of the city was the first to give in, establishing a ten-hour day for all public servants. The master carpenters and master cordwainers followed, and other employers then quickly fell in line until the ten-hour day prevailed throughout the city. "The mechanics of

Philadelphia stood firm and true," Ferral wrote; "they conquered, because they were united and resolute in their actions. The presses which could not retard the progress of public opinion, nor divert it from its just objects, viz. the adoption of the ten-hour system . . . now proclaim the triumph of our bloodless revolution. . . ."

The movement spread to other parts of the country and in many instances won a corresponding success. Soon the ten-hour day had widely replaced, for artisans and mechanics, the former sun-up to sunset. In the factories that were being established for the New England textile industry, and in many other manufacturing industries, the work day was long to remain twelve hours and more. In some trades the gains of the 1830's were to be lost. But a very real victory had been won for the workers by their concerted stand in the strikes of Philadelphia and other cities. Moreover the Federal Government was soon to be induced to establish a ten-hour day for all public works. Congress had refused to take any notice of the frequent memorials addressed to it on the subject, but when striking shipwrights directly appealed to President Jackson in 1836, the system was installed at the Philadelphia navy yard. Four years later, Van Buren even more directly admitted his debt to the workingmen for their political support by an executive order which established ten hours as the work day on all government projects.

The employers held out as long as they could in combatting the workers' demands both for higher wages and a shorter working day. They continued whenever possible to undermine their employes' bargaining power by drawing upon cheaper sources of labor. But where skilled artisans and mechanics were concerned, they found it increasingly difficult to maintain their position. The craft unions succeeded in enforcing a closed shop which tied the employers' hands. Through public cards listing as "unfair" any journeyman who did not join a union and designating as "foul" any establishment where an "unfair man" was given work, they largely controlled the labor market. This was not of course always true, but the records of the time reveal an unexpected power on the part of the organized workers in the skilled trades.

Under these circumstances the employers turned more and more to mutual protective associations which were prepared to act together in opposing "every injurious combination" of the workingmen. In New York a group of Employers, Curriers and Leather Dealers took up arms against the General Trades' Union and mutually agreed that they would not employ "any man who is known to be a member of that or any other society which has for its object the direction of terms or prices for which workmen shall engage themselves." In Philadelphia the master carpenters took the lead in calling for formation of an Anti-Trades' Union Association. A set of resolutions was adopted declaring the trades' union to be arbitrary, unjust, mischievous and a powerful engine of the leveling system that would reduce masters to the status of journeymen. Employers had every right, it was maintained, to make whatever contract with their employes they chose without the interference of any workingmen's society.

When the employer associations were again unable to hold out against the labor societies, court action was once more in order. The drive to break up unions as conspiracies in restraint of trade was vigorously renewed, and as in the opening years of the century, the employers found willing allies among conservative members of the bench.

The case of the *People* v. *Fisher*, decided in the New York Supreme Court in 1835, was a first important demonstration in this period that the opposition of the courts to labor unions had not changed. A society of journeymen cordwainers in Geneva, New York, was prosecuted for conspiring to raise wages and thereby, as claimed by the plaintiffs, committing an act injurious to trade and commerce and a misdemeanor under existing laws. The presiding judge ruled in the employers' favor. On the theory that the interests of society were best served when the price of labor was left to regulate itself, he declared that in combining to raise wages the cordwainers were working a public injury because "a conspiracy for such an object is against the spirit of the common law."

"Competition is the life of trade," the decision concluded. "If the defendants cannot make coarse boots for less than one dollar per pair, let them refuse to do so; but let them not directly or indirectly undertake to say that others shall not do the work for a less price. . . . The interference of the defendants was unlawful; its tendency is not only to individual oppression, but to public inconvenience and embarrassment."

The effect of this decision was to encourage other employers to seek to suppress the trade societies even though they did not engage in strikes, and when the courts continued to follow a flagrantly anti-labor policy, a storm of protest arose among workingmen and their sympathizers. It came to a head in New York after a further case in 1836 where the presiding judge strongly charged the jury to find a society of journeymen tailors guilty of conspiracy in restraint of trade.

"They were condemned," William Cullen Bryant wrote in vehement defense of the tailors in the *New York Evening Post*, "because they had determined not to work for the wages offered them! Can any thing be imagined more abhorrent. . . . If this is not Slavery, we have forgotten its definition. Strike the right of associating for the sale of labor from the privileges of a freeman, and you may as well at once bind him to a master or ascribe him to the soil. . . ."

The outraged labor leaders of New York distributed throughout the city circulars, inscribed with a coffin, that called upon all workingmen to attend court on the day set for sentencing the convicted tailors.

"On Monday, June 6, 1836," the circulars read, "these Freemen are to receive their sentence, to gratify the hellish appetites of the Aristocracy. On Monday, the Liberty of the Workingmen will be interred! Judge Edwards is to chant the requiem! Go! Go! every Freeman, every Workingman, and hear the melancholy sound of the earth on the Coffin of Equality! Let the court-room, the City Hall—yea, the whole Park, be filled with Mourners!" The crowd which actually turned out does not appear to have reached the hoped-for proportions and it was entirely peaceful. A week later, however, after the tailors had been duly sentenced, another mass meeting was held which drew some 27,000 persons and the offending judge was dramatically burned in effigy.

The reaction against these trials was in fact so strong that juries could not fail to be influenced by it, and in two other conspiracy cases the same summer verdicts of not guilty were returned. Finally, in 1842, Chief Justice Shaw of the Massachusetts Supreme Court rendered an important decision in the case of *Commonwealth* v. *Hunt*, which appeared to provide a firm basis for the legality of unions.

The case was that of the Journeymen Bootmakers' Society of Boston, whose members had agreed not to work for any person employing a journeyman who did not belong to their organization. Chief Justice Shaw stated that the manifest purpose of the society was to induce all those engaged in the same occupation to become members, and that this could not be considered unlawful. Nor could he see that in attempting to accomplish it by refusing to work for any employer who engaged a journeyman not a member, the bootmakers were employing criminal means. He cited as a possible parallel a society whose members might undertake to promote the highly laudable cause of temperance by agreeing not to work for anyone who employed a user of ardent spirits. In other words, agreement for common action to achieve a lawful object was not necessarily a criminal conspiracy. "The legality of such an association," the decision concluded, "will . . . depend upon the means to be used for its accomplishment. . . ."

So far as the labor societies might still have to prove that the means they adopted to attain their ends were in every case lawful, this decision was not a complete victory for labor. It had, indeed, turned upon certain technicalities in the indictment. But both union organization and even the principle of the closed shop had nevertheless received substantial support. It would not be until a much later period that labor again found itself on the legal defensive, fighting renewed conspiracy charges under the anti-trust laws and the arbitrary use of injunctions against strikes and boycotts.

In the ten-hour movement, the revolt against the conspiracy laws, and in their strikes, the workingmen of the 1830's had the full and active backing of their general trades' unions. These organizations were ready to render whatever assistance they could, both in supporting the local societies in their demands and in extending financial assistance when workers went out on strike. In New York, Philadelphia, Boston—wherever general trades' unions had been formed—there was close cooperation among the workers as a result of this leadership. Monthly dues were paid in to the central organization, making possible the creation of a strike fund, and in many instances, additional union appropriations were made to aid the members of other societies out on strike. Occasionally such aid was extended from one city to another. When a delegation of Philadelphia bookbinders appealed to New York's General Trades' Union for aid in February, 1836, a resolution favoring such action was at once adopted. It called upon all members to support "their fellow mechanics who are at this inclement season driven to a stand for their rights against aristocratical tyranny." Varying sums of money were sent to the book-binders not only by unions in New York but also by those of Washington, Baltimore, Albany and Newark.

The National Trades' Union, which had met first in 1834 and held conventions in the next two succeeding years, did not have the close organization of the general trades' unions. It remained little more than an annual conference which debated labor issues and occasionally addressed memorials to Congress—on the ten-hour day, prison labor or public lands. It also went on record, although refusing to enter upon direct political action, in support of many of the reforms being promoted by the Jackson Democrats. It attacked "this American banking system, this rag-money system, this sysem of legalized monopolies which makes the rich richer and the poor poorer." It was in no sense a class conscious movement, however. "Our object in the formation of the Trades' Union," declared its organ, *The Union*, on April 21, 1836, ". . . was not to create a feeling of enmity against the non-producers; . . . [but] to raise in the estimation of themselves and others, those who are the producers of the necessaries and luxuries of life."

Perhaps the greatest contribution of the National Trades' Union to the cause of labor was that of bringing together the workingmen's leaders from various parts of the country. It gave them a sense of common purpose and of support for their activities which encouraged them, as in the case of the ten-hour movement, to keep up their local struggles for labor's rights.

John Ferral, the aggressive handloom weaver who led the successful ten-hour strike in Philadelphia, was a prominent figure at union conventions. No one more strongly urged direct economic action by the labor societies or warned more often of the danger of their being diverted from their main purposes by political blandishments. "The office holders and office seekers of all parties have tried to lure us into the meshes of their nets," he wrote, "but experience came to our aid, and, coy as the young deer, we shied off from their advances; we felt grateful for their proffered aid, but told them 'we knew our own rights, and knowing dared maintain them.'" His initiative and energy were perhaps the most important factors in the organization of the Philadelphia General Trades' Union. He served as chairman of one of its original organizing committees, was constantly involved in its activities, and references to his "spirited addresses" run through all the proceedings of the union.

Another Philadelphia delegate was William English, for a time secretary of the General Trades' Union. He was a journeyman shoemaker, and both a radical and highly erratic champion of the workers' cause. His critics declared he did not have an idea that he had not borrowed or stolen from someone else, but his impassioned addresses always held popular attention.

The principal representative of the New England workingmen was Charles Douglas, one of the founders of the New England Association of Farmers, Mechanics and Other Workingmen, and editor of the *New England Artisan*. His opposition to political activity, although the New England Association had become directly involved in state campaigns in Massachusetts, was no less pronounced than that of John Ferral. His special interest was the status of the factory operatives in the textile mills, and he was one of the first spokesmen for this class of workers.

Attending at least one National Trades' Union meetings was his co-worker in this cause, Seth Luther, the so-called "Traveling Agent" of the *Artisan* and a prototype of many later labor agitators. He was one of the most picturesque of the leaders of this period, a tall, lanky, tobacco-chewing Yankee, habitually wearing a bright green jacket, who toured through the factory towns calling upon the workers to defend their rights. "You cannot raise one part of the community above another unless you stand on the bodies of the poor," he repeatedly declared, and in support of this thesis, he issued a stream of pamphlets depicting the harsh life of the women and children working in the cotton mills under the lash of factory managers. His style was grim, sardonic, highly colored. "While music floats from quivering strings through the perfumed and adorned apartments . . . of the rich," Luther wrote, "the nerves of the poor woman and child, in the cotton mills, are quivering with almost *dying agony*, from *excessive labor* to support this splendor."

The first president of the National Trades' Union was Ely Moore. Originally a student of medicine, he had abandoned the profession to become a journeyman printer, and then entered actively into the labor movement. He suffered from ill health, which was eventually to force his retirement from the political scene, but not before he had proved himself both an able organizer and effective administrator in union activities. Tall, handsome, with curly black hair brushed back over a broad forehead, invariably well dressed and habitually carrying an ivory-headed cane, he was possessed, according to contemporaries, with a thrilling power of eloquence. He headed the General Trades' Union in New York before taking over his post in the National Trades' Union, and in the former capacity had sounded the keynote of the developing labor movement in addressing the workingmen as Pioneers in the Great Cause.

"To you, then, gentlemen, as the *actual* representatives of the Mechanic interests throughout the country," Moore declared, "the eyes of thousands and thousands are turned; for should the experiment succeed here, and the expectations of the friends of the 'Union' be realized, other Unions of a kindred character will be formed, in every section. . . ." But should they fail, he then went on to warn his audience, "the haughty aristocrats of the land will hail the event with exulting hearts and hellish satisfaction."

Moore soon made his position in labor circles the springboard for entry into active politics, and with the support of the unions and Tammany Hall, he was sent to Congress the same year that saw him chosen head of the National Trades' Union. There he won national prominence as a spokesman for the interests of labor and played a notable part in introducing the various memorials addressed to Congress by the union. Whenever he spoke he seems to have commanded rapt attention for his pleas in behalf of workingmen's rights and his vehement attacks upon "the heartless cupidity of the privileged few."

During the aftermath of the popular excitement aroused in New York by the conspiracy trial of the journeymen tailors, he rose on one occasion in April, 1836, to defend labor under unusually dramatic circumstances. A representative from South Carolina had warned of a possible workingmen's insurrection. Although he was so ill that he had to steady himself by leaning on his cane, Moore addressed his audience in a ringing voice that reached to every corner of the House. How could the interests and safety of the state be plotted against, he asked peremptorily, by a group composing three-fourths of the state? "Sir," he declared, glaring at the Speaker as his audience listened intently and one southern congressman was heard to murmur that the high priest of revolution was singing his swan song, "there is much greater danger that capital will unjustly appropriate to itself the avails of labor, than that labor will unlawfully seize upon capital."

"My eye was fixed upon him," wrote a reporter describing the scene for the *Democratic Review;* "I saw him grow paler than ever; till a deadly hue swept over his face; his hands were arrested in the air—he grasped at emptiness—a corpse seemed to stand with outstretched hands before the agitated crowd—his eyes were closed—he tottered, and amid the rush and exclamations of the whole house, fell back insensible into the arms of one of his friends."

Moore recovered from this attack of illness but he would not again address the House. His friends felt that he was in too poor health to undergo the strain that public speaking imposed upon one of his excitable, nervous temperament. But his oration went rapidly through four editions and played its part in arresting the drive to outlaw unions by court action. Public opinion was more and more swinging to their support. "What but a general revolt of all the laboring classes is to be gained," William Cullen Bryant asked in the *New York Evening Post,* "by these wanton and unprovoked attacks upon their rights?"

The labor movement of these years cannot be compared with that of a century later. It grew out of conditions in American society that still had only a remote parallel with those of a period in which the great mass of workingmen are wage earners in mass production industries. The members of the early labor societies were, as we have seen, largely mechanics and artisans, relatively independent, who did not like to think of themselves as belonging to a permanent and distinct wage earning class.

In considering contemporary divisions in American society, the lines they saw were those between aristocracy and democracy, between the rich and the poor, rather than between employers and employes. They were greatly aroused, as stated in an address of the New England Association, by "the low estimation in which useful labour is held by many whose station in society enable them to give the tone to public opinion." They resented the trend whereby all those who could, sought to find some means of living without hard work and condemned the more use-

ful and industrious portion of the community to a life of constant toil—
"stripped of the better share of their earnings, holding a subordinate, if
not degraded situation in society, and frequently despised by the very
men, and women and children who live at ease upon the fruits of their
labour." The dignity of labor, and the respect due workingmen, were as
much the concern of the labor unions of the 1830's as improvement in
actual working conditions.

Whatever may be said of the high purpose of the labor unions of the
1830's, and whatever progress they made in achieving both their broader
and more immediate aims, their days were numbered. In 1837 the
prosperity that had provided the background for their growth and accomplishments came to a sudden end. The bubble of speculation was
rudely punctured. As prices plunged precipitately downward, hard
times again swept over the entire nation. Trade and commerce dried up,
manufacturing sharply declined, and business stagnated in the formerly
prosperous towns and cities of both the Atlantic seaboard and the west.

The workingmen again faced what depression has always meant for
labor—declining wages and unemployment. When the alternative to
work was starvation for themselves and their families, they deserted the
unions as they had in 1819 for fear of employer retaliation, and did not
dare strike to protect the gains they had won when things were going
well. With few exceptions, the journeymen societies that had seemed so
powerful completely folded up. They were crushed by economic circumstance, and in their collapse their newspapers and their federations
also disappeared almost overnight. The depression of 1837 brought the
emerging labor movement to a halt, as that eighteen years earlier had
broken up the original trade societies. Unionism would not regain a
comparable measure of strength and vitality for another half century.

Had organized labor survived this financial and economic panic, its
subsequent history might have followed a quite different course. For
strong unions would perhaps have been able to cope with the new needs
and new problems confronting labor when the full impact of the industrial revolution made itself felt in American society. Its long shadow
was falling over the land in the 1830's and the new class of factory operatives was constantly growing. The skilled workers already organized
were prepared to cooperate with these weaker wage earners, and they
could have helped to promote at this early stage of industrialization the

establishment of effective unions among the unskilled. But this was not to be. As the steady expansion of manufactures tended to depress the wage-earning class, labor failed to develop for the workers as a whole any program that could successfully uphold their interests.

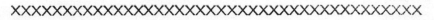

V: THE IMPACT OF INDUSTRIALISM

IN THE COURSE of his American tour in 1842, Charles Dickens visited Lowell, Massachusetts where the new textile manufacturers of New England had established one of the country's first factory towns. The young women and girls who made up most of the working force appeared to him as paragons of virtue—happy, contented and exemplary in their conduct. With their neat and serviceable bonnets, warm cloaks and shawls, "they were all well dressed, but not to my thinking above their station; . . . from all the crowd I saw in the different factories that day, I cannot recall or separate one face that gave me a painful impression."

The English traveler also admired the well-ordered rooms in the factories, some of them with plants growing in the windows, and the fresh air, cleanliness and comfort; he was impressed with the boarding houses where the young women lived under careful chaperonage, and he was particularly struck with what he reported as three startling facts: there were joint-stock pianos in many of the houses, nearly all of the young ladies subscribed to circulating libraries, and a magazine was published—the *Lowell Offering*—that was entirely made up of stories and articles by the factory operatives. Gazing happily upon this industrial paradise, Dickens compared it with the manufacturing centers of England and earnestly begged his countrymen "to pause and reflect upon the difference between this town and those great haunts of misery."

Although it could also have been pointed out, even in 1842, that the factory girls worked incredibly long hours, were badly overcrowded in their boarding houses, and found their lives wholly ordered and controlled by the paternalistic factory owners, the picture that the enthusiastic Dickens drew of Lowell was not wholly out of keeping with the facts. Other visitors confirmed his general impressions. They too wrote of the pleasant atmosphere, of the cultural opportunities of circulating libraries and lecture rooms, and of the gay appearance of the young ladies, not only with neat bonnets over the carefully curled ringlets of their hair, but wearing silk stockings and carrying parasols. Lowell may not have been amusing as the French traveler, Michael Chevalier, wrote, but it was "clean, decent, peaceful and sober."

In these early stages of the industrial revolution, at least some parts of the United States seemed to have escaped the more unlovely aspects of its advent in Europe. The Massachusetts capitalists who established the first textile mills, wanted to prevent the oppression of the workers that had so notoriously resulted from the development of the factory system abroad. They intended to draw their labor supply from the New England farming population, to a very great extent young women and girls, and attractive conditions helped them to secure the type of workers they wanted. In the Rhode Island mills, where whole families were induced to move to town with husband, wife and children all playing their part in tending the looms and spindles, the situation was quite different. Factory hands were callously exploited. The idea behind Lowell, however, was virtually that of a female boarding school, except that the young women worked in the mills rather than at their studies.

Everything possible was done to safeguard their health, and even more particularly, their morals. They had to live in the boarding houses, where they were under strict supervision and the doors were closed at 10 P. M. They were expected to attend church. Not only was discharge an immediate consequence of immodesty, profanity or dancing, to say nothing of more serious lapses from morality, but insofar as male workers were concerned, the Lowell Manufacturing Company stated that it would not "continue to employ any person who shall be wanting in proper respect to the females employed by the company, or who shall smoke within the company's premises, or be guilty of inebriety."

The long hours of work were long but not as oppressive as they might appear. Tending the looms was not so arduous as other types of factory work were to become, and the young ladies had frequent opportunities to rest, to read, to talk among themselves, and to water the plants on the window sills. After paying for their board and lodging, they seldom had more than $2 a week left out of their wages, but for members of farm families for whom any cash income was almost unknown, even this small sum seemed like riches. It generally went into the bank and there was a time when the deposits of the Lowell girls were said to average as much as $500.

The most important distinction between conditions in this early period and later years, however, was that the workers still did not in any sense consider themselves permanently employed. Most of the young women came in from the country to work at Lowell for only the few years necessary to save up money to get married, or enough to go out to Ohio and other parts of the new west as schoolteachers. Moreover, if they did not like the work, or should be laid off in slack times, they could easily return to their farm homes. They were neither firmly attached to the mills nor wholly dependent upon them.

The relatively happy circumstances of this life did not last, however, for very long. Far-reaching changes were already well underway at the time of Dickens' visit to Lowell. As competition increased in the textile industry, the benevolent paternalism of the millowners gave way to stricter controls which had nothing to do with the well-being of the workers. Wages were reduced, the hours of work lengthened, and the equivalent of the speed-up was introduced into factory processes. For a work day from 11½ to 13 hours, making up an average week of 75 hours, the women operatives were generally earning less than $1.50 a week (exclusive of board) by the late 1840's, and they were being compelled to tend four looms whereas in the 1830's they had only taken care of two. When the manager of one mill at Holyoke, Massachusetts, found his hands "languorous" because they had breakfasted, he ordered them to come before breakfast. "I regard my work-people," an agent at another factory said, "just as I regard my machinery. So long as they can do my work for what I choose to pay them, I keep them, getting out of them all I can."

Embittered complaints began to take the place of earlier satisfaction as these conditions grew steadily worse. "These ladies have been imposed upon egregiously by the aristocratic and offensive employers, assuming to be their lords and masters," wrote the *Lynn Record*. Orestes Brownson, radical friend of labor, declared that "the great mass wear out their health, spirits and morals without becoming one whit better off." In the *Voice of Industry*, a new labor newspaper devoted to the cause of mill workers, there were frequent attacks upon the policies that the employers were following.

"Your factory system is worse by far than that of Europe," stated an open letter in this journal addressed to Abbott Lawrence. "You furnish your operatives with no more healthy sleeping-apartments than the cellars and garrets of the English poor. . . . The keepers are compelled to allow . . . but one room for six persons and generally crowd twelve and sometimes sixteen females into the same hot, ill-ventilated attic. . . . You shut up the operatives two or three hours longer a day in your factory prisons than is done in Europe. . . . You allow them but half an hour to eat their meals. . . . You compel them to stand so long at the machinery . . . that varicose veins, dropsical swelling of the feet and limbs, and prolapsus uter, diseases that end only with life, are not rare but common occurrences."

The factory girls themselves more and more resented "the yoke which has been prepared for us," and tried to combat the reductions in wages and increase in work. Even in the 1830's, as we have seen, they had experimented with strikes, and now a decade later they pledged themselves not to accept additional looms without wage increases and called for shorter working hours. But they could make no headway, and as a consequence began to return to their farm homes. The so-called "slavers"—long, low black wagons which cruised about the countryside as far afield as Vermont and New Hampshire—could no longer recruit mill hands with promises of easy work and high wages that were known to be false. The New England farm girls were quitting the mills.

Their place was taken by a new class of workers even less able to protect their interests. A rising tide of immigration had by mid-century made available a great reservoir of Irish and German girls, and some French-Canadians, who had no other alternative than to accept work in the mills no matter what the wages or hours. Conditions grew worse rather than better under these circumstances. The infusion of cheap immigrant labor, as a committee of the Massachusetts legislature noted in 1850, was causing "an entire modification and depression of the state of society in and about manufacturing places."

While the textile trade provides a striking example of what happened to working conditions with increasing industrialization, the same thing was taking place in other trades. The Lynn shoemakers had enjoyed a high degree of independence in the 1830's with their own work shops and the opportunity to fall back on farming or fishing should trade fall off. "When the spring opened," read one perhaps too idyllic account of a worker's life, "the horizon of his hopes expanded. Less clothing and fuel were needed. The clam banks discounted more readily; haddock could be got at Swampscott so cheap that the price wasn't worth quoting. The boys could dig dandelions. . . . Then if the poor man had his little 'spring pig' that he had kept through the winter, 'pork and dandelions' were no small item in the bill of fare while 'greens' lasted." But the masters steadily tightened their control over manufacturing and wages were reduced and paid in store orders rather than cash. The shoemakers gradually found themselves forced from their own work shops, from their fishing and farming in off hours, into the new factories with whose machine processes they could no longer compete.

In the pages of *The Awl*, a journeymen shoemakers' paper, resentment was repeatedly expressed against manufacturers who pretended to pay the workers a living wage but "did by other means reduce them to degradation and the loss of that self-respect which had made the mechanics and laborers the pride of the world." The protesting shoemakers of Lynn called upon their fellow artisans in the larger cities to take concerted action to demonstrate "that we are not menials or the humble subjects of a foreign despot, but free, American citizens." Nothing came of this agitation. A way of life was inevitably passing, and the shoemakers as well as the textile workers were inextricably caught in the toils of the factory system.

The printers' trade was also being revolutionized by the invention of new presses and the use of steam power. These developments not only tended to throw men out of work and to depress wages, but encouraged the transfer of control over their trade from the printers themselves to outside management. A highly independent profession was transformed through the widened gulf between employer and employe. Their long record of organization helped the printers, and they were to continue to enforce union rules governing apprentices and working conditions with considerable success, but they were facing new forces that made it increasingly difficult to maintain either their wages or their general status.

Among other trades, the introduction of power looms worsened conditions for the hand-loom weavers whose weekly wages, never very high, were virtually halved by the mid-forties; the relatively well paid journeymen hatters suffered a decline in their pay, between 1835 and 1845, from about $12 to $8 a week, and the cabinetmakers found themselves compelled to work longer and longer hours to earn as much as $5 a week in the face of competition from the wholesale production of German immigrants who were said to "work rapidly, badly and for almost nothing."

The greater supply of cheap labor, indeed, was as important as the introduction of machinery in cutting wages, not only in the New England cotton mills but throughout industry. In the first half century of our national history, approximately one million immigrants entered the country, but in the single decade from 1846 to 1855, the total was almost three million. Famine in Ireland and suppression of the revolutionary uprisings on the continent accounted for a swelling stream of workers crossing the Atlantic, and there was an increasing proportion of mechanics and laborers, as contrasted with farmers, among these newcomers. They tended to settle in the east, drawn to the rapidly growing cities and manufacturing centers, and were available for all kinds of work, more often unskilled than skilled, at wages greatly reduced from anything which native artisans and mechanics considered essential for decent living conditions. Immigration, that is, was perhaps for the first time providing a labor surplus which counteracted the effect of cheap land and the frontier in drawing workers off from the eastern states. A pattern that was to become even clearer in the 1880's and 1890's, when the trend of immigration showed still greater gains and a further shift toward the ignorant, unskilled and poverty-stricken peasants of southeastern Europe, was already outlined in the 1850's.

The general conditions among workers in the seaboard cities graphically revealed the effect of such immigration. Two separate estimates of a workingman's family budget in the early 1850's, the one in the *New York Times* and the other in the *New York Tribune*, gave a minimum for essential expenditures, for rent, food, fuel and clothing, that amounted to approximately $11 a week. "Have I made the workingman's comforts too high?" asked Horace Greeley in commenting on this budget. "Where is the money to pay for amusements, for ice-creams, his puddings, his trips on Sunday up or down the river in order to get some fresh air?" But except for those in the building trades, whose relatively high wages just about met this budget, there were few urban workers who even approached it—not the factory operatives, not the workers, men and women, employed in the clothing trades, and most assuredly not the common laborers. Shortly before publishing his budget, Greeley had actually estimated that "the average earnings of those who lived by simple labor in our city—embracing at least two thirds of our population—scarcely, if at all, exceed one dollar per week for each person subsisting thereon."

Contemporary descriptions afford ample evidence of the part that inadequate wages played in creating the slum areas of such cities as New York, Philadelphia and Boston. Over-crowding, lack of sanitary conveniences, dirt, filth and disease already stood in stark and glaring contrast to the comfortable, spacious, well-furnished homes of the wealthy. There was in New York a cellar population, estimated to total over 18,000, crowded into damp, unlighted, ill-ventilated dens with anywhere from six to twenty persons—men, women and children—living in a single room. In the notorious Five Points, hundreds of families were squeezed into ramshackle buildings, their only sanitary conveniences outside privies. Boston had equally depressing and unhealthful slums. "This whole district," a Committee on Internal Health reported in 1849, "is a perfect hive of human beings without comforts and mostly without common necessaries, in many cases huddled together like brutes without regard to sex, age or a sense of decency, grown men and women sleeping together in the same apartment, and sometimes wife, husband, brothers and sisters in the same bed."

The situation that Thomas Jefferson had foreseen when he spoke of the mobs of great cities adding just as much to pure government "as sores do to the strength of the human body," appeared to have developed. The workers themselves began to protest against immigration as creating "a numerous poor and dependent population." The abject condition they had known in their own countries, the *Voice of Industry* declared, made such immigrants all the more helpless victims of exploitation in the United States, satisfied to work "fourteen and sixteen hours per day for what capital sees fit to give them."

The harsh effect of industrialism and the mounting tide of immigration served in large measure to prevent any reconsolidation of the ranks of labor. The workingmen did not resume on a comparable scale either the political or trade union activity that had had such dynamic drive before the panic of 1837. Baffled by the new forces let loose by industrialism, they seemed to be frantically seeking means of escape. Organization was almost forgotten. Instead, the workers became involved in the more general reform movements of the day that reflected a middle-class, humanitarian revolt against the changes being wrought in American society by machines and factories. The 1840's were pre-eminently a period of vague, idealistic, utopian reforms, each one of which was held forth by its zealous advocates as a complete panacea for all the evils of the day. Communism and land reform, abolition and feminism, temperance and vegetarianism . . . there was no end to the agitation and propaganda which marked the ferment of social change.

The reformers themselves were forever seeking to win the support of workingmen for their various causes. They descended in droves upon every meeting or convention that might be summoned to consider labor issues, and sometimes succeeded in wholly dominating it. The first formal meeting of the New England Workingmen's Association in 1844, called to inaugurate a revived ten-hour movement, had only a scattering of delegates from labor societies in comparison with the brilliant array of reformers. George Ripley, of Brook Farm; Horace Greeley and Albert Brisbane; Wendell Phillips and William Lloyd Garrison; Charles A. Dana, William H. Channing, and Robert Owen were all on hand, eagerly seeking to win new disciples. The meeting was thrown open in sweeping enthusiasm "to all those interested in the elevation of the producing classes and Industrial Reform and the extinction of slavery and servitude in all their forms." However generous the impulses behind such activity, they could not have been more vague and diffusive.

The imagination of some of the workers during this period was caught by the glowing promises of the "Associationists." Through the formation of independent, socialistic communities, all of whose members were working toward a common end, the Associationists promised an escape from the consequences of the industrial revolution and actually hoped to recreate the simpler society of an earlier day. This idea was primarily derived from the utopian socialism of Charles Fourier, with its elaborate system of phalanxes, designed both to dignify labor and increase production, which had been introduced to America by Albert Brisbane. In 1840 Brisbane published "The Social Destiny of Man," a detailed exposition of Fourier's program, but far more important in spreading the gospel of Association were his writings in the column which Horace Greeley placed at his disposal in the *New York Tribune*.

Greeley was, indeed, to do everything possible to promote this tempered form of socialism as one phase of his general support for the interests of workingmen. An idealistic Yankee, who had come to New York as a farm boy to enter the printing trade, he was a familiar figure at labor gatherings and his round moon face, with its fringe of whiskers, was known to thousands of workers. "Why should those by whose toil ALL commodities and luxuries are produced or made available," he asked, "enjoy so scanty a share of them?" He realized perhaps more than any of his contemporaries among public men the effects of the exploitation of the workingmen resulting from the industrial revolution, and he felt that any lasting betterment for society depended upon their organization. He not only opened the columns of the *Tribune* to Albert Brisbane but ran a weekly letter dealing with socialism from a European correspondent—Karl Marx.

Fourierism, in any event, won many converts through the *Tribune* and even before Brisbane laid out his own plan for a North American phalanx, a group of workingmen launched the Sylvania phalanx in western Pennsylvania. Other communities quickly followed on the heels of this experiment and even the idealistic founders of Brook Farm, whose colony represented an intellectual revolt against the spirit of the times, were persuaded to adopt the form and organization of a Fourierite community. In all, some forty phalanxes, with perhaps 8,000 members, were established during the 1840's.

They were not a success. One by one they fell by the wayside, the North American phalanx itself ceasing operations in 1854. Community living and community production did not prove practical. Nor did they in any way meet the needs of labor. In spite of the enthusiastic propaganda, the answer to industrialization did not lie in an attempt to escape from it. The hopeful dreams of the Associationists foundered on the rock of economic and social forces that could not be so easily withstood or diverted.

As the phalanxes collapsed, some attempt was made to provide a partial substitute in the interests of the workingmen by establishing both consumers' and producers' cooperatives. "The direction and profits of industry," the proponents of cooperation declared, "must be kept in the hands of the producers." In Massachusetts, in New York and in other parts of the country, protective unions were organized which undertook to set up self-employing workshops whose products were to be sold at wholesale prices for the benefit of the union's members. There were other instances of cooperatives such as the Journeymen Molders' Union Foundry, which established a plant near Cincinnati, the Boston Tailors' Associative Union, and a Shirt Sewers' Cooperative Union Depot in New York. But whether consumers' or producers' cooperatives, these early ventures were no more successful than the phalanxes. Various factors accounted for their failure, but basically the conditions of American life, perhaps the American temperament, did not provide a fertile soil for the growth of cooperation. They lent themselves rather to competition and individualistic striving to make the most of the opportunities a young and growing country afforded. Cooperation was to be revived again and again in the future and to have some limited success, but neither in the 1840's nor later could it provide any real solution to the problems confronting the laboring classes.

Another and more significant reform which won widespread labor support was a new agrarianism. The original workingmen's parties had been in part wrecked by the internal friction and external attacks resulting from their flirtation with the radical agrarian ideas of Thomas Skidmore, but the new revelation did not involve the assault upon all property which Skidmore had launched so vigorously in "The Rights of Man to Property." The agrarianism of the 1840's and 1850's was far more moderate. Its thesis was that the people as a whole had a natural right to the existing public lands, and that they should be equally distributed in farm lots of 160 acres which would be both inalienable and exempt from seizure for debt. Through such a program, it was maintained, the workingmen would be assured of his just share in the national wealth and be freed from his complete dependence on the masters of capital.

The high priest of this reform was George Henry Evans. After the dissolution of the Workingmen's Party in New York, he had retired in 1836 because of ill-health to a farm in New Jersey, and only emerged with his new message in 1844. Re-establishing the *Working Man's Advocate,* his old paper, he dedicated himself to agrarianism and in season and out demanded action by Congress to promote his program. "This is the first measure to be accomplished," he wrote in the *Advocate*, "and it is as idle to attempt any great reforms without that as it is to go to work without tools. Place the surplus mechanics on their own land in the west in Rural Townships with their large Public Square and Public Hall in the center of each, leaving full employment to those who remain in the cities. . . ." There was hardly a labor meeting at which he did not appear to present this plan, wholly disregarding the practical question of whether the workers, even if they could, would want suddenly to pull up stakes and take up farming in the distant West.

The climax of his activities was the establishment of the National Reform Association in 1845. His earlier experience had led him to distrust third party political action, and the purpose of the new organization was to demand support for his program from all candidates for public office as the condition for securing the workingmen's votes. The strategy was that which the American Federation of Labor was to adopt almost half a century later: reward your friends, punish your enemies. Evans hoped to make it effective by demonstrating that the agrarians meant business. "We, whose names are annexed, desirous of restoring to man his Natural Right to Land," the membership pledge of the National Reform Association stated, "do solemnly agree that we will not vote for any man, for any legislative office, who will not pledge himself, in writing, to use all the influence of his station, if elected, to prevent all further traffic in the Public Lands of the states and of the United States, and to cause them to be laid out in Farms and Lots for the free and exclusive use of actual settlers."

Although support for this program was by no means limited to the workingmen, their close ties with the National Reform Association were clearly revealed in the membership of the original central committee. It included four printers, two cordwainers, a chair maker, a carpenter, a blacksmith, a bookbinder, a machinist, a picture frame maker, and a clothier. Associated with Evans, moreover, were such trade union leaders of the 1830's as John Commerford, who had been president of the General Trades' Union in New York, and John Ferral, leader of the Philadelphia Trades' Union. The new labor journals, re-emerging after the panic of 1837, almost universally made land reform one of their basic demands.

The movement was strongly opposed by capitalists and employers in the eastern states. "By your policy you strike down our great manufacturing interests," one of their spokesmen declared in Congress, ". . . You turn thousands of our manufacturers and labourers out of employment. . . . You depreciate the value of real estate. You make a bid for our population, by holding out inducements for our productive labourers to leave their old homes, under the seductive promise of land for nothing, and railroads without taxes, thereby decreasing our population and consequently increasing the burden of those that remain in the old states." But farmers and other settlers in the West joined forces with the eastern workingmen in supporting the movement. With its alluring slogan of "Vote Yourself a Farm," the National Reform Association appeared to be making substantial headway.

The workingmen of the 1840's were not to profit from its program and its relevancy to their relief from industrial oppression may also be questioned. The movement instituted by Evans, however, was to lead directly to passage of the Homestead Act in 1862. While it did not provide for either inalienability or exemption from seizure for debt, it granted free land to all bona fide settlers.

Land reform was closer to the interests of the workingmen than many of the mid-century humanitarian movements, but the most immediately practical undertaking was the renewed drive for the ten-hour day. While it had been widely won for artisans and mechanics in the 1830's, factory employes, as we have seen, were not generally affected. The new movement was primarily for the relief of this new group of wage earners. Unlike the earlier drive it did not take the form of trade union activity—the factory operatives were unorganized—but of political pressure upon state legislatures to establish a ceiling on hours in private industry. The National Reform Association even unbent sufficiently to make the demand for a ten-hour day one of its subsidiary planks, and it was taken up by many other workingmen's associations formed for this specific purpose.

The most protracted struggle took place in Massachusetts where the development of the textile industry created both the greatest need for reform and the strongest opposition to it. A call for concerted action on the part of the workers, seeking to bring together various local associations, was first issued in 1844 and was responsible for formation of the

New England Working Men's Association. Both Fourierites and land reformers tried to take over control of this organization, and for a time appeared to have succeeded in diverting attention from the ten-hour issue, but the agitation in favor of the latter reform nevertheless gained increasing headway. Almost swamped with petitions (one from Lowell being 130 feet long with some 4,500 signatures), the Massachusetts General Court felt compelled to make an official investigation.

Its committee reported that the average working day in the textile factories ranged from 11 hours and 24 minutes to 13 hours and 31 minutes, according to the season, and that there was no question but that shorter hours and more time for meals would benefit the workers. It also asserted the right and duty of the legislature to regulate hours whenever public morals or the well-being of society were menaced. In spite of such premises, however, it concluded, largely on the grounds that industry would be driven from the state, that no action should be taken. "The remedy is not with us," the committee stated, casually brushing aside legislative responsibility. "We look for it in the progressive improvement of art and science, in a higher appreciation of man's destiny, in a less love for money, and a more ardent love for social happiness and intellectual superiority."

The factory operatives attacked the report as clearly reflecting "a cringing servility to corporate monopolies" and renewed a struggle which now crossed state lines and aroused the workers throughout the country. New arguments and counter-arguments were advanced. Labor did not emphasize, as it had in the 1830's, the need for more time for self-education and fulfillment of the duties of citizenship. It stressed instead the improvement in the quality of work that should result from shorter hours. The employers, however, were more concerned over production costs. In combatting the workingmen's views they stated that shorter hours would have to mean a lower day's wage. At the same time they reasserted a paternalistic attitude toward the workers' welfare. "The morals of the operatives will necessarily suffer," one of them stated, "if longer absent from the wholesome discipline of factory life, and leaving them thus to their will and liberty, without a warrant that this time will be well employed."

While the debate still raged over conditions in Massachusetts, the reformers succeeded in winning at least partial victories in a number of other states. New Hampshire passed the first state ten-hour law in the nation's history in 1847; Pennsylvania adopted a bill the next year providing that no person should work more than a ten-hour day or sixty-hour week "in cotton, woolen, silk, paper, bagging and flax factories," and during the 1850's, Maine, Connecticut, Rhode Island, Ohio, California and Georgia also fell in line with some sort of ten-hour laws. There was a catch, however, in almost every case. The ten-hour provision could be circumvented by "special contracts." The employer could virtually disregard the law, that is, by refusing to hire anyone unless he were willing to accept a longer working day, and through combining with other employers he could effectively blacklist any worker who attempted to stand up for his legal rights.

The inclusion of the special contract clause was defended by employers as necessary to protect the right of a citizen to sell his services as he himself saw fit. It was an argument to be advanced even more aggressively in later years when the Fourteenth Amendment was interpreted as specifically safeguarding individual freedom of contract from any infringement by state laws. Its speciousness, although he had originally opposed hour legislation, was exposed by Horace Greeley.

"To talk of the Freedom of Labor, the policy of leaving it to make its own bargains, etc.," he wrote in the *Tribune* on September 18, 1847, "when the fact is that a man who has a family to support and a house hired for the year is told, 'If you will work thirteen hours per day, or as many as we think fit, you can stay; if not you can have your walking papers: and well you know no one else hereabout will hire you'—is it not most egregious flummery?"

The workers in Massachusetts undoubtedly thought so, and in continuing their struggle through a series of Ten-Hour Conventions, they insistently demanded effective legislation that would not mean simply a standardization of the working day but a real—and enforceable—abridgment of the hours of labor. ". . . We do declare, explicitly and frankly," it was stated in 1852, "that our purpose, and our whole purpose, is, the enactment of a law which shall prohibit, in stringent and un-mistakeable terms, and under adequate penalties, the corporations, chartered by the laws of the State, from employing any person in labor·

ing more than ten hours in any one day. This is just the law—and all the law—we want on this subject."

This straightforward demand was not realized in Massachusetts— nor in any other state. The inclusion of the special contract clause rendered such laws as were passed unenforceable, and factory workers remained subject to whatever conditions their employers chose to impose upon them. "The ten-hour law will not reduce the hours of labor," one newspaper emphatically stated in regard to the New Hampshire bill. ". . . Its authors did not intend any such result. It will also fail, we think, to humbug the working-men—the only object had in view by the demagogues who originated it."

A final effort to keep the ten-hour movement alive was undertaken through a series of industrial congresses, a further outgrowth of such organizations as the National Reform Association and the New England Working Men's Association. They were first set up on a national basis, and then in the form of state or other local conventions. Instead of furthering practical labor aims, however, they proved to be somewhat vague and ambiguous assemblages, once again attracting reformers rather than trade union delegates. They tried to influence legislation in favor of free land and cooperation as well as the ten-hour day by promising political support to those who would advocate these reforms, but no real progress was made. Moreover while it was again hoped to "eschew partyism of every description," as George Henry Evans had advocated for the National Reform Association, the politicians were soon successfully taking over. The Industrial Congress in New York, for example, originally sought to limit membership to delegates of labor organizations, but Tammany Hall was before long in almost complete control.

The old story of the workingmen's inexperience in politics and the intriguing guile of the professional politicians was being repeated. James Gordon Bennett predicted the fate of the New York Industrial Congress in 1850. "It will fall into the hands of a few wire-pullers, who will turn it to their own advantage and sell the trades to the highest bidder," he wrote prophetically in the *New York Herald*. "Then will be acted over again the farces already played in this city, in which the trades have been made the ladder of needy or ambitious politicians, who kicked them away the moment they gained the summit of their aspirations."

It was not until well into the 1850's that labor began to free itself from its absorption in the hazy garrulity of reform associations and conventions and return to straight-forward trade union activity. An improvement in economic conditions, although interrupted by another brief depression in 1857, promoted this shift from the ineffectual pursuit of vaguely humanitarian panaceas. Once again the bargaining position of the workers was strengthened and the way opened to effective action through the practical weapon of strikes. The unions of this period, however, were to reveal in one important respect a somewhat different philosophy from that held by the earlier societies of the 1830's. They were much less concerned over the solidarity of labor, and fastened their attention far more narrowly on the needs of their own individual membership. Little effort was to be made to form city centrals or any other labor federations comparable to the general trades' unions.

The unions of both periods were primarily made up of artisans and mechanics; that is, skilled craftsmen, and they were largely concentrated in the old established trades. But whereas those in the earlier period were wholly sympathetic toward the organization of unskilled workers and factory operatives, and prepared to cooperate with such societies as they might form, there was little interest in these groups of workers on the part of the trade unions of the 1850's. New lines were being drawn between skilled and unskilled workers and the former were already reluctant to link their activity in any way with the latter.

The more limited scope of the labor movement during these years resulted from a growing realization of the almost insuperable difficulties in trying to organize the mass of workers who were being drawn into factories and mills. Such hopes as there had once been that this could be done appeared to be quenched by two basic considerations. In the first place, many of these factory workers at the time were women and children who were willing and able to work at much lower wages than male employes; and in the second, the ranks of male workers were being constantly swelled by the immigrants who accepted jobs regardless of the working conditions involved. The idea of the solidarity of all labor was not entirely forgotten, and was to be revived after the Civil War. The attitude of the unions in the 1850's, however, seemed to foreshadow that of the American Federation of Labor when it placed its organizational emphasis on the development of strong unions among the skilled workers rather than the more nebulous goal of unity for all labor.

While the revived unions of the 1850's consequently stressed the maintenance of apprenticeship rules, the closed shop and higher wages and shorter hours for their own members, they did not promote with any vigor the labor movement as a whole. They lacked the dynamic drive of their predecessors. In accepting the impracticability of trying to establish by political pressure or reform the equality that had been so much the concern of the workers in the 1830's, they were perhaps realistic. They recognized, as a resolution of one society frankly stated, that under existing conditions "there exists a perpetual antagonism between Labor and Capital . . . one striving to sell their labor for as much, and the other striving to buy it for as little, as they can." But their efforts to combat capital on these grounds were not to be very successful.

The most interesting development of the time was the first real attempt to form national trade unions. The National Typographical Union, the National Molders' Union and the Machinists' and Blacksmiths' National Union were organized, and a National Protective Association was founded by railway engineers with delegates representing fourteen states and fifty-five railways. Other embryonic national unions were also started by cordwainers, upholsterers, plumbers, stone cutters and cotton mule spinners. None of these organizations was too successful but they helped pave the way for more effective activity in later years.

In other respects, the general organization of labor conformed to familiar patterns. The local unions still retained various benefit features, collected dues from their members and sought to maintain strike funds, engaged in collective bargaining with employers, and were prepared to call strikes when their legitimate demands were not met. At times strikes were widely prevalent. "Each spring," the *New York Tribune* declared on April 20, 1854, "witnesses a new struggle for enhanced wages in some if not most of the trades of this and other cities." Public opinion recognized that there was real reason for the restlessness of the workers in the already customary failure of wages to keep pace with advancing

living costs, and the unions' demands often received sympathetic support in the press. "Men should always have a fair compensation for their
labor," the *Trenton Daily State Gazette* stated on April 24, 1857 in commenting on an agreement newly reached among master and journeymen
carpenters in that city, "and we believe it is seldom that they demand
more."

One strike toward the close of the period, breaking out early in
February, 1860, awoke widespread concern and was to prove the most
extensive yet recorded in American history. It was called by the shoemakers of Natick and Lynn, Massachusetts, and spread throughout New
England. With the formation of mechanics' associations in some twenty-
five towns, close to 20,000 workers were ultimately reported to have
turned out. In making the demand for higher wages responsible for this
strike, the shoemakers declared that they were acting in the interests of
the manufacturers as well as in their own interest "inasmuch as the
wealth of the masses improves the value of real estate, increases the
demand for manufactured goods, and promotes the moral wealth and
intellectual growth of society." Their emphasis upon the purchasing
power of wages did not, however, convince their employers of the
desirability of meeting their demands.

The strike was described in newspaper headlines as "Revolution in
the North," "Rebellion Among the Workmen of New England," and
"Beginning of Conflict between Capital and Labor." For almost the
first time, the police and militia were called out in a labor disturbance.
But there was no violence and in many towns the workers had the sympathy and support of their fellow citizens. Many female employes took
part in the strike and in their demonstrations and parades, they proved
to be zealous advocates of the cause. "They assail the bosses," a reporter
for the *New York Herald* wrote from Marblehead, "in a style which
reminds one of the amiable females who participated in the first French
Revolution."

Before the end of the second week the employers began to come to
terms with the strikers. While refusing in most cases to recognize their
unions or to sign written agreements with them, they granted wage
increases substantially meeting the workers' demands. The strike had
proved successful.

As the 1850's drew to a close, the slavery issue began to impinge on the labor movement as it did on every phase of economic or political activity throughout the country. Among northern workingmen, the same divisions of opinion were evident as among other elements of the population. In New England there was strong abolitionist sentiment, especially among operatives in the cotton mills, but in other parts of the country there was little disposition to allow sympathy for the Negro to be carried so far as to favor a war to effect his freedom. It was felt in the growing industrial centers that the slavery of the white wage earner was often quite as degrading as the slavery of the Negro and that reform might better begin at home. Even after Lincoln's election in 1860, many unions vigorously supported the various compromise proposals that were being put forward to reconcile northern and southern differences.

Thirty-four leading trade unionists, indeed, banded together for action early in 1861 and with the slogan "Concession not Secession," summoned a National Workingmen's Convention to protest against the government's course. "Under the leadership of political demagogues and traitors," they vehemently stated in the *Mechanics' Own*, ". . . the country is going to the devil as fast as it can, and unless the masses rise up in their might, and teach their representatives what to do, the good old ship will go to pieces." Their meeting was held in Philadelphia on February 22 with parades, speech-making and resolutions upholding the Crittenden Compromise. It was not a very impressive affair, however, and it could not in any event exercise any appreciable influence on the forces that were so soon to plunge the country into war.

Once hostilities were declared, the workers enlisted in great numbers in response to President Lincoln's call for troops, and many of those who had been most strongly opposed to war were among the early volunteers. In a number of cases, the members of unions entered the service as a group. "It having been resolved to enlist with Uncle Sam for the war," read a typical resolution by one such organization, "this union stands adjourned until either the Union is safe or we are whipped."

The war was to bear heavily upon labor. The workers were subject to the draft, while the wealthy could escape service by paying bounties, and they suffered severely from an inflation that for manufacturers and tradesmen meant rising profits. There were rumblings of discontent as the issuance of greenbacks whirled the cost of living ever higher. "What would it profit us as a nation," the workers asked, "were we to preserve our institutions, save our constitution, and sink the masses into hopeless poverty and crime?" They were prepared to play their full part in the war effort, but their resentment flared against profiteers and speculators.

By 1863 the situation in New York shockingly reflected what a good thing war could be for those in a position to make money out of it. The hotels, theaters, jewelry establishments and other luxury stores were doing a phenomenal business. The "shoddy," as the profiteers were called, were spending fortunes with reckless, shameless extravagance. "The men button their waistcoats with diamonds of the first water," said *Harper's* "and the women powder their faces with gold and silver dust." The hard-hit workingmen earned no such profits and strikes soon spread as they demanded that wages be kept in some reasonable relation to rising prices.

The bricklayers in Chicago insisted on a rise; conductors and horse-car drivers walked out in New York; the union printers in St. Louis struck for higher wages; carpenters, painters and plumbers were everywhere threatening to throw down their tools unless their demands were met; the iron molders sought a fifteen per cent advance; shipwrights and longshoremen went on strike, and the locomotive engineers called out their members.

In occasional instances, martial law was proclaimed to combat such disturbances with troops acting as strikebreakers. But labor had a friend in the White House. While Lincoln may not have fully understood the implications of an organized labor movement, his sympathies were with the workers. With one possible exception, he would not support strike intervention by the government. "Thank God we have a system of labor where there can be a strike," he had declared prior to the war, and he steadfastly maintained his faith in labor and respect for labor's rights throughout the national emergency. The democracy which he affirmed was predicated on his belief that "working-men are the basis of all government." In his first annual message to Congress he had declared that labor was prior to, and independent of, capital which could never have been created without labor's first existing. Meeting a delegation from the New York Workingmen's Democratic Republican Association in 1864, he reiterated these views: "Labor is the superior of capital, and deserves much the higher consideration."

Under these circumstances, the strength of labor increased during the Civil War and the trade unions took a fresh lease on life. Between 1863 and 1864, the number rose from 79 to 270, and it was estimated that the total of organized workers was over 200,000—still fewer than thirty years earlier but more than at any time in the 1840's or 1850's. Moreover there were among these unions 32 organized on a national basis which showed far greater stability than those of the 1850's. The most prominent among them was the reorganized Iron Molders' International Union,[1] but the Machinists and Blacksmiths, the Locomotive Engineers, the American Miners' Association and the Sons of Vulcan (iron puddlers) were other strong organizations which also revealed the changing character of the labor movement.

The wartime revival of unionism was accompanied by the re-emergence of an influential labor press that began to put forward organized labor's views and advocate labor reform. *Fincher's Trades' Review,* the organ of the Machinists and Blacksmiths, was the most important of these papers and with representation on its editorial board from other unions, it became a national spokesman for the whole labor movement. Its editor, Jonathan Fincher, was an able and indefatigable reporter, and a forthright commentator on labor issues. Other labor journals were a new *Workingman's Advocate,* published in Chicago; the New York *Trades' Advocate* and the *Weekly Miner.*

A further advance was the establishment of new trades' assemblies, corresponding to the old general trades' unions. The local unions of Rochester, New York, first revived this form of organization and within a short time almost every city had a trades' assembly. They became a source of very real strength and introduced a new labor weapon, the boycott, as a means of coercing employer compliance with union demands. "All the trades unite for this purpose," read a contemporary report of the boycott, "and when a case of oppression is made known a committee from the Trades' Assembly calls upon the offender and demands redress. If the demand is not complied with every trade is notified, and the members all cease trading at the obnoxious establishment." The trades'

---

[1] The international union, introduced by the Molders, was so-called because of the inclusion of Canadian locals.

assemblies also sponsored picnics, balls and other social activities, and in some instances maintained libraries and reading rooms.

Labor emerged from the Civil War on the offensive. It was prepared to move into fields of even broader national organization, seeking to bring the new unions together in a unified movement that could meet more effectively the consolidated forces of capital. But it still had a weary road to travel.

XXXXXXXXXXXXXXXXXXXXXXXXXXXXXXXXXXXXXXXXXXX
VI: TOWARD NATIONAL ORGANIZATION
XXXXXXXXXXXXXXXXXXXXXXXXXXXXXXXXXXXXXXXXXXX

BETWEEN THE CIVIL WAR and the close of the nineteenth century, the United States underwent phenomenal industrial expansion. The railroads flung out new networks of rails to span the continent and knit the country into an economic whole. The burning stacks of steel mills lighting the skies over Pittsburgh symbolized the growth of a gigantic industry made possible by the discovery of the incalculable iron resources of the Mesabi range. Oil gushed from the wells being driven in western Pennsylvania and Ohio. In the great slaughterhouses of Chicago and St. Louis, thousands of cattle and hogs were butchered daily. The textile mills of New England hummed with activity and a ready-made clothing industry grew up out of the sweatshops of New York and other eastern cities. Everywhere new factories and mills reflected the triumphs of the machine and the growth of mass production. As cities and manufacturing towns mushroomed along the Atlantic seaboard and in the Middle West, the face of America was transformed.

The basic factors behind these developments were the nation's illimitable resources, its great labor reserves and an insatiable demand for the products of the new industries, but the immediate driving force of industrial expansion was provided by a group of visionary, ambitious and ruthless business leaders and financiers. Jay Gould, E. H. Harriman and James J. Hill fashioned an empire of railroads, Carnegie an empire of steel, Rockefeller an empire of oil. The corporation became the accepted form of business organization and under the leadership of such men, mercilessly crushing their competitors, mergers and consolidations were effecting the further nationalizing of business. Gigantic trusts sprang up in scores of industries—in oil and steel, sugar, linseed oil, stoves, fertilizers. Monopoly was the goal of the industrialist and a complacent government and complacent courts, wedded to the economic doctrines of laissez faire, gave free rein to policies that rapidly created a concentration of economic wealth and power that the country had never before known.

The laboring forces were swept along on this tide of expansion. Although such development would have been wholly impossible without them, they had no voice in determining the course of economic growth. The workingmen became almost helpless pawns in the hands of corporate employers. As the onetime independent craftsmen were drawn into the factories, mills and foundries where their special skills had little value, and where they were called upon to perform only single, automatic steps in the complicated processes of mass production, they lost the bargaining powers they had previously enjoyed. Industry looked upon labor as a commodity, to be bought as cheaply as possible. Little more sense of responsibility was felt toward the workers than toward the raw materials of manufacture.

"Before this concentration began, while as yet commerce and industry were conducted by innumerable petty concerns with small capital, instead of a small number of great concerns with vast capital," Edward Bellamy was to write in *Looking Backward*, his famous Utopian romance, "the individual workman was relatively important and independent in his relations to the employer. Moreover, when a little capital or a new idea was enough to start a man in business for himself, workingmen were constantly becoming employers and there was no hard and fast line between the two classes. Labor unions were needless then and general strikes out of the question. But when the era of small concerns with small capital was succeeded by that of the great aggregations of capital, all this was changed. The individual laborer, who had been relatively important to the small employer, was reduced to insignificance and powerlessness over against the great corporation, while at the same time the way upward to the grade of employer was closed to him. Self-defense drove him to union with his fellows."

With the laws of supply and demand so completely determining wages, everything possible was done by industry to make certain that the supply of labor would be plentiful. During the Civil War the business interests of the country had taken a first step in enlisting the support of Congress to make assurance doubly sure on this point. There was passed, in 1864, a contract labor law which permitted the advance of passage money to prospective immigrants in return for a lien upon their wages. With such encouragement the American Emigrant Company, capitalized at $1,000,000 and backed by such prominent figures as Chief Justice Chase, Secretary of the Navy Welles, Senator Sumner and Henry Ward Beecher, undertook to meet the requirements of an expanding economy by building up the resources of available workers. Its announced program was "to import laborers, especially skilled laborers, from Great Britain, Belgium, France, Switzerland, Norway and Sweden, for the manufacturers, rail-road companies, and other employers of labor in America." Its advertisements declared it was prepared to provide, at short notice and on reasonable terms, miners, puddlers, machinists, blacksmiths, molders and mechanics of every kind.

The agents of the American Emigrant Company, together with those of the railroads, the steamship companies, and many industrial corporations, were soon drumming up trade in this new form of contract labor almost as had the "newlanders" two centuries before in their continental quest for indentured servants. "These men, when they arrive," stated an alarmed report to a labor convention, "as a general rule, have but little money; consequently they are compelled to work at starvation prices. . . . We stand no chance of competing with these men. . . ."

In California and in the construction of the first trans-continental railway, labor needs were met by importing Chinese coolies and the West Coast was to have its own peculiar problems. The abortive experiment was even made, although on a very small scale, of employing them for the shoe industry in Massachusetts. "They are with us!" exclaimed the *Boston Commonwealth* in June, 1870, "the 'Celestials'—with almond eyes, pigtails, rare industry, quick adaptation, high morality, and all—seventy-five of them—hard at work in the town of North Adams, making shoes."

As time went on the number of European immigrants mounted steadily—almost half a million entered the country in 1880 and in the following decade over five million, or nearly twice the total for the previous ten years. Moreover there was a gradual shift in the source of supply. The great bulk of the new immigration no longer came from northwestern but from southeastern Europe. The steerage of the trans-Atlantic steamships was crowded with Italians, Poles, Czechs, Slovaks,

Hungarians, Greeks and Russians—ignorant, unskilled, penniless peasants. They provided an apparently inexhaustible reserve of cheap labor for mines, mills and factories.

Immigration had always impinged upon the efforts of American labor to raise living standards, but by the close of the century its influence in holding down wages was more pronounced than ever before. For not only was the supply of unskilled workers constantly augmented by importation from Europe, but the gradual disappearance of available free land in the West was shutting off the escape valve that the frontier had traditionally represented in times of unemployment and economic depression. However indirect the effect of the western movement may actually have been in relieving the pressure in earlier years, the closing of the frontier meant that an entirely new epoch had begun in American history. There was still opportunity but it was to be far more limited than in the expansive days of western settlement.

In the 1840's and 1850's the workers had already felt that the conditions under which they lived were deteriorating, but the skilled artisans and mechanics could still maintain standards that deeply impressed all foreign visitors. As more and more wage earners were now drawn in their search for work into factories, mills and shops, they wholly lost their former independence and were also paid relatively lower wages. Crowded together in cities and towns growing far too rapidly to absorb them, they labored under the constant shadow of pay cuts and unemployment. For the occasional few there was still opportunity to climb the economic ladder—many of industry's leaders were to rise from the ranks of labor—but the great bulk of industrial workers, alien or native, could no longer expect to escape from the wage-earning class and by becoming employers, join the aristocracy of wealth. "The hope that the workingmen may enter this circle," the *Workingman's Advocate,* of Chicago, declared as early as 1866, "is a glittering delusion held up before him to distract his attention from the real object of his interests."

The cruel paradox of "progress and poverty," which Henry George noted in the 1870's, was not even then anything new and it became increasingly apparent as the years went by. Economic growth and expansion were undeniable facts, and so were the rise in the national income and the improvement in living standards for the country as a whole. Yet at the same time many millions lived in abject poverty in the densely packed slums. They were all too often without the most simple comforts and conveniences which their own labor made possible for others. They struggled merely to maintain their families above the level of actual hunger and want. While circumstances were better for those who still retained special skills, the great majority worked such long hours for such little pay that their status was a tragic anomaly in the light of the prosperity so generally enjoyed by business and industry.

As the introduction of machinery caused an increasing division of labor, permitting more and more of the work of manufacture to be done by the semi-skilled or unskilled, employers were able to use "green hands" rather than the artisans and mechanics of an earlier day. Migratory workers threatened the jobs of local workers, and periodic unemployment undermined the onetime security of established craftsmen. As business became nationwide, moreover, the competition of different manufacturing areas meant that prices and wages were no longer determined by local conditions. They fluctuated as a consequence of economic changes wholly beyond the control of the employers or workers immediately concerned.

In this new national market, for example, the makers of stoves in Troy and Pittsburgh, Philadelphia or Detroit, had to meet the competition of manufacturers in Chicago and St. Louis. Wage scales in the East were linked with those in the West. If the iron molders in Troy or St. Louis wished to protect themselves from wage cuts in time of business recession, they had to look beyond merely local conditions and search out means to uphold the wages of comparable workers in other parts of the country.

It became increasingly clear under these new conditions that labor had to meet the challenge of nationwide industry by itself organizing on a nationwide basis. This meant in the first instance, an attempt to build up national unions which would enable the workers in any trade to safeguard their wage scales against competition from whatever quarter, and in the second, an effort to confront the community of interests growing up among all employers by a like community of interests among all workers. There was to be much talk of the solidarity of labor as a new group of leaders sought to bring the national unions, political labor parties, cooperatives and other labor reform associations into what might be termed a united front to combat the rising power of organized capitalism.

In seeking to effect this broader national organization in the years immediately following the Civil War, labor was nevertheless still so confused by the new forces of industrialism as to be wholly uncertain as to what course it should follow. It was drawn into various political movements, beguiled by new promises of reform, and caught up in controversy over socialist theory and radical concepts of class struggle. There was continued debate over the relative benefits of political as against economic action, and the advantages of craft unions as opposed to more all-inclusive unions.

On many occasions, the workers took matters in their own hands regardless of the fine-spun theories being discussed at labor conferences. Feeling themselves ground down more and more heavily under the heel of capitalist exploitation, they ignored a leadership that appeared to be out of touch with the actualities of economic circumstance and rose in spontaneous revolt to protect their rights. Before the Civil War, strikes had been local, short-lived and generally peaceful, but in the latter half of the century their character was drastically to change. The country was to experience widespread and violent industrial strife.

The initial step toward a national organization of labor was taken in 1866. A group of union leaders, wholly forgetful of similar moves in the 1830's, summoned what they called "the first National Labor Congress ever convened in the United States." It was held in Baltimore and attended by some seventy-seven delegates from various local unions, trades' assemblies and national unions. The avowed purpose of the conference was to create a new unity within the ranks of labor as a whole. In organizing what was to become the National Labor Union, provision was made for the membership not only of the skilled workers enrolled in existing trade unions, but of unskilled workers and also farmers. At last all those who toiled were "to rise in the majesty of their strength" and challenge the employing class to acknowledge their rights and privileges.

From the outset the National Labor Union was reformist and politically minded. It was the first broad attempt to bring all labor together on a common program, but it still reflected the utopianism of pre-Civil War days and the feeling then so current that the producers could make over society in their own image in spite of the gathering forces of industrialism. The independence and individualism of a frontier society made it almost impossible for the nineteenth century American workingman, for all the evidence to the contrary, to accept the permanence of a wage-earning class.

The leaders of the National Labor Union were not greatly interested in such practical objectives as concerted trade union pressure for the immediate improvement of working conditions. They declared that the labor movement was dependent on trade unions and urged every workingman to join one. Meeting at Baltimore, however, they upheld political action as the most effective means of promoting the workers' interests and they strongly deprecated resort to strikes. The advocates of economic rather than political action were able to defeat a motion for the immediate formation of a straight-out political labor party, but the conference nevertheless agreed that one should be set up "as soon as possible."

The general aims of the National Labor Union were set forth in an "Address to the Workingmen of the United States." It primarily emphasized, as "the first and grand desideratum of the hour," a demand for the adoption of laws establishing eight hours as a legal day's work in every state in the union. As we shall see, this represented a reform with deeper implications than the earlier drive for a ten-hour day and for a time it appeared to dominate labor activity. The National Labor Union, however, also sought to promote both consumers' and producers' cooperatives, reviving the old movement of the 1840's, and partly as a means to make capital more readily available for such enterprises, it was to become more and more absorbed in currency and banking reform. The abolition of convict labor; the restriction of immigration, particularly of Chinese coolies on the West Coast, in order to safeguard the living standards of native workers; the disposal of public lands only to actual settlers, and the establishment by the national government of a Department of Labor, were further objectives set forth in 1866.

These largely political goals were supplemented by appeals for the broader organization of working people. The interests of women in industry were recognized, the new union pledging individual and undivided support to "the sewing women, factory operatives, and daughters of toil," and the head of the Troy Laundry Workers, a union of female workers, was made one of the association's assistant secretaries. The organization of Negroes was also encouraged, but in this first recognition of their possible role in the labor movement, they were urged to form their own unions rather than invited to join the National Labor Union.

The formation of this new organization was for the first time to create a national labor leadership and among the men figuring most prominently in its activities—chosen its president in 1868—was William H. Sylvis. Commenting on the gathering of labor leaders that attended the convention that chose him president, the *New York Sun* bore witness to the prominence he had won throughout the country by declaring that his "name is familiar as a household word."

Sylvis was at this time a man of forty, medium-sized and strongly built, with a florid complexion, light beard and mustache, and "a face and eyes beaming with intelligence." Few labor leaders have been more devoted to the cause, more willing to sacrifice every personal consideration in working for labor's interests, or commanded more loyalty and affection on the part of his fellow workers. He was very literally to wear himself out in their behalf. "I love this Union cause," he declared on one occasion. "I hold it more dear than I do my family or my life. I am willing to devote to it all that I am or have or hope for in this world."

His views on the policies labor should promote underwent marked shifts and changes. He was erratic and highly inconsistent in his thinking. But whatever his position at a particular moment, he defended it aggressively. He once assailed his critics as a "two-faced, snarling crew, who act the part of puerile wiffets." His most telling shafts were always reserved, however, for the new capitalist class that he so strongly felt was seeking only to exploit the workers—"a monied aristocracy—proud, imperious, and dishonest . . . blasting and withering everything it comes in contact with."

Sylvis was born, the son of a wagon maker, in Annoph, Pennsylvania, in 1828 and as a boy worked in the local iron foundry. It was some time in the 1840's that he graduated from his apprenticeship and was duly invested with the "freedom suit" that marked his new status as a journeyman molder—a fine broadcloth coat, white shirt, woolen hose, calfskin boots and high silk hat. Continuing to work at his trade in and about Philadelphia, he joined the local Stove and Hollow-Ware Molders' Union and at once became an active labor organizer. He was inspired with the idea of bringing all molders together in a single organization and it was largely through his efforts that a convention was held in Philadelphia, in 1859, at which forty-six delegates from eighteen locals established the National Molders' Union.

It collapsed with the outbreak of the Civil War and Sylvis himself enlisted for a short period of army service. In 1863, however, he was again back at his chosen work and was elected president of the revived Iron Molders' International Union. His only interest was in building up this organization and through his unflagging zeal, he introduced new methods and techniques in labor organization. Traveling back and forth across the country, often begging a ride in the engineer's cab because he had no money for railway fare, he met with groups of local molders in city after city, helped them organize locals and admitted them to membership in the national union. Returning for the annual convention in 1864, he was able to boast that "from a mere pigmy, our union has in one short year grown to be a giant." With fifty-three locals and a total membership of 7,000 (soon to rise to 8,500), the Iron Molders' International Union had by 1865 become the strongest and most closely knit labor organization in the country.

Sylvis was to look back upon this period when he traveled so widely and came in such intimate contact with so many workingmen in New England, the seaboard states, the Midwest and Canada as the happiest in his life. But he exhausted the slight capital at his disposal and was wholly dependent upon small funds given him by the molders. "He wore clothes until they became quite threadbare and he could wear them no longer," his brother wrote of these days. ". . . The shawl he wore to the day of his death . . . was filled with little holes burned there by the splashing of molten iron from the ladles of molders in strange cities, whom he was beseeching to organize."

Sylvis also proved himself to be as capable in administration as he was in organization. Control was effectively centralized in the national union, a per capita tax on all union members provided a revenue which built up a substantial strike fund, and the issuance of union cards and publication in the labor press of a "scab album" made possible general enforcement of a closed shop. Sylvis believed strongly in collective bargaining and did not encourage strikes, but when they proved to be the workers' only resource, he was ready to back them up to the hilt—"the results will depend on who can pound the hardest."

Until the winter of 1867–1868, the policies pursued by the Molders' Union were uniformly successful but during that difficult season the National Stove Manufacturers' and Iron Founders' Association launched an all-out counter-attack. Wages were cut and members of the union laid off. When the workers went out on strike, the employers were then in a strong enough position to lock them out. The embattled molders fought back for months as best they could but their strike funds became exhausted, internal dissensions eventually broke their united front, and they began to straggle back to work on the employers' terms. Sylvis was able to save the union from complete extinction, but with the failure of the strike it largely lost the strength and influence it had once exerted.

He was so discouraged by this experience that he increasingly shifted his attention from trade unionists to more general labor reform and thus found in the new National Labor Union broader scope for his activities. He was ready to support, as vigorously as he had formerly supported union organization, the drive for the eight-hour day by legislative enactment, the formation of cooperatives and currency reform. Reversing his earlier views, he threw all his influence behind the trend within the National Labor Union to promote these reforms by political action. "Let our cry be REFORM," he demanded in his first circular as its president. ". . . Down with a monied aristocracy and up with the people."

Meetings of the National Labor Union clearly revealed the growing absorption with political reform. Among the delegates at the convention in 1868 (whose "philosophic and statesmanlike views of the great industrial questions" were warmly commended by the *New York Herald*) were representatives of eight-hour leagues, land reform associations, anti-monopoly societies and many other political causes. Conspicuous among them were two advocates of woman suffrage, Elizabeth Cady Stanton and Susan B. Anthony. Their presence created something of a furor for while Sylvis and other leaders supported woman suffrage, the delegates as a whole were not prepared to go this far. They agreed to seat the suffrage leaders only after making it plain that in so doing they were not endorsing their "peculiar ideas." The *Herald* nevertheless noted that Miss Anthony was "delightfully insinuating and made no mean impression on the bearded delegates."

The National Labor Union took a step at this same convention which clearly foreshadowed its own transformation into a third party. It encouraged the formation of labor reform parties in the several states and urged them to undertake direct political action. The trade unionists found their interests increasingly subordinated to the promotion of causes that concerned them only indirectly, if at all. The old story of the labor congresses of pre-Civil War days was being repeated. The only difference in the experience of the National Labor Union was that it was not so much captured by the reformers (in spite of the "delightfully insinuating" Miss Anthony) as controlled by labor leaders who had themselves turned reformers. Sylvis was the outstanding example of this trend, but other onetime trade unionists were by the close of the 1860's no less zealous partisans of reform and political activity.

The impetus given to the National Labor Union by the election of Sylvis as its president was to prove short lived. On the eve of its annual convention in 1869, he was suddenly overtaken by death. The blow was a harsh one for the labor movement and "cast a veil of despondency upon the whole working class." There was scarcely a union that did not adopt laudatory resolutions, and the labor press published innumerable editorials upon the irreparable loss of a great leader in the zenith of his fame. "Sylvis! The National Calamity," one paper headed its comment upon his death; the *Working Man's Advocate* appeared with black borders.

From Europe came further condolences from the leaders of the International Workingmen's Association—the First International—with which Sylvis had sought to establish an alliance in the "war between poverty and wealth." A letter signed among others by Karl Marx declared that the world could ill afford the loss of "such tried champions in the bloom of life as him whose loss we mourn in common."

The contributions that Sylvis had made to the labor cause were the example and inspiration of his organizing zeal in building up the Molders' International Union, and his stalwart support of the rights of the workers on the national stage. He had made himself a true spokesman for labor and his words commanded attention and respect. Short as his life was, he stands out as the first really national labor leader the country had known.

Whether the history of the National Labor Union would have been much different had he lived is problematical. It had already gone off on a somewhat dubious political tangent, and Sylvis had encouraged rather than sought to restrain the diversion of its energies to reform. In any event its days were numbered. Richard F. Trevellick, a coworker with Sylvis and head of the International Union of Ship Carpenters and Caulkers, succeeded him as president. He too had moved away from an early interest in trade unionism to mounting concern with politics. Under his presidency the National Labor Union made the final plunge and at the annual convention in 1872 transformed itself into the National Labor Reform Party. A program primarily emphasizing currency reform was adopted and Judge David Davis of Illinois was nominated for the presidency. When Davis withdrew his name, the political movement largely collapsed and with that collapse, the National Labor Union ended its days.

Although the National Labor Union was both so short lived and so unsuccessful, certain of the issues with which it was concerned demand further consideration. The first of these was that campaign for a legislative eight-hour day that in 1866 was declared to be "the question of all others, which at present engrosses the attention of the American workman." It was based upon theories that went much deeper than the old arguments that upheld a shorter working day in order to promote the health, the moral well-being or the educational opportunity of workers. The eight-hour day, according to its advocates, was to transform the existing organization of society by raising both the wages and status of the workers, thereby gradually narrowing the gap between employer and employe "until the capitalist and laborer are one."

The high priest of the eight-hour movement was Ira Steward, a Boston machinist and loyal union member, who was so deeply convinced that his ideas were the solution for all labor's problems that he could not be swerved from his self-appointed task of promulgating them at all times and in all places. "Meet him any day as he steams along the street," wrote a contributor to the *American Workman*, ". . . and, although he will apologize and excuse himself if you talk to him of other affairs . . . if you only introduce the topic of 'hours of labor,' and show a willingness to listen, he will stop and plead with you till night-fall."

He addressed innumerable workingmen's audiences on the eight-hour day, testified before the Massachusetts legislature, wrote pamphlets and articles for the labor press, and organized first the Labor Reform Association and then the Grand Eight Hour League of Massachusetts. His ideas seized upon the imagination of the workers. Eight-hour leagues sprang up all over the country and in making their program its own, the National Labor Union was reflecting a nationwide interest in this proposed reduction of labor's working day.

Steward's basic theory clearly pointed to ideas and practices that in the twentieth century were to be even more widely accepted. In favoring the reduction of the working day to eight hours, he assumed that it would not mean any loss of wages. The workers would demand pay at least equal to what they had been receiving for ten and twelve hours work, and since such a demand would be universal, the employers would have no valid ground for refusing it. Any resistance "would amount to the folly of a 'strike' by employers themselves, against the strongest power in the world, viz., the habits, customs and opinions of the masses." With their increased leisure, the workers would then be in a position to enjoy, and consequently would want to purchase, more of the products of industry. Maintaining that it was a "mechanical fact, that the cost of making an article depends almost entirely upon the number manufactured," Steward then asserted that the manufacturers would immediately profit from an expansion of their markets because onetime luxuries could be widely sold to the working population.

The major point stressed by Steward was that the reduction of working hours could be effected without any cut in wages, and this idea was popularized by a jingle attributed to his wife:

Whether you work by the piece or work by the day
Decreasing the hours increases the pay.

It was at least problematical whether employers would actually pay their old wages for a legislative eight-hour day in the hope of building up purchasing power for their goods. The eight-hour leagues were highly successful, however, in promoting this optimistic view of a complete regeneration of capitalistic society. Both the national government and a number of states, moreover, were induced to take action to meet the workers' demands. The former established an eight-hour day for all its employes in 1868, and six states also made eight hours "a legal day's work."

As in the case of the earlier legislative drive for a ten-hour day, however, the action taken by the states was to prove illusory. The new laws were again subject to the reservation "where there is no special contract or agreement to the contrary," and there appeared to be no way to circumvent such limitations. A contemporary report to the National Labor Union was wholly discouraging. "Your committee wishes also further to state," it read, "that Eight Hour laws have been passed by six states, but for all practical purposes they might as well have never been placed on the statute books, and can only be described as frauds on the laboring class."

Faced with these actualities, the movement lost the support it had temporarily commanded. Maximum-hour laws were to remain an objective of social reformers. They were eventually to be adopted by the states without qualifying clauses, and in the 1930's Congress approved comparable legislation for all employes engaged in interstate trade. But during the last quarter of the nineteenth century, labor gave up the attempt to secure a shorter working day by political action and returned to economic pressure. The eight-hour movement of the 1880's and 1890's found the unions making demands directly upon employers, as had the original trade societies, and seeking to enforce compliance through strikes.

As the maximum-hour drives of the 1860's subsided, a new enthusiasm for cooperation as the solution of labor's problems took its place and was in turn whole-heartedly supported by the National Labor Union. Again more was involved than in comparable agitation in the 1840's. The sponsors of cooperation envisaged the complete renovation of society as had the proponents of the eight-hour day. Through the establishment of producers' cooperatives in every trade, the workingmen were to set up a system of self-employment which would ultimately do away with the wage system, provide practical means for an equitable distribution of the profits of industry, and wholly free labor from its bondage to capital.

Sylvis had himself taken the lead in this movement with the establishment of cooperatives by the iron molders. Not only had their local unions set up foundries at Troy, Rochester, Chicago, Cleveland, Louisville and other cities, but after its disastrous strike experiences, the national union itself went directly into cooperation in 1868. Impulsively changing its name to the Iron Molders' International Cooperative and Protective Union, it embarked on an ambitious project, at a cost of $15,000, for a large foundry at Pittsburgh. So enthusiastic was Sylvis over this program that at one time in 1868 he appeared to be ready to give up everything else to promote it. "The time has come," he stated, "when we should abandon the whole system of strikes and make co-operation the foundation of our organization and the prime object of all our efforts."

Other unions followed the molders' example. The machinists set up a number of shops on a joint stock basis; the shoemakers established both producers' and consumers' cooperatives; the coopers organized some eight shops in Minneapolis, and comparable projects were started by bakers, printers, hatters, carpenters and shipwrights.

For a time some of these cooperatives appeared to be successful but one by one they gradually failed. There was strong opposition to them on the part of the business community, which attacked such "Frenchy theories of communism," and they faced cut-throat competition. But the real trouble was in their own business operation. The union officials lacked managerial skill and the cooperatives were run inefficiently, sometimes even dishonestly, with the result that they got into increasing difficulties. Moreover, there was a basic handicap, in a day when large capital outlays had already become necessary for any productive enterprise, in the unions' lack of available funds and the virtual impossibility of their obtaining credit.

The latter consideration, indeed, caused the National Labor Union to turn its attention to currency reform as a basic factor in any move by labor to help itself. On the surface there was nothing more to this agitation, growing out of the proposed retirement of the greenbacks issued during the Civil War, than a demand for an inflationary policy to combat falling prices. It seemed to be a strange shift of emphasis from the days when the workers had favored hard money. The theories underlying Greenbackism, however, went deeper than any mere change in the price level. Labor aligned itself with the farmers on this issue because it promised radical reform of the whole financial, economic system. Like the eight-hour day and cooperation, currency reform also looked toward the creation of a producers' commonwealth to replace capitalism.

Taking their ideas in large part from the proposals for a new monetary system that had been advanced as early as 1848 by Edward Kellogg, the currency reformers urged the transformation of the public debt into bonds bearing three per cent interest, and interconvertible at will with a legal tender currency based not upon gold but upon the physical wealth of the country. Such a program, it was believed, would break down the monopoly of "irresponsible banking associations," abolish the "robbery of interest rates," and free the economic system from that dependence upon gold whereby "the very heart's blood of the workingman was mortgaged from the cradle to the grave."

Here was a final panacea for assuring labor its natural rights. "It would effect," the National Labor Union declared in already familiar phrases, "the equitable distribution of the products of labor between non-producing capital and labor, giving to laborers a fair compensation for their products, and to capital a just reward for its uses, remove the necessity for excessive toil and afford the industrial classes the time and means necessary for social and intellectual culture."

Once again Sylvis, who had been swept along in turn by trade unionism, the eight-hour movement, and cooperation, eloquently preached this newest reform. Everything else was forgotten. "There are about three thousand trades' unions in the United States," he wrote. ". . . We must show them that when a just monetary system has been established, there will no longer exist any necessity for trade unions."

It was through adopting this program and allying itself with the political Greenback movement, however, that the National Labor Union lost the support of trade unionists and then collapsed after trying to run a political campaign in 1872. Still, currency revision had its impassioned devotees among both farmers and workers, and local Greenback-Labor parties were formed throughout the country in succeeding years to press the demand for legal tender currency and interconvertible bonds. Eventually such parties coalesced to set up a national Greenback-

Labor Party, and in the mid-term elections of 1878 succeeded in polling over a million votes and sending fourteen representatives to Congress.

The pressure this party exerted helped to bring to a halt the further retirement of greenbacks, but the basic measures for which the currency reformers agitated were passed by. The outstanding notes were made redeemable in gold in the resumption act of 1878. With the adoption of this measure the Greenback-Labor Party, which appeared to have temporarily aligned labor and agriculture on a common program, soon disappeared. Greenbackism had won the support of reformist-minded labor leaders, but it may well be doubted whether it had ever evoked very much enthusiasm among the rank-and-file workers. They could hardly be expected to understand its implications, and so far as they supported it, they did so largely as an expression of their discontent with existing conditions and willingness to accept any program which promised them relief.

After the collapse of the National Labor Union in 1872, various efforts were made to set up some new organization that would eschew politics and get labor back on the straightforward path of trade unionism and economic action. A series of industrial congresses were held between 1873 and 1875 whose delegates declared that "the great desideratum of the hour" was no longer the eight-hour day, currency revision or any other reform but "the organization, consolidation, and cooperative effort of the producing masses." Two secret societies were also formed—the Industrial Brotherhood and the Sovereigns of Industry—with the same general aims. These efforts, however, represented moves on the part of a few leaders to impose some sort of control over labor from the top down, and they did not have any really substantial backing. They provided little more than forums for discussion and debate.

Moreover economic conditions at this time had once again cut the ground out from under the labor movement and created seemingly insuperable barriers to any effective activity. In 1873 the country was swept by a panic that ushered in an even more prolonged and severe depression than that of the 1830's. There was a repetition of the old story of falling prices, business stagnation, curtailed production, wage cuts and unemployment. As mines, mills and factories reduced operations or actually closed up, some three million persons were thrown out of work. Hard times not only brought an abrupt end to such nebulous strivings for labor unity as the National Labor Union and the industrial congresses, but again they almost completely shattered the existing national unions. They could no more survive the harsh impact of wage cuts and mounting unemployment than the promising unions forty years earlier had been able to survive the disrupting consequences of the panic of 1837.

There were some thirty national unions when the crisis developed. The *Labor Standard* listed only nine in 1877 and the total strength of unionized labor was reported to have declined from 300,000 to perhaps 50,000. Union after union had the same experience. The Knights of St. Crispin was a remarkable organization of shoemakers which had been established on industrial lines, rapidly built up a membership of 50,000, and proved itself to be amazingly effective in enforcing the closed shop through a series of successful strikes. But it collapsed as quickly as it had risen and by 1878 had completely disappeared. The Machinists and Blacksmiths lost two-thirds of their members and the Coopers almost three-fourths. Even the more stable National Typographical Union suffered a loss of half its members, while the newly organized Cigar Makers' National Union fell from almost 6,000 to little more than 1,000. Trade unionism was not entirely crushed, but with employers taking every advantage of hard times to combat it, and the workers unable to protect themselves, it was virtually forced underground.

In the decade since the Civil War, labor had failed to adjust itself to the new conditions of an industrialized society and had not yet attained the underlying strength to withstand depression. Its leaders advanced innumerable ideas and programs, but their shifting, changing attitude toward trade union activity, reform and politics did not command the popular support of the great mass of workers or inspire any real feeling of cohesion. For all the wordy talk at labor conventions, and the articles and appeals of the labor press, there appeared to be an increasingly wide gap between the handful of active participants in the labor movement and their nominal followers.

As far as there had been any definite philosophy behind the activities promoted by the National Labor Union, it was based upon the reform thesis that the producers could somehow take over and direct the economic system. There was as yet no general realization that the machine, mass production and large scale capital investment made it impossible for the workers to control the means of production by such simple expedients as producers' cooperatives. The reformers were looking backward instead of forward. A permanent wage earning class was an actuality which the leaders of labor were still highly reluctant to accept. The eight-hour movement, Greenbackism and cooperation sprang from middle class concepts of how society might be regenerated rather than from any real understanding of the immediate needs of the workers in a capitalistic order.

VII: AN ERA OF UPHEAVAL

THE DEPRESSION of the 1870's ushered in one of the most confused periods in American labor history. Against the somber background of hard times, the workers rose to protest violently what they considered their ruthless exploitation by employers. Demonstrations by the jobless were held in city after city, often calling out forceful intervention by the police; strikes among miners led to bloodshed and killing, and in 1877 a spontaneous uprising on the part of railway workers caused such widespread rioting that the country seemed to be facing a general labor insurrection.

Even after these disturbances subsided, the unrest and dissatisfaction of the workers continued to simmer dangerously below the surface and when in the 1880's the country again experienced depression, with the usual cycle of wage cuts and unemployment, so many strikes broke out that the period has been called that of "the Great Upheaval." As never before the nation came to realize the explosive force inherent in the great mass of industrial workers that were the product of its changing economy.

It was not surprising that the public, as well as conservative business interests, felt the country endangered as these disturbances flared up. Among the hordes of immigrants entering the country, there were foreign radicals who sought to fasten upon American labor the socialistic and even anarchistic ideas widely prevalent in Europe in these years, advocating direct action rather than the slow processes of reform. Fear of their influence colored many reports of unemployment demonstrations and of strikes, and came to a head in the tragic Haymarket Square riot of 1886. The opprobrium of radicalism and violence was cast over the entire labor movement.

In their outcries against communism and anarchism, however, the conservatives were greatly exaggerating the radicalism of American

114

labor. In spite of its left-wing elements, it remained basically conservative. The improvement of existing conditions rather than the overthrow of capitalism was still labor's goal. In holding foreign radicals responsible for the disturbed labor scene of the 1870's and 1880's, the newspapers of that era, as those of many later periods, tended to disregard the underlying factors of low wages and unemployment that were basically responsible for the workingmen's discontent.

The violence that marked such a dramatic revolt as the great railway strike of 1877 must be set against the background of a long depression unrelieved by any public consideration of the plight of those whose wages were cut or who were unable to earn any wages whatsoever, the unfeeling attitude of such great employers as the railroads which were controlled by bankers and financiers interested only in profits, and the lack of any organization among the workers to direct their protests against injustice in effective form. The smoldering discontent among the railway workers did not need the spark of radical agitation to burst into open revolt. It flared up naturally as wage cut added to wage cut drove the frustrated workers to strike out blindly in a gesture of embittered defiance.

These years of labor strife were also to witness the slow growth of the Knights of Labor and of those national unions which in mounting rivalry with the Knights were later to band together in the American Federation of Labor. But these basically more important developments were for a time overshadowed by the unorganized violence and radical agitation which reflected labor's growing pains in a capitalistic society where the human factor in industrial relations was still so largely ignored.

As the effects of the panic of 1873 deepened and widened, there were scenes of disorder in cities throughout the country. In New York, Chicago, Boston, Cincinnati and Omaha, crowds of unemployed workers gathered in huge meetings to protest against the intolerable circumstances in which they found themselves with factories and workshops closed down. Unemployment in an industrialized society was far more serious than it had ever been in the less complex agrarian society of the first half of the nineteenth century. Homeless, hungry and despairing, the workers refused to disperse when the police sought to break up their gatherings. They fought back in defense of what they considered their right of free assembly and challenged society to meet their demands.

The most noted of these outbursts was the Tompkins Square riot in New York on January 13, 1874. A meeting of the unemployed had been called to impress upon the city authorities the need for relief and it was at first approved, the mayor himself promising to speak. Evidence that radical agitators were prepared to address the proposed gathering, members of the American section of the International Workingmen's Association having participated in the arrangements, then caused a last minute cancellation of the police permit. At the scheduled hour, Tompkins Square was nevertheless densely packed with working people who knew nothing about the change in the official attitude toward the meeting. Suddenly a squadron of mounted police appeared on the scene. Without warning, they charged into the crowd, indiscriminately swinging their clubs and hitting out at everyone within reach. Men, women and children were ridden down as they fled in panic and scores of innocent bystanders were severely injured in trying to escape the police charge.

The *New York Times* reported the next day that the police applied their clubs with "reasonable but not excessive severity" and that "the scrambles of the mob as the officers advanced were not unamusing." Ignoring the underlying causes for the workingmen's discontent, and whatever rights they had in seeking unemployment relief, it took the attitude that the demonstration was wholly the work of alien radicals. "The persons arrested yesterday," it editorialized, "seem all to have been foreigners—chiefly Germans or Irishmen. Communism is not a weed of native growth."

There was one young laboring man who took very much to heart the lesson that the Tompkins Square riot appeared to teach of the risks trade unions ran in accepting radical leadership. The youthful Samuel Gompers was on hand when the mounted police charged the crowd, barely saving his own head from being cracked open by jumping down a cellarway.

"I saw how professions of radicalism and sensationalism," he wrote years later in his autobiography, "concentrated all the forces of society against a labor movement and nullified in advance normal, necessary activity. I saw that leadership in the labor movement could be safely entrusted only to those into whose hearts and minds had been woven the experience of earning their bread by daily labor. I saw that betterment for workingmen must come primarily through workingmen. . . ."

In the wake of such disturbances as the Tompkins Square riot and unemployment demonstrations in other cities, outbreaks of violence in the anthracite coal fields of eastern Pennsylvania next awoke public attention. The workers in this industry, following the lead of the soft coal miners who had established the Miners' National Association, had formed a union of their own in the Miners' and Mine Laborers' Benevolent Association. It succeeded in reaching a trade agreement with the Anthracite Board of Trade but in December, 1874, the operators independently cut wages below the agreed upon minimum. The miners at once walked out of the pits and in what became known as "the long strike," they tried to compel the operators to restore the wage cuts. As hunger and want began to exact their toll among the workers and compelled many of them to return to the pits, something like open war developed between the remaining strikers and the coal-and-iron police sent into the area by the operators to protect strikebreakers.

Into this troubled situation there was then projected another element whose exact role in the long strike it is still impossible to determine. At the time, however, sensational reports appeared in the press of the operations of a secret organization among the miners, the Ancient Order of Hibernians, more popularly known as the Molly Maguires, which was said to be terrorizing the coal fields and preventing those miners who wished to return to work from doing so. The members of this society were also charged with attempting to intimidate the coal operators, as they had once sought to intimidate Irish landlords under the leadership of the redoubtable widow named Molly Maguire from whom they took their name, by violent threats against foremen and superintendents, sabotage and destruction of mine property, outright murder and assassination. It has subsequently been revealed that the operators themselves instigated some of these attacks on the mines in order to provide an excuse for moving in, not only to crush the Molly Maguires but also all union organization. This interpretation of the wave of violence that swept over eastern Pennsylvania would appear to be substantiated at least in part by the steps taken to suppress the disorders.

The bitterly anti-labor head of the Philadelphia and Reading Railroad, which controlled many of the mines, took the initiative in this campaign. He hired a Pinkerton detective, one James McParlan, to get proof of the criminal activity of the Molly Maguires at any cost. Posing as a fugitive from justice, McParlan won his way into their confidence, and under circumstances not entirely clear,[1] finally succeeded in turning up evidence in the fall of 1875 that lead the authorities to make a series of arrests. His testimony on the stand and that of other witnesses turning state's evidence was in many instances suspect, but the trials resulted in the wholesale conviction of twenty-four of the Molly Maguires. Ten of them were hanged for murder and the others sentenced to jail for terms from two to seven years.

Peace and order were restored in the coal fields. Whatever the power and influence of the secret society had really been, it was shattered by this attack. But the operators had also succeeded in breaking the Miners' Benevolent Association and forcing the strikers back to work on their own terms. The long strike ended in complete failure for the workers and the virtual collapse of their union.

Unemployment riots and violence in the anthracite coal fields were but a prelude to the railroad strikes of 1877 which led to disorders and rioting that called for the intervention of federal troops before they could be suppressed. The workers at first commanded public sympathy. Their wages had been arbitrarily cut while high dividends were still being paid on watered stock, and the railways were in any event highly unpopular in the 1870's. "It is folly to blink at the fact," the *New York Tribune* reported, "that the manifestations of Public Opinion are almost everywhere in sympathy with the insurrection." But as the violence continued uncontrolled, the choice appeared to become one between civil law or chaos. Although not everyone agreed with the *Nation's* blunt statement that the strikers should have been confronted by "trained bodies of men sufficient to overawe or crush them at the first onset," it was recognized that the government could not evade its responsibility to restore public order.

The strikes, breaking out early in July, 1877, in protest against the

[1] A recent study of this confused episode is Wayne G. Broehl, Jr., *The Molly Maguires*, Cambridge, 1964.

wage cuts, were spontaneous. The first one was on the Baltimore and Ohio and it was at once followed by similar moves on the part of railway workers on the Pennsylvania, the New York Central and the Erie. Within a brief time all lines east of the Mississippi were affected, and the movement then spread to the Missouri Pacific, the St. Louis, Kansas and Northern, and other western lines. Railroad traffic throughout the country was interrupted and in sections completely paralyzed. As rioting flared up dangerously in Baltimore and Pittsburgh, Chicago and St. Louis, and even San Francisco, the country was confronted with its first industrial outbreak on a national scale. "It is wrong to call this a strike," the *St. Louis Republican* exclaimed, "it is labor revolution."

The strikers on the Baltimore and Ohio were the first to clash with authority at Martinsburg, West Virginia and order was restored at that point only after two hundred federal troops had been sent to the scene. Rioting on a much larger scale occurred in Baltimore. There the strikers stopped all trains, refused to allow them to move, and began to seize railroad property. When the militia, called out by the governor of Maryland, marched from their armory to the railway station, a gathering crowd of workers and their sympathizers attacked them with brickbats, stones and clubs. The troops opened fire and broke for the station, but the rioters had had a taste of blood. They kept up the assault and set fire to the station. When police and firemen arrived, the mob for a time tried to prevent them from putting out the blaze but finally gave way. Disturbances continued through a wild and riotous night, and only the arrival of federal troops the next morning brought any real return of order. By then the toll of victims had mounted to nine persons killed, and more than a score (of whom three later died) gravely injured.

In the meantime a still more serious outbreak took place in Pittsburgh, where the strikers also stopped the trains and took possession of railway property. Here popular sympathy was wholly with the railway workers because of a deep seated resentment against the policies of the Pennsylvania. The local militia, openly fraternizing with the strikers, refused to take any action against them. The arrival of a force of 650 soldiers dispatched from Philadelphia to protect railway property, consequently precipitated a pitched battle in which the troops opened fire and after killing some twenty-five persons, and wounding many more, took over possession of the roundhouse and machine shops.

The infuriated strikers, their ranks swelled by miners, mill hands and factory workers, returned to the attack with arms seized from near-by gun shops and laid siege to the troops. As night fell, freight cars were set afire and pushed into the roundhouse until it too was blazing. The troops, surrounded by flames and nearly suffocated with smoke, fought their way out amid a hail of bullets and retreated across the Allegheny River.

The field was now left clear to what had become a mob of four or five thousand persons, swelled by hoodlums and tramps. Railway tracks were torn up, freight and passenger cars broken open, and what could not otherwise be destroyed, set afire. Some two thousand cars, the machine shops, a grain elevator and two roundhouses with one hundred and twenty-five locomotives went up in flames. The Union Depot itself was burned down. As the rioting continued unchecked, the more unruly and criminal elements broke into the liquor stores and began to pillage at will without regard to whose property they were robbing. They carried off furniture, clothing, provisions.

"Here a brawny woman could be seen hurrying away with pairs of white kid slippers under her arms," read one contemporary description; "another carrying an infant, would be rolling a barrel of flour along the sidewalk, using her feet as the propelling power; here a man pushing a wheelbarrow loaded with white lead. Boys hurried through the crowd with large-sized family Bibles as their share of the plunder, while scores of females utilized aprons and dresses to carry flours, eggs, dry goods, etc. Bundles of umbrellas, fancy parasols, hams, bacons, leaf lard, calico, blankets, laces and flour were mixed together in the arms of robust men, or carried on hastily constructed hand barrows."

It was not until after a weekend of drunken pillaging, in which the damage was estimated at from five to ten million dollars, that the police, reinforced by bands of armed citizens, began to restore some semblance of order. In the meantime, the entire state militia had been called out and following an emergency cabinet meeting, President Hayes ordered all federal troops in the Atlantic Department made available to cope with the emergency. Only when the regulars arrived in Pittsburgh, was full protection finally accorded railway property.

Headlines and editorials declared that communism was at the bottom of the strike and responsible for its violence in Baltimore, Pittsburgh and other parts of the country. It was described as "an insurrection, a revolution, an attempt of communists and vagabonds to coerce society, an endeavour to undermine American institutions." The *New York Tribune* stated only force could subdue this "ignorant rabble with hungry mouths"; the *Times* characterized the strikers as "hoodlums, rabble, bummers, looters, blacklegs, thieves, tramps, ruffians, incendiaries, enemies of society, brigands, rapscallions, riffraff, felons and idiots," and the *Herald* declared that the mob was "a wild beast and needs to be shot down." Reading such headlines as "Pittsburgh Sacked—The City Completely in the Power of a Howling Mob," and "Chicago in the Possession of Communists," an alarmed public was swept by hysterical fears.

As the federal troops reached the scene in city after city, however, the rioting subsided as quickly as it had flared up. The strikers not only made no further attempts to interfere with the railroads' operations, but gradually went back to work. They knew when they were beaten; they knew they had no chance with government upholding the railroads. By the end of July, the trains were generally running again and the strikes were over.

The outbreaks of violence and mob action had demanded vigorous enforcement of law and order, but in the suppression of the strikes, the original grievances of the railway workers appeared to have been completely overlooked. The *New York Tribune*, which had at first admitted that public opinion was largely with the workers, took the position that they should have been willing to practice greater self-denial and economy until conditions had settled down. It was not impossible to sustain life on two dollars or even one dollar a day, it editorialized, and if the railway employes were unwilling to work for such wages, they had no right to prevent others from taking jobs they spurned. In adopting such an attitude, "they deserve no sympathy, but only punishment."

This attitude reflected a view widely held during these years as to the need for workingmen to submit to whatever conditions prevailed in industry. "God intended the great to be great and the little to be little," the noted preacher, Henry Ward Beecher, once wrote. ". . . I do not say that a dollar a day is enough to support a working man. But it is enough to support a man! Not enough to support a man and five children if a man insists on smoking and drinking beer. . . . But the man who cannot live on bread and water is not fit to live."

The month of July, 1877 had, in any event, been one of the most turbulent in American history and the long-term consequences of its disorder and rioting were to be highly important. The business community was aroused as never before to the potential power of industrial workers and embarked on an aggressive program to suppress all labor activity, reviving the old conspiracy laws, seeking to intimidate the workers from joining unions, imposing the "iron clad" oath, and enlisting strikebreakers whenever trouble threatened. The lesson driven home for labor was the need for organization and authority that would prevent strikes from developing into uncontrolled mob action which inevitably invited suppression by state or federal troops. Capitalism had won this first round of industrial strife, but was fearful of the future. Labor had lost, but it had a new realization of its latent strength.

The violence that marked both unemployment demonstrations and railway revolt in the 1870's had its counterpart in another round of strikes during the next decade, but the Haymarket Square riot in 1886 served more than any other outbreak of these years to arouse and alarm the public. The anarchists were held responsible for this tragic affair, and while only a tiny segment among the workers in Chicago were at all influenced by their violent "propaganda by the deed," the repercussions of the riot affected the entire labor movement. The foes of unionism made the most of this dramatic incident in trying to discredit organized labor and fasten upon it the stigma of being radical, revolutionary, and un-American.

The left-wing groups within the labor movement were in this as in other periods constantly shifting their alignments and organizing new parties which reflected the vagaries of the revolutionary European factions from which they largely sprang. The American section of the International Workingmen's Association had been dissolved in 1876 as a result of a split within the parent body abroad, and the socialist forces in the United States had formed a new Working Men's Party. It was

not important, its small membership largely drawn from among German and other European-born immigrants, but it had been active
during the railway strike in 1877, instigating violence and trying to
foment a general strike.

Its ranks were soon split by further internal quarrels. There was embittered rivalry between the Marxian socialists, who sought to promote
trade unionism as a base for the revolutionary activity that was eventu
ally to overthrow the capitalist state, and the Lassalleans, who urged
direct political activity as a far more effective means of achieving the
same end. In addition to these two groups, a third flirted with the far
more radical doctrines of anarchism which were being preached in this
country by Johann Most, a big, black-bearded German immigrant who
had formerly been a socialist but arriving in the United States in 1882
had become a fiery exponent of revolutionary violence. The radicals
who espoused his brand of anarchism established an International
Working People's Association, to become known as the Black International, which succeeded in winning control of the Central Labor Union
in Chicago. It had some 2,000 members drawn from German and
Polish metal workers, cabinet makers and packing-house employes, and
through the pages of its organ, the *Alarm*, openly called for immediate
revolution.

Nothing could have been less representative of American labor than
this little coterie of foreign-born revolutionaries, and there was even
less chance than in the case of the communists of their views winning
support among the rank and file of the workers. But there was always
the risk of the anarchists precipitating some form of violence, and the
Chicago newspapers were constantly stressing a danger which they
were quick to discover in every demonstration of labor militancy.
"The Nihilistic character of the procession," read one report of a labor
parade in which members of the Central Labor Union apparently
participated, "was shown by the red badges and red flags which were
thickly displayed throughout it."

When in 1886 a movement spread across the country for general
strikes in favor of the eight-hour day, the Chicago anarchists were
ready to take advantage of every opportunity to preach their own doctrines of revolutionary violence. The day set for the strike itself—
May 1—passed off very quietly, but two days later a clash between

strikers and strikebreakers at the McCormick Harvester plant in Chicago led to police intervention and the death of four men. Here was the sort of situation for which members of the Black International were waiting. That night leaflets were circulated through the city calling upon the workers to avenge their slaughtered comrades.

"The masters sent out their bloodhounds—the police," this incendiary appeal read; "they killed six of your brothers at McCormick's this afternoon. They killed the poor wretches because they, like you, had the courage to disobey the supreme will of your bosses. . . . To arms we call you, to arms!"

A protest meeting was summoned for Haymarket Square the next evening, May 4, and some three thousand persons gathered to hear impassioned and inflammatory speeches by the anarchist leaders. But it was an entirely peaceful meeting for all these alarms (the mayor himself attended it and left upon finding everything so quiet), and when a cold wind began to blow gusts of rain through the square, the crowd gradually melted away. The meeting had, in fact, virtually broken up when a police detachment of two hundred men arrived and their captain peremptorily ordered such workers as remained to disperse. Suddenly there was a sharp explosion. Someone had hurled a bomb into the ranks of the police, killing one outright. They at once opened fire and there were answering shots from the workers. During the affray seven police in all were either killed or fatally wounded, and some sixty-seven injured; four workers were killed and fifty or more injured.

Not only Chicago but the entire country was outraged by the bomb throwing. The anarchists were at once blamed and there was universal demand that they be hunted down and brought to trial. The police combed the city for suspects, and finally eight known anarchist leaders were arrested and charged with murder. In a frenzied atmosphere compounded equally of fear and the desire for revenge, they were thereupon promptly found guilty—seven of them sentenced to death and the eighth to fifteen years' imprisonment. There was no evidence whatsoever connecting them with the bombing. They were condemned out of hand for their revolutionary views and the incitements to violence which had supposedly caused the bombing. "Convict these men, make examples of them, hang them," urged the state's attorney, "and you save our institutions. . . ."

Two of the convicted men pleaded for executive clemency and were given life imprisonment. Six years later Governor John Peter Altgeld pardoned them, together with the eighth man who had been sentenced to fifteen years' imprisonment, on the ground that they had not been granted a fair trial. So violent was the feeling against the anarchists even at this late date, that Altgeld was assailed throughout the country for what has since been universally recognized as an act of simple justice.

Organized labor was in no way associated with the Haymarket Square bombing and had at once denied any sympathy whatsoever for the accused anarchists. The Knights of Labor were as violent in condemning them as the most conservative newspapers. "Let it be understood by all the world," their Chicago organ declared, "that the Knights of Labor have no affiliation, association, sympathy or respect for the band of cowardly murderers, cut-throats and robbers, known as anarchists. . . . ." Wholly disregarding the complete failure of the prosecution to connect the accused men with the actual crime with which they were charged, the Knights clamored for their conviction. "Better that seven times seven men hang," it was declared, "than to have the millstone of odium around the standard of this Order in affiliating in any way with this element of destruction."

The reason for such an outburst was obvious. The capitalistic enemies of labor were seeking to hang upon the labor movement this "millstone of odium" by charging that the Knights of Labor and the unions generally were permeated by the spirit of anarchism and communism. An hysterical public appeared ready to believe it. The whole labor movement was blackened by the bomb tossed by some unknown hand into the police squad at Haymarket Square. It did not matter that its responsible leaders and the overwhelming mass of the workers were as opposed to both anarchism and communism as any other group in society. All labor was thrown on the defensive.

This whole episode was to have an important influence on the developing trend of trade unionism, but it has taken us beyond our account of the growth of the labor movement as a whole. As already noted, the rise of the Knights of Labor during the 1880's was far more significant than the activities of the radical fringe that was always present in the labor movement, but never deeply affected its native philosophy.

VIII: RISE AND DECLINE OF THE KNIGHTS OF LABOR

IT WAS SEVENTEEN YEARS before the Haymarket Square riot and eight years before the great railway strike that the first step had been taken in the organization of what was to become the Noble and Holy Order of the Knights of Labor. Nevertheless it was the years of labor unrest and industrial strife that intervened between these two events which saw its rise to an unprecedented pinnacle of power. Even though there was at the same time a slow revival of national unionism, and Samuel Gompers was stubbornly promoting the policies that were to come to fruition with the formation of the A.F. of L., the future of American labor in the mid-1880's appeared to lie with the Knights of Labor. For the first time a labor association seemed strong enough to challenge industry on its own grounds. "It is an organization," one contemporary writer stated emphatically, "in whose hands now rests the destinies of the Republic. . . . It has demonstrated the overmastering power of a national combination among workingmen."

The Knights were to be accused in the feverish atmosphere of these days of promoting the radical ideas being preached by foreign agitators, and the repercussions of the Haymarket Square riot contributed to a decline in their strength almost as rapid as had been their rise to power. But the Noble and Holy Order was in reality quite in the American tradition and its underlying philosophy did not differ very much from that of the National Labor Union. Its leaders looked toward the ultimate creation of some sort of industrial commonwealth, whose outlines were always somewhat hazy, but the emphasis was invariably placed upon the need for a long process of education and agitation to attain this goal rather than direct action. And in the meantime the Knights were prepared to work within the existing economic system, originally going even so far as to oppose all strikes.

More significantly they sought to promote a unionism that would embrace all workers, the skilled and the unskilled, in a single labor organization. They recognized the vital importance of the role of industrial workers in our emerging capitalist system, and were convinced that trade unionism as it had been known had to give way to labor organization on a much broader basis. Their attitude in some measure foreshadowed the industrial unionism of a later day, but rather than a federation or congress of individual unions, the Knights continually emphasized the solidarity of labor and looked toward a centralized association which would include the workers in all industries and occupations. Their ideal of a pervasive unity among workingmen everywhere—"an injury to one is an injury to all"—was a high-minded concept, but had it been attained, it would have been fraught with grave risks both for labor and for society as a whole. The concentration of power resulting from a single, unified labor organization would have gravely endangered democratic institutions.

Regardless of such possible considerations, the Knights of Labor did not succeed in realizing their aims. Their efforts to bring the unskilled workers within the fold of organized labor won only temporary success. However right in theory they may have been as to the importance of the organization of the unskilled, they were ahead of the times. The great mass of such workers, largely drawn from the ranks of the newly arrived immigrants, were separated by almost insuperable barriers of race, language and religion. Employers were quick to take advantage of every opportunity to stir up the friction and animosities that blocked any real cooperation. Moreover as the workers' ranks were constantly swelled by new arrivals, a tremendous reservoir of potential strikebreakers was always at hand to furnish cheap replacements for those who dared to take part in any union activity. The unskilled, industrial workers did not have in the 1880's either the cohesiveness or the bargaining power to make their inclusion in the organized labor movement practicable. In the face of unrelenting employer opposition it was not, indeed, until after the restriction of immigration in the 1920's and government support for labor organization in the 1930's that industrial unionism—with some few notable exceptions such as in coal mining—was successfully promoted.

The members of the traditional trade unions—the counterpart of the mechanics and artisans of an earlier day—realized this in the 1880's, and became increasingly unwilling to link their fortunes with such weak allies as the unskilled workers proved to be. They felt driven to sacrifice the solidarity of labor as preached by the Knights in order to protect their own interests by organizing more exclusively along craft lines. The national unions vigorously combated the Knights of Labor and the A.F. of L. became the embodiment of a "new unionism" concerned only with the immediate needs of its own membership.

Nine inconspicuous tailors, meeting in the hall of the American Hose Company, in Philadelphia, founded the Knights of Labor on December 9, 1869. Members of a local Garment Cutters' Association which had been forced to dissolve because of lack of funds to maintain its benefit program, they decided to form a new association which originally differed little from any other craft union except that it was a secret society and its activities were centered about an elaborate ritual. But one of the group had a far broader vision of labor organization and his fellow members were soon caught up by his idealistic enthusiasms. This was the concept of a new labor solidarity that would make it possible to include in a single unified order, without regard to nationality, sex, creed or color, all the nation's workers.

There was no idea of class struggle in the thinking of the founders of the Knights of Labor. They did not plan any attack upon the citadels of industry—"no conflict with legitimate enterprise, no antagonism to necessary capital." While they looked forward ultimately to "the complete emancipation of the wealth producers from the thralldom and loss of wage slavery," this was to be gradually brought about by mitigating the evils of the existing economic system and establishing producers' cooperatives. In time a new industrial commonwealth would then be created in which moral worth rather than material wealth would be accepted as the true standard of individual and national greatness.

The leader of the nine tailors who met in Philadelphia and the principal exponent of these ideas was Uriah S. Stephens. He was born in Cape May, New Jersey, in 1821 and educated for the Baptist ministry. Forced to abandon his studies after the panic of 1837, he became apprenticed to a tailor and the 1840's found him working at his trade in Philadelphia.

Some time later he traveled extensively—to the West Indies, Mexico and California—but on the eve of the Civil War he was back again in Philadelphia. He attended the workers' anti-war convention in 1861 and the next year helped to organize the Garment Cutters' Association. Never a trade unionist in any strict meaning of the term, believing unions to be too narrow in their outlook and circumscribed in their operations, Stephens drew from his religious background that vision of the universality of labor which was symbolized in the mysticism of the Knights of Labor's secret ritual.

"Cultivate friendship among the great brotherhood of toil," he was to advise his followers; "learn to respect industry in the person of every intelligent worker; unmake the shams of life by deference to the humble but useful craftsman; beget concert of action by conciliation. . . . The work to which this fraternity addresses itself is one of the greatest magnitude ever attempted in the history of the world. . . . It builds upon the immutable basis of the Fatherhood of God, and the logical principle of the Brotherhood of Man. . . ."

This was the strain that ran through all his writing and addresses. In pursuing the ultimate goal of consolidating "all branches of labor into a compact whole," he dismissed the idea of organizing separate trades or callings and would have done away with both boycotts and strikes whose benefits he felt were "partial and evanescent." His vision embraced all mankind. "Creed, party and nationality," he wrote, "are but outward garments and present no obstacle to the fusion of the hearts of worshippers of God, the Universal Father, and the workers for man, the universal brother."

Stephens' role in the foundation of the Knights of Labor was all important, and he became the first Grand Master Workman when it was nationally organized. Nevertheless he did not stay with it for very long. He turned to politics, as had so many labor leaders of the mid-century period; and, becoming interested in currency reform, he ran unsuccessfully for Congress on the Greenback ticket in 1878. Resigning his post in the Knights, he then drifted away from the labor movement altogether and died in 1882 without witnessing the Order's unexampled rise to prominence. Yet his influence lived on. "All through our rituals and laws," the *Journal of United Labor,* organ of the Knights, wrote upon announcement of his death, "will be found the impress of his brain, and inspiration of his keen insight into the great problems of the present hour."

In the meantime, the original Philadelphia assembly of the Knights of Labor grew very slowly. The secrecy which had been adopted to enhance the mystical appeal of ritual and ceremony, as well as to protect members from possible employer retaliation, was rigidly maintained. A prospective new member would be invited to attend a meeting of the group without being told what it was, and only after having given satisfactory answers to various questions as to his opinion upon "the elevation of labor" would he be considered eligible for initiation. The ritual was passed on by word of mouth and outsiders had no way of knowing the existence of the Order, let alone its purposes. In all public documents or notices, the name was designated by five asterisks.

Provision was made for expansion through the admission of "sojourners," workers in other crafts than that of tailoring, on the payment of an initiation fee of $1. When their number became sufficient they could "swarm" and form an assembly of their own. But it was not until 1872 that a second assembly, made up of ship carpenters, was actually established. The pace of growth then speeded up. In the next two years some eighty locals were formed in and about Philadelphia, and in 1874 the first assembly outside this immediate area was established in New York. These groups were all composed of workers in distinct crafts— garment cutters, ship carpenters, shawl weavers, masons, machinists and blacksmiths, house carpenters, tin plate and iron workers, stone cutters and gold beaters.

The next step in the evolution of the Knights—pointing toward the ultimate goal of labor unity—was the formation of district assemblies made up of delegates from the local assemblies. The first of these units was established in Philadelphia in 1873, and the next year one was set up in Camden, New Jersey, and another in Pittsburgh, a first step toward invasion of the West. Soon there were district assemblies in Ohio, West Virginia, Indiana and Illinois as well as Pennsylvania, New York and New Jersey, with a membership that included unskilled and semi-skilled workers in addition to craft workers.

As time went on, many local assemblies were established as mixed assemblies made up of workers in different trades. Miners, railway workers and steel workers joined the Knights in increasing numbers, and wherever there were not enough members of a single trade to form a trade assembly, especially in small towns and rural areas, the mixed assembly became a general catchall. Eventually the mixed assemblies outnumbered the trade assemblies and with their inclusion of unskilled workers gave the Knights their distinctive character. In all, some fourteen district assemblies, with a total membership of about nine thousand, had been formed when the leaders of the movement decided that the time had come to send out a call for a general convention to form a national body.

This meeting was held in Reading, Pennsylvania, in January, 1878 with thirty-three delegates. After long discussion a constitution was adopted setting up a General Assembly as the supreme authority of the Knights with control over both the district and the local assemblies. In theory the new organization was highly centralized, but the district assemblies had authority within their own jurisdictions and were never subject to as rigid control as the constitution theoretically contemplated. The Order became, however, a truly national organization in a sense never attained by its predecessors, and it further differed from them in that the membership remained on an individual basis rather than through affiliated unions. The workingman anxious to join simply applied for membership in a local assembly, was duly initiated, paid chapter dues, attended meetings and so became an accredited Knight of Labor.

Membership was open to all wage earners and to all former wage earners (although the latter could not exceed one-fourth of the membership in any local assembly) with the exception of lawyers, doctors, bankers and those who sold or made their living through selling liquor—to which excluded group were later added stockbrokers and professional gamblers. "It gathers into one fold," stated a later provision in the constitution, "all branches of honorable toil."

The preamble to the constitution, taking over the general principles that had been put forward by the earlier Industrial Brotherhood, called attention to "the recent alarming development and aggression of aggregated wealth" and stated that unless it were checked, it would inevitably lead "to the pauperization and hopeless degradation of the toiling masses." Only through unification could labor be assured of the fruits of its toil, the Knights declared, and to bring this about, "we have formed * * * * * with a view of securing the organization and direction, by cooperative effort, of the power of the industrial classes. . . ."

The constitution itself set forth many of the traditional demands of organized labor and also outlined certain new goals. It called for the establishment of cooperatives, the reservation of public lands for actual settlers, the eight-hour day, and a fiat currency in very much the same terms as had the National Labor Union. It demanded abolition of the contract system for prison labor, the prohibition of child labor, equal pay for the sexes, establishment of bureaus of labor statistics, and, by later amendment, government ownership of the railways and telegraphs, and adoption of a graduated income tax.

These provisions were largely reformist or political. In so far as industrial action was concerned, the Knights of Labor supported boycotts, which were to become increasingly important, but they strongly favored arbitration rather than resort to strikes which they at first wholly opposed. While a resistance fund was eventually set up for use in certain carefully defined contingencies, it was provided that only thirty per cent of the money collected could be directly used for strikes, with sixty per cent set aside for cooperatives and ten per cent for education. The Knights had had to recognize that strikes might sometimes be necessary, but they were unwilling to support them except when definitely approved by their Executive Board. "Strikes at best afford only temporary relief," the revised constitution of 1884 was to state, "and members should be educated to depend upon thorough education, cooperation and political action, and through these the abolition of the wage system."

This cautious attitude was in part due to the experience of the workers during the railway strikes of 1877. The lawlessness to which these strikes had led, with consequent intervention by federal troops, seemed to make such direct action a very dubious expedient in the minds of the leaders of the Knights of Labor. But they had no solution to the problem of how arbitration was to be enforced should employers refuse to deal with their representatives. The Knights consequently became involved in strikes in spite of themselves, and when the local assemblies were threatened by retaliatory measures on the part of industry, the Executive Board felt bound to come to their aid.

The ambiguities of its position on the strike issue might also seem to mark the stand of the Noble and Holy Order on political questions. The contemplated reforms went in some respects even beyond those put forward by the National Labor Union, and yet the Knights sought to remain primarily an industrial rather than a political organization. While they engaged in lobbying activities and in time entered even more directly into politics, they made no attempt to set up a labor party. "Politics must be subordinated to industry," the General Assembly declared in 1884, and made it clear that "this Order is in no way bound by the political expression of its individual members."

The basic policies of the Knights of Labor, in short, remained somewhat vaguely idealistic and humanitarian, in the pattern originally set forth by Uriah Stephens, and they sometimes appeared to be highly contradictory. The Knights sought to emphasize their industrial character, and yet agitated an all-inclusive program of social reform; they discouraged strikes and yet became deeply involved in them; they called for political action and denied that they had any direct concern with politics. Moreover while the Order was theoretically highly centralized, leading to charges that its policies were dictatorially determined by a handful of leaders, its membership actually took things very much in their own hands and went their own way.

The first General Assembly set the stage for further expansion. A membership of 9,287 rose to 20,100 a year later, and then declined to 19,422 in 1881. The secrecy that had at first provided a protective screen safeguarding members from employer attack began to react upon the Order as a whole. It became associated in the public mind with such other secret societies as the Molly Maguires, and aroused such suspicion on the part of the Catholic Church that in Canada all Catholics were forbidden to join it. Measures were consequently taken to make the name of the Order public, remove the oath from the initiation proceedings, and eliminate all scriptural passages from the ritual. Through the intercession of Cardinal Gibbons, who was persuaded that there was nothing about the revised ritual offensive to religious doctrine, the Pope was then induced to withdraw his condemnation and uphold the propriety of Church approval. The membership rapidly recovered its losses after these moves to do away with secrecy. It had doubled in 1882, to a total of over 42,000, and within the next three years rose to more than 100,000.

Upon Stephen's retirement in 1879, only a year after formation of the General Assembly, Terence V. Powderly was chosen as his successor in the exalted post of Grand Master Workman. This young labor agitator, for he was only thirty at the time, had been born at Carbondale, Pennsylvania, in 1849. The son of Irish Catholic parents who had emigrated to this country in the 1820's, he worked while a young boy as a switch tender in the local railway yards but soon decided that he wanted to become a machinist. When seventeen, he was apprenticed to this trade, and three years later got a journeyman's job in the shops of the Delaware and Western Railroad in Scranton.

In the next few years he successively joined the International Union of Machinists and Blacksmiths, became the Pennsylvania organizer for the Industrial Brotherhood, and, in 1874, was initiated into the Knights of Labor. After a brief period of "sojourning," he organized and became Master Workman of Assembly No. 222 and corresponding secretary for District Assembly No. 5. His mounting interest in labor politics also led to participation in the activities of the Greenback-Labor party and in 1878 he was elected on its ticket as the labor mayor of Scranton.

Powderly was to continue to hold this latter post until 1884, even though he had in the meantime been elected Grand Master Workman of the Knights. He always had many and varied interests. He studied law and later practiced at the bar, served as a county health officer, was part owner and manager of a grocery store, became vice president of the Irish Land League. At one time he applied, unsuccessfully, for the post of head of the Bureau of Labor Statistics in Washington, established largely through the efforts of the Knights, and after he finally lost the presidency of the Order in 1893, he obtained a government post in the Bureau of Immigration. He was at first Commissioner General and then chief of the Division of Information, living until 1924 when his stormy career as a labor leader was almost forgotten by a generation far removed from the turbulent industrial strife of the 1880's.

Powderly did not look like a labor leader. Slender and under average height, he had wavy light brown hair; a blond drooping mustache, and mild bespectacled blue eyes. He dressed conventionally and well, his usual costume a double-breasted broadcloth coat, stand-up collar, plain tie, dark trousers and small, narrow shoes. His manners were formal and polite, giving every appearance of a man of breeding and refinement. "English novelists take men of Powderly's look," commented John Swinton, a labor journalist, "for their poets, gondola scullers, philosophers and heroes crossed in love but no one ever drew such a looking man as the leader of a million of the horny-fisted sons of toil."

He was strait-laced, almost puritanical in his point of view. A convinced total abstainer, he warred incessantly against the saloon and had little toleration for those who liked to drink. While he inspired both affection and loyalty among his followers, he was never an easy mixer or really at home in labor gatherings. He had his own sense of humor, as shown in his autobiographical writings, but there was no natural give and take about the man.

On assuming his post as Grand Master Workman, he did yeoman work in building up the Knights of Labor's membership. He was an eloquent and persuasive speaker and an indefatigable letter writer. Yet even in these early days of enthusiasm, he never dedicated himself to the labor movement with the wholehearted devotion of such a leader as William Sylvis. He continually protested that his other interests did not allow him to give full time to his job as Grand Master Workman, and on occasion petulantly complained that his health (which, it is true, was never very good) was not equal to the heavy demands being made upon it. He not only resented the incessant requests for him to speak, but with a sense of his own importance that time would not diminish, he insisted that when he did speak, it should be under circumstances suitable to his high office in the Order.

"I will talk at no picnics," he once wrote exasperatedly in the *Journal of United Labor*. "When I speak on the labor question I want the individual attention of my hearers and I want that attention for at least two hours and in that two hours I can only epitomize. At a picnic where . . . the girls as well as the boys swill beer I cannot talk at all. . . . If it comes to my ears that I am advertised to speak at picnics. . . . I will prefer charges against the offenders for holding the executive head of the Order up to ridicule. . . ."

For all his prima donna attitude, or perhaps because of it, there was no gainsaying his skill as an organizer, while his able handling of the dispute with the Catholic Church was largely responsible for Cardinal Gibbons' intercession with the Pope in the Knights' behalf. He was also a past master at labor politics and built up a personal machine that enabled him to keep close control over the General Assembly during these years of growth and expansion. There were times when he declared that there was nothing he wanted more than to hand over his post to someone else, but this did not prevent him from vigorously combatting any opposition to his policies, sharply assailing his opponents, and clinging firmly to office.

Powderly's ideas and theories were closely in accord with the underlying aims of the Knights of Labor as expressed in their original First Principles—and they had the same idealistic, broadly humanitarian and often contradictory scope. He believed in education rather than direct economic action, but it was not always clear for what he was agitating. He was given to uttering vague generalities, clothed in the most grandiloquent phrases.

"The Knights of Labor is higher and grander than party," he declared on one occasion. "There is a nobler future before it than that which clings to its existence amidst partisan rancor and strife. . . . We seek and intend to enlist the services of men of every society, of every party, every religion, and every nation in the crusade which we have inaugurated against these twin monsters, tyranny and monopoly; and in that crusade we have burned the bridges behind us; we have stricken from our vocabulary that word fail; we aim at establishing the complete rights of man throughout the world. . . ."

Cooperation was the means whereby he apparently hoped to achieve these idealistic aims. At times he seemed to be ready to place major emphasis on some other reform "In my opinion," he told the General Assembly in 1882, "the main, all absorbing question of the hour is the land question. . . . Give me the land, and you may frame as many eight-hour laws as you please yet I can baffle them all and render them null and void." His zeal for temperance also led him to emphasize this campaign. "Sometimes I think it is the main issue," he wrote while engaged in one of his periodic attacks on the "rum seller" and the "rum drinker." But sooner or later he would return to cooperation as the ultimate solution for labor's problems.

The Knights of Labor became very active in various ventures along these lines. Many of the district assemblies set up both consumers' and producers' cooperatives, some 135 in all, and the national organization itself purchased and for a time operated a coal mine at Cannelburg, Indiana. These undertakings, whether in mining, cooperage, shoe manufacturing, printing or other industries generally failed, however, for the same reasons as had most previous experiments along these lines. The Knights of Labor were no more successful than the National Labor Union in meeting the competition of private enterprise, securing the capital funds necessary for the expansion of their undertakings, or in providing them with efficient management.

Their funds were to be greatly dissipated in these ventures and their failure played an important part in the Order's ultimate collapse. Powderly nevertheless clung to his conviction that cooperatives represented the only way in which labor could establish the self-employment that was its ultimate salvation.

"It is to cooperation . . ." he told the General Assembly in 1880, "that the eyes of the workingmen and working women of the world should be directed, upon cooperation their hopes should be centered. . . . There is no good reason why labor cannot, through cooperation, own and operate mines, factories, and railroads. . . . By cooperation alone can a system of colonization be established in which men may band together for the purpose of securing the greatest good to the greatest number, and place the man who is willing to toil upon his own homestead." He likened the movement to the Revolution and long after it had been abandoned by the Knights, he continued to assert his faith in the ultimate creation of a cooperative commonwealth. "My belief that cooperation shall one day take the place of the wage system," he wrote years later in his autobiographical *The Path I Trod*, "remains unshaken."

Although these long-term aims were his real concern, as head of the Order he had to deal with such immediate and practical issues as shorter hours and higher wages—objectives in which the Knights themselves were far more interested. This raised the question of strikes. As an idealistic man of peace, Powderly opposed them. "The tendency of the times is to do away with strikes," he wrote in 1883; "that remedy has been proved by experience to be a very costly one for employer and employe." He was later to boast that "not once did I, during my fourteen years' incumbency of the office of General Master Workman, order a strike." But in his attitude on this vital issue of the 1880's, lay perhaps his greatest weakness. As the Knights of Labor repeatedly became involved in strikes, both with and without the approval of their governing body, the Grand Master Workman had a responsibility in supporting them which he could not avoid. There were times when Powderly did so courageously in spite of his own inner conviction that they were futile, but in other instances he seemed to be so timid as to be ready to conclude any sort of settlement with employers. His vacillating attitude often led to confusion, and broke down the united labor front that under more forthright leadership might have carried the strikes through to real success.

Powderly was at heart a humanitarian, thinking in terms of the general elevation of the producing class to a higher level in contemporary society. "If I had the right to give myself a name," he later wrote in his autobiography, "I would call it equalizer." Nothing could have more clearly portrayed his impatience with the immediate, short-run objectives that most interested the great majority of workers in their growing acceptance of their status as wage earners.

"Just think of it!" he once wrote in self-pitying explanation of his position. "Opposing strikes and always striking. . . . Battling with my pen in the leading journals and magazines of the day for the great things we are educating the people on and fighting with might and main for the little things. Our Order has held me in my present position because of the reputation I have won in the nation at large by taking high ground on important national questions, yet the trade element in our Order has always kept me busy at the base of the breastworks throwing up earth which they trample down."

It was when hard times again hit the country in the 1880's, leading to widespread wage cuts and unemployment in the traditional pattern of the economic cycle, that the Knights of Labor became involved in the strikes that were first to promote their spectacular growth and then precipitate their gradual decline. Powderly was to be tried and found wanting. But both the rise of the Noble and Holy Order and its ultimate collapse were in reality due to economic and social forces far beyond his control.

As restive workers sought to combat the exactions of employers trying to reduce operating costs, there were walkouts in 1883-1884 by glass workers' unions, telegraph operators, cotton spinners in Fall River, Philadelphia shoemakers and carpet weavers, miners in both Pennsylvania and the Hocking Valley in Ohio, Troy iron molders and shopmen on the Union Pacific. Knights of Labor participated in each of these strikes and in four of them, played a major role. What was most significant was that while the other strikes were crushed by the employers, those in which the Knights engaged most actively resulted, with a single exception, in victories for the workers. The most important of these strikes was that of the railway shopmen, which succeeded in forcing the Union Pacific to restore wage cuts all along the line.

The victory of the workers in this strike was in large part due to the aggressive leadership of Joseph R. Buchanan, a militant labor agitator who had joined the Knights in 1882. A onetime prospector in Colorado, he typified the new west—a large, rough, domineering type of man. His success in leading the shopmen's strike was primarily due to the creation of a feeling of unity among the workers through organization of the Union Pacific Employes' Protective Association and the subsequent establishment of local assemblies of the Knights of Labor.

A year after the Union Pacific affair another strike of railway shopmen broke out on the lines making up the so-called Southwest System—the Missouri Pacific; the Missouri, Kansas and Texas; and the Wabash. It had no sooner got underway through spontaneous work stoppages than Buchanan hurried to the scene, as a representative of the Knights of Labor assemblies on the western railroads, and repeated his earlier success on the Union Pacific by organizing the disaffected workers of the Southwest System into local assemblies. With the support of the trainmen, the striking shop workers were able to put up such a strong front that again they won their demands.

These victories, so surprising in the light of the disastrous experience of the railway strikes in 1877, redounded to the credit of the Knights of Labor and their prestige began to soar even though so far only local assemblies had been involved in the strikes. But an even more sensational success was won a little later in 1885 when the Noble and Holy Order clashed directly, as a result of further disputes on the Wabash, with Jay Gould, the powerful, astute and unscrupulous financier who controlled the entire Southwest System. The Wabash had begun in April and May to lay off shopmen who were members of the Knights of

Labor in what appeared to be a determined effort to break the local unions. The district assembly that had been organized the previous year in Moberley, Missouri at once called a strike and appealed to national headquarters for help. The executive board was still seeking to maintain a general anti-strike policy but it was forced to recognize that the very existence of the Order was at stake in this challenge to the organization of railway workers. When the Wabash bluntly refused to halt its lay-offs, the board consequently felt driven to take action. All Knights of Labor still working on the Wabash were ordered out, and those on other railways in the Southwest System and on the Union Pacific were instructed not to handle any Wabash rolling stock. The workers responded enthusiastically. Trains were stopped and the cars uncoupled, engines were "killed," and widespread sabotage, in some cases leading to disorder and violence, spread throughout the Southwest.

The threat to his entire transportation system, which the Knights appeared to be strong enough to tie up completely, forced Gould to consider coming to terms. A series of conferences was held in New York and the country was treated to the amazing spectacle of the management of one of the nation's greatest railway systems negotiating with the executive board of a nationwide labor organization. Nothing like it had ever before happened. Moreover the result was an understanding. Gould agreed to end all discrimination against Knights of Labor on the lines he controlled, reputedly saying that he had come to believe in labor unions and wished that all his railroad employes were organized. Powderly called off the strike and promised that no further work stoppages would be authorized until conferences had been held with the railway officials.

"The Wabash victory is with the Knights," exclaimed the *St. Louis Chronicle* in astonishment. "No such victory has ever before been secured in this or any other country."

For the nation's workers generally, Gould's apparent capitulation was the signal for an overwhelming rush to join an organization which had proved itself to be so powerful. During the next few months, more local assemblies of the Knights of Labor were formed than in the previous sixteen years. The new membership came largely from the unskilled or semi-skilled workers on the railroads, in mines and in the mass production industries, strengthening particularly the so-called mixed assemblies. But all trades and occupations were represented including many persons who were not wage earners at all—farmers, shopkeepers and small employers—while thousands of women and Negroes also joined the Order. Between July 1, 1885 and June 30, 1886, the number of local assemblies rose from 1,610 to 5,892 and total membership shot up from around 100,000 to over 700,000. "Never in all history," exulted the editor of one labor paper, "has there been such a spectacle as the march of the Order of the Knights of Labor at the present time."

So great was the influx that harassed organizers found themselves initiating new members so rapidly that they wholly lost control of the situation and were for a time compelled to suspend the formation of new assemblies. There was no question that the Order was expanding much too rapidly. Powderly was later to state that "at least four hundred thousand came in from curiosity and caused more damage than good." Nevertheless in the spring of 1886, the Knights of Labor appeared to have taken over control of the entire labor movement and to be virtually all-powerful.

Wild rumors magnified even the astounding growth that had actually taken place. The membership was said to be almost 2,500,000 with a war chest of $12,000,000. The conservative press conjured up the frightening prospect of the Order wholly dominating the country. It was prophesied that it would name the next president, or even more fearfully that it would overthrow the whole social system.

"Five men in this country," an article in the *New York Sun* stated, "control the chief interests of five hundred thousand workingmen, and can at any moment take the means of livelihood from two and a half million souls. These men compose the executive board of the noble order of the Knights of Labor of America . . . They can stay the nimble touch of almost every telegraph operator; can shut up most of the mills and factories, and can disable the railroads. They can issue an edict against any manufactured goods so as to make their subjects cease buying them, and the tradesmen stop selling them. They can array labor against capital, putting labor on the offensive or the defensive, for quiet and stubborn self-protection, or for angry, organized assault as they will."

As the head of this powerful organization, Powderly was said to have become an absolute czar of labor, ruling his followers with "despotism and secrecy." Actually he was overwhelmed by the uncontrolled expansion of the Order and the tremendous responsibility suddenly thrust upon him. "The position I hold," he ruefully commented, "is too big for any ten men. It is certainly too big for me. . . ."

But the public saw in the Knights of Labor a closely controlled and disciplined organization that could apparently win any contest against employers to which it gave its aggressive support. The Knights of Labor were at the peak of their astounding prestige.

Everywhere workers were singing:

> Toiling millions now are waking—
> See them marching on;
> All the tyrants now are shaking,
> Ere their power's gone.
>
> *Chorus:*
> Storm the fort, ye Knights of Labor,
> Battle for your cause;
> Equal rights for every neighbor—
> Down with Tyrant laws!

The very scope of early victories, however, held the seeds of dissolution. Success had gone to the Knights' head. Although the *Journal of United Labor* warned of the danger that "in the excess of joy, our members may imagine themselves invincible," and the executive board plaintively declared that far too many strikes were taking place at the same time, the rank-and-file workers were not to be restrained. The huge, unwieldly membership of the Order recognized no disciplinary control and had no sense of responsibility. Making the most of what were thought to be the weak points of industry, the workers continued to press their demands upon employers and to count upon the Order in supporting them. Out of this situation were to come a succession of defeats, as discouraging for the Knights as their original triumphs had been stimulating.

A first setback resulted from another strike on the part of the railway workers on the Southwest System. The employes of the Missouri Pacific and the Missouri, Kansas and Texas were still discontented. They had been ready to strike in support of the shopmen on the Wabash in 1885, and with highly exaggerated ideas of the strength of the Knights of Labor were seeking a pretext the following spring to walk out in demand for higher pay. When a Knights of Labor foreman on the Texas and Pacific Railway was fired, the Master Workman of District Assembly No. 1, a local leader named Martin Irons, promptly called a strike without awaiting any official authorization. It quickly spread from the Texas and Pacific to workers on the other lines.

"Tell the world that men of the Gould Southwest system are on strike," read one grandiloquent appeal. "We strike for justice to ourselves and our fellowmen everywhere. Fourteen thousand men are out. . . . Bring in all your grievances in one bundle at once, and come out to a man, and stay out until they are all settled to your entire satisfaction. Let us demand our rights and compel the exploiters to accede to our demands. . . ."

Such extravagant demands were all that Gould, and the officials of the railways he controlled, needed in order to convince them that the Knights of Labor should be crushed. There is no reason to believe that Gould ever really favored unionization in the slightest. He retreated in 1885 only to gather force for a counter-attack in 1886. Powderly, indeed, was later to charge that the management of the Texas and Pacific had instigated the new strike, actually coercing Irons into calling out the men against his will. However that may be, the southwest railroads now fought the strikers with all the weapons at their command. When the workers again uncoupled cars and killed engines, management hired strikebreakers and Pinkerton guards, and appealed to the state governors for military protection. This time there were to be no concessions and no compromises.

Powderly felt himself to be in an impossible situation. He did not approve the strike and had nothing to do with calling it, but he found himself accused by the railways of violating the pledge he had made not to authorize any work stoppage without previous conferences. He sought out Gould and tried to find a basis for settlement the strikers could accept. But the railway magnate now had no idea of negotiating with the Knights and the conversations were entirely fruitless.

In the meantime, things were going badly for the workers. Only some 3,000 out of 48,000 employes on the Gould system were reported to have actually turned out, and in their battles with the scabs, they were being worsted. Public opinion was also against them. "They are, in fact," the *Nation* declared, "trying to introduce into modern society a new right— that is, the right to be employed by people who do not want you and who cannot afford to pay what you ask." There was general condemnation for "the forcible resistance of the strikers, to the conduct of the business by anybody but themselves."

Finally, with the railroads refusing all concessions, a congressional committee investigating the strike, and public opinion becoming more and more outraged at the interruption to railway service, Powderly in effect washed his hands of the whole affair. He recognized the importance of the controversy for the prestige of the Noble and Holy Order and was unwilling to capitulate to Gould, but he saw no way in which the strike could be carried through successfully. Left with the responsibility the Grand Master Workman evaded, the executive council then gave way and ordered the men back to work. The Knights of Labor had suffered their first serious reverse and their organization among the workers on the Gould system collapsed.

There were to be further defeats as other employers, following Gould's lead, marshaled their forces to crush every workers' uprising and permanently break the power of the Knights. During the latter half of 1886, some 100,000 wage earners were involved in labor disputes, and in the great majority of these strikes and lockouts, they were wholly unsuccessful.

The Knights suffered most severely from a strike in the Chicago stockyards. The eight-hour day was the issue at stake and the associated meat packers not only refused to meet this demand but declared that they would no longer employ any members of the Order. The strike, nevertheless, tied up the packing houses completely and there seemed to be some chance of a compromise agreement when suddenly and without warning, Powderly ordered the men back to work with the threat of taking away their charters if they refused. He was to be accused both of selling out to the employers and of being unduly influenced by the intercession of a Catholic priest in this maneuver. His own account of the episode states that the strikers were bound to be defeated and that he took such action as he did to prevent further suffering and possible bloodshed. In any event, the Knights lost control of the situation as a result of their leader's erratic attitude. With the collapse of the strike, their prestige suffered another irremediable blow.

It was clear that the tide had turned. The aggressive counter-attack of industry, quick to take advantage of every opportunity, rolled back labor's earlier gains. As early as July, 1886, John Swinton had declared that while at the opening of the year the Golden Age appeared to be on hand, it already looked as if the workers "had been deceived by the will-o'-the-wisp." Now he was wholly convinced of it—"the money power had swept all before it and established its supremacy beyond challenge."

"Jay Gould, the enemy's generalissimo," Swinton continued, "had squelched the railroad strikes of the Southwest and this was followed by the failure of hundreds of other strikes. . . . The union men had been blacklisted right and left and a vast conspiracy against the Knights of Labor has shown itself in many localities. The laws had been distorted against boycotting. Pinkerton thugs had been consolidated into petty armies for the hire of capital. . . . The constitutional rights of citizens had been invaded, labor meetings broken up and labor papers threatened or suppressed."

The onslaughts of industry and consequent loss of strikes were not the only developments that now served to undermine the strength of the Knights of Labor. Its leadership seemed to become more and more bungling. Powderly sought to minimize industrial strife and direct attention toward cooperatives, and increasingly lost the confidence of the workers themselves. They felt that he no longer understood their real interests and was unwilling to support their legitimate demands upon their employers.

An example of what was considered his pusillanimous attitude was the policy he adopted when the reviving national unions, already associated in the Federation of Organized Trades and Labor Unions, predecessor to the American Federation of Labor, sought in 1886 to promote the general strike for an eight-hour day that provided the background for the Haymarket Square riot. Although the Knights of Labor strongly favored an eight-hour day, Powderly would not associate the Order with the strike call. "No assembly," he stated in a secret circular, "must strike for the eight-hour system on May 1st. under the impression they are obeying orders from headquarters, for such an order was not, and will not be given. . . ." Instead of such direct action, he suggested that the local assemblies have their members write short essays on the eight-hour day for simultaneous publication in the press on Washington's Birthday! Many of the district assemblies nevertheless adopted resolutions to support the general strike in spite of Powderly's attempt to dissuade them, and when May 1 arrived, thousands of Knights took part in this first mass demonstration on the part of the nation's workers to impress their demands upon industry.

It was not a success. Some 340,000 workers were estimated to have participated in the eight-hour movement and over half of this total actually went out on strike on May 1. But while 200,000 were said to have secured employer recognition of the eight-hour day, their gains proved to be short-lived. It was reported by the close of the year that employers had retracted for all but some 15,000 workers such concessions as they had temporarily felt compelled to grant. The anti-labor reaction that followed the Haymarket Square affair was perhaps largely responsible for this debacle, but the failure of the Knights of Labor to support the movement in the first instance was felt to be an important contributing factor.

When the Knights of Labor met for their convention in the fall of 1886, appearances still belied the inner weaknesses that were leading to dissolution. The National Assembly at Richmond was the most impressive labor gathering that the country had ever witnessed and the seven hundred delegates were formally welcomed by the governor of Virginia. But this strong showing was little more than a bright façade and there was something empty in the impassioned eloquence of the assembly speakers who attacked "the lash of gold" that was falling upon "the backs of millions." The failure of so many strikes, the collapse of the eight-hour movement, the unhappy consequences of most of the cooperative ventures, and the after-effects of the Haymarket Square riot, together with the widening breach between leaders and members, had started the Knights of Labor on a decline from which it would never recover.

Many of the local assemblies simply dissolved and others made up of skilled craftsmen threw their support behind the movement that was leading to formation of the American Federation of Labor. For the Knights were already deeply involved in that decisive struggle with the emerging forces of the new unionism that was to complete their downfall. A membership of 700,000 dropped to 200,000 within two years. In 1893, it had further fallen to 75,000. The conservative press rejoiced at the disintegration of an organization which had once been thought to hold the destinies of the republic in its power. "The only wonder," one editor commented with relief, "is that the madness lasted so long."

For a time the leaders of the Knights of Labor sought to combat this trend by turning toward political as opposed to industrial activity. Powderly urged the workingmen to protect their interests by making their concerted pressure felt "upon that day which of all days is important to the American citizen—ELECTION DAY." The support of the Order was thrown behind local labor candidates for political office in a dozen cities in the fall of 1886, and the Grand Master Workman himself campaigned energetically for Henry George and his single tax program in the mayoralty election in New York. For while Powderly still did not believe in a third party movement, his feeling of frustration over the failure of economic action led him more and more to politics as a last resort. In 1889 he was urging the Knights "to throw strikes, boycotts, lockouts and such nuisances to the winds and unite in one strike through the legislative weapon in such a way as to humble the power of the corporations who rule the United States today."

In the final stages of decline, the agrarian elements within the Knights of Labor, which had always been present with the admission of farmers to membership, began to overshadow the influence of industrial workers. Powderly was ousted in 1893 and his post of Master Workman taken over by James R. Sovereign, of Iowa, who was exclusively interested in reform politics.

"It is not founded on the question of adjusting wages," Sovereign stated in 1894 in describing the functions of the Order, "but on the question of abolishing the wage system and the establishment of a cooperative industrial system. When its real mission is accomplished, poverty will be reduced to a minimum and the land dotted with peaceful happy homes."

The words had a familiar ring—Sylvis, Stephens, Powderly himself might have uttered them—but Sovereign had forgotten that mitigation

of the wage system was to be a step toward its ultimate abolition, and
that the workers themselves had flocked to join the Order not because
of its vague and idealistic ultimate goals, but because of the support
they thought it was prepared to give for immediate wage and hour
demands. And the strength of the Knights of Labor had been in its
militant membership. Now that assembly after assembly had drifted
away, the Order reverted to something like the status of the old labor
congresses. A handful of political-minded leaders occasionally met to
urge measures which they were wholly unable to carry through.

In spite of its sorry end, the Noble and Holy Order had given a tremendous impetus to the organization of labor and both its successes
and its failures were to be of continuing significance for the growth of
the labor movement as a whole. For the Knights had, indeed, created
a solidarity among the workers that had been but dimly felt before
their advent, and they offered a challenge to the power of industry that
revealed as never before the inherent strength of organization. After
all, the growth within less than twenty years from a little secret society
of seven journeymen tailors to a nationwide organization of seven hundred thousand workers was in itself an almost incredible achievement.

Failure was due to the interrelated effects of irresponsibility on the
part of the membership and fumbling leadership; participation in
poorly organized and consequently unsuccessful strikes; the dissipation
of energy and funds in cooperative ventures doomed to collapse, and
above all to the impracticality of trying to draw the unskilled, industrial
workers into a single, unified labor organization and the consequent
withdrawal of support by the national trade unions.

Powderly well realized before his final retirement that the Order was
in the throes of final dissolution, and he felt that whatever the faults or
virtues of its leadership, internal contradictions made its impending
fate inevitable.

"Teacher of important and much-needed reforms," he wrote in 1893,
"she had been obliged to practice differently from her teachings. Advocating arbitration and conciliation as first steps in labor disputes she
had been forced to take upon her shoulders the responsibilities of the
aggressor first and, when hope of arbitrating and conciliation failed, to

beg of the opposing side to do what we should have applied for in the first instance. Advising against strikes, we have been in the midst of them. Urging important reforms we have been forced to yield our time and attention to petty disputes until we were placed in a position where we have frequently been misunderstood by the employee as well as the employer. While not a political party we have been forced into the attitude of taking political action. . . ."

The Knights of Labor had failed. Yet it was also true, as Powderly went on to state, that the Order had stamped deep its impression on the country and even in collapse could point "to its splendid achievements in forcing to the front the cause of misunderstood and downtrodden humanity."

XX

IX: THE AMERICAN FEDERATION OF LABOR

XXXXXXXXXXXXXXXXXXXXXXXXXXXXXXXXXXXXXXXXXXXX

QUESTION: You are seeking to improve home matters first?

ANSWER: Yes, Sir, I look first to the trade I represent . . . the interest of the men who employ me to represent their interests.

CHAIRMAN: I was only asking you in regard to your ultimate ends.

WITNESS: We have no ultimate ends. We are going on from day to day. We fight only for immediate objects—objects that can be realized in a few years.

IN THIS OFTEN QUOTED TESTIMONY given by Adolph Strasser, president of the International Cigar Makers' Union before the Senate Committee on Education and Labor in 1885, we find the core of the philosophy that underlay the revival of trade unionism and was to inspire the formation of the American Federation of Labor. The new leaders of organized labor were not interested in the reformation of society through creation of a cooperative commonwealth. While they did not wholly abandon the humanitarian, idealistic goals of their predecessors, they prided themselves above all else on being "practical men." They were primarily concerned with the improvement of wages, hours and working conditions for their own trade union followers within the framework of the existing industrial system.

While the old national trade unions had been almost wholly broken up during the somber days of depression in the 1870's, the very years

150

that witnessed the dramatic rise of the Knights of Labor found them slowly coming back to life. In some instances they were associated with the Knights, joining the Order as national trade assemblies; in other cases they held wholly aloof and maintained a complete independence. Their role in the labor movement appeared in either event to be largely overshadowed by that of the Knights throughout the greater part of the 1880's. A public impressed with the apparent unity and strength of the Noble and Holy Order little realized that the future was to lie with the trade unions rather than with the inchoate masses of skilled and unskilled workers who were believed to be so completely at the beck and call of Terence V. Powderly.

The history of the national unions during these years conforms to no set pattern. Their revival after the 1870's was marked by rivalry and conflict, and all the intricate maneuvering of labor politics. But the "new unionism" which Strasser had in mind with his emphasis upon immediate and practical goals, gradually took shape and form as events demonstrated that the program of the Knights of Labor was failing.

This practical approach to labor problems was not of course entirely new. The original trade societies half a century earlier had stressed organization on a strictly craft basis, job protection and such forthright objectives as higher wages and shorter hours. The national unions of the late 1860's and early 1870's had these same ends in view, and an immediate progenitor of the new program could be found in the Molders' International Union in the days before William Sylvis was converted from trade unionism to reform. Nevertheless there was to be in many respects a fresh approach to the basic problem of the organization of labor born of the unhappy experience of the national unions during earlier periods of depression.

Among such unions one which had narrowly escaped complete extinction was the International Cigar Makers' Union. Its membership had dwindled to little more than a handful when its reorganization was undertaken by three militant leaders—Adolph Strasser, Ferdinand Laurrell and, most conspicuously, Samuel Gompers—who undertook to put it back on its feet with the adoption of sound, efficient practices. A New York local was established in 1875, Gompers taking over the presidency, and in 1877 Strasser was elected president of the international. A strike among the New York cigar makers in protest against the sweatshop system failed disastrously this latter year, but defeat merely strengthened the determination of the new union officials to carry their program through and give the cigar makers an organization that could effectively protect their interests. "Trade unionism," as Gompers wrote, "had to be put upon a business basis in order to develop power adequate to secure better working conditions."

Initiation fees and high dues, together with a system of sickness and death benefits, were adopted to ensure the stability and permanence of the new union. The principle of equalization of funds, whereby a local in a strong financial position could be ordered to transfer some part of its reserves to any local in distress, was borrowed from the practice of British trade unions. A highly centralized control gave the international officers virtually complete authority over all local unions and guaranteed both strict discipline in the promotion of strikes and adequate support when they were officially authorized. The Cigar Makers laid paramount stress on responsibility and efficiency. While they were prepared to use the strike as the most effective weapon in enforcing a demand for trade agreements, it was to be employed only when the union commanded the resources to make it successful.

"With the administration of Strasser," Gompers wrote of these days in his autobiography, "there began a new era for the Cigar Makers and for all trade unions—for the influence of our work was to extend far. There was the beginning of a period of growth, financial success, and sound development for the International Cigar Makers' Union of America, a period during which uniform regulations, high dues, union benefits, union label, better wages, and the shorter work-day were established."

Other unions adopted these procedures, notably the Brotherhood of Carpenters and Joiners under the able leadership of Peter J. McGuire, but the cigar makers were the real pioneers and they carried their reorganization through so successfully that they became the model for the new unionism. Their experience graphically illustrated what could be done on a firm foundation of financial stability and centralized authority. There was no nonsense about producers' self-employment, a cooperative commonwealth or any other utopian goal. "Necessity has forced the labor movement to adopt the most practical methods," it was stated emphatically. "They are struggling for higher wages and shorter hours. . . . No financial scheme or plan of taxation will shorten the hours of labor."

This pragmatic approach was a revolt against both the middle class concepts of reform which had in the past appeared to lead labor down so many unproductive byways, and also against socialists theories which the leaders of the new unionism considered equally harmful. Both Strasser and McCuire had been socialists; Gompers was at one time under their influence. But the first two had become disgusted with socialist rivalry and dissension, and we have seen how his own experience turned Gompers against all radicalism. Convinced of the futility of seeking the salvation of labor from any such source, these leaders fell back strongly on "pure and simple" trade unionism. Their philosophy was based upon wage consciousness rather than class consciousness. They had no idea of trying to change the economic system, let alone seeking to overthrow it.

This is not to say that there were no radicals in the reorganized labor movement. The revolutionary element which had had a part in the rioting and disorder of the 1870's and 1880's was not entirely eliminated. The adherents of both Marxian and Lassallean socialism continued "to bore from within" in their attempts to swing labor into their respective camps and they were to win their converts among members of unions affiliated with the American Federation of Labor. But the responsible leaders of the new unionism strongly and successfully opposed all such influences, and were to become more and more conservative in their approach to economic and social issues.

If the driving force behind the new unionism came largely from the International Cigar Makers, it was Samuel Gompers above all others who was its most able spokesman and the principal architect of the national organization that was to promote its basic principles. He was not only to become the first president of the American Federation of Labor, but with the exception of a single year, he held that post until his death in 1924. The reorientation of the labor movement upon the decline of the Knights of Labor, and the success of the A.F. of L. in surviving the depression of the 1890's, were in large part the work of this stocky, matter-of-fact, stubborn labor leader whose character and philosophy were in such glaring contrast to the character and philosophy of Powderly.

Gompers was born in London's East End in 1850. His father, of Dutch-Jewish stock, was a cigar maker and at the age of ten the young Samuel was apprenticed to this trade. When the family emigrated to America in 1863, he first helped his father in making cigars in their tenement home in New York's East Side, but soon branched out to get a job of his own and as early as 1864 joined a local union.

The cigar making shops at this time were schools of political and social philosophy as well as manufactories, and there was no more avid student than the young immigrant from London already steeped in the background of British trade unionism. As he sat at his bench in the dark and dusty loft, dexterously fashioning cigars, he listened with eager attention to the talk of socialism and labor reform among his fellow workers. Most of them were European-born and many of them members of the International Workingmen's Association. They had the custom of having one of their number read the labor periodicals and other magazines aloud to them (chipping in to make up the pay he would otherwise have lost) and Gompers was often given this assignment.

As already suggested, his thorough exposure to Marxist philosophy did not, however, have the effect of making the young cigar maker a theorist. On the contrary it appears to have confirmed his hard-headed, practical approach to the problems of labor. He was perhaps greatly influenced in maintaining this point of view by Ferdinand Laurrell, who was a tough-minded Swedish immigrant experienced in all phases of radicalism. Laurrell advised him to read Marx and Engels, but to be constantly on guard against being carried away by their theorizing. He warned him not to join the Socialist Party. "Study your union card, Sam," he told Gompers, "and if the idea does not square with that, it ain't true."

It was with such a background that Gompers plunged into the task, in cooperation with Strasser and Laurrell, of rebuilding the Cigar Makers' Union. Looking back upon the experiences of those days, Gompers was always to think of them as responsible not only for his own career but for the future course of American labor. "From this little group," he wrote of the men with whom he had thrashed out his ideas in endless discussion, "came the purpose and initiative that finally resulted in the present American labor movement. . . . We did not create the American trade union—that is the product of forces and conditions. But we did create the technique and formulate the fundamentals that guided trade unions to constructive policies and achievements."

Gompers was twenty-nine when the International Cigar Makers' Union was reorganized and from this early period he followed an undeviating path. Unlike both Sylvis and Powderly, he stuck closely to his last and never admitted any other interests. He was neither a reformer nor an intellectual, and he scorned their pretensions to show labor the course it should pursue. In his complete distrust of such theorists, whom he considered "industrially impossible," he never tried himself to elaborate any philosophy of labor. He liked to talk about moral influence and intuition, but his approach to every question was wholly pragmatic.

His ideas tended to be narrow and limited, and his program was invariably one of immediate opportunism. While he once spoke vaguely of favoring abolition of the wage system, he did not actually look beyond the bounds of higher wages and shorter hours for the skilled workers of the craft unions. In breaking completely with such panaceas as currency reform, land settlement and cooperation, which had so intrigued the leaders of the National Labor Union and the Knights of Labor, he also abandoned their goal of labor solidarity. Gompers' realistic attitude was to place the labor movement, at least as far as the skilled workers were concerned, on a firmer and more stable basis than it had ever before attained, but his lack of breadth and vision was greatly to limit the role of the American Federation of Labor in advancing the cause of labor as a whole. He at one and the same time saved the trade union movement from possible complete breakdown, and threw away the opportunity for developing it along those broader lines which had been the highly idealistic dream of his predecessors.

In promoting the interests of his own union and then of the American Federation of Labor, his zeal was reenforced by an apparently inexhaustible fund of energy. There were never to be any complaints of being unable to meet the demands made upon his time. As an organizer and administrator, Gompers was tireless, traveling all over the country to address labor meetings and conventions. Once known as "Stuttering Sam," he outgrew any hesitations in his speech and eloquently boomed forth the exhortatory platitudes that were so much his stock in trade. His speeches, it is true, were sometimes rather vague and confused, for he had no real gift for oral expression. His manner was often solemn and pontifical. But with a flair for the dramatic that would also distinguish an even more theatrical labor leader of later days, he knew well how to hold the center of the stage.

Off the platform and outside the conference room, Gompers was friendly, easy-going and very much one of the boys. His nature was warm and open-hearted. He liked beer parlors, the theater, music halls, show girls and the Atlantic City boardwalk. He completely shed his official character when he foregathered with a group of friends for the evening, comfortably relaxed in the congenial atmosphere of the back room of a saloon, a big black cigar gripped in his teeth and a foaming stein of beer on the table. His conviviality shocked his strait-laced, puritanical rival in the Knights of Labor. "The General Executive Board," stated a pamphlet issued by the Knights in the midst of their struggle with the American Federation of Labor, "has never had the pleasure of seeing Mr. Gompers sober." It was an unfair comment by an ardent temperance advocate, but there was no question that Gompers hugely enjoyed his beer.

In appearance, Gompers looked far more like a labor leader than the somewhat effete Powderly. His short, thick-set, sturdily built body —he was only five feet, four inches tall—seemed to justify his boast that "the Gompers are built of oak," and the strong jaw beneath a broad forehead revealed both the force and stubborness of his character. In the early 1880's he had dark, unruly hair and wore a drooping walrus mustache with a little tuft of hair on his chin. In later years, he was to be clean shaven with a glittering pince-nez shielding his dark, snapping eyes. He dressed well, was quite accustomed to a silk hat and Prince Albert on important occasions, and his manners were gracious. Business leaders somewhat patronizingly spoke of his being "very much of a gentleman."

For all his later hobnobbing with the great—captains of industry, Wall St. bankers, senators and presidents—he never lost touch with the workers themselves and liked to refer to himself as "one who had not grown up from the ranks but still is proud to be in the ranks." He was intensely loyal and always ready to sacrifice his personal well-being and comfort for the cause for which he worked. Impeccably honest, he was to die a poor man and in later years his widow had to accept work from the W.P.A.

None of this is to say that Gompers was not ambitious. He felt himself born to leadership and clung tenaciously to the presidency of the American Federation of Labor. He built up both a powerful political machine and a closely knit labor bureaucracy. He was something of a dictator in pushing his policies and never one to give way before younger, more progressive leadership as time went on and he grew older. But his ambition for power and a public career did not lead him to seek either riches or political preferment. He was to remain wholly content with "serving his class" by making trade unionism and the A.F. of L. his life work.

"I look back over the years of work for my trade," he wrote in his autobiography, "and I rejoice in the conviction that the bona fide trade union movement is the one great agency of the toiling masses to secure for them a better and higher standard of life and work."

The first move leading toward the alliance of national and international unions that eventuated in the American Federation of Labor was made at a Pittsburgh meeting of labor leaders in 1881. Attended by delegates from both the trade unions and the Knights of Labor, the original purpose of the conference was to set up an association that might embrace all labor. "We have numberless trade unions, trades' assemblies or councils, Knights of Labor and other various local, national and international unions," the call for the meeting stated. "But great as has been the work done by these bodies, there is vastly more that can be done by a combination of all these organizations into a federation of trades." The growing rivalry between adherents of the new unionism and the leaders of the Knights of Labor, however, was to make achievement of such a goal impossible, and the Federation of Organized Trades and Labor Unions that grew out of the Pittsburgh meeting was to be short-lived.

Although some of the national unions, as we have seen, were affiliated with the Knights as trade assemblies, they were becoming increasingly opposed to the doctrines of the Noble and Holy Order. More and more of them were breaking away altogether, and they naturally resented any attempted interference in their affairs or infringement on territory they felt to be within their jurisdiction. Their attitude was frankly expressed by McGuire of the Carpenters. "While there is a national or international union of a trade," he stated, "the men of that trade should organize under it and . . . the Knights of Labor should not interfere."

The Knights nevertheless did interfere. Recognizing the importance of the skilled workers belonging to the trade unions, and their strategic position in the labor world, the Order was anxious to hold their allegiance. Powderly, for example, promised the newly organized Amalgamated Association of Iron, Tin and Steel Workers, a craft union, that if it would join the Knights it could retain its separate identity and maintain its own system of government. But the skilled workers in this and other organizations saw themselves pulled down to the level of unskilled workers in submission to the Knights' control. They declared that they would maintain their autonomy against all outside pressure "to protect the skilled trades of America from being reduced to beggary."

Gompers attended the Pittsburgh meeting in 1881 as a delegate of the Cigar Makers and was chosen chairman of the committee on organization. Although he was actually a member of the Knights of Labor, having joined the Order in the 1870's, his opposition to its basic principles led him to make every effort to keep the proposed new federation a strictly trade union affair. His proposals were defeated after vigorous debate. "There seems to be something singular about the manner in which we are changing base," one delegate stated on the floor. "This Congress was widely advertised as a labor congress and now we are talking about trades. Why not make the Knights of Labor the basis for the federation?" While this was not done, the new organization did not draw any line between skilled and unskilled workers, and was theoretically to include all labor without distinction of creed, color or nationality.

The Federation of Organized Trades and Labor Unions was in many ways a transitional stage in labor's swing toward the restricted program of the new unionism. While the ideal of solidarity was upheld, the Federation was primarily concerned with such immediate gains as the wage earners might be able to win rather than fundamental reforms in the economic system. Its legislative program, for whose support it asked all trade bodies to seek representation in the legislature, called for the legal incorporation of trade unions, the abolition of child labor, enforcement of the statutory eight-hour day, prohibition of contract labor, uniform apprentice laws and repeal of the conspiracy laws.

The Federation did not, however, win any active support. The representatives of the Knights withdrew almost at once, and most of those of the national unions soon followed them. There were only nineteen delegates at the second annual convention and twenty-six at the third. Gompers was elected president in the latter year—1883—but he did not even attend the next meeting. Out of touch with the workers themselves, the new organization soon became, like the old National Labor Union, little more than an annual conference. Its only significant action was its promotion of the eight-hour strike on May 1, 1886, but as we have seen, it was unable to carry this movement through successfully without the support of the Knights of Labor.

The Federation was, indeed, about to give up the ghost entirely in 1886. The leaders of the national unions had become convinced that it did not hold out any hope of meeting their problems. In the face of the continued attacks being made on their form of organization by the Knights of Labor, who in the flush of victory were now stating that there was no place in the labor movement for independent trade unions, they decided to take a more forthright stand in their own defense. Another meeting of national unions was consequently called for May 18, 1886, in Philadelphia with the express purpose of seeking means "to protect our respective organizations from the malicious work of an element who openly boast that 'trades unions must be destroyed.'"

The ire of the trade unionists had been especially aroused by the interference of the Knights in the affairs of the Cigar Makers' International Union itself. As a result of internal dissensions in the New York local, involving the related issues of admitting unskilled workers and promoting socialism, a dissident faction had withdrawn from the parent body to form the Progressive Cigar Makers' Union. Strasser strongly condemned this move, refused to recognize the rebels in any way, and caustically described them as "tenement house scum." In the face of this situation, District Assembly 49 of the Knights of Labor jumped into the fray, aggressively supported the rebel union, and campaigned for its admission into the Order.

When the Philadelphia conference met, one more effort was made, at least in theory, to discover a common ground of understanding that might persuade the Knights to cease their hostility toward national unions. A "treaty" was proposed to reconcile the divergent aims of the two groups within the labor movement and bring their feuding to an end. The Knights were to agree that they would not initiate into the Order any trade unionist member without the permission of his union, or any other wage earner who worked for less than the prescribed wage scale of his craft, and they were also called upon to revoke the charter of any local assembly organized by workers in a trade where there was already a national union.

Was this actually a treaty? Its one-sided terms appeared rather a demand for the Knights' complete capitulation to the national unions. Some of the delegates at Philadelphia may have considered it the statement of a position from which they would be willing to retreat if the Order proved to be conciliatory. There can be little question, however, that in the minds of the adherents of the new unionism, it was a declaration of war. Their real aim was to swing the support of the national unions behind still another federation which would break away from the Knights of Labor altogether and concentrate wholly upon protecting the interests of the skilled craft workers. Gompers had wished to do this five years earlier, but the time had not been ripe. Now the increasing hostility between the Knights and the national unions, emphasized by the struggle over dual unionism among the Cigar Makers, provided the opportunity for decisive action.

The Noble and Holy Order played right into the hands of those favoring a complete break. In spite of some professions of willingness to explore means of reconciling the issues in dispute with the national unions, no official action whatsoever was taken in regard to the proposed treaty. Even though the failure of their strikes and the repercussions of the Haymarket Square affair were already weakening their position, the Knights were determined to adhere to their own program and saw no need to make any concessions. Powderly did not even submit the treaty for consideration at the Richmond assembly in October. The national unions were defied by the establishment of new national trade districts; the Progressive Cigar Makers were formally admitted to the Order, and no gesture whatsoever was made toward settling other jurisdictional quarrels.

The answer of the national unions was to meet again, at Columbus, Ohio, on December 8, 1886, and at this conference they were joined by the handful of delegates still representing the almost defunct Federation of Organized Trades and Labor Unions. Altogether there were present some forty-two representatives of twenty-five labor groups. Among the national unions participating were the Iron Molders, Miners and Mine Laborers, Typographers, Journeymen Tailors, Journeymen Bakers, Furniture Workers, Metal Workers, Granite Cutters, Carpenters and Cigar Makers. Their total membership approximated 150,000. The sole concern of the delegates had now become the promotion of the interests of the crafts which they respectively represented, and after due deliberation they formed a new organization for this purpose and elected Samuel Gompers as its first president. Here at last was the American Federation of Labor. Its date of origin was subsequently to be pushed back to 1881, the year in which the Federation of Organized Trades and Labor Unions was established, but although the A.F. of L. took over the treasury and records of its predecessor, the two groups were quite distinct and the history of the American Federation of Labor really begins in 1886.

A first principle of the new organization, growing out of the circumstances of its birth, was "strict recognition of the autonomy of each trade." The executive council set up to handle affairs on a national level was given no power whatsoever to interfere in those that fell within the jurisdiction of member unions. The unity of labor was to be promoted through education and moral suasion rather than through the centralized controls inherent in the structure of the Knights of Labor. Nevertheless the executive council had important functions. It issued the charters for constituent unions, and as a means for stamping out the dual unionism that was felt to be so threatening to the labor movement as a whole, was authorized to settle all jurisdictional disputes. A per capita tax was imposed on all member unions in order to build up the financial reserves that would enable the A.F. of L. to extend practical assistance in strikes and lock-outs, and a legislative program drawn up in the approved fashion of all labor organizations. Finally, there were to be formed under the general authority of the executive council, both city centrals and state federations further to influence the passage of labor legislation.

Major emphasis was definitely placed upon economic or industrial action. The A.F. of L. was to support the national and international unions in winning recognition from employers, entering into collective bargaining agreements, and maintaining a position which would enable them to strike effectively when other measures failed. The legislative program, which included most of the objectives that had been sought by the old Federation of Organized Trades and Labor Unions, was subordinated to this basic line of attack in frank recognition of the inadequacy of the policy of its predecessor. Moreover from the very first, the A.F. of L. was determined to refrain from direct participation in politics or support for any single party. It was to act upon the principle of rewarding labor's friends and punishing its enemies without regard to political affiliations.

In its early years, the American Federation of Labor was almost entirely Samuel Gompers. He had loyal associates but it was he who gave the new organization life and direction. "There was much work, little pay, and very little honor," he was later to write of these days, but such considerations did not daunt him. Setting up his headquarters in an eight-by-ten-foot office made available by the Cigar Makers, with little furniture other than a kitchen table, some crates for chairs, and a filing case made out of tomato boxes, he set about breathing vitality into the new organization with a zeal, devotion and tireless energy that largely accounted for its survival. He wrote innumerable letters, always in his own hand, to labor leaders throughout the country; for a time edited the *Trade Union Advocate* as a means of publicizing his campaign; issued union charters, collected dues, handled all routine business; managed conventions and went on speaking and organization tours, and slowly but persistently transformed the American Federation of Labor from a purely paper organization into a militant and powerful champion of labor's rights. He felt himself to be engaged in a holy cause and from the day the A.F. of L. came into being until his death thirty-eight years later, it was his entire life.

While the long-term struggle of the Federation was to be with the forces of industry, its early years were also marked by the continuing feud with the Knights of Labor. Further efforts were made in the late 1880's and early 1890's to draw the two organizations together, but these proved to be completely unsuccessful. The situation was not unlike that which would develop almost half a century later when the American Federation of Labor found itself in turn challenged by the dissident unions that were to form the Congress of Industrial Organizations. There were principles at stake but they were often overshadowed by the political rivalries and ambitions of contesting leaders.

Powderly moved steadily toward complete scorn of national unions. "I will tell you frankly," he wrote an associate in 1889, "I don't care how quick the National Trade Assemblies go out. They hinder others from coming to us and I am strongly tempted to advise them all to go it alone on the outside and see how it will go to turn back the wheels of the organization for the benefit of a few men who want to be at the head of something." Gompers grew no less caustic in his opinion of the Knights of Labor, their aims and aspirations. "Talk of harmony with the Knights of Labor," he was to say in 1894, "is bosh. They are just as great enemies of trade unions as any employer can be, only more vindictive. It is no use trying to placate them or even to be friendly."

Under such circumstances the possibility of labor unity faded away and the gradually dwindling strength of the Knights was counteracted by the slow growth of the American Federation of Labor. The latter was anything but spectacular. The original membership of 150,000 had increased to only 250,000 six years later. The violent counter-attack of industry upon all unions during these years, the generally repressive attitude of the government and the courts, and finally the trying times of the depression that developed in 1893 made it highly difficult to hold any labor organization together, let alone promote its growth and expansion. But Gompers stuck grimly to his task. He refused to allow the Federation to be drawn away from its immediate, practical aims and at the annual convention in 1893, he was able to look with pride upon what had already been accomplished.

"It is noteworthy," he told the assembled delegates, "that while in every previous industrial crisis the trade unions were literally mowed down and swept out of existence, the unions now in existence have manifested, not only the powers of resistance, but of stability and permanency."

The importance of the A.F. of L. in promoting the practical concepts of the new unionism should not obscure the fact that the national unions were the real basis for the revived labor movement—both at the close of the nineteenth century and in later years. They could exist without the A.F. of L., but the A.F. of L. had no meaning without them. Their autonomy was complete, and it was they who controlled the local unions that made up the membership of the labor movement. Their functions were to direct the activities of the locals, extend union organization through the trade or industry over which they had jurisdiction, provide such assistance as they could in collective bargaining and strikes (for which per capita taxes were levied for a general defense fund), and participate in the more general program of the A.F. of L.

With time the original craft unions were greatly to extend their jurisdiction and their names often reflect the history of this expansion. Many examples might be given, but one often cited as illustrating this trend is the International Association of Marble, Slate and Stone Polishers, Rubbers and Sawyers, Tile and Marble Setters Helpers and Terrazo Helpers. The introduction of new techniques and other economic changes, were to make the settlement of jurisdictional problems one of the major concerns of the A.F. of L. from the days of its foundation.

One important group of unions that did not affiliate with the A.F. of L. was the railway brotherhoods. The organization of railroad employes has followed its own course, and while based on craft lines has for reasons peculiar to itself differed considerably in other respects from that of other workers. The Locomotive Engineers organized as early as 1863, the Railway Conductors five years later, the Trainmen in 1873, and a decade later the Firemen. Although involved in the railway strikes of 1877, the four brotherhoods became increasingly conservative in subsequent years, and because of the hazardous nature of their members' work, the insurance and benefit features of their union programs have always been of primary importance. The permanent organization of other railway employes was to develop more slowly. After an attempt by Eugene V. Debs to form an all-inclusive American Railway Union in the 1890's, to which we shall return, separate unions of Shop Workers, Switchmen, Yardmasters, Signalmen, Telegraphers, and Railway and

Steamship Clerks were formed as affiliates of the A.F. of L. despite the continuing independence of the four brotherhoods.

The fact that the international unions survived the depression of the 1890's did not mean that labor was beginning to have its own way or that even the most strongly organized unions were able to meet employers on anything like equal terms. Wages remained low and hours long for the skilled workers in the 1890's, while the great mass of unskilled existed on the barest subsistence level. Labor was still considered a commodity to be bought at the cheapest rate possible, and its right to organize and bargain collectively had by no means been accepted. As industry sought to break the power of the unions with blacklisting, iron-clad oaths, strikebreakers and Pinkerton detectives, and in combatting strikes was able to call upon state militia and federal troops in the name of law and order, the workers found themselves struggling against what were still overwhelming odds.

The vitality of the American Federation of Labor held out hope for the future. In spite of Gompers' optimism, however, the continuing depression of the 1890's was to bear down heavily on the nation's wage earners and in the industrial warfare of these years, they were to suffer some of their most decisive defeats.

X: HOMESTEAD AND PULLMAN

WHILE THE LASTING SIGNIFICANCE of the 1890's in labor history is found in the final triumph of the American Federation of Labor over the Knights of Labor and the demonstrated strength of the new unionism, the decade was more dramatically marked by its great strikes. Never before had labor and capital been engaged in such organized private warfare as would develop at Homestead in 1892, nor had the public ever become more alarmed over the dangers of industrial strife than during the great Pullman strike two years later. These two outbreaks differed from the uprising of railway workers in 1877 primarily because they were strikes by powerful unions rather than spontaneous expressions of revolt, but they were marked by almost comparable violence and bloodshed. The gravity of the labor problem as it existed in the 1890's could hardly have been more heavily underscored.

Moreover the general discontent among industrial workers which was reflected in these strikes had its political repercussions as the depression of the 1890's deepened and urban unrest was linked with agrarian revolt in the rise of Populism. The alliance between midwestern farmers and eastern workingmen was not to be firmly cemented, in part because of the continued reluctance of the A.F. of L. to engage in direct political activity, but there was widespread fear in 1896 among conservatives that an election victory for the radical doctrines advanced by the Populists would undermine the capitalist system.

In the early morning of July 6, 1892, two barges were being towed slowly up the Monongahela River toward Homestead, Pennsylvania. There had been trouble at the local plant of the Carnegie Steel Company. The skilled workers at Homestead, members of the Amalgamated Association of Iron, Steel and Tin Workers, had refused to accept new wage cuts and were supported in their stand by the rest of the labor force. The company's general manager, tough-minded, stubbornly anti-labor Henry Clay Frick, thereupon peremptorily shut down the entire plant and refused any further negotiations with the union. Special deputy sheriffs had been sworn in to guard company property, which was enclosed by a high board fence topped with barbed wire, but the locked-out workers had run them out of town in the conviction that these preparations foreshadowed the use of strikebreakers. It was a challenge to his authority that Frick was only too glad to accept. Here was his chance to crush the Amalgamated once and for all. Aboard the two barges being towed up the Monongahela were three hundred Pinkerton detectives, armed with Winchester rifles.

As the steel company's private army drew alongside the Homestead mills and prepared to land, there was a sudden exchange of shots between the barges and the shore. The workers had entrenched themselves behind a barricade of steel billets and as the Pinkertons tried to take possession of the plant, they were beaten back in a raging battle that swirled along the river front. All that day, from four in the morning until five in the afternoon, the fusillade of shots continued. The strikers set up a small brass cannon behind a breastwork of railroad ties and opened a direct fire on the barges. Failing to sink them, they poured barrels of oil into the river and set the oil afire. With three men already dead and many more wounded, the Pinkertons were trapped. Deserted by the tug which had towed them upstream, helplessly crowded into the barge which lay farthest from the shore, they finally ran up a white flag and agreed to surrender. In return for a guarantee of safe conduct out of the community, they gave up their arms and ammunition.

But feelings were running too high at Homestead, where the casualties had included seven killed, for any easy re-establishment of order. When the Pinkertons came ashore, they were again attacked and had to run the gantlet of an infuriated mob of men and women, armed with stones and clubs, before they were safely entrained for Pittsburgh. An uneasy calm then settled over the little town as the Homestead workers, victorious in this first round, awaited the next moves by the company.

It was not until six days later that there was any further development. Then on July 12 the state militia, mobilized eight thousand strong by the governor of Pennsylvania upon Frick's appeal for aid, marched in quietly to take over control of Homestead under martial law. With such protection the Carnegie Company began bringing in scabs—the "black-sheep" whom the locked-out workers knew were being hired to take their jobs—and proceeded to file charges of rioting and murder against the strike leaders for the attack on the Pinkertons. The plant was then reopened with militia protection and non-union men given the Amalgamated members' jobs. When the strike was officially called off in November, two thousand strikebreakers had been brought in and only some eight hundred of the original Homestead working force of nearly four thousand were reinstated.

In the aftermath of the original battle another act of violence had occurred. On July 23, a Russian-born anarchist, Alexander Berkman, who had no connection whatsoever with the strikers but had been aroused by the Carnegie Company's employment of Pinkerton operatives, forced his way into Frick's office in Pittsburgh and tried to assassinate him. Although shot and stabbed, the steel executive was not fatally injured and his assailant was captured. The assault had been planned by Berkman and his woman companion, Emma Goldman, a no less ardent advocate of "propaganda by deed," and only lack of funds to make the trip to Pittsburgh, as she later revealed in her autobiography, had prevented her from accompanying Berkman on his mission. He was sentenced to twenty-one years in prison for assault with intent to kill. Released after thirteen years of his term, he was later deported, together with Emma Goldman, to Soviet Russia.

These shocking events aroused the country in some ways even more than had the Great Upheaval of the 1880's or the railway strikes a decade earlier. For the Homestead affair was not a spontaneous uprising on the part of unorganized workers. It was war between one of the most powerful of the great modern corporations and what was then one of the strongest unions in the country. Each party to the dispute had taken the law into its own hands. The *Chicago Tribune* gave over its entire front page on July 7 to a vivid account of what was described as "a battle which for bloodthirstiness and boldness was not excelled in actual warfare."

Until the Homestead strike, relations between the Carnegie Company and the union had been uniformly friendly and working conditions had been governed by a three-year contract for the skilled workers that provided for a sliding wage scale based on the price of steel billets.

Carnegie had professed himself to be wholly in favor of unions, stating in an article in the *Forum* some years earlier that the right of workingmen to combine was no less sacred than that of manufacturers. Moreover he had expressed real sympathy for workers threatened by the loss of jobs through the use of strikebreakers. "To expect that one dependent upon his daily wage for the necessaries of life," he had written, "will stand by peacefully and see a new man employed in his stead is to expect too much." But when the old union contract at Homestead expired in 1892, Carnegie himself was in England and negotiations were wholly in Frick's hands.

Had Carnegie been on the ground, the course of events might have been quite different, and yet the fact remains that he had given Frick a free hand and he could hardly have been unaware of his general manager's anti-labor attitude. Indeed, he told a reporter in the course of the strike that "the handling of the case on the part of the company had my full approval," and in a letter to Gladstone, the British statesman, he declared that his firm had offered the workers generous terms and "they went as far as I could have wished." Yet he also stated in this same letter that in seeking to enforce his terms by operating the Homestead plant with new men, Frick had made a false step. "The pain I suffer," he told Gladstone, "increases daily. The Works are not worth one drop of human blood. I wish they had been sunk."

Frick, however, was in control and his intention in bringing in strikebreakers and Pinkerton guards, for which arrangements had been made even before the failure of wage negotiations, was clearly to smash the union. And he succeeded. It collapsed completely at Homestead and was greatly weakened in other steel mills in the Pittsburgh area where sympathetic strikes led to sharp reprisals. The Amalgamated was to make some further effort to organize the steel workers, but in the face of continued opposition by the Carnegie Company and its successor, the United States Steel Corporation, it steadily lost ground. An effective steel union would not be established until some forty years later when the Steel Workers' Organizing Committee was formed with the revival of industrial unionism in the 1930's.

The Amalgamated was affiliated with the American Federation of Labor and Gompers strongly expressed his sympathy for the strikers and aided in raising funds for the defense of those charged with responsibility for the attack on the Pinkertons. But the Federation was not in a position to offer any effective assistance and Gompers' grandiloquent phrases must have been cold comfort for the strikers.

"You Homestead steel workers," he was quoted as saying in the *Pittsburgh Leader;* "if there is a rose bush blooming it is your work; if there is anything under the sun which shines upon you, which makes Homestead valuable, it is your work. You refused to bow down to this wonderful autocrat, and the first answer he gave you was to send that band of hirelings into this peaceful community to force you to bow down to him, and ultimately drive you from your peaceful homes. I know not who fired the first shot on that memorable morning of the 6th. of July, but I do know the hearts of the American people beat in unison and sympathy with the brave men of Homestead. I am a man of peace and I love peace, but I am like that great man, Patrick Henry, I stand as an American citizen and, 'give me liberty or give me death.' "

Homestead was to take its place in the annals of labor history as one of the great battles for workers' rights, and its immediate repercussions were nationwide. There was agitated discussion in Congress over what such industrial warfare meant for the nation. Senator Palmer of Illinois declared that the Pinkerton army had become as distinctly recognized as the regular army—"the commander in chief of this army, like the barons of the Middle Ages, has a force to be increased at pleasure for the service of those who would pay him or them"—and he maintained that the workers had the right to resist its attack in defense of their jobs and homes. "The owners of these properties," he further stated in reference to such corporations as the Carnegie Company, "must hereafter be regarded as holding their property subject to the correlative rights of those without whose services the property would be utterly valueless."

Outside the ranks of labor itself, however, such progressive ideas found little support. Politics governed many expressions of opinion. Democratic newspapers opposed to a protective tariff seized the opportunity to show that for all the claims made for high duties as safeguarding the wages of the American workingmen, the steel industry was nevertheless reducing wages and exploiting its employes. They condemned the use of Pinkerton mercenaries and expressed sympathy for the locked-out workers. Some Republican papers, resenting the injection of the tariff issue, urged the Carnegie Company to follow a more conciliatory course to refute Democratic charges. But more generally the press took the stand that even though the Homestead employes did not want to work for the wages offered them, there was no justification for their seeking to prevent others from accepting such terms. "Men talk like anarchists or lunatics," the *Independent* stated, "when they insist that the workmen at Homestead have done right." The steel company was upheld in asserting its power to provide protection for whomever it chose to employ.

"If civilization and government are worth anything," the *Cleveland Leader* declared, "the right of every man to work for whom he pleases must and will be maintained." In an article in the *North American Review*, George Ticknor Curtis further developed this theory. "The first duty of the legislative power," he stated, "is to emancipate the individual workman from the tyranny of his class. The individual workman should not be permitted to commit moral suicide by surrendering his liberty to the control of his fellow-workmen." To protect an illusory right to decide the terms on which he could individually sell his services, the workingman's right to associate with others in collective bargaining was denied. The anti-union attitude of conservative employers could not have been more clearly expressed.

There were a number of other violent strikes during these dark days when the forces of the new industrialism were riding roughshod over the right of workers to organize and protect their interests. Metal miners at Coeur d'Alene, Idaho; switchmen in Buffalo, New York; and coal miners in Tennessee walked out in defiance of their employers, and in each instance their strikes were forcibly broken through the intervention of state militia. As depression settled ominously over the land and the army of unemployed swelled to some three million, labor disputes reached a peak involving even more workers—some 750,000—than the strikes in 1886. Of all these conflicts, however, the Pullman strike of 1894 stood out most vividly.

The employes of the Pullman Palace Car Company were in one respect in a quite different situation from the great mass of industrial workers. They had the privilege of living in a model town. The head of the company, George M. Pullman, had established a community for his employes with neat brick houses grouped about a little square where bright flower beds alternated with green stretches of lawn. The whole was "shaded with trees, dotted with parks, and pretty water vistas and glimpses here and there of artistic sweeps of landscape gardening." In the exuberant enthusiasm of the company press agent, Pullman was "a town, in a word, where all that is ugly and discordant and demoralizing is eliminated and all that which inspires self-respect is generously provided."

But were these happy attributes of life in Pullman actually so "generously provided?" The employes had no choice but to live within this feudal domain, renting their homes or apartments from the company, buying their water and gas from the company, paying the company for such other services as garbage removal and the daily watering of streets, buying supplies from the company store, subscribing to the company rental library. And rents for apartments in the model town, which in most instances had no bathtubs and one water faucet for every five families, were some twenty-five per cent higher than in near-by communities. A high premium was also charged for public utility services. "Oh, Hell!" the forthright Mark Hanna was quoted as commenting on his brother industrialist's baronial domain. "Model—. Go and live in Pullman and find out how much Pullman gets sellin' city water and gas ten per cent higher to those poor fools!"

With the depression of 1893, the Pullman Company was for a time hard hit and after laying off more than 3,000 of its 5,800 employes, it cut the wages of those kept on from twenty-five to forty per cent without any corresponding reduction in rents for the company houses. The consequences were disastrous. A worker seldom earned as much as six dollars a week after the company had made its deductions. In one instance, an employe found that after payment for rent was taken out, his pay check came to two cents. "He never cashed it," the Reverend W. H. Carwardine, of the Pullman Methodist Episcopal Church reported. "He has it framed." And yet at the same time such things were happening, the Pullman Company kept on paying dividends. Even after business began to improve, enabling the company to take back some 2,000 of its employes, no steps were taken to restore the wage cuts or to reduce rents.

Finally in May, 1894, a committee of employes asked for some consideration of their grievances. Pullman flatly refused to consider any wage adjustments on the ground that the company was still losing money, and he would take no action in regard to rents. There was no relationship whatsoever, he lightly declared, between the company's dual functions as employer and landlord. Almost immediately after the interview, in spite of definite assurances that there would be no discrimination against the grievance committee, three of its members were summarily discharged.

During this year of hardship and suffering, the Pullman workers had been extensively organized in locals of the American Railway Union. This new association, independent of all other labor federations, had been formed only the year before by Eugene V. Debs as an industrial union open to all white employes of the railroads. Upon the dismissal of the three members of the grievance committee, who were also members of the American Railway Union, the Pullman locals called a strike. When the company countered by laying off all workers and closing the plant, an appeal was made to the national convention for assistance. Attempts were made to submit the issues in dispute to arbitration, but when Pullman met these overtures with the uncompromising statement: "there is nothing to arbitrate," the American Railway Union prepared for action. On June 21 it adopted a resolution that if arbitration was not accepted within five days, its members would be ordered not to handle any Pullman cars.

When this boycott went into effect, involving not only the Pullman Company but railroads using its cars, the challenge of the union was promptly taken up by the General Managers' Association, a group made up of executives of twenty-four railways entering Chicago which altogether controlled some forty thousand miles of track. It ordered the discharge of any worker "cutting out" a Pullman car from any train. But the membership of the American Railway Union was not so easily frightened. Every time a man was fired for refusing to handle a Pullman car, the entire train crew would quit. By the end of July, the strike had become so general that nearly every railroad in the middle west was affected and the nation's entire transportation system seriously threatened.

"The struggle," Debs declared in a ringing appeal to the railway workers, ". . . has developed into a contest between the producing classes and the money power of the country. We stand upon the ground that the workingmen are entitled to a just proportion of the proceeds of their labor. . . ." But while there was sympathy for the strikers in some quarters, Mark Hanna again privately expressing his scorn for Pullman's refusal to arbitrate, the conservative press solidly supported the General Managers' Association. "The necessity is on the railroads to defeat the strike," the *Chicago Herald* declared, while the *New York World* stated that it was "war against the government and against society."

As leader of the railway workers' revolt, Eugene V. Debs sprang overnight into nationwide fame. The American Railway Union was only a year old and yet under his shrewd and capable leadership, it had already gained a membership—some 150,000—which was greater than that of the four railway brotherhoods and rivaled both the declining Knights of Labor and the slowly emerging American Federation of Labor. Both management and the trade unions feared that should he carry it to success in this contest with the railroads, the principle of industrial unionism which it embodied might win a victory that would set the pattern for future labor organization.

Debs was the son of French-Alsatian immigrants who had settled in Terre Haute, Indiana where his father kept a grocery store. Born in 1855, he had gone to work in the railway yards at the age of fourteen and become an engineer at sixteen. For a time he left the yards to work as a grocery clerk and play about with politics, but in 1878 he turned to the labor movement and two years later, at the age of twenty-five, was elected both national secretary-treasurer of the Brotherhood of Locomotive Firemen and editor of the *Locomotive Firemen's Magazine*. It was largely through his efforts that this union was built up during the next dozen years into a flourishing and financially sound organization.

However, Debs grew increasingly concerned over the exclusive attitude maintained by the brotherhood and the complete lack of cooperation between its members and other railway employes. He became convinced that only through the union of all workers on the nation's railroads in a single association could the interests of this important branch of labor be successfully promoted. In 1892 he suddenly resigned his well-paid post in the Brotherhood of Locomotive Firemen and undertook almost single-handedly to form the American Railway Union.

Debs was an able organizer, shrewd and practical; he was an eloquent and forceful speaker, and he was also an idealist prepared to make
any sacrifice for a cause in which he believed. Throughout his life, he
commanded an amazing measure of respect and loyalty. He was to be
villified and abused as few men have been during the Pullman strike,
attacked as a labor dictator, a criminal, an anarchist, a lunatic, a madman, but with time even those who continued to denounce the things
for which he stood, could not help honoring the man. There could be no
doubting his unflinching honesty and sincerity, whether in the 1890's
as an aggressive labor leader or in later years as the spokesman of American socialism. No one ever identified himself more closely with the
struggling masses in our national life or was a more passionate defender
of the underprivileged.

"While there is a lower class I am in it," Debs once said in a much-
quoted statement. "While there is a criminal element I am of it; while
there is a soul in prison I am not free."

Tall and gaunt, nearly bald even at the time of the Pullman strike
when he was thirty-nine, with high forehead and candid eyes, his manner
was quiet and modest. Something about him not only awoke confidence
but inspired affection. "There may have lived some time, somewhere,"
Clarence Darrow was to write, "a kindlier, gentler, more generous man
than Eugene Debs, but I have not known him."

Debs had not desired the strike that was forced upon the American
Railway Union by the appeal of the Pullman workers. Even though it
had already won a surprising strike victory on the Great Northern Railway, he knew that his young organization was not yet strong enough for
such a formidable encounter with the united railway corporations. But
when Pullman refused to arbitrate, he felt that the union could not stand
aside without betraying the Pullman employes. Forced to back them
up, Debs consistently counseled moderation and restraint. He ordered
the strikers to remain wholly passive and in no way to injure railroad
property, and during the first phase of the strike these orders were rigidly obeyed.

The General Managers' Association, however, could not afford a peaceful strike. It was soon importing strikebreakers from Canada, secretly
instructing them to attach mail cars to Pullman cars so that when the
strikers cut out the latter, they could be accused of interfering with the

mails. Conjuring up a still non-existent danger of violence, it induced Attorney General Olney, avowed friend of the railroads, to have 3,400 men, who were actually hired by the railroads and paid by the railroads, sworn in as special deputies to help keep the trains running. These tactics were successful. There were clashes between strikers and deputies; rioting broke out and railway property was destroyed. Promptly asserting that such violence had already become uncontrollable, the Managers' Association thereupon appealed to President Cleveland to send federal troops to restore order, safeguard the mails and protect interstate commerce. Four companies of the Fifteenth Infantry were sent to Chicago.

Governor Altgeld of Illinois immediately protested this move. The situation was not out of hand, he wired the President, and local officials were entirely capable of handling it. "The Federal Government," he stated, "has been applied to by men who had political and selfish motives for wanting to ignore the State government. . . . At present some of our railroads are paralyzed, not by reason of obstruction, but because they cannot get men to operate their trains . . . as Governor of the State of Illinois, I ask the immediate withdrawal of Federal troops from active duty in this State." But Altgeld's protest went unheeded. He had recently pardoned the anarchists involved in the Haymarket Square affair and the newspapers fiercely attacked him as the "friend and champion of disorder." Even though Cleveland had in an earlier message to Congress called for the investigation and arbitration of wage disputes, he looked no further on this occasion than maintenance of order. He stoutly maintained the position he had assumed and justified the use of federal troops, in spite of charges of usurping the functions of the state, on the ground that it was his constitutional duty to keep the mail trains operating.

"If it takes every dollar in the Treasury and every soldier in the United States to deliver a postal card in Chicago," he was reported as saying, "that postal card should be delivered."

Still the ranks of the strikers held firm and in spite of strikebreakers, special deputies and the army, three-fourths of the railroads running into Chicago were almost at a standstill. Moreover the strike was spreading. Sympathetic walkouts by engineers, firemen, repairmen, signalmen, yardmasters and other workers occurred on many lines in both the east and far west. At the same time violence was also increasing. As the struggle became intensified, the strikers could no longer be held in check by Debs' peaceful persuasions. When trains began to move under the protection of the troops, angry mobs sought to stop them. Tramps and hoodlums were soon taking advantage of the situation, as they had in the railroad strikes in 1877, and railway stores were looted, freight and passenger cars burned, and damage inflicted on other property.

As disorder spread, newspapers and magazines rang all the changes on the danger to society in what the *New York Tribune* declared to be "the greatest battle between labor and capital that has ever been inaugurated in the United States." It was almost universally insisted that "this rebellion must be put down" regardless of every other consideration. The attempt was made to draw a line between the railway workers and strike agitators. The former were said to be "the victims of selfish, cruel and insolent leaders" and all honest workingmen were called upon to free themselves from such "insufferable tyranny." The *New York Times* attacked Debs as "a lawbreaker at large, an enemy of the human race" and the *Chicago Herald* asserted that "short work should be made of this reckless, ranting, contumacious, impudent braggadocio . . ."

News stories carried alarming accounts of mob action and battles with the police and troops. With such a newspaper as the *Washington Post* screaming in its headlines that "Chicago Is at the Mercy of the Incendiary's Torch," the general impression given was that the entire city was in the throes of revolution and anarchy. However a correspondent for the *New York Herald,* somehow keeping his balance amid such exaggerated fears and alarms, reported to his paper on July 9 that business was going on as usual, the stores were crowded with shoppers, and "there is no sign of mob or riot or strike, even, about the main part of the city."

But the railroads had already played their trump card. They had persuaded Attorney General Olney to intervene directly and on July 2 a blanket injunction was obtained from Judge Peter J. Grosscup, of the federal district court, forbidding any person from interfering with the operation of the mails or other railroad transportation in interstate commerce, and from seeking to induce any employes of the railroads to refuse to perform their normal services. With the whole force of government and the courts thrown against him, Debs was desperate. For a time he hoped to win labor support for a general strike, only to be rebuffed by the American Federation of Labor. Gompers felt constrained to call a labor conference to consider the issue but he was entirely opposed to a strike. It was, indeed, hardly surprising that an organization that had been founded in opposition to industrial unionism should be unwilling to throw its support behind the American Railway Union.

"We declare it to be the sense of this conference," a statement issued by Gompers on July 13 read, "that a general strike at this time is inexpedient, unwise and contrary to the best interests of the working people. We further recommend that all connected with the American Federation of Labor now out on sympathetic strikes return to work, and those who contemplate going out on sympathetic strike are advised to remain at their usual vocations."

Without help from any quarter, Debs then offered to call off the strike and boycott if the Pullman Company would agree to reinstate all workers without discrimination. With the courts swinging into action, the railroads had no further cause for concern. They bluntly rejected Debs' peaceful overtures: there would be "no recognition of anarchism."

Judge Grosscup now summoned a special jury to hear charges that the strike leaders were guilty of conspiracy in obstructing the mails, and under instructions from the court Debs and three of his aids were promptly indicted. Arrested on this count, they were released on bail, but within a week were rearrested for contempt of court in disobeying the original injunction. This time they went to jail. Other injunctions were enforced against individual strikers and nearly 200 were arrested on federal charges in addition to the several hundred jailed by local police. Deprived of all leadership and direction, completely demoralized, the railroad workers gave up what had become a wholly futile struggle and gradually drifted back to work. The troops were withdrawn on July 20. Government by injunction had won its first victory by completely crushing the Pullman strike.

After some delay the contempt charges brought against Debs were sustained in the circuit court on the ground that under the terms of the recently enacted Sherman Anti-Trust Act, the strike leaders had engaged in a conspiracy to restrain interstate commerce. The following spring the Supreme Court, while not expressly ruling on the applicability of the Sherman Act, upheld the lower court. The federal government was declared to have inherent authority to intervene to protect any obstruction to interstate commerce or the transportation of the mails.

Debs went to jail in Woodstock, Illinois, for six months. The action of the courts had made him a martyr and on returning to Chicago after expiration of his sentence he was wildly acclaimed by a crowd of over 100,000 sympathizers. At a gigantic mass meeting he was hailed by Henry Demarest Lloyd as "the most popular man among the real people today . . . the victim of judicial lynch law." Debs had become convinced while in jail that the cause of labor was hopeless under capitalism. He became a socialist and was to dedicate his life from this time forward to struggle against a system that enabled employers, as he repeatedly declared, to call upon government in enforcing their dictate, "work for what we want to give you, or starve." Until his death in 1926, he campaigned ceaselessly for labor's rights under the socialist banner and was five times candidate of his party for the presidency.

Labor and its sympathizers bitterly denounced the intervention of federal troops and use of the injunction in the Pullman strike, but the policy of the government was vigorously upheld in other quarters. Both the Senate and the House adopted resolutions supporting President Cleveland, there were innumerable statements from public leaders praising his handling of the situation, and the conservative press hailed him as a national hero for so vigorously suppressing what was universally called the "Debs Rebellion." The power of government had been asserted in no doubtful fashion. "To Cleveland and to Olney," the historian James Ford Rhodes wrote, "we in this country of reverence for just decisions, owe a precedent of incalculable value."

Perhaps the most important consequence of the Pullman strike was its revelation of the power that the injunction placed in the hands of industry in combatting the demands of labor. What chance had wage earners when their employers could so easily go into court and obtain injunctions against both strikes and boycotts; when government was ready to throw all its force against labor regardless of right or wrong in the issues under dispute? The workers' hands appeared to be completely tied. The campaign for abolition of government by injunction that at once got underway, taken up by the American Federation of Labor in spite of its reluctance to run any risks in supporting the American Railway Union, became from that day on one of labor's primary concerns. It was still to be a vital issue in the 1940's as it had been in the 1890's.

The forceful suppression of such strikes as those at Homestead and Pullman fanned the mounting discontent of the workers, but unemployment created even greater discouragement and despair. Throughout the country "industrial armies" took to the road and began to march on Washington to demand relief. The most famous of them was Coxey's Army, which actually reached the capital only to be dispersed after its leader was arrested for trespassing on the White House lawn. But there were other groups of ragged, down-at-heel workers on the march. Throughout the country local authorities were called upon to break up these demonstrations and maintain law and order in the face of a constant danger of mob action.

In the meantime, the growing unrest among the nation's farmers, who also found themselves increasingly hard-pressed in a period of falling prices that cut the value of agricultural products almost in half, was fanning the sparks of agrarian revolt. Populism swept through the prairies and while it was to remain primarily an uprising of midwestern and southern farmers, eastern workingmen who felt that the hand of government was everywhere against them could not fail to be attracted by its tenets. For Populism challenged the whole concept of government by organized wealth. In very much the same pattern as Jacksonian Democracy, it strove to recover for the common people the political power that was felt to have been usurped by the business community.

The Populist Party, formally organized in 1892, accepted as its basic premise the idea that wealth belonged to those who produced it, and called for a union of all the laboring elements in the nation to uphold their rights. Every effort was made to win the adherence of industrial workers. While the demand for the free and unlimited coinage of silver was a reflection of agrarian discontent, other demands put forward were wholly industrial in character.

"The urban workmen," the Populist platform stated, "are denied the right to organize for self-protection, imported pauperized labor beats down their wages, a hireling standing army, unrecognized by our laws, is established to shoot them down, and they are rapidly degenerating into European conditions." To combat this situation, the Populists supplemented their program for currency and other general reforms by taking over many of the demands traditionally pressed by the National Labor Union, the Knights of Labor and even the A.F. of L. They called for restrictions on immigration, enforcement of the anti-contract labor law and of the eight-hour day on government projects, an end to the use of injunctions in labor disputes, and the outlawing of the "army of mercenaries known as the Pinkerton system."

The Knights of Labor were ready to throw their enfeebled strength behind the Populists, eighty-two delegates attending the convention in 1892. The workingmen groups which supported Henry George in his campaign for the single tax, and Edward Bellamy in the formation of Nationalist clubs dedicated to socialist reform, formally allied themselves with the People's Party. Eugene V. Debs, fresh from his conversion to socialism while brooding over the failure of the Pullman strike, wholeheartedly backed a program which he believed provided ground for the common people to unite against the money power. Only the American Federation of Labor, once again reflecting the influence of Samuel Gompers, officially held aloof.

A determined effort on the part of socialists within the Federation to swing it in favor of a labor third party on a platform demanding "collective ownership by the people of all means of production and distribution" had been defeated only a short time before. Gompers won out, but in the process had been defeated in 1894 for the presidency. John McBride, of the United Mine Workers, was elected to this post and the headquarters of the Federation removed to Indianapolis. Gompers' eclipse, however, was only temporary. At the next convention he was not only restored to the presidency, but the stand he had taken against socialism was emphatically reaffirmed. When the demand was voiced for the A.F. of L. to take a partisan position in support of Populism, its re-elected president was all the more determined to steer clear of any direct participation in politics. The American Federation of Labor was not prepared to endorse the party of free silver. "These Middle Class issues," Gompers declared in re-emphasizing the importance for wage earners of concentrating all their energies upon the problems of unionism, "simply divert attention from their own interest."

When the Democrats took over the Populist program in 1896, challenging not only the Republicans but the conservatives within their own party, they nevertheless commanded widespread support among industrial workers. Both parties fully recognized the importance of the labor vote. William Jennings Bryan went so far as to state in one speech that if elected president, he was prepared to make Gompers a member of his cabinet—a gesture that nonetheless failed to move the A.F. of L. chieftain. The Republican high command, with Mark Hanna astutely managing William McKinley's campaign from the wings, tried a different tack. The workers were warned by notices in their pay envelopes that a Democratic victory would mean the further closing of factories and the loss of jobs. Every effort was made to keep them in line by the most dire prophesies of economic disaster should "the socialistic and revolutionary forces" led by Bryan, Altgeld and Debs win the election.

In the event, the organized forces of capitalism, represented by the Republican Party, hurled back this onslaught of farmers and workers campaigning under Democratic banners. McKinley was elected. The alliance had not been powerful enough, or strongly enough welded, to create a farmer-labor party that could carry through successfully a program of economic and social reform. Samuel Gompers had kept his organization out of politics and perhaps saved it from going the way of earlier labor associations that had been wrecked on the shoals of partisanship, but the election victory in 1896 went to the conservative defenders of a social order that supported strikebreaking, the Pinkerton system and government by injunction.

As the excitement of the campaign of 1896 subsided, labor had reason for discouragement in taking stock of the situation in which it found itself. The gains that had been made in wages prior to the depression had been largely wiped out. The average annual earnings for manufacturing employes were estimated at no more than $406. Except in a few of the highly skilled trades, working time was far longer than the eight-hour day for which labor had been so long struggling. It generally ranged between fifty-four and sixty-three hours a week—and even more in steel mills, textile factories, and the tenement house sweatshops where women and children in the garment industry toiled endless hours for a mere pittance. Nowhere was there any real economic security for the industrial worker.

While there was a beginning of labor legislation, little progress had really been made in attaining the goals first put forward in the late 1860's by the National Labor Union. A Bureau of Labor Statistics had been set up by the federal government, and comparable bureaus by some thirty-two states; an Alien Contract Labor Law had been enacted; the Chinese Exclusion Acts were on the statute books, and in 1898 President McKinley was to recommend the creation of an Industrial Commission. There were also various state laws regulating certain phases of industrial activity and looking toward the improvement of working conditions in mines and factories. But over against such moderate gains was the weakened position of the unions in general. The old conspiracy laws had, in effect, been revived through the application to unions of the Sherman Act's ban on combinations in restraint of trade and the use of the injunction in suppressing strikes and boycotts.

Moreover the number of organized workers had declined from the peak figures of the 1880's. A total of approximately a million had fallen to little more than a third of this figure. Even though Gompers had been able to boast in 1893 that the national unions had for the first time withstood depression, the American Federation of Labor had only some 250,000 members in 1897, and there were perhaps another 100,000 workers in the Railway Brotherhoods and other unaffiliated unions. This was a more compact and effectively organized nucleus than in earlier years, but in total union strength it was not very much greater than organized labor had claimed in either the early 1830's or the late 1860's.

The great mass of unskilled industrial workers remained unorganized. With their employers able to draw upon limitless replacements from the continuing stream of immigrant labor and obtain support for strike-breaking from the government and the courts, they were wholly defenseless against long hours, low wages and arbitrary dismissal. The crushing defeat of both the Homestead and Pullman strikes had been a bitter lesson in the overwhelming power that could be mustered to smash the efforts of industrial employes to organize in protection of their rights. The only prospect of any promise for labor as a whole appeared to be the further strengthening of the old-line trade unions brought together within the protective fold of the A.F. of L.

XI: THE PROGRESSIVE ERA

THE PROGRESSIVE ERA, extending from Theodore Roosevelt's accession to the presidency in 1901 to our entry into the first World War sixteen years later, saw a quickening of the liberal spirit throughout the United States. The popular discontent with business domination which had boiled over in the campaign of 1896 had not subsided with the defeat of Bryan. It found new expression in a more general and less radical movement that hammered away at political and social reforms through the agency of both major parties. In a determined quest for a larger measure of social justice, the nation demanded an end to "invisible government" and special privilege in whatever form. If liberal aims were not to be wholly realized, there was effective advance in many sectors and "a bracing of the moral sense of the country" that gave the progressive era a distinctive character in sharp contrast to the climate of public opinion in either the 1890's or the 1920's.

On the national stage, strenuous efforts were made to control the trusts, regulate the railroads, reform the monetary system and reduce tariffs, while at the same time the states embarked on individual programs of economic and social reform seeking to mitigate the evils of the slum, safeguard the health of women and children in industry, and generally improve factory conditions. Nineteenth-century concepts of a laissez-faire economy gave way to an awakened sense of social responsibility that accepted the need for action by government to meet the mounting problems of industrialization and urban growth. Moreover these gains were made against a background of peace and prosperity that led to a substantial rise in living standards. Popular faith and confidence in democratic capitalism, dealt such severe blows in the mid-1890's, were once again renewed in a spirit of buoyant optimism.

Labor participated in these general gains and eventually was to benefit materially from the remedial legislation of both Congress and the states. Yet the status of the great bulk of workingmen did not improve during these years of the progressive era in terms commensurate with the national advance as a whole. The real wages of industrial workers; that is, wages in terms of purchasing power, actually declined. Moreover the increasing introduction of labor-saving machinery on the one hand, and the rising tide of immigration on the other, inter-acted to maintain a constant surplus of labor. Not only did this situation hold down wages, but it heightened the feeling of insecurity among workers over whom always hung the dread shadow of unemployment.

And in spite of the new legislation, actual working conditions for the great majority of wage earners were slow in showing any real change. The factory codes were still inadequate and all too often ineffectively enforced. In the coal mines, steel mills, packing houses; in the textile factories still callously exploiting women and children, and in the sweatshops of the urban clothing industry, the harsh circumstances of life were a sad commentary on the prosperity enjoyed by the country as a whole.

As far as labor organization itself was concerned, the gains of these years were uneven and somewhat equivocal. For a time a new era of industrial relations appeared to have opened with bright promise of labor peace, but as the unions grew in strength, industrial counter-attack soon led to further strife and sharp setbacks for labor in the courts and on the picket line. Only toward the close of the period was this early advance renewed with substantial gains in union membership and enhanced bargaining power.

The organized labor movement was almost wholly dominated by the American Federation of Labor—to the radical eruption of the I.W.W. we shall return—and its concern was still the well-being and status of its affiliated unions whose membership was principally made up of skilled or semi-skilled workers. This was to remain a basically important consideration in forthcoming years. While the A.F. of L. unions in coal mining, the garment industry, and textiles were industrial in character, and others included some unskilled workers, the overwhelming number of employes in the great mass production industries—largely foreign-born, ignorant, unassimilated in the American culture—remained outside union ranks. As we follow the course of organized labor during the progressive period, it should be remembered that less than ten per cent of the nation's wage earners were directly involved.

At the close of what Secretary of State John Hay called our "splendid little war" with Spain, the favorable turn in relations between national unions and employers was so pronounced that the years from 1898 to 1904 have been called "the honeymoon period of capital and labor." Strikes occasionally disrupted such harmony, but at least in comparison with the turbulent industrial strife of the 1890's, there was great improvement. In many industries employers and wage earners alike seemed determined to seek out peaceful solutions to their problems. Responsible labor leaders had become convinced of the certainty of failure in such struggles as those epitomized by the Pullman strike, and many industrialists had come to realize the dangerous economic and political implications of strikes even when they were successfully suppressed. The country generally, sobered by past experience, increasingly demanded some way of dealing with industrial disputes that would safeguard the public interest.

This new approach to labor problems was best represented by the National Civic Federation. It had been first set up in Chicago in 1896, but with the turn of the century was operating on a nationwide basis with the avowed object of bringing capital, labor and the public together in a joint campaign to maintain industrial peace. In sharp contrast to the prevailing attitude in the 1890's that tended to identify all labor agitation with anarchy, it was founded on the premise that "organized labor cannot be destroyed without debasement of the masses." Anti-union employers were declared to be as great foes to national stability as radical or socialistic labor leaders. The National Civic Federation accepted unionization and trade agreements as basic principles, and was prepared to offer its services "in establishing right relations between employers and workers" whenever both parties were willing to submit their disputes to its arbitration.

The leaders in this movement were Mark Hanna and Samuel Gompers, and associated with them in the National Civic Federation were a group of outstanding public figures. Grover Cleveland, President Eliot of Harvard, Archbishop Ireland were among the representatives of the public; John D. Rockefeller, Jr., Charles M. Schwab and August Belmont were included in the employer group, and John Mitchell of the United Mine Workers, James O'Connell of the Machinists, and James Duncan of the Granite Cutters were among the spokesmen for labor. The membership list was an impressive one and for a time the influence exercised by the National Civic Federation appeared to be a highly hopeful augury for labor-capital cooperation.[1]

Several important employer groups came to terms with the unions on the basis of mutually acceptable trade agreements. Pacts were concluded between the National Founders' Association and the International Association of Machinists. The Newspaper Publishers' Association and the International Typographical Union entered upon a series of agreements. Railroad operators recognized and negotiated with the railway brotherhoods. There were of course exceptions to this apparent progress toward industrial peace and the acceptance of collective bargaining. A final attempt on the part of the Amalgamated Iron and Steel Workers to organize the steel industry, for example, failed completely when the United States Steel Corporation, whose board of directors had secretly adopted a resolution stating its unalterable opposition to any extension of union labor, crushed a hard-fought strike in 1901. This was an important and highly significant defeat, but the growing number of trade agreements that were the fruit of the A.F. of L.'s program and policies seemed to indicate a change in general employer attitudes that greatly encouraged labor. "It was the harvest," Gompers happily declared, "of the years of organization which were beginning to bear fruit."

The unions flourished under these circumstances and in many parts of the country attained a new position of importance. They were strongest, and showed the greatest gains, in those trades that had the longest history of labor activity. The Miners, the Printers, the Cigar Makers, the Carpenters, the Molders, the Longshoremen, the Brewers, and the Machinists stood in the forefront of international unions affiliated with

---

[1] At a meeting in 1902 Charles Francis Adams read an interesting paper in the light of present-day labor laws, on "Investigation and Publicity as Opposed to 'Compulsory Arbitration'" in which he proposed legislation to set up a commission to investigate and report to Congress whenever a labor dispute threatened to disrupt interstate commerce. It was to be without coercive powers.

the American Federation of Labor, and in each instance they showed substantial gains in membership.

The exposures of the muckrakers, delving during these years into every phase of our industrial life, aroused a certain measure of popular sympathy for labor's efforts to improve its bargaining position. "Capital must make up its mind to get along with organized labor," the *Springfield Republican* declared in 1902. "Such labor is here to stay, and the law is more likely to compel the unionization of labor than it is to outlaw the labor union. The sooner this fact is recognized, the sooner will the country be placed on the way toward attaining a permanent industrial peace." Several years later as spokesman of the new progressivism, Herbert Croly was equally emphatic in upholding labor organization. "Labor unions," he was to write in *The Promise of American Life*, "deserve to be favored because they are the most effective machinery which has yet been forged for the economic and social amelioration of the laboring classes."

Indicative also of changing popular attitudes was the role that government assumed in the most important strike of these years. For when the anthracite coal miners became locked in a bitter struggle with the operators in 1902, President Roosevelt exercised his influence not to crush the strikers, as had President Cleveland when he sent federal troops to Chicago in 1894, but to enforce arbitration. While his primary concern was to avert a possible coal famine, it did not blind him to the legitimate grievances of labor.

Since the 1870's, the turbulent days of the Long Strike and the Molly Maguires, there had been periodic outbreaks in the coal fields as the miners struggled to improve working conditions. But not until the organization of the United Mine Workers in 1890 were they able to present a solid front against the combined strength of the operators. This new union succeeded, however, in organizing the workers in the bituminous mines of Pennsylvania, Ohio, Indiana and Michigan, and won full recognition from the operators in an agreement governing both wages and hours. Fresh from this victory, it then moved in at the close of the 1890's upon the anthracite area of eastern Pennsylvania.

Its task here was more difficult. The operators were organized in a virtual trust under railroad domination and could hardly have been more opposed to union recognition, while there was such a large element of Poles, Hungarians, Slovaks, Italians and other newly arrived immigrants among the workers that they lacked all cohesive unity. Moreover the operators made the most of this lack of homogeneity, doing everything possible to stir up mutual animosities and frictions.

The United Mine Workers made slow progress in the face of such handicaps but while their membership in the anthracite area was still less than 10,000, ten times this number responded to a first strike call in 1900. The operators were ready to meet this attack but Mark Hanna intervened and persuaded them to avert a prolonged conflict. His motive was wholly political. The Republicans were campaigning in 1900 on a platform of prosperity symbolized by the full dinner pail, and a coal strike would have sounded an unfortunate note of discord in the theme song of party orators. The operators reluctantly concluded an unwritten understanding with the miners which did not mean recognition of their union but partially met their immediate demands through a ten per cent wage increase.

This was a truce, however, and not a settlement. The strikers had not won their real objectives and the operators regretted even the slight concessions they had been forced to make. With no real improvement in conditions, the United Mine Workers consequently put forward further demands in 1902 and this time the operators, resolved not to let any further political pressure postpone a showdown, bluntly refused to consider the miners' new proposals or to deal in any way with the union. Another strike call was issued and 150,000 workers now walked out of the mines.

Their grievances were very real. The pay was low by any standard, the ten hours of work a day were hard and dangerous, and a lack of steady employment through frequent lay-offs cut down average earnings to less than $300 a year. Accidents were common, with a death toll of 441 in 1901, and the mine owners did nothing whatsoever either to ensure greater safety or to compensate their employes for injuries. But even more galling to the workers than low wages and poor working conditions, was the rigid feudal system maintained by the operators through their control over the company towns. The workers, Samuel Gompers was later to write, "were brought into the world by the company doctor,

lived in a company house or hut, were nurtured by the company store
. . . laid away in the company graveyard."

With the outbreak of the strike on May 9, 1902, the operators at once
threw 3,000 coal and iron police into the area, together with 1,000 other
special deputies, and began moving in strikebreakers. They trumped-up
charges of violence, sabotage and rioting against the workers and demanded the further protection of state militia. The strike was to be
fought as another anarchistic, revolutionary uprising against property
rights and public order.

In spite of such provocation, there was relatively little resort to
violence. It was on the whole a more orderly strike than the coal fields
had perhaps ever experienced. The workers simply stayed away from
the pits and maintained a completely passive attitude. Their ranks held
firm for all the suffering and hardship which the strike entailed for their
families. If it was to be a fight to the finish, they were ready for it; they
would not mine coal until their demands were met.

This solidarity and order were in large part due to the able conduct
of the strike, and the strong hold exercised over the men, by the president of the United Mine Workers. Since 1898 this post had been held by
John Mitchell. He had started work in the mines as a boy of twelve,
thrown in his lot with the union during its darkest days, and risen to
leadership while still only twenty-eight in large part through his skill
in organizing the many nationalities working in the mines. Slight and
wiry, with his brown eyes and swarthy face giving him somewhat the
appearance of an Italian, he had a modest—almost diffident—manner.
His strength was in his patience, his conciliatory attitude both in union
politics and in employer relations, and his willingness to compromise
on anything but what he thought were major issues.

No labor leader of the period was more conservative in his social and
political attitudes, more willing to accept arbitration, or more disap-
proving of radicalism and violence. He had originally opposed the strike
in 1902, consistently refused to call out the bituminous miners in support of those in the anthracite fields because the former had signed a
contract with the operators, and was ready at any time to submit the
issues in dispute to settlement by any impartial body. He suggested a
committee of five to be appointed by the National Civic Federation,

or one composed of Archbishop Ireland, Bishop Potter and any third person they might choose.

"If they decide that the average annual wages received by the anthracite miners," he stated, "are sufficient to enable them to live, maintain and educate their families in a manner conformable to established American standards and consistent with American citizenship, we agree to withdraw our claims for higher wages and more equitable conditions of employment, providing that the anthracite mine operators agree to comply with any recommendations the above committee may make affecting the earnings and conditions of labor of their employees."

In contrast to the moderation displayed by Mitchell was the truculent attitude of George F. Baer, the tough, hard-boiled spokesman of the operators. His reply to Mitchell's proposals was that "anthracite mining is a business and not a religious, sentimental or academic proposition." He was out to break the union at whatever cost. There was to be no submission of the dispute, as he never hesitated to make clear, to any outside group, let alone direct negotiations with the union. He believed whole-heartedly in the paternalistic controls maintained by the operators. Answering an appeal that he should seek to bring the strike to an end as his Christian duty, he stated his position in terms that seemed even to the *New York Times* to "verge very close upon unconscious blasphemy."

"I beg you not to be discouraged," Baer wrote his correspondent. "The rights and interests of the laboring man will be protected and cared for—not by the labor agitators, but by the Christian men to whom God in His infinite wisdom has given the control of the property interests of this country. . . ."

As the strike dragged on, a growing scarcity of coal, reflected in steadily rising prices, began to create mounting public concern and a popular demand for settlement. Whereas popular sympathy had originally been with the miners, the conservative press now felt free to blame them for the continued halt in production, and whenever any disorders were reported in the coal fields, it made the most of them. The *Journal of Commerce* declared in a familiar vein that what was taking place was "insurrection, not a strike," and the *New York Evening Post* called for "stern measures of suppression."

With the continued failure of the operators to make a single conciliatory gesture, however, public support soon began to swing back in the miners' favor. Editorials and cartoons singled out Baer for strong condemnation after his assertion of "divine right" with rising criticism in many quarters for his stubborn obduracy. But the primary interest of the country was not in either the workers or the operators. It simply wanted coal. Perhaps public opinion was more aptly reflected in a cartoon in the *New York Herald* depicting the public stretched on a wrack with the operators pulling at one end, the miners at the other. Its caption read: "The victim is not particular which quits first."

President Roosevelt felt the force of this demand for peace in the coal fields. His own position on labor issues was somewhat equivocal but his concern now was in getting the mines open. He felt compelled to act to protect the public interest and, as his correspondence reveals, because he feared the political repercussions of a coal famine. His program was not to crush the strike, although the operators were demanding an injunction against the United Mine Workers as a conspiracy in restraint of trade under the Sherman Act, but to compel arbitration. To that end, he summoned a conference of both operators and strike leaders which was held at the White House on October 3.

While Mitchell declared himself willing to accept the findings of any commission appointed by the President, Baer once again bluntly refused to have anything to do with arbitration. His intransigeant stand, as contrasted with the conciliatory attitude of the miners' leader, infuriated Roosevelt. Baer not only attacked the strikers but angrily rebuked the President for seeking to negotiate "with the fomenters of . . . anarchy and insolent defiance of the law." The conference was stormy. "If it wasn't for the high office I hold," Roosevelt is reputed to have said of Baer, "I would have taken him by the seat of the breeches and the nape of the neck and chucked him out of that window."

Still, almost no coal was being mined. Although 10,000 state troops were thrown into the territory to protect the strikebreakers, the men would not go back to work. The public grew more and more restive. Even conservative newspapers now stated that the operators had forfeited their claim to popular support and should settle the strike on the basis of negotiations with the United Mine Workers. "And the public," the *Chicago Evening Post* declared, "will not wait very long either. . . ."

Roosevelt decided to intervene even more directly. He secretly drew up a plan to put the army in the field with orders to its commanding general to dispossess the operators and run the mines as a receiver, and dispatched Secretary of War Root to inform J. P. Morgan, as the real power behind the operators, that this was his alternative if arbitration was still refused. Under such direct governmental pressure, the mine owners were finally induced to capitulate. They requested the President to set up an arbitration commission. Even at this point, however, they still balked at going the whole way and declared that they would not accept a labor member on the commission. Negotiations again hung in the balance until Roosevelt overcame this last obstacle by the appointment of the Grand Chief of the Railway Conductors, not as a labor representative but as "an eminent sociologist"! On October 23, after more than five months in which their lines had held almost without a break, the miners went back to work.

The award of the President's commission, announced in March, 1903, granted a ten per cent wage increase, reduced the working day to eight and nine hours for different classes of workers, and set up a special board to settle disputes arising during the three years in which the award was to remain in force. The miners had not won recognition of their union. They had failed to achieve their full aims and accepted the award reluctantly. But in the face of the operators' stubborn opposition, they had made real and important gains greatly strengthening the position of the United Mine Workers in the anthracite area.

For all the advances made in the opening years of the century, total union membership rising from 868,500 in 1900 to over 2,000,000 in 1904, and in spite of the more generally sympathetic public attitude shown during the coal strike, there was trouble ahead for organized labor. Employers who had for a time seemed willing to recognize unions, now became alarmed at their growing power. Largely abandoning the program for industrial peace originally sponsored by the National Civic Federation, they were beginning by 1903 to join forces in a vigorous campaign to block any further labor gains.

They encouraged the use of "yellow-dog" contracts obligating employes, as in the old iron-clad oaths, to agree that they would not join
any union. They played upon the natural rivalries of immigrant groups
to discourage any cooperative action, employed labor spies to inform on
labor agitators who would then be summarily fired, and exchanged
blacklists of workers charged with radical views. The great employing
corporations were ruthless in this renewed anti-union drive and were
able, moreover, to bolster its force by successfully calling upon the
courts for support in conspiracy indictments and injunctions.

The earlier accords in the machinery and metal trades broke down as
employer associations in both instances reverted to their original anti-
labor attitudes. Following the action of United States Steel in bluntly
refusing to deal with union labor under any circumstances, there was
open warfare in the structural iron industry with the workers resorting
to violence and dynamite. The packing houses suppressed a strike in
which their employes sought collective bargaining; delivery firms in
Chicago joined forces to crush completely a teamsters' strike for recognition. In almost every area, organized labor appeared to have been
set back as employers who a few years earlier had appeared willing to
bargain with the workers, now refused to do so.

There was a change of heart on the part of the National Civic Federation itself. In the face of the increasing breakdown of trade agreements,
it appeared to lose its early enthusiasm for unionization. The employer
members still professed their friendship for labor but directed their
energies primarily toward combatting socialism and the closed shop.
Gompers continued to work with them, being no less opposed to socialism, but in spite of his defense of the National Civic Federation's activities, labor lost confidence in its impartiality in industrial disputes.

Openly opposed to all labor organization were the Industrial Alliances that met in national convention in 1903 to form the Citizens'
Industrial Association. Their lobbying and propaganda were highly
successful in swinging public opinion against labor. After a meeting
in 1906 that brought together some 468 delegates, representing almost
as many employers' associations, President C. W. Post reported enthusiastically on the progress that he felt was being made. "Two years
ago the press and pulpit," he declared, "were delivering platitudes
about the oppression of the workingmen. Now all this has been changed

since it has been discovered that the enormous Labor Trust is the heaviest oppressor of the independent workingman as well as the common American Citizen. The people have become aroused and are now acting. . . ."

The anti-union campaign was at the same time carried forward even more conspicuously by the National Association of Manufacturers, organized in 1895 but embarking on its first real attacks on organized labor about 1903. Its slogan and war cry was "the open shop," a guarantee of the right to work regardless of union affiliation. This appeal in the name of individual freedom, however, thinly disguised an all-out drive against both union recognition and collective bargaining. The N.A.M. stood for industry's sole and exclusive right in determining both wages and conditions of employment.

"Since the principles and demands of organized labor are absolutely untenable to those believing in the individualistic social order," delegates at the annual convention in 1903 were told by President Parry, "an attitude of conciliation would mean an attitude of compromise with regard to fundamental convictions. . . . The greatest danger lies in the recognition of the union." And one of the early pamphlets of the N.A.M., widely distributed in a propaganda campaign reaching out to the schools and churches as well as to the press and industrial organs, flatly stated that "our government cannot stand, nor its free institutions endure if the Gompers-Debs ideals of liberty and freedom of speech and press are allowed to dominate."

The principle of the open shop, often sustained with a conviction that went beyond all purely economic considerations, was used to justify or condone the most drastic measures in seeking to crush unions. This was perhaps most graphically illustrated in the suppression of the strike of employes of the Colorado Fuel and Iron Company in 1913. The real issue at stake in this dispute was recognition of the United Mine Workers, who had sent their organizers into the territory. Rather than make this concession, the company fiercely fought the strikers with hired detectives, special deputies and the state militia.

Open warfare continued for months in the Colorado mine fields and finally reached a bloody climax when the militia attacked a colony of the strikers at Ludlow. After several rounds of indiscriminate machine-gun fire, the tents in which the workers' families were living were soaked in oil and put to the torch. Women and children huddled in pits to escape the raging flames, and in one of them eleven children and two women were later found burned or suffocated to death. The nation was horrified by this massacre, but still the Colorado Fuel and Iron Company refused to consider negotiations with the union to end the strike.

The company was controlled by the Rockefeller interests and in the investigation of the strike by the House Committee on Mines and Mining, John D. Rockefeller, Jr., was called to the witness stand. In reply to questions as to whether he did not feel that "the killing of people and shooting of children" should not have led to efforts to re-establish labor peace, he implied that rather than give in to the miners, his company was prepared to go to whatever lengths were necessary. The only way that the strike could be settled, he stated, was through unionization of all the mines, which could not be accepted because "our interest in labor is so profound and we believe so sincerely that that interest demands that the camps shall be open camps, that we expect to stand by the officers at any cost." He resented particularly the idea that outside organizers should seek to stir up men who were "thoroughly satisfied with their labor conditions." There could be no surrender. "It was upon a similar principle that the war of the Revolution was carried on," Rockefeller declared. "It is a great national issue of the most vital kind."

This was not an isolated instance of uncompromising opposition to allowing employe organization, and the courts generally sustained employers in making non-membership in a union a condition of employment.

In 1898 Congress had passed a law, the Erdman Act, which prohibited any discrimination against workers by the interstate railways because of union membership. Ten years later, in *Adair* v. *United States*, the Supreme Court held this provision of the Erdman Act unconstitutional as an invasion of both personal liberty and the rights of property. A comparable state statute was outlawed in *Coppage* v. *Kansas* in 1915, and the Supreme Court then proceeded to uphold an injunction granted at the request of the Hitchman Coal and Coke Company, in West Virginia, which prohibited the United Mine Workers from seeking to organize company employes who had been compelled to agree not to join the union under yellow-dog contracts.

These legal obstacles to unionization did not pass uncriticized even in the Supreme Court. Justice Oliver Wendell Holmes strongly dissented. "In present conditions," he argued in the Coppage case, "a workman not unnaturally may believe that only by belonging to a union can he secure a contract that shall be fair to him. . . . If that belief may be held by a reasonable man, it seems to me that it may be enforced by law in order to establish equality of position between the parties in which liberty of contract begins. Whether in the long run it is wise for the workingmen to enact legislation of this sort is not my concern, but I am strongly of the opinion that there is nothing in the Constitution of the United States to prevent it. . . ." His brethren on the Supreme Court were not convinced, however. The decisions upholding and enforcing yellow-dog contracts stood until passage of the Norris–La Guardia Act in 1932 finally reversed public policy.

The courts also sustained the employers in their counter-attack upon union boycotts. The American Federation of Labor had found this weapon highly effective in promoting union recognition. By persuading its members to refrain from buying any goods that did not bear a union label, many recalcitrant employers were brought into line. To meet this situation the American Anti-Boycott Association was established to aid employers in going to court on the ground that such boycotts were conspiracies in restraint of trade and subject to injunction as "malicious" interference with the "probable expectancies" of property rights. Two important cases involving these issues dragged through the courts between 1902 and 1916, and in each instance resulted in a decisive defeat for labor.

In 1902 the United Hatters declared a nationwide boycott of the hats of D. E. Loewe & Company, of Danbury, Connecticut, in support of a strike by a local union to win recognition. The company at once instituted suit charging the United Hatters with conspiring to restrain trade in violation of the terms of the Sherman Act, and claimed triple damages from the individual members of the local union who had gone on strike. After a long period of legal wrangling, the company was upheld in 1916 and allowed total damages and costs assessed at $252,000. The bank accounts of the union members were attached and foreclosure proceedings introduced against their homes, but the fines were eventually paid through contributions from the national union and the A.F. of L.

The Danbury Hatters' case particularly awoke the resentment of labor because of its effect in bringing secondary boycotts under the ban of the Sherman Act and subjecting individual members to damage suits. But even while it was making its tortuous way through the courts, the American Federation of Labor itself became involved in another dispute which had even wider repercussions. In 1906 the metal polishers employed by the Buck's Stove and Range Company, of St. Louis, went on strike for the nine-hour day and appealed for aid. The A.F. of L. responded by placing the company on its "We Don't Patronize" list in the *American Federationist* and advising all union members to boycott its products. J. W. Van Cleave, president both of the Buck's Stove and Range Company and of the National Association of Manufacturers, a bitter enemy of all unions, promptly secured an injunction not only restraining the officers and members of the A.F. of L. from placing his firm on the "We Don't Patronize" list, but also from in any way calling attention to the metal polishers' strike either in writing or orally.

The A.F. of L. refused to heed this sweeping court order. While the offending company was taken off its unfair list, Gompers continued to state that union men could not be coerced into buying Buck stoves and ranges. He was thereupon found in contempt of court and sentenced to a year's imprisonment, two other officers of the Federation also being adjudged guilty and given somewhat lighter sentences. He was never to serve this sentence. Court proceedings continued even after the death of Van Cleave and withdrawal of the original injunction, but the case was finally dismissed by the Supreme Court. Although the A.F. of L. leaders consequently escaped jail, their conviction was nevertheless a shock that aroused labor even more against injunction law than its earlier defeats on this score. Gompers could not be reconciled to the position in which he found himself—a conservative, the friend of employers, the arch foe of labor radicalism, attacked by the government as though he were a revolutionary or an anarchist.

The effect of these decisions, and others in which injunctions were freely granted to employers, appeared to labor to represent a revival of the old conspiracy laws against which it had so often fought. The principles at stake closely paralleled those set forth in the legal cases of the early nineteenth century. Labor felt itself to be fighting again for the basic right to organize and strike against courts which had wholly gone over to the employers' camp in banning union activity as being in restraint of trade. The onetime accepted theory that possible injury to property rights through strikes or boycotts was only incidental to their legitimate purpose of seeking to improve working conditions, was being denied under conditions that seemed to threaten the very existence of unions.

The American Federation of Labor considered it imperative to seek legislative relief from such restrictions. It still did not wish to enter directly into politics, and had no idea of seeking even modification of the economic system. Rejecting renewed proposals of the socialists for adopting their program of government ownership of the means of production, Gompers declared in 1903, "economically, you are unsound; socially you are wrong; industrially you are an impossibility"—and was upheld by a vote of 11,282 to 2,147. But somehow the unions had to be freed from the disabilities under which they were suffering. Protection for the right to organize, to bargain collectively, to strike, to boycott, and to picket had become of immediate and vital concern.

A first step in trying to exercise more effective political pressure in support of such aims was made in 1906 when the A.F. of L. submitted a Bill of Grievances to the President and to Congress. It included most of the traditional demands that labor had been voicing since the Civil War, and sponsored various of the more general measures being promoted by progressives throughout the country. Most important, however, were the demands for exemption of labor unions from the Sherman Act and relief from injunctions which were said to represent a judicial usurpation of power properly belonging to the legislature. "We have waited long and patiently and in vain for redress," the Bill of Grievances concluded. ". . . Labor now appeals to you, and we trust it may not be in vain. But if perchance you may not heed us, we shall appeal to the conscience and support of our fellow citizens."

Congress did not heed labor's spokesmen. With the bills labor sought to introduce sidetracked or pushed aside, the A.F. of L. consequently entered actively into the congressional campaign of 1906. It not only called for the support of all congressional candidates friendly to labor's aspirations, but where neither party had named an acceptable candidate, it advised the nomination of a trade unionist. Two years later

Gompers appealed to both party conventions for support. The Republicans completely ignored him but the Democrats adopted an anti-injunction plank in their platform. The *American Federationist* thereupon took the further step of openly opposing William Howard Taft, assailed as the injunction judge, and coming out definitely in favor of William Jennings Bryan. When Taft was elected and the Republicans continued to pass over labor's demands, further support appeared to be forthcoming for the Democrats. While the A.F. of L. again attacked Taft in the election of 1912, however, it maintained a careful neutrality between Roosevelt and Wilson.

These political tactics were stoutly defended by Gompers as in no sense departing from the A.F. of L.'s traditional non-partisan stand of rewarding labor's friends and punishing its enemies. Legislation was needed to free the unions from existing restrictions, according to his thesis, and the Democrats had shown themselves to be more open-minded and sympathetic than the Republicans. "In performing a solemn duty at this time in support of a political party," the A.F. of L. chieftain declared in 1908, "labor does not become partisan to a political party but partisan to a principle."

How successful such political activities were prior to the Wilson administration was highly dubious. State legislatures adopted a number of measures which materially improved conditions for industrial workers, with special reference to women and children, but as already suggested, they were a response to the awakened sense of social responsibility that typified the whole progressive era rather than the result of political pressures exerted by organized labor. They had grown out of a humanitarian feeling which was not so much concerned over labor's rights—union recognition and collective bargaining—as with the more general aspects of an industrial society that harbored so much poverty, disease and crime.

While labor supported these reforms, moreover, they were not of primary consideration according to the philosophy of the A.F. of L. and Samuel Gompers. Suspicious of the state, Gompers was unwilling to rely upon government for the protection of labor's interests. He favored laws safeguarding women and children in industry, but did not want laws governing either hours or wages for union members. The only effective means for improving general working conditions, in his opinion, was the economic pressure of organized labor. All he asked of the state were guarantees of the right to exercise such pressure.

There was, indeed, no more staunch defender of laissez faire among conservative industrial leaders than the head of the A.F. of L. In 1915 Gompers came valiantly to its defense in an editorial in the *American Federationist,* and the phrases he employed have a strange familiarity in the light of political debates in the 1930's.

"Whither are we drifting," he asked. ". . . If there is no market for cotton those interests demand a law. If wages are low, a law or commission is the remedy proposed. What can be the result of this tendency but the softening of the moral fibre of the people? Where there is unwillingness to accept responsibility for one's life and for making the most of it, there is a loss of strong, red-blooded, rugged independence and will power. . . . We do not want to place more power in the hands of the government to investigate and regulate the lives, the conduct and the freedom of America's workers."

The economic and social reforms enacted during the progressive era were nevertheless important, and directly or indirectly they greatly benefited all workingmen. Child labor laws, placing restrictions on the age at which children might be employed, limiting their hours of work, and otherwise safeguarding health and safety had been adopted in some thirty-eight states by 1912, and protection was afforded women in industry through legislation in twenty-eight states setting maximum hours. More importantly, there had been widespread adoption—in at least thirty-five states by 1915—of workmen's compensation laws providing for compulsory benefit payments for industrial accidents. These latter measures were often inadequate and not always effectively enforced, but they demonstrated significant progress toward ensuring employer responsibility for the health and safety of workers in mines and factories.

A beginning was also made in the passage of general maximum hour laws. The demand for such legislation by the states, that had been pressed so vigorously in the 1840's and again in the 1860's, was not taken up by labor as it had been in these earlier periods. Collective bargaining rather than legal limitation were the means on which the unions principally relied to reduce the working day. As a result of progressive rather than special labor agitation, however, some twenty-five states enacted laws during this era which in the interests of public health and safety limited hours of work for men as well as women. They differed sharply from the earlier maximum hour legislation in that the old clause exempting "special contracts" was finally eliminated. For the first time, state hour laws were enforceable.

The courts had originally blocked the passage of much of this labor legislation, taking the stand that exercise of the state's police power could not be carried so far as to interfere with either the property rights of the employer, or the individual freedom of the worker to conclude whatever contract he desired. In *Lochner* v. *New York*, a case in which a maximum hour law for bakery workers was declared unconstitutional in 1905, the Supreme Court stated that such legislation was barred by the guarantees of liberty in the due process clause of the Fourteenth Amendment. However, the court gradually swung over to a more liberal interpretation of constitutional safeguards, and it finally upheld the maximum hour laws for both men and women, and also accepted the new workmen's compensation laws. When the further attempt was made to enact minimum wage laws, however, the Supreme Court divided evenly on their constitutionality and the validity of such legislation, as passed in seven states, remained in doubt. The issue did not again come up for determination until 1923 and it was then ruled, in *Adkins* v. *Children's Hospital*, that wage restrictions could not be reconciled with liberty of contract. This decision was to stand until 1937 when the Supreme Court finally acknowledged that, under existing conditions of employment, liberty of contract was a fiction which in no way preserved the individual worker's freedom in determining either his hours of work or his wages.

In general, state legislation in behalf of industrial workers, while still lagging far behind contemporary European experiments with both old age pensions and unemployment insurance, had substantial achievements to its credit during the Roosevelt and Taft administrations. On the national stage, as already suggested, there was far less cause for satisfaction. The Bill of Grievances submitted by the A.F. of L. in 1906 appeared to have been permanently tabled by hostile committees in both the House and the Senate. No progress whatsoever was being made in enacting its general provisions for union security. As action in so many cases demonstrated, the injunction and union prosecutions under the

Sherman Act became increasingly powerful weapons in the hands of labor's foes. The attitude of the Democratic House chosen in 1910 was a first sign of a more favorable attitude toward labor. An effective eight-hour day for workers on public contracts was finally passed, an Industrial Relations Commission was set up "to discover the underlying causes of dissatisfaction in the industrial situation," and provision made for establishing a Department of Labor particularly designed to promote the wage earners' welfare. But it was not until the election of 1912 that a real turning point was reached so far as broader legislation by the national government was concerned.

Wilson had attacked what he called "the antiquated and impossible" laws currently governing the relations of employers and employes in "The New Freedom." His inaugural further emphasized the need for legislation that would not only safeguard the workers' lives, improve conditions under which they worked, and provide rational and tolerable hours of labor, but also give them "freedom to act in their own interest." He denied that such laws could be considered class legislation and asserted that they were in the interests of the whole people. Labor rejoiced in such a defense of its position and confidently looked forward to the remedial legislation in respect to injunctions and conspiracy prosecutions for which it had striven so long and so unsuccessfully. "We are no longer journeying in the wilderness," Gompers proclaimed. "We are no longer in the season of mere planting. We are in the harvest time."

The results appeared for a time to bear out this optimism. In 1914 Congress passed the Clayton Act which both strengthened earlier anti-trust legislation and incorporated important clauses affecting the rights of labor. Specifically declaring that "the labor of a human being is not a commodity or article of commerce," the new law stated that nothing in the anti-trust laws should be construed to forbid the existence of unions, prevent them from "lawfully" carrying out their legitimate objects, or hold them to be illegal combinations or conspiracies in restraint of trade. Furthermore, it outlawed the use of injunctions in all disputes between employers and employes "unless necessary to prevent irreparable injury to property, or to a property right . . . for which injury there is no adequate remedy at law."

Gompers hailed this statute as the "Magna Carta" of labor—a final guarantee of the workers' right to organize, to bargain collectively, to

strike, to boycott, and to picket. Other opinion varied as to the real
efficacy of the new law. Although the *Wall Street Journal* described
Congress as "a huddled mob of frightened cowards . . . watching for
the labor boss to turn down his thumb," many newspaper editorials,
political leaders and even some labor spokesmen pointed out that
the cautious phraseology of the Clayton Act showed that labor had
really won no new rights and that injunctions had not actually been
outlawed. Gompers chose to ignore all such practical considerations as
he spread the glad tidings of what he insisted was a great labor victory.
Perhaps in order to justify the policies he had followed and to build
up the prestige of the A.F. of L., he admitted no doubts as to the full
freedom that the unions had theoretically won.

The skeptics were soon shown to have been justified. The guarantees
of the Clayton Act proved to be largely illusory once they were subjected
to interpretation by the courts. Loopholes were discovered in the supposed exemption of unions from the anti-trust laws; the provisions in
regard to the use of injunctions were so interpreted as to provide no
real relief. The statement of principle that labor was not a commodity
remained, and it had a real significance as marking a change in public
attitudes, but it had no practical effect on employer-employe relationships.

Yet there were substantial gains for labor during the Wilson administration and in spite of disappointment over the later interpretation of
the Clayton Act, these years were to find organized labor driving ahead
on many fronts. It won legislative support on three important issues.
Passage of the La Follette Seamen's Act in 1915 remedied many of the
most glaring abuses in the employment of sailors and immeasurably
improved conditions in the forecastles of American merchant vessels.
A demand by railway workers for shorter hours was met the next year
when the Adamson Act established an eight-hour day, with time and
a half for overtime, for all employes of interstate railways. And congressional enactment of a literacy test for all European immigrants in
1917 was a first step toward the policy of immigration restriction which
labor had so long demanded.

The growth of labor unions during the first decade of the new century
had been temporarily halted by the industrial counter-attack launched

about 1904. The membership of the American Federation of Labor actually declined in 1905 and for the next five years remained almost stationary. It was only 1,562,000 in 1910 in comparison with 1,676,000 six years earlier. Between 1910 and 1917, however, the A.F. of L. gained some 800,000 new members and trade union enrollment as a whole rose to over 3,000,000. It was almost four times what it had been at the opening of the century.

The urge to join a union, in these years as in other periods, came not only from expectation of economic gain through collective action. The hope that he would attain greater security—a square deal and protection from arbitrary discipline—was always highly important, but there was also an often unconscious desire on the part of the individual wage earner to strengthen his feeling of individual worth and significance in an industrialized society. Machinery was more and more making the worker an automatic cog in a process over which he had no influence or control. The complete impersonality of corporate business, with management far removed from any direct contact with employes, further accentuated this loss of individual status. The wage earner could find a satisfaction in membership in such a meaningful social organization as a labor union that was denied him as one among many thousands of depersonalized employes. The desire to take part in some group activity was, indeed, particularly strong during the progressive era. It was a period marked by the rapid growth of social clubs, lodges and fraternal associations. The unions, often including some of the ritual of the fraternal lodges, met a very real need entirely apart from the support they provided for collective bargaining.

The expansion in union ranks, in any event, was brought about both by the increase in membership in old unions and the establishment of new ones. The United Mine Workers had built up a membership of 334,000, by far the strongest union in the country; the building trades— carpenters, painters, masons, bricklayers—had over 300,000 workers in their various unions, and important additions to the organized labor movement were the unions among garment workers.

Activity in this industry had received dramatic impetus from the "uprising of the twenty thousand" among the shirtwaist makers in New York. This strike in the fall of 1909 had so sensationally dramatized the intolerable conditions prevailing in the sweatshops that popular sympathy had swung wholly over to the strikers. Under the leadership of the International Ladies' Garment Workers, they had been able to win all their major demands except a closed shop. This strike was only a preliminary, however, to a further struggle the next year which broke out among the even more sweated workers in the cloak and suit trade. They were largely unorganized but again direction of the strike was taken over by the I.L.G.W.U. With Louis D. Brandeis, later to become an associate justice of the Supreme Court, serving as a mediator, a favorable settlement was again concluded. The garment workers not only won their wage and hour demands but negotiated a "protocol" with their employers which set up machinery for the conciliation of future disputes. The International Ladies' Garment Workers became one of the nation's strongest and most enterprising unions. It was largely made up of immigrants with a heavy majority of women, was somewhat socialistic in its outlook, and greatly concerned over the individual welfare of its members.

The key union among workers in men's clothing was for long the United Garment Workers. In 1914 internal quarrels led a majority of its membership to break away from the A.F. of L. and form the independent Amalgamated Clothing Workers. This union steadily grew in strength and succeeded in concluding trade agreements with manufacturers in all large centers of industry. Like the I.L.G.W.U., it was socialistic in theory but its day-by-day policy was one of increasing cooperation with employers under constructive, broad-minded leadership.

The United Mine Workers, the International Ladies' Garment Workers and the Amalgamated Clothing Workers were industrial unions, including in their membership all workers in the industries which they represented. They remained, however, outstanding exceptions to the general rule of labor organization. There were no unions of any significance in steel, in automobiles, in agricultural machinery, in electrical manufactures, in public utilities, in tobacco manufacture or in meat packing. The very industries that were becoming most important in the economic development of the country, and employed an increasing proportion of industrial workers, were unaffected by the labor activity of these years because the corporations controlling them were so stubbornly anti-union and so powerful that every effort to organize their employes was doomed to failure.

It was the continued low wages and long hours for workers in these mass production industries that largely accounted for the unevenness of the gains that may be attributed to labor during the progressive era. The social legislation of the period, wage advances for skilled workers banded together in the unions comprising the A.F. of L., a changing public attitude and public policy toward unionization, were counteracted by the depressed circumstances of the great hordes of unorganized industrial workers who still accounted for approximately ninety per cent of the total labor force.

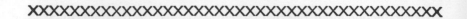

XII: THUNDER ON THE LEFT

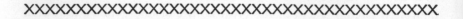

WHILE THE WAGE EARNERS in the national and international unions were generally willing to accept an economic system under which they appeared to be making slow but definite gains, disturbing currents of a deeper discontent developed during the progressive era among the workers who were outside the bounds of existing trade unionism. New demands were voiced for organization on industrial lines or for the all-inclusive union structure abandoned after the collapse of the Knights of Labor; the adherents of socialism grew in strength and redoubled their efforts to build up an effective political party, and there was radical agitation among the unorganized workers for direct action to secure their share of the benefits made available by an expanding economy.

"The labor men are very ugly and no one can tell how far such discontent will spread," Roosevelt was somewhat fearfully writing Henry Cabot Lodge as early as 1906. "There has been during the last six or eight years a growth of socialistic and radical spirit among workingmen and the leaders are obliged to play to this or they lose their leadership."

The upsurge of radicalism appeared somehow out of place in a period in which the spirit of the country was one of buoyant confidence and such general advance appeared to be underway for the people as a whole. It was a direct reflection, however, of the extent to which the interests of the unskilled workers were being ignored. As the American Federation of Labor continued to neglect industrial organization and fought every radical movement as vigorously as industry itself, the embers of discontent were fanned still more strongly. Fertile ground was provided for a revival of revolutionary activity whose aim was the immediate abolition of the wage system and the complete overthrow of capitalism. For a brief time this movement appeared to threaten the stability and basic conservatism of the entire labor movement. Its spearhead was the Industrial Workers of the World.

Miners, lumberjacks and migratory harvest hands in the West joined forces with socialistic groups representing the unorganized industrial workers of the East in the formation of this new association. The I.W.W. denied that there was anything in common between the working class and the employing class. Viciously attacking the policies of the A.F. of L. and all trade unionism, they called upon the workers to take over themselves possession of the machinery of production.

"Instead of the conservative motto, 'A fair day's wage for a fair day's work,'" their ringing manifesto declared, "we must inscribe on our banner the revolutionary watchword, 'Abolition of the wage system.' It is the historic mission of the working class to do away with capitalism."

The I.W.W. grew out of a secret meeting in Chicago in 1905 which drew together all the radical and dissident elements in the labor movement. These militant western miners, socialists of various persuasions, advocates of industrial unionism and anarchistic exponents of direct action closed their ranks for a unified and direct attack upon capitalism. Events were to prove that they agreed upon little else than their mutual scorn for the program and tactics of the A.F. of L. Accepting the thesis of class struggle as their common starting point, however, they set up an economic organization whose aim was to work on both the political and industrial front for the final emancipation of labor.

The most important group behind the organization of the I.W.W. was the Western Federation of Miners. It had once been affiliated with the A.F. of L. but had withdrawn in 1897 in resentment against what was felt to be the effete East's betrayal of the workers' cause. Permeated with the independent and often lawless spirit of the frontier, the miners had then engaged in a series of strikes in the gold, silver, lead and copper mines of the western states, and in 1903–1904 waged open warfare against the operators in the Cripple Creek area of Colorado. They fought the introduction of strikebreakers; the owners counter-attacked through local vigilance committees and state militia. With each side equally committed to violence, the struggle was dramatically marked by mine explosions, the wrecking of trains, mob outbreaks, individual killings, arrests, imprisonments, and the machine gunning of miners' assemblies. After thirteen months of intermittent fighting, the strike was finally crushed and the vigilantes, deputized sheriffs, police and militia restored something like order to Cripple Creek.

After this defeat, the Western Federation of Miners realized it could not stand alone. It had already formed what was first called the Western Labor Union and then the American Labor Union in an effort to bring together all workers in the western states in a single industrial organization, and the Federation's leaders were now ready to welcome any move toward even broader organization. They hopefully answered the call for the Chicago convention that was to result in formation of the I.W.W. Their delegates numbered only five out of a total of some two hundred at this meeting, but with 27,000 members the western miners were far and away the strongest union represented.

The socialists were the other principal group to send delegates. The Working Men's Party had long since been succeeded by the Socialist Labor Party. Under the domineering leadership of Daniel De Leon, a brilliant orator and pamphleteer known as "the socialist pope," incessant warfare had been waged for a decade against what were considered the timid and pusillanimous policies of the A.F. of L. A master of personal invective, De Leon called the Federation "a cross between a windbag and a rope of sand," while Gompers was intermittently a "labor faker," "an entrapped swindler," and "a greasy tool of Wall St." Unity was never possible in the socialist camp, however, and in 1900 a further split within the ranks led to the creation of still another in the long series of parties professing the socialist faith in one form or another. This faction, which was known simply as the Socialist Party, was to exercise far more influence than any of its predecessors, and under the leadership of Eugene V. Debs polled heavy votes in the presidential elections of the progressive era. The Socialist Labor Party and the Socialist Party were naturally always at odds, but that did not prevent both their leaders being present at Chicago.

While other independent radical unions were officially represented, including the American Labor Union, the United Metal Workers and the United Brotherhood of Railway Employes, individuals rather than organizations were primarily responsible for the establishment of the I.W.W. and the convention was enlivened by the clash of their divergent personalities. In addition to De Leon and Debs, other delegates were William D. Haywood, of the Western Federation of Miners; Father

T. J. Hagerty, a big, black-bearded Catholic priest who was the editor of the American Labor Union's official organ and a militant advocate of industrial unionism; A. M. Simons, the socialist intellectual and editor of the *International Socialist Review;* Charles O. Sherman, the general secretary of the United Metal Workers; William E. Trautmann, a radical leader of the United Brewery Workers and editor of its German language paper, and Mother Jones, a fiery, intrepid, little old lady of seventy-five, with curly white hair and kindly gray eyes, whose zeal as an agitator kept her in the front lines of labor's fighting front for almost half a century.

Among these varied and colorful figures, the most arresting was Haywood. A massive, stoop-shouldered, lumbering giant, his generally tough appearance given an almost sinister cast as a result of the loss of one eye, "Big Bill" Haywood was a powerful and aggressive embodiment of the frontier spirit. He had been cowboy, homesteader and miner, but at the turn of the century left the mines of Silver Creek, Idaho to become an active organizer for labor and the Socialist Party. Described as "a bundle of primitive instincts," Haywood accepted violence as a necessary phase of the labor struggle. He stood forthrightly for direct action. On calling to order the first convention of the I.W.W., he addressed it as "the Continental Congress of the working class" and from the onset clearly revealed that his real interest was in organizing the forgotten unskilled workers and especially the migratory laborers of the West—the "bums" and "red-blooded working stiffs." "We are going down in the gutter," Haywood shouted, "to get at the mass of workers and bring them up to a decent plane of living."

Except for Haywood, none of these convention delegates had more than a corporal's guard of followers to bring into the I.W.W. They spoke for themselves and their individualistic attitudes on labor policy appeared to be irreconcilable in the excitement of convention debate. After giving full vent to their opposition to what they derisively called, "the American Separation of Labor," they nevertheless agreed upon a general program for the I.W.W.

Gompers had nothing but scorn for these leftist maneuvers and the attempt to revive a form of labor organization which he roundly condemned as "fallacious, injurious, reactionary." He struck out particularly at his old foe De Leon whose adherence to the I.W.W. he hoped would "bring unction to the soul" of its other promoters. "So the trade union smashers and the rammers from without and the 'borers from within,'" he wrote, "are again joining hands; a pleasant sight of the 'pirates' and the 'kangaroos' hugging each other in glee over their prospective prey."

His belief that such strange bedfellows could not long work together soon appeared to be substantiated. Faction and controversy split the ranks of the I.W.W. almost immediately. At the 1906 convention a conflict between the more moderate elements, primarily represented by the Socialist Party, and the outright proponents of revolution led to wholesale desertions by right-wingers. The next year the Western Federation of Miners itself withdrew, reducing the actual membership of the I.W.W. to less than 6,000, and then in 1908 a final struggle broke out over the basic issue of political or economic action. The group favoring the former policy was led by De Leon and the latter by Trautmann, but the decisive element at the convention was a delegation of western rebels—"the Overalls Brigade"—which beat its way to Chicago on freight trains and had scant interest in doctrinaire squabbling.

This faction ousted the De Leonites, who promptly held a rival convention to form a new organization, and then proceeded to amend the Chicago constitution to their liking. All idea of employing the weapon of politics was given up. The overthrow of capitalism was to be sought solely through direct economic action. Openly revolutionary in theory and practice, committed to strikes, sabotage and violence, the I.W.W. was pledged never to accept peace with the enemies of the workers.

Only through One Big Union, breaking through all craft lines, it was now declared, could the workers present an effective united front in the class struggle. The A.F. of L. had betrayed labor and fallen under the complete domination of employers.

"Tie 'Em Up," sang the Wobblies:

We have no fight with brothers of the old A.F. of L.
But we ask you use your reason with the facts we have to tell.
Your craft is but protection for a form of property,
The skill that you are losing, don't you see.
Improvements on machinery take your skill and tools away,
And you'll be among the common slaves upon some fateful day.

Now the things of which we're talking we are mighty sure about.—
So what's the use to strike the way you can't win out?

> Tie 'em up! tie 'em up; that's the way to win.
> Don't notify the bosses till hostilities begin.
> Don't furnish chance for gunmen, scabs and all their like;
> What you need is One Big Union and One Big Strike.

Refusing to abandon the right to strike at any time or on any occasion, the I.W.W. did not approve of trade agreements. Everyday struggles for wages and hours were only the first line of attack; the decks had to be kept clear for the final assault. Industrial unions were to provide the "structure of the new society within the shell of the old" and a workers' government replace what in a capitalistic society was "simply a committee employed to police the interests of the employing class."

The I.W.W. made its greatest appeal to western miners, construction gangs, lumberjacks and migratory harvest hands who were not interested in political action since they seldom had the vote. Ill-paid, homeless, unmarried; drifting from job to job, largely cut off from the usual ties of society, they considered themselves victims of an economic system designed solely to exploit them. They were ready to strike, to resort to violence, to wage open warfare—not for the nebulous dream of "pie in the sky" but for down-to-earth ownership of the means of production. Converts were also won among the immigrant workers of steel mills, packing plants and textile mills whom the I.W.W. was prepared at all times to aid. This group was not as rough and ready as the western rebels. Eastern factory workers did not necessarily accept the revolutionary implications of the I.W.W. program. But whether they did or not, they were grateful for the support given to their strikes.

Membership in the I.W.W. never became very great—probably no more than sixty thousand at its peak. Several hundred thousand union cards were issued, but casual workers did not remain very long in the ranks. The significance of the I.W.W., as already suggested, was its revolutionary leadership. The Wobblies themselves as they came to be called in the West, often appeared to welcome violence, enjoying a brawl for its own sake, and they fought the forces of law and order without too much concern over the validity of the issues involved. "Hanging is none too good for them," the San Diego Tribune exploded on one occasion in 1912, "they would be much better dead, for they are absolutely useless in the human economy; they are the waste material of creation and should be drained off into the sewer of oblivion there to rot in cold obstruction like any other excrement." Yet without this class of workers, however obstreperous, the West would hardly have developed so rapidly. They did the rough and heavy work: cut the timber, harvested the crops, dug out the minerals. And however mistaken their views may have been, however hopeless their often blind struggle against society, they had courage and militancy that were colorful and exciting.

Their spirit found expression in the I.W.W. songs sung at their union meetings, in harvest camps, on the picket line: "Are you a Wobbly?" "Dump the Bosses Off Your Back," "Paint 'Er Red," "What We Want," "The Red Flag" and "Hallelujah! I'm a Bum!"

> O! I like my boss,
>   He's a good friend of mine,
> And that's why I'm starving
>   Out on the picket-line!
> Hallelujah! I'm a bum!
>   Hallelujah! Bum again!
> Hallelujah! Give us a hand-out
>   To revive us again!

There were I.W.W. strikes in the mining fields, on lumbering projects, in the construction camps of the Northwest; in Pacific coast canneries, eastern textile mills, midwestern steel and meat packing plants, and among streetcar workers, window cleaners and longshoremen. The I.W.W. leaders, and notably "Big Bill" Haywood, who had stayed with the I.W.W. in spite of the withdrawal of the Western Federation of Miners, were ready to back up the unorganized workers—anywhere, anytime. They directed strike activity, manned picket lines, provided relief for the workers' families, agitated and organized with a reckless ardor that made the tactics of the A.F. of L. seem pale and insipid.

When local authorities tried to suppress the activity of the I.W.W. and threw its organizers into jail, "free speech" fights broke out from Walla Walla, Washington to New Bedford, Massachusetts. There was no sooner news of arrests in some particular town than the Wobblies would arrive upon the scene by the hundreds to exercise their constitutional rights and defy the police. When the first contingents were jailed, others took their place until the harassed authorities found the burden upon the community so great that they had no alternative to setting their prisoners free. The Wobblies would pour from the jail triumphant, ready again to agitate, to picket, to battle for their rights.

The West was the scene of the most spectacular strikes and free speech fights waged by the Wobblies, but one of their greatest victories was won in a struggle of textile workers in Lawrence, Massachusetts, in 1912. In spite of eastern fears of an intrusion of frontier violence, however, this strike was marked by rigid discipline. The I.W.W. realized in this instance the importance of winning public sympathy for the workers and did everything possible to maintain order. All idea of revolutionary activity was subordinated to the immediate job. Without any support from other unions, which were jealous of their invasion of an eastern factory town, the I.W.W. leaders in Lawrence directed all their energies toward maintaining the united front among the strikers that ultimately forced the employers' submission.

A reduction in wages for the 30,000 workers in the Lawrence textile mills, about half of whom were employed by the American Woolen Company, brought on the strike. The earnings of the mill hands, largely Italians, Poles, Lithuanians and Russians, averaged less than $9 a week —when the mills were running full time. Moreover in addition to insufficient wages and long hours, a premium system had been introduced to speed up the work under conditions that imposed terrific pressure and tension. The pay cuts were the last straw. The angry workers began spontaneously to walk out on January 12, 1912, as the bells of the city hall rang a general alarm, in a concerted protest that soon involved some 20,000 men and women.

There were some union members in the mills. A few belonged to the United Textile Workers, an A.F. of L. affiliate, and something like a thousand to the I.W.W. The rest were unorganized. Foreseeing the strike, the I.W.W. members had already sent to headquarters for help and Joseph J. Ettor, a member of the general executive board, hurried to Lawrence and was soon joined by another I.W.W. leader, Arturo Giovannitti. These two men at once took over virtual control of the strike, organized it on a wholly realistic basis, and imposed strict discipline. Ettor arranged great mass meetings to keep the strikers united, established picket lines, and saw that relief was given to the needy and suffering families whose sole sources of income had been abruptly cut off. Relief was, indeed, his greatest problem for over half of the city's population of 85,000 were either strikers or their dependents. General committees were formed for each separate national group to distribute supplies, maintain soup kitchens, and provide other aid.

The first suggestion of lawlessness was the discovery, announced in scare headlines in the press, of dynamite planted in various parts of the city. The I.W.W. was at once accused of importing its terroristic methods and such sympathy as had at first been aroused for the strikers turned to angry resentment. "When the strikers use or prepare to use dynamite," the *New York Times* declared editorially, "they display a fiendish lack of humanity which ought to place them beyond the comfort of religion until they have repented."

The strikers protested at once that the dynamite planting was none of their doing. Events were wholly to vindicate them. Before the strike was over it was proved that a local undertaker had planted the dynamite, in an obvious effort to discredit the strikers and particularly the I.W.W., and that the plot had been contrived by persons closely associated with the mill owners themselves. With the arrest of the head of the American Woolen Company, on the charge of being implicated in this scheme, even the most conservative newspapers strongly assailed the strategy of trying to involve the workers in pretended bombing plots. The *Iron Age* spoke of "betrayal of the cause of employers generally," and the *New York Evening Post* condemned "an offense on the part of capitalism which passes the worst acts ever committed by labor unions."

In the meantime the American Woolen Company, still refusing even to consider the workers' demands, tried to reopen the mills. This move caused a violent clash between strikers and police and during the rioting an Italian woman was shot and killed. The authorities promptly declared martial law, twenty-two militia companies were called out to patrol the streets in order to prevent any public meetings or talks, and Ettor and Giovannitti were arrested as accessories to murder.

Neither the strike committee nor the I.W.W. allowed these developments either to drive them into unwarranted counterviolence or to lessen their determination to see the strike through. "Big Bill" Haywood took charge after the arrest of Ettor and Giovannitti, and in spite of his own and the I.W.W.'s revolutionary policies, he continued to insist upon an attitude of passive resistance. With such control the workers held firm. The protection offered by the militia to employes desiring to return to their jobs did not encourage any defections from the ranks. "In the spinning room every belt was in motion, the whir of machinery sounded on every side," wrote a newspaper reporter visiting one of the mills, "yet not a single operative was at work and not a single machine carried a spool of yarn."

The problem of feeding the strikers became increasingly difficult, however, and early in February the committee evolved a plan which had the double objective of helping to meet immediate needs and dramatically calling public attention to them. Labor sympathizers in other cities were asked to provide temporary homes for the children of the strikers. The response was immediate and several hundred children were sent to other communities. Alarmed at the effect of this move, which the head of the United Textile Workers took the lead in denouncing as made solely "to keep up the agitation and further the propaganda of the Industrial Workers of the World," the Lawrence authorities stated that no more children would be allowed to leave the city. When the strike committee undertook to send another group away, the police forcibly interfered under circumstances that were more successful in creating sympathy for the strikers than anything else could possibly have been.

"The station itself," read a report of the Women's Committee of Philadelphia, which was to take care of the children, "was surrounded by police and militia. . . . When the time approached to depart the children, arranged in a long line, two by two, in orderly procession, with their parents near at hand, were about to make their way to the train when the police, who had by that time stationed themselves along both sides of the door, closed in on us with their clubs, beating right and left, with no thought of the children, who were in the most desperate danger of being trampled to death. The mothers and children were thus hurled in a mass and bodily dragged to a military truck, and even then clubbed, irrespective of the cries of the panic-striken women and children. . . ."

This was perhaps the turning point in the strike. Neither the Lowell authorities nor the mill owners could withstand the flood of protests from every part of the country. There were to be further attacks on the strikers and further arrests—the latter totaled 296 during the two months of the strike—but with the picket lines holding firm the American Woolen Company finally admitted defeat and on March 12 offered terms which virtually met all the workers' demands. Wages were to be increased from five to twenty-five per cent, with time and a quarter for overtime; the premium system equitably adjusted, and there was to be no discrimination in rehiring the strikers. At a great mass meeting on the Lawrence Common, Haywood advised acceptance of this offer and the mill operatives agreed to return to their jobs.

A final episode was the trial of Ettor and Giovannitti. For a time it appeared that they would not be given a fair hearing and were likely to be convicted in spite of the lack of any evidence directly implicating them in the murder with which they were charged. The I.W.W. organized a defense committee which collected $60,000 and the workers in Lawrence, declaring that unless the authorities opened the jail doors they would close the mill doors, went on a twenty-four hour protest strike—15,000 strong. In the final outcome, both men were found innocent, and on being released were wildly greeted by crowds who held them in no small part responsible for the victory that the Lawrence textile employes had won under their direction.

Before the trial ended, the two accused men made speeches to the jury setting forth their position, in which they frankly avowed the revolutionary aims of the I.W.W. and their refusal to be intimidated by the police. That of Giovannitti, a poet in his own right whose revolutionary verses are to be found in many anthologies, was eloquent and moving.

"Let me tell you," he declared, "that the first strike that breaks again in this Commonwealth or any other place in America where the work and help and the intelligence of Joseph J. Ettor and Arturo Giovannitti will be needed and necessary, there we shall go again, regardless of any fear or of any threat. We shall return again to our humble efforts, obscure, unknown, misunderstood soldiers of this mighty army of the working class of the world, which, out of the shadows and darkness of the past, is striving towards the destined goal, which is the emancipation of human kind, which is the establishment of love and brotherhood and justice for every man and every woman on this earth."

The I.W.W. had won an astounding triumph in Lawrence. Its membership among the textile workers jumped almost overnight to 18,000, and this renewed vitality appeared to promise still further growth. Alarm was created within the A.F. of L. as to the future development of its aggressive strike tactics, while even greater fears were aroused in the business community over the possible spread of radical doctrines among American workers. "Are we to expect," an article in the *Survey* asked, "that instead of playing the game respectably, or else frankly breaking out into lawless riot which we know well enough how to deal with, the laborers are to listen to a subtle anarchistic philosophy which challenges the fundamental idea of law and order, inculcating such strange doctrines as those of 'direct action,' 'syndicalism,' 'the general strike,' and 'violence'? . . . We think that our whole current morality as to the sacredness of property and even of life is involved in it."

These fears soon proved to be groundless. The I.W.W. had reached the height of its power and influence. As with the old Knights of Labor, its greatest victories were the forerunners of disastrous defeats and of a decline which within a few years would lead to virtual collapse. The I.W.W. was too revolutionary to attract the support of the basically conservative forces of American labor, and in spite of the violence of its propaganda, too cautious to be successful as revolution. The only thing in which it fully succeeded was in arousing popular fears of violence that could not be allayed even by the relatively peaceful tactics of Lawrence.

The next important strike in which the I.W.W. participated was a harbinger of its decline. Trouble developed in 1913 in the silk mills of Paterson, New Jersey, and among other leaders of the Wobblies, Haywood and Ettor were again on hand. This strike was a prolonged and embittered struggle. The Paterson authorities were determined to crush the revolutionary menace of the I.W.W., and it in turn felt that too much depended on a victory in this strike to give in. The brutality of the police in arresting strikers on any pretense, clubbing them into insensibility when they resisted, and breaking up their picket lines was notorious. Yet the strike went on. Among others who were won to sympathy for the silk workers was John Reed, the young Harvard-educated revolutionary who was to write *Ten Days that Shook the World* and be buried beside the walls of the Kremlin. Describing the scene at Paterson, he said that he could never forget "the exultant men who had blithely defied the lawless brutality of the city and gone to prison laughing and singing." But after five grueling months, the exhaustion of their funds and the growing need of their families forced the strikers to surrender. The I.W.W. had to admit defeat.

Succeeding years saw the Wobblies engaged in scores of minor strikes, while their membership greatly fluctuated as local unions broke up and the migratory construction workers and harvest hands drifted in and out of the organization. There were clashes with authority in many instances, and in the western states a mounting tendency to suppress strikes by any means and at any cost. A free-speech fight at Everett, Washington, for example, resulted in seven deaths when deputized sheriffs opened fire on a boatload of Wobblies landing in the harbor.

Upon the outbreak of the European conflict in 1914, the I.W.W. took a decisive stand against war. "We, as members of the industrial army," read a resolution adopted at its convention that year, "will refuse to fight for any purpose except for the realization of industrial freedom." When the United States joined the Allies three years later, it did not modify its position and refused to support the national war effort at the expense of the class conflict. The interests of the workers in their continuing struggle against capitalism were held superior to those of the country as defined by a government which the I.W.W. considered no more than a committee of the employing class. Critical strikes by metal miners at Butte, Montana, and lumber workers in the Northwest dangerously impeded the war program, but the Wobblies maintained that they were not trying to sabotage vital industries but to improve conditions for the workers.

The public reaction was to condemn the I.W.W. as unpatriotic, pro-German, treasonable. In the frenzied atmosphere of war, popular feeling was everywhere whipped up to fever pitch against "Imperial Wilhelm's Warriors." And employers seeing their chance to smash the I.W.W. once and for all, did everything possible to add fuel to these blazing embers of hatred with the enthusiastic cooperation of much of the press. "The outrageous eruption of the I.W.W. in the far West," the *Chicago Tribune* declared, ". . . is nothing less than rebellion." "While the country is at war," echoed the *Cleveland News*, "the only room it can afford I.W.W.'s . . . is behind the walls of penitentiaries."

Such sentiments found concrete expression. In 1917–1918 state after state passed criminal syndicalism laws outlawing the I.W.W. and count-less arrests were made under these statutes. The national government also entered the picture under the provisions of the Sedition and Espionage Acts. Federal authorities obtained some 160 convictions against members of the I.W.W. on charges of obstructing the war effort. At a mass trial in Chicago, Haywood and ninety-four others were convicted of sedition and sentenced to jail for terms running up to twenty years. The charges of conspiring against the government were in many instances so flimsy as to be ridiculous, but patriotic fervor was not often restrained by consideration of the constitutional rights of free speech and assembly during the first World War.

When the authorities did not act promptly enough, loyalty leagues and local vigilantes often took the law into their own hands. Brutal clubbings, horse-whippings, tar-and-featherings took place in many communities; there were several instances in which I.W.W. agitators were taken out and lynched by lawless mobs. In July, 1917, some 1200 striking miners at Bisbee, Arizona, of whom less than half were actually I.W.W. members, were forcibly deported from the town by a posse deputized by the sheriff at the instance of a local loyalty league. They were put into cattle cars, taken across the state line and abandoned in the desert. After thirty-six hours without food or water, they were rescued by federal authorities and taken to a detention camp in Columbus, New Mexico.

The energies of the I.W.W. were largely absorbed during these war years in trying to defend what it insisted were its "class war prisoners." Unable to do so successfully, it soon found itself without leaders. Haywood himself eventually skipped bail and fled to Soviet Russia. The organization did not break up—it later experienced recovery of a sort—but it never regained its militant pre-war strength.

Changing economic conditions in the West, marked by the increased use of farm machinery and developing automobile transportation, depleted the ranks of the migratory workers who were such an important element in the membership. The Communist Party, organized as a branch of the Third International in 1919, drew away many of the radical socialists. Finally, what was left of the I.W.W. became far less aggressive with the loss of its old leadership. Emphasis was placed upon preparations for administering control of the means of production rather than revolutionary action to seize such control. "The 'Wobblies' . . . said nothing of revolution or class consciousness, of exploitation . . . or of the necessary overthrow of the capitalist system," a reporter for the *New York World* wrote of an unemployment conference after the war. "They talked instead of 'uninterrupted production,' 'the coordination of industrial processes.' . . ." By the mid-1920's the old fighting I.W.W. had already become a legend.

The impact of the I.W.W. on the labor movement was more important than either its membership or its erratic strike activity would suggest. Apart from such direct results as may have been obtained in improving working conditions in western mines, lumber camps and harvest fields, and occasionally in eastern factories, this revolutionary movement spectacularly centered attention on the desperate needs of vast numbers of unskilled workers and gave a new impetus to industrial unionism which even the A.F. of L. could not entirely ignore. The radical doctrine of class struggle badly shook, for a time at least, the complacency of conservative labor leaders who refused to look beyond the confines of traditional trade unionism.

The I.W.W. was nevertheless a failure. It made no more progress toward abolishing the wage system by inciting class warfare than had the Knights of Labor by their moderate program of education and agitation. The overwhelming bulk of American workingmen remained as fundamentally opposed to I.W.W. philosophy as were their employers or the middle class generally. The American Federation of Labor, which lost no opportunity to discredit and attack its radical rival, continued to dominate the labor movement and revolutionary unionism made no real headway against business unionism. The I.W.W. was a dramatic expression of left-wing sentiment, but it made few converts. American labor could not be convinced that the historic role of the working class was to do away with capitalism.[1]

[1] On February 14, 1965, the *New York Times* awakened dim echoes of a distant past when it reported that the Industrial Workers of the World had petitioned for removal from the Attorney General's subversive list. It appeared that a handful of Wobblies still maintained their identity and while resentful of being classed as subversives, held to their ancient faith. "The things we set out to do in 1905," one of them told the *Times* reporter, "remain to be done and because they remain to be done we have a future."

XX

XIII: THE FIRST WORLD WAR—
AND AFTER

XXXXXXXXXXXXXXXXXXXXXXXXXXXXXXXXXXXXXXXXXX

As THE SHADOW of impending war fell over the United States and events rapidly drove the country toward participation in the European struggle, American labor was confronted with a grave problem. Was the conflict one in which workingmen had anything at stake? Should the war effort be supported or should labor take advantage of the national crisis to promote its own class interests? The I.W.W. had made its choice in 1914 and stuck to it. The socialists were divided, but true to his convictions Eugene V. Debs continued to attack what he declared to be a wholly capitalistic war—and went to jail. The American Federation of Labor, however, carrying with it the great majority of the nation's wage earners, declared and maintained complete loyalty to the government and its entire war program. As the outstanding spokesman for labor, no public figure was more exuberantly patriotic than Samuel Gompers and no one proved himself to be a more faithful adherent of the Wilson administration.

On the eve of hostilities, organized labor was stronger than it had ever been before and had won for the first time what was in effect official recognition of its role in the national economy. The report of the Commission on Industrial Relations, ascribing much labor discontent to denial of the right to organize, definitely upheld trade unionism as an essential institution for the settlement of industrial disputes; the Clayton Act apparently exempted unions from prosecution under the antitrust laws, and President Wilson had both demonstrated his friendliness on many occasions and declared that no future president would ever be able to ignore the organized labor movement.

Moreover the victory won by labor in 1916 when Congress passed the Adamson Act marked an important extension of governmental authority in the field of labor relations. It was true that Congress had acted under the imminent threat of a railway strike that would have paralyzed the national defense program, and there was widespread resentment against the tactics employed by the railway brotherhoods. But the acceptance of an obligation to safeguard the interests of the workers was nonetheless highly significant.

It was with a new sense of both power and responsibility that the spokesmen of some three million wage earners undertook to define the attitude of labor toward war. The issue was first taken up at a conference held on March 1, 1917—almost a month before hostilities, but at a time when war already appeared imminent—that was attended by representatives of seventy-nine international unions, the railway brotherhoods, and the A.F. of L. executive council. At its conclusion the conferees issued a public statement on "American Labor's Position in Peace or in War" that pledged the full support of all labor organizations should the country become directly involved in conflict with Germany.

It was not an unconditional pledge. Organized labor was determined that such gains as had been made in recent years should be protected in the event of war, and in pledging support to the Wilson administration, insisted on full recognition of its newly attained status. The unions were to be the medium through which government would operate in seeking the cooperation of wage earners, and they were to be given representation on all boards dealing with national defense. Labor was to be free to exercise the right to organize, and while prepared to use all possible restraint, did not agree nor intend to surrender the weapon of the strike. These conditions for labor cooperation were said to be necessary because of the very nature of the aims for which the country was prepared to go to war.

"Wrapped up with the safety of this Republic," the labor leaders asserted, "are ideals of democracy, a heritage which the masses of the people received from our forefathers, who fought that liberty might live in this country—a heritage that is to be maintained and handed down to each generation with undiminished power and usefulness."

The administration was prepared to work with labor on this basis and after our actual entry into the war, tried to pursue a policy in respect to industrial relations that would forestall strikes. Agreements with the American Federation of Labor specifically provided for the enforcement of trade union standards in all government contracts, labor representatives were appointed to all appropriate government agencies, and

Gompers was made a member of the Advisory Commission of the National Council of Defense. "While we are fighting for freedom," President Wilson told the A.F. of L. convention in November, 1917, "we must see among other things that labor is free. . . ."

But industrial peace was not to be so easily maintained during 1917. As prices rose under the stimulus of wartime purchasing without a corresponding increase in wages, there was discontent among the workers and general demands for increases in pay. When such demands were not met, strikes broke out on a scale that exceeded even pre-war years. Before 1917 ended, they reached a total of 4,450, involving over a million workers.

Many of these strikes were instigated by the I.W.W. Under its radical leadership there were threatening outbreaks in the lumber camps of the northwest, among shipyard workers on the Pacific coast, and in the copper mines of Arizona. Labor unrest was by no means limited, however, to workers who fell within the radical fringe of the labor movement. Many of the conservative and patriotic unions affiliated with the A.F. of L. felt justified in making wartime demands and backing them up with strikes that seriously interrupted production in defense industries.

By the beginning of 1918 this situation threatened to block the flow of military supplies overseas. While efforts were constantly being made to resolve labor disputes through special wage adjustment boards and a mediation commission that had been set up by President Wilson in August, 1917, the government felt obliged to intervene still further in order to assure essential industrial output. Both the friendliness of the administration toward organized labor and simple expediency dictated a policy that would win the workers' support rather than one of suppressing strikes by force. Representatives of labor and management were consequently appointed to a War Labor Conference Board, and after it had unanimously agreed upon a set of principles to govern future labor relations, the President appointed upon its recommendation, in April, 1918, a National War Labor Board to serve as a final court of appeal to settle all industrial disputes that could not be resolved through other means. It was composed of five representatives of labor and five of management, with two joint chairmen representative of the public: former President Taft and Frank P. Walsh, who had been chairman of the Commission of Industrial Relations. Somewhat later a further agency, the War Labor Policies Board, headed by Felix Frankfurter, was also established to act as a clearing house to unify departmental labor policies on wages and hours in the war industries.

The general principles upon which the National War Labor Board operated were immensely significant as a reflection of new governmental attitudes toward labor, and also foreshadowed those later to be incorporated in the labor legislation of the New Deal. In return for a general undertaking that there would be no further strikes or lockouts for the duration of the war, the Wilson administration was prepared to accord labor full support for virtually all its traditional demands. The right to organize and bargain collectively through "chosen representatives" was definitely recognized, and was not in any way to be abridged or denied by employers; all existing agreements in respect to union or open shops were to be upheld on their pre-war basis; the eight-hour day was to be applied as far as possible; women entering industry were to be given equal pay for equal work, and there was complete acceptance of "the right of all workers, including common laborers, to a living wage . . . which will ensure the subsistence of the worker and his family in health and reasonable comfort."

With these highly important commitments, strikes tended to subside and such disputes as did develop were in most instances quickly settled. They caused few work stoppages interfering with war production. No need consequently developed to consider such drastic measures as a manpower draft, compulsory arbitration or anti-strike laws. Labor generally upheld its side of the bargain into which it had tacitly entered and Secretary of War Baker declared on one occasion that it had proved to be "more willing to keep in step than capital."

As the principal spokesman for labor, Gompers continued to support the war effort in every possible way and succeeded in completely identifying the A.F. of L. with our foreign policy. He vociferously attacked all pacifist or suspected pro-German groups, promoted the American Alliance for Labor and Democracy as a counter-move to socialist propaganda for peace, and staunchly upheld Americanism. "I want to express my admiration," was President Wilson's warm tribute, "of his patriotic courage, his large vision, and his statesmanlike sense of what had to be done." In the fall of 1918, Gompers went abroad to attend an inter-allied labor conference and he was in Paris during the peace negotiations as a member of the Commission on International Labor Legislation.

Labor policy was reflected in the wartime gains of the workers and the growth of unionism. Wages gradually rose until average earnings in manufacturing, transportation and coal mining topped the $1000 mark, and the unions in 1919 had over a million more members than in 1916—a total of 4,125,000. When the government took over control of the railways, the recognition previously granted only the railway brotherhoods was extended to shopmen, yardmen, maintenance-of-way workers, railway clerks and telegraphers. In other industries where unionization had had hard sledding, there were important advances—among packing-house employes, seamen and longshoremen, electrical workers, and machinists. The war had opened up great opportunities, and American labor had made the most of them.

The conclusion of hostilities at once created a new situation. As wartime restraints were removed and government surrendered such controls as had been exercised by the National War Labor Board, both labor and industry prepared for the inevitable renewal of their historic contest. The precarious wartime truce expired. Labor was militantly determined not only to maintain the gains that had been made during the war but to win further recognition of its rights, and industry was no less bound to free itself from all government control, check any further advance of unionization, and reassert its power. No holds were barred by either antagonist as industrial strife broke out in 1919 on a scale greater than the country had ever before experienced. The strikes that year were to be nationwide in their scope and would directly and dangerously affect, as would those somewhat more than a quarter of a century later, the whole process of national reconversion to peace.

Wages were an immediate cause for many of these disputes. The wartime price rises continued unchecked in 1919—the cost of living would ultimately reach twice the pre-war level—and the workers began to feel the pinch despite the high pay they were still able to command. But the basic issue of union security was far less easily settled than wage adjustments. Many employers were willing to grant or at least compromise wage demands, but saw in any extension of collective bargaining a threat to their management of their own business. They refused to recognize union spokesmen, and concessions that had been made under the pressure of war were widely withdrawn.

The vital importance of this issue of union recognition was brought out in the one attempt the Wilson administration made in post-war years to reconcile the differences between management and labor. The various agencies for handling labor disputes had been promptly scrapped after the Armistice, but as the number of strikes increased, the President summoned a National Industrial Conference, this time composed of representatives of labor, industry and the public, in the hope that some basis could be found for labor peace. Fundamental disagreements at once developed over the nature of collective bargaining and the obligation of an employer to deal with men or groups of men who were not his own employes. The labor representatives insisted on the right "to organize without discrimination" as the only means of assuring recognition of national unions, and the conference collapsed when the public representatives, a group somehow including John D. Rockefeller, Jr., and Elbert H. Gary, chairman of the United States Steel Corporation, upheld those of industry in refusing to grant this concession.

In the meantime, the extent and character of the strikes of 1919 began more and more to alarm the public. They were felt to be not only endangering economic reconversion but threatening the stability of American institutions. The attitude of many people was greatly affected by almost frantic fears of the spread of communism aroused by the Bolshevik Revolution in Russia. Indeed, the influence of the red scare in molding public opinion toward labor strikes in 1919 can hardly be exaggerated. Popular hysteria over the supposed role of Moscow in fomenting disorder in the United States led a great part of the public to believe that most strikes were instigated by Communists on direct orders from the Kremlin. The legitimate rights and justified grievances of the workers were forgotten in a fearful eagerness to make Bolshevism the cause of all labor unrest. Employers made the most of these fears and alarms, waging a ceaseless campaign to identify all strikers as reds. After the high hopes born of the war, labor found itself everywhere on the defensive, hard-pressed to maintain its position, let alone improve it.

There were some grounds for the attitude of the public. The Communist International preached world revolution and had its adherents in the United States. The local Communist Party formed in 1919 attracted many of the radical elements in the labor movement that had formerly been associated with the I.W.W. and other left-wing groups. Its members infiltrated into a number of unions, exercised an influence out of all proportion to their actual numbers, had a part in fomenting several strikes, and occasionally incited violence. But as on previous occasions when an alarmed public saw a radical threat to society in labor uprisings—the railway strikes of 1877, the Pullman strike, and even the coal strike of 1902—communist influence was greatly overemphasized.

Moreover the attempt of conservative employers to fasten the charge of Bolshevism on the labor movement as a whole could not have been wider of the mark. The leadership of the A.F. of L. was as violently hostile to communism as the governing board of the National Association of Manufacturers. Gompers was in the very forefront of the red-baiters who were helping to create the hysterical intolerance of this period. Indeed, his attempt to absolve the labor movement from industry's charges of radical and subversive activity by continually attacking Bolshevism, proved to be something of a boomerang. His irresponsible exaggeration of the red menace intensified the public's fears of social conflict and consequent demand for the forceful suppression of strikes.

In any event, newspaper reports of strike activity, editorial comment, cartoons and the statements of public leaders, all revealed a hardening of the public attitude toward labor as the year progressed. The more sympathetic feeling of the progressive period evaporated as reaction set in against the whole concept of Wilson's New Freedom. There was derisive talk of factory employes riding to work in their cars, buying silk shirts for themselves and silk stockings for their wives, at the very time that they were demanding higher wages. The strikes awoke "unstinted condemnation from almost every walk of life," one newspaper stated; another declared that the only One Big Union the nation would tolerate was "the one whose symbol is the Stars and Stripes."

Popular demand grew for a national policy of strike suppression in the name of economic and social stability. By the close of 1919, strike after strike was collapsing, the *Literary Digest* pointed out, because the power of public opinion had strongly and definitely crystallized in favor of federal, state and local police intervention in support of the employers and against the workers.

A first strike to arouse public opinion in the post-war period was the so-called general strike that broke out in Seattle in February, 1919. It was not actually to prove very important, but the background of violence out of which it grew and the very effort to call out all workers, created national concern and evoked what were already becoming the inevitable charges of Bolshevism.

The incident leading to this strike was a demand on the part of shipyard workers in Seattle for higher wages. When it was bluntly rejected by their employers, the men walked out. The Central Labor Committee in Seattle at this time was controlled by James A. Duncan, a member of the Machinists Union who had risen to power amid the embittered industrial strife promoted throughout the northwest by the I.W.W. He was an outspoken opponent of the conservative labor policies followed by the A.F. of L., had strongly opposed our entry into the war, and was sympathetic toward Soviet Russia. Seizing the opportunity to make trouble, he called a general strike of all workers in Seattle. Some 60,000 responded and for five hectic days the industrial life of the city was almost paralyzed and its citizens deprived of most of their normal services.

A general strike was a new phenomenon for the United States and the gathering public opposition, both in the Northwest and throughout the country, soon made the participating unions realize that in pursuing such tactics they were forfeiting all popular sympathy. They withdrew their support from the Central Labor Committee and the strike completely collapsed. In the meantime, however, Mayor Ole Hanson had burst into the nation's headlines with sensational statements that the whole thing had been a Bolshevist plot which was crushed only by his own heroic measures.

Even more disturbing was the strike some months later of the Boston police. Discontented with low wages and other aspects of their jobs which they considered unfair, the police had formed a union, which was called the Boston Social Club, and applied to the American Federation

of Labor for a charter. Police Commissioner Curtis promptly stated that
no members of the force would be allowed to join a union, suspended
nineteen of the men who had done so, and began recruiting volunteers
to take over should any union activity continue. Outraged at what they
considered such unwarranted and arbitrary action, the police took matters in their own hands and on September 9 suddenly went on strike.
Boston found itself wholly without police protection that night and its
nervous citizens hardly knew what outbreaks of crime and violence to
expect. In the event there was a good deal of rowdyism by bands of
hoodlums, but no such general lawlessness as had been feared. The
next day volunteers and state guards took over the duties of police and
complete order was restored.

Settlement of the highly involved issues at stake was not so easy.
Charges and counter-charges flew back and forth over responsibility
for the strike and the failure to place on duty immediately the volunteer
force which had supposedly been trained for just such an emergency.
The police commissioner and the mayor were at odds. While the former
refused to consider the grievances that had led to the strike or to reinstate any of the men who had taken part in it, the latter showed a good
deal more sympathy for the strikers and charged that the whole affair
had been miserably mishandled. From A.F. of L. officials came accusa-
tions that the police commissioner was more interested in trying to discredit labor than in solving the controversy, and that he had virtually
goaded the police on to strike.

Whatever was brought out in support of the police, however, the
public generally condemned them for deserting their posts and upheld
Commissioner Curtis in his refusal to re-employ them. A "crime against
civilization" was President Wilson's sharp comment on the strike, and a
future President won nationwide fame by an even more positive statement. Calvin Coolidge, then governor of Massachusetts, was requested
by Gompers to remove the police commissioner. He refused. "There is
no right to strike against the public safety," read his terse telegram, "by
anybody, anywhere, anytime." The public cheered such sentiments to
the echo, the Boston police were not reinstated, and Coolidge was
started on the road to the White House.

Although the Seattle general strike and the Boston police strike attracted the attention of the entire country, they were local affairs. A

great deal more significant in their national, industry-wide implications were strikes in steel and coal. They were defeated under the conditions prevailing in 1919, but they foreshadowed a new pattern of industrial conflict that was to be greatly accentuated after the second World War. The steel strike was especially important. If the steel workers had been successful, the whole labor history of the 1920's might have followed a completely different course. Suppression of the strike, however, postponed effective organization of the workers in this basic industry for another eighteen years.

Conditions in the steel mills fostered universal discontent and underscored what labor leaders declared was an imperative need for unionization if the workers expected any consideration of their grievances. Wages remained low in spite of wartime advances and were steadily falling further behind the continued rise in living costs. A twelve-hour day, six days a week, was still in effect for something over half the labor force, and the average working week was just under sixty-nine hours. Among the highly diversified immigrant groups that made up the majority of employes, living conditions were a bitter travesty upon the promise of a more abundant life which had drawn them to the Land of Opportunity.

Organizational progress on other sectors of the labor front had no parallel in the steel industry. Since suppression of the strikes of the old Amalgamated Association of Iron, Steel and Tin Workers in 1901 and 1910, no further efforts had been toward unionization. While the Amalgamated was still in existence, it was a small craft union that did not touch the interests of the great mass of unskilled workers.

The first step leading toward the strike was the formation, in the summer of 1918, of an organizing committee made up of representatives of twenty-four unions having jurisdiction in the steel industry. Its objective was not only improvement of conditions in the mills but the conquest of this key industry by union labor. The guiding spirit was William Z. Foster, a radical exponent of direct economic action whose early experience in industrial conflict was won in the ranks of the I.W.W. and who later was to become a leading communist. His organizational skill was outstanding and as secretary-treasurer of the associated union committee, he was put in charge of this "one mighty drive to organize the steel plants of America."

Within a year the number of organized workers in the steel mills jumped to 100,000 and an attempt was made to open negotiations with Chairman Gary of the United States Steel Corporation for a trade agreement. When he completely disregarded this request, a strike vote was taken and in behalf of the steel workers, the union committee demanded collective bargaining, the eight-hour day and an increase in wages. Gary's reply to further overtures for the discussion of these demands was blunt and unequivocal. "Our corporation and subsidiaries, although they do not combat labor unions as such," he stated, "decline to discuss business with them." The strike was then officially set for September 22 and by the end of the month close to 350,000 men had quit work in nine states.

The steel industry—the strongest capitalistic power in the world—was ready to meet this challenge and in its determined efforts to break the strike received the full cooperation of local, state and even federal authorities. Thousands of strikebreakers were brought in, particularly large numbers of Negroes; labor spies were hired to do everything possible to stir up animosity and racial antagonism among the different foreign elements in the mills, and deputized guards, local police and state constabularies smashed picket lines and broke up strike meetings with little regard for civil liberties. Violence was held down by the enforcement of martial law in many localities, troops being dispatched to Gary, Indiana, under Major General Wood, but some twenty persons were killed—eighteen of them workers—before the strike was over.

The steel companies also opened up a terrific barrage through newspaper advertisements to discourage the strikers and convince public opinion that the whole thing was a plot hatched in Moscow for the overthrow of American capitalism. The strike was not between the workers and their employers, the steel companies proclaimed, but between revolutionists and America. It could not win for the United States would "never stand for the 'red' rule of Bolshevism, I.W.W.ism or any other 'ism' that seeks to tear down the Constitution." Rumors were even circulated "that the Huns had a hand in fomenting the strike, hoping to retard industrial progress."

So great were the excitement and controversy stirred up under these circumstances that a Commission of Inquiry was set up by the Interchurch World Movement, an organization of Protestant churches, to investigate the strike. It could find no evidence whatsoever of the sinister intrigues the steel companies alleged they had uncovered, and stated that it was far more profitable to consider the workers' uprising in the light of industrial history than "in the glare of baseless excitement over Bolshevism." The repeated emphasis upon the radical, anarchistic, communist aspects of the strike, however, and Foster's left-wing views, succeeded in alienating much popular sympathy for the steel workers in spite of uncontradicted disclosures of the harsh conditions in the mills. The public was all too ready to see Bolshevism at work. The very fact that so many of the steel workers were "hunkies," "dagoes" and "wops," was taken as convincing evidence that they were un-American, revolutionary and controlled by Moscow.

The strike committee could find no way to combat this propaganda successfully. There were withdrawals of support on the part of the sponsoring unions, Foster's leadership was repudiated by the A.F. of L., and discouragement spread through the ranks of the strikers themselves. Late in November the union committee consequently asked the Interchurch Commission to mediate and agreed to accept whatever plan it might suggest for ending the dispute. Gary refused to listen to any peace proposals. The strikers sought "the closed shop, Soviets, and the forcible distribution of property," he declared: ". . . there is absolutely no issue." The strike dragged on but the disheartened men now began to drift back to work. In January, 1920, the leaders gave up. The strike was called off and such men as had not in the meantime been blacklisted returned without having won a single concession.

"The United States Steel Corporation," the Interchurch Commission declared in a final report, "was too big to be beaten by 300,000 workingmen. It had too large a cash surplus, too many allies among other businesses, too much support from government officers, local and national, too strong influence with social institutions such as the press and the pulpit, it spread over too much of the earth—still retaining absolutely centralized control—to be defeated by widely scattered workers of many minds, many fears, varying states of pocketbook and under a comparatively improvised leadership."

The organization of steel was decisive if labor was to unionize other mass-production industries from which it had so far been barred. The business and financial community fully recognized the significance of the 1919 strike as a showdown between the open shop and industrial unionism. The United States Steel Corporation was backed to the hilt. J. P. Morgan assured Gary of his full approval of the stand he had taken in refusing to deal with the unions. Every effort was made—and made successfully—to hold out the bogey of Bolshevism as a justification for refusing even to consider the demands of the workers. The results of the strike were not only back to the twelve-hour day, but back to uncontrolled paternalism and anti-unionism in the country's most important industry.

Even before the end of the steel strike, the conflict in the bituminous coal fields came to a head. The United Mine Workers had concluded a contract with the operators covering the war period, and with the higher prices of 1919 asked for an adjustment in wages that had not been raised since 1917. They proposed a sixty per cent increase in pay and adoption of the thirty-hour week in order to combat the unemployment resulting from the falling-off of wartime need for fuel. The operators not only refused to consider the miners' demands, admittedly excessive, but they insisted that the old contract was still in effect because the war was not yet technically over. A strike that was to involve 425,000 miners was then called for November 1.

The danger to the national economy of any prolonged stoppage in the mining of coal, as on other occasions both before and since 1919, was a matter of grave public concern. The government had already warned that a strike would be illegal under wartime legislation governing the coal industry. To the consternation not only of the United Mine Workers but of American labor generally, the onetime friendly Wilson administration now took the drastic step of securing an injunction, granted by Judge Albert B. Anderson of the federal district court in Indianapolis, which prohibited any further strike activity by union officials and called upon them to cancel the strike order.

Intervention by the government, in the face of what had been taken by labor as a pledge not to use its wartime authority to suppress strikes, aroused a storm of protest. The American Federation of Labor condemned the injunction as "an outrageous proceeding . . . which strikes at the very foundation of justice and freedom." It called upon the miners not to give in to government pressure and promised them full support in continuing their struggle.

The acting president of the United Mine Workers in 1919 was a forty-year old labor leader who during the war years had been the union's chief statistician and who was wholly unknown to the public. But John L. Lewis was at once to step into the popular limelight. He did so by calling off the strike. Although he strongly attacked President Wilson for countenancing the use of an injunction, he was unwilling to follow the militant advice of the A.F. of L., and in what later years would seem to make very uncharacteristic action, advised surrender. "We are Americans," Lewis told newspapers in this first instance of his strike leadership, "we cannot fight our government."

The miners themselves, again in what seems an unusual role, refused to follow his orders. They stayed away from the pits in spite of cancellation of the strike order. Before they could be induced to return, further conferences were held in Washington and an understanding reached whereby the operators granted an immediate fourteen per cent wage increase and agreed to leave final settlement of wage demands and other issues in dispute to a special Bituminous Coal Commission. The final award raised the wage increase to twenty-seven per cent, almost half of what the miners had originally asked, but ignored altogether the demand for a thirty-hour week.

The strike had been ended by government action. Even though the miners won considerable gains, the important aspect of the controversy was the application of injunction law. A vital precedent had been established. In his willingness to comply with the government's orders, however, Lewis showed a keener realization of how far public opinion was prepared to go in suppressing strikes than the leaders of the A.F. of L. The resentment that had been displayed in the case of the steel strike was even more intensified when the coal miners threatened the nation with a fuel famine just as winter drew on.

President Wilson declared the coal strike to be "wrong both morally and legally." Congress endorsed his position, and editorials throughout the country applauded the use of the injunction. "Neither the miners nor any other organized minority," the *Chambersburg Public-Opinion* commented, "has the right to plunge the country into economic and social chaos. . . . A labor autocracy is as dangerous as a capital autocracy." "When enormous combinations of workingmen," the *Philadelphia Public Ledger* said, "deliberately enter upon a country-wide plan to take the country by the throat and compel the employers in that particular field of industry to yield to the demands of the men, they are engaged in an unlawful conspiracy." And the *Chicago Daily News* bluntly stated: "The public is weary of industrial strife. It is determined to protect itself."

The issue of Bolshevism was of course raised again. Senator Poindexter said that the strike was the penalty paid for an over-lenient governmental policy towards "anarchists and murderous communists." After its settlement the *New York Tribune* declared that the firm policy finally adopted by the administration was both an example and a warning: "Tell this in Russia, proclaim it on the streets of Moscow, sear it into the mind of all domestic disintegrators."

Although the strikes of 1919 resulted in a sharp setback for labor and there was a feeling of embittered disillusionment with what was regarded as betrayal at the hands of the Wilson administration, the wartime advance in unionism was not yet halted. Labor was still militant in spite of defeats. In many important areas it succeeded in winning the wage increases for which it fought, and there was continued expansion in union membership. Among the 110 unions now affiliated with the A.F. of L., machinists, non-operating railway workers, textile operatives and seamen showed especially important gains, and in such industries as food and clothing both unskilled and semi-skilled workers were being organized.

The A.F. of L. nevertheless found itself in an increasingly difficult position. The government support on which it had counted in pursuing its program of business unionism had given way to a revival of injunction law, and consequently there was strong pressure to adopt more aggressive tactics. The Federation leadership still refused, however, to be drawn into political action and in the face of new suggestions for a labor party, expressly reaffirmed the traditional non-political objectives that had always governed A.F. of L. policy. At a conference in December, 1919, a new "Labor's Bill of Rights" was proclaimed that called for union recognition, a living wage and restrictions on the use of injunctions, but beyond this the Federation would not go.

Circumstances soon made such a program more than ever difficult.

Before the close of the next year, a sudden, sharp depression struck the country. The collapse of the inflationary post-war boom led to tumbling prices all along the line, business failures, industrial stagnation, universal wage cuts, and unemployment on a large scale. By midsummer 1921, an estimated five million workers had lost their jobs. Industry took quick advantage of these circumstances to intensify its anti-union campaign. Injunctions and arrests broke a strike of the seamen's union and subsequent blacklisting reduced it to less than a fifth of its wartime strength. The packing house employes were so badly defeated that the industry reverted to the open shop. And in 1922 the railway shopmen, under fire from all sides, suffered an even more significant reverse.

The latter strike broke out when the Railway Labor Board, set up to govern employe relations after the railroads had been returned to private ownership in 1920, abrogated agreements that had been negotiated during the war, abolished overtime, and authorized wage cuts totaling $60,000,000. The railway brotherhoods were not affected by these pay reductions and the maintenance-of-way workers agreed to arbitration, but the members of the six shop craft unions were incensed at the board's apparent submission to employer pressure. A strike was called and on July 1,1922, the shopmen walked out, 400,000 strong.

From the very first they found the going hard. With the Railway Labor Board declaring their action an outlaw strike, the brotherhoods cooperating with management to keep the trains running, and President Harding warning against any interference with the mails, public sympathy was almost entirely against the shopmen. The popular attitude was perhaps most graphically revealed by the fact that among the strikebreakers brought in under the protection of deputized guards and militia, were hundreds of college boys. But this was not all. On September 1, as the strike appeared in any event about to collapse, the government stepped in to deliver the coup de grace. Attorney General Daugherty obtained from Judge James H. Wilkerson, of the federal district court in Chicago, what has often been described as "the most sweeping injunction ever issued in a labor dispute."

It prohibited picketing of all sorts, strike meetings, statements to the public, the expenditure of union funds to carry on the strike, and the use of any means of communication by the leaders to direct it. No one was permitted to aid the strikers "by letters, telegrams, telephones, word of mouth . . ." or to persuade anyone to stop work by "jeers, entreaties, arguments, persuasion, rewards or otherwise." Daugherty intended to break the strike at any cost. "So long and to the extent that I can speak for the government of the United States," he told the press, "I will use the power of the government within my control to prevent the labor unions of the country from destroying the open shop."

This drastic move caused vehement debate throughout the country. Not only newspapers sympathetic to labor but many others, perhaps influenced by partisan considerations in a good many cases, assailed the injunction as wholly unwarranted and a denial of freedom of speech. The *New York Evening Post* declared that it had been watching the impending defeat of the strike with a sense that it was well deserved, but that this was "a blow below the belt." The *Newark News* referred to the injunction as "gag law" and the *New York World* criticized it severely as "a clumsy step." On the other hand, conservative Republican papers tried to defend administration policy. The *New York Tribune,* the *Philadelphia Inquirer,* the *Boston Transcript* and the *Chicago Daily News* agreed that however broad the injunction, it was no broader than the lawlessness of the shopmen in threatening to paralyze all railroad transportation. The last word on the part of labor's enemies was perhaps spoken by the *Manufacturers' Record.* The injunction, it declared, merely commanded the workers "to cease their adulterous intercourse with lawlessness."

For the railway shopmen government intervention was the final straw. They eagerly seized upon a proposal by President Willard of the Baltimore and Ohio for separate settlements with individual roads and came to terms as best they could. The more friendly attitude of some lines enabled them to retain their organization for some 225,000 workers, but 175,000 were forced into company unions. Government intervention had swung the scales in favor of the employes and railway labor had suffered a disastrous blow.

The whole labor movement continued to lose ground during the 1921–1922 depression, and under the demoralizing influence of unemployment was unable to command the strength to defend itself as the capitalistic counter-attack, reinforced by injunction law, gathered steady momentum. Some unions were completely crushed; others suffered heavy losses. Labor had come out of the war strongly organized, determined to extend its gains, and confident that with friendly government protection it would be able to raise the standard of living for all American workers. Between 1920 and 1923, however, union membership as a whole fell from its peak figure of a little over 5,000,000 to approximately 3,500,000.

XIV: LABOR IN RETREAT

THE SEVEN YEARS from 1922 through 1929 were a period of expanding production, further concentration of economic power, rising national income and a conservative retreat to the laissez-faire principles governing our economy in the nineteenth century. Business largely dominated government and there were no new advances along the path of social and economic reform plotted out by pre-war progressives. Prosperity and a soaring stock market, speculation and two cars in every garage, were all that seemed to matter. A complacent people happily accepted in 1928 President Hoover's confident pronouncement that "we in America are nearer to the final triumph over poverty than ever before in the history of any land."

The 1920's were also "the era of wonderful nonsense." The younger generation was in revolt; speakeasies, bottleggers and gangsterism flourished mightily, and newspaper sensationalism fastened public attention upon million dollar prize fights, long distance marathons, the Scopes monkey trial, Lindberg's trans-Atlantic flight, bathing beauty contests. . . . The American scene was vivid, colorful, exciting.

The country's thirty-odd million non-agricultural workers played their full part in national development and generally shared in the mounting prosperity. Wages rose, and while two cars in every garage may have remained a distant dream, there was more left over in the average workingman's budget after payment for food, shelter and clothing than ever before in all our history. Wage earners were swept along with the general public in the orgy of installment buying of automobiles, vacuum cleaners, washing machines and electric refrigerators; and they paid their share of the cool $10,000,000,000 that was being spent annually for amusements and recreation. They even made their occasional flyers on the stock market, with William Green broadcasting upon "The

Worker and His Money" for the Wall Street investment firm of Halsey, Stuart and Company.

"A workman is far better paid in America than anywhere else in the world," wrote an enthusiastic French visitor, André Siegfried, in 1927, "and his standard of living is enormously higher. This difference, which was noticeable before the War, has been greatly accentuated since, and is now the chief contrast between the old and the new continents. . . ."

Looking upon the American scene as a whole, indeed, more and more wage earners appeared in the process of being absorbed into what was commonly called the middle class. With not only higher pay making possible conveniences and luxuries heretofore beyond their reach, but shorter working hours providing new leisure for the enjoyment of other aspects of life, working people were no longer set off in a distinct category as they perhaps once had been. Their recreation and amusements conformed increasingly to a general nationwide pattern. The automobiles that every Sunday crowded the country's motor roads; the huge weekly attendance at moving picture theaters; the growing audience for the new phenomenon of radio broadcasting were all manifestations of this growth of a more uniform society. If factory employes did not pay as much for their clothes as those in higher income brackets, they wore the same models. The sons and daughters of working people went to the great state universities in closer fulfillment of the century-old dream of equal education. In scores of ways, the workers were taking over the customs, the mores and the aspirations of the people generally. Social democracy appeared to have attained a new validity as the American way of life.

This process was aided by the curtailment of immigration. The status of industrial workers had been traditionally depressed by the annual influx of ignorant, penniless and unskilled immigrants. The adoption of the quota system in the mid-1920's, cutting down the annual number of alien arrivals from some five million to a bare 150,000, had an immense effect not only economically but also socially on the position of the worker. New paths of advancement were opened up by this curtailment of the traditional labor surplus, not necessarily paths leading out of the wage earning class to the employer class, but nevertheless promising a more assured status in our evolving society.

It was largely overlooked in the 1920's, however, that there were still
glaring inequalities in the way these material and social gains were
distributed among the workers, just as there were in the general distribution of prosperity in the country at large. Many segments of labor did
not appear to have been invited to the feast of plenty that was provided
by economic expansion, and even those groups of workers who profited
most from the upward trend of wages, could still feel that their share of
the awards of prosperity were by no means commensurate with the far
greater profits being made by business.

More important, unemployment was by no means banished from the
land and in some areas was unusually high. Technological advance,
which was constantly enabling industry to produce more goods with
fewer workers, led to declines in factory pay rolls in many basic industries. New machinery and labor saving devices in road construction,
textiles, the rubber industry and electrical equipment, to cite a few instances, cut the necessary labor for given output anywhere from twenty-
five to sixty per cent. It was estimated that in manufacturing, railroads
and coal mining, the labor of 3,272,000 fewer workers was necessary
to maintain old rates of production, and that increased economic activity
called for the addition of only 2,269,000. This left a net decline in employment in these industries of over 1,000,000. New opportunities in
trade and service industries helped to offset this situation, but there
was nevertheless persistent unemployment throughout the 1920's which
was estimated to have ranged in terms of man-years from ten to thirteen
per cent of the total labor supply. At least two million persons were
probably out of work even in 1928.

The insecurity of the industrial worker in respect to his job which
resulted from such conditions could never be wholly compensated by
high wages while he was at work. In their study of *Middletown*, the
Lynds found the fear of being laid off a constant obsession among the
working-class families they interviewed even though the community was
a prosperous one. The job was the thing in which they were interested
much more than wages or hours. Whatever the general statistics of
employment, the individual out of work faced the always bleak prospect of trying to find something else to do before his meager savings
melted away altogether.

As for the status of organized labor—rather than that of wage earners

generally—conditions in the 1920's had a paradoxical effect. In flat contradiction of what had been its record in every previous period of national prosperity, the labor movement lost ground. Not only was no
further progress made in organizing the unskilled workers in the mass
production industries, but existing trade unions steadily declined in
membership. We have seen that under the impact of the depression
in 1921, the total enrollment in American unions fell from over 5,000,000
to approximately 3,600,000. What was far more significant, however,
was the failure during succeeding years to make up any of these losses.
At the peak of 1929 prosperity, total union membership was 3,443,000—
less than it had been in any year since 1917.

In the happy light of continued good times and generally rising wages
for those who had work, this did not seem to matter. While job insecurity may have deterred some employes from joining unions in the
face of employer opposition, many of them apparently felt that unions
were no longer as necessary as they had formerly believed them to be.
What profit strikes or other agitation for collective bargaining when
the pay envelope was automatically growing fatter and a more abundant
life seemed to be assured with our rapid approach to the final triumph
over poverty?

There was no way for the workers to foresee in the halcyon atmosphere
of these days that just over the horizon was another depression, a more
devastating, long-lived depression than even those of the 1830's, the
1870's or the 1890's, when fifteen million helpless workers would find
themselves thrown on the streets, selling apples at corner stands, queue-
ing up before soup kitchens, crowding the breadlines. But its gathering
shadows were soon to extinguish the "golden glow" of the 1920's and
startlingly reveal the inherent weakness in labor's position. While the
entire country was to suffer grievously from the sudden collapse of the
New Economic Order, the impact of depression was once again to fall
most heavily upon wage earners.

The economic recovery that succeeded the brief collapse of 1921
found industry determined to prevent organized labor from recapturing
the position it had attained during the war. The anti-union campaign
revived in 1919 was intensified, and a new emphasis placed upon up-

holding the open shop. Theoretically, the open shop still implied nothing more than the right of the employer to hire whomever he chose, regardless of membership or non-membership in a union. But as in the early 1900's, it actually meant not only a policy whereby union members were almost invariably subject to discrimination, but refusal to recognize the union even if a majority of the employes belonged to it. The open shop, that is, became more than ever a recognized technique for denying the whole process of collective bargaining in the relations between employer and employe.

To promote the drive against unions, open shop associations were formed throughout the country in the 1920's, as they had been during earlier periods of industrial counter-attack. Fifty such employer groups were set up in New York, eighteen in Massachusetts, twenty in Connecticut, forty-six in Illinois, seventeen in Ohio and twenty-three in Michigan. Local chambers of commerce, manufacturers' associations and citizens' alliances further supported the campaign, and behind them stood the National Association of Manufacturers, the National Metal Trades Association and the League for Industrial Rights. With an inspiration born of the heightened nationalism of these postwar years, a conference of these various associations, meeting in Chicago in 1921, formally named the open shop the "American Plan." The traditional values of rugged individualism were set against the subversive, foreign concepts of collectivism. "Every man to work out his own salvation," the proponents of the American Plan proclaimed, "and not to be bound by the shackles of organization to his own detriment."

Full advantage was also taken of every indication of corrupt union leadership and racketeering to convince both workers and the public that they were being duped by the supposed advantages of collective bargaining. And both corruption and racketeering could be found in some unions during the feverish days of the 1920's. Unlawful collusion between union leaders and employers, extortion by labor bosses, and outright graft were exposed in the building trades and service industries of such cities as New York, Chicago and San Francisco. In some instances gangsters, sensing an opportunity for even greater profit than bootlegging, moved in on the unions and fleeced both employers and employes by intimidation and violence. The conservatives' attack upon labor unions, however, made no distinction between these occasional examples of corrupt and anti-social policies and the over-all picture of responsible leadership in the great majority of unions. When labor leaders were not luridly depicted as Bolsheviks plotting revolution, they were described as conscienceless spoilsmen, taking advantage of union members in every possible way to build up their own power and wealth.

"The palatial temples of labor," John E. Edgerton, president of the N.A.M. grandiloquently declared in 1925, "whose golden domes rise in exultant splendor throughout the nation, the millions of dollars extracted annually by the jewelled hand of greed from the pockets of wage earners and paid out in lucrative salaries, tell the pitiful story of a slavery such as this country never knew before." The employers of the nation were summoned to fulfill their duty "to break the shackles that have been forged upon the wrists of those who labor" and to free their employes from "the false leadership of designing pirates who parade in the guise of the workingmen's friend."

Nor was propaganda the only weapon employed in fighting unionism and promoting the open shop. Many employers continued to force yellow-dog contracts upon employes, to plant labor spies in their plants, to exchange black lists of undesirable union members, and openly follow the most discriminatory practices in hiring workers. It was the old story of intimidation and coercion, and when trouble developed in spite of all such precautions, strong-arm guards were often employed to beat up the trouble-makers while incipient strikes were crushed by bringing in strike-breakers under protection of local authorities.

In the coal fields, for example, unionism found itself particularly hard-pressed with factionalism and conflict within labor's own ranks making it highly vulnerable to employer attacks. Coal was a sick industry, failing to share in the country's general prosperity as a result of competition from new sources of power, and the mine owners were doubly determined to meet the problem of cutting production costs by beating down labor. They sought to undermine wage agreements already signed with the miners, and even more dangerously for unionism, began shifting production from the central bituminous field to non-unionized mines in such states as West Virginia, Kentucky, Tennessee and Alabama where they could operate without union restraints upon wages and hours.

The United Mine Workers were confronted with a knotty dilemma.

When strikes broke out in the non-unionized fields, there were insistent demands for help. Should the union violate its contracts in the central bituminous field by declaring a sympathetic strike, or should it stand by passively and allow conditions to deteriorate in the non-union mines and ultimately drag down the entire industry? John L. Lewis insisted upon maintaining contractual agreements. He refused assistance to all strikes not authorized by the union and proposed to meet the problem of the non-union mines by organizing the workers in the south and bringing them under disciplined control.

His program failed. The United Mine Workers steadily lost ground in the unionized fields, even though it concluded and maintained further agreements with operators, and organization in the non-unionized mines made no headway. The union agents were received in a manner somewhat at variance with traditional southern hospitality. They were tarred-and-feathered, ridden out of the company controlled mining towns on rails, beaten up by armed guards and sometimes murdered. Increasing strikes and disorder led in some mining communities to virtual civil war with an ugly record of violence, shootings and assassination.

The more radical elements among the United Mine Workers bitterly resented the failure of Lewis to call a general strike in support of the non-union miners. They helped to stir up discontent against a policy that was said to be both betraying the unorganized workers and destroying the union itself. There was rebellion among his own lieutenants and outlaw strikes even within union ranks. When Lewis countered by violently attacking his opponents as Communists, insisting upon complete submission to his authority and expelling local leaders who countenanced unauthorized walk-outs, there was widespread dissatisfaction among the rank and file who saw in his maintainence of contracts only surrender to anti-union operators.

Lewis managed during these difficult days to retain control of the union but it was badly split and in no position to maintain the influence that it had formerly exercised in the mine fields. The operators were able to whittle away the gains won through earlier national strikes, and the demoralization that marked the non-union mines spread into the organized areas of the central bituminous field. In 1922 the United Mine Workers had attained a strength of 500,000—some seventy per cent of all coal miners. The story of decline is perhaps most graphically revealed in a membership that had shrunk ten years later to 150,000.

In seeking to combat the anti-union campaign of employers, whether in the coal fields or elsewhere, labor could not look for any aid or support from government or the courts. The validity of yellow-dog contracts, so widely enforced in the southern coal mines, was still upheld; there was no legal redress for discrimination against union members, and successive court decisions wholly invalidated the supposed safeguards of the Clayton Act against injunction law.

Early in 1921, the Supreme Court stated in *Duplex Printing Press* v. *Deering* that nothing in the act legalized secondary boycotts or protected unions from injunctions that might be brought against them for conspiring in restraint of trade. Later that same year, in the notable case of *Truax* v. *Corrigan*, any hope of legal relief for labor was even more effectively killed. Arizona had passed a law that sought to do away altogether with injunctions in labor disputes and the Supreme Court in effect declared it to be unconstitutional. In preventing an employer from obtaining an injunction, it was decreed, the state took away his means of securing protection and thereby deprived him of property without due process of law. With such encouragement, employers resorted to injunctions even more frequently than in the days before passage of the Clayton Act. In 1928 the American Federation of Labor submitted a list of 389 that had been granted by either federal or state courts in the preceding decade, and this was obviously far from complete because of the large number unrecorded in the lower courts.

Perhaps the most revealing of all court decisions in this period was that in the previously noted case of *Adkins* v. *Children's Hospital* which was handed down in 1923. In invalidating a minimum wage law as a violation of constitutional safeguards of liberty of contract, it marked an abrupt reversal of the earlier trend toward sustaining such legislation, but it was even more significant because of a reassertion of the old concept that labor was a commodity. While the Supreme Court conceded "the ethical right of every worker, man or woman, to a living wage," it declared that the employer was not bound to furnish such a wage and that there was no warrant for the state to seek to establish it by legislation. Since in principle "there can be no difference between the case of selling labor and the case of selling goods," the court said, any attempt to compel the employer to pay a stated wage "is so clearly the product of a naked, arbitrary power that it cannot be allowed to stand under the Constitution of the United States."

Even Chief Justice Taft—the "injunction judge"—protested this conclusion and pointed out that individual employes were not on a level of equality in contracting with employers and were "peculiarly subject to the overreaching of the harsh and greedy employer." Associate Justice Holmes also dissented, with sharp criticism of the court's one-sided support of "the dogma Liberty of Contract."

Although both government and courts theoretically recognized the desirability of labor unions, even President Harding declaring that the right of workers to organize was "not one whit less absolute" than that of management and capital, they were consistently restricting the activity for which unions were formed. The one exception to such repressive policies during the 1920's was the passage and approval of the Railway Labor Act of 1926. This measure provided for the formation of unions among railway workers "without interference, influence or coercion," and set up special machinery for the settlement of all railway labor disputes. In upholding this law, the Supreme Court declared that the legality of collective action on the part of employes would be "a mockery if representation were made futile by interferences with freedom of choice." But rights upheld for railway workers were not extended to other classes of employes until the 1930's.

Confronted with legal restrictions on union activity and adverse court decisions, organized labor once again began to feel, as it had when it submitted its "Bill of Grievances" in 1906, that more direct political pressure would have to be exercised if it was to win any freedom of action in combatting the employers' anti-union campaign. The drive for a labor party that had first developed in 1919 when "Labor's Bill of Rights" was drawn up, gathered increasing force with further revelations of the Supreme Court's attitude. Even the A.F. of L. was unable wholly to resist the pressure for some sort of unified political action.

This agitation had first come to a head in 1922 when a Chicago meeting of some 128 delegates from various farm, labor and other liberal groups formed the Conference for Progressive Political Action. William H. Johnston of the powerful International Association of Machinists was a leading figure in this movement; the railway brotherhoods, smarting under the restrictions of the old Railway Labor Board and the revival of injunction law, backed it vigorously, and support was also forthcoming from twenty-eight national unions, eight state labor federations, several mid-western farmers' parties, the Women's Trade Union League, and the Socialists. When two years later both the Republicans and the Democrats nominated highly conservative candidates, Calvin Coolidge and John W. Davis, these progressives offered an independent nomination to Senator La Follette of Wisconsin. On the condition that no attempt be made to run candidates for other offices than the presidency and vice-presidency (Senator Wheeler of Montana being given the latter nomination), La Follette accepted this proposal and the Conference for Progressive Political Action formally entered the 1924 campaign.

The platform, declaring that the principal issue before the country was the control of government and industry by private monopoly, was in large measure a carry-over of the progressive principles of pre-war years. It called for public ownership of the nation's water power and of railroads, the conservation of natural resources, aid for farmers, tax reduction on moderate incomes, downward tariff revision, and remedial labor legislation. "We favor abolition of the use of injunctions in labor disputes," it was stated, "and declare for complete protection of the right of farmers and industrial workers to organize, bargain collectively through representatives of their own choosing, and conduct without hindrance cooperative enterprises."

The American Federation of Labor was at first opposed to the Conference for Progressive Political Action, but when both major parties ignored labor's demands, it took the unprecedented step of endorsing the La Follette candidacy. The Republican and Democratic parties, declared the executive council, have "flouted the desires of labor" and are "in a condition of moral bankruptcy which constitutes a menace and a peril to our country and its institutions." In spite of this attack on the major parties, however, the A.F. of L. aligned itself with the Progressives of 1924 very cautiously. In keeping with his policy during the political flirtations of pre-war years, Gompers tried to make it clear that the Federation made no commitments except to support La Follette as "a friend of labor" in this single campaign and was not countenancing a third party as such. While recognizing the need for legislation to free labor from the restrictions represented by injunction law, he reaffirmed his faith in "voluntarism" by declaring that "we do not accept government as the solution of the problems of life."

Even with these qualifications and reservations, many A.F. of L. leaders refused to go along with the action of the executive council. John L. Lewis and William Hutcheson, of the Carpenters, gave their support to Coolidge, and George L. Berry, of the Printing Pressmen, at the last moment shifted over to the camp of John W. Davis. Although the A.F. of L. had so far departed from its traditional policy as to come out openly for a presidential candidate of a third party, its support was somewhat left-handed and only $25,000 was raised as a campaign fund.

La Follette secured nearly five million votes—a substantial indication of popular discontent with both Republican and Democratic conservatism—but he carried only his home state of Wisconsin. The labor vote had not been delivered and the progressives' failure was widely interpreted as labor's failure. "The radical movement of this year," wrote the Washington correspondent of the *Seattle Times*, "represented the first attempt on the part of organized labor, through its governing bodies, to secure separate political action. The radical failure seems likely to end the possibility, for a good many years, of labor endorsement of a third-party presidential ticket." There was "no such thing as a labor vote," the *New York Herald Tribune* stated in analyzing the election returns, and the *Washington Star* agreed that "the workingmen of this country have not joined the insurgency against the established parties." More succinctly and colloquially, the *Philadelphia Bulletin* simply stated that "labor's incursion into politics was a dud."

The A.F. of L. apparently read very much the same meaning into the election. It promptly withdrew its support from the Conference for Progressive Political Action and reasserted its opposition to a third party. The entire movement collapsed. While in succeeding years labor continued to press for relief from injunctions, no further direct forays were made into politics. With even the Socialist vote falling off heavily, wage

earners appeared ready to accept, with the rest of the country, the conservative political pattern that continued to characterize the national
scene until the advent of the New Deal.

It was shortly after this unsuccessful campaign—in December, 1924—
that the grand old man of the A.F. of L., Samuel Compers, died at the
age of seventy-four. In his later years it had become increasingly difficult
for him to carry on his work. Nothing except death, however, could make
him surrender the power he had held so securely ever since the Federation had been established forty years earlier. His control had momentarily
appeared to be threatened in 1921 when Lewis entered the lists as a
presidential candidate, but Gompers had put down this incipient rebellion as he had so many others. He was the acknowledged leader of
organized labor and there was no real rival to his pre-eminence in this
field. Both the successes and the failures of the A.F. of L. largely reflected the application of the conservative, pragmatic philosophy he so
consistently upheld.

Labor mourned his death and so also did the business community.
Newspaper editorials were an interesting commentary on the extent to
which his moderate policies had won confidence and were accepted as
forestalling more radical tendencies on the part of the nation's workers.
Gompers was said to have held trade unionism to a straightforward,
non-political path by the sheer force of his personality, and he was
generally applauded for having consistently tried to bridge the gap between capital and labor. His death was termed a loss to America primarily because it opened up the possibility of a split within the A.F. of L.
that might enable extremist elements to come into power.

When the choice of the Federation for its new president fell upon
William Green, the business community consequently breathed a sigh
of relief. For Green too stood for conservatism in labor policies, and
assurance seemed to be made doubly sure by an immediate statement
to the press that it would be his "steadfast purpose to adhere to those
fundamental principles of trade-unionism so ably championed by Mr.
Gompers." The country at once felt that there was no need for concern
over possible socialistic or other third party deviations from the traditional A.F. of L. program. "Labor is safe under his leadership," the

Richmond Times Despatch declared in a typical comment upon Green's election; "capital has nothing to fear, and the public is fortunate in having him as spokesman of a highly important group of citizens."

Green was born in Coshocton, Ohio, in 1873. Like so many labor leaders, he was a second generation American, the son of Welsh immigrants, and as a boy had followed his father into the coal pits in Ohio. Joining the United Mine Workers, he was chosen a sub-district union president in 1906 and started upon a gradual climb to the high councils of organized labor. As leader of the miners in Ohio, he was sent to the state legislature as a trade union representative, and then elected secretary-treasurer of the United Mine Workers in reward for his faithful services. When in 1913 Gompers decided that the miners should be represented on the executive council of the A.F. of L., he turned to Green and appointed him an eighth vice-president. As death one by one removed the higher officers, Green slowly rose in scale to third vice-president. It was from this post, with the backing of Lewis, that he was raised to the pinnacle of the A.F. of L. presidency.

He appeared in 1924 a rather undistinguished figure without the forceful, dramatic characteristics that in different ways marked Gompers, Mitchell and Lewis. Sober and sedate—he had taught Sunday School as a young man and originally hoped to train for the ministry—he was not one to drink beer with the boys in the Gompers' tradition. His teetotalism was rather a reminder of Terence Powderly. Secretary of Labor Perkins was later to describe him as "the mildest and most polite of men" and his plump figure, round, humorless face, soft voice and quiet manner did not add up to a very arresting personality. But Green was a great joiner, belonging to the Elks, the Odd Fellows and the Masons, and his pleasant, affable manner and general friendliness made him popular. He was also respected for his unquestioned integrity and conscientious, hard-working devotion to the concerns of union labor.

In 1917 Green had declared himself, as a result of his own experience with the United Mine Workers, to be wholly in favor of industrial unionism, and this was one reason for the support Lewis gave him. "The organization of men by industry rather than by craft," Green had stated, "brings about a more perfect organization, closer cooperation. . . . It is becoming more and more evident that if unskilled workers are forced to work long hours and for low wages, the interests of the skilled are constantly menaced thereby." But in his new office all this was forgotten. Craft unionism as opposed to industrial unionism was to remain the basic policy of the A.F. of L., and no real attempts would be made during the 1920's to press for union recognition among the unskilled workers in mass-production industries.

In proving himself to be quite as conservative as Gompers had been, Green appeared no more willing than his predecessor to recognize the possible need for changes in the A.F. of L. policy to meet changing circumstances. He continued to uphold the concept of voluntarism which Gompers had so stoutly defended with that emphasis upon "strong, red-blooded, rugged independence" which might well have come from President Hoover himself. It was not until 1932, when the impact of the depression had undermined many A.F. of L. principles, that Green finally gave up his opposition to such forms of state intervention as old-age pensions and unemployment insurance.

The conservatism if not timidity of the A.F. of L. weakened all organized labor in the face of the anti-union drive of employers in the 1920's. But yellow-dog contracts and injunctions were not the only barriers in the path of unionization. The labor movement was also being killed by kindness. Industry complemented its aggressive enforcement of the open shop with a developing program of welfare capitalism. It sought to discourage trade unionism by making working conditions so favorable that the workers would no longer consider unions of any value, at the same time increasing production and industrial efficiency through closer labor-management cooperation.

Industry had long since tried to promote greater production per worker, to reduce labor turnover, and generally to improve technical standards through a process of "rationalization" in industrial management. During the progressive era, a program developed by Frederick W. Taylor had begun to be widely adopted. Time and motion studies, the development of piece work, increased productivity on the assembly line, and "scientific" adjustment of employe relations were the subject of universal experimentation. In the post-war era "Taylorism" won even wider attention in the constant search to reduce manufacturing costs. Trade unionism had no place in this program of industrial efficiency, but employers recognized the need for some substitute that would help to create the idea of "one big family" working cooperatively in the mutual interests of industry and labor. They thought they had found it in shop councils, employe representation plans, and most specifically, company unions.

An early move along such lines was a program adopted by the Colorado Fuel and Iron Company after the strike that had culminated in the bloody massacre at Ludlow in 1914. The Rockefeller interests had refused to recognize the United Mine Workers, and instead instituted a company union that was to provide "industrial democracy" without the dangerous implications of any association with the organized labor movement. The Rockfeller experiment was followed by many other corporations, 125 setting up company unions in one form or another during the war, and the open-shop campaign of post-war years led to still further emphasis upon this trend toward employer-controlled substitutes for outside unions. By 1926 the number of company unions had increased to over 400, with a membership of some 1,369,000, or about half the membership of unions affiliated with the A.F. of L.

As personnel managers made further studies of the labor problem (almost three thousand books on the subject were published in the first five years after the war) other measures were adopted to strengthen the role of the company unions and win employe allegiance. Scores and then hundreds of corporations set up profit-sharing schemes, paid out bonuses in company stock, or otherwise sought to give the workers a direct financial interest in corporate activities. It was estimated in 1928 that over a million employes owned or had subscribed for over a billion dollars worth of stock in the companies by which they were employed. Group insurance policies, which were forfeited should the employe change his job, were also introduced and some five million industrial workers were insured under such plans by 1926. At the same time, various old-age pension programs were established, free clinics set up to help maintain health standards, and employe cafeterias and lunchrooms installed. Under the direction of personnel departments or company unions, picnics, glee clubs, dances, sports events and other recreational activities were also sponsored for plant employes, while hundreds of company magazines rang all the changes on goodwill and friendly human contacts between labor and management.

The amplifications of welfare capitalism knew no limits and it succeeded to a very considerable extent in improving working conditions and indirectly increasing employe income. Its immediate benefits for the worker were very real. Yet the entire program remained wholly subject to the control of the corporation sponsor, and there was no reality to employe representation under such conditions. It was not without significance that those corporations which most generously provided for the workers' welfare were also those most strongly anti-union in their basic policies. How quickly welfare capitalism might collapse—and especially its stock distribution program—should prosperity give way to depression was hardly realized at the time. Few of the members of company unions understood how dependent they had become upon their employers for the favors they were receiving in lieu of union recognition and the advantages of genuine collective bargaining.

This lesson would be learned after 1929, but in the meantime welfare capitalism won many victories. "The assertion may be boldly made," S. B. Peck, chairman of the Open Shop Committee of the National Association of Manufacturers, declared, "that the decreasing membership in most of the unions and the great difficulty they are experiencing in holding their members together, is due to the fact that the employers—notably the once so-called 'soulless corporations'—are doing more for the welfare of the workers than the unions themselves." The Committee on Education and Labor of the Seventy-Sixth Congress reported, in 1926, that the N.A.M. had done its work in combatting unionism so well that it was able to settle back "to the quiet enjoyment of the fruits of their efforts during the years of prosperity."

The consequences of the double-edged program of seeking to suppress bona fide labor unions and building up employe allegiance through the benefits of company unions and welfare capitalism, were seen not only in declining membership for the A.F. of L. but in a greater measure of industrial peace than the country had enjoyed for many years. This does not mean there were no strikes. Those on the part of the depressed textile workers, for example, were persistent, hard-fought and marked by violence and bloodshed. In such southern mill towns as Gastonia and Marion, North Carolina, and Elizabethton, Tennessee, open clashes between strikers and state troopers led to heavy death tolls. The overall record, however, was one of a steadily declining number of labor disputes. During the war period, the total number of strikes had averaged over 3000 a year and involved well over a million workers annually. By the mid-1920's, such figures had been halved. At the close of the decade, the annual number of strikes was around 800 and engaged only some 300,000 workers, or slightly more than one per cent of the aggregate labor force.

Far from seeking to revive labor militancy, the American Federation of Labor made every effort to encourage labor-management cooperation. Green was destined to accept proudly in 1930 the gold medal of the Roosevelt Memorial Association for his outstanding services in allaying industrial strife. While the A.F. of L. could not countenance company unions, it passively acquiesced in many other aspects of welfare capitalism. Content with the gains that its own membership was making as wages rose in response to the demand for skilled workers, little effort was made to broaden the scope of union activity. At the close of the 1920's the organized labor movement appeared to be accepting as complacently as any other element in our national economy the promise of assured economic advance.

It has been said that the nation's workers generally experienced a greater rise in wages during the 1920's than in any comparable period. Annual earnings, indeed, rose between 1921 and 1928 from an average of $1,171 to $1,408. In terms of actual purchasing power, for there was no comparable rise in living costs, this has been estimated to represent a gain of more than twenty per cent.

Both actual wages and their rate of increase were nevertheless very uneven. The hourly rate for bricklayers in New York rose, between 1920 and 1928, from $1.06 to $1.87 and that of newspaper compositors from 92 cents to $1.20, but in the case of bituminous miners, there was a decline in the hourly rate from 83 cents to 73 cents, and for mule spinners in the cotton mills a drop from 83 cents to 63 cents. The gains of the 1920's went primarily to the skilled workers and trade union members. Millions of working class families still had incomes of less than $1000 a year even in 1929.

As far as hours of work were concerned, the general picture shows substantial improvement. The eight-hour day generally prevailed and

It was estimated that since the opening of the century, the working week for wage earners had been cut from fifteen to thirty per cent. But wide discrepancies appear when available statistics are broken down. While a 43.5 hour week was the average in the building trades, for instance, a 60-hour week was still being maintained for blast furnace workers in the steel mills.

Factors other than wages and hours also affected the well-being of the nation's workers in these as in other years. The speed-up in industrial processes added to the strain and nervous tension under which men operating machines and working on the assembly line constantly labored. For many factory employes the substitution of wholly mechanical operations for the exercise of individual skills meant monotony and boredom that were not always compensated by higher wages and shorter hours. While this was nothing new in the history of industrialization, it was more than ever true during the 1920's.

With the march of the machine also holding over the worker's head the constant threat of losing his job, the industrial workers of the country were consequently still far from attaining that security and well-being that was the goal of organized labor. The gains that had been made were more precarious than impersonal statistics might suggest, especially since those that might be attributed to welfare capitalism were wholly unprotected by any contractual understanding. So far as organizational strength and aggressive trade unionism had been sacrificed in accepting labor-management cooperation in place of genuine collective bargaining, the wage earners had seriously undermined their hard-won capacity to protect their own interests. They were almost wholly dependent on the continued willingness and ability of employers to treat them fairly.

This was the situation when depression gradually engulfed the country after the sudden collapse of the stock market in 1929. The story is a familiar one: the shock to national confidence as billions of dollars of security values melted away, the frantic assertions that conditions were fundamentally sound, and the slow strangulation of business as the cracks in our industrial system slowly widened and the whole structure seemed threatened with collapse. The depression was another historic turn in the economic cycle, but its impact on society was greater than that of any depression in the past.

Before it had run its course, farm prices fell to forty per cent of their previous levels, the value of exports declined to a third of their former peak, industrial production was almost halved, and the balance sheet of corporate enterprise revealed a deficit of $5,650,000,000. In three years, a national income estimated at $82,885,000,000 had dropped to $40,074,000,000. Even more significant—and far more devastating—unemployment rose to over seven million by the close of 1930, and then in another two years to something like fifteen million.

Statistics, however, give only an inadequate idea of the dire effects of the depression. They can hardly depict the scrimping and saving forced upon millions of middle-class families, the privations and hardships caused those in lower income groups, and the cruel suffering of the unemployed workers and their families. The bread lines, the tramp jungles so ironically called Hoovervilles that sprang up in the outskirts of countless cities, the army of young men and boys wandering back and forth across the country in hopeless search for jobs, were a tragic commentary upon the glowing mirage of the era that was to abolish poverty.

The country's wage earners stood by helplessly as the depression cut into production and paralyzed normal trade, causing many factories, mines and workshops to close down altogether. Early in 1930 a series of industrial conferences had been held in Washington at which employers promised to uphold wages and maintain employment. The workers accepted these pledges in good faith. Like the rest of the country, they could not believe that prosperity had so suddenly collapsed and were still hopeful that recovery was just around the corner. But there were no collective bargaining agreements in the mass production industries —steel, automobiles, electrical equipment—to compel observance of wage scales. Pay checks were gradually cut, and then all too often replaced by blunt notices of dismissal.

The whole program of welfare capitalism also went abruptly by the board as employers were forced to withdraw the benefits that in the piping days of prosperity had often been granted in the place of wage increases. Profit-sharing schemes, employe stock ownership, industrial pensions and even workers' health and recreational projects were rapidly discarded. Circumstances forced retrenchment, but in many cases it was carried out at the expense of the workers while full dividends were still being paid on common stock. The company unions were powerless to protect their members' interests. Reliance upon welfare capitalism had proved to be a delusion.

Organized labor seemed to be completely demoralized. The national unions did not even try to exercise any direct pressure upon the government in favor of recovery measures, and their strength had been so sapped by the retreat before welfare capitalism that concerted action along economic lines was out of the question in the face of nationwide unemployment. Strike activity was at a minimum and in 1930 fell to a new low point when less than 200,000 workers were involved in all work stoppages. Continued declines in union membership were also the general rule. The total number of organized workers fell by 1933 to less than 3,000,000—or the approximate level of 1917.

In some ways the most surprising phenomenon of the depression years was this apathetic attitude on the part of industrial workers while the unemployment figures steadily mounted and the bread lines lengthened. There was no suggestion of revolt against an economic system that had let them down so badly. There was no parallel of the ugly railway strikes of 1877 or Debs' Rebellion in 1894. In Park Avenue drawing rooms and the offices of Wall Street brokers, there was a great deal of talk of "the coming revolution," but the unemployed themselves were too discouraged and too spiritless to be interested.

Writing in *Harper's* in mid-summer 1932, George Soule found that while there was a distinct drift on the part of intellectuals into the radical camp, with rising interest in communism, no such trend could be discovered in the ranks of labor. "The masses are in a desperate condition all right," he wrote, "but unfortunately there is no sign that they feel the slightest resentment. They just sit at home and blame prohibition. . . . Like the Republican administration, they are awaiting nothing more drastic than the return of prosperity." In another article in the same magazine, Elmer Davis also commented with astonishment on "the quiet acceptance of the situation by men who have lost their jobs and everything else through the operation of the policies that were to abolish poverty."

There was one unexpected occasion when Green, addressing the A.F. of L., "dropped his gentle manner," as described in the *Literary Digest*, "to let loose a verbal blast as thunderous as a crash of coal in the Ohio mine where he used to swing a pick." Unless a shorter work day and shorter work week were adopted to increase employment, he told a cheering audience, "we will secure it through force of some kind." Asked by eager reporters just what he meant by force, he quickly explained that he meant economic force. Even this vague hint of labor militancy, however, awoke concern. "Is this the time for industrial war?" asked the *Boston Transcript*. Any suggestion of trying "to coerce industry by the strike method" was deeply deplored by the *Washington Post*. The *Herald Tribune* felt that Green had suffered "an attack of nerves."

But this outburst was an exception to the generally cautious attitude of the American Federation of Labor. Maintaining until the end of 1932 its strong opposition to unemployment insurance, it urged nothing more concrete in the way of government action to promote recovery or relieve unemployment than "the stabilization of industry" through adoption of its program for increasing jobs by a shorter work week.

The press praised this attitude. "Today labor stands patient and hopeful," the *Cleveland Plain Dealer* wrote. ". . . Never has there been a period of depression so free from labor strife. Unemployment has harassed it. Closed factories have taken away its livelihood. But, in the face of enormous hardship, labor has showed its good citizenship and sturdy American stamina. Labor deserves a salute." Whether the workers themselves were satisfied with this generous salute instead of jobs may be open to question. The *Philadelphia Record*, reflecting a more realistic attitude than that of the *Plain Dealer*, declared that the Federation's stand against unemployment insurance was a ghastly jest. "Liberty to starve?" it asked, "Is that what Mr. Green fights for?"

The consequences of government inaction and labor passivity were with every passing month more graphically reflected in the increasing number of jobless workers dependent upon state or private charity. The vaunted campaign to spread the work did not seem to have any effect other than to reduce the workers' income, seldom opening up any opportunities for those who had already been laid off.

Some of the states attempted to pass legislation that would improve working conditions. New workingmen's compensation laws were adopted in a number of instances, fourteen states approved old age pensions, and Wisconsin pioneered with a new Labor Bill of Rights and unemployment insurance. Early in March, 1932, a highly significant victory for organized labor as a whole was won through the passage by Congress of the Norris–La Guardia Act. This measure at long last declared it to be public policy that labor should have full freedom of association, without interference by employers; outlawed yellow-dog contracts, and prohibited federal courts from issuing injunctions in labor disputes except under carefully defined conditions. Although at least one congressman rose to state that this bill represented a "long march in the direction of Moscow," it was overwhelmingly supported in both the House and Senate and received widespread popular approval. For all the importance of the Norris–La Guardia Act in pointing the way to the labor policies of the New Deal, however, it did not meet the immediate problem of the nation's wage earners. It held no solution for unemployment.

As conditions reached their nadir in the summer of 1932, the presidential campaign offered a first practical opportunity for political protest against the failure of the Hoover Administration to cope adequately with the depression. Franklin D. Roosevelt, as Democratic nominee, clearly demonstrated his sympathy for the working masses of the country and for "the forgotten man at the bottom of the economic pyramid." He repeatedly stressed the imperative need to provide direct relief and vigorously advocated unemployment insurance. Yet the American Federation of Labor declared its neutrality in the presidential campaign. Willing to endorse friends of labor among the congressional candidates, it refused to announce itself in favor of either Hoover or Roosevelt. There can be no question that industrial workers helped to swell the great popular majority that Roosevelt won in 1932, but the A.F. of L. did not officially have any part in his election.

The campaign over, no further developments took place in respect to labor problems and economic conditions continued to deteriorate. The American Federation of Labor urged a thirty-hour week and expanded public works; it finally came out in favor of unemployment insurance. But no positive action was taken to promote such measures. Labor was waiting, like the rest of the country, to see what the new President would do.

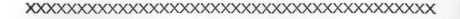

XV: THE NEW DEAL

"... A HOST OF UNEMPLOYED CITIZENS face the grim problem of existence, and an equally great number toil with little return. Only a foolish optimist can deny the dark realities of the moment. . . . Our greatest primary task is to put people to work."

When Franklin D. Roosevelt came into office in March, 1933, his stirring inaugural held out a promise of action in coping with the national emergency that created throughout the nation a new feeling of hope and confidence. The government was at long last prepared to accept the responsibility of extending that measure of direct aid to agriculture and labor, as well as industry, which alone could restore the disrupted balance of our national economy. As the President spiritedly declared that "the only thing we have to fear is fear itself," the country felt that it had found the leadership for want of which it had been floundering helplessly in the deepening morass of depression.

There was nothing in Roosevelt's immediate program that applied directly to labor except his promise to put people to work. Social security —with unemployment and old-age insurance—was already under consideration, but the labor provisions that were to be written into the National Recovery Administration codes, the Wagner Act and the Fair Labor Standards Act were not envisaged when he entered upon office. They evolved gradually out of the needs of the times. A basic understanding and sympathy for the rights of labor were nevertheless inherent in the emerging philosophy of the New Deal. For the first time in our history a national administration was to make the welfare of industrial workers a direct concern of government and act on the principle that only organized labor could deal on equal terms with organized capital in bringing about a proper balance between these two rival forces in a capitalistic society. Heretofore labor unions had been tolerated, they were now to be encouraged.

The advent of the New Deal was thus to prove a momentous watershed in the history of the labor movement. Age-old traditions were smashed; new and dynamic forces released. Greater gains were to be won by wage earners than in any previous period in our history, and both the economic and the political power of labor was immeasurably enhanced. The struggles, hardships and defeats of a century appeared to have culminated in the possibility of complete attainment of the workers' historic objectives.

The premise upon which New Deal policy toward labor was based had already been set forth in the general recognition of its right to organize written into the Norris–La Guardia Act. When the Roosevelt administration adopted the over-all experiment in economic control of the National Industrial Recovery Act, somewhat dubiously based upon the powers of Congress to regulate interstate commerce, a first step was taken toward implementing this right to organize in the famous—or as viewed in some quarters infamous—Section 7(a).

This important move in support of labor's interests was an end result of highly complicated manoeuvering. In March, 1933, a bill was introduced into Congress by Senator Black and Representative Connery to establish the thirty-hour week that the A.F. of L. had been demanding as a means of spreading work and relieving unemployment. Roosevelt was very skeptical of its value unless there was included in it some provision for maintaining wages. In behalf of the President, Secretary of Labor Perkins consequently suggested amendments that would have combined with the reduction in work hours a guarantee of minimum wages. The theory underlying the new bill was not unlike that promoted by Ira Steward in the 1860's—except that increasing the pay through decreasing the hours was subordinated to wage stabilization. There was as yet no idea of going any further. "When I talked with the President in April, 1933, about the Black bill," Secretary Perkins has recorded, "his mind was as innocent as a child's of any such program as N.R.A."

The idea of minimum wages awoke a storm of opposition from business interests and was not too enthusiastically supported by labor. In place of such a limited approach to the problems of depression, it was urged in both camps that the administration raise its sights and institute a far broader recovery program. The United States Chamber of Commerce proposed that business should be freed from the restrictions of the anti-trust laws and encouraged to work out its own salvation. As a spokesman for labor, John L. Lewis advocated that the controls over production, prices and wages that he had been demanding in coal mining should be extended to industry as a whole. As scores of such plans began to arouse increasing interest both in and out of Congress, several independent groups of presidential advisers began to try to work out specific measures. Little real progress was being made, however, and Roosevelt decided to intervene. Withdrawing administration support from the Black–Connery bill, in which at best his interest had been lukewarm, he called upon his advisers to get together on a common program, shutting themselves up in a locked room if necessary until they could come to agreement.

The plan finally adopted and incorporated into the National Industrial Recovery Act was to allow industry to write its own codes of fair competition, but to compensate labor for granting industry such a free hand by providing special safeguards for its interests. Section 7(a) of the new measure, drawing in part from provisions of the Railway Labor Act of 1926, stipulated that the industrial codes should contain three important provisions: employes should have the right to organize and bargain collectively through representatives of their own choosing, free from interference, restraint or coercion on the part of employers; no one seeking employment should be required to join a company union or to refrain from joining any labor organization of his own choosing; and employers should comply with maximum hours, minimum rates of pay and other conditions of employment approved by the President. Considering the new law as a whole, the ideas underlying the Chamber of Commerce program, labor's traditional demand for union recognition, and certain modified provisions of the Black–Connery bill were brought together in a single omnibus measure, and to this over-all plan was further added, under a separate title, a vast public works program authorizing appropriations of $3,300,000,000.

The basic purpose of the National Industrial Recovery Act, as approved in June, 1933, was in the President's words, "to put people back to work." It was at once to ensure reasonable profits for industry by preventing unfair competition and disastrous overproduction, and living wages for labor by spreading work through shorter hours. Roosevelt termed the law "the most important and far-reaching legislation ever enacted by the American Congress."

The N.R.A. was virtually to collapse through internal stress and strain even before it was finally outlawed by the Supreme Court—a generally unlamented victim of early New Deal enthusiasm. Nevertheless its implications for labor went far toward justifying Roosevelt's statement. The guarantee of collective bargaining and establishment of wage and hour controls by congressional action, in spite of loopholes that were to develop in enforcement of the law, represented the most forward steps ever taken by government in the field of industrial relations. And these steps were not to be retraced even when other provisions of the N.R.A. went by the board. The New Deal picked up the shattered fragments of Section 7(a) and put them together again, far more carefully, in the Wagner Act and the Fair Labor Standards Act. There was to be no retreat under Roosevelt from this progressive advance in safeguarding the interest of industrial workers.

In June, 1933 the N.R.A. was hailed enthusiastically throughout the country. It is true that such a conservative organ as the *Manufacturer's Record*, looking with a jaundiced eye upon any concessions to labor whatsoever, was soon to state that "labor agitators . . . are trying to establish a labor dictatorship in this country," but this critical note was lost in the general chorus of excited approval for the new recovery program. In the bright dawn of its inception, the N.R.A. started off under the dynamic direction of General Hugh Johnson amid a fanfare of patriotic oratory and popular demonstrations. As symbols of code acceptance, Blue Eagles were soon being proudly displayed the length and breadth of the land.

Labor joyfully acclaimed Section 7(a). "Millions of workers throughout the nation," William Green declared, "stood up for the first time in their lives to receive their charter of industrial freedom." Countless unions were overnight aroused from the doldrums of depression lethargy. Confident in the protection of the law, organizers set out to restore the depleted strength of moribund locals, form new ones, and invade territory from which they had formerly been barred. In the coal fields, placards at the mine pits announced "President Roosevelt wants you to join the union." The workers themselves often did not wait for the official emissaries from A.F. of L. headquarters but set up their own locals, and then applied for charters from the parent organization. The burst of labor activity had no precedent except perhaps the dramatic growth of the Knights of Labor half a century earlier.

When the A.F. of L. met for its annual convention in October, President Green confidently announced that an unofficial count showed over 1,500,000 new recruits added to its ranks, recouping the losses of over a decade and bringing total membership to close upon four million.[1] He envisaged a goal of ten millions, eventually twenty-five.

The greatest gains were in the so-called industrial unions,[2] and particularly in those that had suffered most heavily during the depression. Within a few months the United Mine Workers recouped 300,000 members and concluded new agreements in the formerly non-union coal fields of Kentucky and Alabama; the International Ladies' Garment Workers added 100,000 to its rolls, recapturing lost territory in New York and runaway shops in other parts of the country, and the Amalgamated Clothing Workers made up its earlier losses with some 50,000 recruits. But this was not all. Under the spur of Section 7(a), the A.F. of L. even appeared to be ready, with the new slogan of "Organize the Unorganized in the Mass Production Industries," to invade territory from which it had formerly held aloof. Nearly 100,000 workers were said to have been organized in the automobile industry, 90,000 in steel, 90,000 in lumber yards and sawmills, and 60,000 in rubber.

It was soon to develop, however, that this burst of activity among the unorganized workers had a very precarious foundation and the proud boasts of President Green were not wholly justified. The traditional skepticism of the A.F. of L. toward industrial unionism, reinforced

---

[1] These figures were a broad estimate. It might be noted at this point, however, that all general statistics on union membership are only approximate because of widely different practices in reporting enrollment. Real exactitude is never possible. See Leo Wolman, *Ebb and Flow in Unionism*, National Bureau of Economic Research, Washington, 1936.

[2] In distinction to craft unions, whose jurisdiction was limited to one or several allied trades, industrial unions exercised a jurisdiction over all or most occupations, skilled or unskilled, within an entire industry. They were sometimes called vertical unions at this time.

by the determination of old-line craft union leaders to retain control of the labor movement, blocked any campaign to organize the workers in mass production along industrial lines. The accepted technique was to form so-called federal unions, directly affiliated with the A.F. of L. itself, until jurisdictional problems could be worked out and the new union membership in steel, automobiles, rubber and other industries gradually absorbed into existing unions. Between 1932 and 1934, the number of federal charters outstanding rose from 307 to 1798. This was not the form of organization, however, that met the real need of unskilled workers and very soon the initial flurry of activity in the mass production industries began to subside.

Such evidence of failure gave rise to an insistent demand on the part of the more progressive leaders within the A.F. of L. for a change of tactics. They called for a more aggressive campaign to bring the unorganized workers into the fold and the immediate granting of industrial union charters in automobile and steel, in rubber, aluminum and radio. When the conservative oligarchy in control of the A.F. of L. rejected these demands, a widening breach between adherents of craft unions and industrial unions led to what was to prove a critical split in the ranks of labor. Its unity was shattered at the moment of its greatest opportunity. The labor insurgents set up their own Committee for Industrial Organization, under circumstances to which we shall return, and a new chapter was opened in labor history.

In the meantime, the older unions had also discovered that the high promise of their new charter of liberties was not to be realized without further struggles. Pending adoption of the N.R.A.'s industrial codes, all employers were asked to subscribe to the President's Re-Employment Agreement—a blanket code in which a forty-hour week was prescribed, minimum wages were set at either $15 a week or 40 cents an hour, and child labor abolished for all those under sixteen. More permanent agreements were then to be drawn up by the trade associations, with the workers' interests supposedly protected by a labor advisory board in each industry. In the final analysis, however, the trade associations generally acted independently and employes had no real part in the formulation of the permanent codes. A majority of them established the forty-hour week, with minimum wages from $12 to $15 a week, but while some ninety-five per cent of the nation's industrial workers were ultimately given this protection, labor's rights in other respects were largely ignored. The safeguards for collective bargaining were either not definitely recognized or were gradually whittled away. The automobile manufacturers, for example, succeeded in having inserted in their code a clause that enabled them to select, retain or advance their employes "on the basis of individual merit." In theory such a right could hardly be disputed, but for anti-union employers it provided the means to discriminate against union members on any convenient pretext. President Roosevelt subsequently ordered that interpretations of Section 7(a) should not be included in any code. It did not interfere with the bona fide right of the employer to hire whom he chose, he asserted, but it clearly prohibited the exercise of this right as a device to keep employes from joining a union.

As industry began to recover and fearful employers crept cautiously out of the cyclone cellars into which they had been driven by the depression, further resentments developed over the concessions granted labor in return for management's freedom to control production and fix prices. The *Iron Age* warned of the dangers of what it chose to call "collective bludgeoning" and *Steel* stated that with organized labor "baring its teeth," every effort should be made to retain the open shop. Viewing fearfully predictions of a membership of 10,000,000 in the A.F. of L., the *Commercial and Financial Chronicle* declared that the country would then have "an organized body, or class within the State, more powerful than the State itself. That in itself would mean the extinction of freedom and independence. In the end oppression would prevail everywhere. . . ." Responding to such dire warnings, some employers bluntly refused to comply at all with the labor provisions of the codes and others sought every possible means to evade the spirit if not the letter of the law.

One of the principal weapons used in combatting the clear intent of Section 7(a) was the company union. Employes could not be required to join such an organization, but their employers were still free to exercise every possible kind of pressure in making it seem advisable. And this was done so effectively that enrollment in company unions rapidly rose from 1,250,000 to 2,500,000. The N.R.A. not only tacitly approved such unions, stating that the government had not endorsed "any particular form of organization," but encouraged them by allowing proportional representation in collective bargaining. Even when a national union enrolled a majority of workers in a plant, it was not accepted as spokesman for the whole labor force and management could still deal with any other employe group. Such an interpretation of the law was attacked by labor as completely nullifying the whole principle of collective bargaining. The N.R.A. was bitterly assailed as the National Run Around and the Blue Eagle was said to have changed into a vulture.

As the old lines of industrial strife were again tightened, the N.R.A. thus found itself caught between two fires: the recalcitrant attitude of many employers and the militant demands of labor. First a National Labor Board, then special boards in certain industries, and finally in July, 1934, a National Labor Relations Board were set up to handle the growing volume of industrial disputes. They failed to win the confidence of either management or labor and often appeared to be working at cross purposes with the N.R.A. itself. The National Labor Relations Board stood for important principles. Its support for majority representation, secret elections and bona fide collective bargaining, together with its refusal to acknowledge company-dominated unions, were to provide a basis for the policies of the later board under the same name. The original N.L.R.B., however, was hampered and restricted under the operation of the National Recovery Administration and had no power to enforce its decisions.

To defend their interests, the workers felt more and more driven to strikes. The number of industrial disputes rose precipitately in the latter half of 1933—almost as many in this six month period as in all of 1932 —and the next year saw the total rise to 1,856. Almost 1,500,000 workers —more than seven per cent of the total labor force—were involved. In steel, automobiles, and textiles, among the longshoremen of the Pacific coast and the lumber workers of the northwest, in scores of other industries, strikes were either threatened or broke out on a scale comparable to that of the early 1920's. Many of these strikes were for wage increases but a great number of them, at least a third, were for union recognition.

Government did what it could to allay this unrest, setting up special advisory boards and mediation commissions which tried to get the strikers back to work while further investigations were made in the industries concerned. The outbreaks among steel and automobile workers were prevented from developing into national strikes at the last moment; mediation settled the longshoremen's strike after San Francisco had been briefly gripped by what was fearfully called a general strike. But the workers went back to their jobs dissatisfied and highly skeptical of government policy.

The most serious and violent strike was that of the textile workers. Employers were widely disregarding code provisions and the Cotton Code Authority did nothing to enforce them. Demanding a thirty-hour week without reduction in the minimum $13 wage, abolition of the stretch-out and recognition of the United Textile Workers, the mill employes walked out in mass during August, 1934—110,000 in Massachusetts, 50,000 in Rhode Island, 60,000 in Georgia, 28,000 in Alabama. By the end of the month, somewhere between 400,000 and 500,000 men and women were estimated to be on strike in twenty states—the largest single strike in labor history to that time. In the south, where "flying squadrons" rushed from one mill town to another to call out the workers and set up picket lines, there were inevitable clashes with the police and special sheriff deputies. At the height of the struggle some 11,000 national guardsmen in eight states were under arms to preserve order.

On September 7, after President Roosevelt intervened and promised the appointment of a new Textile Labor Relations Board to study conditions in the industry, the union leaders called the strike off. Was it strategic retreat or surrender? Opinion was varied and the labor policy makers were both praised and assailed for ordering the textile workers back. But it was soon apparent that there was to be no real peace in the industry. The employers continued to discriminate against union members, returning strikers were often barred from the mills in southern towns, and demoralization spread further throughout the workers' ranks.

The gains that labor had made in the early days of the N.R.A. seemed to be fading away. The obdurate attitude of employers unwilling to accept code provisions or carry out bona fide collective bargaining, the failure of the government to safeguard the workers in strike settlements, and the inability or reluctance of the A.F. of L. to give the mass production workers the support that might have enabled them to organize effectively, combined to dash labor's high hopes. Although union membership in 1935 was a million greater than it had been two years earlier, it was below the four million mark that Green had so proudly announced for the A.F. of L. alone at the close of 1933. Hundreds of thousands of the new recruits had fallen by the wayside and some six hundred federal unions disbanded. The organized strength of the automobile workers dwindled to 10,000; the burst of activity in steel subsided with a residue of only 8,600 members in the Amalgamated Association of Iron, Tin and Steel Workers, and of the several hundred thousand who had joined the United Textile Workers during the textile strike, only 80,000 remained with the union. The dramatic movement touched off with the adoption of Section 7(a) had lost its momentum.

By the beginning of 1935 the failure of the N.R.A., not only to solve the problem of labor relations but to provide for successful business organization, could no longer be disguised. It was being openly attacked on all fronts in sad contrast to the exuberant fervor of the parades and flag waving with which it had first been greeted. An original impetus had been given to recovery, but the psychological effect of that shot in the arm had worn off. Big business was generally in revolt against the labor provisions in the codes. Little business felt itself squeezed to the wall both by the revival of monopoly and by union demands. Labor was convinced that it had been betrayed. With the whole program bogging down because of inner contradictions, the country was no longer willing to support a system of economic controls that could not be successfully administered and appeared to bear most heavily on the consumer. It was with relief rather than regret that the public accepted the announcement in May, 1935, that the Supreme Court had delivered the coup de grace to the entire set-up by declaring, in the famous Schechter poultry case, that the National Industrial Recovery Act was unconstitutional.

This development completely swept away such safeguards for labor as had been written into Section 7(a). However, an amendment to the Railway Labor Act had definitely extended them to railroad employes, and a drive to secure them on a firmer basis for all other workers had already been launched. As early as March, 1934, Senator Wagner introduced a bill to close the loopholes that enabled industry to cripple labor's strength by setting up company unions and refusing to bargain collectively with any other group. He had temporarily withdrawn this measure on the President's plea for a further trial period under existing legislation, but reintroduced it early in 1935. Just eleven days before the N.R.A. was declared unconstitutional, it passed the Senate.

The Wagner bill had strong support from labor and the collapse of the N.R.A. naturally intensified the demand for its immediate acceptance by the House. "I do not mind telling you," an unusually militant Green testified before one congressional committee, "that the spirit of the workers in America has been aroused. They are going to find a way to bargain collectively. . . . Labor must have its place in the sun. We cannot and will not continue to urge workers to have patience, unless the Wagner bill is made law, and unless it is enforced, once it becomes law."

Roosevelt had no part in developing this new measure and on the evidence of both Secretary Perkins and Raymond Moley, he did not particularly like it when it was described to him. It was Senator Wagner's work. But with the N.R.A. out of the picture, Moley has reported, the President "flung his arms open" and suddenly embraced it. Labor could not be completely let down and here were the means to re-enact a stronger Section 7(a) so far as collective bargaining was concerned. With administration support, the measure now promptly passed the House. It was signed by Roosevelt on July 5.

Although the general policy of the Wagner Act—or as it was officially called the National Labor Relations Act—had been foreshadowed by Section 7(a) of the National Industrial Recovery Act, the new law heavily underscored the basic change in governmental attitude toward labor. Not only were old ideas of a laissez-faire attitude in industrial relations again ignored; the Roosevelt administration now upheld the right of wage earners to organize without making any such corresponding concessions to management as had been incorporated in the N.R.A. It was prepared to strengthen the bargaining position of the workers, and consequently their ability to obtain a larger share of the national income, over against whatever claims might be put forward by industry. The justification for this position was that only through government support could labor meet management on anything like equal terms in our industrialized society, and that the time had come when the scales, always so heavily weighted in favor of industry, should be redressed in favor of the workers. Every unfair labor practice banned in the Wagner Act applied to employers and it imposed no restraints whatsoever on the unions.

Roosevelt declared the purpose of the law to be the creation of a better relationship between labor and management but he tacitly acknowledged its one-sidedness. "By preventing practices which tend to destroy the independence of labor," he stated, "it seeks, for every worker within its scope, that freedom of choice and action which is justly his."

To assure such freedom, labor's right to organize was not only expressly reaffirmed, but all employer interference was explicitly forbidden. It was to be an unfair labor practice for an employer to restrain or coerce his employes in exercising their rights, to try to dominate or even contribute financially to the support of any labor organization, to encourage or discourage union membership by discrimination in hiring and firing, or to refuse to bargain collectively. Moreover, representatives designated for collective bargaining by a majority of the employes in an appropriate unit, whether it was an employer, craft or plant unit, were to have exclusive bargaining rights for all employes. The new legislation, that is, definitely undertook to outlaw the company-dominated unions that had flourished under the N.R.A., and to foster and to promote the growth of a bona fide unionism.

The administration of the Wagner Act was placed in the hands of a new National Labor Relations Board, made up of three members, with sole authority to determine the appropriate bargaining unit and to supervise the elections wherein employes chose their exclusive representatives for dealing with employers. The board could also hear complaints of unfair labor practices, issue "cease and desist" orders where they were found to be justified, and petition the courts for enforcement of its orders. The N.L.R.B. was not concerned with the substance of disputes over wages and hours, or any other issues affecting conditions of work, but solely with the practical encouragement and facilitation of collective bargaining.

"It should be clearly understood," President Roosevelt said in explaining the quasi-judicial functions of this administrative agency, "that it will not act as mediator or conciliator in labor disputes. The function of mediation remains, under this Act, the duty of the Secretary of Labor and of the Conciliation Service of the Department of Labor. . . . It is important that the judicial function and the mediation function should not be confused. Compromise, the essence of mediation, has no place in the interpretation and enforcement of the law."

At the time of its passage, the Wagner Act had widespread support. Conservative elements within the business community criticized the one-sidedness of the law, freely predicted union irresponsibility under its provisions, and were generally alarmed at what they considered the dangers to management control. But public opinion polls repeatedly emphasized popular sympathy for labor's aspirations in these days. There was a general feeling that the workers were fully entitled to government protection even at the expense of management, and confidence that they would not abuse their new privileges.

Whatever the pro's and con's of the new legislation, however, its implications were tremendous. At long last the general expressions upholding labor's right to organize—in the Clayton Act, the Norris–La Guardia Act, the National Industrial Recovery Act—were given reality. Labor had for over a century fought for freedom from legal restraints which hampered its activity. It had struggled against conspiracy laws, against enforcement of yellow-dog contracts, against judicial interpretations of liberty that actually nullified the individual worker's freedom, against the arbitrary use of injunctions. The Wagner Act not only removed past obstructions to union activity but erected substantial barriers to any interference on the part of employers to the full mobilization of labor's economic strength.

The battle to realize the full benefits of the new law, however, had still to be fought. While many employers were ready to accept its provisions and bargain collectively with their employes in good faith, there were others so implacably opposed to unionization that they were determined to continue their resistance to it at all cost. In many quarters labor had to push its campaign for organization against as fierce opposition as it had ever faced. The workers again fell back on strikes to win the union recognition that many companies withheld in spite of all governmental guarantees.

The excuse often advanced for refusing to meet the new legal requirements of collective bargaining was that the Wagner Act was unconstitutional. Advised by their lawyers that the Supreme Court would almost certainly invalidate it as going beyond the powers of Congress over interstate commerce, on which its provisions were based, anti-union employers did not hesitate to violate the law and instituted scores of injunctions to prevent the National Labor Relations Board from enforcing it. They launched an attack on labor which was especially aimed at unionization in steel, automobiles, rubber and other mass production industries. They still tried to maintain their control over company unions. Labor spies, stool pigeons and agents provocateurs were hired to ferret out any evidence of union activity, sow seeds of distrust and suspicion among the workers themselves, and furnish the information which would enable the employers to get rid of all those who might be classed as agitators. Strong arm squads were maintained in some instances to discourage union membership by more forcible methods, and outside organizers were beaten up, run out of town and threatened with further violence should they ever show up again.

The report of the La Follette Civil Liberties Committee was a shocking revelation of the disregard of legal and constitutional rights that so widely characterized industrial relations between 1933 and 1937. A first installment, made public in December, 1937, disclosed that some 2,500 corporations, the list reading "like a bluebook of American industry," had long followed the practice of hiring labor spies from agencies specializing in industrial espionage. The records of such firms as the Pinkerton and Burns agencies, the Railway and Audit Inspection Company, and the Corporations Auxiliary Company showed that they had furnished in the three year period under review a total of 3,871 agents to report on union activities, stir up discontent among employes and generally block labor organization. In carrying out their secret activities, individual operatives had become affiliated with ninety-three unions, and a third of the Pinkerton detectives had actually succeeded in becoming union officials. It was further stated that a selected list of companies, representative but not inclusive, had spent from 1933 to 1936 a total of $9,440,000 for spies, strikebreakers and munitions, the General Motors Corporation alone footing a bill of $830,000.

"The public cannot afford to let this challenge presented by industrial espionage go unnoticed," the La Follette committee concluded. "Through it private corporations dominate their employes, deny them their constitutional rights, promote disorder and disharmony, and even set at naught the powers of the government itself."

When this same committee investigated the Little Steel strike of 1937, disclosures of the weapons that had been accumulated for industrial war were even more startling than those of industrial espionage. The Youngstown Sheet and Tube Company had on hand 8 machine guns, 369 rifles, 190 shotguns and 450 revolvers, with 6,000 rounds of ball ammunition and 3,950 rounds of shot ammunition, and also 109 gas guns with over 3,000 rounds of gas ammunition. The Republic Steel Corporation had comparable equipment, and with purchases of tear and sickening gas amounting to $79,000, was described as the largest buyer of such supplies—not excepting law enforcement bodies— in the United States. Senator La Follette declared that the arsenals of these two steel companies "would be adequate equipment for a small war."

There was also brought to light one especially notorious example of industrial techniques in combatting unionism, first developed by the Remington Rand Company and then widely publicized by the National Association of Manufacturers under the name of the Mohawk Valley formula. This formula blueprinted a systematic campaign to denounce all union organizers as dangerous agitators, align the community in support of employers in the name of law and order, intimidate strikers by mobilizing the local police to break up meetings, instigate "back to work" movements by secretly organizing "loyal employes," and set up vigilance committees for protection in getting a struck plant again in operation. The underlying purpose behind the Mohawk Valley formula was to win public support by branding union leaders as subversive and threatening to remove the affected industry from the community if local business interests stood by and allowed radical agitators to win control over workers otherwise ready and anxious to cooperate with their employers.

The evidence made public by the La Follette Committee unveiled previously hidden aspects of industrial warfare. Even the most conservative newspapers, while suggesting that the committee's investigation had been one-sided and its report undoubtedly exaggerated, recognized a state of affairs that could not be condoned and came to the defense of labor's civil liberties. The disclosures, indeed, played a highly important part in convincing many corporations of the wisdom of abandoning practices which could not stand the light of day.

Labor was in the meantime combatting this anti-union campaign with its own militant tactics. Widespread industrial unrest continued throughout the whole period in which the basic principles underlying the Wagner Act were at stake. In 1937 strikes rose to a peak even higher than that of 1934. They totaled 4,720 and engaged almost two million workers.

The constitutionality of the Wagner Act was still undetermined as this new wave of unrest rose to a dramatic climax in the sit-down strikes of General Motors automobile workers, but the Supreme Court finally acted on April 12, 1937. In a series of decisions, of which the most important was that rendered in the case of *National Labor Relations Board* v. *Jones and Laughlin Steel Company*, the law was sustained. This was a spectacular victory for the New Deal and for organized labor, reflecting the change in the attitude of the court that dramatically punctuated the struggle over its reorganization initiated earlier in the year by President Roosevelt. The regulation of labor relations as they might affect interstate commerce was declared to be clearly within the province of Congress under the commerce clause, and the contention that the rights of either employer or employe were invaded by the provisions of the act was flatly rejected.

"Employees have as clear a right to organize and select their representatives for lawful purposes," Chief Justice Hughes stated in the five-to-four decision in *N.L.R.B.* v. *Jones and Laughlin,* "as the respondent has to organize its business and select its own officers and agents. Discrimination and coercion to prevent the free exercise of the right of employees to self-organization and representation is a proper subject for condemnation by competent legislative authority. Long ago we stated the reason for labor organizations. We said that they were organized out of the necessities of the situation; that a single employee was helpless in dealing with an employer; that he was dependent ordinarily on his daily wage for the maintenance of himself and his family; that if the employer refused to pay him the wages he thought fair, he was nevertheless unable to leave the employ and resist arbitrary and unfair treatment; that union was essential to give laborers opportunity to deal on an equality with their employer. . . ."

Its authority established, the National Labor Relations Board was finally in a position to apply the law effectively. It interpreted broadly the provision that it was an unfair labor practice for an employer to interfere with, restrain or coerce employes in the exercise of their rights. Not only were such old practices as yellow-dog contracts, blacklisting and other overt forms of discrimination outlawed, but the employment of labor spies and anti-union propaganda were prohibited. Company-dominated unions were disestablished, both union shops and closed shops upheld, interference forbidden with peaceful picketing.

The majority of cases coming before the board in regard to unfair labor practices were actually handled without prejudice to the interests of industry. It of course remained true that wholly unjustified charges might often be brought up, and that management could not counter with any complaints of unfair practices on the part of the unions. The over-all record of the N.L.R.B. was nevertheless quite a different one from that presented by a generally hostile press which lost no occasion to attack the board for its supposed partiality to labor.

Between 1935 and 1945, a total of 36,000 cases involving charges of unfair labor practices and 38,000 concerned with employe representation were handled. Considering them as a whole, 25.9 per cent were withdrawn without any action being taken, 11.9 were dismissed by regional directors, 46.3 were settled by informal procedures leading to mutual agreement, and only 15.9 required official hearings. The latter cases led to the disestablishment of some 2,000 company unions and the reinstatement of 300,000 employes, with back pay aggregating $9,000,000, where employers were found guilty of discrimination against bona fide union members.

In addition to hearing cases of unfair labor practices and issuing cease and desist orders when it found them justified, the National Labor Relations Board during this period from 1935 to 1945 also held some 24,000 elections, in which 6,000,000 workers participated, to determine collective bargaining units. The C.I.O. won 40 per cent of these elections, the A.F. of L. 33.4 per cent, independent unions 10.5 per cent, and in 16.1 per cent no bargaining unit was chosen. It should be remembered that the board had nothing whatsoever to do with disputes over wages and hours, but in respect to the issues that it was authorized to handle, its activities greatly helped to stabilize industrial relations.

The protection given labor's right to organize and bargain collectively was the most important phase of the pro-labor policy that was generally followed under the New Deal. Once embarked on its course, the Roosevelt administration went far beyond any previous administration in encouraging the growth of unions and accepting the basic role they played in the development of our national economy. But the Wagner Act was not the only New Deal measure which aided labor or contributed to the improved status of industrial workers.

The insistence of the President, from his earliest days in office, upon the obligation of government to cope directly with the fundamental problems of unemployment and relief clearly demonstrated a sympathetic understanding of the needs of the nation's wage earners that was in line with the most progressive principles of American democracy. The public works program included in the National Industrial Recovery Act was principally intended as a means to prime the pump of industry, but both the Civilian Conservation Corps and the Federal Emergency Relief Administration had as their direct objectives relief for the great army of unemployed. They represented an approach to the vital problem of human needs that differed sharply from that of President Hoover, who had long held out against direct relief as undermining individual initiative and self-respect. The Roosevelt administration was to be much more realistic in recognizing the position in which the unemployed found themselves and the necessity of government aid until a revived industry could provide normal opportunities for employment.

This was further borne out in the program that culminated in the Works Progress Administration. This agency was set up not only to aid the unemployed but to provide them with jobs that would enable them to retain their self-respect. The slow pace of recovery, and the recession that developed in 1937, were to involve the government far more deeply in this undertaking than had been originally contemplated. The well-being of industrial workers was nevertheless considered more important than possible economies, and the administration held to its course in spite of all criticism of the tremendous expense involved.

A much more far-reaching measure, considered by Roosevelt "the cornerstone of his administration," was the Social Security Act with its comprehensive provision for unemployment insurance, old age insurance, and other aid for the needy. The principles underlying this law had been opposed by the American Federation of Labor, as we have seen, until the reversal of its traditional policy on unemployment insurance at the 1932 convention. It then came out in support of governmental action. The President's own interest, however, most effectively sustained the drive for social security. "In his own mind," Secretary Perkins has written, "it was *his* program."

Roosevelt instituted studies on the best method of providing for social security early in 1933, talked continually with his advisers of what he termed "cradle to the grave" insurance long before the phrase became current in England, and appointed a Committee on Economic Security in his cabinet to reconcile differing views on how the whole program should be handled. A proposed bill was placed upon his "must list" in 1934 and when Congress failed to act that year, he renewed his insistence upon its adoption at the next session. Final action was then taken and in August, 1935 the Social Security Act was overwhelmingly approved.

The new law had three major parts: First, unemployment compensation was to be handled through the states by remission of ninety per cent of a national payroll tax to every state adopting an insurance program meeting federal specifications. Second, old age pensions were to be administered directly by the federal government from funds secured through equal taxes upon employers and employes which were to start at one per cent of the latter's wages and gradually rise to three per cent. Third, other assistance for the needy was to be provided through grants to the states for the aged and blind, dependent children, and the crippled and disabled, while federal funds were also allocated for maternal and child health services, child welfare work, the rehabilitation of the disabled, and general public health.

This social security program was limited in its scope because of the exclusion of several categories of employes; its benefit payments were not over-generous by any standards, and it fell far short of the "cradle to grave" insurance about which Roosevelt liked to talk. The United States still lagged behind other countries that had long since developed more comprehensive plans. The new law was nevertheless another epochal development in the history of a nation so long wedded to laissez-faire concepts of the role of government in economic and social matters. That social security won the support of industry, labor and the public was a highly significant indication of how the stress of economic circumstances had changed popular attitudes since the depression.

"The experience of these years," Green wrote, "showed that the very disaster of the crisis compelled the government to assume responsibilities and discharge functions within the field of private endeavour which had been regarded as outside its scope. The national government, acting in behalf of all the people, was compelled to care for the needy and unemployed."

In addition to direct relief for the unemployed and social security, the New Deal was also committed to the improvement of working conditions first attempted in the wage and hour provisions of the N.R.A. codes. Other means to attain this goal were at once sought when the National Industrial Recovery Act was declared unconstitutional. A first step was passage of the Walsh-Healey Public Contracts Act, establishing the forty-hour week and minimum wages for all employes of contractors making supplies for the government. But this measure was obviously limited in its scope and the real question was how a more general measure could overcome the constitutional objections that had been brought not only against the N.R.A. but also against minimum wage legislation by the states. Secretary Perkins explored the possibilities of a new approach to the problem but the attitude of the Supreme Court seemed an insuperable barrier.

The issue entered into the 1936 campaign. The Republicans came out in favor of minimum wage legislation through state laws or interstate compacts, but the Democrats declared they would continue to seek national legislation "within the constitution." It was not until the Supreme Court battle had been fought out early in 1937, however, that Roosevelt gave the go-ahead signal for the introduction of a bill providing for maximum hours, minimum wages and, as an almost last minute addition, the abolition of child labor which had first been sought in the N.R.A. codes.

The Fair Labor Standards bill, as it came to be known, met vigorous opposition, reflecting in part the political animosities growing out of the court struggle, and it was at first given only very equivocal support even by labor. Many of the conservatives in the A.F. of L. were still opposed to wage legislation in principle, fearing that minimum wages

would become maximum wages, and President Green took an unyield-
ing stand against what he considered important shortcomings in the
administration's proposals. With spokesmen for the American Federation of Labor and the National Association of Manufacturers in dubious
alliance, few New Deal measures faced harder sledding.

Roosevelt repeatedly and emphatically stressed the importance of
the bill both in messages to Congress and in fireside chats to the country.
"A self-supporting and self-respecting democracy," he declared in May,
1937, "can plead no justification for the existence of child labor, no
economic reason for chiseling workers' wages or stretching workers'
hours." But entirely apart from justice to the wage earners themselves,
the provisions of the proposed bill were supported as an essential means
for sustaining and building up national purchasing power.

The importance of high wages from this point of view was of course
no new idea. Labor had always maintained that only when the workers
were paid enough to enable them to buy the products of their own industry could our economic system function successfully. The assertion
of this principle goes back at least as far as the statement of the Mechanics' Union of Trade Associations in 1827 on wages, consumption and
manufacturing output. But the argument made slow headway and in
the early 1930's was only gradually beginning to gain the acceptance that
is today almost commonplace. The purchasing power theory in support
for high wages had been traditionally overshadowed by the counter
argument that by increasing costs of production, high wages actually
narrowed the market for manufactured goods and consequently slowed
down production.

When Congress failed to act on the Fair Labor Standards bill in the
summer of 1937, Roosevelt returned to the attack on this broad front
and after calling a special session in November, again demanded prompt
passage.

"I believe that the country as a whole," he stated, "recognizes the
need for congressional action if we are to maintain wage increases and
the purchasing power of the nation against recessive factors in the
general industrial situation. The exploitation of child labor and the
undercutting of wages and the stretching of the hours of the poorest
paid workers in periods of business recession has a serious effect on
buying power. . . . What does the country ultimately gain if we en-

courage businessmen to enlarge the capacity of American industry to produce unless we see to it that the income of our working population actually expands sufficiently to create markets to absorb that increased production?"

After successive delays, redrafts of the original bill to meet labor's objections, and the exercise of strong administration pressure, the opposition finally gave way. The Fair Labor Standards bill was passed in June, 1938. It established a minimum wage of 25 cents an hour rising to 40 cents an hour in seven years, a forty-four-hour week to be reduced to forty hours in three years, and prohibited the labor of children under sixteen in industries whose products entered into interstate commerce. A movement whose origins may be traced back to the demands for a legislative ten-hour day voiced by labor over a century earlier had come to fruition. The state had entered more directly and comprehensively into the control of wages and hours than would have been believed even remotely possible prior to the depression. It was a development in its way as far-reaching as the government's new support for collective bargaining. Again nothing could have more directly contravened the principles of laissez-faire economy, which such labor leaders as Samuel Gompers, and even William Green, had upheld no less zealously than the most conservative of capitalists. But maximum hour and minimum wage legislation was now generally approved—accepted as necessary—by most people.

Government had swung over to the support of the interests of labor and so had the courts. The series of cases in which the Wagner Act, Social Security and the Fair Labor Standards Act were upheld marked a judicial reversal of earlier decisions which gave the final stamp of approval to New Deal policies. The view that laws affecting union membership or prescribing minimum wages violated constitutional guarantees of liberty of contract was abandoned when the Supreme Court stated that "regulation which is reasonable in relation to its subject and is adopted in the interests of the community," could not be construed as violating the due process clause of either the fifth or fourteenth amendments.

Moreover the courts now went on wholly to exempt unions from prosecution under the anti-trust laws and to reverse other restrictive policies by generally upholding the right to strike, to boycott and to picket. Whereas during even the progressive era labor found supposedly guaranteed privileges repeatedly curtailed by the Supreme Court, its position was now being constantly bolstered by favorable decisions. Peaceful picketing was declared in one notable case, *Thornhill* v. *Alabama,* for example, to be a legitimate exercise of free speech within the area guaranteed by the constitution.

So far, indeed, did the Supreme Court go that in 1945 a majority decision in *Hunt* v. *Crumboch* upheld the right of a union, under highly complicated circumstances, to exercise a boycott that virtually drove the firm against which it was directed out of business. To Justice Jackson this case gave occasion for a significant review of judicial policy toward labor.

"With this decision," he stated in a vigorous dissenting opinion, "the labor movement has come full circle. The workingman has struggled long, the fight has been filled with hatred, and conflict has been dangerous, but now workers may not be deprived of their livelihood merely because their employers oppose and they favor unions. Labor has won other rights as well, unemployment compensation, old-age benefits and, what is most important and the basis of all its gains, the recognition that the opportunity to earn his support is not alone the concern of the individual but is the problem which all organized societies must contend with and conquer if they are to survive. This Court now sustains the claim of a union to the right to deny participation in the economic world to an employer simply because the union dislikes him. This Court permits to employes the same arbitrary dominance over the economic sphere which they control that labor so long, so bitterly and so rightly asserted should belong to no man."

Whatever the validity of Justice Jackson's views and the later problems that would arise in regard to the sometimes arbitrary assertion of labor's rights, the general program of the New Deal in encouraging the growth of strong unions and otherwise sustaining the position of organized labor was still applauded by the nation as a whole in the mid-1930's. Repeated public-opinion polls revealed strong support for each of the successive labor measures adopted by Congress between 1933 and 1938. President Roosevelt was undoubtedly justified at this time in asserting his belief that a majority of the people were glad "that we are slowly working out for labor greater privileges and at the same time greater responsibilities."

The continued strikes of these years, and particularly those of 1937, clearly showed that no final solution had been found for industrial relations and a pronounced reaction to the pro-labor policies of the New Deal was soon to set in. In spite of both labor disturbances and a growing demand for modification of the Wagner Act, however, Roosevelt was to remain convinced that the increased strength of unionism would in time lead to greater industrial stability. He believed thoroughly in the principle of collective bargaining. "It must remain," he declared, "as the foundation of industrial relations for all time." He was prepared not only to help labor to maintain its gains but to advance them still further.

"Only in free lands," he stated in an important address to the convention of the International Brotherhood of Teamsters in 1940, "have free labor unions survived. When union workers assemble with freedom and independence in a convention like this, it is a proof that American democracy has remained unimpaired; it is a symbol of our determination to keep it free."

Labor was still suffering from growing pains, in his opinion, and more responsible leadership was bound to emerge and make possible a larger degree of cooperation with equally responsible management. When warned on one occasion that the unions might become too powerful, he was quoted as replying, "Too powerful for what?" His attitude was that their power should prove an antidote for that of big business. His faith in labor and in the vital importance of free labor unions was not to be shaken.

The basic importance of the New Deal program did not lie in immediate gains or losses for labor but in its recognition that this whole matter of working conditions was no longer the concern of employe and employer alone, but of society as a whole. Democratic capitalism could hardly hope to survive unless the great army of workers could obtain through concerted effort the freedom and the security that as individuals they were powerless to defend in an industrialized society. The New Deal's policy was pro-labor, but it was pro-labor in order to redress the balance that had been tipped in favor of industry. It looked primarily toward the wellbeing of the workers, but in the conviction that upon their wellbeing rested that of the entire country.

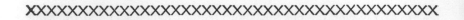

XVI: RISE OF THE C.I.O.

WHILE ORGANIZED LABOR was making such pronounced gains during the period of the New Deal, conflict within its own ranks shattered the relative unity that it had formerly maintained. As the controversy over industrial versus craft unionism within the American Federation of Labor led to insurgent revolt and establishment of the Committee for Industrial Organization, the ground was laid for a continuing rivalry which in some measure may actually have stimulated union growth, but also served to diffuse labor's energy through internal feuds and dissension.

The issues in dispute were comparable to those which had arisen when the A.F. of L. challenged the Knights of Labor half a century earlier. Should union organization be pursued principally in the interests of the skilled workers, or should it aim to include more effectively the great mass of unskilled workers? The Knights had sought to meet the problem by promoting one all-inclusive union, but economic circumstance gave far greater validity to the program of the new unionism of the A.F. of L. with its emphasis on closely disciplined crafts. Industrial unionism could not be successfully promoted in any form in the 1880's because the unskilled workers, their ranks constantly replenished by immigration, had such meager bargaining power. But changed conditions in the 1930's underscored both the importance and the practicality of building up out-and-out industrial unions. Failure to meet the needs of unorganized workers in the mass production industries had greatly weakened the whole labor movement, and the opportunity to organize them was better than ever before with government support and the curtailment of immigration greatly enhancing their potential bargaining power.

Craft unionism versus industrial unionism, however, became increasingly overshadowed in the quarrel between the A.F. of L. and the C.I.O.

by the drives for power on the part of the two factions and the mounting rivalry between their leaders. The issues originally at stake gave way to the fierce interplay of union politics and the clash of ambitious personalities. Charges and countercharges flew back and forth between William Green and John L. Lewis.

"In the midst of our common effort to better the welfare of all workers," Green was to write, "came forth a man who sought other ends. Consumed with personal ambition, he gave the lie to the democratic process after it had rejected his leadership. He raised the voice of dualism and disunity, a voice which while pretending to unite sought to disrupt; a voice which while declaiming democratic ideals sought dictatorship."

Lewis struck back savagely at what he considered the obstructive attitude of the A.F. of L. and the blind conservatism of its leadership. The organizing efforts of the Federation were said to represent "twenty-five years of unbroken failure," and its president was charged with being unable to either understand what was happening to the national economy or to rise to the opportunities of the hour. "Alas, poor Green," Lewis told reporters as the verbal brickbats were flying back and forth in 1936, "I knew him well. He wishes me to join him in fluttering procrastination, the while intoning *O tempora, O mores!*"

In taking over command of the campaign for industrial unionism and directly defying the oligarchy in control of the A.F. of L., Lewis soon revealed himself to be the most aggressive and colorful figure that American labor had ever known. His spectacular success in reviving the United Mine Workers during the early days of the New Deal, increasing its membership from 150,000 to 400,000, attracted nationwide attention. The magazine *Fortune* wryly commented that "he made a noise like the whole labor movement," and in time the noise was to rise to a deafening roar. It was characteristic of popular attitudes toward Lewis in this period that he was invariably described, whether by friend or foe, in gaudy superlatives. He was either an unexampled hero or an unspeakable villain.

Philip Murray, destined to succeed him as president of the C.I.O., declared that he was "without a peer in the realm of America"; in the days of the united front with communism, Earl Browder hailed him not merely as the greatest of American trade union leaders but "as a leader of world democracy," and Huey Long could pay him no higher compliment than to single him out as "the Huey Long of labor." The chorus of condemnation, on the other hand, reached its peak during the days of war. When *Fortune* held a poll in 1943 on who were the most harmful individuals in the United States, seventy per cent of the ballots bore the name of John L. Lewis.

Both his family background and early life were closely associated with the labor movement. His parentage, like that of William Green, was of Welsh mining stock and when his father emigrated to the United States in 1875, the family settled in the small coal town of Lucas, Iowa, where Lewis senior promptly joined the Knights of Labor. John L. was born in 1880 and went into the pits at the age of twelve. After restlessly roaming the mining regions in several states as a boy and young man, he took up labor politics in 1909. Elected president of a United Mine Workers local in Panama, Illinois, he became state legislative agent for the union, then a field representative for the A.F. of L., and successively chief statistician, first vice-president and finally president of the United Mine Workers. At the time of the coal crisis in 1919, as we have seen, he won national headlines for his refusal to lead the miners in a strike against the government. Subsequent years found Lewis desperately on the defensive as the coal operators hammered away at his union, radical elements promoted a revolt against his leadership, and the strength of the U.M.W. gradually dwindled. It was his prompt seizure of the chance presented by the N.R.A. to recoup both his and his union's fortunes that first demonstrated the shrewd tactical sense and astute opportunism, reenforced by defiant courage, which were to make him a national leader.

No public figure other than President Roosevelt was more familiar to the American people as he pursued his stormy, turbulent career after 1933—militantly challenging the world of industry ("They are striking me hip and thigh . . . right merrily shall I return their blows"), vilifying his enemies within the labor movement, making and breaking alliances as he shifted the grounds of his attack, and defying the government in self-centered pursuit of his own ambitions. Innumerable articles attempted to find the answer to the question he once asked: "What makes me tick? Is it power I am after, or am I a Saint Francis in disguise, or what?" An elemental force, a consummate actor, a consecrated leader, a self-willed opportunist . . . what was John L. Lewis? If the answer was indeed a Saint Francis, the disguise could hardly have been more complete. Cartoonists had a happy field day drawing the jutting jaw, the glowering scowl, the bushy eyebrows of this mighty protagonist of labor.

No consistent philosophy could be discerned in the tortuous windings of his career. He paid eloquent tribute at one time to Herbert Hoover's "genius for constructive industrial statesmanship"; eagerly embraced the New Deal and threw the full weight of his influence behind Roosevelt in 1936; dramatically broke with the President four years later to stake retention of his office in the C.I.O. on the election of Wendell Willkie. In politics and within the labor movement, it was "off ag'in, on ag'in, gone ag'in—Finnigin" for this erratic individualist whose only definite lodestar so often appeared to be the interests of John L. Lewis. Whether he believed in a laissez-faire or a regulated economy might often be in doubt, but there was no question but that he always believed in himself.

To the interviewers who flocked to discuss national problems with him in 1936 and 1937, he talked pompously of industrial democracy, but completely failed to clarify what the term meant. It was apparent only that he had no idea of trying to overturn or seriously disturb the existing economic system. He had no long range program or ultimate ideal, and from that point of view his policy conformed to the traditional opportunism of Samuel Gompers and the A.F. of L. rather than the reformist zeal of Terence V. Powderly and the Knights of Labor. He believed that labor should play a greater role in affairs of government but his flirtations with the idea of a third party seemed to be inspired not so much by the desire to promote any specific program as the desire to promote John L. Lewis. When asked about the future of labor, his answers were lost in hazy and verbose platitudes. "It would be unwisdom to paint a picture that would only alarm our adversaries of tomorrow," he told one inquiring reporter. "Neither can I bond the purity of motive or the administrative rectitude of the labor movement of tomorrow."

On the platform, in public meetings and over the radio, Lewis showed a flare for the dramatic that inevitably arrested public attention. He well knew his ability as an actor ("My life is but a stage," he said on one occasion) and he would alternately cajole, denounce, threaten, pontificate with equal self-assurance. His sense of his own importance was magnificent.

He performed prodigies of valor in building up the United Mine Workers and in organizing the C.I.O. Labor was to owe him an immense debt. But his insatiable lust for power helped to betray the solidarity of trade unionism and his defiance of government during the Second World War was a highly important factor in alienating the public sympathy that labor enjoyed in the early days of the New Deal. Whatever the losses he suffered in either public or labor support, however, Lewis could never be relegated to the background. With his miners standing firmly behind him, accepting his dictatorial control of their union because he got results, he continued to play an important role in labor politics.

The discontent with the fumbling policies of the A.F. of L. that was to give Lewis his chance to lead the movement for industrial unionism came to a head at the annual convention of the Federation in San Francisco in 1934. With the drifting away of union members in textiles and steel, in automobiles and rubber, the demand for industrial charters to replace federal charters became increasingly vocal. The leaders of industrial unions within the A.F. of L. attacked the policy that required new unions to be subordinated to the jurisdictional claims of existing craft unions. They vigorously reasserted their conviction that only the organization of all workers—the skilled and the unskilled—in single industry-wide unions could meet the needs of workers engaged in mass production.

The old-line craft union leaders were not convinced. The very fact that in previous years the membership in existing industrial unions had increased 130 per cent, while that of craft unions had gained only 10 per cent, simply emphasized for them the dangers of granting the new industrial charters which the insurgents demanded. They insisted that such a departure from traditional practice would destroy the foundations upon which the A.F. of L. had been built. Wage earners could not be successfully organized, it was reiterated, except by bringing them into "the respective national and international unions where jurisdiction has been established."

The controversy was temporarily resolved at San Francisco by a compromise engineered by moderates on both sides of the issue. It was agreed that charters would be granted for unions in automobiles, rubber, cement, radio and aluminum, and an intensive drive initiated to organize the steel industry, but that the rights of existing craft unions would be fully protected and all jurisdictional disputes submitted to an executive council enlarged to include representatives of the industrial unions.

This was at least a partial success for the insurgents and a hopeful augury for labor, but the succeeding year saw little or nothing done to carry out the agreement. The A.F. of L. leadership had not in reality been aroused from its complacent conservatism. The craft union leaders, and especially those of the building trades, had not been persuaded of the need for industrial unionism. They still saw only dangers to their own hold on power in any broadening of the bases of the labor movement. They continued to postpone and delay any action along the lines to which they had supposedly agreed. The next convention of the Federation, held at Atlantic City in 1935, met against a background of growing union demoralization in the mass production industries and an executive council report that "we did not deem it advisable to launch an organizing campaign for the steel industry."

Lewis came to Atlantic City demanding action. The situation in steel was for him one of particular concern. He had succeeded in organizing the workers in the captive coal mines belonging to that industry and was convinced that this new union redoubt could not be held unless the steel workers were also organized. This time he was determined, together with other leaders favoring industrial unionism, to compel the executive council to live up to its promises—or else.

The issue was placed fairly before the convention in majority and minority reports submitted by its resolutions committee. The former declared that since it was a primary obligation of the A.F. of L. "to protect the jurisdictional rights of all trade unions organized upon craft lines," industrial charters would violate the agreements that had always existed between the Federation and its craft affiliates. The latter insisted that in any industry where the work performed by a majority of the workers fell within the jurisdictional claim of more than one craft union, industrial organization was "the only form that will be acceptable to the workers or adequately meet their needs."

On the one side in this embittered controversy were William Green, cautiously following the policies bequeathed him by Samuel Gompers in spite of earlier advocacy of industrial unionism; the hard-boiled and hard-hitting head of the carpenters, William L. Hutcheson, firmly resolved to keep all workers in wood or its substitutes within the comfortable fold of his own union; Daniel J. Tobin, the pugnacious leader of the teamsters who scornfully characterized the unskilled workers in the mass-production industries as "rubbish;" Matthew Woll, of the photoengravers, whose conservatism was exemplified by his role as acting president of the old and moribund National Civic Federation, and the dignified, scholarly John P. Frey, head of the Metal Trades Department of the A.F. of L. This was the Old Guard, ready to fight industrial unionism with all the weapons at its command.

Lewis led the insurgents and had the support of some of the most progressive and forceful labor leaders of the day. Among them were Charles P. Howard, calm, persuasive head of the Typographical Union and the actual author of the minority report; Philip Murray, the somewhat retiring and soft spoken, but extremely able, *alter ego* of Lewis in the United Mine Workers; Sidney Hillman, the Lithuanian-born needle trades leader, who harbored a fund of nervous energy and ambition beneath his quiet manner and who had just brought the formerly independent Amalgamated Clothing Workers into the A.F. of L., and David Dubinsky, one of the shrewdest of trade unionists and president of the effervescent International Ladies' Garment Workers.

The debate among these chieftains over A.F. of L. policy continued for several days, the issue sharpened by attack and counterattack on the floor of the convention. Its peak was reached when Lewis, excoriating tactics that resulted in the new unions "dying like the grass withering before the autumn sun," vehemently assailed what he regarded as the betrayal of the promises made at the preceding convention.

"At San Francisco they seduced me with fair words," he thundered, "Now, of course, having learned that I was seduced, I am enraged and I am ready to rend my seducers limb from limb, including delegate Woll. In that sense, of course, I speak figuratively." He called upon the convention delegates to make a contribution to the welfare of their less fortunate brethren, to heed their cry from Macedonia, to organize the unorganized and make the Federation into the greatest instrument that had ever been forged to befriend the cause of humanity. And he solemnly warned that if they let slip this opportunity, the enemies of labor would be encouraged "and high wassail will prevail at the banquet tables of the mighty."

But for all his eloquence, his appeals and his warnings, Lewis was unable to make the delegates see why they should modify traditional policies. The majority were unmoved by the threat of being rended limb from limb, even figuratively. Their ears were closed to all cries from Macedonia. They were not disturbed by the picture of high wassail at the banquets of the mighty. When the final vote was taken, the program for industrial unionism went down to defeat through a vote of 18,024 to 10,933 in favor of the majority report of the resolutions committee favoring craft unions.

Shortly afterward an incident occurred which appeared to symbolize the break that this crucial vote meant. The details are somewhat obscure. But in the course of further wrangling over procedure, Hutcheson so far departed from parliamentary decorum as to call Lewis a term which bystanders identified as "bastard." The rejoinder of the miner's chieftain was an uppercut, with all the force of some 225 pounds behind it, which caught the equally burly czar of the carpenters squarely on the jaw. The assailants were separated and the danger of a free-for-all happily averted, but the altercation hardly served to placate feelings, already so touchy, in the two camps into which labor had been divided.

Immediately after the A.F. of L. convention, the advocates of industrial unionism met to consider further action. They were unwilling to accept a decision that once again put off any effective organizational work in the mass production industries and on November 9, 1935 took the first steps to set up their own Committee for Industrial Organization. As originally constituted it was made up of Lewis, Howard, Hillman and Dubinsky, together with Max Zaritsky, of the Cap and Millinery Department of the United Hatters; Thomas F. McMahon of the United Textile Workers; Thomas H. Brown of the Mine, Mill and Smelter Workers, and Harvey C. Fremming of the Oil Field, Gas Well and Refining Workers. It was the declared intent of this committee to work within the framework of the A.F. of L. rather than to set up an independent organization. Its functions were to be "educational and advisory" in an effort to promote the recognition and acceptance of "modern collective bargaining" in the mass production industries. In spite of such statements, however, the leaders of the C.I.O. were at once accused by Green of going against the majority decision of the A.F. of L. convention. Their sole motive, he was repeatedly to declare, was to force acceptance of their own views. The answer of Lewis was to bid further defiance to the executive council.

"Dear Sir and Brother," he wrote Green on November 23: "Effective this date I resign as vice-president of the American Federation of Labor."

The C.I.O. at once began to lay plans for its own organizing campaign and early in January, 1936, submitted to the executive council of the A.F. of L. for a final time the old demand for industrial charters in steel and automobiles, rubber and radio. But there was no break in the ranks of the Old Guard. More fearful than ever of what the aggressive tactics of the new committee might mean to the established position of craft unions in the A.F. of L., the members of the executive council now countered with an order for the immediate dissolution of the C.I.O. It was fomenting insurrection, they charged, and was a dual organization created only to serve the interests of "a few self-seeking individuals."

Throughout the next few months angry controversy raged between the leaders of the A.F. of L. and those of the C.I.O. and the cleavage in labor's ranks steadily widened. Green alternately pleaded and threatened in trying to bring the rebels back into the fold. Lewis adamantly went his own way. Finally in late summer, the A.F. of L. executive council suspended the ten unions that had in the meantime affiliated with the C.I.O. Far from submitting to such discipline, however, Lewis declared that the council had acted without authority. "I fear his threats," was his answer to Green's charges on one occasion, "as much as I believe his promises." When the Federation met for its 1936 convention at Tampa, Florida, delegates from the C.I.O. unions were conspicuously absent. The countermove of the A.F. of L. was to vote by an overwhelming but meaningless majority that their suspension should remain in effect until "the breach be healed and adjusted under such terms and conditions as the Executive Committee may deem best."

The C.I.O. marched ahead with its own organizing program. New unions in steel, automobiles, glass, rubber and radio joined the original members. In increasing alarm, the A.F. of L. again denounced the movement as threatening to destroy the whole basis of labor federation and assailed its leaders for betraying the union cause. In March, 1937, amid the nationwide excitement caused by organizational drives in both steel and automobiles, the executive council made the decisive move of ordering all C.I.O. unions expelled from state and city federations of the A.F. of L.

Toward the close of 1937, again under the influence of moderate leaders in both camps, belated efforts were made to find some basis for peace. They were foredoomed to failure. The A.F. of L. proposed the return of the original C.I.O. unions and the merger of its new ones with existing A.F. of L. unions. The C.I.O. demanded admittance of its entire membership, now grown to some thirty-two unions, with full voting power. Each organization was looking toward domination in any proposed merger and neither A.F. of L. nor C.I.O. leaders were willing to make the concessions that might have enabled them to work together. The issue was no longer, if it ever had been in reality, industrial unionism versus craft unionism. It was a contest for power. The welfare of labor as a whole was sacrificed to the rivalries of stubborn, self-willed ambition.

In the opinion of many observers, it was at this time that Lewis first dangerously overplayed his hand and lost what might have been the chance to control a united labor movement. For the C.I.O. membership had actually outstripped that of the A.F. of L. At the close of 1937 it totaled some 3,700,000 as against its rival's 3,400,000, and whatever the terms of merger, the industrial unions would have dominated a reconstituted A.F. of L. But the growing power of the C.I.O. apparently convinced Lewis that he could win even greater victories without sharing responsibility, and he was stubbornly determined to go his own way. Not again would such a favorable opportunity present itself for restoring labor unity.

After the failure of these peace negotiations in the fall of 1937, the A.F. of L. confirmed the action of its executive council in expelling all C.I.O. members, except for the Ladies' Garment Workers who were soon to return to the fold. Then in May, 1938, Lewis and his lieutenants took the final steps to transform what had originally been only an organizing committee into a permanent Congress of Industrial Organizations. These moves, however, were only formalities. The rift in the house of labor was already complete.

The C.I.O. was to continue to promote industrial unionism and uphold the interests of the great mass of unskilled workers but it did not in actual fact differ very much from the A.F. of L. In spite of the attacks made upon it, and the charges that it was fostering communism, it was no less conservative in its basic principles than the parent organization. Unlike such earlier opponents of craft unionism as the Knights of Labor, the Socialist Trade and Labor Alliance and the I.W.W., the C.I.O. was wholly committed to advancing the interests of wage earners through collective bargaining within the existing structure of democratic capitalism. It was prepared to put more emphasis on political action than the A.F. of L. had in the past, but this was a logical outgrowth of the larger role that government was playing in the regulation of labor relations. There was no reflection of a radical or revolutionary demand for any change in our political system.

In actual structure the C.I.O. also followed the general pattern of the A.F. of L. except that it did not have special departments. The older organization had long since found it necessary to set up a Building and Construction Trades Department, a Metal Trades Department, a Railway Employees' Department and a Union Label Trades Department, but with its major unions industrial in scope, there was no need for such divisions within the C.I.O. It did, however, establish state and city industrial union councils comparable to the A.F. of L. state federations of labor and city centrals. The authority of the C.I.O. in dealing with the member unions has proved in practice to be more extensive than that of the A.F. of L. and its executive council has intervened far more often in local union affairs.

Generally speaking, the C.I.O. conformed to the established traditions of American labor, rather than the more class-conscious traditions of European labor. Its startling impact on the labor movement was primarily due to the fact that it was more alert to the needs of the unskilled workers than the A.F. of L. and more active and aggressive in promoting them.

The response to the C.I.O.'s vigorous campaign for industrial unionism, set in motion soon after its revolt against the dilatory and delaying tactics of the A.F. of L. in 1935, was immediate and nationwide. Here was what the great body of workers in mass production industries had been waiting for and they flocked to join unions that really met their needs and freed them from the discriminatory controls of federal unions. As organizers went out from the new C.I.O. headquarters, supported by funds made available through contributions from the miners, needle workers and other sympathetic unions, they were greeted with enthusiasm. With the energetic, skillful leadership of Lewis and Murray, Hillman and Dubinsky, progress was phenomenal.

The key drive of the C.I.O. among the nation's steel workers was launched in June, 1936 with the establishment of the Steel Workers' Organizing Committee. Under Murray's direction it took over the nearly defunct Amalgamated Association of Iron, Steel and Tin Workers, set up district headquarters in Pittsburgh, Chicago and Birmingham, and soon had some four hundred organizers distributing union literature, holding mass meetings, canvassing from house to house in the steel towns of Pennsylvania, Ohio, Illinois and Alabama. With average annual wages among the workers as low as $560, compared with a minimum $1500 standard of living budget, they found fertile ground for effective union propaganda. The steel industry, whose obdurate anti-unionism could be traced from Homestead through the great steel strike of 1919, was prepared to meet this new challenge with full recognition of its significance. Page advertisements were inserted in papers throughout the country by the Iron and Steel Institute which declared that the companies' own employe representation plans fully met the needs of the workers, that the C.I.O. was trying to intimidate and coerce them into joining the union, and that radical and communist influences were again at work.

Lewis took to the radio in a nationwide hook-up to counteract this propaganda barrage and warned not only the steel operators but all industry that the drive sponsored by the C.I.O. to unionize the industrial workers could not be withstood.

"Let him who will, be he economic tyrant or sordid mercenary," he shouted into the ether, "pit his strength against this mighty upsurge of human sentiment now being crystallized in the hearts of thirty million workers who clamor for the establishment of industrial democracy and for participation in its tangible fruits. He is a madman or a fool who believes that this river of human sentiment . . . can be dammed or impounded by the erection of arbitrary barriers of restraint."

Within a matter of months, the industry which had successfully beaten back unionism on so many occasions found itself on the defensive. Thousands of workers flocked to join the Steel Workers' Organizing Committee. Former company unions in many instances simply transformed themselves into locals of the new union, and when management sought to regain control by promising wage increases tied to the cost of living, their members bluntly rejected any such agreements. By the close of 1936, the S.W.O.C. could boast of the establishment of some 150 union lodges with a total membership of over 100,000. It had become strong enough to demand recognition and collective bargaining, strong enough to threaten a nationwide strike should the steel industry refuse to heed the workers' demands.

While preparations for such a move were still underway, however, an unexpected and dramatic announcement was made on March 1, 1937. As a result of secret negotiations which had been proceeding for some time between Lewis and Myron C. Taylor, chairman of the board of directors of the United States Steel Corporation, an agreement had been reached whereby "Big Steel" recognized the S.W.O.C. as the bargaining agent for its members, granted a ten per cent wage increase, and accepted an eight-hour day and forty-hour week. Even though the company still maintained a technical open shop policy, it was a tremendous victory for unionism and one that had few if any parallels in the whole history of the organized labor movement. A citadel had fallen before the onslaught of the C.I.O. and its submission graphically revealed what was to become the new pattern of labor relations in the mass production industries as a whole.

"Big Steel" had surrendered, it was believed, under the pressure of banking interests that had clearly read the handwriting on the wall ever since passage of the Wagner Act. With a majority of the company's employes (more accurately, those of its chief subsidiary, the Carnegie-Illinois Steel Company) already enrolled under the banners of the Steel Workers' Organizing Committee, they foresaw a strike that would cripple operations at a time when production was just getting back into stride and new orders were piling up on the company's books. The corporation that had at one time declared its unalterable opposition to union labor was induced to accept peacefully a trend which could no longer be successfully withstood. Enlightened self-interest triumphed over stubborn prejudice.

Over a hundred independent companies followed the lead of United States Steel and by May the S.W.O.C. membership had leaped ahead to over 300,000. But there were still important hold-outs. The companies known as "Little Steel"—Republic, Youngstown Sheet and Tube, Inland Steel and Bethlehem—refused to come to terms with the S.W.O.C. and began to mobilize their forces to resist any further union pressure. Under the leadership of Tom M. Girdler, the tough, reactionary, virulently anti-labor president of Republic, the battle lines were drawn.

The reply of the leaders of the S.W.O.C. was a strike call and during May some 75,000 workers in the plants of "Little Steel" walked out in a concerted move to compel recognition of their union. The companies fought back and through their strong control over the steel towns did so successfully. Citizens' committees were formed to support a campaign of intimidation and violent coercion; back-to-work movements were organized with the protection of local police and special deputies; and attacks upon the picket lines, tear gassing of union headquarters, arrests of strike leaders, and the use of militia to protect strikebreakers gradually broke down the morale of the workers.

Violence flared up in a score of steel towns and reached a peak in a bloody clash at the South Chicago shop of the Republic Steel Company. On May 30 a line of some three hundred pickets was halted by the police, some missiles were thrown, and the police opened fire. The unarmed workers broke ranks and frantically fled for safety from the hail of bullets, but they left ten of their number dead on the street and over a hundred injured. While some twenty-two of the police were also wounded in the affray, not a single one suffered any critical injury.

The "Memorial Day Massacre," as it was at once called by union labor, awoke widespread public sympathy for the strikers. Later investigations, including careful study of moving picture films, clearly revealed that they had not provoked the attack. But the sentiment in the steel towns themselves still remained strongly anti-union and with such support the companies were too well entrenched for the workers to hold out. Propaganda, force and terrorism broke the strike and the C.I.O. suffered its first defeat.

It was to prove a Pyrrhic victory for "Little Steel." Four years later the National Labor Relations Board ordered the companies concerned to recognize what had by then become the United Steelworkers of America, reinstate all employes who had lost their jobs through participation in the strike or because of union membership, and to accept collective bargaining. Stubbornly resisting labor pressure up to the last moment, "Little Steel" was finally forced to capitulate through government intervention. By then—1941—the C.I.O. had succeeded in organizing 600,000 steel workers and virtually the entire industry was covered by union contracts.

In the meantime an even more dramatic and violent revolution had taken place in the automobile industry. There had been seething unrest among its workers since the advent of the N.R.A. and the failure of the incipient strikes of 1934. In spite of high hourly rates, seasonal lay-offs held down annual wages to an average of less than $1,000 while another widely held grievance was the speed-up on the assembly line. For the worker whose sole task was to stand by a conveyor belt and put a wheel on a passing chassis, set a fender or simply tighten a bolt, the tense strain of working under increasing pressure sometimes became almost unbearable. But every attempt to secure modification of such conditions by concerted protest was beaten down by management. The automobile industry had developed its spy system so extensively that union activity appeared to be blocked before it could get started.

Nevertheless unionization was not given up. The United Automobile Workers had been established through a merger of the federal unions originally set up by the A.F. of L. and its organizers were actively at work. Still, progress was slow. Growing discontented with the meager support of the Federation, the new union thereupon broke away from the A.F. of L. in 1936 and threw in its lot with the C.I.O. Homer S. Martin was elected as president and preparations made for a revitalized organizational campaign that was eventually to make the United Automobile,

Aircraft and Agricultural Implement Workers the largest industrial union in the country.

Martin was young and idealistic, with little experience as either a worker or union member. After graduating from a small Missouri college, he had entered the Baptist ministry and in 1932 become pastor of a small church in a Kansas City suburb. His outspoken sympathy for the workers soon led to his losing his position, and he took a job in a Chevrolet factory where he began to preach unionism with evangelical zeal. Fired as a trouble maker, he devoted all his time to union work and rose to be vice-president of the struggling U.A.W. Described in appearance and manner as an almost typical Y.M.C.A. secretary— friendly, quiet, bespectacled—Martin took over control of the union after his election to the presidency and infused it with a new spirit. What he lacked in experience, he made up in energy. Under the impact of his inspirational appeals, which turned union meetings into something very much like old-fashioned revivals, the automobile workers joined up in rapidly increasing numbers.

There were some scattered strikes during the summer of 1936 and by late fall the United Automobile Workers—some 30,000 strong—was coming out in the open, prepared to demand recognition from the giants of the industry—General Motors, Chrysler, and Ford. "We don't want to be driven; we don't want to be spied on," was the workers' new refrain. But the companies, defying the provisions of the Wagner Act, were not yet willing to make any concessions. When Martin asked the officers of General Motors for a conference on collective bargaining, William S. Knudsen, vice-president, merely suggested that if the workers had any grievances they should take them up with local plant managers. The reply of the union was a strike which began in the Fisher Body plants of the company at Flint, Michigan, in January, 1937 and then gradually spread to Detroit, Cleveland, Toledo, and other parts of the country. Production in General Motors came to a standstill with some 112,000 of its 150,000 workers idle.

This strike was something new under the sun. It took the form in Flint of a sit-down. There had been some earlier use of this radical technique, notably among the rubber workers at Akron, but the General Motors strike marked its first use on a really wide scale. The automobile workers refused to leave the plant; they just sat at their work benches.

It was not an act of violence but one of passive resistance, doubly effective in that such a strike could be broken only by the forcible removal of the workers from company premises.

Excitement ran high in Flint and neighboring Detroit. General Motors management and the Flint Alliance, a company-sponsored association supposedly made up of loyal employes, assailed the sit-down as an unlawful invasion of property rights and called for the immediate ejection of the strikers. Martin countered with charges that General Motors proposed to invade the property rights of the workers.

"What more sacred property right is there in the world today," he demanded, "than the right of a man to his job? This property right involves the right to support his family, feed his children and keep starvation away from the door. This . . . is the very foundation stone of American homes . . . the most sacred, most fundamental property right in America."

The C.I.O. at first looked upon the strike with misgivings and was anything but enthusiastic over the sit-down. Deeply involved in the organizing drive in steel, whose success was considered basic to the whole program of industrial unionism, the outbreak in automobiles was highly embarrassing. But support could not be withheld and the C.I.O. undertook to do everything it could to aid the General Motors employes. "You men are undoubtedly carrying on through one of the most heroic battles that has ever been undertaken by strikers in an industrial dispute," Lewis declared. "The attention of the entire American public is focussed upon you. . . ."

The latter part of his statement was unquestionably true, and became even more so as violence broke out in Flint and the strikers showed their stubborn determination not to be dislodged from the occupied plants. The cutting off of all heat—even though it was the dead of winter—made no difference. When the police tried to rush Fisher Body Plant No. 2, they were met by a hail of missiles—coffee mugs, pop bottles, iron bolts and heavy automobile door hinges. When they then returned to the attack with tear-gas bombs, the strikers retaliated by turning streams of water on them from the plant fire hoses. The forces of law and order were finally compelled to make a hasty retreat in what the exultant workers promptly termed the "Battle of the Running Bulls."

The strike dragged on from week to week as the General Motors employes continued to sit it out with food and other supplies brought in to them through the picket lines. Discipline was rigid. "Brilliantly lighted," reads a contemporary description by a union organizer, "this vast plant was heavily guarded inside and outside—to keep strikebreakers and other interlopers from entering and to protect the building and its contents. Especially did these strikers guard the company's dies. No liquor was permitted on the premises, and smoking was prohibited on all production floors. Forty-five men were assigned to police patrol duty inside. Their word was law."

Both the company and the Flint Alliance now demanded that the state militia be mobilized to clear the plants since the police had failed to do so. But Governor Murphy of Michigan, sympathetic with the automobile workers and fearful of the bloodshed that would certainly result, refused to take this step. Finally, however, General Motors obtained a court order setting 3:00 P. M. on February 3 as the deadline for evacuation of the plants under penalty of imprisonment and fines. The strikers were undismayed. "We the workers," they wired the governor, ". . . have carried on a stay-in strike over a month to make General Motors Corporation obey the law and engage in collective bargaining. . . . Unarmed as we are, the introduction of the militia, sheriffs or police with murderous weapons will mean a blood-bath of unarmed workers. . . . We have decided to stay in the plant."

Realizing that the strikers meant what they said, Murphy frantically summoned a peace conference. John L. Lewis rushed to Detroit ("Let there be no moaning at the bar when I put out to sea," he cryptically told reporters as he entrained in Washington) and began negotiations with Vice-President Knudsen, whom Governor Murphy had prevailed upon to meet him. But the morning of February 3 arrived without any settlement having been reached. The sit-downers were barricaded in the factories, armed with iron bolts and door hinges, and protected against the expected tear and vomiting gas with slight cheesecloth masks. Outside the besieged plants, thousands of sympathetic workers and members of women's emergency brigades milled about as sound trucks blared forth the slogan of "Solidarity Forever."

The zero hour approached—and passed. Governor Murphy refused to order the national guardsmen to enforce the court order. In spite of mounting popular pressure, he remained unwilling to make a move that would have precipitated violence on an unpredictable scale.

The next day President Roosevelt added his request for a continuation of negotiations to that of Governor Murphy, and the Lewis-Knudsen talks (with other representatives of both General Motors and the strikers present) were resumed. For a full week, while the sit-downers grimly held the fort, the conference proceeded until at long last, the weary, haggard governor was able to announce that agreement had been reached. General Motors undertook to recognize the United Automobile Workers as the bargaining agent for its members, to drop injunction proceedings against the strikers, not to discriminate in any way against union members, and to take up such grievances as the speed-up and other matters.

It was not a complete victory for the union. The U.A.W. had sought sole bargaining privileges for all General Motors employes, a uniform minimum wage and the thirty-hour week. But as in the case of the S.W.O.C. settlement with "Big Steel," another anti-union stronghold had been captured. Organized labor had taken the first step toward what was to become the complete unionization of the entire automobile industry. Whatever might be said of the legality or ethics of a sit-down strike, the results spoke for its effectiveness.

With the success of the automobile workers in General Motors, sit-down strikes spread through union ranks in all parts of the country. The employes of the Chrysler Corporation soon followed suit, and after a relatively brief sit-down in comparison with the forty-four day strike at General Motors, succeeded in winning recognition for the union and a collective bargaining agreement comparable to that exacted from General Motors. Indeed, only Ford continued to hold out among the automobile companies, successfully resisting all attempts of the United Automobile Workers to organize its plants for another four years.

Other industries also felt the impact of labor's new weapon. Between September, 1936, and June, 1937, almost 500,000 workers were involved in sit-down strikes. Rubber workers, glass workers and textile workers sat at their benches; striking Woolworth clerks stayed behind their counters but would not wait on customers; pie bakers, opticians, dress-makers and apartment house janitors sat down. The longest strike of this kind was that of some 1800 electrical workers in Philadelphia. Two bridegrooms sat out their honeymoons and the wives of six other married strikers greeted their returning husbands with newly born babies.

As workers throughout the country eagerly took up this militant strategy to force anti-union employers into line, they enthusiastically sang their song of revolt:

> When they tie the can to a union man,
> Sit down! Sit down!
> When they give him the sack, they'll take him back,
> Sit down! Sit down!
>
> When the speed-up comes, just twiddle your thumbs,
> Sit down! Sit down!
> When the boss won't talk, don't take a walk,
> Sit down! Sit down!

These strikes aroused increasing popular resentment. Conservative newspapers grew hysterical in condemning such a flagrant invasion of property rights and there was little support for the sit-downs from any quarter. While Upton Sinclair wrote from California that "for seventy-five years big business has been sitting down on the American people, and now I am delighted to see the process reversed," even among labor sympathizers there were few to echo this sentiment. The A.F. of L. explicitly disavowed the sit-down and while the C.I.O. had supported the automobile workers, official approval was never given to its general use. After lively and acrimonious debate, the Senate resolved that such strikes were "illegal and contrary to public policy," and the courts eventually outlawed them as constituting trespass on private property.

For all the excitement it occasioned during the first half of 1937, the sit-down strike in fact proved to be a temporary phenomenon and was abandoned almost as quickly as it had been adopted. It had been the quick and ready response of new and impatient union members fighting for recognition in the strongholds of anti-unionism and embittered by the refusal of employers to comply with the provisions of the Wagner Act. When the law was sustained and the N.L.R.B. empowered to hold elections for collective bargaining units, the sit-downs were given up.

Before this happened, however, the strikes of early 1937 had greatly aroused public opinion and labor as a whole bore the brunt of popular condemnation of the sit-down. Gallup poll reports showed that an overwhelming majority of persons interviewed opposed the use of labor's new weapon, while seventy per cent of those questioned were convinced that new regulatory laws were needed to curb the unions. Sit-down strikes might be explained as no more contrary to law than the refusal of industry to heed cease-and desist orders issued by the N.L.R.B., but they awoke fears and alarms that were not easily stilled.

The immediate consequences of C.I.O. activity throughout 1937 were, in any event, immense gains for all affiliated unions. If the dramatic victories won in steel and automobiles were the most important fruits of the general assault upon the mass production industries, there were other developments that played their part in revolutionizing the labor scene. Organized drives among the rubber workers, radio and electrical workers, lumbermen and longshoremen, among others, served to build up strong and powerful unions. The campaign of a new Textile Workers' Organizing Committee, under the skillful management of Sidney Hillman, was particularly significant in that it succeeded in organizing many southern mills where the A.F. of L. had failed to make any appreciable headway. Thousands of new converts for unionism were won in company towns where labor organizers had never before dared to show themselves, and within a year the union had signed hundreds of collective bargaining agreements throughout the industry.

More important than the actual strength of C.I.O. unions at the close of 1937—600,000 mine workers, 400,000 automobile workers, 375,000 steel workers, 300,000 textile workers, 250,000 ladies' garment workers, 177,000 clothing workers, 100,000 agricultural and packing workers— was the broader base for organized labor as a whole that its campaign had finally achieved. The C.I.O. had successfully organized the unskilled workers into industrial unions, and broken through the narrow lines of craft unionism fostered by the A.F. of L. It had welcomed as the Federation had never done, immigrants, Negroes, and women, disregarding lines of color, sex or nationality.

The C.I.O. influence, moreover, extended to the entire labor front. The A.F. of L., as previously suggested, soon found that it could not ignore the unskilled workers while its rival made such giant strides in organizing them. It had, of course, never done so altogether. The lines between skilled, semi-skilled and unskilled workers had, indeed, become so blurred with the advance of the machine and the assembly line that many A.F. of L. unions included all types. There had also always been industrial unions in the Federation, as we have seen in tracing the growth of organization among coal miners and workers in the garment industry. But the example of what had been done in steel, automobiles and other mass production industries aroused the A.F. of L. to the need of expanding its own organization to prevent the C.I.O. from wholly monopolizing the new opportunities for unionization. Thousands of workers whose skill was no greater than that of the rank and file of the industrial unions were drawn into such multiple-craft or semi-industrial A.F. of L. unions as the machinists, the boilermakers, the meat cutters, the restaurant employes, the hod carriers and common laborers, and the teamsters. Galvanized into more strenuous activity than ever before, the Federation admitted new recruits wherever it could find them, and if its development was not as dramatic as that of the C.I.O., there were large gains in membership. Even with the defection of the unions that went over to the rival organization, A.F. of L. enrollment at the close of 1937, as we have seen, was about a million greater than in 1933.

The A.F. of L. and the C.I.O. continued to strive to build up their strength in jealous competition. The former reached out to set up new industrial unions, the latter did not hesitate to charter craft unions. As labor leaders increasingly realized that there was no one formula for organization, and that different working conditions demanded different approaches to union problems, debate over the old issues that had led to the split in the labor movement became wholly academic. While the C.I.O. had a majority of industrial unions in the mass production industries and the A.F. of L. included by far the larger proportion of what might still be called craft unions, old distinctions were largely broken down and both organizations, becoming more and more alike, were prepared to welcome all comers.

The unhappy by-product of these developments was the spread of

jurisdictional quarrels between competing unions. The A.F. of L. carpenters fought the C.I.O. woodworkers, the C.I.O. automobile workers
fought the A.F. of L. machinists, and A.F. of L. and C.I.O. longshoremen, textile workers, electrical workers, packing house workers and
retail clerks battled indiscriminately. The heavens rang with charges
of union raiding, scabbing, and mutual betrayal. The bitterness of
these family squabbles often exceeded that of labor-capital disputes.
The recriminatory attacks of the two organizations upon one another,
and sometimes union battles within either the A.F. of L. or C.I.O., were
on occasion more violent than labor attacks upon industry. Strikes broke
out again and again for no other cause than a quarrel over jurisdiction,
to the great loss of the workers immediately concerned and to the immense harm of all organized labor.

In their efforts to win recognition for their respective unions, the
A.F. of L. and the C.I.O. brought the National Labor Relations Board
into their feud. The goal of this agency was absolute impartiality in
handling elections for the unions to be designated as employe bargaining
agents, but it was hampered again and again by attacks made upon it
not by industry but by labor. The very fact that it was criticized so
severely in both labor camps was perhaps the best proof of its success
in maintaining impartiality, but such criticism nevertheless provided
ammunition to those who were assailing it on the broader grounds of
exceeding its authority and displaying an anti-industry bias. Labor's
internal squabbles were not only dissipating its own strength, but
threatening to undermine the governmental agency set up to encourage
union recognition.

The solidarity which had been the bright dream of nineteenth century
labor leaders was lost. It may well be argued that a too closely unified
labor movement would have held out the risks of over-centralized
authority and the nationwide control of the workers by dictatorial leaders who would have ignored democratic procedures. Diversity in the
ranks of labor is an assurance against such a dangerous development.
Nevertheless the position of organized labor, from either its own or the
public point of view, was not as securely established as it might have
been had statesmanship prevailed in the original dispute over craft
versus industrial unionism, or in the later efforts for reunion between the
A.F. of L. and the C.I.O. It was widely felt at the close of the 1930's that

not until a greater measure of unity was restored would organized labor be able to act with the responsibility that was so highly important if it was to play its full part in upholding the stability of our economic system and broadening the bases of social democracy.

XVII: LABOR AND POLITICS

THE ROLE OF LABOR in politics took on a new significance with the New Deal. With government intervention in industrial relations on such a broad scale, the maintenance in office of a national administration and congress sympathetic toward labor's aspirations became of more vital import than ever before. The limited objectives sought by the lobbying activities of the A.F. of L. in the days when Samuel Gompers opposed minimum wages, old age pensions and unemployment insurance as "softening the moral fibre of the people," no longer met the needs of the nation's workers. The new industrial unions were especially dependent upon the protection afforded them by New Deal legislation and were consequently ready to do everything in their power to assure the continuance of a pro-labor administration in Washington.

The pronounced swing toward more extensive participation in politics was not, however, entirely due to this desire for effective enforcement of the new labor laws. There was a growing awareness of the larger issues involved in the Roosevelt program. Labor generally felt that the New Deal represented the progressive forces in American democracy, carrying forward a tradition of popular government in the interests of the common people that stemmed from the days of Jackson. All the implications of democratic capitalism were accepted in this support for the New Deal. Labor did not think in terms of an industrial commonwealth or a socialist state. Its goal was to bring about those conditions in our economic and social life that would enable the system of free enterprise to operate successfully with the largest possible degree of social justice.

It was natural that in this burst of political activity, the C.I.O. should be far more aggressive than the A.F. of L. The liberal and insurgent spirit characterizing its advocacy of industrial unionism was carried over to the promotion of social reform. While there was not actually any far departure from the old tradition of rewarding labor's friends and punishing its enemies, the C.I.O. was to go much farther in trying to make this policy effective. Unlike the A.F. of L., which continued in upholding non-partisanship in presidential elections, it was prepared to come out in vigorous support of Roosevelt.

There was also greater recognition by the industrial unions making up the C.I.O. membership than on the part of the more strongly established craft unions in the A.F. of L. of the extent to which all wage earners had become dependent upon government. The experience of the depression had convinced them of the need for additional controls over the economic life of the nation.

"With the guarantee of the 'right to organize,' such industries may be unionized," Lewis wrote in regard to mass-production enterprises, "but, on the other hand, better living standards, shorter working hours and improved employment conditions for their members cannot be hoped for unless legislative or other provisions be made for economic planning and for price, production and profit controls. Because of these fundamental conditions, it is obvious to industrial workers that the labor movement must organize and exert itself not only in the economic field but also in the political arena. . . ."

To carry forward such a program, the C.I.O. leadership was instrumental in establishing Labor's Non-Partisan League in 1936, and also supported the formation of the American Labor Party in New York. The primary purpose behind these moves was the re-election of Roosevelt, and every effort was made to win the support of both A.F. of L. and C.I.O. unions. The first president of the Non-Partisan League was George L. Berry, of the Printing Pressmen's Union, an A.F. of L. affiliate. But while many state labor federations and member unions did cooperate with the league, the A.F. of L. itself would not officially have anything to do with it. The executive council was divided on political issues. William Hutcheson headed the Republican Labor Committee and Daniel Tobin the Democratic Labor Committee. While Green personally backed Roosevelt, he condemned the Non-Partisan League as a dual movement in politics just as the C.I.O. was a dual movement in economic organization.

There was never any question, however, as to where either the C.I.O., or the new industrial unions stood. Heavy contributions were made to the Non-Partisan League's campaign fund, the United Mine Workers alone advancing $500,000, and Lewis called for unequivocal support for the New Deal. "Labor has gained more under President Roosevelt," he declared, "than under any president in memory. Obviously it is the duty of labor to support Roosevelt 100 per cent in the next election."

The Democrats had appealed for labor's backing and had every reason to expect it. The Roosevelt administration had grappled directly with the issues created by the depression and shown a primary concern with getting people back to work, raising wages and promoting union organization. "We will continue to protect the worker," the Democratic platform pledged, "and we will guard his rights, both as wage earner and consumer. . . ." The Republicans also promised to uphold the right to organize, but neither their previous record nor general attitude were any assurance that labor's broader aims would receive from them the support which had been obtained under the New Deal.

The campaign of 1936 was a bitter one. The divisions of opinion created in American society crossed party lines and aligned class against class as had not happened since Populism challenged the conservative rule of the dominant business community forty years earlier. With former President Hoover and the Liberty League charging that the administration sought "to introduce the foreign creeds of Regimentation, Socialism and Fascism," Roosevelt struck back no less vigorously with the counter-charge that the "economic royalists" considered government as a mere appendage of their own affairs. "Government by organized money," he declared, "is just as dangerous as government by organized mob."

The votes of labor—of A.F. of L. as well as C.I.O. union members—played an important part in enabling Roosevelt to sweep the country in 1936. The wage earners had aligned themselves with other liberal elements in the country in a nationwide popular response to a dynamic program of recovery and reform. Labor was endorsing agricultural relief and business reform as well as a new order of industrial relations and social security; it was endorsing a measure of economic recovery reflected in rising business activity and higher farm income as well as lessening unemployment and increased wages.

The campaign activities of the Non-Partisan League and the vote won for Roosevelt in New York by the American Labor Party appeared to demonstrate the value of direct labor action in politics. The

C.I.O. developed a broad and comprehensive legislative program, and in a new Declaration of Purpose, the Non-Partisan League stated that it would attempt in future elections to insure both the nomination and the election of candidates pledged to support labor and other progressive measures. It was ready to work "with every progressive group whose purpose is to secure the enactment of liberal and humanitarian legislation."

The Non-Partisan League entered into local elections in several states during the next few years, seeking to capture control of the Democratic Party in Pennsylvania, playing an active role in New Jersey politics, and throwing its support behind a campaign for a labor administration in Detroit. In New York, the American Labor Party drew largely from the socialist-minded members of the needle trades unions, but it also attracted enough liberal supporters outside the ranks of labor to rally 500,000 votes for the re-election of Mayor La Guardia in 1937. On the national stage, there was continued activity in backing up New Deal legislation, supporting Roosevelt's program for the reorganization of the Supreme Court, and promoting further reform measures all along the line. The Non-Partisan League entered into the congressional elections of 1938 and energetically tried to defeat all opponents of the New Deal and to elect its adherents regardless of party affiliation.

An important part was played in this political activity of the late 1930's—although his role was to be even more significant with the formation of the C.I.O.'s Political Action Committee in 1944—by Sidney Hillman. A strong proponent of "constructive co-operation" between labor and management, he also urged broad participation by wage earners in politics to assure the basic conditions that would make such cooperation feasible. Few unions have been more politically conscious than his Amalgamated Clothing Workers. Sometimes characterized as the very embodiment of "social engineering" union leadership, at once highly practical and idealistic, Hillman was one of the foremost labor strategists of the day with a broad and visionary view of the society he believed could be created in America.

"Having realized our dreams of yesterday," he told a union convention in 1938, "let us dedicate ourselves to new dreams of a future where there will be no unemployment; a future where men and women will be economically secure and politically free."

The possibilities of developing an even more active political role for labor than represented by the Non-Partisan League were widely debated at this time. The old issue of formation of a labor party, which had so often been raised in the past, was once again revived. The League was seen in some quarters as the possible nucleus for a movement in which labor, the farmers and other liberal groups might be brought together in a coalition that would either capture control of the Democratic machine or set up an independent third party should it prove desirable.

These ideas did not make any real headway, however. The A.F. of L. would have none of them and the C.I.O., while repeatedly calling for a constructive program of economic security, did not go so far as to endorse independent political action. Past experience with third party movements was discouraging for further experiment along these lines, and the friendly attitude toward labor of the New Deal appeared in any event to make it inadvisable. The workers as a whole appeared to endorse Green's stand that labor was not a sect or a class, but a cross-section of the nation with such diverse interests that a labor party would have no real validity. As throughout the nineteenth century, there was no binding tie like a common belief in socialism or any other positive philosophy. The possible threat of a third party was always in the background, however, should wage earners find that they could not exercise sufficient influence on the major parties—and especially the Democrats—to assure support for their basic aims.

Third party or no third party, conservative and anti-New Deal forces became increasingly alarmed over the effect of the political pressure labor was exerting in the late 1930's. To combat such influences, the program of the C.I.O. was singled out as radical and un-American. Charges were made that left-wing elements were wholly in control of the Non-Partisan League and forcing it to follow the Communist party line. The National Association of Manufacturers and other employer groups seized every opportunity to press such attacks. One pamphlet widely circulated by various anti-union groups had the engaging title "Join the C.I.O. and Help Build a Soviet America." The active leaders of the Non-Partisan League and the American Labor Party, including

Hillman and Lewis, were assailed for their supposed sympathies with communism and willingness to promote policies dictated from Moscow.

There were some fitfully burning embers where the opponents of the C.I.O. saw such dense clouds of smoke. The radical elements always present in the labor movement, and which in the past had been represented by Chicago anarchists, left-wing socialists and the I.W.W., were now generally enrolled in the Communist camp. Their labor front had originally been the Trade Union Educational League, founded by William Z. Foster after the failure of the steel strike in 1919, and subsequently the Trade Union Unity League set up some ten years later to promote industrial unionism independently of the A.F. of L. The shift in the Moscow party line in the mid-1930's, which swung Communist support to a united democratic front against fascism, then led to abandonment of dual unionism and a return to older socialist techniques of boring from within. The Communists were prepared to do everything they could to encourage industrial unionism and hoped to win control, or at least to dominate, the C.I.O. and its political affiliates.

Lewis did not hesitate to draw upon their experience and organizing skill in building up the C.I.O. and the Non-Partisan League. He needed help from every quarter. "We have to work," he stated, "with what we have." While he fully recognized that the Communists would seek to use the new unions for strengthening their own position, he nevertheless thought that he could disregard their politics so long as they were aiding him in promoting industrial unionism. As a result of such hospitality, Communists or fellow travelers won important positions in some unions and even in the high councils of the C.I.O. itself. There was to be continued internal strife within the United Automobile Workers as the left-wing and conservative factions struggled for power, and Communist sympathizers largely succeeded in winning control in the Electrical, Radio and Machine Workers; the Transport Workers, the Maritime Union, the State, County and Municipal Workers, the Fur and Leather Workers, and the Woodworkers of America. Their zeal and enterprise —in parliamentary strategy, organizational "leg-work," and the pressures exerted by "goon squads" of toughs in local elections—gave them an influence out of all proportion to their actual numbers.

There was no more question at this time than in previous periods of the basic conservatism and loyalty of the great bulk of union members, whether allied with the A.F. of L. or the C.I.O. Communist leadership in a union did not mean that its members conformed to the party line, but rather that they accepted direction from any quarter which brought results. Just as anti-revolutionary workers had welcomed the aid of I.W.W. organizers twenty-five years earlier, so those engaged in the strikes of the 1930's were quite willing to accept Communist help. The high command of the C.I.O. distrusted the Communists because it well knew that they put the welfare of the party ahead of everything else, but so long as they were cooperating in promoting labor's aims, it continued to take advantage of their assistance. If Lewis appeared to be flirting too dangerously with them at times, if not actually working in close alliance, other leaders in the C.I.O., such as Murray and Hillman, were strenuously to combat their influence. They fully realized that however small the Communist nucleus in the labor movement might be, it was so tightly knit and so closely disciplined that it was always a threat to democratic unionism.

The political support that the left-wing was prepared to give Roosevelt and the New Deal as part of the program for a united front, added further confusion to the labor scene. The anti-New Deal forces made the most of Communist backing for Roosevelt in attacking his administration for what they declared were its socialistic and radical policies. But while the President could repudiate Communist support as such, he continued to need that of organized labor. It was consequently greatly to his interest to have a united movement strong enough to throw out the Communists, dominate the radical minority, and independently rally the progressive forces of the nation behind his policies. Since 1937 he had continually urged a reconciliation between the A.F. of L. and the C.I.O. with such ideas in view, and in 1939 he again called upon both organizations to make a real effort to settle their differences.

Upon Roosevelt's insistence, peace negotiations were resumed that year and representatives of the A.F. of L. and the C.I.O. tried to get together. The issue of craft unionism versus industrial unionism had long since lost any real validity, as we have seen, but the rival drives for power had been intensified by the conflicts of the past few years. Lewis put forward an ambitious proposal for the merger of the A.F. of L., the C.I.O. and also of the railway brotherhoods. It was wholly impractical, for the railway brotherhoods were not remotely interested in such a project, and Lewis was immediately charged with not acting in good faith.

The A.F. of L. counter-offer was for readmission of the C.I.O. unions in the parent organization but without recognition of their extended jurisdiction. Lewis adjourned the meeting without giving a definite answer to this proposal, but was soon declaring that peace was "impossible" because of the obstructive attitude of the A.F. of L. leaders who were pursuing a policy of "rule or ruin." The truth of the matter was that neither side was willing to make real concessions. In spite of their professed acceptance of the need for labor unity, both the A.F. of L. and the C.I.O. put their own interests first. Green continued to express his "passion for peace," but it was to be upon his own terms. Lewis was perhaps more frank in stating, "we must expand our movement."

The internal difficulties confronting labor, whether born of Communist intrigue or jurisdictional squabbling, were in no way resolved in 1939. In the meantime, however, far more important developments on the world scene were to have their inevitable repercussions on both labor and national politics. Russia and Germany concluded their famous pact in late August and immediately afterward Europe was plunged into war by Hitler's attack on Poland. The United States found itself menaced by the growing possibility of being drawn into the raging struggle against fascism, and popular attention was increasingly diverted from domestic problems to the larger issues of foreign policy. The country was critically divided into opposing camps on the overshadowing question of whether aid to the allies could keep war from our shores, or whether we should seek to maintain an isolationist position as the only means to safeguard our own peace.

As expressed in resolutions adopted by both the A.F. of L. and the C.I.O., labor was wholly opposed to our entering the war but was prepared to back up Roosevelt's policy of extending aid to the allies and building up our own national defense. There were differing viewpoints within union ranks, however, as among other elements in the population, while the Communist party line had abruptly shifted from the united democratic front to virulent isolationism. The Roosevelt administration was attacked as vigorously as it had formerly been defended. With the approach of the election of 1940, the question of how labor would vote consequently became of utmost importance. In these circumstances the position of Lewis was to attract nationwide attention, and it was a strange, unpredictable role that he chose to play.

In the aftermath of Roosevelt's re-election in 1936, Lewis had grandiosely assumed that the Democrats had won their sweeping victory not merely because of labor's support but because he—John L. Lewis—had been largely instrumental in delivering the labor vote. The C.I.O. and its Non-Partisan League, according to this thesis, had saved the New Deal and Roosevelt consequently was under a direct obligation to pay off his political debt by subscribing fully to C.I.O. policy. Success had gone so much to Lewis' head that he appeared to think that the President should be at his beck and call, and in the midst of the sit-down strikes at the General Motors plants early in 1937, he made his position clear.

"For six months the economic royalists represented by General Motors," Lewis told reporters, "contributed their money and used their energy to drive this administration out of power. The administration asked labor for help and labor gave it. The same economic royalists now have their fangs in labor. The workers of this country expect the administration to help the workers in every legal way and to support the workers in General Motors plants."

It was an arrogant statement and Roosevelt showed his resentment at the assumption that he stood in any way committed to the C.I.O. He did not let it interfere with his efforts to bring about peace in the automobile industry, which he felt to be in the public interest, but he rejected the idea of political bargaining in what had been his close cooperation with Lewis in the past. Smarting under at least an implied presidential rebuke, the C.I.O. leader began to nurse a grudge and it was deepened when in the course of the fierce struggle between the S.W.O.C. and the "Little Steel" companies, Roosevelt flared out in a statement calling down a "plague o' both your houses." After brooding over this further rebuff, Lewis took the occasion of a Labor Day radio speech, in which he recounted the deaths and injuries suffered during the steel strike, to return to the attack.

"It ill behooves one who has supped at labor's table and who has been sheltered in labor's house," he pontifically proclaimed, "to curse with equal fervor and fine impartiality both labor and its adversaries when they become locked in deadly embrace."

There was another aspect, however, to this growing rift between Roosevelt and Lewis. With the continuing triumphs of the C.I.O. and his own mounting fame, Lewis began to have political ambitions. Some time after the third term possibilities for Roosevelt had become a matter of widespread discussion, in late 1939 or early 1940, he went to the President with a proposal. Frances Perkins has related the story in an account of a conversation in which Roosevelt told her and Daniel Tobin, of the A.F. of L. teamsters' union, of how Lewis had proposed a way to get around all objections to a third term.

"Mr. President, I have thought of all that and I have a suggestion to make for you to consider," Mrs. Perkins quotes Roosevelt, who in turn was quoting Lewis. "If the vice-presidential candidate on your ticket should happen to be John L. Lewis, those objections would disappear. A strong labor man would insure the full support, not only of all the labor people, but of all the liberals who worry about such things as third terms."

It was a suggestion that did not appeal to the President. He let it slide. But there is another account of this incident, probably apocryphal. It has Lewis proposing to Roosevelt that as the "two most prominent men in the nation" they would make an invincible ticket, and the President blandly asking, "Which place will you take, John?"

Whatever part frustrated ambition may have played in Lewis' political stand, he had allowed himself to become convinced by 1940 that Roosevelt was no longer the great champion of industrial democracy to whose support he had summoned all labor four years earlier. He now charged the administration with betraying the workers' cause and refusing to give labor representation in either the cabinet or any policy-making government agency. At a United Mine Workers convention in January, he dramatically broke all former ties with the President. "Should the Democratic National Committee," he told his startled audience, "be coerced or dragooned into renominating him, I am convinced . . . his candidacy would result in ignominious defeat."

Lewis was playing a dangerous game. His course appeared to suggest that having failed to transform the Democratic Party into an out-and-out labor party, with himself as possible successor to Roosevelt, he had formed the idea that Labor's Non-Partisan League might develop into a third party which could provide the necessary vehicle for his own political preferment in 1944. The whole issue was deeply involved in his feuding with other C.I.O. leaders and his close association with left-wing and Communist groups. It was also bound up with the position he had taken on foreign policy. For with the outbreak of war in Europe, Lewis had swung over to the isolationist camp and was in angry opposition to the whole program of aid to the allies. The extent to which foreign policy rather than personal pique and political frustration accounted for his desertion of Roosevelt remains, however, a question which perhaps even Lewis himself could not honestly answer.

In any event, he openly opposed the President as the 1940 campaign got underway. The New Deal had completely failed to bring about economic recovery, he declared, and it was in fact entirely responsible for the prolongation of the depression. For a time he did not indicate whether opposition to Roosevelt meant support for Wendell Willkie, nominated by the Republicans, but such doubts as to where he stood were resolved in a radio speech on October 25th which had been carefully timed for full dramatic effect.

"I think the re-election of President Roosevelt for a third term would be a national evil of the first magnitude," Lewis stated. "He no longer hears the cries of the people. I think that the election of Mr. Wendell Willkie is imperative in relation to the country's needs. I commend him to the men and women of labor. . . .

"It is obvious that President Roosevelt will not be re-elected for a third term unless he has the overwhelming support of the men and women of labor. If he is, therefore, re-elected, it will mean that the members of the Congress of Industrial Organizations have rejected my advice and recommendation. I will accept the result as being the equivalent of a vote of no confidence and will retire as president of the Congress of Industrial Organizations in November."

The men and women of labor were not, however, to have their political opinions made up for them by Lewis. The labor vote could no more be delivered in 1940 than in previous years. Ignoring the warnings of the C.I.O. president, many of his associates came out openly for the Democratic candidate, and union after union adopted resolutions favoring a third term. The majority of the A.F. of L. leaders and unions also endorsed the President, and there can be no question that the votes of wage earners contributed heavily, as they had in his two earlier elections, to Roosevelt's third triumph. The vote in mining districts where the leadership of Lewis was generally followed automatically, showed that even members of the United Mine Workers refused to heed his advice in national politics.

In happy contradiction of the Lewis pronouncement, Green declared after the election that working men and working women had voted for Roosevelt because "they believe he is the friend and the champion of social justice and economic freedom."

Lewis had completely over-reached himself. In gambling the presidency of the C.I.O. on the willingness of labor's rank and file to follow him, he had not only taken himself completely out of politics but had sacrificed control of the organization he had done so much to build up. For he fulfilled his pledge to retire from the presidency of the C.I.O. at its next convention. He was still able to exert a powerful influence in labor councils, but it was the close of a chapter in his spectacular career. For all the defiant independence and dramatic posturing that were to mark his later activities, and in spite of the excitement he was to cause as a war and post-war strike leader, he could not recapture the power and prestige of his days as president of the C.I.O.

He remained, of course, head of the United Mine Workers and its members continued to follow wherever he led so far as union affairs were concerned. It was a merry chase. Lewis was soon to take them out of the C.I.O. and then in time back into the A.F. of L. The miners could never be sure just where they stood. Lewis made up his own mind and gave short shrift to the ideas of associates or followers. At the close of 1947, the miners were again to find themselves in the labor wilderness when their erratic chieftain walked out of the A.F. of L. for the second time with a casual abruptness that was startling even for him. Reporters summoned to the United Mine Workers headquarters were shown a message scrawled in blue crayon on a two-by-four inch slip of paper which read: "Green, AFL. We disaffiliate, Lewis. 12/12/47."

The new C.I.O. president in 1940 was Philip Murray, the hero of the S.W.O.C. organizing campaign and for so many years the able and loyal lieutenant of Lewis in the United Mine Workers. His background had a marked similarity to that of both Green and Lewis in that his family was

of British coal mining stock. Murray, however, was himself born abroad
—in Lanarkshire, Scotland in 1886—and did not come to the United
States until he was sixteen. He then followed the family tradition of
entering the mines. Two years later he had his first difficulties with
management and lost his job as a result of taking part in a strike. "I've
never had a doubt since then," he has written, "of what I wanted to do
with my life."

In 1916 he was chosen president of District Number 5 of the United
Mine Workers and four years later vice-president of the international
union. He was known as an extremely able administrator and organizer,
but perhaps most of all for his faithful support, in good times and bad,
of the policies laid down by his chief. He had shown no great interest in
broad ideas of social reform, but believed thoroughly that something
that went with any system of free enterprise was the right of the worker
to a decent wage. Labor organization and collective bargaining were
essential, in his opinion, to secure this goal.

Quiet and self-effacing, Murray was for long considered little more
than a shadow of Lewis. When he became president of the C.I.O. he
was to reveal, however, a tough-minded and stubborn independence that
enabled him to set his own course and to follow it even when it led to a
break with the man whom he most admired and for whom he continued
to profess a deep affection. Murray had qualities, as time was to show,
that made him stand out as a labor leader of strong convictions who
was also able to inspire great personal loyalty.

He gave a first and unexpected demonstration of his independence
when he insisted as a condition for assuming the C.I.O. presidency that
the convention adopt a forthright resolution condemning communism
and all foreign ideologies. In view of the shadowy alliance that Lewis
had maintained with the left wing, Murray was determined to set the
record straight. He did not intend to embark upon a purge of all Communists and fellow travelers, nor did he desire to disrupt the labor movement by extravagent red-baiting. But he was wholly opposed to communism and refused to let the C.I.O. become a front for subversive
political activity. In the same independence of spirit, he rejected the
isolationism that was being preached by both Lewis and the Communists. While still opposing American entry into the war, he was prepared
to support Roosevelt's foreign policy and program for national defense.

It was his own decision. "The convictions which I recommend," he was to tell the C.I.O. convention a year later, "have not come to me as a result of pressure from any group within or without. I am one individual, as you know, who resents the exercise of pressure from individuals or groups. I stand upon my individual integrity as a man."

After the election of 1940, the country in general swung more strongly behind the program of national defense. The successive measures taken by the Roosevelt administration to extend aid to the allies, particularly the adoption of lend-lease, became the all-important issues confronting the nation. The division between isolationists and interventionists grew even more embittered, but the imperative necessity to build up our own security could hardly be denied by any school of thought other than outright pacificists. Mounting war orders from abroad had long since provided a spur to the economic recovery that the New Deal had been unable to achieve, and the demands of the defense program were now to stimulate even greater production all along the economic front. The United States felt itself in imminent danger of being drawn into the war, but it was in the meantime beginning to enjoy unparalleled prosperity.

Labor felt the impact of these developments in many ways. Increased production brought about a rapid decline in unemployment, which had remained at dangerously high levels in spite of everything done by the Roosevelt administration, and also served to stimulate wage increases. The growing need for skilled workers in the defense industries was a new characteristic of the labor market contrasting sharply with conditions that had prevailed for over ten years. Between April, 1940, and December, 1941, total non-agricultural employment rose from thirty-five to over forty-one million, and wage rates generally increased about twenty per cent. In the durable goods industries that were basic to the defense program, average earnings spurted from $29.88 to $38.62 a week. War had come to the rescue of American industry and the strength of organized labor, as enrolled in both the A.F. of L. and C.I.O. unions, enabled wage earners to share substantially in the mounting profits of wartime business.

Labor was prepared to cooperate fully in building up the United

States as "the great arsenal of democracy," but remembering the defeats and setbacks of the 1920's, was also insistent that the benefits attained under the New Deal should not in any way be prejudiced. Further than that, it asserted the right to press forward the campaign to extend union recognition and collective bargaining, and as the cost of living rapidly rose under wartime conditions, demanded further wage increases to maintain the purchasing power of labor income. With industry booming and union strength growing, the stage was consequently set for further struggles between management and labor over their respective roles in our expanding economy. The year 1941 was to prove one of the most tumultuous in labor history.

In most instances labor was pursuing reasonable and constructive policies; and industry, accepting the principles of collective bargaining, met it half way in concluding mutually advantageous agreements on wages, hours and working conditions. The "Little Steel" companies and the United Steelworkers of America finally came to terms, and Henry Ford completely reversed his anti-union policies to sign a contract unreservedly recognizing the United Automobile Workers and even going so far as to grant it a closed shop. But such progress in allaying the causes of industrial strife was soon overshadowded by the outbreak of fresh disputes. In some instances they arose out of excessive and unwarranted union demands, but in others from the obduracy of employers refusing to accept the implications of the new industrial order.

Almost hysterical fear of the growing strength of the unions led a few companies not only to refuse new wage demands but to try in every possible way to clip labor's wings. This group refused further concessions looking toward union recognition, attacked the closed shop as undemocratic and un-American, and circumvented the legal requirements of collective bargaining wherever they could. They covered their anti-union activity in many instances with a mantle of patriotism, insisting that their objectives were merely to maintain uninterrupted industrial production.

The needs of national defense, indeed, tended to make the public impatient of labor's demands and its cause was in no way helped by widespread internal squabbling. The angry recriminations of rival leaders, jurisdictional strikes and highly publicized exposures of a few instances of union racketeering and graft weakened public confidence in the responsibility of organized workers in the face of the mounting national emergency. And it was true that some of the new, insurgent unions were unable to maintain discipline among their thousands of freshly recruited members. Their belligerent attitude toward employers and insistence upon wage increases and other concessions were on occasion as destructive of industrial peace as the anti-union policies of reactionary business.

The number of labor disputes in 1941 reached a higher total than in any previous year with the single exception of 1937. There were strikes in the automobile industry, in the shipyards, in transportation, in the building trades, in textiles, steel and coal mining. Hardly an industry escaped work-stoppages which at least for a time seriously interfered with production. In all, there were 4,288 strikes involving over 2,000,000 workers—almost twice the number of disputes and four times the number of workers as in the previous year. Approximately 8.4 per cent of the nation's employed industrial wage earners took part in these outbreaks and 23,000,000 man-days of work were lost.

A number of strikes were fomented by Communists. Until Germany's invasion of Russia, the party line remained one of virulent opposition to aid to the allies and there were radical left-wing efforts to sabotage the program of national defense. After June, 1941, this attitude was to change in another overnight shift of policy, but Communist-instigated strikes, which responsible labor leadership did its best to control, accounted for no small part of the labor disturbances in the first half of the year.

The threat to the defense program in these work stoppages led to the creation, as early as March, 1941, of the National Defense Mediation Board. This was a tripartite body, representative of labor, management and the public, with authority to seek the adjustment of disputes in the defense industries through either mediation or voluntary arbitration. Its powers did not include enforcement of its decisions, and while it was successful in restoring industrial peace in many instances, more drastic action was to prove necessary on several notable occasions.

A strike on the part of aviation workers at Inglewood, California, led to seizure of a North American Aviation plant by the War Department before a negotiated compromise could be effected, and the Navy Department moved in on a strike of shipyards workers at Kearny, New Jersey, after the Federal Shipbuilding and Dry Dock Company rejected a proposed settlement granting the union maintenance of membership. The climax both of labor disputes and of the troubles of the National Defense Mediation Board was to be reached, however, in a coal strike that so seriously interrupted production as to threaten the whole defense program.

The major issue at stake was establishment of the union shop in the so-called "captive" coal mines operated by the steel industry. The Defense Mediation Board had wavered on the validity of incorporating such a demand in union contracts and when the mining dispute came before it for action in the fall of 1941, it refused to accept the union shop as a basis for a contract. Lewis consequently ignored the board and in the face of President Roosevelt's plea that as a loyal citizen he should come to the aid of his country, called a strike in the captive coal mines on October 27 that threatened to close down almost the entire steel industry.

His defiance of the government had wider significance than protection of the rights of coal miners. Lewis was seeking to win back his shattered prestige by a dramatic labor victory, and he was also demonstrating the opposition which as an outspoken isolationist he felt toward the whole Roosevelt program in foreign affairs. He had pitted himself against the President in the political arena in 1940, and now a year later he was prepared to challenge him in the economic sphere. The fight for the union shop was to be made a test of power, and in complete disregard of the needs of the country and public opposition to his tactics, Lewis was ready to go his own way.

Roosevelt promptly went on the air after the strike was called to declare that the country had to have coal and that national production could not be hampered "by the selfish obstruction of a small but dangerous minority of labor leaders." There were suggestions that he was finally ready to accept anti-strike legislation already being proposed in Congress. But in the meantime Lewis had been negotiating with Myron C. Taylor, of the United States Steel Corporation, and an agreement was reached whereby the union shop issue was again to be reviewed by the Defense Mediation Board without either party obliged to accept its rulings. Lewis was confident that his demands would now have to be approved because of the country's urgent need for coal, and he called off the strike for a temporary truce period while the board again took the case under consideration.

It gave its decision on November 10—and it was nine to two against the union shop. Only the two C.I.O. members dissented from a report which was upheld not only by the representatives of management and the public, but by those of the A.F. of L. Ninety-five per cent of the 53,000 workers in the captive coal mines were already members of the United Mine Workers, but the position taken was that a union shop was a matter for collective bargaining rather than government order, and it was unjustifiable for the Defense Mediation Board to force 2,500 men to join a union against their will.

A principle was at stake and a showdown between Lewis and the President appeared to be unavoidable. The miners' leader refused to modify orders renewing the strike at the expiration of the truce, and he was backed up by the C.I.O. in spite of the internal feuds within that organization. Its representatives on the Defense Mediation Board promptly resigned, and a resolution of the convention then in session upheld Lewis' stand. For his part, Roosevelt declared that under no circumstances would the government order a union shop, insisted upon further negotiations between the miners and the steel companies, and at the same time made preparations for government seizure of the mines should an agreement not be reached. Congress was currently debating amendments to the neutrality legislation and partly to assure support for his foreign program by Congressmen who felt he was dealing too leniently with labor, the President pledged that regardless of what Lewis might do, coal would be mined—"the government proposes to see this thing through."

There was a week of feverish negotiations with the country clamoring for a settlement but neither the miners nor the steel companies would give in on the union shop. On November 17 the strike was again on. The workers in the captive mines laid down their tools and soon sympathetic strikes in other areas swelled the total of idle men in the coal pits to some 250,000. The steel industry was hamstrung in the face of a national emergency rapidly coming to a climax. It was reported that Roosevelt was finally ready to act, with 50,000 troops ordered to take over the mines, and the situation grew hourly more tense. Then suddenly and unexpectedly, on November 22, the strike was called off. Lewis had accepted a proposal of the President for binding arbitration of the union shop issue by a three man tribunal—Lewis himself, President Fairless of the United States Steel Corporation, and as the impartial member, John R. Steelman of the United States Conciliation Service.

Had Lewis capitulated? The secret of his abrupt move was the position of the third man on the tribunal. Steelman was a friend of labor and he was known to be sympathetic toward the union shop. The miners' chieftain felt certain of what his decision would be—and events were to prove him wholly justified. It was Roosevelt who had given in. The appointment of the new arbitration tribunal was in effect repudiation of the Defense Mediation Board and acceptance of Lewis' demands. The strike had been called off, coal would be mined, but governmental authority had been brazenly flouted. The grave national emergency had convinced the President that the defense program could not be further jeopardized, even if it meant letting Lewis have his way. The precedent established was to have grave consequences.

Public reaction to the coal strike was a growing intensification of the anti-labor feeling that had been sweeping the country ever since the early strikes had broken out in defense industries. The work stoppages of the first half of the year, and especially those that were felt to be Communist-inspired, had greatly aroused a nation feverishly arming for a threatened war. Newspaper editorials, the statements of national leaders and public opinion polls, all showed a pronounced stiffening of attitudes toward labor. In and out of Congress, there was a demand for new legislation to restrict the power of the unions and safeguard the public interest against further interruptions to industrial production. The coal strike, and the shocking spectacle of Lewis arrogantly defying the National Defense Mediation Board and the authority of the President, merely brought matters to a head. Anti-labor laws of varying severity had already been passed in twenty-two states and some thirty bills to curb unions were introduced in Congress.

Against the background of uncertainty over the coal strike, and other labor disturbances including a narrowly averted railroad strike, the House approved one of these anti-labor measures on December 3 by a vote of 252 to 136. It would have banned all strikes in defense industries involving the closed shop or growing out of jurisdictional disputes, and any others unless approved by a majority of workers in government-supervised elections after a thirty-day cooling off period. The bill was denounced by Green as "an instrument of oppression"; Murray declared that "nothing more subversive to American democracy has ever been prepared." It appeared probable that its terms would be modified by the Senate, and the President was believed to favor a milder measure, but there was little doubt that some law would be speedily enacted to meet what was generally being called "the national menace" of continued strikes paralyzing defense.

The country was angry. Even the friends of labor, fearing that the popular feeling against unions might lead to curtailment of basic rights guaranteed by the Wagner Act, called for greater moderation on the part of both A.F. of L. and C.I.O. leaders. "The union movement in this country is no longer an infant requiring protection," the *New Republic* editorialized. "It has grown up physically, and if it is to conduct itself like a responsible adult it must be controlled by the same social discipline which governs the rest of the community."

How far the pendulum might have swung against labor in the face of this public reaction in 1941 can hardly be known. For new events suddenly interposed with dramatic force. On December 7—the very day that the arbitral tribunal announced that Lewis had been granted a union shop in the captive coal mines and while the House anti-strike bill was pending in the Senate—Japan struck at Pearl Harbor. The nation found itself at war.

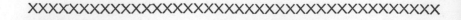

XVIII: THE SECOND WORLD WAR

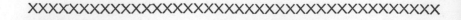

THE SECOND WORLD WAR constituted an immense challenge to every segment of American society—a challenge that was met magnificently in marshaling the country's resources and carrying through the war itself to a final and decisive victory over the enemy powers. In this great effort, American labor played its full part. No less than farmers, businessmen, the professional classes, or members of the armed forces, the industrial workers were prepared to subordinate their own immediate concerns to the national interest.

This is not to say that organized labor did not also remain constantly alert during these grim years to safeguard the gains that unionism had achieved in the 1930's. Its leaders were well aware of the possible erosion of these gains as the development of a wartime economy wholly upset the normal balance of the nation's economic life. They were deeply concerned over the maintenance of union security, the relationship between wages and prices in a rigidly controlled economy, and adequate labor representation on the burgeoning government agencies which directed the war effort on the home front. Throughout the period of hostilities and the subsequent difficult days of conversion to a peacetime economy, both the A.F. of L. and the C.I.O. exercised all the influence they could muster to assure full protection for the interests of both union members and industrial workers generally.

Even before the outbreak of hostilities, labor had insisted on its right to full representation on the economic agencies created to deal with the mounting emergency. And President Roosevelt had recognized the justice of such demands. In first setting up the Office of Production Management in 1941, he had appointed Sidney Hillman (choosing him among other labor leaders on the ground that he stood "just half way between John Lewis and Bill Green") to serve as its co-director with William S. Knudsen, a General Motors vice-president. Labor representatives were also appointed to the subsequent War Production Board, and to the Office of Civilian Defense, the Office of Price Administration, the Office of Economic Stabilization and the War Manpower Commission. Yet something more than this role in helping to order the economy was obviously needed to assure labor's full support for the war effort and to guard against the ever-present danger of strikes that might curtail the production of essential military supplies.

To this end the President summoned a conference of labor and business leaders just ten days after Pearl Harbor to plan new measures for industrial cooperation. After prolonged discussion the conferees agreed upon a three-point program: no strikes or lockouts for the duration of hostilities, peaceful settlement of all industrial disputes, and more concretely, the creation of a tripartite board, with labor, management and the public each represented by four members, which would be empowered to handle all labor controversies affecting the war effort that otherwise failed of settlement. In return for assurances that it would have a voice in determining such conditions and terms of employment as might be required by wartime necessity, this meant that labor had agreed in the national interest to surrender for the time its right to strike.

A sharp decline in work stoppages throughout the country was the immediate consequence of this agreement. In comparison with the 23,000,000 man-days lost in 1941, the total for 1942 fell to 4,180,000. But as the pressures and tensions of war mounted, this record could not be sustained. Labor's leaders charged that the workers' interests were being ignored in the controls government now exercised over wages and prices. William Green declared that it was on the basis that collective bargaining would be sustained that labor had foregone the right to strike and that the course Washington was following could not be reconciled with its earlier pledges. John L. Lewis was far more belligerent in his stand and soon showed that he was ready to defy all governmental authority in protecting the interests of the United Mine Workers. In such circumstances strikes notably increased during 1943 with a total of 13,500,000 man-days lost; and while they again declined somewhat the next year, rose again as the war drew to an end in 1945.

Nevertheless labor continued on the whole to support the war effort conscientiously and a great majority of unions sought in every possible way to restrain strike activity. The man-days lost actually averaged only about one-tenth of one per cent of the total working time in industry as a whole, and were estimated to be the equivalent of no more than one day per worker for the four war years. Many of the strikes were no more than unauthorized "quickies." Their grievances intensified by the strain of long hours and other hardships resulting from wartime conditions, the workers took matters in their own hands. They laid down their tools or quit their jobs in frustrated protest, but once they had let off steam by asserting themselves, went back to work without serious interruption to production. A few more threatening strikes also occurred, but they were the exception rather than the rule.

As the war finally drew to an end, there was hardly a political or military leader who did not take occasion to pay glowing tribute to the role labor had played. It was the determination of American workers to preserve their heritage for coming generations, President Roosevelt declared, that had made possible "the greatest production achievement in the world's history."

The key to labor's wartime history was the agency created to implement and carry through the agreements which had been reached at the labor-management conference summoned by President Roosevelt in the wake of Pearl Harbor. This was the National War Labor Board which officially came into being, under the chairmanship of William H. Davis, former head of the National Defense Mediation Board, by executive order in January, 1942. Its primary function was to take over all unsettled industrial disputes certified by the Secretary of Labor as likely to "interrupt work which contributes to the effective prosecution of the war." Its decisions were to be binding in such cases on both management and labor, and since they were made on a tripartite basis, this in effect gave the public representatives a determining voice on all issues where labor and management could not be brought into accord.

A first and vital problem faced by the War Labor Board was the issue of union security which had wrecked the old Defense Mediation Board. It met this problem successfully with adoption of the principle of maintenance of membership. There would be no attempted enforcement of either a closed shop or a union shop in contract negotiations, but union members, or those who subsequently joined the union, would be required to keep up their membership for the contract's life. Should they fail to maintain good union standing, they were subject to dismissal from their employment. The labor members of the Board accepted this solution of the problem without qualification; those representing management acquiesced very reluctantly. Once it had been agreed upon, however, the principle of maintenance of membership was consistently upheld throughout the war. It ultimately applied to some three million workers, or approximately 20 per cent of those covered by collective bargaining agreements.

The assurances embodied in this program for both union security and individual freedom of action contributed immensely to industrial peace and were greatly responsible for the low level of strikes during 1942. At the end of that year labor's leaders could boast without fear of contradiction that the country's workers had maintained "the finest record of continuous, uninterrupted production ever achieved." Addressing the A.F. of L. convention, Roosevelt stated that labor's cooperation spoke for itself—"it is splendid."

However, the War Labor Board soon found itself facing an even more troublesome problem than union security. Rising prices, induced by the inevitable inflationary pressures of wartime, led the unions to demand wage increases at least commensurate with the rise in the cost of living, and when they threatened to strike if necessary to enforce their claims, something had to be done. The Board first sought to meet this issue on a union-by-union basis. But when the government, gravely concerned over the effects of a price-wages spiral on the national economy, adopted an over-all stabilization program, it was clear that a more consistent and comprehensive policy would have to be worked out. Some sort of formula was needed which would at once hold wages as a whole in line and yet allow such increases as were clearly justified by the rise in the cost of living that had already occurred.

The War Labor Board seized the opportunity to work out and apply such a formula when, in July, 1942, the employees of the Little Steel companies demanded a wage increase of $1 a day. After lengthy hearings it was decided that a rise in wages was justified, but that it should be limited to an equivalent of the increase in living costs between January, 1941, a time of relative price stability, and May, 1942, when the government had instituted its stabilization program. According to the reports of the Bureau of Labor Statistics, the cost of living index had risen some 15 points during this period, and consequently any wage increase would have to be held to this same percentage over existing levels. The War Labor Board consequently awarded the workers at Little Steel plants a raise of 44 cents a day rather than the $1 they originally demanded.

The Little Steel formula now became the basic yardstick for the settlement of all wartime wage disputes. It had been adopted, however, on the assumption that the new stabilization program had brought to an end "the tragic race between wages and prices" and that a 15 per cent wage increase was therefore fair and equitable. This soon proved to be a false assumption. Prices could not be held completely in line. The War Labor Board found itself in the unenviable position of trying to reconcile its formula for wage increases with a further rise in living costs that progressively exceeded the figures on which the formula was based.

Moreover its troubles were compounded when passage of the Economic Stabilization Act in October, 1942, giving congressional sanction to the government's program, expanded its authority beyond the dispute cases which were its original concern. The Board was now obliged by government directive to restrict all wage increases, except where flagrantly substandard conditions existed, to the 15 per cent increase in straight-line hourly wages that had been granted in the steel industry. For the remainder of the war it consequently had two distinct functions: settlement of dispute cases and supervision of voluntary wage agreements. And in both classifications the Little Steel formula was frozen as the official limitation on all wage adjustments.

Organized labor promptly and vigorously protested this broadening of the application of the Little Steel formula as an arbitrary and unwarranted interference with the processes of collective bargaining completely undermining the bases of labor's no-strike pledge. As consumer prices continued to rise, reaching an index figure of 124 by the spring of 1943, these protests became more vehement and a feeling of angry resentment flared up among the rank and file of industrial workers. They believed that government was forcing the wage earners to bear the brunt of an inflationary price rise from which farmers and other producers were actually profiting. Compelled to take some action, the government chose to try to roll back prices rather than permit further wage increases. While a hold-the-line order issued by the President in April was to prove relatively successful in blocking any further increase in living costs, there was no rollback. Labor's grievances still remained as the rise in living costs continued to exceed the allowable increase in wages under the Little Steel formula.

These were the circumstances that encouraged strikes in 1943. For the most part, as already noted, they were of brief duration and did not seriously impede the production of essential wartime goods. Moreover the leaders of both the A.F. of L. and the C.I.O., in spite of continuing criticism of the government's wage policy, did everything they could to keep things under control. But quite a different situation developed in the coal industry. John L. Lewis bluntly stated that the War Labor Board had breached its contract with labor in establishing the Little Steel formula and that he had no intention whatsoever of submitting to its authority so far as the miners were concerned. In stubborn defiance of both the government and an angry public, he was to engineer a series of strikes that provided the most dramatic—if not the most salutary—chapter in labor's wartime history.

The expiration in April, 1943, of the annual contract between the United Mine Workers and the coal operators initiated this drawn-out controversy. Lewis demanded on behalf of the union not only a wage increase of $2 a day but what was termed portal-to-portal pay for the time the miners spent traveling underground. He refused to compromise these exorbitant demands and when the dispute was referred to the War Labor Board contemptuously stayed away from the hearings of an agency which he attacked as "prejudiced" and "malignant." He said that he would not of course call a strike in wartime, but blandly announced "the miners were unwilling to trespass upon the property of the coal operators in the absence of a contract."

The members of his union needed no further instructions. They began to quit work even before the final expiration of the old contract and the country found itself faced with an even graver crisis than that confronted in 1941. Fully aware of the disastrous effects of a stoppage in coal production, President Roosevelt gave immediate orders for the seizure of the coal mines and on May 2 went on the air to appeal to the strikers to return to work.

Placing full responsibility for the breakdown in contract negotiations on the officials of the United Mine Workers, he declared that every man who stopped mining coal was directly obstructing the war effort, gambling with the lives of American soldiers and sailors, and endangering the security of the entire people. He expressed his sympathy for the miners, promising that any new agreement would be made retroactive, but insisted that production must continue pending further negotiations. "Tomorrow the Stars and Stripes will fly over the coal mines," the President concluded. "I hope every miner will be at work under that flag."

The workers returned to the mines. It was, however, on the orders of the president of their union rather than the appeal of the President of the United States. Just twenty minutes before Roosevelt had gone on the air, Lewis had announced a fifteen-day truce (later extended to thirty days) to try to work out a new agreement with Secretary of the Interior Ickes, under whose direction the mines were to be placed. He made no concessions or promise of what might happen after the expiration of the truce. He stood firmly on his original demands.

The next six months were a hectic period alternatively punctuated by temporary truces and renewed work stoppages. At one point the government returned the mines to private operation, but when contract negotiations still made no headway and the miners once again laid down their tools, the government moved in for a second time. Roosevelt now ordered Secretary Ickes to conclude a special wage agreement, subject to approval by the War Labor Board, which would be limited to the duration of the government's operation of the mines.

Throughout this period it was Lewis who held the reins, whatever Washington might say or do, and he continued to insist that the national emergency was no excuse for what he characterized as a policy of callous exploitation of the miners. He declared that their right to higher wages was a matter of simple justice and overrode every other consideration even in time of war. He completely controlled his union. When he told the miners to work, they worked; when he suggested they might stay home or go fishing, they stayed home or went fishing. They ignored both the appeals of President Roosevelt and mounting popular resentment of their wilful attitude. Hard-pressed by the rise in living costs so far outstripping their pay, realizing that every gain they had made in the past had been in defiance of all governmental authority, and generally isolated from the impact of public opinion in their scattered little coal towns, the miners were blindly ready to follow Lewis's lead.

Reflecting the mounting anger of the country as a whole, the press criticized Roosevelt for failing somehow to get the coal mines back into steady production, but its most vehement attacks were leveled against John L. Lewis. He was charged with want of patriotism for placing the interests of the miners above those of the country, assailed for his arrogance, and castigated in season and out for endangering national security. Even other labor leaders criticized the miners' embattled chieftain. There was sympathy for the workers and in some quarters their strike was even welcomed for dramatizing the government's failure to hold down prices. Nonetheless the C.I.O. executive committee condemned Lewis for his supercilious attitude toward the War Labor Board and for what it described as "his personal and political vendetta against the President of the United States."

The situation could not endure indefinitely. After the second seizure of the coal mines a compromise was finally hammered out between Ickes and Lewis, but it was one which went very far toward meeting the union leader's original demands. On the basis of some increase in the miners' working hours and the inclusion of portal-to-portal time, this new agreement provided for an increase of $1.50 a day in the prevailing wage rates. By such expedients it conformed at least nominally to the Little Steel formula, and the War Labor Board, although very reluctantly, approved it. Lewis ordered the miners back to work. He had forced the government's hand. If his victory was not quite as complete as he triumphantly claimed, his stubborn, intractable stand had served the miners well.

The coal strike had greatly aroused the public and fearful that other union leaders might be tempted to follow what were felt to be Lewis's outrageous tactics, a new demand rose for legislative action to curb labor's power. Other work stoppages in the spring of 1943, which anti-union employers seized upon to illustrate labor's irresponsibility, strengthened this demand, but the threatened breakdown in coal production was the single most important factor in creating the popular mood.

A number of restrictive bills were introduced in Congress in response to such gathering pressure, but the one which acquired strongest support was a measure jointly sponsored by Representative Smith and Senator Connally. In the first instance it provided definite statutory authority for the National War Labor Board, but it then went on to incorporate a series of provisions which in tone and content were definitely anti-labor. The President was empowered, whenever government mediation in a labor dispute proved unsuccessful, to take over control of any plant or industry where a halt in production threatened the war effort and thereupon to enforce criminal penalties against any persons who instigated or promoted a strike. It did not place any ban on strikes where the government had not felt compelled to intervene. In contradiction to what had heretofore been a complete no-strike policy, the Smith-Connally bill in such cases sought merely to restrain possible work stoppages by providing for a thirty-day cooling-off period during which the National Labor Relations Board was to hold a strike vote among all employees concerned. Finally, among several other minor provisions, union contributions to political campaign funds were expressly forbidden.

In the heat of the excitement occasioned by the coal strikes, Congress passed this measure by decisive majorities in both the Senate and the House. Labor was incensed. Its spokesmen declared that the bill ignored the widespread observance of the no-strike pledge through its criminal provisions, and at the same time undermined this voluntary commitment by providing under general circumstances for a strike vote. The A.F. of L. executive committee bitterly attacked the proposed law as "born of hatred and malice on the part of reactionary congressmen"; President Murray told the C.I.O. convention that the country was witnessing "the most vicious and continuous attack on labor's rights in the history of the nation."

President Roosevelt vetoed the Smith-Connally bill. Although recognizing the need to control irresponsible unionism, he agreed with labor that the provision for a cooling-off period with strike votes ran wholly counter to the no-strike program. The proposed law, he stated emphatically, would be conducive to labor unrest rather than industrial peace. In the temper of the times Congress paid no attention whatsoever to his reasoned arguments and on June 25, 1943, overrode his veto. Even the *New York Times* now described what was officially called the War Labor Disputes Act as "a hasty, ill-considered and confused measure." Nonetheless it remained on the statute books for the duration of the war.

Whatever the influence of the new legislation, which was hard to assess, strike activity followed an erratic course in succeeding years. As we have noted, it was to decline in 1944 and then, in spite of the new law, to increase in 1945. The most disturbing situation apart from that in the coal industry, however, developed in an area which fell outside the jurisdiction of the Smith-Connally Act or other wartime legislation. This was a threatened strike on the part of railway workers, subject to controls provided in the amended Railway Labor Act of 1926, which created a serious crisis in the fall of 1943.

Following a breakdown of contract negotiations between the unions and the railway operators, President Roosevelt appointed an Emergency Board under the Railway Act's provisions to settle the dispute. Its award, however, went beyond the limits on wage increases incorporated in the Little Steel formula, and the Office of Economic Stabilization consequently disapproved it. The railway unions thereupon prepared to strike.

Faced with an emergency quite as dangerous to the war effort as the strikes in the coal fields, Roosevelt promptly intervened in this confused situation and proposed that he should act as an arbitrator between the opposing positions assumed by the Emergency Board and the Office of Economic Stabilization, with his decision binding on all parties concerned. Although the railroads and most of the railway unions accepted this plan, the Locomotive Firemen, the Railway Conductors, and the Switchmen's unions refused to withdraw their strike orders. The President gave instructions for immediate seizure of the railroads. "The war cannot wait and I cannot wait," he declared. "American lives and victory are at stake."

Before the strike orders actually went into effect or any direct confrontation had developed between the government and the railway workers, announcement was made of the presidential decision in the conflict between the Emergency Board and the Office of Economic Stabilization. It upheld the former. In spite of an apparent violation of the Little Steel formula in the wage award, the President sustained it on the ground that the wage increases for the railway workers were made in lieu of overtime and vacation pay to which they would otherwise have been entitled. In the light of a settlement going so far toward meeting their original demands, the unions which had refused presidential arbitration now reversed their position and withdrew their strike orders. There had been no interruption of service. On January 18, 1944, the government thereupon restored the railways to private operation after only a brief period of nominal control and no further troubles developed on the transportation front during the remainder of the war.

The role of the National War Labor Board had been generally ignored or bypassed in the settlement of the labor disputes in both the coal industry and the railroads. Its authority under these circumstances appeared to have been significantly diminished. Nevertheless it was still charged with settling other disputes and approving wage agreements reached through collective bargaining. But with every passing month it was more than ever caught in the tightening squeeze between its legal responsibilities under the Little Steel formula and the inequity of limiting wage advances to a percentage that had been far outrun by further increases in the cost of living. Moreover, the approval of wage adjustments for coal miners and railroad workers that actually went beyond the Little Steel formula, however disguised as being made in compensation for travel time or in lieu of vacation pay, made the Board's position all the more difficult. It somehow had to devise an escape from an impossible dilemma if it were to exercise any sort of influence in maintaining industrial peace.

The Board found the answer by authorizing on an ever-broadening scale new fringe benefits which substantially supplemented the workers' take-home pay without violating any limitation on increases in straight-time hourly rates. It approved in the collective bargaining agreements coming under its review, provision for holidays and vacations with pay, allowances for travel time and lunch periods, new adjustments for shift differentials, and the establishment of various systems of incentive and bonus payments. It also in effect encouraged insurance and hospitalization benefits for employees by ruling that the setting up of funds for such purposes through collective bargaining was not subject to its supervision or control. As these fringe benefits became more and more widely granted by employers, wage earners were at least partially compensated for the restrictions on wage increases. Labor unrest was substantially allayed.

Altogether during the war years the War Labor Board imposed settlements in 17,650 dispute cases, affecting over 12,000,000 employees, and in 95 per cent of these cases successfully averted any further threat to production. It also approved 415,000 voluntary wage agreements, involving about 20,000,000 workers. This was a gigantic and time-consuming task, for which there was no parallel in all the history of labor relations, but on the whole the Board operated very efficiently.

Both management and labor repeatedly criticized the Board's policies. Industry's complaint was that it did not uphold the Little Steel formula as rigidly as it should have, and, through approving fringe benefits, had in effect granted wholly unjustified wage increases. From the opposite tack, labor insisted that the cost of living index, on which the Little Steel formula was based, was both inaccurate and unfair, and the Board's interpretation of the formula had become "a thumbscrew with which to torment the working people of America and their families."

The attacks from both sides suggested that the Board at least had been vigilant in its protection of the public interest, and actually the great majority of its awards were accepted voluntarily. It had the authority, should a decision in a war industry be disputed, to recommend to the President seizure of the affected plants and the consequent application of direct sanctions to compel compliance with its orders. But this proved necessary on only 40 occasions. The President took action 26 times when unions would not cooperate, 23 times when management proved recalcitrant, and once when neither the union nor management would agree to a Board decision.

The most dramatic instance of defiance was the refusal of the Montgomery Ward Company to accept the Board's jurisdiction on the ground that the mail order business did not directly affect the war effort. President Roosevelt promptly ordered seizure of the company's plants. Before the issue was finally settled the country was treated to the engaging spectacle of Montgomery Ward's violently anti-labor president, Sewell Avery, being carried bodily from his office by two stalwart members of the army detachment sent to take over company property.

The full record of the National War Labor Board, for all its difficulties and for all the criticism it aroused, constituted a very real success for this unprecedented experiment in tripartite labor arbitration. The Board helped materially in maintaining labor peace and played an important role in sustaining the government's wage and price stabilization program. Through its sponsorship of maintenance of membership agreements in protecting union security and its approval of fringe benefits as part of the collective bargaining process, it also safeguarded labor's basic rights and significantly promoted its long-term interests. "The performance of the War Labor Board," so astute a labor historian as Philip Taft has written, "was one of the more notable accomplishments of a government agency dealing with economic problems during World War II. Its ability to gain compliance of decisions, which were frequently objectionable to one of the parties, is one of the remarkable examples of 'voluntarism' in our history."

Organized labor remained active on the political as well as on the economic front during the war years. The expanding role of government agencies and passage of the Smith-Connally Act drove home with compelling force the indubitable fact that union interests were greatly affected by the measure of sympathy and support labor could command in Washington. As the presidential campaign of 1944 approached, union leaders launched a determined drive in support of President Roosevelt and the election of congressional candidates who might be counted upon to support the labor cause. While the A.F. of L., maintaining its traditional nonpartisanship, did not officially endorse the Democratic Party, most of its member unions worked actively for Roosevelt's re-election. Without any such restraining legacy,

the C.I.O. not only endorsed a fourth term for the President by a resolution of its executive committee, but formed a nationwide Political Action Committee with the avowed purpose of getting out the labor vote
in his support.

Under the energetic leadership of Sidney Hillman, the P.A.C. laid
plans for a national doorbell-ringing campaign to educate the workers
in their political responsibilities, publicize the labor records of members of Congress, and encourage a heavy registration. It also sought
hearings at both party conventions, as indeed labor groups had done
ever since the days of Gompers, and used all its influence in favor of
pro-labor planks in their platforms. Its influence was greatest with the
Democrats and the P.A.C. was reputed to have played an important
role in the selection of Roosevelt's running mate. While unable to secure the nomination of Henry Wallace, its first choice for the vice-
presidential candidacy, it successfully blocked that of James F. Byrnes
and opened the way for Harry Truman. Hillman was the key labor
figure in this behind-the-scenes political maneuvering and his supposed
ascendancy was highly dramatized by the published story—denied by
all concerned but given nationwide publicity—that in the vice-presidential struggle Roosevelt had ordered his aides to "clear everything
with Sidney."

During the campaign itself, the P A C. not only carried through
vigorously its door-to-door canvass to get out the vote, but published
and distributed a great mass of pro-labor literature—millions of copies
of pamphlets, leaflets, and fliers. Declaring that the first task facing the
nation was complete victory in the war, these pamphlets further outlined a postwar domestic policy based on full employment, fair wages,
adequate housing, social security, and further protection of the interests of workers, farmers and veterans. To attain these objectives, labor's
campaign literature constantly reiterated, it was essential to elect a
President and a Congress fully committed to progressive ideals. The
magazine *Time* wryly commented: "Far and wide the slickest political
propaganda produced in the U.S. in a generation."

Such aggressive tactics created great alarm in conservative and anti-
labor circles. The P.A.C. was assailed as radical, un-American, and
dominated by Communists. The president of the Union Pacific Railroad solemnly warned that it was "a pernicious innovation that has

literally snaked its way into American politics," and Senator Bricker of
Ohio declared that it was seeking "to dominate our government with
radical and communistic schemes." Sidney Hillman struck back angrily,
saying that the smear campaign was "lies on the top of lies." Nonetheless the Dies Committee was to charge in a lengthy report that the
P.A.C. had engaged in "a subversive Communist campaign to subvert
the Congress of the United States to its totalitarian program."

In cooperation with other pro-labor groups, the P.A.C. undoubtedly helped to swell the majority whereby Roosevelt was once again
swept into office. Every survey indicated that labor was probably more
united behind a single presidential candidate than ever before. A ques-
tionnaire sent to 140 union newspapers indicated that only one of them
had supported the Republican candidate, Thomas E. Dewey, while
even more revealing, only eleven upheld the A.F. of L.'s official policy
of neutrality.

As the war finally drew to an end, the fundamental problem facing
the nation was the readjustment of the economy to the needs of peace
without allowing unemployment to create a depression or permitting
inflation to set off a chain reaction of rising prices and rising wages that
might bring about an equally dangerous cycle of boom and bust.
Organized labor was convinced that a breakdown in the economy
could be avoided only if the government took a strong position in support of full employment and further wage increases in order to sustain
national purchasing power and thereby create an expanding market for
industrial goods. It was prepared to fight for such a program both in
the interests of wage earners and in the interests of the country as a
whole. Underlying all such economic considerations, moreover, was a
further issue. After the close of the First World War, labor had seen
the gains made during the period of hostilities gradually whittled away
by the aggressive counterattack of industry in breaking the turbulent
strikes of 1919. As the guns fell silent in Europe and the Pacific a quarter century later, it was determined there should be no recurrence of
this setback for union security. Labor would militantly defend its
rights.

This resolve was strengthened by the immediate consequences of peace. There were widespread lay-offs in the latter half of 1945 as industry closed its factories to re-tool for normal production, and even workers holding their jobs found their take-home pay reduced with a return to the forty-hour week. Moreover, prices once again began to rise and the limited wage adjustments allowed by the still functioning War Labor Board were wholly inadequate to meet higher living costs. But in answer to union demands that wages be increased, industry retorted that labor was treating "the economic pool as a grab-bag" and refused any concessions. The lines of battle were being drawn.

President Truman hoped that the issues at stake could be resolved and the reconversion program speeded up by a return to the normal processes of collective bargaining. He was prepared to relax many of the wartime controls over the economy and to transfer the functions of the War Labor Board to a new tripartite National Wage Stabilization Board. Moreover he stated his conviction that the unions were entitled to safeguards that would counteract their feeling of insecurity in the postwar era, and that industry could afford reasonable pay concessions without having to raise prices on manufactured goods. "Wage increases are imperative," he said on October 20, 1945, "to cushion the shock to our workers, to sustain adequate purchasing power and to raise national income. . . . Fortunately there is room in the existing price structure for business as a whole to grant increases in rates."

The country's industrial leaders promptly attacked this statement as indicating the administration's intent to continue the favoritism for labor that had marked the New Deal era. In the Senate, Taft declared that the President had surrendered to the C.I.O. Whatever the political implications of Truman's stand, there could in fact be no denying that he had accepted labor's main contentions. His administration appeared ready to act on the premise that the national government had a direct responsibility in trying to safeguard the nation's millions of industrial workers from unemployment and otherwise promote their economic well-being. But he was also emphasizing the vital importance of maintaining national purchasing power, as Roosevelt had before him, for the benefit of the entire country.

The validity of his thesis that wages could be raised without compensating price increases for industry was more debatable than his general theories about purchasing power. Governmental reports bolstered his position in showing that corporation profits during the war period had been two and one-half times the prewar average and were heading toward the highest levels in all history. Business economists, however, flatly denied the accuracy of these government surveys. In a quite different analysis of the prevailing situation, they insisted that higher wages would mean added costs that could not possibly be absorbed by industry within the existing price structure.

It soon became apparent in these circumstances that collective bargaining could not be relied upon to settle the mounting number of industrial disputes. Neither management nor labor showed any disposition to work out their problems in a conciliatory spirit. With a basic power struggle underlying the controversy over wages and prices, there was little room for maneuver and the government saw the whole reconversion program dangerously threatened. As petitions for strike votes submitted to the National Labor Relations Board under the terms of the Smith-Connally Act steadily rose (the pending total was 800 in October), President Truman, as had President Wilson under similar circumstances in 1919, turned to a labor-management conference in the hope of bringing the two sides together.

This conference met in Washington on November 5 to try to formulate "a broad and permanent foundation for industrial peace and progress." The representatives of labor and management duly met, conferred, and then adjourned—without making any appreciable progress whatsoever. They accepted the validity of collective bargaining, which was more than labor and management had been able to do in 1919, but they could not agree on any procedures which might break the impasse in current negotiations. The failure of the conference was to give a new impetus to the rising tide of strikes throughout the country. Even as the labor and management representatives were discouragedly packing their bags to leave Washington, it came into full flood.

Machinists and shipyard workers in San Francisco went on strike; building service operators and longshoremen in New York broke off their contract negotiations; truck drivers in the Midwest quit their jobs, and in other parts of the country oil refinery workers, lumberjacks, and glass workers walked out. Picket lines in city after city, the strikers carrying placards demanding union security and take-home pay the equivalent of wartime wages, brought home vividly to the public the extent and gravity of industrial unrest. With the close of 1945 the strikes began to assume even greater proportions as the major C.I.O. unions launched an all-out attack against the mass production industries. Some 200,000 employees of General Motors struck in November, two months later 300,000 meat packers and 180,000 electrical workers quit their jobs, and then with even more devastating impact on the economy, 750,000 steel workers walked out. At the beginning of the new year, the staggering total of almost 2,000,000 industrial workers were simultaneously on strike.

There was little violence. What was taking place was a grim endurance contest between the forces of labor and industry rather than a slugging match. But newspaper headlines from coast to coast underscored the mounting gravity of the crisis and the public clamored for decisive action to restore industrial peace. Steel held the spotlight. The halt in production in this vital industry was also causing the lay-off of additional thousands of workers in other plants as they felt the harsh effects of spreading economic paralysis.

President Truman was confronted with the complete collapse of a postwar labor policy predicated on the resumption of peaceful collective bargaining. While he still hoped to keep governmental interference at a minimum, he nonetheless realized that he had to act to restore labor peace and safeguard his economic stabilization program. What he now proposed was a policy providing for a thirty-day cooling-off period before any strike could take place and in each instance the submission of the issues in dispute to a presidential fact-finding board. This board would seek to resolve the controversy before it through a formula that would permit wage increases commensurate with the rise in the cost of living and yet hold the line against further inflation.

Neither labor nor management welcomed this plan but on his own initiative Truman proceeded to set up his fact-finding boards. Estimating that since 1941 there had been a 33 per cent increase in living costs, they evolved a general policy for strike settlements providing a comparable wage increase, with price relief for any company whose earnings fell below prewar averages. Application of this policy in individual cases meant that over and above wage increases already permissible under the Little Steel formula, further advances might be authorized averaging from 17½ to 20 per cent. This compared with the 30 per cent increases being generally demanded by the unions, but nevertheless amounted to an average rise of 18½ cents in straight-line hourly rates.

Agreements along such lines were gradually worked out in all the major disputes beginning with those in oil refining, meat packing, and electrical equipment manufacture. In applying the new formula to the steel industry, provision was made for an advance in prices averaging $5 per ton, and after a three-week strike the workers were back on the job. The most serious hold-out occurred in the automobile industry when the General Motors Corporation, resenting President Truman's statement that "ability to pay is relevant," withdrew from the fact-finding board's hearings. Only after a work stoppage of some four months was a settlement finally reached within the framework of governmental policy. By mid-March, however, strikes had largely subsided and the number of workers still on the picket line had fallen to 200,000. The crisis facing the nation at the opening of the year had been resolved.

The question remained whether too heavy a price had been paid for industrial peace. While the resiliency of the national economy rapidly asserted itself, the wage advances granted under the terms of the President's program induced dangerous inflationary pressures. In addition to the settlements made in the strike disputes, the National Wage Stabilization Board found itself compelled to approve comparable wage increases in some 4,000 voluntary agreements. "A bulge in the line," Truman stated in commenting on the consequences of his wage-price policy, "but if you all cooperate with me, there will be no break-through."

The end was not yet however. Even as the major strikes in other sectors of the economy were reaching settlement, a new conflict developed in the coal industry. John L. Lewis could hardly be expected to stand aside as the C.I.O. unions made such substantial gains. He not only demanded further wage increases for the miners but establishment of a general welfare fund to which the operators would contribute seven cents a ton for all coal mined. When the operators balked, Lewis promptly broke off further negotiations. "Good day, gentlemen," he was reported as saying. "We trust that time, as it shrinks your purse, may modify your niggardly and anti-social purposes." On April 1 some 400,000 miners were once again on vacation from shaft, tipple, and breaker house in the small, drab coal towns of Pennsylvania and West Virginia, Kentucky and Alabama, Illinois and Iowa.

The coal strike continued intermittently for the rest of the year 1946 with Lewis in customary fashion defying the operators, the government, and the public. Once again government took over the mines under the terms of what Lewis called "the infamous Smith-Connally statute," but soon after a highly favorable agreement had been reached with Secretary of the Interior Krug, Lewis arrogantly declared its provisions inadequate. When Krug refused to consider their revision, the strike was resumed.

Under the circumstances the government applied for a federal injunction to restrain all strike activity. Judge Goldsborough of the federal district court in Washington, characterizing the strike as "an evil, demoniac, monstrous thing," granted the government's request. Lewis refused to acquiesce in what he called "the ugly recrudescence of government by injunction," and ignored the court's orders. He was thereupon cited for contempt and after a formal trial found guilty. The United Mine Workers was fined $3,500,000 and Lewis himself $10,000.

The case was carried to the Supreme Court and in a five-to-four decision it sustained Judge Goldsborough on the ground that in spite of the provisions of the Norris–La Guardia Act prohibiting the use of injunctions in industrial disputes, the government could indeed obtain one where a strike threatened the national welfare and security. Lewis had for once suffered a sharp reverse. He agreed to call off the strike, the Supreme Court on such assurances reducing the fine against the United Mine Workers to $700,000, and the miners returned to their jobs. Still and all, the union's power had by no means been broken. When the mines were returned to private operation on the expiration of the Smith-Connally Act in June, 1947, Lewis succeeded in winning a new contract that met virtually all his demands both in respect to wages and contributions to the welfare fund.

A further major strike was narrowly averted in May, 1946, following a breakdown in wage negotiations between management and workers on the nation's railways. The elaborate machinery of the Railway

Labor Act failed to bring about a settlement and the government once again had recourse to a special emergency board. It finally hammered out a settlement acceptable to the carriers and most of the unions, but this time the Railroad Trainmen and the Locomotive Engineers— 300,000 strong—refused to go along and sent out strike orders.

In this new emergency President Truman promptly seized the railroads and when the trainmen and engineers began to quit work, ignoring his warning that it would be a strike against the government, he went on the air on May 24 to deliver an uncompromising ultimatum. Unless all employees returned to their jobs the next day, the government would operate the railroads and provide the protection of the country's armed forces "to every man who heeds the call of his country in this hour of need." When there was no move to call off the strike on the expiration of this deadline, he went before Congress and at a tense and expectant session asked specific authority not only to apply for an injunction, but for further powers to deprive the strikers of their seniority rights and draft them into the armed forces should they continue on their course.

As the President reached the dramatic climax in this speech, he was suddenly interrupted. A clerk handed him a message and in the hushed silence, he quietly announced: "Word has just been received that the rail strike has been settled on the terms proposed by the President." Almost hysterical cheers greeted this announcement but when they finally died down, Truman deliberately went on with his prepared text. The legislation he sought was still necessary, he stated, in order to fully resolve the crisis.

The House promptly responded to the President's appeal, but with the strike now over the Senate let the bill die in committee. The whole atmosphere was one of anticlimax. In both congressional and popular debate, however, Truman found himself strongly attacked for proposing such an unprecedented and forceful measure. He was not only assailed by labor and liberal spokesmen but, in ironic reversal of their usual positions, conservatives led by Senator Taft attacked the President's plan as unfair to the railway workers and a violation of their civil liberties.

In union circles opposition could hardly have been more vehement. In spite of everything he had done to uphold labor's cause in the earlier disputes of this tumultuous year, Truman found himself universally condemned for his attitude during the railway crisis. He was accused of having turned completely against the unions and at the C.I.O. convention was scornfully labeled "the Number One strikebreaker of the American bankers and railroads."

The record of the twelve-month period since the end of the war had been a shattering one—4,630 work stoppages and a total of 5,000,000 strikers piling up 120,000,000 days of idleness. Nevertheless the economy had successfully withstood such heavy battering. Instead of the feared depression and consequent unemployment, the reconversion program was forging ahead and at the close of the year the civilian labor force had risen to an all-time high of 55,000,000 workers.

In the meantime, however, inflation had got out of hand. The whole issue of government regulation of wages and prices had become deeply enmeshed in politics and the result was first the suspension and then abandonment of all controls. Prices began to spiral upward and as 1946 came to a close, the consumer price index stood at 153. This was a figure no less than 20 points above what it had been in midsummer, when wage settlements were based on the fact-finding boards estimate of a 33 per cent increase since 1941, and constituted a greater rise in six months than in the entire three-year period in which government controls had been in effect. Faced with this unexampled situation, the unions inevitably insisted on further wage increases and the stage was set for a second round in the continuing battle between labor and industry.

There were a number of strikes in 1947. The telephone operators walked out, a work stoppage on the part of marine and shipbuilding workers shut down shipyards for 135 days, unionized airplane pilots struck, and the coal miners had their annual turnout—though this time for only eight days. In general, however, the new wage disputes were settled without major strikes, and man-days lost dropped from the 1946 total of 116,000,000 to 34,600,000. The underlying issue of union security had in effect been settled as a consequence of labor's postwar victories. Freed of government regulation of the economy, the way was once again open to collective bargaining. In consequence in-

dustry and the major unions concluded a series of settlements that provided for another increase of about 15 per cent in straight-line hourly
wages. Continued inflation was partially to nullify these union gains,
but with the new fringe benefits added to the wage increases, organized labor had once again materially improved its position and industrial workers throughout the country were enjoying a higher standard
of living than ever before.

The major unions had demonstrated a cohesive force that would not
be denied in their postwar confrontation with industry. They had built
up their power during the war, and in its aftermath had shown that
they were readly to use it, ruthlessly if necessary, in safeguarding their
security and their members' economic interests.

XIX: TAFT-HARTLEY TO THE A.F.L.-C.I.O. MERGER

WHILE LABOR HAD COME THROUGH the reconversion period with its wartime gains intact and the position of the nation's wage earners greatly improved, its very success had elements of danger. A public that had helplessly watched the great industrial unions threaten to paralyze the entire economy as they insisted on their rights and demanded ever higher wages for their members, was fearful of their vast economic power. The postwar strikes in the steel and coal industries, on the part of automobile workers, and on the railroads, for a time so gravely endangering the national welfare, intensified the powerful anti-union sentiment that had led to passage of the Smith-Connally Act. The feeling was widespread that in self-centered defense of its own interests, organized labor was totally ignoring those of the people as a whole. This latent hostility was fanned by reactionary, anti-labor forces within the business community which were basically opposed to all union organization. Yet the fact remained that repeated public opinion polls showed that the nation was deeply concerned over the militancy of labor's rank-and-file and the seeming lack of responsibility of its leaders.

In the past government had been compelled to assert its authority over Big Business. The question now arose as to whether it should not do so more rigorously over Big Labor. There was a growing popular conviction, strongly reflected in Congress, that it had become essential to prevent the arbitrary domination of the country's economic life by any minority, even though that minority might be as widely representative as the forces of labor.

At no time were there any suggestions from responsible quarters that the unions should be deprived of the basic rights guaranteed them under the terms of the National Labor Relations Act. A congressional majority was nevertheless convinced that the time had come when a measure which had been concerned only with unfair practices on the part of management, should be amended to single out and penalize unfair practices on the part of the unions. It was felt that something should be done, that is, to redress a balance which under the pro-labor administrations of the 1930's had been allowed to swing much too far in support of unions. The end result of this mounting agitation in favor of more restrictive legislation was the enactment, in June, 1947, of the Taft-Hartley Act.

Before this basic measure became law, Congress had adopted an earlier bill introduced by Representative Case which clearly revealed its temper. This bill had first been passed by the House during the industrial union strikes of early 1946. As they were settled under President Truman's program, further action lagged. With the subsequent crises in coal and on the railroads, however, the Senate hurriedly fell in line and approved the Case bill. This measure set up a Federal Mediation Board, prescribed a sixty-day cooling-off period before any strike could be called, and decreed loss of all their rights under the Wagner Act for workers who quit their jobs during the cooling-off period. It also banned secondary boycotts and jurisdictional strikes, and authorized the use of injunctions to prevent violent or obstructive picketing.

This was a Draconian measure which hit hard at labor's historic right to strike. President Truman promptly vetoed it. He argued persuasively that it dealt with the symptoms rather than the causes of industrial unrest and urged Congress to take a more thorough look at the whole problem. What was really needed, he stated, was a long-range program that would face up to the unresolved issues of labor relations and at the same time continue to safeguard the basic principle of union security.

The anti-labor forces in Congress could not muster the votes to override this veto, but they had no idea of letting restrictive legislation go by the board. The mid-term elections of 1946 strengthened their hand. The Republicans won decisive control of Congress and their landslide victory was interpreted as a direct popular mandate to take drastic action on the labor issue in spite of President Truman's position. Some thirty states were to adopt various forms of restrictive legislation and in such circumstances it was hardly surprising that Congress should hasten to fall in line. The leaders of both the A.F. of L. and the C.I.O. assailed what they termed a "deliberate and monstrous movement . . . to cripple if not destroy, the labor movement," but they were unable to rally the support, either in Congress or in the country as a whole, to combat the anti-labor trend.

The Taft-Hartley Act had a stormy passage through Congress. The more severe provisions first incorporated in the measure by the House were to be somewhat liberalized by the Senate, but in its final form the bill very definitely reflected the conservative reaction. President Truman vetoed it as he had the Case bill. He condemned it as primarily designed to weaken the unions, declared that it would in fact, encourage rather than discourage strikes, and deplored what he said would be its effect in making government "an unwanted participant at every bargaining table." The bill's provisions, he emphatically concluded, were "shocking—bad for labor, bad for management, bad for the country."

This time his opposition was to prove unavailing. Vehemently attacking the President for his pro-labor sympathies, the bill's proponents baldly charged that he had completely misrepresented its provisions. They succeeded in winning the necessary support in both the House and the Senate to override his veto and the Taft-Hartley Act duly became the law of the land.

It was a long and immensely complicated measure whose declared purpose was to restore that equality of bargaining power between employers and employees which it was contended had been sacrificed in the Wagner Act. The rights guaranteed labor in that earlier law were matched by specific safeguards for the rights of management. Employers were guaranteed full freedom of expression in respect to their views on union organization, short of threats of reprisal or promises of benefits, and they were authorized themselves to call for elections to determine the appropriate bargaining units in wage negotiations. At the same time it was declared an unfair labor practice for the unions in any way to attempt to coerce employers, engage in either secondary boycotts or jurisdictional strikes, or in their turn to refuse to bargain collectively.

These clauses might well be justified as more nearly equalizing the positions of management and labor, but the law also incorporated a number of provisions directly affecting union security. It expressly banned the closed shop, required highly complicated voting procedures for establishment of the union shop, and, perhaps most significantly, left the door open to even more severe anti-union legislation by the states. In Section 14 (b) it permitted the states to bypass federal legislation allowing the union shop by themselves banning it. This provision made possible the so-called state "right-to-work" laws which were to hamper further union organization more directly than anything in the Taft-Hartley Act itself.

There were further restrictions. Unions were required to give 60-day notice for the termination or modification of any agreement and were made suable in the federal courts for breach of contract. They were not allowed to make contributions or otherwise expend any of their funds in political campaigns. Their officers were required to file affidavits affirming that they were not members of the Communist Party or of any organization supporting it.

In Title II the Taft-Hartley Act broke entirely new ground with an elaborate formula for dealing with strikes that created a national emergency. It gave the President the authority, after making an investigation through a special board of inquiry, to apply for what in effect constituted an 80-day injunction against any strike that was found to be imperiling the national health or safety. Should negotiations during this period still fail to solve the controversy, the President was to submit a report to Congress "with such recommendations as he may see fit for consideration and appropriate action." Finally, Taft-Hartley made a number of significant administrative changes in existing legislation. It provided for the enlargement of the National Labor Relations Board, with appointment of a new General Counsel, and established an independent Federal Mediation and Conciliation Service with authority to step into any labor dispute threatening a substantial interruption of interstate commerce.

The debate over the bill had been impassioned. The temper of the House was revealed in the report of its Committee on Education and Labor which declared that as a result of union activity, the individual worker's "mind, his soul, and his very life have been subjected to a tyranny more despotic than anyone could think possible in a free country." The committee would have abolished the National Labor Relations Board, eliminated the requirement of management obligation in collective bargaining, and required a vote of all workers involved before a strike could be called. The position of the Senate Committee on Labor and Public Welfare was a more moderate one. It recommended that the social gains which employees had received under previous legislation should be maintained and that Congress seek to remedy existing inequities between employers and employees by precise and carefully drawn legislation. The views of the Senate committee were more nearly to prevail, partly through common sense and partly to assure a majority that could override President Truman's expected veto. In the meantime, however, representatives of industry and of labor fought out their own battle in the public forum.

The full strength of employer associations, spearheaded by the National Association of Manufacturers, was thrown behind enactment of a stiff bill. The A.F. of L. and the C.I.O. opposed any new legislation whatsoever. Both industry and labor sent their spokesmen to the congressional hearings, inserted full-page advertisements in the country's newspapers presenting their contrasting philosophies, and bought radio time to air their views. While the bill's proponents maintained that the proposed legislation went no further than to equalize bargaining power, its opponents characterized it as a vindictive attack on unionism instigated by those who wished to do away with collective bargaining altogether.

In the light of the prevailing popular mood, labor's position was very weak. In refusing any compromise in respect to the proposed legislation and seeking to hold reactionary employees wholly responsible for the drive to modify the pro-labor provisions of the Wagner Act, both the A.F. of L. and the C.I.O. were ignoring public opinion. Their leaders failed to take into consideration the almost universal sense of frustration among the people as a whole when industrywide strikes interfered with basic public services or otherwise threatened a breakdown in the national economy. And in refusing to suggest any alternative measure to meet the recognized inadequacies, if not unfairness, of the Wagner Act, they reinforced the widespread view that organized labor had become increasingly irresponsible in the exercise of monopolistic power.

There was still much latent support for the labor cause. Some three months after final passage of the Taft-Hartley Act, public opinion polls showed that 53 per cent of the persons questioned who knew of its enactment believed that it should be repealed or at least revised. But the campaign to block anti-labor legislation had been started too late and had been too uncompromising to overcome the momentum of the conservative reaction that had been building up since 1946. In unjustified self-assurance, union leadership had failed to adjust itself to new times and new circumstances. At the peak of its economic power, labor had suffered a severe setback on the political front.

The passage of the Taft-Hartley Act did not by any means bring to an end the impassioned controversy over its merits. While neither the hopes of its adherents nor the fears of its critics were in practice to be realized, it remained a bone of embittered contention among the pro-labor and anti-labor forces in the country. Congress faced no more sensitive political issue in the whole range of domestic legislation. As the 1948 presidential campaign approached, neither party was able to ignore it. The Republicans cautiously called for continuing study to improve labor-management legislation; the Democrats more forthrightly pledged Taft-Hartley's immediate repeal.

The unexpected and dramatic re-election of President Truman raised high labor's hopes that repeal would actually be effected. They were disappointed. A conservative coalition of Republicans and southern Democrats remained in control of Congress and it had little sympathy with organized labor. One amendment to the law was adopted. The required elections for the union shop had in every case shown such overwhelming workers' support (an average 87 per cent among those voting) that it was henceforth provided that such agreements could be concluded without employee polls. Otherwise every move to revise or repeal the law was beaten back. Taft-Hartley remained on the statute books.

Labor continued to attack it as a "slave labor" bill. This it certainly was not. There was little question that certain of its provisions, and most notably Section 14(B) with its encouragement of state right-to-work laws, impeded union organization in the South and perhaps some other parts of the country. Nevertheless there was to be further growth in union membership during the next few years and the proportion of the nation's workers whose terms of employment were governed by collective bargaining agreements rose steadily.

Where Taft-Hartley proved most disappointing and ineffective was in the application of its provisions for settling strikes that endangered the public welfare. Title II, which labor condemned as reestablishing "the abhorrent principle of government by injunctions," afforded no real solution to the problem such strikes created. In succeeding years its provisions were invoked only with great reluctance and often served to confuse rather than clarify the issues in dispute.

A first major strike that led President Truman to take action under the injunction proceedings occurred in the perennially restless coal fields. In spite of the settlement reached in 1947, intermittent work stoppages continued and a new controversy developed between the miners and the operators when the ever-aggressive John L. Lewis charged that the latter had "dishonored" their contract in respect to the health and welfare fund. This dispute was finally ironed out, but two years later the miners' chieftain again began to agitate in favor of higher wages. His new technique was to avoid the charge of directly calling a strike but to bring comparable pressure on the operators by periodically ordering out the miners in a series of so-called "memorial" work stoppages protesting against the high rate of deaths and injuries in the coal mines.

As these work stoppages went on, President Truman finally felt compelled under public pressure to invoke Title II of Taft-Hartley and on February 6, 1950, he obtained a temporary injunction against any further strikes. When the union officials sent out instructions ordering the miners back to work, they were largely ignored. The government then instituted contempt proceedings against the United Mine Workers on the ground that the orders calling off the strike had been given only "token compliance." A federal court, however, refused to sustain these proceedings. It asserted that the government had not proved its charge of lack of good faith in the union's issuance of its orders.

In this impasse Truman turned rather desperately to Congress for authority—as in wartime—to seize the coal mines. While Congress hesitated, a new agreement was finally reached—in March—between the union and the operators, and the work stoppages came to an end without the necessity of further government intervention. The experience with Taft-Hartley had proved, to say the least, very inconclusive.

Another strike involving the law's emergency provisions—though they were not actually invoked—took place in the steel industry in 1952. It was to last nearly two months—the longest and costliest work stoppage that the industry had up to that time ever experienced—and taking place as it did against the background of the Korean War, aroused a measure of public concern comparable only to the strike crises during World War II. There could be no disputing the fact that the breakdown in steel production created a national emergency.

Wages and hours had at this time once again been brought under government control as a result of the Korean hostilities, and when negotiations for a new contract between the United Steelworkers and the industry broke down at the close of 1951, the dispute was referred to a new Wage Stabilization Board. The union agreed to hold any strike activity in abeyance until the Board made its report; when the Board did so some three months later, the union agreed to accept its recommendations. However, the steel industry denounced the report for advocating recognition of the union shop and refused to accept the proposed wage settlement unless it was allowed to make compensatory increases in the price of steel. When the Economic Stabilization Director denied the price increases, the industry rejected the settlement as a whole and the union thereupon made ready to strike.

There was an immediate and widespread demand that President Truman should seek an injunction under the Taft-Hartley Act. He bluntly refused to do so. He took the position that the steel workers had already refrained from striking for three months while the Wage Stabilization Board was making its investigations, and to enjoin them further was not warranted. Instead of an injunction he took the drastic step, on April 8, 1952, of seizing the steel plants on his own authority as the only way to maintain production vital to the war effort. "I feel sure," he stated, "that the Constitution does not require me to endanger our national safety by letting all the steel mills close down at this particular time."

His action created a storm of protest. While the steel workers remained on the job, the industry promptly took the matter to the courts. The legal issue was fought out against a confused background of preliminary injunctions against government operation, temporary stays of the court orders, and a final appeal to the Supreme Court. On June 2 it ruled that the seizure of the mills was an unconstitutional exercise of executive authority. The President perforce returned them to private operation, whereupon the steel workers—560,000 strong—resumed their strike and brought production to a complete halt.

As the popular controversy over Truman's refusal to invoke the Taft-Hartley Act and his arbitrary seizure of the steel mills continued to rage throughout the country, the union and the industry renewed their contract negotiations. It was not, however, until July 26 that they came to terms. The settlement at last reached generally conformed to that originally proposed by the Wage Stabilization Board, but in the meantime the strike had cost the industry $350,000,000 and the workers had lost $50,000,000 in wages. More important, the strike had not only crippled the steel industry itself but had caused the shutdown of many steel-using plants and brought automobile assembly lines to a temporary halt. It had seriously endangered the flow of essential military materials to Korea and only the gradual cessation of hostilities had prevented an even more grave crisis.

A third major strike, which in this instance led to action under the Taft-Hartley Act, occurred the next year on the docks and wharves of New York when the International Longshoremen's Association and the New York Shipping Association found themselves unable to come to terms over wages and hiring practices. This dispute was to become even more complicated than the strikes in the coal fields or in steel. With the work stoppage tying up all shipping in New York, the A.F. of L. expelled the union on charges of racketeering and chartered a new longshoremen's organization; the state authorities of New York and New Jersey intervened in the interests of law and order; and a Senate investigating committee angrily reported that the waterfront had become "a lawless frontier" plagued by corruption, Communism, and gangsterism. President Eisenhower, who had now succeeded President Truman, finally invoked the emergency provisions of Taft-Hartley but in spite of a federal injunction a series of wildcat strikes continued as a result of the bitter fight between the old and new longshoremen's unions.

Elections under the auspices of the National Labor Relations Board ultimately confirmed the right of the original union, in spite of all the charges that had been brought against it, to represent the longshoremen in bargaining with the shipping industry. Negotiations then were resumed and a settlement reached barring both strikes and lockouts for a two-year period. Something like peace temporarily descended on the embattled waterfront, but once again government intervention under Taft-Hartley had proved to be wholly unsatisfactory.

There were other strikes in the aftermath of the law's passage and they always made good newspaper copy. Communications workers, textile workers, automobile workers, and construction workers among others had relatively brief work stoppages; the railway workers staged a series of "sick" walkouts in 1951 that led to government threats to dismiss all employees who did not stay on the job, and the next year the coal miners had still another strike. What passed largely unnoticed, however, was that in spite of all the furor over the coal miners, steel workers, longshoremen and other restive unionists, there was actually a sharp decline in work stoppages. The annual total of man-days lost in the years 1947–51 averaged 40,000,000 in comparison with 116,000,000 in 1946.

This falling-off in strike activity did not mean that the workers had been cowed into submission or that they found their unions crippled by the restrictions of Taft-Hartley. What they still called a "slave labor" bill did not prevent their winning their major demands in these strikes or, even more significantly, keep them from obtaining additional wage increases and other benefits without being forced to resort to strikes. Organized labor enjoyed a highly favorable bargaining position as the national economy forged ahead; nothing in the existing laws precluded the major unions from making the most of their advantages.

In the mid-1950's something like two-thirds of all nonagricultural workers—an approximate 30,000,000—were covered by collective bargaining agreements. The earnings of those in the manufacturing industries had risen to an average of $75 a week, and this figure, after being adjusted to changes in the price level, represented an advance in real wages of about 50 per cent since 1939. And these increases did not include the steadily expanding fringe benefits which were every year becoming more the rule than the exception in union contracts.

Labor's advance on the economic front did not lead it to ignore the less favorable battleground of politics. It had learned a bitter lesson in the passage of the Taft-Hartley Act. The campaign for the repeal of this measure continued unabated and on a broader front every effort was made to promote new social legislation. "Labor has long recognized," President Murray of the C.I.O. declared, "that the gains which it wins through economic action can be protected, implemented and extended only if it develops a progressive program of legislation and secures its enactment through effective participation in the political life of the nation."

The Republican victory at the polls in 1952 dashed all hopes for the repeal of Taft-Hartley but its revision still seemed possible. In a message to Congress on February 2, 1953, President Eisenhower stated that experience had shown the need for corrective measures in existing legislation. Moreover he appointed Martin P. Durkin, former president of the United Association of Journeymen Plumbers and Steamfitters, as his Secretary of Labor (it was said the cabinet was made up of nine millionaires and a plumber!), and this appeared to be a further good augury for the advancement of labor's interests.

Yet nothing was done. Durkin drew up 19 proposed amendments to Taft-Hartley and, in the belief that he had the President's approval for them, gave out the draft of a message for their submission to Congress. Eisenhower, however, denied he had promised his support. Resenting what he interpreted as repudiation of an agreed-upon policy, Durkin thereupon resigned from the cabinet. Although the President tried to justify his policy and reassure labor of his continuing sympathy, union leaders were convinced that the conservative elements surrounding him had forced him to go back on his promises. He was to declare at the A.F. of L. convention in September that he had "a very great comprehension of what organized labor had done for this country," but such vague rhetorical phrases hardly compensated for his failure to back up his own Secretary of Labor in support of remedial legislation.

The leadership of both the A.F. of L. and the C.I.O. realized anew under these circumstances that labor would have to build up its political strength if it were not to face the danger of further restrictive legislation. The A.F. of L. had already set up a League for Political Education paralleling the C.I.O.'s Political Action Committee. The two organizations had done yeoman work in the 1952 election, even though not too successful, and they were now prepared to cooperate fully in exerting all possible pressure on Congress in organized labor's interest.

Their lobbying activities helped to bring about a further expansion in the Social Security program. It was extended to cover an increasing number of workers in respect to old-age and survivors' insurance benefits, and the monthly payments on such accounts were substantially increased. In 1955 Congress also raised the minimum wage levels established under the Fair Labor Standards Act from 75 cents to $1 an hour. On another front, although unsuccessful for another decade, union lobbies worked consistently for the old-age health program, which became known as Medicare.

Organized labor's political interests were not limited by social welfare legislation. They extended beyond domestic horizons as the harsh impact of the cold war convinced the leadership of both the A.F. of L. and the C.I.O. that foreign policy had become increasingly important for the nation's workers. With the country's great expectations for a durable peace so cruelly shattered by the continuing conflict with Communism, no segment of American society was more alert to the dangers threatening the stability of the democratic world. An enduring belief that a system of free enterprise offered more opportunities for the advancement of American wage earners than any other possible economic system gave a definitely conservative cast to labor's position on international affairs. Its leadership—outside a few left-wing unions —could hardly have been more militantly anti-Communist.

Through a series of forthright resolutions adopted at their annual conventions, the A.F. of L. and the C.I.O. asserted their full support for the policy of containment initiated by President Truman and still further developed during the Eisenhower Administration. They upheld the original program of military and economic aid to Greece and Turkey, endorsed the Marshall Plan, fully backed American participation in the North Atlantic Treaty Organization, urged continued extension of foreign aid, and supported without hesitation the United Nations' action in Korea. Moreover labor's leaders stood in the very forefront of those emphasizing the gravity of the Communist threat and repeatedly called for more effective common action in combatting it.

Writing in the *American Federationist* in January, 1948, George Meany, at that time secretary-treasurer of the A.F. of L., emphasized that in order to win the peace so essential for American security the United States should make every effort to keep its sister democracies free. He declared that the Marshall Plan was the best means of halting the surge of totalitarianism in Europe and cogently argued that its annual cost would be no more than the nation spent in a single 16-day period during World War II. In a later article he supported the North Atlantic Treaty even more emphatically. "In this grave hour," he stated, "the people of America can be fully assured that in American labor the cause of democracy at home and abroad has a devoted, determined, and dynamic champion."

Within the ranks of the C.I.O., both Philip Murray and Walter Reuther were equally forthright in pledging labor's vigorous support for the Truman-Acheson policy, especially foreign aid. An article in the *C.I.O. News* singled out for praise President Truman's Point Four program of technical assistance for the underdeveloped countries. In providing help for other people, it succinctly noted, Point Four would also create additional jobs for American workers. On one occasion Reuther called for more effective social action "to back the country's defense and foreign aid programs."

In reaffirming support of the Truman policies after the outbreak of the Korean War, both national labor federations adopted new resolutions. In the light of the conflagration in eastern Asia, that of the A.F. of L. stated, the paramount task confronting the free labor movement was to deter and, if need be, decisively defeat Soviet imperialism. The C.I.O. declared that it fully backed the American government and the United Nations in the struggle being waged against Communist aggression.

Within the sphere of its own responsibilities organized labor undertook to break all ties with Communism and to purge the unions of all possible Communist influence. It withdrew its representatives from the World Federation of Trade Unions when it appeared to be falling under Communist domination and cooperated in the formation of a new International Confederation of Free Trade Unions. On the home front, steps were taken to disqualify Communists from any positions of union leadership and to expel from the national organizations any unions following the Communist line.

This internal problem affected the C.I.O. rather than the A.F. of L., as a consequence of the former's acceptance in the 1930's of help from any quarter in building up the new industrial unions. It faced squarely up to this issue at its 1949 convention and revised its constitution to make Communists ineligible for any executive office within the C.I.O. and to provide for the expulsion by a two-thirds vote of any national union following the Communist line. After investigations by a special committee, it expelled 11 unions, constituting something like a fifth of its membership, within the next year.

Their officials, President Murray declared, had been following a policy of "harassment, of opposition and obstruction" in their adherence to the Communist program. New unions (most notably that of the electrical workers) were chartered to replace those expelled. In announcing these developments Murray also sought to reassure the public of labor's basic loyalty. Characterizing the Communist-dominated unions as "a small but noisy clique" within the ranks of the C.I.O., he declared that the overwhelming majority of its union membership had no sympathy whatsoever with subversive activity.

If there was never any question of labor's support for American intervention in Korea, the continuing hostilities there did raise questions comparable to those confronted during World War II. As the government moved to reinstitute its former controls over the national economy, setting up the new Wage Stabilization Board as an arm of a revamped Economic Stabilization Agency, organized labor insisted on full representation on all policy-making boards. Acting in close concert, the A.F. of L. and C.I.O. established a United Labor Policy Committee to advise the government on appropriate measures to assure industrial peace and to work out a joint program among the major unions in regard to manpower problems, production, wages, prices, and the appointment of union officials to public office.

There were to be the inevitable difficulties in carrying through a cooperative program and labor repeatedly charged that government was paying slight attention to its view. On one occasion, when the Wage

Stabilization Board refused to allow wage increases of more than 10 per cent over the levels existing in 1950, the United Labor Policy Committee underscored its protest by calling for the withdrawal of labor representatives both from the Board and all other government agencies. This "walkout" lasted some two months. However, the issues at stake were finally settled and labor representation restored on a new National Advisory Board on Mobilization Policy and a reorganized Wage Stabilization Board.

In spite of these troubles, strike activity was kept at a minimum during 1951, with only 23,000,000 man-days, or .23 per cent of total working time lost. While this figure was somewhat greater the next year, largely as a consequence of the long steel strike, it fell again in 1953. There was no serious interruption in the production of military or other supplies. The economy boomed with further gains for labor in employment and in wages.

Throughout these years which were at once marked by further economic advances and the setback on the political front caused by passage of the Taft-Hartley Act, the forces of American labor remained divided. Of the estimated total of something over 17,000,000 union members in the mid 1050's, the A.F. of L. claimed 9,000,000, the C.I.O. some 6,000,000, and an approximate 2,500,000 belonged to the United Mine Workers, the Railway Brotherhoods, and other independent unions. There were repeated efforts to establish an organic unity among these divisive elements, and a number of committees were set up to discuss the complicated issues involved. But in spite of general agreement that "the economic, social and industrial interest of labor can best be served through the establishment of a united labor movement," no satisfactory formula for bringing it about could be found.

The original conflict between the A.F. of L. and the C.I.O. over industrial unionism had subsided. Both federations had long since recognized that industrial unions had their place alongside rather than in opposition to craft unions. There had also been increasing cooperation in many phases of labor activity, most notably creation of the United Labor Policy Committee during the Korean War, and the unions generally worked together on such political issues as their continuing battle against Taft-Hartley. It was perhaps the persistence of old rivalries among the leaders of the A.F. of L. and the C.I.O. as much as anything else that brought every move toward an effective merger to a dead end.

In 1952 a change in leadership in both federations gave a fresh impetus to the reunification movement. Within the brief span of 12 days in November of that year, Willam Green, president of the A.F. of L. for nearly 30 years, and Philip Murray, president of the C.I.O. since the resignation of John L. Lewis, both died with dramatic unexpectedness. Their sudden passing from the scene was in many ways a harsh blow for the American labor movement, confronting both the A.F. of L. and the C.I.O. with the difficult task of choosing new leaders who could face up to the pressing problems of the 1950's. At the same time, handing over responsibility to men who had not played major roles in the original split between the A.F. of L. and the C.I.O. provided a unique opportunity for bringing old and outworn rivalries to an end.

After a sharp struggle among contending factions, the C.I.O. elected to its presidency Walter Reuther, the brilliant, hard-hitting, dynamic head of the United Automobile Workers. Having begun as an apprentice die and tool maker, he had played an important part in the organization of his union during the 1930's, at one time being brutally beaten up by the "brass-knuckle-men" of the Ford Company's service department, and had risen to the presidency in 1946. He was a skillful organizer, a persistent, stubborn negotiator in his relations with management, and highly articulate in presenting his views to the public.

In appearance Reuther looked far more like a successful businessman than a hard-fighting labor leader. He was invariably well dressed and somewhat fastidious. Neither a smoker nor a drinker, he was little given to social diversions. Throughout his whole career he had worked at the job with a concentrated, single-minded energy that largely accounted for his gradual emergence as one of labor's strongest, as well as most ambitious, leaders.

His ideas of labor's role in society were broad and comprehensive, carrying him far beyond the immediate problems of business unionism. They owed something to socialist theory but his approach to politics was completely pragmatic. Labor should work within the existing party structure, which in the circumstances of the time meant support for the Democrats, and he never believed in a possible third party. No labor leader was more strongly opposed to Communism, which he had seen in action in Soviet Russia, and he vigorously fought and ultimately drove out the Communist faction within his own union. At the same time his imagination led him to envisage social goals for labor that went far beyond its traditional objectives.

"The kind of labor movement we want," he once stated, "is not committed to a nickel-in-the-pay-envelope philosophy. We are building a labor movement, not to patch up the world so men can starve less often and less frequently, but a labor movement that will remake the world so that the working people will get the benefit of their labor."

There was never any question of Reuther's complete devotion to labor's cause. At once idealistic and eminently practical, a veteran in union warfare and an experienced leader, he was in every way a logical candidate for the post first held by Lewis.

The A.F. of L. chose as its new leader a man of quite a different stripe—George Meany, its secretary-treasurer. Relatively little known outside union ranks, he had had a long career of activity within the organized labor movement ever since his early days as an apprentice plumber. He first became a union business agent and then went on to serve as secretary of the New York Building Trades Council and president of the New York State Federation of Labor before taking over his post in the national organization in 1939. A large, heavily built man, weighing some 228 pounds, he was once described as "a cross between a bulldog and a bull." He looked like the old-fashioned, conventional labor leader of an earlier era, generally pictured either smoking a big cigar or chewing determinedly on an unlighted one. But he hardly conformed to type in the breadth of his interests. Fond of dancing, a fair pianist, he was also very much interested in sports—the first A.F. of L. president to be a golfer.

In his contacts with other union leaders and the representatives of management, Meany was aggressively outspoken, sometimes truculent. "Blunt as the plumber's wrench," a labor writer characterized his public addresses. One of the few A.F. of L. officials both willing and able to stand up to Lewis, he had successfully challenged the latter's stand against signing the anti-Communist affidavits required by the Taft-Hartley Act. He could be as tough as circumstances demanded.

Throughout his career Meany had always stood for progressive principles—not always conforming to the more conservative position of the A.F. of L. officialdom—and he fought hard for every cause he favored. He was a consistent opponent of racial or religious discrimination in union membership, and again in contrast to many of his colleagues, believed strongly in labor's need to play an active role in politics. Moreover he felt that unions should enter more actively into community affairs and seek to exercise their influence on the local level as well as on state and national issues.

The new heads of both federations, and this might also be said of many other contemporary union leaders, were in many ways a different breed of men than the conventional leaders of the past. They had had only relatively brief experience as actual wage earners (one remembers Samuel Gompers working for years at his cigar maker's bench), had a broader education than had been the rule in an earlier era, made a distinctive career of labor politics, and in comparison with the more narrow proponents of business unionism, kept their sights constantly raised. Indeed, labor leadership as a whole had by the 1950's become increasingly comparable to leadership in industry itself as the unions became more institutionalized. Not only the officers of the two federations, but those of the international and national unions, had far more administrative duties than in the past, had an important public role to fulfill, and were accustomed to meet their counterparts in industry and also the highest government officials on equal terms. They were not as close to the rank-and-file of workers as their predecessors. With high salaries and imposing offices, they moved in a rarefied atmosphere that conspicuously underlined how far the labor movement had progressed since its early days.

Nevertheless as their backgrounds and temperaments both suggested, Reuther and Meany were determined to do everything they could to build up the strength of organized labor. They were prepared to institute new organizing campaigns among the unorganized and seek every opportunity to marshal the political support of union members behind further progressive legislation. To this end they were also committed to the cause of labor unity, ready to break new ground in trying to settle the differences that had divided the A.F. of L. and the C.I.O. for nearly two decades. A first step was their conclusion in June,

1953, of a two-year no-raiding agreement among the constitutent unions of the two federations, and the next year both the A.F. of L. and the C.I.O. conventions duly ratified it. Union piracy and jurisdictional strikes had long been recognized as a disruptive force within labor ranks and perhaps the greatest continuing obstacle to reunification. But it was Meany and Reuther who had both the vision and the authority to tackle the issue directly and to point the way toward a settlement that held out some promise of an end to this costly and futile inter-union warfare. "The signing and ratification of the No-Raiding Agreement between our two organizations," they jointly announced, "is an historic step. We are confident that the No-Raiding Agreement may function in a spirit of understanding and fraternal friendship."

By 1955, 80 affiliated unions of the A.F. of L. and 33 C.I.O. unions had accepted the agreement's terms. While it was to prove impossible —either then or in later years—to eradicate jurisdictional strikes entirely, their frequency was sharply reduced and a better atmosphere created among rival unions.

In the meantime, the two federations had also set up a Joint Unity Committee, headed by their new presidents, which undertook to explore possible ways to effect a merger. Its deliberations were kept secret and outside official labor circles (except so far as the no-raiding agreement was a straw in the wind), little was known as to what progress the committee might be making. The underlying politics were extremely complicated. John L. Lewis, whom Meany would not permit to take part in the negotiations ("Good Lord, he's the fellow that split the A.F. of L. He's the fellow that tried to split the C.I.O."), was playing a divisive role, and the influential William Hutcheson, one-time head of the Carpenters Union, was in the opposition camp. The long history of earlier discussions did not inspire any great optimism over the new Joint Unity Committee's ability to surmount the many obstacles in its path.

It was consequently with great dramatic impact that the committee announced, on February 9, 1955, that full agreement had been reached for the merger of the A.F. of L. and the C.I.O. into a unified federation. In a joint statement Meany and Reuther further declared that in the new A.F.L.-C.I.O. the identity of each affiliated national or international union would be preserved, the no-raiding agreement would be continued on a voluntary basis, and special departments within the old A.F. of L. would remain, although supplemented by a new Industrial Union Department. In this way explicit recognition was given to the need for both craft and industrial unions within the ranks of organized labor and every encouragement offered to promoting the most effective forms of organization among American workers as a whole.

The program for the new federation, in addition to plans for greater efforts to organize the unorganized, embraced a new approach to the three greatest internal problems plaguing the labor movement: corruption, racial discrimination, and possible Communist infiltration. A sustained campaign would be launched on the part of unified labor against the racketeering and gangsterism that had become rife in a number of unions. The federation would insist that the benefits of union organization be extended to all workers regardless of race, creed, or color—a victory for the more tolerant stand of the C.I.O. And, finally, it was forthrightly stated that every effort would be made to protect the American trade union movement from "the undermining efforts of the Communist agencies and all others who are opposed to the basic principles of our democarcy and of free and democratic unionism."

The difficult problem of leadership in the new federation was resolved by the willingness of the C.I.O., in the person of Walter Reuther, to step aside in favor of the A.F. of L., which was allowed to provide both the president and the secretary-treasurer. After ratification of the merger agreement at meetings of the two organizations, a first convention of the A.F.L.-C.I.O., held in early December, 1955, thereupon elected George Meany president and William Schnitzler secretary-treasurer, with Walter Reuther serving as a vice president in charge of the Industrial Union Department.

In their historic statement announcing the final agreement for the consolidation of the A.F. of L. and the C.I.O., Meany and Reuther jointly declared: "We feel confident that the merger of the two union groups which we represent will be a boon to our nation and its people in this tense period. We are happy that, in our way, we have been able to bring about unity of the labor movement at a time when the unity of all American people is most urgently needed in the face of the Communist threat to world peace and civilization."

The general public accepted the implications of this broad statement of purpose. Throughout the country the press almost universally welcomed the prospect that labor unity would encourage labor responsibility and promote the cause of free and democratic unionism to the benefit of the entire nation. There were of course exceptions to such a sympathetic response by anti-union forces which fearfully saw in reunification the creation of a dangerous labor monopoly. The president of the National Association of Manufacturers bluntly expressed this conservative reaction in stating that the merger "should be outlawed." Far more significantly, the responsible organs of the business community were hopeful that the move would make for industrial peace. The *Wall Street Journal* did not believe that the merger would in itself enhance the monopoly status of labor, and *Nation's Business*, while suggesting that it might create "a political powerhouse," nonetheless pointed out its potential benefits to industry in minimizing jurisdictional disputes.

Among leading newspapers, the *New York Times* characterized the merger as a "feat of statemanship," the *Washington Post and Times-Herald* referred to it as an "effective demonstration of the maturity and responsibility labor has attained," and, in like vein, the *Christian Science Monitor* also spoke of labor's "growing maturity and sense of responsibility." Echoing papers in many other parts of the country, the *Washington Star* expressed its belief that apart from all other considerations, the merger should contribute substantially "to a long-term stability of labor-management relations."

This generally favorable response to the creation of the A.F.L.-C.I.O. did not mean that the public had suddenly abandoned the critical attitude toward labor that had led to passage of the Taft-Hartley Act. As later developments were soon to show, it still remained somewhat fearful of the unions' mounting power and deeply resentful of the threat to economic stability in industry-wide strikes. But it was clear that the adamant opposition to organized labor of earlier days had given way to general acceptance of the unions and recognition of the important part they played in the nation's economic life. What the American people so clearly hoped in welcoming the merger was that in its newfound unity labor would indeed develop its future policies with the public interest as well as that of union members constantly in mind.

Shortly after these developments, George Meany wrote a significant article in *Fortune* outlining organized labor's goals and aspirations. It was perhaps most interesting in revealing the continuity in the development of the labor movement and the persistence of the hard-headed pragmatism that had been brought to it by Samuel Gompers. Meany emphasized the need for further improvement in the status of industrial workers and the consequent importance of further economic and political activity in their behalf. He made no suggestion of a labor party, but he did declare emphatically that because of an ever-increasing stake in governmental policies, "we shall remain in politics." Summarizing labor's traditional position, he then wrote: "We do not seek to recast American society in any particular doctrinaire or ideological image. We seek an ever rising standard of living. Sam Gompers once put the matter succinctly. When asked what the labor movement wanted, he answered, 'More.' If by a better standard of living we mean not only more money but more leisure and richer cultural life, the answer remains, 'More.'"

In concluding his article Meany reviewed the past with a sense of great achievement. Largely through the efforts of the national and international unions, he declared, American wage earners had since 1900 doubled their standard of living while their working time had been reduced by one-third. He looked forward confidently, he told his readers, to further progress within the framework of that system of free enterprise which had made possible labor's favorable status in American society.

XX: DISAPPOINTED HOPES

THE MERGER OF THE A.F. of L. AND THE C.I.O. appeared to hold out in 1955 the highest prospects for the still further growth and development of unionism. The leaders of the new federation were confident that the unity finally achieved would enable labor to put its house in order and resolve its nagging internal problems. They hopefully envisioned a doubling of union membership within ten years and a consequent increase in both economic and political power that might be exerted in strengthening the security of all industrial workers. They also believed that it would at last be possible to bring about either the repeal of the Taft-Hartley Act or substantial modification of its restrictive provisions, encouraging recruitment from the ranks of non-unionized workers and broadening the scope of collective bargaining agreements.

These bright expectations were not fulfilled. The problems facing organized labor proved to be far more intractable than they appeared to be in 1955, and over the horizon were new developments that served to impede the progress so confidently anticipated. As the nation's economic progress continued, subject only to a temporary recession in the late 1950's, the nation's wage earners fully shared in the benefits of an "affluent society." At the same time they were increasingly haunted by the spectre of possible unemployment due to technological advance and automation. Moreover, the organized labor movement itself was to experience a decline in membership and potential power which before the end of the 1950's created an atmosphere of deep discouragement in labor circles.

The establishment of the A.F.L.-C.I.O. did not of itself create all-embracing unity within the labor movement. The difficult and ticklish problem remained of bringing together the state and local organizations of the two federations and strengthening the procedures which would prevent jurisdictional quarrels among their constituent unions. In spite of the no-raiding agreements, disputes over what workers belonged in what unions continued to plague the labor movement in the 1950's as they had throughout all its turbulent history.

As president of the new federation George Meany proved to be an effective leader of the combined labor force, at once flexible and tough-minded. Many problems were handed over to him with the easy assurance, "let George do it." But he could not always command the full co-operation of officials in either the state federations or the international unions.

The A.F.L.-C.I.O. at its best, moreover, was still no more than a federation of wholly autonomous individual unions. Its executive committee could only recommend action, rather than exercise any coercive power, when jurisdictional or other disputes threatened to block the course of reunification. Historic rivalries did not disappear overnight and negotiations often proceeded at a snail's pace. It was not until the close of the 1950's that the processes of federation were completely achieved in all state organizations, and even then agreements had not been reached in many instances at the local level. Complete unity remained a frustratingly elusive goal.

Nor did the A.F.L.-C.I.O. ever include all national or international unions. The Railway Brotherhoods, even though at one time it had been hoped they might join a national federation, held back for the time being. John L. Lewis and the United Mine Workers were outside the fold. Within a few years the Teamsters Union, largest in the country, would be expelled on the grounds of internal corruption. Although the dominant element in the labor movement as a whole, the A.F.L.-C.I.O. could not speak for all unions without qualification.

There remained also the large number of workers still completely unassociated with the organized labor movement, let alone with the unions affiliated with the A.F.L.-C.I.O. Apart from those in the white collar and professional categories who resisted unionism on their own volition were the unorganized among day laborers and other unskilled workers. Through their disproportionate concentration in this grouping, Negroes did not have a representation in union ranks comparable to that of whites. Even further removed were the nation's agricultural

workers, white or colored. Their number had progressively declined
with the mechanization of agriculture, totaling only some 8,000,000 in
1955, and they were completely unorganized. At one time migrant
workers had found a temporary home in the I.W.W., but otherwise
those who labored on farms had always been wholly outside the labor
movement and played no part in its history.

A year after its formation the federation was to attain what proved
to be its greatest membership—a total of some 15,500,000 in affiliated
unions. Succeeding years saw a steady attrition in this figure and in
1964 it had fallen to an approximate 13,500,000. While the expulsion of
the Teamsters accounted for the greater part of this decline, there had
also been substantial losses in the membership of other important industrial unions which continued their affiliation with the parent body.
The A.F.L.-C.I.O. had far from attained its optimistic hopes of either
representing all labor or experiencing a steady growth in membership.

Even more significant than any such shifts or changes within the national federation, however, was what proved to be the failure of union
membership as a whole to continue its record of steady growth. The
peak was reached in 1956 with an over-all total of 17,500,000, or 33.4
per cent of the non-agricultural employment. Eight years later this total
had fallen to 16,800,000, or, in percentage terms, only some 30 per cent
of the increased labor force and the lowest figure since 1952.

This actual decline and even more drastic drop in percentage terms
was to continue in succeeding years. The contrast with the hopes in
1955 that union membership would be doubled in a decade could
hardly have been more glaring. In weight of numbers at least, the
labor movement appeared to have wholly lost its momentum. In 1960
Walter Reuther bluntly declared: "We are going backward."

Many factors accounted for what was from labor's point of view
such an unhappy situation. The A.F.L.-C.I.O. encountered unexpected
obstacles in developing the new organizing campaign in which its leadership had such confidence. In a number of industries, partly due to
prosperity and the more generous wage policies followed by enlightened employers, there was simply little interest in unionization.
Outright opposition remained strong in such geographic areas as the
South, where the unions had never obtained any real foothold, and organizers were hampered by the state right-to-work laws. In many

instances the labor leaders themselves, both at the top and at local levels, appeared to have lost something of the zeal that had marked their organizing activity in the past. It appeared to be impossible to awaken the enthusiasm or inspire the action that had first given such vitality to the campaign to organize the unorganized.

Over and beyond all such considerations, however, were the changes that had taken place by mid-century in the structure of the civilian labor force. More than anything else they accounted for the drop in union membership and the seemingly insuperable obstacles which organized labor faced in seeking to combat it. For the number of blue collar workers, who provided the bulk of union membership, was declining in contrast to a steady rise in the number of non-unionized white collar workers. In traditional terms, the labor pool from which the unions could hope to draw their members was steadily shrinking, and as yet no way had been found to effectively organize the growing number of those workers who for social rather than economic reasons had always resisted unionism.

More specifically, what had happened since the close of World War II was that the proportion of the nation's workers engaged in mining, manufacturing, and transportation had fallen, while that of employees in wholesale and retail trade, the service industries, and government had increased. Technological advance, making possible increased industrial production with fewer workers, accounted for the one phenomenon, and a popular demand for expanded services, both private and public, explained the latter. The effect on the relative proportions of blue collar and white collar workers in the total labor force was statistically reflected, between 1947 and 1963, in the former's decline from 40.7 per cent to 36.4 per cent of the total, and in the latter's rise from 45.3 per cent to 57 per cent.

As a consequence, membership in such basic industrial unions as those of the steel workers, automobile workers, and miners was falling, and there were no compensating gains in the relatively weak unions which represented the retail clerks, department store and office workers, or government employees. An exception was the vigorous growth of the Teamsters, the country's largest union, but the over-all picture was clear. Unless labor could more successfully organize the white collar workers, the trend toward declining union membership that had begun in 1957 seemed likely to continue.

The disappointments labor suffered so far as union membership was concerned were paralleled in the field of political action. The A.F.L.-C.I.O. was militantly determined to marshal the full support of labor behind all candidates for public office who showed a sympathy for union aims and aspirations. To this end it established a new Committee on Political Education. While this committee reaffirmed labor's traditional attitude in stating that it would maintain "a strictly nonpartisan attitude," it was hardly surprising that in practice this nonetheless meant, as in every year since 1936, virtually all-out support for the Democratic ticket in national elections. C.O.P.E. campaigned vigorously for Stevenson in 1956, and again for Kennedy in 1960. It generally supported Democratic candidates for Congress. In the light of congressional gains by the liberals in these years (in spite of the reelection of Eisenhower in 1956), efforts were thereupon renewed through the most intense lobbying activities to get some action on Taft-Hartley's repeal and to promote further legislation favorable to labor and the nation's workers.

Such efforts were unsuccessful, and before the close of the 1950's Congress had enacted another piece of labor legislation that the unions attacked as being quite as obstructive to their interests as Taft-Hartley itself. The only political achievement that could be credited to organized labor during this period was that of holding the line against the further proliferation of the state right-to-work laws.

In 1955, 17 states had such laws barring not only the closed shop but the union shop. They were largely in the South or Far West, but conservative business interests mounted an intensive campaign to win over some of the more heavily industrialized states. While labor continued to feel that the only resolution of this issue was repeal of Section 14 (b) of the Taft-Hartley Act, it conducted a hard-hitting war against any further state legislation. In only two instances did it fail to defeat proposed new right-to-work laws, and in 1958 decisively threw back anti-union forces in the five important states of California, Ohio, Colorado, Idaho, and Washington.

In the meantime, however, labor had suffered that reverse in the field of national legislation which the A.F.L.-C.I.O. roundly denounced as the fruit of an anti-union design "to destroy labor" and "the most severe setback in more than a decade." The background for this new law was the dramatic disclosure of corruption and racketeering in a number of unions and an irate public reaction to labor's apparent inability to clean its own house.

The problem of corruption had a long history which may be traced back at least as far as the disclosures of extortion and other improper activities on the part of local union officials made before the United States Industrial Commission in 1902. Then, as half a century later, the unions most deeply involved were those in the building trades, long-shoremen, truck drivers, laundry and dry cleaning employees, and other service workers. The opportunities for racketeering had always been much greater in such unions than in those embracing the workers in productive industry and corruption could never be wholly stamped out.

A further development followed the close of the prohibition era. Gangsters increasingly invaded the field of labor relations to exploit both employers and employees in collusion with corrupt union officials. The A.F. of L. became greatly aroused by this threat to the whole labor movement. It repeatedly condemned "racketeering and gangsterism of all forms," but, as a federation based on the complete autonomy of all member unions, it held back from any outright intervention in local affairs. As evidence of corruption continued to increase in postwar years as a result of governmental investigations and newspaper campaigns, it nevertheless felt driven to take more effective action than periodic resolutions by the executive committee.

A first instance of such action was the move made in 1953 to expel the longshoremen's union as a result of the dramatic revelations of racketeering and gangsterism on the New York waterfront. The federation's position in demanding reforms was based on the proposition, as set forth in communicating with the union, that "your relationship with the American Federation of Labor demands that the democratic ideals, clean and wholesome free trade unionism, must be immediately restored within your organization and all semblance of crime, dishonesty

and racketeering be forthwith eliminated." Although the A.F. of L. encountered insuperable obstacles in trying to carry through its reform
program, its efforts to bring the longshoremen in line marked a new
departure in its policy.

Even though the number of unions actually involved in racketeering
or other illegal practices was very small, the leaders of the merged
A.F.L.-C.I.O. realized even more than had their predecessors that
every disclosure of corruption undermined the public image of organized labor as a whole. Consequently one of their first moves, in line
with the federation's original statement of principles, was the establishment of an Ethical Practices Committee. It was authorized to draw up
and seek to enforce rules of conduct aimed against racketeering and
malfeasance on the part of union officials, other corrupt practices in the
conduct of union affairs, and especially any misuse of union money
which was invested in the pension and welfare funds that in recent
years had been growing enormously.

The federation's hope was that through such means labor could circumvent possible government interference in union affairs. However,
further examples of the strong grip that racketeers had won over a
number of unions awoke increasing public concern. Neither the public
nor Congress was willing to leave the matter entirely to the relatively
gentle ministrations of the A.F.L. C.I.O., and the demand grew for a
thorough governmental investigation and possible legislation.

In response to such pressure the Senate established in 1957 a Select
Committee on Improper Activities in the Labor or Management Field
which was headed by Senator McClellan of Arkansas and had as its
vigorous chief counsel a youthful Robert F. Kennedy. This committee
promptly instituted a series of public hearings, nationally televised,
that were to shock and alarm the entire country. The evidence spread
upon the public record revealed a larger degree of dictatorial union
leadership, violating every democratic principle, and of corruption,
racketeering, and gangsterism on the part of union officials, than even
labor's most severe critics had suspected. Witness after witness testified
to rigged elections, the misuse of union funds, embezzlement, and
theft. It was true that these disclosures involved only a handful of
unions. Nevertheless they served to cast suspicion on the entire labor
movement and placed its leaders very much on the defensive.

One of the chief targets of the congressional investigation was the Teamsters Union. Probing deeply into its internal affairs, the Mc-Clellan Committee brought out innumerable cases of political chicanery in the locals, extortion on the part of union officials in their dealings with employers, and close associations (particularly in New York) with known gangsters. Racketeering was rife, with inevitable terrorism and violence. Even more sensationally, the hearings disclosed that corruption extended to the top leadership. The Teamsters' president, David Beck, was running the union very much as he chose and had diverted large union funds to his own private purposes. Self-assured and arrogant, completely disdainful of the Senate committee's powers, Beck repeatedly refused to answer the questions asked him and when threatened with contempt proceedings, insolently took refuge in the Fifth Amendment. The evidence brought out against him nevertheless forced him to give up the presidency of his union and led to his indictment—and ultimate conviction—on charges of tax evasion and grand larceny.

The downfall of Beck did not, however, lead to any clean-up in the Teamsters' affairs. He was succeeded in office by James R. Hoffa, whose rise in union ranks since his early organization of a warehouseman's union in 1932 had brought him to the Teamsters' vice-presidency. An able, efficient organizer, his career had nonetheless been marked, according to testimony before the McClellan Committee, by undercover business relationships with the firms with which his union was negotiating and other private dealings with companies handling its health and welfare funds.

It soon became apparent that the new union president was. if anything even more determined than Beck had been to defy any interference with how he ran things. After a group of union officials had unsuccessfully contested his election as illegal, the McClellan Committee sought to oust him on charges that he was the source of a "cancer" that spread continuing corruption and gangsterism throughout his union. But when his case was taken to the courts and a federal district judge appointed a Board of Monitors to supervise temporarily the conduct of the Teamsters' affairs, Hoffa fought back with every possible legal device and continued to hold his office.

A bitter feud thereupon developed between the Teamsters' chief and the Department of Justice, which was accentuated when Robert Kennedy became Attorney General. The former McClellan Committee counsel continued through repeated prosecutions for malfeasance and corruption to try to break Hoffa's power. The latter nonetheless was re-elected to his presidency in 1961 (with a salary of $75,000), successfully combatted or appealed every legal move made against him (even when found guilty in 1964 of tampering with a jury), and continued to dominate what Kennedy called his "hoodlum empire."

The hearings involving the Teamsters were the most sensational of those held by the McClellan Committee but only a little less so were the disclosures of corruption in a number of smaller unions. The Hotel and Restaurant Employees, the Bakery and Confectionery Workers, the Laundry Workers, the Operating Engineers, the Allied Industrial Workers, and the United Textile Workers all came under attack. Union witnesses again reported cases of the misuse of union funds, of collusion between union officials and employers, and of extortion and violence. Once more there was spread upon the record the picture of a relationship between union officials and underworld elements which made employees and employers alike, as well as the public, victims of a network of festering corruption.

As this evidence came to light the Ethical Practices Committee of the A.F.L.-C.I.O. was galvanized into new action. It called the unions accused of such improper activities to account and placed them on probation, so far as their membership in the federation was concerned, until they met prescribed terms for internal reform. When the Teamsters Union, the Bakery and Confectionery Workers, and the Laundry Workers signally failed to clean house, the A.F.L.-C.I.O. officially expelled them. It was seeking to do what it could, however limited its powers, to demonstrate that responsible labor leadership was deserving of public confidence.

In spite of such moves on the part of the A.F.L.-C.I.O., the first report of the McClellan Committee insisted that its fully documented disclosures of union corruption called for governmental action. President Eisenhower agreed. On his urging Congress began to consider various proposals to stop "corruption, racketeering and abuse of power in labor-management relations." There was widespread support for some measure along these lines, but congressional debate soon opened up the broader question of legislation affecting the unions' legal rights with a demand for tightening the provisions of the Taft-Hartley Act rather than liberalizing them.

Organized labor at once took alarm. Admitting the need for a bill safeguarding welfare funds, it strongly opposed using the investigations of the McClellan Committee as "a basis for legislative proposals designed to weaken all unions, rather than eliminate corruption." As this was exactly what labor's foes in Congress seemed determined to do, the battle was fairly joined. During the next seven months pro-union and anti-union forces fought fiercely over the issues involved, both in the halls of Congress and in the newspapers.

The contesting forces in the Senate were led by John F. Kennedy and Barry Goldwater. The former brought in a bill limited to safeguarding the pension and welfare funds; the latter strongly opposed it as a complete surrender to organized labor. It was a "sweetheart type of bill," the Arizona senator declared, "so we can get in bed with labor and not make anyone mad." The Republicans thereupon submitted a series of tough amendments, but Democratic lines tightened to oppose their passage. With the strong support of Senator Johnson, the majority leader who was somewhat later to confront Goldwater on an even more important stage, the Democratic forces won out. But Johnson had helped secure passage of the relatively innocuous Welfare and Pension Plans Disclosure Act, signed by the President on August 28, 1958, only by promising the immediate submission of a more general anti-corruption bill. Kennedy then presented such a measure but it still fell far short of the strict legislation which the Republicans declared necessary not only to combat union corruption but to curb labor's economic power. While the Senate passed the Kennedy bill, the House would have none of it. A conservative coalition of Republicans and southern Democrats marshaled the strength to reject it in a dramatic roll call by the narrow margin of eight votes.

The issue was not dead, however. It was put over to the next Congress and the mounting public indignation over the further findings of the McClellan Committee served in the meantime to strengthen greatly the hands of labor's foes. The tide began to run heavily against the moderate legislation favored by the Democrats and in favor of the rigid union controls which the Republicans, with full administration support, were so stridently demanding. In spite of strenuous union lobbying, the stage was being set for another labor defeat.

The Landrum-Griffin Act, which Congress now adopted rather than the Kennedy bill and which President Eisenhower signed on September 14, 1959, was the measure of this defeat. The first sections of this new law dealt with the corruption issue and incorporated a Bill of Rights for union members. These provisions embodied specific safeguards for democratic procedures in the conduct of union affairs, protected union funds with the imposition of fines and prison sentences for any official guilty of their misuse, made any forceful interference with the rights of union members a federal offense, and prohibited persons convicted of certain crimes, and also members of the Communist Party, from serving as union officials for five years after their release from prison or after termination of Communist membership. Such regulations were patently in the interest of responsible unionism. The Landrum-Griffin Act, however, went beyond them to amend Taft-Hartley by severely tightening a number of its provisions governing union activities.

The existing ban on secondary boycotts was broadened to prevent a union from bringing any pressure to bear on an employer to make him cease doing business with another employer. A new curb was placed on picketing to outlaw any action whereby a union sought to coerce a company where a rival union was lawfully recognized. And most seriously from the labor point of view, the new legislation stated that in the so-called "no-man's-land"—an area where disputes were judged too unimportant or localized for consideration by the National Labor Relations Board—the states could assume jurisdiction. This latter provision strongly militated against further union organization in the South, where only 2,000,000 out of a possible 12,000,000 workers were organized, because of the wide prevalence in that region of right-to-work laws.

The Landrum-Griffin Act did not entirely please anyone. While management felt that it did not go far enough, organized labor was especially resentful of the new curbs on boycotts and picketing, and the "no-man's-land" provisions. Fears of the possible consequences of the new restrictions were to prove exaggerated, as in the case of the anti-union clauses in Taft-Hartley. But the A.F.L.-C.I.O. leadership felt that the unions had not only suffered a severe political defeat, but saw in passage of the law ominous portents for the future. There was no question that it reflected a strong popular reaction against unionism which was largely due to the disclosures of corruption by the Mc-Clellan Committee.

In its provisions to safeguard democratic procedures in union affairs, the new law was impinging upon an issue which in the final analysis could only be resolved by the unions themselves. Their growth in and of itself, the concentration of power in the hands of a few officials as contract negotiations became increasingly complicated, and an inevitable trend toward bureaucratization more and more tended to remove direct control of union business from the hands of the union members themselves. Entirely apart from possible corruption, this spreading gap led in some instances to a feeling of restlessness and discontent among the rank-and-file which was to find expression in a number of unions in popular revolts against existing leadership. One notable example was the narrowly contested election in 1965 in which the United Steelworkers forced David McDonald out of office because they felt that he was working too closely with management, successful though his negotiations had been, and was getting out of touch with union members.

Apart from such issues and whatever else might be said of the Landrum-Griffin Act as being anti-labor or pro-labor, perhaps its greatest importance lay in the further extension of governmental influence, if not control, in the whole field of labor relations. The underlying justification for such legislation was the protection of the public interest. The new law was designed to do so by attacking the abuses in the management of union affairs. Its sponsors could therefore claim that it would help to provide a stronger basis for the development of more responsible collective bargaining.

In general terms, subsequent investigations and enforcement under the act showed that corruption within the labor movement was by no means as widespread as the spectacular hearings of the previous year had suggested. Misuse of funds, collusion between union officials and management, and racketeering might still be found in some few unions, but the idea that labor organizations as a whole were shot through with corruption was clearly refuted. "One of the great contributions of the Landrum-Griffin Act," Philip Taft has written, "is to demonstrate the basic falsehood of such beliefs, and to show that for probity and integrity the labor movement compares favorably with other American institutions."

During this period of legislative battling over the position of organized labor, the nation's wage earners themselves continued to enjoy the progressive gains they had so consistently achieved since World War II. Moreover they had been won with a minimum of work stoppages. The downward trend that has been previously noted in the incidence of strikes continued in the late 1950's and the total of man-days lost fell to the lowest levels since 1944. The restive longshoremen again walked out on a number of occasions, the automobile workers in one year struck successively against Ford, General Motors, and Chrysler, and employees in atomic energy plants created a new problem affecting national security when they briefly went on strike. But none of these walk-outs seriously contradicted the general picture of improving industrial relations. The one exception to such relative stability was the great steel strike in 1959. It went even beyond that of seven years earlier in its threat to the national economy and in its highly significant consequences.

Wages and fringe benefits of course entered into this controversy between the union and the industry, but underlying all this were the new and ominous issues raised by the rapid pace of technological advance and automation. The strike was in effect a renewed power struggle between labor and management. The steel workers sought to maintain their jurisdiction over work rules, which could help safeguard their jobs, while their employers strove to win a completely free hand in introducing and controlling new methods of production.

It was perhaps natural that this contest should take place within the steel industry. The strike recalled those major conflicts of the past— Homestead, the steel strike of 1919, the Little Steel strike of 1937—in which labor had fought so bitterly for its rights against the entrenched power of the country's most gigantic industry. And in 1959, as in these earlier strikes, the forces of all organized labor and those of all industry felt that their interests were deeply involved in the outcome of the struggle—this time a grim endurance contest rather than a flare-up of violence and intimidation.

The real nature of the conflict was not apparent at first. The negotiations for a new contract between the United Steelworkers and the steel industry appeared to be no more than another chapter in the endless bargaining over wages, and it was generally believed that the ultimate outcome would be the sort of compromise settlement that had marked every postwar contract. A helpless public expected a further increase in steel wages followed by another mark-up in steel prices—and a consequent spur to the upward spiral of living costs.

The industry's position, as developed in the early stages of the negotiations, revealed an apparent determination this time to call a halt to any further increase in wages. Its spokesmen insisted that this was the only way to control inflation and their arguments commanded a good deal of popular support. The union, on the other hand, declared that the workers were entitled to higher pay in the light of both increased productivity and higher living expenses, and stoutly maintained that the profits of the steel companies made a reasonable wage increase possible without raising steel prices. Agreement on this issue was difficult enough in itself, and it only gradually became apparent that more was at stake. But when industry also demanded modification of the existing work rules, the union stiffened its resistance all along the line. It refused any concessions on what was a more vital issue than wages.

In these circumstances the contract negotiations broke off in mid-July and steel workers throughout the country walked out on strike. Subsequent attempts to reconcile the divergent positions of labor and industry failed with monotonous regularity; as the strike dragged on for seemingly endless weeks and steel supplies reached near exhaustion, the nation's entire economy began to falter even more dangerously than in 1952. An outraged public, still not understanding the issues at stake, but merely seeing the steel union and the steel industry battling over wages at the public expense, began to demand governmental intervention in the interests of industrial peace and national prosperity. The Eisenhower Administration moved very slowly and very reluctantly. The last thing the President wanted was to become involved in a labor dispute. Finally he felt compelled to act and on

October 9 invoked the emergency provisions of Taft-Hartley. Declaring that the continuing strike imperiled the national health and safety, he appointed a special board of inquiry, and when it duly reported that it could discover no basis for the strike's settlement, he ordered the Department of Justice to seek an injunction against the union. A federal district court granted the government's plea, and although the union appealed on the ground that the strike had not created a national emergency (undertaking to provide whatever steel was necessary for national defense), the Supreme Court sustained the lower court's decision by an 8 to 1 vote on November 7. The strikers thereupon returned to work but the officers of the United Steelworkers bitterly attacked the administration for strike-breaking and, without conceding a point, appeared to be fully prepared to resume the strike when the injunction had run its course.

The deadlock appeared to be insurmountable. There was much talk of the wage issue, but the real stumbling block, on which neither side was willing to give way at all, remained the dispute over work rules and their possible relationship to automation. As the year drew to an end the prospect of a renewal of the strike, with even more serious consequences for the economy, became insupportable. Still, the union's lines held firm with the workers' determination to renew the strike strengthened by the industry's obdurate stand on the work rules. For a time the latter's front seemed to waver when the Kaiser Company withdrew from the corporate coalition, reaching an independent agreement with the union, but it was soon reestablished. The industry's spokesmen reiterated their insistence upon changes in the work rules as a necessary condition for any contract.

Then on January 5, 1960, came the announcement of a sudden and dramatic breakthrough. In the face of steadily mounting economic and political pressure, and its fear that if the strike were renewed government would force an unsatisfactory settlement, the steel industry in effect surrendered. It came to terms with the union and signed a new agreement. It provided for increased pension and insurance payments, with a subsequent wage rise, but most importantly it incorporated maintenance of the existing work rules. David McDonald, president of the United Steelworkers, declared it was the best contract the union had ever concluded.

Over and beyond its more specific provisions, the agreement also had a new and unique feature. It set up two special committees under neutral chairmen. One was to undertake a study of human relations within the steel industry, and the other was designed to investigate local working conditions. The idea behind the creation of these committees was that continuing study of labor problems could provide a basis for future contract negotiations that would at least ameliorate the crisis atmosphere in which they were so often held.

The victory won by the United Steelworkers in the face of such stubborn opposition on the part of management was far more significant in its implications for future union controls over work rules than for its wage increases. And it was a victory important for organized labor as a whole since it had been won in the face of the resistance of industry as a whole. Labor had successfully reasserted its compelling economic power in the protection of the interests of union members. In spite of the setbacks on other fronts, and whatever might be read into the Landrum-Griffin Act, it had again demonstrated an underlying strength and vitality.

The steel strike nevertheless drove home another lesson. From the point of view of both labor and industry, and even more from that of the American public, the consequences of another such strike might well be disastrous for the economy. The injunction proceedings of the Taft-Hartley Act had once again proved to be wholly inadequate and any real solution of the basic problem of industry-wide strikes appeared to be as distant as ever. President Eisenhower summoned a new conference of labor and industrial leaders. But their discussions were wholly inconclusive. And while Congress talked a great deal about the issue, in an election year it remained politically fearful of really coming to grips with the situation.

In spite of victory in the steel strike, the 1950's came to a close, as had the 1940's, with organized labor in a highly vulnerable position. The Executive Committee of the A.F.L.-C.I.O. was to declare that the movement had barely survived "some of the worst storms in trade union history." The major unions might still wield tremendous economic power, but, as a result of the growth of anti-union sentiment revealed in passage of the Landrum-Griffin Act, their future seemed imperiled. At the annual convention of the A.F.L.-C.I.O. in the autumn of 1959, the atmosphere was thick with gloom. The dominant theme in every discussion was the imperative need for greater unity in meeting what was characterized, with customary exaggeration, as a new conspiracy on the part of industry to weaken or destroy the entire labor movement.

A first necessity in the minds of the federation leaders was to win back public confidence. This was the essential prerequisite if the downward trend in union membership was to be halted and organized labor was to strengthen its position in collective bargaining. The picture of irresponsibility and corruption drawn in the revelations of the Mc-Clellan Committee had somehow to be erased. Organized labor had to be depicted as a social force—what President Meany described as "an instrumentality for good"—which was devoted to the broad interests of the American people as a whole rather than exclusively concerned with the wages and hours of union members. The new propaganda line was to emphasize the role that organized labor had played in supporting such progressive domestic policies as social security, improved housing, better education, and civil rights, and in consistently backing a foreign policy aimed at averting the global threat of Communist imperialism.

The importance of gaining greater popular sympathy was heavily underscored, in the eyes of labor leaders, by the grave uncertainties of the future. Looming over the horizon was that deepening problem, already so strongly accented in the struggle over work rules in the steel industry and in several other disputes, of how organized labor could effectively combat the threat of technological unemployment in a booming economy. Job security was every year becoming a graver issue. This situation primarily engaged the labor movement but obviously affected the country as a whole. For the inevitable consequences of unemployment were a paradoxical and tragic continuance of poverty in the midst of plenty.

XX

XXI: THE CHALLENGE OF THE 1960'S

XXXXXXXXXXXXXXXXXXXXXXXXXXXXXXXXXXXXXXXXXXXX

THE BASIC PROBLEM of job security which so importantly affected labor-management relations as the 1950's gave way to the 1960's, was not of course a new one. It had always been a matter of grave concern to wage earners throughout the country. But the changes that had taken place in the economy since the close of World War II had immensely accentuated its significance. Increasing automation in many industries and the consequent lay-off of workers even as production mounted appeared to be the key factor in the situation.

The recession of 1957–58 had brought about unemployment as high as 6.8 per cent of the civilian working force and even as the economy gradually righted itself, this heavy burden of joblessness stubbornly persisted. President Johnson would emphatically state on December 4, 1964, that "the Number 1 in priority today is more jobs. This is our dominant domestic problem, and we have to face it head-on." There was abundant evidence that union labor faced a compelling new challenge in trying to meet this dangerous threat to the otherwise greatly improved position of the nation's wage-earners.

Against this background of emergent new problems, the status of the organized labor movement in the early 1960's, as developments in the previous decade so clearly suggested, offered something of a paradox. From one point of view the major unions were stronger than ever before. They were still able to win the successive wage increases which had marked contract negotiations, as we have so repeatedly seen, throughout the previous two decades. Whenever forced to strike, they almost invariably secured the major share of their demands. A booming economy and ever higher industrial profits enabled them to do so without blocking further economic progress, but the fact remained that they often appeared to have very much their own way.

On the other hand, the failure of organized labor to maintain existing union membership, let alone make the gains anticipated in 1955, gave new substance to those fears on the part of labor leaders that the movement as a whole was losing its drive and its working class support. In spite of every effort to push new organizing campaigns, they remained on dead center. There was little recovery from the losses sustained in the late 1950's and indeed total enrollment in all unions in the United States was in 1965 still estimated at no more than about 17,000,000.

The shift in the labor force which marked the growing ascendancy of white collar workers over blue collars still largely accounted for this persistent failure to build up membership. It was highly significant that only some 2,300,000 workers among the 22,000,000 who fell within the white-collar category were union members. But the apathy of wage earners generally, which Walter Reuther sought to explain on the ground that in a traditional sense they were no longer "hungry," also impeded every effort to organize them. Facing this situation labor's leaders found little relief from the discouragement that had marked the convention of the A.F.L.-C.I.O. in 1959. In spite of further wage gains, they envisaged a progressive weakening of the broad base—union membership—on which organized labor's economic and political strength ultimately rested.

Moreover there was often a feeling of frustration and even helplessness as the unions tried to meet the problems of the 1960's. While George Meany as recently as 1955 had felt justified in saying that, as in the days of Samuel Gompers, organized labor's primary objective remained "more," such a simplified goal was no longer wholly relevant with the new technology forcing more and more men out of their jobs altogether. Higher wages were no longer the issue that most concerned workers in the mass production industries; what they wanted was firmer assurance of continuing to have any wages at all.

If the cure for unemployment in earlier periods had been a return of prosperity, this no longer appeared to be the answer when higher production could be attained with fewer workers. Yet it seemed almost impossible to adapt the processes of collective bargaining, so successful in winning wage increases and fringe benefits, to maintaining job security. In some instances they had helped to guarantee work for members of strategically placed unions, but in too many other cases they proved to be almost completely ineffective. And what might be the future of strikes, labor's final weapon in seeking to protect its interests, should strike-proof automated factories dominate ever larger areas of national production?

Some new approach seemed essential in meeting the intensified problem of technological unemployment. Where direct economic action was unavailing, there was the possibility of more effective political pressure. It was still far from the thinking of union leaders that labor should have its own party. The question nevertheless remained of finding a way to play a more persuasive role in directing national policy along lines that would meet the needs of both organized labor and the nation's workers as a whole.

At the opening of the 1960's "frozen leadership and static membership" did not seem to hold out great hopes that labor could command such influence at Washington. One commentator wrote that its political prestige stood "at the lowest ebb in 30 years." He declared that public disenchantment was perhaps largely due to "the recent revelations of gross immorality in some unions," but that it also stemmed from the fear of the economic consequences of collective bargaining which ignored the public interest. Another observer would write in 1963 that the unions were undergoing "a crisis of public confidence unmatched since Franklin D. Roosevelt's New Deal."

Organized labor was at once too strong and too weak. It could wreck havoc through an industry-wide strike, but in so doing sacrificed the public sympathy and support on which it was basically dependent. It wielded great economic power, but the persistent erosion of union membership was undermining the source of such power. It could still win progressively higher wages for the employed, but could not guarantee them any real security in their jobs.

As the decade advanced all the old and recurrent clichés of labor standing at the crossroads, labor at the turning point, labor in crisis, were endlessly repeated at union meetings, in symposia among economists, and in magazine articles and special studies. In 1963 a survey of the opinions of 38 union presidents and 47 staff personnel singled out what were considered the most discouraging features of the current scene. They first listed such basic factors as automation and consequent unemployment, the weakness of union structure, and the loss of public sympathy. There was also a heavy emphasis in many of the replies on the lack of the old sense of dedication to the labor movement. What was primarily needed, one respondent wrote, was "smaller waist lines, more vigor, and above all, a better educated and more literate leadership."

Whatever the future might hold, existing circumstances for those wage earners who did have steady jobs were more highly favorable than ever before. If the advance in real wages had been 50 per cent above prewar levels in the mid-1950's, a decade later it was approaching 70 per cent. The increase in wages for those engaged in manufacture—from a weekly average of $44 in 1945 to $105 in 1965—far outstripped the rise in the cost of living. The average hourly rate for production workers in the latter year was $2.50, but in certain occupations was far higher. Longshoremen earned $3.62 an hour, members of the Teamsters Union $3.28, and steel workers as high as $4.40. Even more significant than all such figures was the general increase in what economists called "discretionary income." Wage earners were finding that they had more money available than ever before after payment of all their essential family expenses.

A still more unprecedented advance was the continued extension of the fringe benefits which supplemented weekly wages. The new collective bargaining agreements of the 1960's went even further than those a decade earlier. They not only included escalator clauses for further rises in the costs of living. They invariably incorporated provisions for life, sickness and accident insurance, survivor benefits, generous pensions, welfare funds, and supplementary unemployment benefits.

A contract signed by the United Automobile Workers and General Motors in 1964 added to these customary provisions coverage for "short-term psychiatric therapy," tuition for job related education courses, severance pay, and an incentive program for early retirement. A worker with 30 years of service could ordinarily retire at age 65 with a stipend of $316 a month, but should he retire at 62, his monthly check would be $381.

If unionized workers had come a long way so far as their pay was concerned, equally important was what was happening in respect to leisure time. The average workweek had not itself greatly changed since the general adoption of the 40-hour week in the 1930's. While in a few industries it had been further cut to 35 hours (a contract signed in 1962 by construction engineers in New York provided a 25-hour week!), the national average in 1965 was about 41 hours. However, virtually every union contract marked a further advance in paid holidays and vacations.

The former ranged between six and ten every year (the General Motors contract previously noted made one of these holidays the worker's birthday), and the latter, depending on length of service, were anywhere up to four weeks annually. In one instance, a local Teamsters contract in New York had a "vacation security" clause providing seven weeks off with pay for all workers with over 25 years of service. In comparison with conditions prevailing as recently as the 1930's, nothing stood out more conspicuously than this increase in leisure time.

Indeed such leisure, which was estimated over and beyond the usual two-day weekend to amount to an average of 20 days a year for some 85 per cent of all the country's wage earners, had ironically enough become something of a social problem. Economists and sociologists were worried. How was this free time in the hands of industrial workers to be spent? "The burden of leisure, long the exclusive curse of the rich," a contributor to the *Nation* wrote in April, 1963, "is now the darkest threat to the well-being of the working man and the subject of increasing concern on the part of organized labor."

He was not referring to the leisure consequent upon unemployment, in which case his point would have been well taken, but to the free time at the disposal of workers who had jobs. His article reflected the persistence of the age-old puritan attitude toward the inherent evils of idleness. The fact was that popular mores had changed. Holidays and vacations had been given social sanction in the twentieth century, and also they had their economic importance both in helping to spread work and in encouraging the spectacular postwar growth of a vast amusement industry. It was nonetheless widely felt that such enhanced leisure should at least be spent "constructively." Otherwise, in the phraseology of one sociologist, it would tend to debase rather than elevate the American way of life.

Higher wages and more leisure time, in any event, had materially altered the status of the great majority of the country's wage earners. The increase in discretionary income was particularly important in narrowing the gap between the living standards of blue collar and white collar workers, or between wage earners and salaried employees. More and more unionized workers owned their own homes, could afford automobiles, television sets, and sometimes motor boats, and were able to travel and take vacation tours. Sharing in the country's general prosperity, they raised their living standards, sent their children to college, took up the current fads in recreation and amusements, and otherwise conformed to the prevailing customs of the middle-class society of which they were becoming a part.

Many such wage earners were moving to the new housing developments springing up everywhere throughout the country, and they tended to take on the more conservative coloration of their salaried or professional neighbors in suburbia. They occasionally shifted their political allegiance, swinging over to vote a Republican ticket, and in other ways revealed the long distance they had traveled from their working-class origins. The general status of wage earners in the United States in the 1960's could hardly have afforded a more striking denial of the major tenets of Marxism or more convincingly justified the American unionist's traditional faith that a system of free enterprise held the promise of great rewards for the army of labor.

Yet there was another side to this Utopian picture—the dark, tragic picture of poverty in the midst of plenty, of stagnation and even decay that stood in glaring contrast to the shining march of progress. Not only the unhappy situation of the unemployed, but that of wage earners not protected by collective bargaining agreements (the great number of unskilled workers outside the ranks of organized labor) was a harsh reminder that the glowing attributes of an affluent society were still far from universal. Union members in their new-found prosperity could never be wholly secure as long as such contrasting conditions persisted.

The broadened concepts of the welfare state made some amends for the failure of the national economy to meet this problem. In 1961 the provisions of the Fair Labor Standards Act were amplified to cover an increased number of workers and also to raise the minimum wage to $1.25 an hour. But while this established a floor for the pay of all those engaged in industry affecting interstate commerce, it was an exceedingly low one. It meant annual earnings of no more than some $2,600, or less than half the average earnings of production workers generally and a figure well below that accepted as a minimum subsistence income for an average-size family. For the temporarily unemployed there were the benefits of unemployment insurance while the elderly were entitled to old-age pensions and other welfare benefits made available through the expanded provisions of the Social Security Act. Finally, in 1965, Congress at long last passed Medicare with its sickness benefits for those over 65.

Organized labor had strongly supported these measures and they reflected an added emphasis on the responsibility of government to meet the needs of the people. However, they offered no real cure to the malaise of continued unemployment and of substandard wages in many areas. For those workers who had exhausted their benefits under the Social Security program, and for others unable even to find a place for themselves in the labor market, the situation remained a shocking travesty on all the boasts of national property.

The number of unemployed throughout the country in 1960 was still at about the total of the recession days of 1957–58. It very gradually declined in succeeding years and by the autumn of 1965 had fallen below the seemingly persistent level of 4,000,000 to a more encouraging 3,600,000. But this figure still represented 4.5 per cent of a civilian labor force which had grown to 75,000,000. The basic problem remained, and it was seriously worsened by the heavy incidence of such unemployment among three special groups: unskilled workers, teenagers seeking to enter the labor market, and Negroes.

Every index revealed that the poorer educated and untrained workers were finding it very hard to get jobs, and their unemployment rate was far higher than that of the skilled workers. In the case of teenagers, joblessness was three times the national average for labor as a whole. Negroes made up a quarter of the unemployed even though they constituted little more than one tenth of the labor force, or, to put it another way, the unemployment rate among non-whites was twice as high as among whites.

By 1965 the over-all increase in employment had led to considerable improvement in conditions for blue collar workers and also for teen-agers, but not for the Negroes. "The two-to-one ratio," Daniel Patrick Moynihan, onetime Assistant Secretary of Labor, wrote in the *Reporter* on September 9, 1965, "is now frozen into the economy." The veteran Negro labor leader A. Philip Randolph, of the Brotherhood of Sleeping Car Porters, declared that in the light of the continuing scar-city of unskilled jobs, "black workers face a virtually unsolvable problem."

The implications of this aspect of unemployment were of utmost importance to the whole movement of these days to secure the civil rights of Negroes. But while organized labor strongly supported legis-lative action to this end, its own record in making jobs as available for Negroes as for whites was marred by many instances of flagrant union discrimination. Even in the late 1950's there was a widespread pattern of exclusion in the building trades, and if this was not the case in the industrial unions, Negro membership still did not necessarily mean equal opportunity. At least in the South there was often a dual system of seniority governing wage scales for the two races. Admitting a situa-tion which he deplored, George Meany on one occasion stated that the A.F.L.-C.I.O. could not in good conscience call upon Congress to act against racial discrimination while some of its own affiliated unions were still guilty of practicing it.

With the establishment of its own civil rights committee in 1955, the federation nevertheless tried to bring union practices more in line with union principles and called upon its affiliates to eliminate any segregation on the basis of color or race. But its control over the inter-national unions, and in turn their control over locals, remained very limited. To spur more effective action a thousand convention dele-gates joined in 1960 to form the Negro American Labor Council, under the chairmanship of A. Philip Randolph, with the stated purpose of keeping "the conscience of the A.F.L.-C.I.O. disturbed." Under such pressure Meany launched a drive to exert increasing economic pressure on employers for more effective implementation of the racial equality clauses written into most labor-management agreements. The challenge was one that somehow had to be met.

While most economists, and particularly those associated with organized labor, held automation primarily responsible for the heavy incidence of unemployment among Negroes and other unskilled workers, this explanation was in other quarters disputed. In a series of articles, published in *Fortune* in the spring of 1965, Charles E. Silberman flatly stated that "it was simply not true that the new technology is eliminating demand for relatively unskilled and poorly educated blue-collar workers." Admitting that between 1956 and 1961 industry had eliminated through the introduction of machinery some 1,700,000 production worker jobs, he nevertheless insisted that the trend toward fewer blue-collar jobs and more white-collar jobs was not likely to continue much longer. Emphasizing the impact of defense production— missiles, electronic equipment, the space program—in increasing the relative demand for skilled workers, he stated that this expansion was becoming stabilized at current levels while new opportunities for unskilled workers in the booming service industries were rapidly compensating for the loss of jobs in other areas. He also sought to explain away the heavy impact of unemployment among teenagers as due to a fortuitous combination of factors wholly unrelated to automation. The increased number of young people entering the labor market (the war babies of the 1940's) had happened to coincide with both a temporary slowdown in the economy and a heavy influx of female workers. Since women made up 34 per cent of the labor force in 1964 as compared with only 20 per cent in 1947, "teenagers were competing for jobs with their mothers." There was every reason to believe, Silberman asserted, that in spite of automation employment for the unskilled would substantially increase with the further expansion of the economy.

The sociologist Daniel Bell also undertook in an article in the *New York Review* to deflate "the bogey of automation." He insisted in his turn that the real reason for continuing unemployment was no more than the failure of the economy "to grow as rapidly as the national rate of productivity, plus the increase in the labor force." He cited a number of instances where automation had not actually displaced workers but rather increased employment.

These arguments were not, however, always persuasive and from the point of view of labor—and even more from that of the individual workers who lost their jobs—they seemed to ignore the human element. As Michael Harrington pointed out in one perceptive article, an employee who found himself a victim of automation might possibly turn up some other low-paying, unorganized job, but with little or no opportunity to rise in the economic or social scale. "Automation has now created an abyss between those with training and education and those without," he wrote. "So a man can be sentenced to life at the bottom of the economy without even becoming a certified, statistical tragedy."

Whatever immediate nationwide gains or long-term statistical projections might suggest, there remained the harsh, irrefutable fact that coal mines, steel mills, automobile plants, packing houses, shipping concerns, and railroads were continuing to lay off workers with the progressive introduction of new machinery, labor-saving devices, and automated equipment. It was reported that more automobiles were made in 1963 than in 1955 with 17 per cent fewer workers. In the steel industry new technological developments enabled management in a number of mills to maintain production levels with just half the number of previous employees. One statement hardly encouraging for labor was made by President Johnson in 1964. He predicted that in the 1970's the United States would be able to match the industrial output of the 1960's with 22,000,000 fewer workers. "The worker's great worry these days," A. H. Raskin, the labor expert of the *New York Times* wrote, "is that he will be cast onto the slag heap by a robot. The reassurances that can be won at the bargaining table are often painfully inadequate."

Unemployment could not be brushed aside. It brought in its train depressed living conditions for those out of work, increased poverty in the urban slums where the rate of joblessness was highest, a pervasive restlessness and feeling of rebellion among teenagers and Negroes, juvenile deliquency, and a rising crime rate. Whether or not automation was the primary factor causing unemployment, organized labor felt that it was. On one occasion George Meany burst out to declare that it was "a curse to society." That impulsive statement, however, did not reflect the reasoned views of union leaders generally. They accepted more realistically the inevitability of further technological advance and of automation's displacement of many workers in existing jobs. Their aim was to try in every possible way to control and mitigate the impact of such developments on their own membership, and to enlist government support in meeting the over-all problem of unemployment as it affected the nation's workers as a whole.

As a consequence of this situation, the story of labor negotiations and industrial strikes in the early 1960's largely centers on union efforts to attain job security. Wage and fringe benefits naturally continued to be of importance in the greatly complicated labor-management contracts of these days, but the protection of union members against arbitrary displacement by machines was invariably a major target in all collective bargaining. Union negotiators stressed seniority rights, retraining programs, incentive payments for early retirement, generous severance pay, and supplementary unemployment benefits. However, the grave difficulties in reaching any agreement on even softening the impact of automation or other technological innovations led to the period's major strikes.

The problem had provided the basic issue in the battle over work rules during the steel strike of 1959–60. It provoked a series of work stoppages on the part of longshoremen and dockyard workers. It underlay a continuing and embittered controversy between the railroads and the operating unions which dragged on from 1960 to 1964. It was the issue in strikes by the printing trades, maritime engineers, electrical workers in the new aerospace industries, meatcutters, airplane pilots, and marine engineers on automated vessels.

There was nevertheless a double irony in the strike record of these years. In spite of the unrest among workers as they sensed the overshadowing threat of automation to their jobs, both the number of strikes and the number of wage earners involved continued the downward course of the 1950's. At the close of 1963 Secretary of Labor Wirtz was able to announce that the country had experienced "the most peaceful 3-year record for labor-management relations since we started keeping records about 30 years ago." In the last year of this period, less than a million workers were involved in strikes and man-days lost was only .13 per cent of total working time. One had to go back to the war year 1944 before finding a lower figure.

At the same time, several of the strikes that did break out endangered the economy as seriously as those in the immediate postwar years. These strikes long baffled every effort to bring about settlements safeguarding the public interest and once again aroused great public indignation. Never before, one commentator wrote with special reference to the printers' strike in New York, had so few disrupted the lives of so many. Given widespread and sometimes sensational publicity, these strikes heightened the feeling that in spite of general industrial peace, the unions holding monopolistic power were heedless and irresponsible in the exercise of that power and were determined to advance their own members' interests at whatever cost to society.

Serious work stoppages did not take place, as in earlier years, in the coal fields, in the automobile industry, or in steel. The position of the unions was so well established that the threat of strikes was often enough to bring about eventual settlements. In the steel industry, however, and such other areas as the railroads and shipping, agreements were not reached without government intervention. Where the national welfare was so directly affected, industry-wide strikes could hardly be tolerated; the public insisted that Washington take action. On occasion the emergency provisions of the Taft-Hartley Act were invoked, but they were no more effective than they had been in the past. Every effort was now made to bring labor and management together before an emergency arose. Through the operations of the Federal Mediation and Conciliation Service, arbitration by special emergency boards, and in several instances direct presidential intervention, government was playing a larger role in labor disputes than ever before. It was compelled to make every possible move to sustain the economy in the light of an always precarious world situation.

The United Mine Workers succeeded without a strike or governmental intervention in winning substantial wage increases in 1964. John L. Lewis had already come to grips with the problems of automation, though at the expense of dwindling jobs reflected in the membership decline in his own union. His concern was high wages and welfare benefits for those still employed, and the remaining coal miners were among the highest paid of all industrial workers.

The automobile industry also escaped a major strike when the time came for a renewal of contracts in 1964. Nonetheless, work stoppages at the local level held up full production at General Motors plants for some time and provided an unusual illustration of the immense complexity of negotiations over work rules. General Motors had to reach agreements with some 130 shop committees, calling for hundreds of hours of hard bargaining, over such small, nagging issues as lunch hours, coffee breaks, relief time, and smoking rules. An example of what this involved was reported to its membership by one local after seemingly endless negotiations: "We at the local level obtained for you at Fisher Livonia in the year nineteen sixty-four a privilege that has been in other plants since World War II, and that is, smoking in our toilets and restrooms. Imagine, boys and girls, you are growing up now."

The situation in steel was very complicated. Largely through the pre-contract negotiations of the industry's Human Relations Committee, the ground was prepared for a peaceful settlement in 1963 that substantially increased wages and welfare benefits, and also incorporated extensive sabbatical leaves. To meet the increased costs of this contract, the steel manufacturers raised prices. President Kennedy thereupon assailed this inflationary move as "irresponsible defiance of the public interest" and the manufacturers were compelled to rescind what they felt to be an entirely justified action.

As the time approached for a new contract in 1965, lines were consequently drawn for a more sustained struggle. Industry was unwilling to make further concessions for which it could not obtain compensation through raising prices; the union nonetheless insisted on "total job security." Neither side was willing to give way and the country was aghast at the prospect of another steel strike comparable to those in 1959 and 1952. However, when all attempts at mediation and arbitration failed, President Johnson directly and personally intervened. His approach was in effect to knock together the heads of both union and management representatives and tell them they had to come to terms. He was successful. It was a costly agreement, although the President termed it fair and designed to prevent inflation, but it did avert a shutdown in steel.

Critics were to state that the settlement, however advantageous for the public, was another classic case of the failure of collective bargaining. "Mr. Johnson let it be known," said the *Chicago Tribune*, "that whenever his administration doesn't like the way collective bargaining is going, he will step in to 'protect the national interest.' Thus responsibility is removed from labor and management. If one side or the other holds out long enough, no matter how outlandish its demands, the government can be counted on to step in with a dictated settlement of its own." There was some exaggeration and anti-administration bias in this comment; nonetheless it pointed up the problem of how a strike endangering the whole economy could otherwise be avoided.

The issue of technological unemployment leading to the longshoremen's work stoppages had first come to a crisis on the West Coast in 1959. The dockyard workers walked out in protest against the introduction of labor-saving machinery, so clearly threatening their jobs, and tied up all shipping in the general area. The consequences soon became so serious that President Eisenhower felt compelled to apply for an injunction under the terms of the Taft-Hartley Act, but upon its expiration the strike was renewed. Only after a further shipping tie-up did the International Longshoremen's Association and the Pacific Maritime Association, with the aid of the Federal Mediation Service, finally come to terms early in 1960. Their agreement on meeting the problems of automation was then termed "epochal." The longshoremen agreed to the introduction of new machinery on the docks in return for establishment of a jointly managed fund to avert its impact on existing jobs. The shipping companies undertook to pay $5,000,000 annually into this fund over a five-and-one-half-year period, to provide supplementary wages to any registered longshoreman deprived of his usual work, and to institute a program of incentive payments for early retirement.

Two years later, and then again in 1964, comparable strikes broke out on the East Coast and in Gulf Coast ports. On both occasions Taft-Hartley injunctions were ineffectively applied, and the work stoppages renewed before any final settlement could be reached. The specific issue in these strikes centered on the reduction in the size of work gangs consequent upon the introduction of new machinery, and the final contract followed a pattern somewhat comparable to that concluded on the West Coast. The longshoremen accepted a reduction in work gangs from 20 to 17 men in return for the shipping companies' guarantee that registered workers would be given either 1,600 hours work annually or the equivalent in wages totaling $5,792 a year. In addition, the contract provided for four-week vacation periods for longshoremen with 12 years of service and once again early retirement incentives.

The problem of automation in this industry was thus at least partially resolved. The jobs of the presently employed longshoremen were safeguarded by the equivalent of a guaranteed annual wage, while the shipping companies could gradually whittle down the dockyard work force through a process of gradual attrition.

An even more threatening and protracted dispute centering on the same sort of issue was the four-year controversy between the railroads and the five operating unions. The operators insisted on changes in the work rules whereby they could cut down on the size of train crews and do away with firemen on Diesel engines. The unions stubbornly resisted any such changes and were prepared to strike—300,000 strong—in protection of their members' interests. To prevent such disruption of the country's transportation system, the government resorted to every possible stratagem to bring about an accord.

It first persuaded the railroads and the unions, in December, 1960, to submit the dispute to a special Presidential Railroad Commission. After a long and thorough investigation this commission recommended, something over a year later, changes in the work rules calling for the eventual elimination of some 33,000 railway jobs. The railroads made ready to put such work-rule changes into effect; the unions adamantly refused to accept them and sent out new strike orders.

The government hurriedly interposed with the establishment of a new Emergency Board as provided by the Railway Labor Act. However, it was unable to bring about any settlement and once again a work stoppage was imminent. In something close to desperation, President Kennedy thereupon turned to Congress. On July 22, 1963, he proposed legislation which would refer the whole controversy to the Interstate Commerce Commission and empower it to make a two-year binding decision on the primary issues involving job elimination. Comgress accepted this general idea but rather than authorizing the I.C.C. to handle the matter, it set up another seven-man emergency board with the authority the President had requested. In what was described as the country's first compulsory arbitration law, this crash legislation decreed that during the two years in which the arbitral award on the primary issues was in effect, no strike or lockout on the railroads would be permitted, while at the same time any work stoppage over secondary issues outside the scope of the emergency board's adjudication was banned for 180 days.

The board made its final ruling in November. It called for the gradual elimination of 90 per cent of the firemen on Diesel engines but under conditions which safeguarded the jobs of those with long years of service, and in other cases provided either transfer to comparable work or generous severance pay. It remanded the question of the size of train crews to further negotiations based on guide lines that through a process of attrition would ultimately abolish an additional 19,000 jobs. This award was challenged in the courts but after procedures dragging on some months, the Supreme Court upheld it.

The unions had no further recourse against the legally binding decisions on Diesel engine firemen and the size of train crews. In the meantime, however, there had been no agreement on the so-called secondary issues involving other aspects of railroad operation, and the 180-day ban on any strike over them had elapsed. As the railroads made ready to put new work rules into effect on these matters, the unions again sent out strike orders.

President Johnson, who had inherited the whole problem from Kennedy, now swung into action. He first wrung from the unions an agreement to postpone their walkout and then launched an almost frantic, last-minute round of new negotiations over the secondary issues. On April 22, 1964, it appeared that through his personal intervention the day had been won. In a nationwide television appearance, he dramatically announced that "a just and fair" settlement had been reached in the last phase of the controversy and a railway strike averted.

Had an agreement not been concluded, further congressional action imposing a solution would almost surely have taken place. What had been at stake was not only maintenance of railway traffic but the whole system of collective bargaining. Both the railroads and the unions were under terrific pressure to come to terms but the President's intervention was decisive. When a reporter asked a union leader how the controversy could have been settled so quickly after it had dragged on for over four years, he replied, "there's your answer," and pointed at Johnson.

The agreement was highly complex in its detailed provisions. What had basically happened, however, was that at long last the unions accepted the elimination of the Diesel engine firemen, reduction in train crews, and other changes in the work rules in return for immediate safeguards and other concessions that improved working conditions for the railway employees generally. Management had won its major point: the imperative need to do away with "feather-bedding" in the operation of the railroads. The reform was to be carried out, however, as in the case of the dockyard workers, through a gradual process respecting the rights of veteran workers rather than by wholesale and indiscriminate firing.

The strike of the printing trades and of the Newspaper Guild in New York (coinciding with a comparable work stoppage in Cleveland) shut down all the newspapers in the country's major city in 1963. The interrelationships among the unions involved, problems of crossing picket lines when agreement had been reached with some but not all of them, and controversy among the various publishers created an incredibly confused situation. Automation lay at the basis of the dispute. Printers, pressmen, engravers, and stereotypers were strongly opposed to the unrestricted introduction of new processes, for example, the replacement of linotype machines with typewriter-linked computers. Only after three months of a mounting crisis in communications were agreements finally reached whereby in general terms—as in the dockyard and railway controversies—the new processes might be introduced, but not at the expense of presently employed union members.

While the threat of dwindling jobs could be partially countered in some industries by the broad application of the principles of attrition, no such formula could resolve the problem of unskilled workers who had only limited bargaining power or were seeking without any union support to find their place in the labor market. From their point of view the need was for the creation of new jobs and had far broader ramifications than the problems of individual unions.

The A.F.L.-C.I.O. was fully aware of this. While it continued to exercise all the political influence it could muster for such traditional goals as revision of the Taft-Hartley Act, broadening the social security program, and a progressively higher minimum wage, it also lobbied vigorously for new legislation dealing with unemployment. It specifically proposed a 35-hour-week and double pay for overtime as one means to spread jobs, and also called for government-sponsored vocational training to aid those workers displaced by machines. In all pronouncements on unemployment the executive committee constantly reiterated that "this is not just a trade union problem, it's a national problem."

To strengthen its influence in promoting legislation along these lines, labor was prepared, as it had been ever since the 1930's, to throw its political support behind the Democrats. Experience under the Eisenhower Administration had deepened the conviction that they were more sympathetic to trade union aspirations than the Republicans. Both the Committee for Political Education of the A.F.L.-C.I.O. and the leaders of the major international unions, not only campaigned vigorously for Kennedy in 1960, but for Johnson in 1964. The labor vote unquestionably helped to build up the majorities which brought these presidents into office and contributed materially to the election of liberal congressmen.

Both Kennedy and Johnson recognized their political debt to labor and also the need for governmental action in facing up to the whole problem of technological unemployment. Kennedy's appointment of Arthur J. Goldberg, the counsel of the A.F.L.-C.I.O., as his Secretary of Labor revealed his sympathies. At the same time he strove in every way to build up a fully cooperative program. "What is good for the United States—for the people as a whole," he declared, "is going to be good for every American company and every American union." Johnson not only accepted unemployment as "our dominant, relentless domestic problem," but he came out in support of labor's drive for repeal of Section 14 (b) of the Taft-Hartley Act. Through other public statements he further demonstrated his understanding of labor's problems and his acceptance of the unions' important role in his entire domestic program.

In these circumstances there was to be broad collaboration between the forces of organized labor and those of the successive Democratic administrations of the 1960's. Kennedy took a first step toward meeting the issue of automation by appointment of a National Advisory Committee on Labor-Management Policy charged with the task of investigating and making recommendations on its impact on the labor force. A first report laid down three basic principles: automation was essential for the national welfare, it should be introduced and developed without sacrifice of human values, and, to fulfill the latter condition, there should be both government and private action. What this meant from labor's viewpoint was that where economic pressure, either through collective bargaining or strikes, proved unavailing in safeguarding job security, national policy should be directed toward alleviating a situation that bore so heavily on unskilled workers.

Apart from the legislation extending the social security program and raising minimum wages, there was consequently enacted at this time a first concrete measure to help workers losing their jobs through the displacement of men by machines. This was the Manpower Development and Training Act, passed in 1962, with an appropriation of $35,000,000 spread over three years.

The election of President Johnson in 1964 brought about a renewed and comprehensive attack not only against the consequences of unemployment but against all poverty as a continuing contradiction of the country's general prosperity. This broad program had organized labor's full support. It was after all to combat the poverty resulting from low wages and unemployment that the unions had originally embarked on their own campaign to raise wages, shorten hours, and create decent living conditions for the country's workers as a whole. If the depression of the 1930's had first driven home the realization that government had a basic role in this area, prevailing conditions in the early 1960's further strengthened this conception of its responsibilities. The war against poverty fitted in with the new philosophy of such union leaders as Walter Reuther when he stated that organized labor's goal was not only to increase wages for union members but "to gear economic abundance to human needs."

The concrete results of the Johnson program were new legislation which ranged from aid to education to urban development, from civil rights to Medicare. The Economic Opportunity Act, with appropriations of nearly $1,000,000,000, set up such new projects as a job corps for young people, work-training assistance, and varied urban and rural community action programs. In 1965 Congress made available more money for social welfare in general than ever before in all its history. All this was greatly in the interests of union members. Their own high wages and their improved status in society would assuredly go by the board if unemployment and poverty were allowed to undermine the basic economic structure of the country. The new legislation held out the promise of a great advance in mitigating, if not eliminating, the economic and social evils that continued to mar the general prosperity that the country as a whole was enjoying.

In the exercise of its political power, labor upheld the foreign as well as the domestic policies of Kennedy and Johnson. In logical sequence to the support it had always accorded a program of containment against the further spread of Communism, it continued to back every administration move to extend economic or military aid to countries threatened by infiltration or external attack. The A.F.L.-C.I.O. remained aggressively anti-Communist; it went even further than Washington in its willingness to uphold bans against trade with countries in the Communist bloc. In October, 1965, its executive council strongly reaffirmed its full support for American policy in Vietnam.

Organized labor's stand on foreign affairs, indeed, disappointed its liberal friends who found no difference between its ideas and those of the Chamber of Commerce. One writer of this persuasion found the unions entirely quiescent so far as international relations were concerned and grieved that their members apparently thought no further on such matters than bland acceptance of "George Meany's 'get tough with the Communists' line."

Even labor's most severe critics among liberals and intellectuals, however, agreed, as they well might, that the organized movement invariably gave decisive support to the continuing national campaign to broaden the bases of social welfare, bolster the economy, combat poverty, improve public education, eradicate urban slums, and strengthen civil rights. And while these goals were obviously in the interests of union members, as already noted, they transcended them in that they so importantly affected the well-being of the nation as a whole. Labor, wrote one observer of the contemporary scene, was "the largest single organized force in this country pushing for progressive social legislations."

In spite of everything that was taking place in the 1960's—apart from foreign affairs—to encourage hopes for a more abundant life for the American people and even the gradual elimination of poverty, the future of the labor movement itself remained clouded. The disquiet that pervaded union ranks at the opening of the decade was not stilled with passing years; a feeling of frustration continued to characterize much of the discussion over where labor was headed. The A.F.L.-C.I.O. convention in 1965 was again a rather gloomy occasion.

There had been repeated times in the past when the movement had been seriously weakened by relentless anti-union campaigns or its strength eroded by the effects of economic depression on union membership. The situation in the 1960's, however, did not conform to conditions responsible for these earlier crises. There was no parallel with the embittered and violent industrial strife of the 1890's, which had led to the collapse of the Knights of Labor and the emergence of an American Federation of Labor committed to a new business unionism. Labor had suffered no sharp reverses comparable to those experienced immediately after World War I. There had been no such catastrophic loss of membership—even though it had somewhat declined—as the unions had suffered in the 1920's, leaving them so helpless during the great depression until passage of the Wagner Act set them on a new course. It was sometimes argued in the mid-1960's that in spite of the economic and political strength the unions could still muster, another phase in labor's long history was drawing to an end. There was no consensus as to what this might really mean, however, and even less agreement as to what new directions the organized movement, primarily as represented by the A.F.L.-C.I.O., might or should take in coming years.

The paradoxes that had marked the domestic scene ever since the close of World War II remained. The wages for unionized labor were higher than they had ever been, fringe benefits continued to expand, and strikes remained at a low level. In the tradition of Samuel Gompers and William Green, the unions were still effectively carrying on their historic mission to provide "more" for their members. In a number of cases they had also succeeded through collective bargaining, as we have seen, in compelling management to follow a policy of gradual attrition in the process of replacing men by machines. However, they had hardly been able to solve the basic problems of technological unemployment and job security. Here it remained quite evident that government would have to play a major role. The task facing organized labor was to build up and apply the political pressures that would result in more effective legislation to help maintain full employment, not only for established union members but for the unskilled, for young people, and for the Negroes.

A further question revolved about labor's responsibility toward the public as well as toward the workers, and the adaptation of bargaining processes to new times and new circumstances. One advance had been the steady growth of voluntary arbitration—labor settlements that did not make newspaper headlines. Moreover, where unions and management had agreed to submit unresolved issues or the execution of collective bargaining contracts to outsiders, the courts had upheld the binding character of their arbitral awards. But there were still no satisfactory procedures, as the experience of the early 1960's so clearly demonstrated, in forestalling industry-wide strikes that threatened the paralysis of the national economy. It seemed to be increasingly clear that government could not stand aside while labor and management fought their private battles at the public expense.

Many labor experts consequently urged that where strikes might have national repercussions, some program for impartial fact-finding and possible compulsory arbitration should be considered, not on an emergency basis as in the railway dispute, but as a predetermined policy with adequate safeguards. It was widely felt that when all the resources of collective bargaining and mediation had been exhausted, governmental action had become absolutely essential to maintain industrial peace in the major industries for the sake of the country as a whole. "The country has outgrown the existing machinery for dealing with big labor disputes," Walter Lippmann warned. "But the country has not yet grown up to a consensus on the machinery to replace it. When a new system of industrial relations is established, it is bound to consist of some form of judicial inquiry and judgment. . . ."

In his State of the Union message at the opening of 1966, President Johnson most significantly emphasized this same issue. He stated his intention to ask Congress "to consider measures which, without improperly invading state or local authority, will enable us effectively to deal with strikes which threaten irreparable damage to the national interest."

This was perhaps the greatest challenge facing organized labor. If its position had somewhat improved since the opening of the decade, critics both within and without the unions nevertheless continued to question its dynamism and creativity in meeting new problems. Could labor's leaders revitalize their thinking to develop a unionism better suited to the structural changes in the nation's economy? Could they develop the techniques that would adequately safeguard the rights of union members without endangering national welfare? Could they regain public confidence in the maturity and reasonable restraint of the labor movement as a whole? "Both labor and management, while they have separate responsibilities," Walter Reuther once wrote, "also have a joint responsibility to the whole of society: the joint responsibility to the whole transcends their separate responsibilities."

In the more general acceptance of such views lay the hope that organized labor would not only continue to play its vitally important role in the nation's economic development, but that it would otherwise exercise a beneficial influence in helping to strengthen a free and secure America.

FURTHER READING

GENERAL

Two general bibliographies in the broad field of American labor history are Gene S. Stroud and Gilbert E. Donahue, *Labor History in the United States: A General Bibliography*, Urbana, Ill., 1961, and Maurice E. Neufeld, *A Representative Bibliography of American Labor History*, Ithaca, N.Y., 1964. The latter has the unusual feature of including, in addition to more conventional material, both novels and plays touching on the labor scene.

A classic source among general histories remains John R. Commons and associates, *History of Labour in the United States*, 2 vols., New York, 1918, which may be supplemented by John R. Commons and others, ed., *A Documentary History of American Industrial Relations*, 10 vols., New York, 1958. The former volumes have been brought more nearly up to date in a supplementary study by Selig Perlman and Philip Taft, *A History of Trade Unionism in the United States, 1896–1932*, New York, 1935.

In many ways the successor of Commons, Taft has also written two volumes on the American Federation of Labor: *The A.F. of L. in the Time of Gompers*, New York, 1957, and *The A.F. of L. from the Death of Gompers to the Merger*, New York, 1959, and more recently a full and comprehensive one-volume textbook on the labor movement as a whole, *Organized Labor in American History*, New York, 1964.

Other general histories of relatively recent vintage include Harold U. Faulkner and Mark Starr, *Labor in America*, New York, 1957; Philip S. Foner, *History of the Labour Movement in the United States*, 3 vols., New York, 1947, 1955, and 1964 (carrying the story, with a Marxist slant, to 1909), Henry Pelling, *American Labor*, Chicago, 1960; Joseph G. Rayback, *A History of American Labor*, New York, 1959; and of rather less value, Thomas R. Brooks, *Toil and Trouble, A History of American Labor*, New York, 1964.

Three theoretical studies of the labor movement are Frank Tannenbaum, *A Philosophy of Labor*, Cambridge, 1955; Selig Perlman, *A Theory of the Labor Movement*, New York, 1928; and Mark Perlman, *Labor Union Theories in America: Background and Development*, Evanston, Ill., 1958.

A volume of highly interesting documents is Eli Ginzberg and Hyman

417

Berman, *The American Worker in the Twentieth Century: A History Through Autobiographies*, New York, 1963, and an even more recent paperback study of historical problems is *Labor in American Society*, edited by R. S. Inman and T. W. Koch, Chicago, 1965.

TO THE 1930s

Two books very useful for the colonial period are Marcus W. Jernegan, *Laboring and Dependent Classes in Colonial America, 1707–1783*, New York, 1960, and Richard B. Morris, *Government and Labor in Early America*, New York, 1946; while, for the beginning of the 19th century interesting material, emphasizing politics, may be found in John B. McMaster, *The Acquisition of Political, Social, and Industrial Rights of Man in America*, reprinted, New York, 1961, and Arthur M. Schlesinger, Jr., *The Age of Jackson*, Boston, 1945. Norman Ware provides valuable accounts of labor later in the century in two books: *The Industrial Worker, 1840–1860*, Boston, 1924, and *The Labor Movement in the United States, 1860–1895*, New York, 1929. Among contemporary accounts published in this period, still interesting, are Richard T. Ely, *The Labor Movement in America*, New York, 1886; John Mitchell, *Organized Labor*, Philadelphia, 1903; and George E. McNeill, ed., *The Labor Movement: The Problem of Today*, Boston, 1887.

A first history of the A.F. of L., Lewis L. Lorwin's *The American Federation of Labor: History, Policies, and Prospects*, Washington, 1933, has been largely superseded by Philip Taft's two books. Of outstanding importance for the early years of the 20th century are two volumes reflecting a more interpretive approach to labor history: Irving Bernstein, *The Lean Years: A History of the American Worker, 1920–1933*, Boston, 1960; and James O. Morris, *Conflict Within the A.F. of L.: A Study of Craft versus Industrial Unionism, 1901–1938*, Ithaca, 1958.

THE NEW DEAL AND WORLD WAR II

The developments of the 1930's produced a large number of contemporary studies. Among the more important are Herbert Harris, *American Labor*, New Haven, 1939, and the same author's *Labor's Civil War*, New York, 1940; Edward Levinson, *Labor on the March*, New York, 1938; Benjamin Stolberg, *The Story of the C.I.O.*, New York, 1938; Mary Heaton Vorse, *Labor's New Millions*, New York, 1938; J. R. Walsh, *C.I.O.—Industrial Unionism in Action*, New York, 1937; and, on government policies, R. R. R. Brooks, *Unions of Their Own Choosing: An Account of the National Labor Relations Board and Its Work*, New Haven, 1939; the same author's

When Labor Organizes, New Haven, 1937; and Carroll R. Daugherty, *Labor Under the N.R.A.,* Boston, 1934.

These contemporary books may be supplemented by such later studies as Walter Galenson, *The C.I.O. Challenge to the A.F. of L.: A History of the American Labor Movement, 1935–1951,* Cambridge, 1960; Milton Derber and Edwin Young, eds., *Labor and the New Deal,* Madison, Wis., 1957; Sidney Fine, *The Automobile Under the Blue Eagle,* Ann Arbor, 1963; and Irving Bernstein, *The New Deal Collective Bargaining Policy,* Berkeley, 1950. A useful pamphlet summary is E. David Cronon, *Labor and the New Deal,* Chicago, 1963.

On the war and immediate postwar period, reference may be made to Joel Seidman, *American Labor from Defense to Reconversion,* Chicago, 1953; Colston E. Warne, ed., *Labor in Postwar America,* Boston, 1949; Jack Barbash, *The Taft-Hartley Law in Action,* New York, 1954; and H. A. Millis and E. C. Brown, *From the Wagner Act to Taft-Hartley: A Study of National Labor Policy and Labor Relations,* Chicago, 1950.

SPECIAL STUDIES

There are many special studies dealing with various aspects of the history of the labor movement. The following represent a highly selective sampling: Robert W. Dunn, *Company Unions,* New York, 1927; Marguerite Green, *The National Civic Federation and the American Labor Movement, 1900–1925,* Washington, 1956; Leo Huberman, *The Labor Spy Racket,* New York, 1937; Felix Frankfurter and Nathan Greene, *The Labor Injunction,* New York, 1930; Joseph Gaer, *The First Round: The Story of the CIO Political Action Committee,* New York, 1944; Fay Calkins, *The CIO and the Democratic Party,* Chicago, 1952; Donald L. McMurray, *Coxey's Army: a Study of the Industrial Army Movement of 1894,* Boston, 1929; Charles O. Gregory, *Labor and the Law,* New York, 1946; Malcom A. Johnson, *Crime on the Labor Front,* New York, 1950; Leo Wolman, *Ebb and Flow in Trade Unionism,* Washington, 1936.

BIOGRAPHY AND AUTOBIOGRAPHY

A highly interesting approach to labor history is through biography and autobiography. Material on William H. Sylvis is available in James C. Sylvis, *The Life, Speeches, Labors and Essays of William C. Sylvis,* Philadelphia, 1872, and in the biography by Jonathan Grossman: *William Sylvis, Pioneer of American Labor,* New York, 1945. Terrence V. Powderly wrote two autobiographical books: *Thirty Years of Labor,* Columbus, Ohio, 1889, and *The Path I Trod,* New York, 1940. Samuel Gompers has a two-volume autobiography, titled *Seventy Years of Life and Labor*, New York, 1925 (a one-volume edition was published in 1957, edited by Philip Taft and John A. Sessions); a standard account of his career is Rowland H. Harvey, *Samuel Gompers*, Stanford, 1935, and Louis B. Reed has examined his basic ideas in *The Labor Philosophy of Samuel Gompers*, New York, 1930. Elsie Gluck wrote *John Mitchell, Miner*, New York, 1929; the best account of Eugene V. Debs is Ray Ginger, *The Bending Cross; A Biography of Eugene V. Debs*, New Brunswick, N.J., 1949. Two autobiographies of radical labor leaders are William D. Haywood, *Bill Haywood's Book*, New York, 1929, and Ralph Chapin, *Wobbly: The Rough and Tumble Story of an American Radical*, Chicago, 1948.

Among the better biographies of more recent labor leaders are Saul Alinsky, *John L. Lewis*, New York, 1949; Matthew Josephson, *Sidney Hillman, Statesman of Labor*, Garden City, 1952; Maxwell Raddock, *Portrait of an American Labor Leader: William L. Hutcheson*, New York, 1955; and Irving Howe and B. J. Widick, *The UAW and Walter Reuther*, New York, 1949. Two very recent accounts of James Hoffa are Ralph and Estelle James, *Hoffa and the Teamsters*, Princeton, 1965; and Clark D. Mollenkoff, *Tentacles of Power: The Story of Jimmy Hoffa*, Cleveland, 1965.

Three group studies of labor leaders are Bruce B. Minton and John Stuart, *Men Who Lead Labor*, New York, 1937; Harold Seidman, *Labor Czars*, New York, 1938; C. Wright Mills, *The New Men of Power: America's Labor Leaders*, New York, 1948; and Charles A. Madison, *American Labor Leaders: Personalities and Forces in the Labor Movement*, New York, 1950.

RADICALISM AND STRIKES

The story of radicalism and strike activity within the labor movement is told in such general studies as Louis Adamic, *Dynamite*, New York, 1931; Samuel Yellen, *American Labor Struggles*, New York, 1936; David J. Saposs, *Left Wing Unionism*, New York, 1926; the same author's *Communism in American Unions*, New York, 1959; Chester M. Destler, *American Radicalism, 1865–1901*, New London, Conn., 1946; and David A. Shannon, *The Socialist Party of America: A History*, New York, 1955.

Anthony Bimba is the author of *The Molly Maguires*, New York, 1932, but it is largely replaced by the more recent study of Wayne G. Broehl, Jr., also titled *The Molly Maguires*, Cambridge, 1964. Radicalism in the early 1900's is recounted in Paul F. Brissenden, *The I.W.W., A Study of American Syndicalism*, New York, 1919 (reprinted, 1957); and John S. Gambs, *The Decline of the I.W.W.*, New York, 1932. More recently Joyce L. Kornbluh has published a fascinating record of the Wobblies' songs and literature in *Rebel Voices: An I.W.W. Anthology*, Ann Arbor, Mich., 1964.

Accounts of individual strikes include Robert V. Bruce, *1877: Year of Violence*, Indianapolis, 1959; Donald L. McMurray, *The Great Burlington Strike of 1888*, Cambridge, 1956; Henry David, *History of the Haymarket Affair*, New York, 1936; Almont Lindsey, *The Pullman Strike*, Chicago, 1942; Robert J. Cornell, *The Anthracite Coal Strike of 1902*, Washington, 1957; and William Z. Foster, *The Great Steel Strike*, New York, 1920; and Leon Wolff, *Lockout: The Story of the Homestead Strike of 1892*, New York, 1965. See also for its material on labor troubles Robert K. Murray, *Red Scare: A Study in National Hysteria, 1919–1920*, Minneapolis, 1955.

LABOR IN FICTION

Labor has not played a great part in American fiction but a few novels may perhaps be noted as providing especially illuminating background material. One of the first was John Hay, *The Breadwinners* (published anonymously), New York, 1884. Two books describing industrial conditions in the early 1900's are Frank Norris, *The Octopus*, New York, 1901, and Upton Sinclair, *The Jungle*, New York, 1906, and there is some comparable material in Ernest Poole, *The Harbor*, New York, 1915.

Among more recent novels might be mentioned Albert Halper, *The Foundry*, New York, 1934; Ruth McKenny, *Industrial Valley*, New York, 1939, and John Steinbeck, *In Dubious Battle*, New York, 1936.

INDIVIDUAL UNIONS

The histories of individual unions provide a special and often rewarding approach to any study of the labor movement as a whole. Among those published in the past quarter century are Jack Barbash, *Unions and Telephones*, New York, 1952; Brailsford Brazeal, *The Brotherhood of Sleeping Car Porters*, New York, 1946; David Brody, *Steelworkers in America: The Non-Union Era*, Cambridge, 1960; David Brody, *The Butcher Workmen: A Study of Unionization*, Cambridge, 1964; McAllister Coleman, *Men and Coal*, New York, 1943; William C. Doherty, *Mailman, U.S.A.*, New York, 1960; David W. Hertel, *History of the Brotherhood of Maintenance of Way Employees*, Washington, 1955; Elmo P. Hohman, *History of American Merchant Seamen*, Hamden, Conn., 1956; Irving Howe and B. J. Widick, *The UAW and Walter Reuther*, New York, 1949; Leo Huberman, *The National Maritime Union*, New York, 1943.

Also Vernon H. Jensen, *Lumber and Labor*, New York, 1945; Robert D. Leiter, *The Musicians and Petrillo*, New York, 1953; Jacob Loft, *The Printing Trades*, New York, 1944; Mark Perlman, *The Machinists, A New Study in American Trade Unionism*, Cambridge, 1961; Reed C. Richardson, *The*

Locomotive Engineer: 1863–1963, Ann Arbor, Mich., 1963; Harold S. Roberts, *Rubber Workers*, New York, 1944; Donald B. Robinson *Spotlight on a Union, The Story of the United Hatters*, New York, 1948; Howard D. Samuel and Lynne Rhodes, *Profile of a Union* (the Amalgamated Clothing Workers), New York, 1958; Joel Seidman, *The Needle Trades*, New York, 1942; Joel Seidman, *The Brotherhood of Railway Trainmen*, New York, 1962, and Benjamin Stolberg, *Tailor's Progress, The Story of a Famous Union and the Men Who Made It*, Garden City, 1944.

THE CONTEMPORARY SCENE

Studies of the labor movement have greatly multiplied since World War II, both on special issues and on its more general aspects. While few of them have significant historical value, a number may be singled out for the light they throw on the contemporary scene.

Arthur J. Goldberg's *AFL-CIO: Labor United*, New York, 1956, is perhaps most interesting because of the eminence of its author; and important for somewhat the same reason are Robert F. Kennedy's *The Enemy Within* (an account of the McClellan Committee Investigations), New York, 1960, and W. Willard Wirtz, *Labor and the Public Interest*, New York, 1965.

A group of books whose titles clearly suggest their contemporaneity are Bert Cochran, ed., *American Labor in Midpassage*, New York, 1959; Paul Jacobs, *The State of the Unions*, New York, 1963; Jack Barbash, *Labor's Grass Roots*, New York, 1961; Paul E. Suttan, *The Disenchanted Unionist*, New York, 1964; Sidney Lens, *The Crisis of American Labor*, New York, 1959; B. J. Widick, *Labor Today: The Triumphs and Failures of Unionism in the United States*, New York, 1964; Maurice R. Franks, *What's Wrong With Our Labor Unions*, Indianapolis, 1963; Richard A. Lester, *As Unions Mature*, New York, 1958; Joseph A. Beirne, *New Horizons for American Labor*, Washington, 1962.

Attention may also be drawn to the issue of the *Monthly Labor Review* in honor of the 50th anniversary of the Department of Labor, June, 1963, as well as its annual reviews of American labor; the special issues on labor of *The Annals of the American Academy of Political Science*, Vols. 333 (1961) and 350 (1963), and the section on "Labor" in *Congress and the Nation*, Washington, 1965.

In the periodical field are among other journals *Labor History, Monthly Labor Review*, the *AFL-CIO News, The Federationist*, and a host of labor journals published by individual unions.

INDEX